Riley McGowan

IOE

2017

HOLT *Traditions*

Warriner's Handbook

Fourth Course

Grammar • Usage • Mechanics • Sentences

Instructional Framework by

John E. Warriner

HOLT, RINEHART AND WINSTON

AUTHOR **JOHN E. WARRINER** taught for thirty-two years in junior and senior high schools and in college. He was a high school English teacher when he developed the original organizational structure for his classic *English Grammar and Composition* series. The approach pio- neered by Mr. Warriner was distinctive, and the editorial staff of Holt, Rinehart and Winston have worked dili- gently to retain the unique qualities of his pedagogy in *Warriner's Handbook*. John Warriner also co-authored the *English Workshop* series and edited *Short Stories: Characters in Conflict*.

ISBN 978-0-03-099003-8

ISBN 0-03-099003-3

12   1083   17
4500671889

CONTENTS IN BRIEF

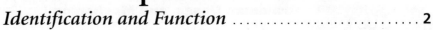

PART 1 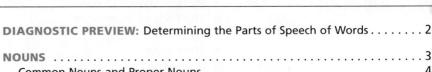 **Grammar, Usage, and Mechanics** 1

The Parts of a Sentence

CHAPTER

2

Subjects, Predicates, Complements **34**

The Phrase

The Clause

Agreement

CHAPTER

5

Subject and Verb, Pronoun and Antecedent **108**

Using Pronouns Correctly

Nominative, Objective, and Possessive Case;

Using Verbs Correctly

Principal Parts, Tense, Voice, Mood **170**

CHAPTER

CHAPTER

Using Modifiers Correctly
Forms, Comparison, and Placement 210

A Glossary of Usage

CHAPTER

9

Capitalization

Punctuation

Punctuation

Spelling

Correcting Common Errors

CHAPTER

Key Language Skills Review **408**

PART 2   Sentences **442**

Writing Complete Sentences **444**

CHAPTER

17

DIAGNOSTIC PREVIEW 444
  A. Identifying Sentences and Sentence Fragments
  B. Revising Sentence Fragments
  C. Identifying and Revising Run-on Sentences

SENTENCE FRAGMENTS 446
  Phrase Fragments 448
    Verbal Phrases 448
    Appositive Phrases 449
    Prepositional Phrases 449
  Subordinate Clause Fragments 450

RUN-ON SENTENCES 454
  Revising Run-on Sentences 454

CHAPTER REVIEW 459
  A. Identifying Sentences, Sentence Fragments, and Run-on Sentences
  B. Revising Run-on Sentences
  C. Revising Sentence Fragments and Run-on Sentences

Writing Effective Sentences **462**

CHAPTER

18

DIAGNOSTIC PREVIEW 462
  A. Combining Sentences
  B. Combining Sentences by Forming Compound and Complex Sentences
  C. Revising a Paragraph to Improve Sentence Style

COMBINING SENTENCES 464
  Inserting Words 465
  Inserting Phrases 467
    Prepositional Phrases 467
    Participial Phrases 467
    Appositive Phrases 468

John Warriner:
In His Own Words

In the 1940s and '50s, John Warriner (1907–1987) published his first grammar and composition textbooks. Mr. Warriner's goal as a teacher and as a writer was to help students learn to use English effectively in order to be successful in school and in life. Throughout the years that followed, Mr. Warriner revised his original books and wrote others, creating the series on which this textbook is based. Included in Mr. Warriner's books were a number of short essays to his students. In these essays, Mr. Warriner explored the role of language in human life, the importance of studying English, and the value of mastering the conventions of standard English.

We could tell you what John Warriner thought about the study of English, but we'd rather let you read what he himself had to say.

Language Is Human

"Have you ever thought about how important language is? Can you imagine what living would be like without it?

"Of all creatures on earth, human beings alone have a fully developed language, which enables them to communicate their thoughts to others in words, and which they can record in writing for others to read. Other creatures, dogs, for example, have ways of communicating their feelings, but they are very simple ways and very simple feelings. Without words, they must resort to mere noises, like barking, and to physical actions, like tail wagging. The point is that one very important difference between human beings and other creatures is the way human beings can communicate with

Warriner's first grammar and composition textbooks, published in the 1940s and '50s.

one another by means of this remarkable thing called language. When you stop to think about it, you realize that language is involved to some extent in almost everything you do."

(from *English Grammar and Composition: First Course*, 1986)

Warriner's English Grammar and Composition: Fourth Course, 1977

Why Study English?

"The reason English is a required subject in almost all schools is that nothing in your education is more important than learning how to express yourself well. You may know a vast amount about a subject, but if you are unable to communicate what you know, you are severely handicapped. No matter how valuable your ideas may be, they will not be very useful if you cannot express them clearly and convincingly. Language is the means by which people communicate. By learning how your language functions and by practicing language skills, you can acquire the competence necessary to express adequately what you know and what you think."

(from *English Grammar and Composition: Fourth Course*, 1977)

Why Study Grammar?

"Grammar is a description of the way a language works. It explains many things. For example, grammar tells us the order in which sentence parts must be arranged. It explains the work done by the various kinds of words—the work done by a noun is different from the work done by a verb. It explains how words change their form according to the way they are used. Grammar is useful because it enables us to make statements about how to use our language. These statements we usually call rules.

"The grammar rule that the normal order of an English sentence is subject-verb-object may not seem very important to us, because English is our native tongue and we naturally use this order without thinking. But the rule would be very helpful to people who are learning English as a second language. However, the rule that subjects and verbs 'agree' (when the subject is plural, the verb is plural), and the rule that some pronouns (*I, he, she, we, they*) are used as subjects while others (*me, him, her, us,*

Warriner's English Grammar and Composition: Third Course, 1982

them) are used as objects—these are helpful rules even for native speakers of English.

"Such rules could not be understood—in fact, they could not be formed—without the vocabulary of grammar. Grammar, then, helps us to state how English is used and how we should use it."

(from *English Grammar and Composition: Third Course*, 1982)

Why Is Punctuation Important?

"The sole purpose of punctuation is to make clear the meaning of what you write. When you speak, the actual sound of your voice, the rhythmic rise and fall of your inflections, your pauses and hesitations, your stops to take breath—all supply a kind of 'punctuation' that serves to group your words and to indicate to your listener precisely what you mean. Indeed, even the body takes part in this unwritten punctuation. A raised eyebrow may express interrogation more eloquently than any question mark, and a knuckle rapped on the table shows stronger feeling than an exclamation point.

"In written English, however, where there are none of these hints to meaning, simple courtesy requires the writer to make up for the lack by careful punctuation."

(from *English Grammar and Composition: Fourth Course*, 1973)

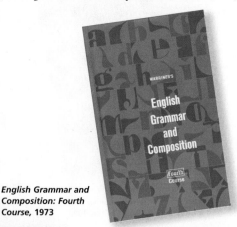

English Grammar and Composition: Fourth Course, 1973

Why Learn Standard English?

"Consider the following pair of sentences:

1. George don't know the answer.
2. George doesn't know the answer.

"Is one sentence clearer or more meaningful than the other? It's hard to see how. The speaker of sentence 1 and the speaker of sentence 2 both convey the same message about George and his lack of knowledge. If language only conveyed information about the people and events that a speaker is discussing, we would have to say that one sentence is just as good as the other. However, language often carries messages the speaker does not intend. The words he uses to tell us about events often tell us something about the speaker himself. The extra, unintended message conveyed by 'George don't know the answer' is that the speaker does not know or does not use one verb form that is universally preferred by educated users of English.

"Perhaps it is not fair to judge people by how they say things rather than by what they say, but to some extent everyone does it. It's hard to know what is in a person's head, but the language he uses is always open to inspection, and people draw conclusions from it. The people who give marks and recommendations, who hire employees or judge college applications, these and others who may be important in your life are speakers of educated English. You may not be able to impress them merely by speaking their language, but you are likely to impress them unfavorably if you don't. The language you use tells a lot about you. It is worth the trouble to make sure that it tells the story you want people to hear."

(from *English Grammar and Composition: Fourth Course*, 1973)

John Warriner

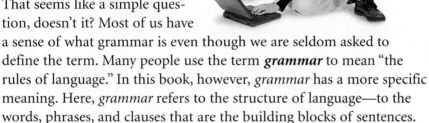

What is grammar?

That seems like a simple question, doesn't it? Most of us have a sense of what grammar is even though we are seldom asked to define the term. Many people use the term **grammar** to mean "the rules of language." In this book, however, *grammar* has a more specific meaning. Here, *grammar* refers to the structure of language—to the words, phrases, and clauses that are the building blocks of sentences. Grammar gives us the labels we use to talk about language.

What about the rules that govern how language is used in various social situations? In this book, these rules are called usage. Unlike grammar, **usage** determines what is considered standard ("isn't") or nonstandard ("ain't") and what is considered formal ("why") or informal ("how come"). Usage is a social convention, a behavior or rule customary for members of a group. As a result, what is considered acceptable usage can vary from group to group and from situation to situation.

To speak standard English requires a knowledge of grammar and of standard usage. To write standard English requires something more—a knowledge of mechanics. *Mechanics* refers to the rules for written, rather than spoken, language. Spelling, capitalization, and punctuation are concepts we don't even think about when we are speaking, but they are vital to effective written communication.

Why should I study grammar, usage, and mechanics?

Many people would say that you should study grammar to learn to root out errors in your speech and writing. Certainly, *Warriner's Handbook* can help you learn to avoid making errors and to correct the errors you do make. More importantly, though, studying grammar, usage, and mechanics gives you the skills you need to take sentences and passages apart and to put them together, to learn which parts go together and which don't. Instead of writing sentences and passages that you hope sound good, you can craft your sentences to create just the meaning and style you want.

Knowing grammar, usage, and mechanics gives you the tools to understand and discuss your own language, to communicate clearly the things you want to communicate, and to develop your own communication style. Further, mastery of language skills can help you succeed in your other classes, in future classes, on standardized tests, and in the larger world—including, eventually, the workplace.

How do I use *Warriner's Handbook*?

The skills taught in *Warriner's Handbook* are important to your success in reading, writing, speaking, and listening.

Not only can you use this book as a complete grammar, usage, and mechanics textbook, but you can also use it as a reference guide when you work on any piece of writing. Whatever you are writing, you can use *Warriner's Handbook* to answer your questions about grammar, usage, capitalization, punctuation, and spelling.

How is *Warriner's Handbook* organized?

Warriner's Handbook is divided into three main parts:

PART 1 The **Grammar, Usage, and Mechanics** chapters provide instruction on and practice using the building blocks of language—words, phrases, clauses, capitalization, punctuation, and spelling. Use these chapters to discover how to take sentences apart and analyze them. The last chapter, **Correcting Common Errors,** provides additional practice on key language skills as well as standardized test practice in grammar, usage, and mechanics.

PART 2 The **Sentences** chapters include Writing Complete Sentences, Writing Effective Sentences, and Sentence Diagramming. **Writing Complete Sentences** and **Writing Effective Sentences** provide instruction on and practice with writing correct, clear, and interesting sentences. **Sentence Diagramming** teaches you to analyze and diagram sentences so you can see how the parts of a sentence relate to each other.

To Our Students

PART 3 The **Resources** section includes **Manuscript Form,** a guide to presenting your ideas in the best form possible; **The History of English,** a concise history of the English language; **Test Smarts,** a handy guide to taking standardized tests in grammar, usage, and mechanics; and **Grammar at a Glance,** a glossary of grammatical terms.

How are the chapters organized?

Each chapter begins with a Diagnostic Preview, a short test that covers the whole chapter and alerts you to skills that need improvement, and ends with a Chapter Review, another short test that tells you how well you have mastered that chapter. In between, you'll see rules, which are basic statements of grammar, usage, and mechanics principles. The rules are illustrated with examples and followed by exercises and reviews that help you practice what you have learned.

What are some other features of this textbook?

- **Oral Practice**—spoken practice and reinforcement of rules and concepts
- **Writing Applications**—activities that let you apply grammar, usage, and mechanics concepts in your writing
- **Tips & Tricks**—easy-to-use hints about grammar, usage, and mechanics
- **Meeting the Challenge**—questions or short activities that ask you to approach a concept from a new angle
- **Style Tips**—information about formal and informal uses of language
- **Help**—pointers to help you understand either key rules and concepts or exercise directions

go. hrw .com

Warriner's Handbook **on the Internet**

As you move through *Warriner's Handbook,* you will find the best online resources at **go.hrw.com.**

Grammar, Usage, and Mechanics

GO TO: go.hrw.com

Grammar

Usage

Mechanics

Parts of Speech Overview

Identification and Function

Diagnostic Preview

Determining the Parts of Speech of Words

Identify the part of speech of each italicized word or word group in the following paragraphs.

EXAMPLES   What were the **[1]** *most* common forms of transportation in North America **[2]** *between* **[3]** *colonial* times and the twentieth **[4]** *century?*

    1. *adverb*

    2. *preposition*

    3. *adjective*

    4. *noun*

Since the [1] *condition* of the roads prevented [2] *extensive* use of wheeled vehicles, the most reliable means of transportation in colonial times was the [3] *saddle horse.* Some [4] *exceptionally* wealthy people kept carriages, but [5] *these* were usually heavy vehicles [6] *that* were pulled by two or more horses. Such carriages were [7] *satisfactory* for short trips, [8] *but* they were not practical for long journeys.

    Stagecoaches were introduced in [9] *America* in about 1750. [10] *By* this time roads ran between such major cities as New York and

Boston. Although these roads [11] *were* little more than muddy tracks, [12] *most* were wide enough for a four-wheeled coach. [13] *Three* or four pairs of horses [14] *were harnessed* to a coach. Generally, however, the vehicles were so heavy that [15] *coach* horses tired [16] *quite* [17] *rapidly* [18] *and* had to be either rested frequently [19] *or* changed at post houses along the route. The design of horse-drawn vehicles soon improved, and until the early years of the twentieth century, buggies and wagons remained a common [20] *form* of transportation.

Nouns

1a. A *noun* names a person, a place, a thing, or an idea.

Persons	hero	teachers	audience	Mai Ling
Places	museum	countries	rain forest	San Diego
Things	stereo	songs	fences	Pacific Ocean
Ideas	sympathy	fairness	generosity	Impressionism

Exercise 1 **Identifying Nouns in Sentences**

Identify the nouns in the following sentences. Treat as single nouns all capitalized names containing more than one word.

EXAMPLE 1. Elizabeth Cady Stanton was born in the state of New York in 1815.

1. *Elizabeth Cady Stanton, state, New York*

1. As a young woman, Elizabeth Cady Stanton studied mathematics and the classics both at home and at Troy Female Seminary, from which she graduated in 1832.
2. Beginning at an early age, she recognized the injustices suffered by women, especially in education and politics.
3. In 1840, she married Henry Stanton, a prominent abolitionist.
4. At an antislavery convention in London, England, Mrs. Stanton was outraged at the treatment of the female delegates.
5. She later helped to organize the first meeting to address the rights of women.
6. At that convention, she read her "Declaration of Sentiments," outlining the inferior status of women and calling for reforms.

HELP
You do not need to include years, such as *1815*, in your answers for Exercise 1.

7. Among these reforms, the most controversial was giving women the right to vote.
8. In 1850, Stanton began working with Susan B. Anthony.
9. These two women did much work for the suffrage movement.
10. Stanton remained adamant about effecting change for the remainder of her life.

Common Nouns and Proper Nouns

Reference Note

For more on **capitalizing proper nouns,** see page 267.

A *common noun* names any one of a group of persons, places, things, or ideas. A *proper noun* names a particular person, place, thing, or idea. Generally, common nouns are not capitalized; proper nouns are.

Common Nouns	Proper Nouns
mountain	Mount McKinley
novelist	Louisa May Alcott
museum	Museum of Fine Arts
ship	*Queen Elizabeth 2*
movie	*Casablanca*

Compound Nouns

Reference Note

For information about **capitalizing the parts of a compound noun,** see page 267.

A *compound noun* consists of two or more words that together name a person, a place, a thing, or an idea. The parts of a compound noun may be written as one word, as separate words, or as a hyphenated word.

One Word	Separate Words	Hyphenated Word
basketball	civil rights	no-hitter
newspaper	Arts and Crafts Club	sister-in-law

NOTE If you are not sure how to write a compound noun, look it up in an up-to-date dictionary. Some dictionaries may give two correct forms for a word. For example, you may find the word *vice-president* written both with and without the hyphen. Generally, use the form the dictionary lists first.

Exercise 2 Replacing Common Nouns with Proper Nouns and Identifying Compound Nouns

For each of the following common nouns, give a proper noun. Then, write *compound* next to each compound noun that you write.

EXAMPLE   **1.** river
         1. *Mississippi River—compound*

1. play	**6.** newspaper	**11.** planet	**16.** actor
2. state	**7.** ocean	**12.** poet	**17.** explorer
3. street	**8.** writer	**13.** country	**18.** scientist
4. song	**9.** poem	**14.** friend	**19.** religion
5. president	**10.** car	**15.** continent	**20.** document

Concrete Nouns and Abstract Nouns

A *concrete noun* names a person, a place, or a thing that can be perceived by one or more of the senses (sight, hearing, taste, touch, and smell). An *abstract noun* names an idea, a feeling, a quality, or a characteristic.

Concrete Nouns	Abstract Nouns
dog	liberty
sunset	beauty
thunder	kindness
silk	success
Nile River	Marxism

Collective Nouns

A *collective noun* names a group of people, animals, or things.

Collective Nouns		
audience	crowd	orchestra
batch	flock	pride
bouquet	gaggle	set
bunch	jury	staff
cluster	litter	swarm

Reference Note

For information on **using verbs with collective nouns,** see page 120.

┌─HELP──

The singular form of a collective noun names a group. Other kinds of nouns must be made plural to name a group.

Classifying Nouns

Identify each of the italicized nouns in the following paragraph as *proper* or *common* and as *concrete* or *abstract*. Also, if the noun is a *compound noun* or a *collective noun*, label it as such.

EXAMPLE   Doesn't the Cajun **[1]** *dish* in the picture look delicious?

1. common, concrete

Cajuns are descended from a **[1]** *group* of French settlers who were expelled from Acadia (a region including parts of present-day Maine and eastern Canada) by the British in 1755. When some of these displaced

people settled in the **[2]** *Atchafalaya Basin* in southeastern Louisiana, they had to invent **[3]** *ways* to use local foods in their traditional French recipes. If you've never tried Cajun food, the crawfish in this picture may be unfamiliar to you. In **[4]** *addition* to the plentiful crawfish, shrimp, and oysters caught in Louisiana waters, freshwater fish, alligator meat, **[5]** *rice*, and many **[6]** *spices* find their way into Cajun cooking. Gumbos are soups flavored with **[7]** *filé*, which is powdered sassafras leaves. **[8]** *Gumbos* often contain okra and sausage, chicken, or seafood. The **[9]** *popularity* of these and other Cajun dishes has spread throughout the **[10]** *United States* in recent years.

Pronouns

1b. A *pronoun* takes the place of one or more nouns or pronouns.

EXAMPLES   Susan watched the monkey make faces at her little brother and sister. **She** laughed at **it** more than **they** did. [*She* is used in place of *Susan, it* in place of *monkey,* and *they* in place of *brother* and *sister.*]

When others saw the monkey, **they** began laughing, too. [*They* takes the place of the pronoun *others.*]

Reference Note

For information about **choosing pronouns that agree with their antecedents,** see page 130.

The word or word group that a pronoun stands for is called the ***antecedent*** of the pronoun. In the first example above, *Susan* is the antecedent of *She, monkey* is the antecedent of *it,* and *brother* and *sister* are the antecedents of *they.* In the second example, *others* is the antecedent of *they.*

Personal Pronouns

A *personal pronoun* refers to the one(s) speaking (*first person*), the one(s) spoken to (*second person*), or the one(s) spoken about (*third person*).

	Singular	Plural
First Person	I, me, my, mine	we, us, our, ours
Second Person	you, your, yours	you, your, yours
Third Person	he, him, his, she, her, hers, it, its	they, them, their, theirs

EXAMPLES   **I** hope that **you** can help **me** with **my** homework.

           He said that **they** would meet **us** outside the theater.

NOTE   This textbook refers to the words *my, your, his, her, its, our,* and *their* as possessive pronouns. However, because these words can come before nouns and tell *which one* or *whose,* some authorities prefer to call them adjectives. Follow your teacher's instructions regarding these possessive forms.

Reflexive and Intensive Pronouns

First Person	myself, ourselves
Second Person	yourself, yourselves
Third Person	himself, herself, itself, themselves

A *reflexive pronoun* refers to the subject of a sentence and functions as a complement or as an object of a preposition.

EXAMPLES   I'm not quite **myself** today. [*Myself* is a predicate nominative identifying *I*.]

           Cecilia let **herself** take a study break. [*Herself* is the direct object of *let*.]

           They chose costumes for **themselves.** [*Themselves* is the object of the preposition *for*.]

Reference Note

For more information about **complements,** see page 48. For more about **objects of prepositions,** see page 24.

TIPS & TRICKS

To tell whether a pronoun is reflexive or intensive, use this simple test: Read the sentence aloud, and omit the pronoun. If the meaning of the sentence stays the same, the pronoun is most likely intensive. If not, the pronoun is probably reflexive.

EXAMPLE
  She changed the tire herself. [*She changed the tire* makes sense. The pronoun *herself* is intensive.]

Reference Note

For more about **demonstrative adjectives,** see page 12.

Reference Note

For more about **relative pronouns** and **subordinate clauses,** see page 94.

An *intensive pronoun* emphasizes its antecedent and has no grammatical function in the sentence.

EXAMPLES   Ray painted the mural **himself.**

The children dyed the eggs **themselves.**

Demonstrative Pronouns

A *demonstrative pronoun* points out a person, a place, a thing, or an idea.

this	that	these	those

EXAMPLES   **This** is our favorite campsite.

The tomatoes we grew in the garden taste better than **these.**

NOTE   The words that can be used as demonstrative pronouns can also be used as adjectives.

  PRONOUN   **This** tastes good.
  ADJECTIVE   **This** hummus tastes good.

Interrogative Pronouns

An *interrogative pronoun* introduces a question.

who	whom	which	what	whose

EXAMPLES   **What** is the address of this house?

Whose is the red truck parked outside?

Relative Pronouns

A *relative pronoun* introduces an adjective clause.

that	which	who	whom	whose

EXAMPLES   The dog **that** you trained is very well-behaved.

She is the candidate **who** promises to listen to the people.

Indefinite Pronouns

An *indefinite pronoun* refers to a person, place, thing, or idea that may or may not be specifically named.

all	each other	most	one another
another	either	much	other
any	everybody	neither	several
anybody	everyone	nobody	some
anyone	everything	none	somebody
anything	few	no one	someone
both	many	nothing	something
each	more	one	such

EXAMPLES **Everything** we will need is packed in the trunk.

Has **anyone** called for Mr. Reynolds?

NOTE Many of the pronouns you have studied so far may also be used as adjectives.

EXAMPLES **that** oyster **whose** pearl **some** shells

Reference Note

For information about **distinguishing between pronouns and adjectives,** see page 12.

Exercise 3 Identifying Pronouns in Sentences

Identify the pronouns in each of the following sentences.

EXAMPLE 1. Let me tell you about one of the camping trips that I took last summer.

1. *me, you, one, that, I*

┌HELP┐

In Exercise 3, if a pronoun is used more than once, note it each time it appears.

1. All of the other members of my family like to go camping, but few of them enjoy the outdoors more than I do.
2. Last summer several of my cousins and I stayed at a rustic camp in the Rocky Mountains, which are not far from our hometown.
3. At camp we learned how to build a campfire and how to keep it going ourselves.
4. A group of us even went beyond that—we learned to cook meals safely over the open fire.
5. One of our counselors showed those who were interested how to cook themselves simple meals.
6. Each of his recipes was delicious and easy to follow, and everyone ate everything in sight.
7. All of us enjoy anything cooked over a campfire.

8. We also enjoy telling stories while sitting around the fire.

9. Often we tell each other eerie stories.

10. Who wants to go to sleep afterward?

Adjectives

1c. An *adjective* modifies a noun or a pronoun.

To modify means "to describe" or "to make the meaning of a word more specific." An adjective is a modifier that tells *what kind, which one, how many,* or *how much.*

What Kind?	Which One?	How Many?	How Much?
spilled ink	**this** park	**twenty** miles	**no** salt
English tea	**these** papers	**two** men	**enough** water
howling winds	**that** house	**several** apples	**some** food

An adjective may be separated from the word it modifies.

EXAMPLES   She is **clever.**

The sky had become **cloudy** suddenly.

NOTE An adjective that is in the predicate and that modifies the subject of a clause or sentence is called a *predicate adjective.*

Articles

The most frequently used adjectives are *a, an,* and *the.* These words are usually called *articles.*

A and *an* are called *indefinite articles* because they refer to any member of a general group. *A* is used before a word beginning with a consonant sound; *an* is used before a word beginning with a vowel sound.

EXAMPLES   **A** park ranger helped us.

Shady Lane is **a** one-way street. [*One-way* begins with a consonant sound.]

They planted **an** acre with corn.

We kept watch for **an** hour. [*Hour* begins with a vowel sound.]

COMPUTER TIP

Using a computer software program's thesaurus can help you choose appropriate adjectives. To make sure that an adjective has exactly the connotation you intend, look up the word in a dictionary.

Reference Note

For more information on **predicate adjectives,** see page 52.

The is called the **definite article** because it refers to someone or something in particular.

EXAMPLES   **The** park ranger helped us.

They planted **the** acre with corn.

The hour dragged by.

Exercise 4   **Identifying Adjectives and the Words They Modify**

For the following sentences, identify each adjective and the word it modifies. (Do not include the articles *a, an,* and *the.*)

EXAMPLE   **1.** In the latter part of the nineteenth century, bicycling became a popular sport in the United States.

   1. latter—part; nineteenth—century; popular—sport

1. By the 1890s, an extraordinary craze for bicycling had swept the nation.
2. Though bicycles had been available for years, the early versions made for an awkward ride.
3. Ungainly cycles like the one in the picture had a very large wheel in the front and a small wheel in the back.
4. In 1885, however, a more sensible model was introduced, one that resembled the modern cycle.
5. Energetic people everywhere took to this kind of bicycle.
6. Bicycling soon became a national sport.
7. Cyclists joined special clubs that took vigorous tours through the countryside.
8. A typical ride might cover twenty miles, with a welcome stop along the way for refreshments.
9. Races were also popular with enthusiastic spectators, who often outnumbered those at ballgames.
10. The fans enjoyed watching these tests of endurance, which sometimes lasted six days.

Pronoun or Adjective?

Some words may be used either as adjectives or as pronouns. In this book, demonstrative, interrogative, and indefinite terms are called pronouns when they stand for other nouns or pronouns. They are called adjectives when they modify nouns or pronouns.

PRONOUN **Which** did you choose, Roberto?
ADJECTIVE **Which** book did you choose to read, Alex?

PRONOUN **Those** are excited fans.
ADJECTIVE **Those** fans are excited.

NOTE The words *this, that, these,* and *those* are called **demonstrative adjectives** when they modify nouns or pronouns and are called **demonstrative pronouns** when they take the place of nouns or other pronouns.

In this book, the words *my, your, his, her, its, our,* and *their* are considered possessive pronouns. However, some authorities consider them to be adjectives. Follow your teacher's instructions on labeling these words.

Exercise 5 Identifying Words as Adjectives or Pronouns

Tell whether each italicized word in the following paragraph is used as a *pronoun* or an *adjective*. For each adjective, give the word it modifies.

EXAMPLES Of ants and wasps, **[1]** *which* do you think are considered **[2]** *antisocial*?

1. *pronoun*

2. *adjective—which*

Although ants are related to wasps, there are [1] *many* differences between [2] *these* two kinds of insects. [3] *All* ants are social insects. They live together in colonies made up of [4] *three* castes: a queen, males, and workers. Unlike ants, [5] *most* wasps are solitary insects. [6] *Most* of the 20,000 known species of wasps are solitary. Of [7] *these,* [8] *many* are hunting wasps [9] *that* make individual nests. [10] *These* wasps usually build their nests in the ground. [11] *Some* nest in wood or mud. However, not all wasps are antisocial; [12] *some* behave more like their cousins the ants. [13] *These* wasps live in permanent colonies of adults and young. While [14] *most* wasps are solitary, there are about 1,000 species of social wasps. Among the best-known social wasps are [15] *those* within a group that, like ants, has a caste system in [16] *its* societies. The queen builds a small nest consisting of a [17] *few* cells, and then she lays eggs. [18] *These* hatch into workers. The workers enlarge the nest, [19] *which* is made of material that has been chewed, regurgitated, and mixed with saliva. [20] *Some* of the best-known social wasps are yellow jackets and hornets.

Noun or Adjective?

When a word that can be used as a noun modifies a noun or pronoun, it is called an adjective.

EXAMPLES   **salad** bowl   **chicken** dinner

                  New England states   **gold** medal

> NOTE Notice in the preceding examples that the proper noun *New England* remains capitalized when it is used as an adjective. An adjective that is formed from a proper noun is called a ***proper adjective.***

Some word groups are considered compound nouns.

EXAMPLES   salad dressing   chicken hawk   New England clam chowder

By checking an up-to-date dictionary, you can avoid mistaking a word that is part of a compound noun for a word that is considered a separate adjective.

Reference Note

For more information about capitalizing **proper adjectives,** see page 267. For more about **compound nouns,** see page 4.

Review B **Identifying Nouns, Pronouns, and Adjectives**

Identify the nouns, pronouns, and adjectives in the following sentences. For each adjective, give the word it modifies. (Do not include the articles *a, an,* and *the.*)

EXAMPLE   **1.** Several different kinds of butterflies flew around us.

         1. nouns—kinds; butterflies

          pronoun—us

          adjectives—Several (kinds); different (kinds)

1. Our teacher, Mr. López, identified the various trees along the nature trail.
2. Many people are working to clean up polluted rivers and streams to make them livable environments for wildlife again.

3. The flag over the hotel was a welcome sight to the two travelers.
4. The antique doll was dressed in a sailor hat and a blue suit.
5. A large bowl of fruit sat in the center of the kitchen table.
6. Along the Hudson River, autumn leaves colored the highway with bright splashes of orange and red.
7. Someone has filled the fruit bowl with dates and walnuts.
8. As a young girl, Susan B. Anthony was taught Quaker religious tenets, which include the belief in the equality of all people.
9. The bird feeder in the elm tree in my yard attracts cardinals, robins, and chickadees.
10. The dust jacket of that literature anthology has certainly seen better days.

Review C Identifying Nouns, Pronouns, and Adjectives

Identify each numbered, underlined word in the following paragraph as a *noun*, a *pronoun*, or an *adjective*.

EXAMPLE The Spanish built the first *ranchos,* or ranches, that were in the **[1]** United States.

1. *noun*

The **[1]** man in this picture is a *vaquero,* but you can call **[2]** him a cowboy. *Vaqueros* got their name from the **[3]** Spanish word *vaca,* which means "cow." In fact, cowboys were at **[4]** home on the range in Mexico long before they gained **[5]** legendary status in the United States. Notice that this *vaquero* wears **[6]** leather chaps (*chaparejos*) to protect his legs and uses a **[7]** lasso (*el lazo*) to rope the steer. **[8]** Many other words that we associate with cowboys came into the English language from **[9]** Spanish. **[10]** These include *rodeo, stampede,* and *bronco.*

Californians Catching Wild Horses with Riata by Hugo Wilhelm Arthur Nahl (1833–1889), Oil on canvas mounted on masonite 19 $\frac{5}{8}$" x 23 $\frac{3}{4}$". Collection of the Oakland Museum, Kahn Collection.

Verbs

1d. A *verb* expresses action or a state of being.

In this textbook, verbs are classified in three ways: (1) as main or helping verbs, (2) as action or linking verbs, and (3) as transitive or intransitive verbs.

Main Verbs and Helping Verbs

A *verb phrase* consists of one *main verb* and one or more *helping verbs* (also called *auxiliary verbs*).

EXAMPLES   I **am reading** Thomas Hardy's novel *Under the Greenwood Tree.* [*Am* is a helping verb. *Reading* is the main verb.]

We **should have been listening** instead of talking. [*Should, have,* and *been* are helping verbs. *Listening* is the main verb.]

Commonly Used Helping Verbs				
Forms of *Be*	am	be	being	was
	are	been	is	were
Forms of *Have*	had	has	have	having
Forms of *Do*	did	do	does	
Modals	can	might	shall	would
	could	must	should	
	may	ought	will	

NOTE   A *modal* is an auxiliary verb that is used to express an attitude toward the action or state of being of the main verb.

EXAMPLE   I **may** go to the concert after all. [The modal *may* expresses an attitude of possibility in relation to the main verb *go.*]

Helping verbs may be separated from the main verb.

EXAMPLE   **Did** she **paint** the house?

NOTE   The word *not* and its contraction, *n't,* are never part of a verb phrase. Instead, they are adverbs telling *to what extent.*

Reference Note

For more about **modals,** see page 197.

Reference Note

For more about **adverbs,** see page 20.

—HELP—

Some sentences
in Exercise 6 have more
than one verb or verb
phrase.

Exercise 6 Identifying Verbs and Verb Phrases

Identify the verbs and verb phrases in the following sentences. Be sure to include all helping verbs.

EXAMPLE 1. The marching band would be performing during half time.

1. *would be performing*

1. Because of the cold weather, the members of the band worried about their half-time performance.
2. Marcia and the other saxophone players were clapping their hands vigorously so that their fingers wouldn't become even more numb in the raw, icy air.
3. They imagined what would happen if their fingers froze to the keys of their instruments.
4. Instead of music, harsh noise would blare out and probably startle the spectators.
5. The other band members would likely skip a beat, and chaos would soon spread across the field.
6. Out of step, the flute players might well stumble into the clarinet players, collide with the trombone players, or even trip over the drummers.
7. When half time was called, Marcia and her friends rolled their eyes and laughed about the dreadful scene they had just pictured.
8. Could such a disaster possibly happen?
9. As the band marched onto the field, large, white snowflakes swirled in the air and settled on the brand-new uniforms and shiny instruments.
10. Some people were leaving the stands when the principal announced over the loudspeaker: "Ladies and gentlemen, the band will now play 'Jingle Bells.'"

Action Verbs and Linking Verbs

An *action verb* expresses either physical or mental activity.

PHYSICAL	bring	say	shout	jump	breathe
MENTAL	ponder	trust	review	evaluate	guess

EXAMPLES   Please **return** this book. [*Return* expresses physical action.]

Do you **know** Han? [*Do know* expresses mental action.]

A *linking verb* connects the subject to a word or word group that identifies or describes the subject. Such a word or word group is called a *subject complement.*

EXAMPLES   Kelp **is** the scientific name for seaweed. [The subject complement *name* identifies the subject *Kelp.*]

Kelp **has been** a good source of iodine. [The subject complement *source* identifies the subject *Kelp.*]

Kelp **tastes** good in salads. [The subject complement *good* describes the subject *Kelp.*]

As it ages, kelp **becomes** brown. [The subject complement *brown* describes the subject *kelp.*]

Reference Note

For more information about **subject complements,** see page 51.

Commonly Used Linking Verbs			
Forms of *Be*			
be	were	shall have been	should be
being	shall be	will have been	would be
am	will be	can be	could be
is	has been	may be	should have been
are	have been	might be	would have been
was	had been	must be	could have been
Others			
appear	feel	look	seem	sound	taste
become	grow	remain	smell	stay	turn

Some of the verbs listed as *Others* in the previous chart can be used as action verbs as well as linking verbs.

LINKING   Emilia **felt** calm at the seashore.
ACTION   Emilia **felt** the waving strands of kelp.

The forms of *be* are not always used as linking verbs. That is, they do not always link a subject to a subject complement. Instead of a subject complement, an adverb that tells *where* or *when* may follow the form of *be.* In such cases, the verb *be* is called a ***state-of-being verb.***

EXAMPLE   My friends and I **were** there yesterday. [The verb *were* is followed not by a subject complement but by *there,* which tells *where,* and by *yesterday,* which tells *when.*]

TIPS & TRICKS

To determine whether a verb in a sentence is a linking verb, substitute a form of the verb *be* for the verb. If the sentence makes sense, the verb is most likely a linking verb.

LINKING
Emilia **felt** calm at the seashore. [The verb *was* can sensibly replace *felt: Emilia was calm at the seashore.*]

ACTION
Emilia **felt** the waving strands of kelp. [The verb *was* cannot sensibly replace *felt.*]

**Identifying Verbs as Action Verbs
or Linking Verbs**

Identify each italicized verb in the following sentences as an *action verb*
or a *linking verb*.

EXAMPLE **1.** The ancient Egyptians *built* a grand temple for Amon-Re,
their chief deity.

1. action verb

1. Situated on the banks of the Nile River in Egypt, these ruins at
Karnak *are* some of the most impressive sights in the world.
2. The largest structure there *is* the Great Temple of Amon-Re.
3. As you can see, its immense size *dwarfs* people.
4. The 42-meter-high gateway *amazes* visitors who follow the avenue
of sphinxes that leads to the entrance.
5. The ceiling of the temple *rests* more than 23 meters above the floor.

6. Of course, the central columns that support
the stone roof *look* enormous.
7. Carvings *decorate* the surfaces of these huge
columns.
8. Even an amateur engineer *can appreciate*
the tremendous efforts that must have gone
into the completion of this temple.
9. We now *know* that inclined planes, combined with levers and blocking, enabled the
ancient Egyptians to raise the large stones.
10. A remarkable technical achievement, the
Great Temple of Amon-Re today *remains* a
monument to the ancient builders' skills.

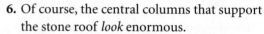

**Writing Sentences Using Verbs as Both
Linking and Action Verbs**

For each of the following verbs, write two sentences. In the first
sentence, use the verb as a linking verb; in the second sentence, use
the verb as an action verb.

EXAMPLE **1.** become

*1. We become older by the day.
That hat becomes her.*

1. appear	**3.** smell	**5.** look	**7.** remain	**9.** taste
2. sound	**4.** grow	**6.** feel	**8.** stay	**10.** turn

Transitive Verbs and Intransitive Verbs

A *transitive verb* has an *object*—a word that tells who or what receives the action of the verb.

EXAMPLES   She **trusts** her friend. [The object *friend* receives the action of the verb *trusts.*]

                Zora Neale Hurston **wrote** novels. [The object *novels* receives the action of the verb *wrote.*]

An *intransitive verb* does not have an object.

EXAMPLES   The audience **applauded.**

                The train **stops** here.

The same verb may be transitive in one sentence and intransitive in another.

TRANSITIVE   Elsa **swam** the channel. [The object *channel* receives the action of the verb *swam.*]

INTRANSITIVE   Elsa **swam** for many hours. [no object]

TRANSITIVE   Miss Castillo **weeds** the garden every day. [The object *garden* receives the action of the verb *weeds.*]

INTRANSITIVE   Miss Castillo **weeds** every day. [no object]

© 1984 by Sidney Harris-Punch.

"I MISS THE GOOD OLD DAYS WHEN ALL WE HAD TO WORRY ABOUT WAS NOUNS AND VERBS."

Reference Note

For more about **objects of verbs,** see page 53.

GRAMMAR

NOTE Action verbs can be transitive or intransitive. All linking verbs are intransitive.

ACTION   I **studied** my geometry notes for an hour. [transitive]

           Luis also **studied** for an hour. [intransitive]

LINKING   We **are** ready for the quiz. [intransitive]

Like a one-word verb, a verb phrase may be classified as *transitive* or *intransitive* and as *action* or *linking.*

EXAMPLES   We **are planting** some cactus dahlias. [transitive action]

           They **should bloom** in about six weeks. [intransitive action]

           The flowers **will be** deep red. [intransitive linking]

┌─**HELP**─

If you are not sure whether a verb is transitive or intransitive, look in a dictionary. Most dictionaries group the definitions of verbs according to whether the verbs are used transitively (*v.t.*) or intransitively (*v.i.*).

Identifying Verbs as Transitive or Intransitive

Read each of the following sentences aloud. Then, identify the verb or verb phrase in each sentence, and tell whether it is *transitive* or *intransitive*.

EXAMPLE   **1.** We eagerly anticipated our trip to the seashore.

        1. anticipated—transitive

  1. The strong winds died down.
  2. We quickly packed a lunch for our adventure.
  3. The whitecaps on the ocean disappeared.
  4. The sunlight sparkled on the splashing surf.
  5. At low tide, Rosita suddenly spotted a starfish.
  6. She noticed its five purplish arms.
  7. She touched a soft, brown sponge floating nearby.
  8. Three shore crabs swam in the tidal pool.
  9. The beach was alive with interesting creatures.
10. Have you seen the ocean?

Adverbs

1e. An *adverb* modifies a verb, an adjective, or another adverb.

An adverb tells *how, when, where,* or *to what extent* (*how much, how long,* or *how often*).

Adverbs Modifying Verbs

EXAMPLES   The bird was chirping **outside.** [*where*]

               The bird chirped **today.** [*when*]

               The bird chirped **loudly.** [*how*]

               The bird **never** chirped. [*to what extent*]

Identifying Adverbs and the Verbs They Modify

Identify the adverbs in the following sentences. For each adverb, give the verb that it modifies.

EXAMPLE   **1.** The Montgolfier brothers worked steadily and earnestly to build the first hot-air balloon.

        1. steadily—worked, earnestly—worked

| TIPS & TRICKS |

Many adverbs end in *–ly.* However, not all words ending in *–ly* are adverbs. For instance, the following words are adjectives: *homely, kindly, lovely,* and *deadly.* To tell whether a word is an adverb, ask yourself these questions:

• Does the word modify a verb, an adjective, or an adverb?

• Does the word tell *when, where, how,* or *to what extent?*

1. Birds, bats, and bugs fly effortlessly.
2. During the eighteenth century, a few creatures involuntarily entered the skies.
3. In 1783, an unpiloted balloon was tested, and a hot-air balloon carrying a sheep, rooster, and duck was launched later in the year.
4. Humans successfully flew for the first time in November of 1783.
5. The first balloonists floated gently above Paris in a hot-air balloon that had been cleverly designed by the Montgolfier brothers.
6. Although their earlier attempts had failed, the Montgolfiers kept trying and finally settled on a balloon made of paper and linen.
7. Early balloons differed significantly from modern balloons like those pictured, which are sturdily constructed of coated nylon.
8. Despite their ingenuity, the Montgolfiers originally thought that smoke, rather than hot air, would effectively push their balloon skyward.
9. In their experiments, they initially produced hot smoke by burning straw and wool.
10. Balloonists greatly appreciated the discovery that dense smoke was not a requirement for flight.

Adverbs Modifying Adjectives

EXAMPLES   It was a **fiercely** competitive game. [The adverb *fiercely* modifies the adjective *competitive*.]

The **exceptionally** brave police officer was given an award. [The adverb *exceptionally* modifies the adjective *brave*.]

Exercise 10 **Identifying Adverbs and the Adjectives They Modify**

In each of the following sentences, an adverb modifies an adjective. Identify the adverb and the adjective it modifies.

EXAMPLE   1. A wagon train traveling to northern California carried a considerably large number of pioneers.

    1. *adverb—considerably; adjective—large*

1. The immensely long wagon train started out from Denver, Colorado.
2. Both oxen and mules were used to pull unusually large wagons.
3. Even in good weather, the long trail through the mountains was fairly hazardous.
4. A moderately hard rain could turn the trail into a swamp.
5. When the trail was too muddy, the heavier wagons became mired.

| STYLE | TIP |

Some of the most frequently used adverbs are *too, so, really,* and *very.* In your writing, try to avoid these overused words. Some adverbs that are less common are given below:
  completely
  dangerously
  definitely
  dreadfully
  entirely
  especially
  generally
  particularly
  rather
  surprisingly
  unusually

6. Wagons that were extremely heavy had to be unloaded before they could be moved.
7. Stopping for the night along the trail was a consistently welcome experience.
8. It offered relief to thoroughly tired bones and muscles.
9. Nights in the mountains could be quite cold.
10. On terribly cold nights, the travelers would roll up in blankets and sleep near their campfires.

Adverbs Modifying Other Adverbs

Reference Note

For information on adverbs used to join words or word groups, see **relative adverbs** on page 95 and **conjunctive adverbs** on page 90.

EXAMPLES   The guide spoke **extremely** slowly. [The adverb *extremely* modifies the adverb *slowly*, telling *to what extent* the guide spoke *slowly*.]

We will go to the mall **later** today. [The adverb *later* modifies the adverb *today*, telling *when* today.]

Noun or Adverb?

Some words may be used as either nouns or adverbs. When identifying parts of speech, classify words that are used to modify verbs, adjectives, and adverbs as adverbs.

NOUN   I was at **home.**
ADVERB   "Be **home** by nine o'clock," Dad said.

NOUN   **Tomorrow** is another day.
ADVERB   Do you want to go to the zoo **tomorrow**?

Exercise 11   Identifying Adverbs and the Words They Modify

Identify the adverb or adverbs in each of the following sentences. After each adverb, give the word it modifies and the part of speech of that word.

EXAMPLE   1. My sister Juana and I had often talked about getting a houseplant for our room.

    1. *often—had talked (verb)*

1. A couple of months ago, Juana and I finally decided to buy a houseplant for the kitchen.
2. The large ones we saw were too expensive for us.
3. Suddenly, Juana had a brainstorm.
4. "Let's buy some seeds and grow them indoors."

5. At the seed store, the owner, Mrs. Miller, greeted us cheerfully.

6. We explained that we wanted to grow a large plant but that our room never gets bright sunlight and that in the winter it can be especially chilly and dark.

7. "These are seeds of the bo tree, an unusually hardy member of the fig family native to India," said Mrs. Miller.

8. "There, this tree is sacred to Buddhists because it is said that the Buddha received enlightenment under a bo tree."

9. When we got back to our house, we planted the seeds.

10. In a short time, they sprouted, and we now have an unusual houseplant that is suited to our environment.

Exercise 12   Using Words as Adjectives and Adverbs

Write a pair of sentences for each word. In the first sentence, use the word as an adjective; in the second, use it as an adverb.

EXAMPLE
    1. kindly
    1. *She had a kindly manner.—adjective*
       She spoke kindly.—adverb

1. daily	**3.** late	**5.** far	**7.** further	**9.** straight
2. fast	**4.** more	**6.** early	**8.** hard	**10.** right

Review D   Identifying Parts of Speech

Identify the part of speech of each italicized word or word group in the following paragraphs. If the word is an adjective or an adverb, be prepared to tell what it modifies.

EXAMPLES
    Without warning, the **[1]** *serenity* of the **[2]** *snow-covered* mountains is assaulted.

    1. *noun*

    2. *adjective*

With a **[1]** *thunderous* roar, a mighty avalanche **[2]** *crashes* **[3]** *headlong* down the mountainside. **[4]** *Some* of these slides travel at speeds of more than 200 miles an hour and pose a **[5]** *deadly* threat to skiers, mountain climbers, and the people **[6]** *who* live and work in the mountains.

One **[7]** *common* suggestion for surviving an avalanche is to make swimming motions to remain on top of the snow. However, people caught in avalanches **[8]** *rarely* can save **[9]** *themselves*. They are **[10]** *usually* immobilized, and the slide **[11]** *forces* snow into their nose and mouth.

HELP

In the example for Review D, the adjective *snow-covered* modifies the noun *mountains*.

Avalanche workers in the [12] *United States* and abroad have [13] *long* realized the [14] *potential* [15] *destructiveness* of certain slide paths. The workers [16] *have concluded* that an avalanche can be [17] *greatly* reduced if [18] *explosives* [19] *are used* to trigger a [20] *series* of [21] *smaller* slides before [22] *one* large mass of snow can build up. [23] *Today,* the detonation of explosives has become a standard [24] *practice* for controlling avalanches in [25] *this* country.

Prepositions

1f. A *preposition* is a word that shows the relationship of a noun or a pronoun, called the **object of the preposition,** to another word.

Notice in the following examples how the prepositions show different relationships between the verb *rode* and *village,* the object of each preposition.

EXAMPLES   I rode **past** the village.   I rode **near** the village.

I rode **through** the village.   I rode **around** the village.

I rode **toward** the village.   I rode **beyond** the village.

NOTE   A preposition, its object, and any modifiers of the object form a *prepositional phrase.*

Commonly Used Prepositions			
aboard	below	from	since
about	beneath	in	such as
above	beside	inside	through
across	besides	into	throughout
after	between	like	to
against	beyond	near	toward
along	but (meaning	of	under
amid	except)	off	underneath
among	by	on	until
around	concerning	onto	up
as	down	out	upon
at	during	outside	with
before	except	over	within
behind	for	past	without

STYLE   TIP

In formal writing and speaking, you should avoid using a preposition at the end of a sentence when possible.

INFORMAL
Jaime asked me to name some people whom I look up to.

Sometimes rearranging such sentences results in an awkward or pretentious construction.

AWKWARD
Jaime asked me to name some people up to whom I look.

In formal situations, therefore, it is often best to reword sentences to avoid using such expressions.

FORMAL
Jaime asked me to name some people whom I **admire.**

Reference Note

For more about **prepositional phrases,** see page 65.

A preposition that consists of two or more words is called a *compound preposition.*

EXAMPLES   The soccer game was delayed **because of** rain.

Who is sitting **in front of** Arturo?

Commonly Used Compound Prepositions		
according to	in addition to	instead of
because of	in front of	on account of
by means of	in spite of	prior to

Preposition or Adverb?

Some words may be used as either prepositions or adverbs. Remember that an adverb is a modifier and does not have an object.

PREPOSITION   Marge climbed **down** the ladder.
ADVERB   Marge climbed **down** carefully.

PREPOSITION   **Above** the dry riverbed, buzzards circled lazily.
ADVERB   **Above,** buzzards circled lazily.

NOTE As a preposition, the word *to* precedes a noun or a pronoun to form a prepositional phrase. Do not confuse such a prepositional phrase with an *infinitive*—a verb form preceded by *to*.

PREPOSITIONAL PHRASES	to the library	to her	to Louisiana
INFINITIVES	to create	to play	to compare

Reference Note

For more information on **infinitives,** see page 77.

Exercise 13 **Writing Sentences Using Words as Prepositions and as Adverbs**

For each of the following words, write two sentences. In the first sentence, use the word as a preposition and underline the prepositional phrase. In the second sentence, use the word as an adverb and circle the word or words the adverb modifies.

EXAMPLE   **1.** in

1. *We are going in the house now.*
   We are going in now.

1. around	3. inside	5. up	7. outside	9. by
2. under	4. on	6. below	8. past	10. aboard

Reference Note

For a discussion of using **conjunctions in sentence combining,** see page 469. For the rules governing the use of **punctuation with conjunctions,** see pages 470, 301, and 322.

Conjunctions

1g. A *conjunction* joins words or word groups.

Coordinating Conjunctions

Coordinating conjunctions join words or word groups that are used in the same way.

Coordinating Conjunctions			
and	but	for	nor
or	so	yet	

┌ TIPS & TRICKS ┐

You can remember the coordinating conjunctions as FANBOYS:

For
And
Nor
But
Or
Yet
So

EXAMPLES   The orchestra played waltzes **and** polkas. [*And* joins two nouns.]

We can walk to the neighborhood pool **or** to the park. [*Or* joins two prepositional phrases.]

I looked for Will, **but** he had already left. [*But* joins two clauses.]

Correlative Conjunctions

Correlative conjunctions are pairs of conjunctions that join words or word groups that are used in the same way.

Correlative Conjunctions	
both . . . and	not only . . . but also
either . . . or	whether . . . or
neither . . . nor	

Reference Note

Another kind of conjunction, the **subordinating conjunction,** is discussed with **subordinate clauses,** on page 96.

EXAMPLES   **Neither** the baseball team **nor** the soccer team has practice today.

Both the track team **and** the volleyball team enjoyed a winning season.

Their victories sparked the enthusiasm **not only** of students **but also** of teachers and townspeople.

Exercise 14 Identifying Coordinating and Correlative Conjunctions

Identify the coordinating conjunctions and correlative conjunctions in the following sentences.

EXAMPLE 1. When did whaling and the whaling industry begin to decline in the United States?

1. *and*

1. Once, Nantucket and New Bedford, Massachusetts, were home ports of huge whaling fleets.
2. Whaling brought tremendous profits into these ports, but the golden days of whaling ended about the same time as the U.S. Civil War.
3. Even when it was successful, a whaling trip was no pleasure cruise for either the captain or the crew.
4. The living conditions were often quite dreadful, so maintaining order was no easy task on a long voyage.
5. Inevitably, the sailors had time on their hands, for they didn't encounter a whale every day.
6. To relieve the monotony and resulting boredom, the crews of whaling ships often would exchange visits.
7. Both the captains and their crew members looked forward to such visits.
8. The sailors enjoyed the opportunity not only to chat but also to exchange news.
9. The decline of whaling and of the whaling industry was signaled by the development of a new fuel.
10. By 1860, the United States no longer needed large quantities of whale oil because kerosene, a cheaper and better fuel, had replaced it.

> **MEETING THE CHALLENGE**
>
> Create a crossword-puzzle grid with clues, using at least two examples of each of the eight parts of speech covered in this chapter. (You should have a minimum of sixteen clues.) For instance, a sample clue for a preposition could be "Grandmother's house is _____ the river and through the woods." The answer is *over*, requiring four spaces on the puzzle grid. Include answers to the puzzle on a separate page.

Interjections

1h. An *interjection* expresses emotion. An interjection has no grammatical relation to the rest of the sentence.

Interjections						
ah	ouch	ugh	wow	oops	hey	oh

> **STYLE TIP**
>
> Interjections are common in casual conversation. In writing, however, they are typically used only in informal notes and letters, in advertisements, and in dialogue.

STYLE   **TIP**

When you write an interjection, make sure the punctuation after it reflects the intensity of emotion you intend.

HELP

Check to see that you have punctuated your interjections with exclamation points or commas as needed and that you have capitalized the sentences correctly.

An interjection is generally set off from the rest of the sentence by an exclamation point or by a comma or commas. Exclamation points indicate strong emotion. Commas indicate mild emotion.

EXAMPLES   **Whew!** What a day I've had!

Well, I'm just not sure.

There must be, **oh my,** a dozen snakes there.

Exercise 15   Using Interjections

Using the interjections from the list provided, complete the following sentences. Be sure to use the words as interjections and not as adjectives or adverbs.

EXAMPLE   1. _____ Wait for me!

1. *Hey!*

| excellent | well | whoa | ouch | wow |
| oops | whew | hey | cool | yow |

1. _____ I stubbed my toe!
2. _____ I forgot to buy bananas.
3. _____ our teacher didn't give a pop quiz today.
4. _____ tomorrow is a holiday!
5. _____ I can't decide; both puppies are adorable.
6. _____ I didn't know you ran cross-country.
7. _____ she won the race!
8. _____ what time are you going home?
9. _____ my name was drawn in the raffle!
10. _____ our runner was passed inches away from the finish line!

Determining Parts of Speech

1i. **The way a word is used in a sentence determines what part of speech the word is.**

The same word may be used as different parts of speech. To figure out what part of speech the boldface word is in each of the following sentences, read the entire sentence. What you are doing is studying the ***context***—the way the word is used in the sentence. From the context, you can identify the part of speech that *light* or *help* is in each of the following sentences.

EXAMPLES   Rich heard the **light** patter of raindrops. [adjective]

The flash of **light** hurt her eyes. [noun]

Use care when you **light** the fire. [verb]

Please **help** your sister with her homework. [verb]

I will provide **help,** but I won't do your work for you. [noun]

If you can't find the answer in the instruction manual, you may have to call the **help** desk. [adjective]

Exercise 16 **Determining the Parts of Speech of Words**

Determine the part of speech of the italicized word in each of the following sentences. Be prepared to explain your answers.

EXAMPLES   **1.** Marisa holds the school *record* for the 100-meter dash.

    1. noun

    2. Marisa ran the race in *record* time.

    2. adjective

1. They decided that the hedge needed a *trim*.

2. Their hedges always look *trim* and neat.

3. We usually *trim* the tree with homemade ornaments.

4. Mom always *shears* a couple of inches off the top of the tree.

5. Later, she uses *shears* to cut straggling branches.

6. I wasn't thirsty, but I did *down* one glass of water before finishing my workout.

7. Dale ran *down* the stairs and hugged his sister.

8. "If heights bother you, don't look *down*," the guide warned.

9. I asked for Tuesday off, *but* my boss gave me Monday off instead.

10. All *but* two of the students voted in the class elections.

┌**HELP**──

In the first example, *record* is a noun functioning as the direct object of the verb *holds*. In the second example, *record* functions as an adjective modifying *time*.

Review E **Writing Sentences Using Words as Different Parts of Speech**

Write two sentences for each of the following words, using the word as a different part of speech in each sentence. At the end of the sentence, write what part of speech the word is in that sentence.

EXAMPLE   **1.** hand

    1. Jesse hurt his hand. (noun)
    Please hand me the biscuits. (verb)

1. long	**3.** back	**5.** iron	**7.** tie	**9.** outside
2. cut	**4.** fast	**6.** some	**8.** for	**10.** empty

Review F Determining the Parts of Speech of Words

Identify the part of speech of each italicized word or word group in the following paragraph.

EXAMPLES   The **[1]** *homes* of many **[2]** *of* the early farmers on the Great
            Plains **[3]** *were* **[4]** *quite* **[5]** *primitive*.

            1. noun   *3.* verb   *5.* adjective
            2. preposition   *4.* adverb

[1] *Early* farmers on the [2] *Great Plains* eked out a rough existence, [3] *for* there were few towns, stores, or other signs of civilization.
[4] *Many* farm homes were constructed mostly of sod bricks, [5] *which*
were cut [6] *out of* the prairie. Trees were in short supply on these wind-
swept lands, but the resourceful settler might find a few [7] *cottonwoods*
growing [8] *along* a creek or river. [9] *These* [10] *could be used* to build
a frame for the roof, which was then covered [11] *lightly* with grassy
earth. Grass, both [12] *on* the roof [13] *and* in the sod, helped to hold

the house together. Some of [14] *these*
rugged homes had a door made of
timber, but [15] *quite* often a cowhide
[16] *was draped* across the entrance.
[17] *Inside* was a dirt floor covered with
a bearskin [18] *or* a buffalo hide. As more
settlers moved [19] *west,* bringing fur-
nishings and [20] *building* materials,
farmers eventually abandoned these first,
primitive dwellings and built homes that
were more conventional.

Review G Writing Sentences with Words Used
             as Different Parts of Speech

Use each of the following words or word groups in a sentence. Then,
indicate what part of speech the word or word group is.

EXAMPLE   **1.** gold
           1. Tamisha bought a gold bracelet. (adjective)

1. novel	**6.** tomorrow	**11.** hiked	**16.** inside
2. Park Avenue	**7.** or	**12.** oh	**17.** under
3. this	**8.** quietly	**13.** tasted	**18.** appeared
4. are laughing	**9.** both . . . and	**14.** but	**19.** whew
5. yesterday	**10.** silver	**15.** often	**20.** in

Chapter Review

A. Identifying the Parts of Speech in Sentences

For each of the following sentences, identify each italicized word as a *noun,* an *adjective,* a *verb,* an *adverb,* a *pronoun,* a *preposition,* a *conjunction,* or an *interjection.*

1. In the late nineteenth century, many men *worked* as cowboys on *cattle* drives.
2. There *were few* comforts on the trail.
3. Some *improvement* came after *Charles Goodnight* put together the first chuck wagon.
4. A hinged lid swung *down* from the wagon to reveal a simple *but* complete kitchen.
5. The *first* chuck wagons were pulled *by* oxen.
6. *These* were later replaced by mules *or* horses.
7. *Most* of the cowhands who took part in the historic cattle drives remain *nameless.*
8. Cowboys were *instrumental* in opening trails that were later used by the men and women who *settled* the frontier.
9. *Railroads soon* began to crisscross the country; the cowboy was no longer needed to drive cattle.
10. *Hey!* Did you know that ranchers still hire *cowboys* to brand and herd cattle, repair fences, and do many other jobs?

B. Identifying the Parts of Speech in a Paragraph

Identify the part of speech of the italicized word or words in each sentence in the following paragraph.

[11] In the *thirty* years following the Civil War, millions of long-horn cattle were driven *over* long trails from ranches in Texas to railroads in Kansas. [12] During this *period,* the cowboy *became* an American hero. [13] Novels *and* magazine articles *glorified* life on the range. [14] The men *who* rode this rugged land, however, had to endure *many* hardships. [15] Cowboys spent most of their *time* in the saddle, rounding up strays and moving the herd *along.* [16] Caring for sick animals, repairing fences, and, *well,* doing what had to be done *were* all part of a normal working day. [17] At the end of such a day, each cow-

boy *not only* had to look after his horse *but also* had to cook dinner for *himself* and do a host of other chores. [**18**] The quiet *evenings* gave cowboys a chance to relax by telling stories and singing *campfire* songs. [**19**] Such details of trail life are *realistically* portrayed in the *popular* paintings of Charles M. Russell. [**20**] *Because of* these images and our need for a *truly* American hero, cowboys have become a colorful part of our history.

C. Identifying Pronouns in Sentences

Identify the pronouns in each sentence as *personal, reflexive, intensive, demonstrative, interrogative, relative,* or *indefinite.*

21. They delivered their supplies themselves.

22. One of the exchange students taught himself French.

23. A few shopped for gifts and decided to give these to Becca.

24. Who has been raking the leaves in the backyard?

25. Anybody who has done the homework could do this exercise.

D. Identifying Words as Nouns, Pronouns, or Adjectives

Tell whether each italicized word in the following paragraph is used as a *noun,* a *pronoun,* or an *adjective.* For each adjective, identify the word it modifies.

[**26**] Nearly *everybody* has heard a Strauss *waltz.* [**27**] The waltz is a form of *ballroom* dance that originated in *Germany* and *Austria* in the *eighteenth* century. [**28**] Johann Strauss was the most famous and, *some* say, the best *composer* of waltzes. [**29**] *He* was born in *Vienna,* the *capital* city of Austria, in 1825. [**30**] Strauss came from a *well-established* family of musicians. [**31**] *His* father and brothers Eduard and Josef were *respected* composers and conductors in their own right. [**32**] Johann toured with an *orchestra* for many years, but in 1870, when his *first* wife said *she* would like *him* to write operettas, he turned his attention to writing *music.* [**33**] His most famous compositions are Die Fledermaus (The Bat), an *operetta,* and "The Blue Danube" waltz, which later became *famous* as one of the *themes* of the 1968 movie 2001: A Space Odyssey. [**34**] Johann Strauss wrote more than *five hundred* orchestral compositions. [**35**] When he died in Vienna in 1899, his *worldwide* reputation as the *"Waltz King"* was assured.

E. Classifying Nouns

Identify each italicized noun in the following sentences as *proper* or *common* and *concrete* or *abstract*. Also, tell if a noun is *compound*.

36. On *Sunday,* the neighbor's dog barked all night.

37. To our *surprise,* the *zebras* cantered noisily across the path.

38. A painting that always gives me a feeling of *serenity* hangs in the *Metropolitan Museum of Art* in New York.

39. "As you know," said *Mr. Cima* proudly, *"knowledge* is *power."*

40. Seeking *solitude,* Kathryn hiked across the hills of *Connemara.*

Writing Application
Using Adjectives in a Poem

Vivid Adjectives   The Czech author Franz Kafka wrote a story about a man who becomes an insect! Imagine that you are changed into an animal or an object. Using at least ten carefully chosen adjectives, write a poem describing your changed self.

Prewriting   Select an object or an animal that you think you would like to be. Next, freewrite descriptive words about the object or animal. You may want to consult an article in an encyclopedia for additional details or pictures of your chosen topic.

Writing   As you write your first draft, concentrate on using the most vivid adjectives that you have listed.

Revising   Read through your first draft, and underline each adjective. For each one, ask yourself whether any other word more precisely describes the noun or pronoun. Be sure that you have used at least ten different adjectives.

Publishing   Check your poem to make sure that all words are spelled correctly, especially any adjectives that you do not use very often in writing. Then, proofread your poem for any errors in grammar and punctuation. Your class may want to share poems by reading them aloud or displaying them on a bulletin board.

The Parts of a Sentence

Subjects, Predicates, Complements

Diagnostic Preview

A. Identifying Subjects, Verbs, and Complements

Identify each of the italicized words and word groups in the following sentences as a *subject*, a *verb*, a *predicate adjective*, a *predicate nominative*, a *direct object*, or an *indirect object*.

EXAMPLE   **1.** Robotics is the *science* or *technology* of robots.

          1. *science—predicate nominative; technology— predicate nominative*

1. Have *you* ever met a robot?
2. In the field of robotics, scientists have built vastly complex *robots.*
3. Today, these machines *are put* to work in factories, laboratories, and outer space.
4. How were these complex *machines* first used?
5. There are a *number* of interesting early examples of robots at work.
6. One of the first robots was a mechanical *figure* in a clock tower.
7. It raised a hammer and struck a *bell* every hour.
8. At the 1939 New York World's Fair, Elektro and Sparko were very popular *attractions.*
9. Elektro was *tall,* more than seven feet high.
10. Electric motors gave *Elektro* power for a variety of amazing tricks.

11. Sparko was Elektro's *dog.*

12. Sparko *could bark* and even *wag* his tail.

13. Today, *some* of the simplest robots are drones in laboratories.

14. Basically, drones are *extensions* of the human arm.

15. They can be *useful* in many different ways.

B. Classifying Sentences According to Purpose

Punctuate each of the following sentences with an appropriate end mark. Then, classify the sentence as *declarative, interrogative, imperative,* or *exclamatory.*

EXAMPLE   **1.** There's a twenty-five-foot robot named Beetle

             1. There's a twenty-five-foot robot named Beetle.— declarative

16. Can you picture a robot twenty-five feet tall

17. Step up and say hello to Beetle

18. Perhaps you have heard of CAM, an even more advanced robot

19. It can travel on long legs across rough terrain as rapidly as thirty-five miles per hour

20. What an amazing creation it is

What Is a Sentence?

In conversation, people can often leave out part of a sentence without confusing their listeners. In formal writing and speaking, though, it is usually better to use complete sentences. They help to make meaning clear to your audience.

2a. A *sentence* is a word group that contains a subject and a verb and that expresses a complete thought.

A *sentence fragment* is a word or word group that is capitalized and punctuated as a sentence but that does not contain both a subject and a verb or that does not express a complete thought.

SENTENCE FRAGMENT	The magazine's essay contest for tenth-grade American history students. [no verb]
SENTENCE	The magazine's essay contest for tenth-grade American history students ends Tuesday.

Reference Note

For information on how to correct **sentence fragments,** see page 446.

COMPUTER TIP

Many style-checking soft-
ware programs can help
you identify sentence fragments. If you have access to
such a program, use it to
help evaluate your writing.

Reference Note

For more about the
understood subject,
see page 45.

SENTENCE FRAGMENT	Was chosen as the best one from over two thousand entries. [no subject]
SENTENCE	Her essay was chosen as the best one from over two thousand entries.
SENTENCE FRAGMENT	When the judges announced the winner. [not a complete thought]
SENTENCE	When the judges announced the winner, everyone applauded.

NOTE Some sentences contain an understood subject (you).

EXAMPLES [You] Wait!

[You] Hold on to the reins.

Oral Practice **Identifying Sentences and
Sentence Fragments**

Read the following word groups aloud. Then, identify each word
group as a *sentence* or a *sentence fragment.* Be prepared to explain
your answers.

EXAMPLES
1. Willa Cather wrote poetry, fiction, and nonfiction.
1. *sentence*

2. Grew up in the Midwest.
2. *sentence fragment*

—HELP—

Example 1 of
the Oral Practice contains
a subject and verb and
expresses a complete
thought. Example 2 does
not contain a subject and
does not express a com-
plete thought.

1. Willa Cather was born in Back Creek Valley in northern Virginia.
2. In 1883, when she was nine years old.
3. Her family moved to the treeless prairie of Nebraska.
4. She tracked buffalo and col-
lected prairie flowers.
5. Fascinated by the wild and
rolling plains.
6. Listening to the stories of
neighboring settlers.
7. They told memorable tales
about the harsh struggles
of the homesteaders.
8. After she graduated from high
school in the village of Red
Cloud, Nebraska.

9. The picture of Red Cloud on the previous page shows shops and people that would have been familiar to Willa Cather.
10. And the Opera House at the end of the street where Cather and her classmates graduated in 1890.
11. In college, Willa Cather discovered her talent for writing.
12. Contributing stories and reviews to local newspapers.
13. At first, her writing failed to reach a wide audience.
14. She succeeded in establishing herself as a writer.
15. After years earning a living as a schoolteacher and an editor in New York City.
16. Although Cather enjoyed living in New York.
17. She never lost touch with the sights and sounds of her childhood.
18. She describes how farmers turned the open plains into orderly fields of wheat and corn.
19. In *O Pioneers!*, her second novel.
20. In a later novel, *My Ántonia*, the immigrant neighbors of her childhood play prominent roles.

Subjects and Predicates

2b. Sentences consist of two basic parts: subjects and predicates.

The *subject* tells whom or what the sentence or clause is about, and the *predicate* tells something about the subject.

Notice in the following examples that the subject may come before or after the predicate or between parts of the predicate.

SUBJECT	PREDICATE
Some residents of the desert	can survive a long drought.

PREDICATE	SUBJECT
Particularly noteworthy is	the Australian frog.

PREDICATE	SUBJECT	PREDICATE
For up to three years	it	can live without rainfall.

PREDICATE	SUBJECT	PREDICATE
How can	an animal	survive that long?

In each example above, all the words labeled *subject* make up the **complete subject**; all the words labeled *predicate* make up the **complete predicate**.

┌─HELP─┐

In Exercise 1,
the subject may appear
anywhere in a sentence.

Exercise 1 Identifying Subjects and Predicates

Identify the complete subject and the complete predicate in each of the following sentences.

EXAMPLE
1. When was the precious metal platinum discovered?

1. complete subject—the precious metal platinum
   complete predicate—When was discovered

1. People from a variety of countries have been credited with the discovery of platinum.
2. Spanish explorers in search of gold supposedly discovered this precious metal in the rivers of South America.
3. However, the explorers considered it a worthless, inferior form of silver.
4. Their name for platinum was *platina,* meaning "little silver."
5. Back into the river went the little balls of platinum!
6. The platinum might then become gold, according to one amazing theory.
7. Europeans later mixed platinum with gold.
8. This mixture encouraged the production of counterfeit gold bars and coins.
9. Platinum commands a high price today because of its resistance to corrosion.
10. Such diverse products as jet planes and jewelry may include platinum in some form.

The Subject

2c. The main word or word group that tells whom or what the sentence is about is called the *simple subject*.

The *complete subject* consists of the simple subject and any words or word groups that modify the simple subject.

EXAMPLES   A dog with this pedigree is usually nervous.

Complete subject   A dog with this pedigree

Simple subject   dog

Both of these cockatiels are for sale.

Complete subject   Both of these cockatiels

Simple subject   Both

The Taj Mahal in India is one of the most beautiful buildings in the world.

Complete subject   The Taj Mahal in India
Simple subject   Taj Mahal

Reference Note

A compound noun, such as *Taj Mahal,* functions as a single unit. For more about **compound nouns,** see page 4.

NOTE In this book, the term *subject* usually refers to the simple subject unless otherwise indicated.

The Predicate

2d. The *simple predicate,* or *verb,* is the main word or word group that tells something about the subject.

The *complete predicate* consists of the verb and all the words that modify the verb and complete its meaning.

EXAMPLES   Spiders snare their prey in intricate webs.

Complete predicate   snare their prey in intricate webs
Simple predicate   snare

Rosa has been looking for you all morning.

Complete predicate   has been looking for you all morning
Simple predicate   has been looking

Have my keys been found?

Complete predicate   Have been found
Simple predicate   Have been found

Notice in the preceding examples that the simple predicate may be identical to the complete predicate. Also, the simple predicate may be a one-word verb or a *verb phrase* (a main verb and one or more helping verbs).

Commonly Used Helping Verbs				
am	did	has	might	was
are	do	have	must	were
can	does	is	shall	will
could	had	may	should	would

Reference Note

For more about **verbs** and **verb phrases,** see page 15.

TIPS & TRICKS

When you are identifying the simple predicate in a sentence, be sure to include all parts of a verb phrase.

EXAMPLE
Should Dad have painted the walls light gray? [The simple predicate is the verb phrase *Should have painted.*]

NOTE In this book, the term *verb* usually refers to the simple predicate unless otherwise indicated.

GRAMMAR

2
c, d

Identifying Verbs and Verb Phrases in Sentences

Identify the verb in each of the following sentences. Be sure to include all parts of any verb phrases.

EXAMPLE   1. The giant panda of China is considered an endangered species.

            1. *is considered*

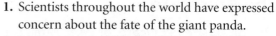

1. Scientists throughout the world have expressed concern about the fate of the giant panda.
2. In recent years this animal's natural habitat has slowly become smaller.
3. Many forests of bamboo, the panda's favorite food, have died.
4. A panda like the one in the picture on this page may devour as much as forty pounds of bamboo daily.
5. However, each tender green shoot of bamboo contains only a very small amount of nutrients.
6. In addition, the large but sluggish panda is not known as a successful hunter.
7. In their concern for the panda's survival, scientists are now studying the habits of this animal.
8. A captured panda is held in a log trap for several hours.
9. During this time, scientists attach a radio to the panda's neck.
10. The radio sends the scientists valuable information about the animal's behavior in the wild.

Finding the Subject

To find the subject of a sentence, find the verb first. Then, ask *Who?* or *What?* before the verb.

EXAMPLES   My cousin from Finland will arrive this afternoon. [The verb is *will arrive*. Who will arrive? *Cousin* will arrive. *Cousin* is the subject.]

            On the other side of the brook stands a cabin. [The verb is *stands*. What stands? *Cabin* stands. *Cabin* is the subject.]

Exercise 3 **Identifying Subjects and Verbs**

Identify the subject and the verb in each of the following sentences.
Be sure to include all parts of any verb phrases.

EXAMPLE   **1.** Our science class has been studying the migratory flights
of different species of butterflies.

    1. subject—class; verb—has been studying

1. Despite their fragile appearance, butterflies have a great deal
   of stamina.
2. They often fly more than one thousand miles during migration.
3. The painted lady butterfly, for example, has been seen in the
   middle of the Atlantic Ocean.
4. In fact, this species was once spotted over the Arctic Circle.
5. During the spring, millions of these insects flutter across
   North America.
6. Huge flocks of colorful butterflies fly from their winter home in
   New Mexico to places as far north as Newfoundland, Canada.
7. The brilliant orange-and-black monarch butterfly flies south each
   September from Canada toward Florida, Texas, and California.
8. The migratory flight of the monarch may cover a distance
   of close to two thousand miles.
9. Every winter for the past several decades, monarchs have
   gathered in a small forest not far from San Francisco.
10. The thick clusters of their blazing orange wings make this forest
    very popular with tourists.

2e. **The subject of a verb is never in a prepositional phrase.**

A ***prepositional phrase*** consists of a preposition, the object of the
preposition, and any modifiers of that object.

EXAMPLES   for the team   of mine   through the years

    on the top shelf   at all times   along with my niece

Do not mistake a noun or pronoun in a prepositional phrase for
the subject of a sentence.

EXAMPLES   One of my cousins has visited Ghana. [Who has visited? *One*
has visited. *Of my cousins* is a prepositional phrase.]

    On top of the building is an up-to-date observatory. [What
is? *Observatory* is. *On top* and *of the building* are
prepositional phrases.]

Reference Note

For more information
about **prepositional
phrases,** see page 65.

HELP

Remember,
the subject is never in a
prepositional phrase.

Exercise 4 Identifying Subjects and Verbs

Identify the subject and the verb in each of the following sentences.

EXAMPLE
1. How much do you know about the Chinese experience in the United States?

1. subject—*you*
   verb—*do know*

1. The people in this picture are celebrating the arrival of the New Year in accordance with an ancient Chinese tradition.
2. These festivities, however, are occurring in the United States.
3. The Chinese New Year celebration, with its dragon parades and festive decorations, is a colorful addition to American culture.
4. In the 1850s, the earliest Chinese immigrants came to the United States for jobs in the gold mines and on the railroads.
5. At first, only men could immigrate.
6. Not until much later could they send home to China for their wives and sweethearts.
7. As a result, not until the 1920s did the close-knit society of America's Chinatowns develop.
8. Have you read about the experience of Chinese immigrants in America?
9. I recommend the book *Longtime Californ': A Documentary Study of an American Chinatown.*
10. In this book, Victor G. Nee and Brett de Bary Nee trace the history of Chinese immigration to the United States and the development of the Chinese American community in San Francisco.

Exercise 5 > Completing Sentences by Supplying Complete Predicates

Finish each of the following sentences by adding a complete predicate. Then, underline the simple subject once and the verb twice.

EXAMPLE   **1.** One of the horses _____.

1. *One of the horses has escaped from the corral.*

1. Those lions _____.
2. A white fence _____.
3. The surf _____.
4. The road by my house _____.
5. Students in our school _____.
6. The school bus _____.
7. The nine-year-old dog _____.
8. Sitting in innertubes, the tourists _____.
9. The stone wall _____.
10. Last month _____.

Review A > Identifying Complete Subjects, Complete Predicates, Simple Subjects, and Verbs

Identify the complete subject and the complete predicate in each sentence in the following paragraph. Then, underline the simple subject once and the verb twice.

EXAMPLE   **[1]** For what is Benjamin Banneker best remembered?

1. *complete subject—Benjamin Banneker*
   complete predicate—For what is best remembered

[1] Benjamin Banneker (1731–1806) was born near Baltimore, Maryland, of a free mother and an enslaved father. [2] Considered free, Banneker could attend an integrated private school. [3] There he began his lifelong study of science and math. [4] Despite having only an eighth-grade education, this young man became a noteworthy astronomer and mathematician. [5] His astronomical research led to his acclaimed pre- diction of the solar eclipse of 1789. [6] A few years later, the first of his almanacs was published. [7] Banneker's almanacs contained tide tables and data on future eclipses. [8] Some bits of practical advice, as well as famous sayings, were also included. [9] These popular almanacs came out every year for more than a decade. [10] In addition to his scientific discoveries, Banneker is known for his work as a surveyor during the planning of Washington, D.C.

TIPS & TRICKS

In many sentences, you can find the subject and the verb more easily if you first cross out any prepositional phrases.

EXAMPLE
The team ~~with the best record~~ will play ~~in the state tournament~~.
Subject   team
Verb   will play

Sentences Beginning with *There* or *Here*

The word *there* or *here* may begin a sentence, but it is almost never the subject. Often, *there* or *here* is used as an adverb telling *where*.

EXAMPLES   There are your **gloves.** [What are? *Gloves* are. *Gloves* is the subject. *There* tells where your gloves are.]

Here is my **nephew.** [Who is? *Nephew* is. *Nephew* is the subject. *Here* tells where my nephew is.]

NOTE   Sometimes, *there* begins a sentence but does not tell *where.* In this use, *there* is not an adverb but an **expletive**—a word that fills out the structure of a sentence but does not add to the meaning.

EXAMPLE   There is not much **time** left. [What is left? *Time* is left. *Time* is the subject. *There* does not add any meaning to the sentence, which may be rewritten without *there: Not much time is left.*]

Sentences Asking Questions

Questions usually begin with a verb, a helping verb, or a word such as *what, when, where, how,* or *why.* In most cases, the subject follows the verb or part of the verb phrase.

EXAMPLES   Where is your **parakeet**?

Did **you** make the team?

In a question that begins with a helping verb, such as *Did you make the team?,* the subject generally comes between the helping verb and the main verb. To find the subject in any question, however, turn the question into a statement, find the verb, and then ask *Who?* or *What?* before the verb.

EXAMPLES   Were your friends early?
                    becomes
             Your friends were early.
             [Who were? *Friends* were. *Friends* is the subject.]

             Where did the horses cross the river?
                    becomes
             The horses did cross the river where.
             [What did cross? *Horses* did. *Horses* is the subject.]

Identifying Subjects and Verbs

Identify the subject and the verb in each of the following sentences.

EXAMPLE　　**1.** There are several thousand asteroids in our solar system.

　　　　　1. subject—asteroids
　　　　　　verb—are

1. There were three questions on the final exam.
2. Here is my topic for the term paper.
3. What did you choose for a topic?
4. Will everyone be ready at eleven o'clock?
5. There will be a study-group meeting tomorrow.
6. When should we go to the library?
7. There were very few books on the subject.
8. Have you outlined the next chapter?
9. Where will our conference be held?
10. Are there many magazine articles about Nelson Mandela?

The Understood Subject

In a request or a command, the subject is usually not stated. In such sentences, *you* is the **understood subject**.

REQUEST　　**[You]** Please rake the yard.
COMMAND　**[You]** Pick up the fallen branches.

When a request or command includes a name, the name is not the subject but a **noun of direct address.** *You* is still the understood subject.

EXAMPLE　　Jason, **[you]** wash the dishes.

Compound Subjects and Compound Verbs

2f. A *compound subject* consists of two or more subjects that are joined by a conjunction and that have the same verb.

The parts of a compound subject are generally joined by the coordinating conjunction *and* or *or.*

EXAMPLES　　**Mr. Olivero** and his **daughter** planted the garden. [Who planted? *Mr. Olivero* and *daughter* planted.]

　　　　　Either **Mr. Olivero** or his **daughter** planted the garden. [The two parts of the compound subject are *Mr. Olivero* and *daughter.*]

Reference Note

For information on using commas with **nouns of direct address,** see page 310.

2g. A *compound verb* consists of two or more verbs that are joined by a conjunction and that have the same subject.

The parts of a compound verb are usually joined by the coordinating conjunction *and, but,* or *or.*

EXAMPLES   At the street festival, we **danced** the rumba and **sampled** the meat pies.

I **have written** the letter and **addressed** the envelope but **have** not **gone** to the post office yet.

Both the subject and the verb of a sentence may be compound.

EXAMPLE   Yesterday, **Jamal** and **I built** a box kite and **painted** it bright yellow and green.

NOTE   There are other cases in which a sentence may contain more than one subject and verb.

	S	V
COMPOUND SENTENCE	The unification of Italy in 1861 was a victory for Giuseppe Garibaldi,	

	S	V
	and the event ended centuries of civil strife.	

	S	V	S
COMPLEX SENTENCE	After the painter finished his self-portrait, he		

	V	V
	went out and ate dinner.	

Exercise 7   Identifying Subjects and Verbs

Identify the subject(s) and the verb(s) in each of the following sentences. If the subject is understood, write *(You).*

EXAMPLE   1. Sarah, please sweep the porch and water the plants.

   1. *subject—(You)*

        verbs—sweep, water

1. Jackets and ties are required in that restaurant.
2. Do any bears or wildcats live in these woods?
3. On our math test, Ann and Mark scored the highest.
4. Bring both a pencil and a pen to the history exam.
5. Miguel neither sings nor plays an instrument.
6. Where do you and Liz buy CDs?

7. The front and back tires are low and need air.
8. Play ball!
9. Humor and wisdom are often used in folk sayings.
10. Either Bill or Jan may stay and help us.

Exercise 8 **Completing Sentences by Supplying Subjects and Predicates**

Complete each of the sentences below with an appropriate complete subject or complete predicate. Underline the subject of each sentence once, and underline the verb twice.

EXAMPLE   **1.** Usually, the _____ leaves on time.

    1. Usually, the northbound <u>train</u> <u>leaves</u> on time.

1. _____ pull sleighs through the snow.
2. Houseplants _____ sunlight.
3. Several of the football players _____ the new sports drink.
4. After sunset, the neighbor's dog _____ .
5. During daylight savings time, Don and Beth _____ their bikes after work.
6. _____ arrive every weekday.
7. The _____ of Congress voted against the bill.
8. _____ enjoyed the beautiful day.
9. Unsure of the correct direction, he _____ the map.
10. _____ laughed.

Review B **Identifying Subjects and Verbs**

Identify the subject(s) and the verb(s) in each of the following sentences. If the subject is understood, write *(You)*.

EXAMPLE   **1.** Most birds and many insects can fly.

    1. subjects—birds, insects
    verb—can fly

1. How do birds fly?
2. Their wings lift and push them through the air.
3. Look carefully at an insect's wings.
4. Most have two sets of wings.
5. The pair in front covers the pair in back.
6. Other animals can move through the air without flying.
7. The flying fish swims fast and leaps out of the water.
8. How does the flying squirrel glide from tree to tree?

9. There are flaps of skin between its legs.
10. Because of its webbed feet, the flying frog can make long, gliding leaps through the air.

Complements

2h. A *complement* is a word or word group that completes the meaning of a verb.

A group of words may have a subject and a verb and still not express a complete thought. Notice how the boldface complements complete the meanings of the verbs in the following examples.

EXAMPLES
           S V   C
           That book is an **autobiography.**

           S V   C
           Bob felt **confident.**

           S V   C
           Joey hit a **home run.**

          V S V C   C
          Did you send **her** a birthday **card**?

          S V   C
          This is **what I want.**

A complement may be compound.

EXAMPLES
           S   V   C   C
           Sandra Cisneros writes **poetry** and **fiction.**

          V S V   C   C   C
          Did you buy paper **plates, cups,** and **napkins**?

A complement may be a noun, a pronoun, or an adjective.

EXAMPLES
           S V   C
           Tino wants a new tennis **racket.** [noun]

            S   V   C
           Aunt Sophie watched **us** fishing. [pronoun]

            S   V   C
           The elephants in the safari park appear **happy.** [adjective]

Do not mistake an adverb for a complement.

ADVERBS   At the next intersection, should we turn right? [*Right* tells *where* we should turn.]

Lucy works hard. [*Hard* tells *how* Lucy works.]

COMPLEMENTS   You have the **right** to express your opinion. [*Right,* a noun, completes the meaning of the verb *have.*]

These pears are **hard.** [*Hard,* an adjective, completes the meaning of the verb *are.*]

Complements are never in prepositional phrases.

EXAMPLES   Christopher quoted from the poem. [*Poem* is part of the prepositional phrase *from the poem.*]

Christopher quoted the **poem.** [*Poem* is the complement.]

Reference Note

For more about **adverbs,** see pages 20 and 212.

Reference Note

For more about **prepositional phrases,** see page 65.

Reference Note

For information about **independent** and **subordinate clauses,** see Chapter 4.

NOTE   Both independent and subordinate clauses contain subjects and verbs and may contain complements.

                S   V   C

EXAMPLES   Although **he appeared sluggish** at the start,

             S   V   C

Ricardo won the **race.**

             S V   C   S   V   C

Josie is an **engineer who designs** computer **hardware.**

Exercise 9   Writing Sentences with Subjects, Verbs, and Complements

Construct ten sentences from the following groups of sentence parts. Add more than only a word or two to each group.

	SUBJECT	VERB	COMPLEMENT
EXAMPLES	**1.** pilot	flew	mission

1. *The pilot flew a scouting mission over the area.*

2. baby   became · sleepy

2. *The baby became sleepy after her bath.*

Subject	Verb	Complement
1. cyclists	planned	trip
2. musicians	performed	duet

(continued)

Subject	Verb	Complement
3. speaker	looked	enthusiastic
4. dancer	tapped	rhythm
5. novel	is	suspenseful
6. Dennis	became	president
7. tambourine	sounds	funny
8. prime minister	gave	speech
9. raccoon	ate	banana peels
10. Girl Scout	built	fire

Exercise 10 Identifying Subjects, Verbs, and Complements

Identify the subject(s) and the verb(s) in the following sentences. Then, identify any complement(s) the sentence contains.

EXAMPLE
1. Have you ever seen the effects of hurricane winds?

1. *subject—you*
   verb—Have seen
   complement—effects

1. A hurricane is a powerful storm, often measuring two or three hundred miles in diameter.
2. Such storms are notorious for their destructive power.
3. To be classified as a hurricane, a storm must have winds of at least seventy-four miles per hour.
4. These winds swirl around the *eye,* an area of calm in the center of the storm.
5. *Wall clouds* surround the eye of a hurricane.
6. Within these clouds the strongest winds and heaviest rain of the storm occur.
7. The winds and rain, along with the force of the sea, often produce enormous waves.
8. In a storm surge, tides rise well above normal.
9. Huge waves produce floods.
10. In fact, most hurricane-related deaths result from drowning in floods.

The Subject Complement

2i. A *subject complement* is a word or word group that completes the meaning of a linking verb and identifies or modifies the subject.

EXAMPLES We may be the only **ones** here. [*Ones,* a pronoun, completes the meaning of the linking verb *may be* and identifies the subject *We.*]

Randy seems **worried**. [*Worried,* an adjective, completes the meaning of the linking verb *seems* and modifies the subject *Randy.*]

Did you know that Lani is a soccer **player**? [In the noun clause *that Lani is a soccer player, player,* a noun, completes the meaning of the linking verb *is* and identifies the subject *Lani.*]

A subject complement may consist of more than one word.

EXAMPLES Michelangelo's full name was **Michelangelo di Lodovico Buonarroti Simoni.** [*Michelangelo di Lodovico Buonarroti Simoni,* a compound noun, completes the meaning of the linking verb *was* and identifies the subject *name.*]

A ring with her birthstone is **what she wants for her birthday.** [*What she wants for her birthday,* a noun clause, completes the meaning of the linking verb *is* and identifies the subject *ring.*]

NOTE Subject complements complete the meanings of linking verbs only. A word that completes the meaning of an action verb is generally a direct object or an indirect object.

There are two kinds of subject complements: the *predicate nominative* and the *predicate adjective.*

(1) A *predicate nominative* is a word or word group that is in the predicate and that identifies the subject or refers to it.

EXAMPLES Some caterpillars become **butterflies.** [*Butterflies* identifies the subject *caterpillars.*]

The winners should have been **they.** [*They* refers to the subject *winners.*]

She is the next **speaker.** [*Speaker* refers to the subject *She.*]

Reference Note

For lists of commonly used **linking verbs,** see page 17. For more about **compound nouns,** see page 4. For a discussion of **noun clauses,** see Chapter 4.

Reference Note

For more about **direct objects** and **indirect objects,** see pages 54 and 55.

STYLE TIP

The use of the nominative case pronoun, as in the sentence *The winners should have been they,* is uncommon in everyday speech. You will often hear such expressions as *That's him* and *It is her.* In formal English, however, you should use the nominative case pronoun in such expressions: *That's* **he** and *It is* **she.**

Reference Note

For more about the **cases of pronouns,** see Chapter 6.

A predicate nominative may be compound.

EXAMPLE   Our cats' names are **Bianca** and **Henry**. [*Bianca* and *Henry* identify the subject *names*.]

A predicate nominative may precede the subject and the verb.

EXAMPLE   What a fine **speaker** you are! [*Speaker* identifies the subject *you*.]

(2) A *predicate adjective* is an adjective that is in the predicate and that modifies the subject of a sentence or a clause.

EXAMPLES   You look **happy**. [*Happy* modifies the subject *You*.]

        When she left, Norma appeared **calm**. [*Calm* modifies the subject *Norma*.]

A predicate adjective may be compound.

EXAMPLE   He said that the yogurt tasted **sweet** and **creamy**. [*Sweet* and *creamy* modify *yogurt*, the subject of the subordinate clause *that the yogurt tasted sweet and creamy*.]

A predicate adjective may precede the subject and the verb.

EXAMPLE   How **silly** that commercial is! [*Silly* modifies the subject *commercial*.]

Exercise 11   Identifying Predicate Nominatives and Predicate Adjectives

Identify the subject complements in the following sentences. Then, tell whether each complement is a *predicate nominative* or a *predicate adjective*.

EXAMPLE   1. Kimchi is a spicy Korean dish of pickled cabbage and peppers.

        1. *dish—predicate nominative*

1. The last scene of the play is very intense.
2. Those two small birds are finches.
3. The music sounded lively.
4. It is difficult to choose a winner when each contestant's costume looks so elegant.
5. My goldfish Alonzo grows larger every day.
6. Andrea's report on digital recording is a highly technical one.
7. When did Uncas become a chief of the Mohegans?
8. Your solution to this algebra problem is clever.

┌HELP────

Do not assume that every adjective in the predicate is a predicate adjective. Remember that a predicate adjective modifies only the subject.

EXAMPLES
  This antique clock is **valuable**. [The adjective *valuable* is a predicate adjective because it modifies the subject *clock*.]

  This antique clock is a valuable timepiece. [The adjective *valuable* is not a predicate adjective. It modifies the predicate nominative *timepiece*, not the subject *clock*.]

┌HELP────

Some sentences in Exercise 11 have more than one subject complement.

9. We felt content after we had eaten Thanksgiving dinner.

10. The setting of the story is a Spanish castle that looks old and deserted.

Review C Identifying Subjects, Verbs, and Subject Complements

Each of the following sentences contains at least one subject complement. Identify each subject, verb, and subject complement. Make a chart like the following one, and fill in the correct words.

EXAMPLE   **1.** Jazz was originally the music of African Americans.

SUBJECT	VERB	SUBJECT COMPLEMENT
1. Jazz	was	music

1. The style of 1920s musicians, such as Jelly Roll Morton, was smooth.

2. With the development of swing, the rhythm of jazz became more regular.

3. Practitioners of swing became known for their solo improvisation.

4. Billie Holiday was one of those practitioners.

5. She became the greatest singer in the history of jazz.

6. A typically American musical form, jazz was the sound of Louis Armstrong, "Count" Basie, Scott Joplin, and Ella Fitzgerald.

7. Created in the early twentieth century, jazz is a blend of elements from African and European music, but its irregular, or syncopated, rhythms are strictly African.

8. Early jazz was a combination of the cakewalk, a dance that was popular with many African Americans in the 1800s, and ragtime, which was mainly instrumental music.

9. After 1917, when jazz phonograph records became popular, the future of jazz appeared bright.

10. People remain fascinated by jazz, perhaps because it sounds new with each playing.

The Object of a Verb

An *object of a verb* is a complement that, unlike a subject complement, does not identify or modify the subject. An object of a verb is a noun, pronoun, or word group that completes the meaning of a *transitive verb*—a verb that expresses an action directed toward a person, a place, a thing, or an idea.

┌HELP┐

A sentence in Review C may have more than one subject, verb, and subject complement.

Reference Note

For more about **transitive verbs,** see page 19.

GRAMMAR

EXAMPLES   The cat was chasing a **moth.** [*Moth* completes the meaning of the transitive verb *was chasing*.]

Jeff's mother gave **him** some **grapes.** [*Him* and *grapes* complete the meaning of the transitive verb *gave*.]

Kevin and I enjoy **playing** chess. [*Playing,* a gerund, completes the meaning of the transitive verb *enjoy*.]

An object of a verb may consist of more than one word.

Reference Note

For more about **compound nouns,** see page 4. For more about **noun clauses,** see Chapter 4.

EXAMPLES   The journalist interviewed the **Secretary of State.** [*Secretary of State,* a compound noun, completes the meaning of the transitive verb *interviewed*.]

Do you know **what this is**? [*What this is,* a noun clause, completes the meaning of the transitive verb *Do know*.]

NOTE   Objects of verbs, like other kinds of complements, can appear in subordinate clauses as well as independent clauses.

EXAMPLE   After she had read **us** the **story,** the teacher gave **us** a **quiz** on it. [*Us* and *story* complete the meaning of *had read* in the subordinate clause. *Us* and *quiz* complete the meaning of *gave* in the independent clause.]

Two kinds of objects of verbs are *direct objects* and *indirect objects.*

2j. A *direct object* is a noun, pronoun, or word group that tells *who* or *what* receives the action of a transitive verb or shows the result of the action.

A direct object answers the question *Whom?* or *What?* after a transitive verb.

EXAMPLES   I took my little **sister** to the parade. [I took whom? *Sister.*]

She loved **the colorful floats.** [She loved what? *The colorful floats.*]

A direct object may be compound.

EXAMPLE   The parrot said **"Good morning"** and **"Cat free to good home."** [The parrot said what? *"Good morning"* and *"Cat free to good home."*]

A direct object may precede the subject and verb.

EXAMPLE   What remarkable **tricks** the illusionist performed! [The illusionist performed what? *Tricks.*]

Direct objects are never found in prepositional phrases.

EXAMPLES   Tom was driving in his car. [*Car* is part of the prepositional phrase *in his car.* The sentence has no direct object.]

Tom was driving his **car.** [*Car* is the direct object.]

Exercise 12 **Identifying Verbs and Their Direct Objects**

Identify the verbs and the direct objects in the following sentences.

EXAMPLE   1. My parents recently bought a 35-mm camera.

1. *verb—bought; direct object—camera*

1. I borrowed my parents' new camera.
2. First, I loaded the film into the camera.
3. Then, I set the shutter speed.
4. I focused the camera on a distant object.
5. I could read the shutter speed in the viewfinder.
6. A flashing red light signals an incorrect setting.
7. Slowly and carefully, I pressed the button.
8. I then advanced the film for the next shot.
9. By the end of the day, I had snapped thirty-six pictures.
10. Have you ever taken photographs?

2k. An ***indirect object*** **is a noun, pronoun, or word group that often appears in sentences containing direct objects. An indirect. object tells** *to whom* **or** *to what* **(or** *for whom* **or** *for what***) the action of a transitive verb is done.**

EXAMPLES   Meli read **us** her poem. [Meli read her poem to whom? *Us.*]

I fed the **horses** some oats. [I fed oats to what? *Horses.*]

Juan left **you** this message. [Juan left this message for whom? *You.*]

Carly knitted her pet **dachshund** a blanket. [Carly knitted a blanket for what? *Dachshund.*]

If the word *to* or *for* is used, the noun or pronoun following it is part of a prepositional phrase and cannot be an indirect object.

PREPOSITIONAL   Jeff wrote a note to me. [*Me* is part of the
        PHRASE   prepositional phrase *to me.*]

        INDIRECT   Jeff wrote **me** a note. [*Me* is the indirect
        OBJECT   object.]

┌─HELP─

An indirect object generally comes between a verb and a direct object.

┌─HELP─

When identifying complements, check first to see whether the verbs in the sentences are action or linking verbs. Remember that only action verbs may have direct objects and indirect objects and that only linking verbs may have predicate nominatives and predicate adjectives.

An indirect object may be compound.

EXAMPLE   Our ski instructor gave **Lucia** and **me** great tips. [Our ski instructor gave tips to whom? *Lucia* and *me*.]

Exercise 13 Identifying Direct and Indirect Objects

Identify the direct objects and indirect objects in the following sentences. Not all sentences contain indirect objects.

EXAMPLE   1. His athleticism has earned Leroy many awards.

           1. *direct object—awards; indirect object—Leroy*

1. Last summer, Leroy told us his plans for the future.
2. He wants a place on the U.S. swim team in the next Olympic games.
3. Of course, this goal demands hours of hard practice.
4. Every day, Leroy swims one hundred laps in the college pool and works out with weights for an hour.
5. Such intense training could limit his social activities.
6. With his rigorous schedule, Leroy doesn't have much time to spend with friends.
7. However, we all understand and give him much encouragement and support.
8. We can't teach him the fine points of competitive swimming.
9. His coach does that.
10. Maybe we'll see Leroy at the next Olympics!

Review D Identifying Sentences, Fragments, Subjects, Verbs, and Complements

Identify each of the following word groups as a *sentence* or a *sentence fragment*. If a word group is a sentence, identify its subject(s) and verb(s). If a sentence has a complement, label the complement as a *predicate adjective*, a *predicate nominative*, a *direct object*, or an *indirect object*.

EXAMPLE   1. Will you be attending the Cinco de Mayo celebration?

           1. *sentence; subject—you; verb—Will be attending; direct object—celebration*

1. Has the planning committee announced the date of the school carnival?
2. Perhaps next week.
3. Linda gave us a summary of her science project.
4. It was long and interesting.

MEETING THE CHALLENGE

Dr. Martin Luther King, Jr., wrote a speech titled "I Have a Dream." What is your dream? Write at least one paragraph describing a goal or dream. Include at least ten complements in your paragraph, and underline each.

5. Books and papers covered the desk and spilled onto the floor.
6. Although it was well written.
7. One of those dogs is not very obedient.
8. Ming Chin gave the children a handful of oatmeal cookies.
9. Kim, Juan, and Tracey were winners at the track meet last Saturday.
10. How happy they were!

Classifying Sentences by Purpose

2l. Depending on its purpose, a sentence may be classified as *declarative, imperative, interrogative,* or *exclamatory.*

(1) A *declarative sentence* makes a statement and ends with a period.

EXAMPLES   Toni Morrison won the Nobel Prize for literature in 1993.

Although we were tired after working all day, we still wanted to go dancing.

(2) An *imperative sentence* gives a command or makes a request. Most imperative sentences end with a period. A strong command ends with an exclamation point.

EXAMPLES   Be careful. [mild command]

Please open the window. [request]

Wait! [strong command]

Notice in the examples above that a command or a request has the understood subject *you.*

(3) An *interrogative sentence* asks a question and ends with a question mark.

EXAMPLES   Can you speak Spanish?

Did you say that you were taking French?

(4) An *exclamatory sentence* shows excitement or expresses strong feeling and ends with an exclamation point.

EXAMPLES   What beautiful fabric this is!

That roller coaster is awesome!

Reference Note

For a discussion of how **sentences** are **classified by structure,** see page 102. For more on **end marks,** see Chapter 11.

STYLE   **TIP**

Sometimes a writer will use both a question mark and an exclamation point to express the combined emotions of disbelief and surprise.

EXAMPLE
"How could you have said that?!" she gasped.

You should limit the use of such combined punctuation to informal writing and dialogue.

NOTE Any sentence may be spoken so that it becomes exclamatory or interrogative. When writing dialogue, use an exclamation point or a question mark to show how you intend a sentence to be read.

EXAMPLES   "It's snowing**.**" [declarative]

"It's snowing**!**" [exclamatory]

"It's snowing**?**" [interrogative]

Exercise 14   Classifying Sentences According to Purpose

Punctuate each of the following sentences with an appropriate end mark. Then, classify the sentence as *declarative, imperative, interrogative,* or *exclamatory.*

EXAMPLE   1. What kinds of music do you like

1. *What kinds of music do you like?—interrogative*

1. The speakers in our living room are small yet powerful
2. Turn down the sound
3. How loud that is
4. Listening to loud music can damage a person's hearing
5. How many watts does your amplifier produce
6. Sound levels are measured in units called decibels
7. Do you know that an increase of ten decibels represents a doubling in the sound level
8. Do not blast your sound system
9. Keep it quiet
10. Music played softly is relaxing

Review E   Understanding the Parts of a Sentence

In your own words, define each of the following terms, and write a sentence in which the term is illustrated.

EXAMPLE   1. a transitive verb

1. *A transitive verb is an action verb that takes an object. Babe Ruth played baseball.*

1. a sentence
2. a complete subject
3. a verb (simple predicate)
4. a verb phrase
5. a complete predicate
6. a simple subject

7. a subject complement   **9.** an understood subject

8. a direct object   **10.** an indirect object

Review F   Identifying Subjects, Verbs, and Complements

Identify each italicized word or word group in the following paragraphs as a *subject,* a *verb,* a *predicate nominative,* a *predicate adjective,* a *direct object,* or an *indirect object.*

EXAMPLE   The photograph below shows the **[1]** *Great Pyramid of Khufu.*

      1. direct object

The Great Pyramid of Khufu is **[1]** *one* of the wonders of the ancient world. **[2]** *It* was once encased with blocks of polished limestone. However, **[3]** *weather and thievery* **[4]** *have combined* to destroy the original structure. As you **[5]** *can see,* the pyramid **[6]** *looks* **[7]** *weather-beaten.* Still, it is an impressive **[8]** *sight.*

Hundreds of years ago, one invading Arab **[9]** *ruler* decided to rob the tomb of Khufu. With many workers at his disposal, he gave the **[10]** *men* his **[11]** *instructions.* The workers **[12]** *hacked* through the incredibly hard solid blocks of granite. Unexpectedly, **[13]** *they* broke into a tunnel. Imagine their **[14]** *excitement!* All too soon, however, they **[15]** *discovered* an enormous **[16]** *plug* of granite blocking their way. They cut around the plug and finally reached the inner **[17]** *chamber.*

Strangely enough, there was no **[18]** *gold.* No vast treasures **[19]** *sparkled* under the light of the torches. The tomb probably **[20]** *had been robbed* many centuries earlier by Egyptians familiar with its secret entrances.

Review G Writing Sentences

Write sentences according to the following guidelines. Underline the subject once and the verb twice in each sentence. If the subject is understood, write *(You)*.

EXAMPLES   **1.** Write a sentence containing a direct object.

     1. <u>(You)</u> <u>Have</u> another glass of milk.

     2. Write a sentence beginning with *Here.*

     2. Here <u>are</u> the missing puzzle <u>pieces.</u>

   1. Write a declarative sentence containing a verb phrase.
   2. Write a sentence beginning with *There.*
   3. Write an interrogative sentence.
   4. Write an exclamatory sentence.
   5. Write an imperative sentence.
   6. Write a sentence containing a compound subject.
   7. Write a sentence containing a predicate nominative.
   8. Write a sentence containing a compound verb.
   9. Write a sentence containing a predicate adjective.
   10. Write a sentence containing an indirect object and a compound direct object.

Chapter Review

A. Identifying Subjects, Verbs, and Complements

Identify the italicized word or word group in each of the following sentences as a *subject*, a *verb*, a *predicate adjective*, a *predicate nominative*, a *direct object*, or an *indirect object*.

1. Native *cactuses* in the Southwest are endangered.
2. Some species are already *vulnerable* to extinction.
3. Cactuses *are being threatened* by landscapers, tourists, and collectors.
4. Many people illegally harvest these wild *plants*.
5. There are many unique cactus *species* in Arizona.
6. Arizona is, therefore, an active *battlefield* in the war against the removal of these endangered species.
7. "Cactus cops" *patrol* the streets of Phoenix on the lookout for places with illegally acquired cactuses.
8. Authorized dealers must give *purchasers* permit tags as proof of legal sale.
9. First violations are *punishable* by a fine of five hundred dollars.
10. Illegally owned cactuses *may be confiscated* by the police.
11. What a thorny problem cactus *rustling* has become!
12. Why are illegal harvesters so *hard* to track?
13. Many work at night and sometimes use permit *tags* over and over.
14. If you purchase a large cactus, always *examine* it for bruises.
15. A legally harvested cactus *should* not *show* any damage.

B. Identifying Subjects and Predicates

┌HELP─
A sentence in Part B may contain more than one subject and predicate.

Identify the complete subjects and complete predicates in each of the following sentences.

16. The invention of motion pictures is attributed to many people.
17. Chief among the inventors are the French brothers Auguste and Louis Lumière.
18. A laboratory assistant of Thomas Edison named Dickson had invented a type of simple "peep-hole" viewing device called the Kinetoscope.
19. The Edison-Dickson Kinetoscope was displayed in Paris in 1894.

20. Auguste and Louis were determined to improve upon it.

21. In 1895, their determination paid off, and the *cinématographe* was patented.

22. The *cinématographe* functioned as a camera and printer as well as a projector.

23. Everyday French life in the 1890s can be glimpsed in the Lumière brothers' first films.

24. Their 1895 film *Workers Leaving the Lumière Factory* is considered the first motion picture.

25. Ironically, *Lumière* means "light."

C. Completing Sentences by Supplying Subjects and Verbs

Complete each of the following sentences with an appropriate subject or verb. Identify your answer as a *subject* or a *verb*.

26. Greyhounds _____ races.

27. A few of the sophomores _____ after class.

28. Many _____ of the Great Plains were nomadic.

29. The audience _____ at the deathbed scene.

30. To get out of the maze, he _____ to where he had started.

31. _____ were blown down by the storm.

32. Dogs _____ to be walked regularly.

33. The wind _____ through the branches.

34. _____ smiled.

35. Every day after school, Maggie _____ pictures.

D. Identifying Predicate Nominatives and Predicate Adjectives

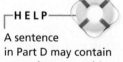

┌HELP┐
A sentence in Part D may contain more than one subject complement.

Write each subject complement in the following sentences, and then identify it as a *predicate nominative* or a *predicate adjective*.

36. We felt exhausted after the marathon.

37. Sitting in the shade was pleasant when the sunlight was so intense.

38. Those dogs are Dalmatians.

39. Your explanation is very clear.

40. My colleague Eric grows calmer every day.

41. Abdullah II became king of Jordan in February 1999.

42. Our neighbor's new car is a sleek and sporty model.

43. The painting looked somber.

44. The first part of the movie is very funny.

45. Their apartment is in a building that looks new and clean.

E. Classifying Sentences as Declarative, Interrogative, Imperative, or Exclamatory

Classify each of the following sentences as *declarative, interrogative, imperative,* or *exclamatory.*

46. Read this article about imperiled cactuses.

47. The author describes a trip into the desert with a legal hauler.

48. Can you imagine a saguaro worth three hundred dollars?

49. A crested saguaro is even rarer and can sell for thousands of dollars.

50. No wonder there is so much illegal harvesting!

Writing Application
Using Varied Sentences in a Letter

Sentence Variety   Your neighborhood association plans to sponsor a summer social event for the teenagers in your area. However, the council is not sure what kind of event teens would like. You have decided to write a short letter to the association to give your opinion. You will mostly use declarative sentences, but try to use at least one of each other kind of sentence for variety and effect.

Prewriting   Jot down a few notes about what kind of event you would like to have. Next, write some different opening sentences. Choose the opener that you think will be the most interesting and effective.

Writing   As you write your letter, refer to your prewriting notes. Use a variety of sentence types.

Revising   Ask an adult you know to listen to your letter. Does he or she think your opening sentence is interesting? Does he or she find your letter persuasive? Revise any sections that are unclear or that lack sentence variety.

Publishing   Proofread your letter for any errors in grammar, punctuation, and spelling. Then, check it for correct letter-writing form. Share your letter with classmates. You may want to compare event ideas and determine which suggestions are most popular or unusual.

The Phrase
Prepositional, Verbal, and Appositive Phrases

Diagnostic Preview

Identifying Prepositional, Verbal, and Appositive Phrases

Identify each italicized phrase in the following paragraphs as a *prepositional phrase*, a *participial phrase*, a *gerund phrase*, an *infinitive phrase*, or an *appositive phrase*.

EXAMPLES An interesting profession **[1]** *to consider as a career* is **[2]** *practicing law.*

1. to consider as a career—infinitive phrase
2. practicing law—gerund phrase

Susana, **[1]** *our next-door neighbor,* wanted **[2]** *to become an attorney.* After she earned a degree **[3]** *from a four-year college,* she took the Law School Admissions Test and was admitted **[4]** *to a prominent law school.* **[5]** *Having completed three full years of law school,* Susana was then awarded a J.D. degree. Before **[6]** *practicing law,* however, she took the state bar exam, **[7]** *a test required by the state board of bar examiners.* Only after **[8]** *passing this exam* had she completed the requirements **[9]** *to be admitted to the bar* and **[10]** *to practice law.*

[11] *Working as an attorney,* Susana provides service and advice **[12]** *relating to legal rights.* Even though she tries hard **[13]** *to keep cases out of court,* Susana enjoys the challenge **[14]** *of presenting cases* to a jury. [15] *Representing a client in court,* however, is only part [16] *of Susana's job.* She devotes hours to [17] *gathering enough evidence* [18] *to defend a client.* She also spends time [19] *on research* and is required [20] *to write numerous reports.*

What Is a Phrase?

3a. A *phrase* is a group of related words that is used as a single part of speech and that does not contain both a verb and its subject.

PREPOSITIONAL PHRASE for you and her [no subject or verb]

INFINITIVE PHRASE to be the best [no subject]

> **NOTE** A group of words that has both a subject and a verb is called a *clause.*
>
> EXAMPLES They will be here soon. [*They* is the subject of *will be.*]
>
> after she leaves [*She* is the subject of *leaves.*]

Reference Note

For more about **clauses,** see Chapter 4.

Prepositional Phrases

3b. A *prepositional phrase* includes a preposition, the object of the preposition, and any modifiers of that object.

EXAMPLES A koala is a marsupial, a mammal **with an external abdominal pouch.** [The noun *pouch* is the object of the preposition *with.*]

To me a koala looks **like a cuddly teddy bear.** [The pronoun *me* is the object of the preposition *To.* The compound noun *teddy bear* is the object of the preposition *like.*]

Koalas, **along with several other marsupials,** are native **to Australia.** [The noun *marsupials* is the object of the compound preposition *along with.* The noun *Australia* is the object of the preposition *to.*]

> **NOTE** Do not confuse a prepositional phrase beginning with *to*—as in *to me* or *to Australia*—with an infinitive, such as *to be* or *to learn.*

Reference Note

For lists of **commonly used prepositions,** see page 24.

Reference Note

For more on **infinitives,** see page 77.

An object of a preposition may be compound.

EXAMPLE   Koalas feed **on only eucalyptus buds and leaves.** [The nouns *buds* and *leaves* are the compound object of the preposition *on.*]

Adjective Phrases

3c. **A prepositional phrase that modifies a noun or a pronoun is called an *adjective phrase.***

An adjective phrase tells *what kind* or *which one.*

EXAMPLES   We ordered a dish **of salsa** and a basket **of tortilla chips.** [*Of salsa* modifies the noun *dish,* telling *what kind* of dish. *Of tortilla chips* modifies the noun *basket,* telling *what kind* of basket.]

No one **in the class** has seen the movie yet. [*In the class* modifies the pronoun *No one,* telling *which one.*]

Two or more adjective phrases may modify the same noun or pronoun.

EXAMPLE   The picture **of their candidate in today's newspaper** is not at all flattering. [Both *of their candidate* and *in today's newspaper* modify the noun *picture.*]

An adjective phrase may also modify the object of another prepositional phrase.

EXAMPLE   The coconut palms in the park **near the bay** were planted a long time ago. [*Near the bay* modifies *park,* the object of the preposition *in.*]

Exercise 1 **Identifying Adjective Phrases**

Identify the adjective phrase(s) in each of the following sentences. After each adjective phrase, give the word it modifies.

EXAMPLE   **1.** Julius Caesar was one of the most successful generals in ancient Rome.

    1. of the most successful generals—one in ancient Rome—generals

---

TIPS & TRICKS

Unlike single-word adjectives, adjective phrases almost always follow the noun or pronoun they modify.

HELP

Remember that adjective phrases modify only nouns or pronouns.

GRAMMAR

1. Roman roads were one reason for Caesar's military successes.
2. The roads of ancient Rome linked the far corners of the empire.
3. Large blocks of hard stone provided a sound foundation for most major routes.
4. Caesar's interest in military roads showed his understanding of the vital importance of communication.
5. Close communication among the empire's provinces strengthened the power of the Roman rulers.
6. The need for roads was addressed in 312 B.C., when the 160-mile Via Appia was begun.
7. The curved surfaces of the road system facilitated drainage.
8. Heavy use of the highways lasted many centuries.
9. Some roads from the old empire still exist.
10. The Romans built nearly 50,000 miles of roads crossing Europe.

Adverb Phrases

3d. A prepositional phrase that modifies a verb, an adjective, or an adverb is called an *adverb phrase.*

EXAMPLES   The mole burrowed **under the lawn.** [*Under the lawn* modifies the verb *burrowed.*]

Althea Gibson was graceful **on the tennis court.** [*On the tennis court* modifies the adjective *graceful.*]

The child speaks quite clearly **for a two-year-old.** [*For a two-year-old* modifies the adverb *clearly.*]

Adverb phrases tell *when, where, why, how,* or *to what extent* (*how much, how long,* or *how far*).

EXAMPLES   **After the storm,** the town grew quiet. [*when*]

He glanced **out the window.** [*where*]

Many street musicians play **for tips.** [*why*]

This summer we're going **by car** to Kansas. [*how*]

She won the contest **by two points.** [*to what extent*]

STYLE   TIP

Be sure to place prepositional phrases carefully so that they express the meaning you intend.

MISPLACED
In its nest at the top of the tree, we could see the great blue heron with binoculars. [The sentence suggests that we are in the heron's nest at the top of the tree and that the heron has binoculars.]

IMPROVED
With binoculars, we could see the great blue heron **in its nest at the top of the tree.**

Reference Note
For more about **misplaced modifiers,** see page 225.

Adverb phrases may come before or after the words they modify, and more than one adverb phrase may modify the same word.

EXAMPLE **In the first inning** she pitched **with great control.** [*In the first inning* modifies the verb *pitched*, telling *when*; *with great control* modifies *pitched*, telling *how*.]

Oral Practice   Identifying Adverb Phrases

Read the following sentences aloud, and then identify each adverb phrase.

EXAMPLE   1. The plane taxied down the runway.

1. *down the runway*

1. The porters hiked toward the summit.
2. The chicken walked across the road.
3. During Ramadan, Muslims fast from sunrise to sunset.
4. Tamara and Dawn floated down the river on a raft.
5. We walked past many beautiful meadows and streams.
6. Beneath the waves, the ocean is calm.
7. We flew across the international date line.
8. After dinner, everyone slept.
9. Spinning out of control, we tumbled into the powdery snow and, laughing, brushed ourselves off.
10. The kayakers rested beside the river.

Exercise 2   Identifying Adverb Phrases

Identify the adverb phrase(s) in each of the following sentences. Then, give the word or word group the phrase modifies.

EXAMPLE   1. For several months no one has lived in the house next to ours.

1. *For several months—has lived in the house—has lived*

1. On Friday, Dad and I were alarmed by plaintive sounds that came from the abandoned house.
2. We searched inside the whole house, from the dusty attic to the cold, damp basement.
3. In the basement we found two stray kittens.
4. They were crying for food.

5. The noises we'd heard had been made by them.
6. I found an empty box in the corner and gently placed both of the kittens in it.
7. They seemed happy with their temporary home.
8. Then, we took the kittens to our house.
9. We lined the box with some soft, old towels and set it in the warm kitchen.
10. Now the plaintive sounds come from our house at all hours of the night and day.

Review A **Sentences with Prepositional Phrases**

Provide a prepositional phrase to complete each of the following sentences. After the sentence, identify the phrase as an *adjective phrase* or an *adverb phrase.*

EXAMPLE   **1.** _____ Mrs. Bowen reads the newspaper.

          *1. In the evening Mrs. Bowen reads the newspaper.—
          adverb phrase*

1. I watched a spider climb _____.
2. _____ the children played hopscotch.
3. We planned a drive _____.
4. Her team played _____.
5. The sky divers jumped fearlessly _____.
6. Hundreds _____ stared.
7. _____ the cyclists unpacked their lunches.
8. There _____ winds a narrow road.
9. This movie will be playing _____.
10. _____ the dancers twirled to the music.
11. Katherine always finishes her homework _____.
12. _____, the children found some coins.
13. The beans _____ are very fresh.
14. Bao wrote a book _____.
15. The group was silent _____.
16. Alice went _____.
17. Everyone _____ was cheering.
18. We traveled _____ to the river.
19. The trees _____ are growing fast.
20. The children _____ are being very cautious.

[handwritten margin notes:]

verbal qualities

• take an object
• formed from verbs and used as adj, nouns, or adverbs

my favorite spot is skiing

He is skiing down the mountain

verb phrase
pres.
participle

He is taller than I am tall.

Verbals and Verbal Phrases

Verbals are formed from verbs and are used as adjectives, nouns, or adverbs. The three kinds of verbals are the *participle*, the *gerund*, and the *infinitive*.

A **verbal phrase** consists of a verbal and its modifiers and complements. The three kinds of verbal phrases are the *participial phrase*, the *gerund phrase*, and the *infinitive phrase*.

The Participle

3e. A **participle** is a verb form that can be used as an adjective.

EXAMPLES   What is the temperature of the **boiling** water? [*Boiling*, formed from the verb *boil*, modifies the noun *water*.]

A **chipped** fingernail can be annoying. [*Chipped*, formed from the verb *chip*, modifies the noun *fingernail*.]

Your **chosen** topic is too broad, I think. [*Chosen*, formed from the verb *choose*, modifies the noun *topic*.]

Two kinds of participles are *present participles* and *past participles*.

(1) Present participles end in *–ing*.

EXAMPLES   The **smiling** graduates posed for the photographer. [*Smiling*, formed from the verb *smile*, modifies the noun *graduates*.]

For an hour we sat there **reminiscing.** [*Reminiscing*, formed from the verb *reminisce*, modifies the pronoun *we*.]

Standing and **applauding,** the audience cheered the cast of the musical *The Lion King*. [*Standing*, formed from the verb *stand*, and *applauding*, formed from the verb *applaud*, modify the noun *audience*.]

(2) Most past participles end in *–d* or *–ed*. Some are formed irregularly.

EXAMPLES   For dinner we prepared **grilled** salmon, **baked** potatoes, and **tossed** salad. [*Grilled*, formed from the verb *grill*, modifies the noun *salmon*; *baked*, formed from the verb *bake*, modifies the noun *potatoes*; and *tossed*, formed from the verb *toss*, modifies the noun *salad*.]

Reference Note

For lists of commonly used **irregular past participles,** see page 174.

For years the treasure had remained **hidden** under tons of **fallen** rock. [*Hidden*, formed from the verb *hide*, modifies the noun *treasure*; *fallen*, formed from the verb *fall*, modifies the noun *rock*.]

3
e, f

> **NOTE** Do not confuse a participle used as an adjective with a participle used as part of a verb phrase.
>
> ADJECTIVE   The shrimp gumbo, **simmering** on the stove, smelled delicious.
>
> VERB PHRASE   The shrimp gumbo **was simmering** on the stove.

Reference Note

For more about **verb phrases,** see pages 15 and 39.

Exercise 3 **Revising Sentences by Adding Participles**

After each of the following sentences is a participle in parentheses. Revise each sentence by inserting the participle next to the noun it modifies.

EXAMPLE   1. We collected funds for the restoration of the building. (*damaged*)

     1. *We collected funds for the restoration of the damaged building.*

1. The space shuttle was greeted with loud cheers. (*returning*)
2. The parents named shows they found unacceptable. (*protesting*)
3. My sister did not hear the doorbell. (*ringing*)
4. The carpenter will show us how to fix this chair. (*broken*)
5. In 1949, Luis Muñoz Marín became Puerto Rico's first governor. (*elected*)
6. The stream crosses the farmer's land at three places. (*winding*)
7. We handed the envelope to the mail carrier. (*crumpled*)
8. This book includes many interesting facts about dinosaurs. (*illustrated*)
9. The Douglas fir behind our house has become a haven for several small creatures. (*fallen*)
10. The plane narrowly missed a radio antenna. (*circling*)

The Participial Phrase

3f. A *participial phrase* consists of a participle and any modifiers or complements the participle has. The entire phrase is used as an adjective.

Verbals and Verbal Phrases   **71**

When writing a sentence that contains a participial phrase, be sure to place the phrase as close as possible to the word or words it modifies.

MISPLACED
The Scouts spotted the white-tailed deer and her twin fawns gathering wood for a campfire. [The sentence suggests that the deer and her two fawns are gathering wood.]

IMPROVED
Gathering wood for a campfire, the Scouts spotted the white-tailed deer and her twin fawns.

Reference Note

For more information on the correct **placement of participial phrases,** see page 226. See page 305 for more on **punctuating participial phrases.**

Reference Note

For more information about **using commas with participial phrases,** see page 305.

In each of the following sentences, an arrow connects the participial phrase with the noun or pronoun the phrase modifies.

EXAMPLES **Climbing the tree,** the monkey disappeared into the branches. [The participial phrase modifies the noun *monkey.* The noun *tree* is the direct object of the present participle *Climbing.*]

I heard him **whispering to his friend.** [The participial phrase modifies the pronoun *him.* The adverb phrase *to his friend* modifies the present participle *whispering.*]

We watched the storm **blowing eastward.** [The participial phrase modifies the noun *storm.* The adverb *eastward* modifies the present participle *blowing.*]

Voted back into office, the mayor thanked her supporters. [The participial phrase modifies the noun *mayor.* The adverb *back* and the adverb phrase *into office* modify the past participle *Voted.*]

The concert **scheduled for tomorrow at the park** has been postponed until next week. [The participial phrase modifies the noun *concert.* The adverb phrases *for tomorrow* and *at the park* modify the past participle *scheduled.*]

NOTE When placed at the beginning of a sentence, a participial phrase is followed by a comma.

Exercise 4 Identifying Participial Phrases

Each of the following sentences contains at least one participial phrase. Identify each participial phrase and the word or words it modifies.

EXAMPLE 1. Robert Scott, commanding a British expedition to the South Pole, learned that another expedition was ahead of him.

1. *commanding a British expedition to the South Pole—Robert Scott*

1. Hoping to be the first to reach the South Pole, Robert Scott (back row, center, in the photograph on the next page) took these four men with him on his final dash to the pole in November 1911.

2. Leading Scott's crew by sixty miles, a Norwegian expedition commanded by Roald Amundsen was moving swiftly, however.

3. Learning about Amundsen, Scott realized a race to the pole was on.

4. Plagued by bad weather and bad luck, Scott fell farther behind Amundsen.

5. Reaching the pole on January 17, 1912, the British found that the Norwegians had already been there.

6. Weakened by scurvy, frostbite, and exhaustion, the five explorers in the photograph set out on the eight-hundred-mile journey back to their base camp.

7. One member of the party, overcome by exhaustion and injuries, died before half the journey had been completed.

8. On March 15 another member, leaving the camp at night, crawled deliberately to his death in a violent blizzard.

9. Eight months later, a rescue mission, sent to find out what had happened, found the bodies of Scott and his companions.

10. Today, the ill-fated Scott expedition, acclaimed for its heroism, is more famous than the successful Amundsen expedition.

The Granger Collection, New York.

Review B   Identifying Participles

Identify the participial phrases and the participles that are used as adjectives in the following sentences. Give the noun or pronoun each participle or participial phrase modifies.

EXAMPLE   1. We have been studying one of the most feared animals in the sea—the killer whale.

1. *feared—animals*

1. Killer whales, long known and feared as wolves of the sea, are not nearly as vicious as many people have thought.

2. Seeking to test the supposedly ferocious nature of the killer whale, scientists studied the whales' behavior.

3. After extensive study, scientists discovered that there is no proven case of an attack on a human by a killer whale.

4. In fact, scientists working with killer whales have confirmed that their charges are intelligent and can be quite gentle.

5. Most killer whales gathered in Johnstone Strait, which is a narrow channel between Vancouver Island and British Columbia in Canada, spend the summer and fall in large family groups.

─HELP─

Sentences in Review B may contain more than one participle or participial phrase.

6. Choosing this spot to observe the mammals, researchers were able to identify more than one hundred whales.

7. The team of scientists, noting the unique shape of each whale's dorsal fin, named each whale in order to keep more accurate records.

8. Impressed by the long life span of killer whales, scientists have estimated that males may live fifty years and females may survive a century.

9. Cruising in groups called pods, most killer whales are highly social animals.

10. During the summer and fall in Johnstone Strait, many pods gather, splashing and playing in "superpods."

The Gerund

Reference Note

For more about **subjects,** see page 38. For more about **predicate nominatives,** see page 51. For more about **direct** and **indirect objects,** see page 54. For more about **objects of prepositions,** see page 65.

3g. A *gerund* is a verb form that ends in *–ing* and that is used as a noun.

A gerund can be used as a subject, a predicate nominative, a direct object, an indirect object, or an object of a preposition.

SUBJECT
Reading will improve your vocabulary. [*Reading,* formed from the verb *read,* is the subject of the verb *will improve.*]

PREDICATE NOMINATIVE
One popular summer sport is **swimming.** [*Swimming,* formed from the verb *swim,* is a predicate nominative identifying the subject *sport.*]

DIRECT OBJECT
Both Dad and Mom enjoy **cooking** together. [*Cooking,* formed from the verb *cook,* is the direct object of the verb *enjoy.*]

INDIRECT OBJECT
Before she decided to become a lawyer, she had given **teaching** thoughtful consideration. [*Teaching,* formed from the verb *teach,* is the indirect object of the verb *had given.*]

OBJECT OF A PREPOSITION
After **studying,** how do you relax? [*Studying,* formed from the verb *study,* is the object of the preposition *After.*]

NOTE Gerunds, like present participles, end in *–ing.* Do not confuse a gerund, which is used as a noun, with a present participle, which may be used as an adjective or as part of a verb phrase.

GERUND	I have enjoyed **reading** about the different species of dinosaurs. [*Reading* is used as the direct object of the verb *have enjoyed.*]
PRESENT PARTICIPLE	I have spent several hours in the library, **reading** about different species of dinosaurs. [*Reading* is used as an adjective modifying the pronoun *I.*]
PRESENT PARTICIPLE	I have been **reading** about the different species of dinosaurs. [*Reading* is used as part of the verb phrase *have been reading.*]

Exercise 5 Identifying Gerunds and Participles

Identify the verbal in each of the following sentences, and tell whether it is a *gerund* or a *participle.* If the verbal is a gerund, tell how it is used—as a *subject,* a *predicate nominative,* a *direct object,* an *indirect object,* or an *object of a preposition.* If the verbal is a participle, tell which word it modifies.

EXAMPLES   **1.** Sleeping on the job is foolish.
  1. Sleeping, gerund—subject

  2. Let sleeping dogs lie.
  2. sleeping, participle—dogs

  1. Their giggling annoyed the other viewers.
  2. Virginia gave cycling a try.
  3. Sneezing, the enemy scout revealed his location.
  4. Fascinated, my sister asked to hear more about our wild plot.
  5. Making friends in a new school can be difficult, but I am getting better at it.
  6. The highlight of the season was watching our team win the regional tournament.
  7. Spinning one full turn, the ballerina gracefully performed a pirouette.
  8. During the summer, Carlota sometimes makes money by walking dogs for her neighbors.
  9. My grandmother and I enjoy digging for clams.
  10. Sensing the danger nearby, he shouted for help.

The Gerund Phrase

3h. A *gerund phrase* consists of a gerund and any modifiers or complements the gerund has. The entire phrase is used as a noun.

SUBJECT	**The sudden shattering of glass** broke the silence. [The gerund phrase is the subject of the verb *broke*. The article *The*, the adjective *sudden*, and the adjective phrase *of glass* modify the gerund *shattering*.]
PREDICATE NOMINATIVE	One of my chores in the summer is **mowing the lawn.** [The gerund phrase is a predicate nominative identifying the subject *One*. The noun *lawn* is the direct object of the gerund *mowing*.]
DIRECT OBJECT	She enjoys **hiking in the mountains occasionally.** [The gerund phrase is the direct object of the verb *enjoys*. The adverb phrase *in the mountains* and the adverb *occasionally* modify the gerund *hiking*.]
INDIRECT OBJECT	Ms. Yashima, a part-time reporter for the local newspaper, is giving **working full time** careful thought. [The gerund phrase is the indirect object of the verb *is giving*. The adverb *full time* modifies the gerund *working*.]
OBJECT OF THE PREPOSITION	By **reading the works of Pat Mora,** I have learned much about Mexican culture. [The gerund phrase is the object of the preposition *By*. The noun *works* is the direct object of the gerund *reading*. The adjective phrase *of Pat Mora* modifies *works*.]

NOTE A noun or pronoun directly before a gerund should be in the possessive case.

EXAMPLES **Eli's** dancing won him first prize in the contest.

His dancing has greatly improved since last year.

Reference Note

For more about the **possessive forms of nouns and pronouns,** see page 356.

Exercise 6 Using Gerunds and Gerund Phrases

Use gerunds or gerund phrases to fill in the blanks of the following sentences.

EXAMPLE 1. The sign on the wall said "No _____."

1. *The sign on the wall said "No Smoking."*

1. _____ daily is a healthy hobby.

2. Fred Astaire was known for his ____.
3. ____ is advised for those who live in sensitive ecological zones.
4. After moving to England, Rick had to get used to many things, such as ____.
5. ____ is one of my favorite pastimes.
6. The ranger enjoys ____.
7. Most dentists recommend ____.
8. One way to increase your aerobic capacity is ____.
9. ____ helps me concentrate.
10. Give ____ your best effort.

The Infinitive

3i. An *infinitive* is a verb form that can be used as a noun, an adjective, or an adverb. Most infinitives begin with *to*.

Infinitives	
Used as	**Examples**
Nouns	**To err** is human. [*To err* is the subject of the verb *is*.]
	His dream is **to travel.** [*To travel* is a predicate nominative identifying the subject *dream*.]
	Betty wants **to act.** [*To act* is the direct object of the verb *wants*.]
Adjectives	The candidate **to believe** is Villegas. [*To believe* modifies the noun *candidate*.]
	She is the one **to ask.** [*To ask* modifies the pronoun *one*.]
Adverbs	Grandmother is coming **to visit.** [*To visit* modifies the verb *is coming*.]
	The favored team was slow **to score.** [*To score* modifies the adjective *slow*.]

NOTE   The word *to* plus a noun or a pronoun (for example, *to Tokyo, to the movies, to her*) is a prepositional phrase, not an infinitive.

Reference Note
For more about **prepositional phrases,** see page 65.

Verbals and Verbal Phrases   **77**

─HELP─

Some sentences
in Exercise 7 contain more
than one infinitive.

| STYLE   TIP |

Placing a word or word
group between the sign of
the infinitive, *to,* and the
verb results in a ***split
infinitive.*** Generally, you
should avoid split infinitives in formal writing and
speaking.

SPLIT
The director wants to,
before rehearsal, speak
with both the stage crew
and the cast.

IMPROVED
The director wants **to
speak** with both the
stage crew and the cast
before rehearsal.

Occasionally, however, you
may need to use a split
infinitive so that your
meaning is clear.

UNCLEAR
He hoped to avoid care-
fully causing delays. [Does
the adverb *carefully* modify the gerund *causing* or
the infinitive *to avoid*?]

UNCLEAR
He hoped carefully to
avoid causing delays.
[Does the adverb *carefully*
modify the verb *hoped* or
the infinitive *to avoid*?]

CLEAR
He hoped **to carefully
avoid** causing delays.

Exercise 7 Identifying and Classifying Infinitives

Identify the infinitives in the following sentences, and tell how each is
used: as a *subject,* a *predicate nominative,* a *direct object,* an *adjective,* or
an *adverb.*

EXAMPLE   **1.** What do you want to do after you graduate from high
school?

1. *to do—direct object*

1. We are waiting to perform.
2. This summer she hopes to travel.
3. I am ready to leave.
4. Do you want to drive?
5. To forgive is sometimes difficult.
6. To excel, one must practice.
7. We are eager to go.
8. A good way to learn is to live.
9. The soup is still too hot to eat.
10. I said to Jo, "One way to improve is to practice."

The Infinitive Phrase

3j. An ***infinitive phrase*** consists of an infinitive and any
modifiers or complements the infinitive has. The entire phrase
can be used as a noun, an adjective, or an adverb.

NOUN **To hit a curveball solidly** is very difficult. [The infinitive
phrase is the subject of the verb *is.* The noun *curveball* is the
direct object of the infinitive *To hit,* and the adverb *solidly*
modifies *To hit.*]

NOUN She wants **to study marine biology.** [The infinitive phrase
is the direct object of the verb *wants.* The noun *biology* is the
direct object of the infinitive *to study,* and the adjective
marine modifies *biology.*]

ADJECTIVE His efforts **to trace his ancestry** led to greater appreciation
of his heritage. [The infinitive phrase modifies the noun
efforts. The noun *ancestry* is the direct object of the infinitive
to trace, and the possessive pronoun *his* is used to modify
ancestry.]

ADVERB I found his explanation difficult **to accept.** [The infinitive
phrase modifies the adjective *difficult.*]

NOTE Unlike other verbals, an infinitive may have a subject. An *infinitive clause* consists of an infinitive with a subject and any modifiers or complements the infinitive has. The entire infinitive clause functions as a noun.

EXAMPLE   I wanted **him to come to our powwow.** [*Him* is the subject of the infinitive *to come.* The entire infinitive clause is the direct object of the verb *wanted.*]

Sometimes *to,* the sign of the infinitive, is omitted.

EXAMPLES   Did you watch her [to] **play** volleyball?

He will help us [to] **paddle** the canoe.

We don't dare [to] **go** outside during the storm.

COMPUTER TIP

Some style-checking software programs can identify and highlight split infinitives. Using such a program will help you eliminate unnecessary split infinitives from your writing.

Exercise 8   **Identifying and Classifying Infinitive Phrases and Infinitive Clauses**

Identify the infinitive phrases and infinitive clauses in the following sentences, and tell how each is used—as a *subject,* a *predicate nominative,* a *direct object,* an *adjective,* or an *adverb.*

EXAMPLE   **1.** Everyone in the class was eager to learn more about the life of Maya Angelou.

1. *to learn more about the life of Maya Angelou—adverb*

1. Our assignment was to read *I Know Why the Caged Bird Sings.*
2. I decided to write a report on Maya Angelou's descriptions of her childhood.
3. To grow up in Stamps, Arkansas, in the 1930s was to know great hardship.
4. Maya Angelou tried to show the everyday lives of African Americans during the Great Depression.
5. To accomplish this purpose meant including many descriptions; one such passage told about the process for curing pork sausage.
6. Angelou has an extraordinary ability to capture vivid details in her writing.
7. She helps us see her grandmother's store through the eyes of a fascinated child.
8. Angelou was eager to experience life beyond her hometown.

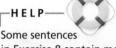

HELP

Some sentences in Exercise 8 contain more than one infinitive phrase or infinitive clause. Remember that the sign of the infinitive, *to,* may be omitted.

9. Her talents and ambition enabled her to achieve success as a writer, a dancer, and an actress.
10. To dramatize her African American heritage was a dream she realized by writing a television series.

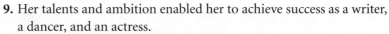

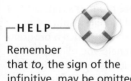
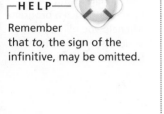

┌HELP┐
Remember that *to*, the sign of the infinitive, may be omitted.

Review C Identifying Types of Verbals and Verbal Phrases

Identify the verbal phrases in the following paragraph. Then, tell whether each verbal phrase is a *participial phrase*, a *gerund phrase*, or an *infinitive phrase*.

EXAMPLE **[1]** Looking at these control panels in the flight deck of a jumbo passenger jet, most of us feel completely lost.

1. *Looking at these control panels in the flight deck of a jumbo passenger jet—participial phrase*

[1] Intensive training is required for pilots. **[2]** Traveling the airways has become much easier because of modern technology. **[3]** Fortunately, in the flight deck sit people trained in the uses of these controls and instruments. **[4]** Sitting in front of identical control panels, both the captain and the first officer can fly the plane. **[5]** The captain, who uses the left-hand panel, operates a lever that controls the wing flaps and helps steer the plane. **[6]** Operating the brake panels is another one of the captain's jobs. **[7]** To the captain's right is the first officer, whose job is to help the captain. **[8]** The throttle, which governs the engines' ability to move the plane forward, is located between the captain and the first officer. **[9]** Some of the other instruments shown here are parts of the plane's navigation, autopilot, and communication systems. **[10]** At another station in the flight deck, the flight engineer monitors gauges and operates switches to control the plane's generators and the pressure and temperature in the cabin.

Review D Identifying Verbal Phrases

Identify the verbal phrases in the following paragraph. Then, tell whether each verbal phrase is a *participial phrase*, a *gerund phrase*, or an *infinitive phrase*.

EXAMPLE   [1] Would you like to have a summer job?

1. *to have a summer job—infinitive phrase*

[1] If you are not offered a job right away, remember that contacting a number of agencies and following up with phone calls and thank-you notes will increase your chances. [2] To persevere in the job hunt is very important. [3] Finding a summer job can be a difficult task. [4] The first step is to scan the classified ads in your local newspaper. [5] After discovering available opportunities, you can embark on the second step, which is matching your skills with the requirements of a specific job. [6] In most cases you can then contact a prospective employer and request an interview by making a phone call or by writing a letter. [7] If you are asked to interview for a job, be sure to prepare for the interview. [8] To make a good impression, be sure to arrive on time, to dress neatly, and to speak courteously. [9] Remember to avoid such nervous habits as constantly checking your watch or shuffling your feet. [10] By presenting yourself as calm, confident, and courteous, you may hear the magic words "We'd like you to work for us."

Appositives and Appositive Phrases

3k. An *appositive* is a noun or pronoun placed beside another noun or pronoun to identify or describe it.

EXAMPLES   My cousin **Bryan** is my best friend. [The appositive *Bryan* identifies the noun *cousin.*]

Our football team has won its first two games, **one** by three points and the **other** by six. [The appositives *one* and *other* identify the noun *games.*]

Soledad, a cautious **driver,** has never had an automobile accident. [The appositive *driver* describes the proper noun *Soledad.*]

3l. An *appositive phrase* consists of an appositive and any modifiers it has.

EXAMPLES   The Vescuzos live on Milner Lane, **a wide street lined with beech trees.** [The appositive phrase identifies the noun *Milner Lane.* Note that the participial phrase *lined with beech trees* is part of the appositive phrase because the participial phrase, like the adjectives *a* and *wide*, modifies the appositive *street.*]

MEETING THE CHALLENGE

A metaphor, one type of comparison, can be expressed in an appositive phrase. For example, the metaphor *The breeze was a soft melody* can be made into an appositive phrase in the sentence *The breeze, a soft melody, whispered in the grove.* Write a descriptive paragraph about a place or event you have enjoyed, and include at least two metaphors. Then, modify the paragraph by expressing the metaphors in appositives or appositive phrases.

Mount Kosciusko, **a part of the Australian Alps,** is the highest peak in Australia. [The appositive phrase describes the noun *Mount Kosciusko.* The prepositional phrase *of the Australian Alps* is an adjective phrase modifying the appositive *part.*]

An appositive phrase usually follows the noun or pronoun it identifies or describes. Sometimes, though, it precedes the noun or pronoun.

EXAMPLE **A diligent and quick-witted student,** Mark always gets good grades. [The appositive phrase identifies the noun *Mark.*]

Appositives and appositive phrases that are not essential to the meaning of a sentence are set off by commas. However, an appositive that tells *which one of two or more* is essential to the meaning of a sentence and should not be set off by commas.

Reference Note

For more information on **how to punctuate appositives and appositive phrases,** see page 309.

NONESSENTIAL Is Karen's sister, **Marcia,** also a sophomore? [The appositive *Marcia* is not essential because Karen has only one sister.]

ESSENTIAL Jorge's sister **Selena** is a sophomore. [The appositive *Selena* is essential because Jorge has more than one sister. Which one of the sisters is a sophomore? *Selena.*]

Exercise 9 Identifying Appositives and Appositive Phrases

Identify the appositive or appositive phrase in each of the following sentences, and give the word it identifies or describes.

EXAMPLE **1.** Dr. Rosen, our family dentist, is a marathon runner.

1. our family dentist—Dr. Rosen

1. Soccer, my favorite sport, is very popular in South America and Europe.
2. The internationally famous soccer star Pelé is from Brazil.
3. Hausa, a Nigerian language, is widely used in western Africa.
4. Have you met my teacher Mr. Zolo?
5. Roseanne's youngest sister, Susan, speaks fluent Spanish.
6. Is your friend Greg getting married?
7. Cindy, a student at the community college, is studying computer-aided drafting.
8. The New York City Marathon, one of the largest spectator sports in the United States, is held each November.

9. The Himalayas, the highest mountains on earth, are magnificent.

10. Always the one to object, Blair said, "No way!"

> **Review E** **Identifying Verbal and Appositive Phrases**

The following paragraph contains ten verbal and appositive phrases. Identify each phrase as a *participial phrase*, a *gerund phrase*, an *infinitive phrase*, or an *appositive phrase*.

EXAMPLE **[1]** Who was responsible for designing the Brooklyn Bridge?

1. *designing the Brooklyn Bridge—gerund phrase*

[1] The Brooklyn Bridge, a remarkable feat of design, spans the East River in New York City. [2] Linking the boroughs of Brooklyn and Manhattan, it was once the longest suspension bridge in the world. [3] Most of the pedestrians who cross the bridge are impressed by the grandeur of its graceful cables, a majesty that the postcard below cannot fully evoke. [4] To support the twin towers on the bridge, the brilliant John A. Roebling, its engineer, designed airtight caissons filled with concrete. [5] Working underwater on the caissons was painstakingly slow and extremely dangerous. [6] The workers also faced great danger when they had to spin the cables from one side of the river to the other. [7] Because of these hazards, the bridge is remembered not only for being a masterpiece of engineering but also for having cost the lives of many of its builders.

> **STYLE** **TIP**
>
> Using too many short sentences will make your writing choppy. By using prepositional, verbal, and appositive phrases, you can avoid the unnecessary repetition of words and improve the flow of your ideas.
>
> CHOPPY
> The Appalachian National Scenic Trail is more than 2,000 miles long. The trail stretches from Mount Katahdin to Springer Mountain. Mount Katahdin is in Maine. Springer Mountain is in Georgia.
>
> SMOOTH
> Stretching from Mount Katahdin in Maine to Springer Mountain in Georgia, the Appalachian National Scenic Trail is more than 2,000 miles long.

Review F **Writing Sentences with Phrases**

Write ten sentences, following the directions below for each sentence. Underline the given phrase in each sentence.

EXAMPLE   **1.** Use *to get there from here* as an infinitive phrase acting as an adjective.

      1. *What is the fastest way <u>to get there from here</u>?*

1. Use *in the garage* as an adjective phrase.
2. Use *for our English class* as an adverb phrase.
3. Use *from an encyclopedia* as an adjective phrase.
4. Use *by train* as an adverb phrase.
5. Use *walking by the lake* as a participial phrase.
6. Use *playing the piano* as a gerund phrase that is the subject of a verb.
7. Use *to hit a home run* as an infinitive phrase that is the direct object of a verb.
8. Use *to find the answer to that question* as an infinitive phrase acting as an adverb.
9. Use *the new student in our class* as an appositive phrase.
10. Use *my favorite writer* as an appositive phrase.

Chapter Review

A. Sentences with Prepositional Phrases

Provide a prepositional phrase for the blank in each of the following sentences. After writing the sentence, identify the phrase as an *adjective phrase* or an *adverb phrase*.

1. The tall building _____ is the art museum.
2. *Brian's Song* is an inspiring story _____.
3. The selection committee was impressed _____.
4. _____, we decided to spend the evening quietly at home.
5. I saw a raccoon _____.
6. Early _____, my family holds a big reunion for all of our relatives.
7. Last Christmas, Mother used a recipe similar to that _____.
8. _____, my father fought as a soldier in the U.S. Army during the Persian Gulf War.
9. After protesting that he wanted to stay up late, my young brother finally went _____.
10. That rosebush _____ had seen better days.

B. Identifying Participles and Participial Phrases

┌HELP┐
Some sentences in Part B contain more than one participle or participial phrase.

Identify the participial phrases and participles that are used as adjectives in the following sentences. Give the noun or pronoun each participle or participial phrase modifies.

11. She heard me sighing loudly.
12. Aided by good weather and clear skies, the sailors sailed into port a day early.
13. Searching through old clothes in a trunk, Ricardo found a map showing the location of a buried treasure.
14. Sparta and Athens, putting aside their own rivalry, joined forces to fight the Persians.
15. I would love to see it blooming; it must be quite a sight!
16. The cat hissed at the dog barking in the yard next door.
17. Waxing his car in the driveway, Joe waved to the neighbors across the street.

18. Known as Johnny Appleseed, John Chapman distributed apple seeds and saplings to families headed west.
19. Locked doors contradicted the "open" sign in the window.
20. Switching its tail, the leopard closed in on its prey.

┌HELP┐

In Parts C and D, you do not need to identify separately a prepositional phrase or verbal phrase that is part of another phrase.

C. Identifying Phrases in Sentences

Identify each italicized phrase in the following sentences as a *prepositional, participial, gerund, infinitive,* or *appositive phrase.*

21. The sundial was one of the first instruments used for *telling time.*
22. *Regarded chiefly as garden ornaments,* sundials are still used in some areas *to tell time.*
23. The shadow-casting object *on a sundial* is called a gnomon.
24. Forerunners of the sundial include poles or upright stones *used as gnomons by early humans.*
25. *To improve the accuracy of the sundial,* the gnomon was set directly parallel to the earth's axis, *the imaginary line running through the planet's poles.*
26. The development of trigonometry permitted more precise calculations *in the construction* of sundials.
27. For everyday use, *owning a watch* has obvious advantages over using a sundial.
28. *In the past,* sundials were used *to set and check the accuracy of watches.*
29. The heliochronometer, *a sundial of great precision,* was used until 1900 *to set the watches of French railway workers.*
30. The difference *between solar time and clock time* is correlated by the use of tables *showing daily variations in solar time.*

D. Identifying Phrases in a Paragraph

Identify each italicized phrase in the following paragraph as a *prepositional, participial, gerund, infinitive,* or *appositive phrase.*

[31] A sundial is not difficult *to make with simple materials.* [32] First find a stick *to use as a gnomon.* [33] At high noon, plant the stick *in the ground,* tilting it slightly northward. [34] To mark the first hour, place a pebble at the tip of the shadow *made by the stick.* [35] An hour later, put another pebble at the tip *of the shadow.* [36] Continue this process *throughout the afternoon.* [37] *Starting the*

next morning, repeat the hourly process. **[38]** Be sure *to place the last pebble at high noon.* **[39]** Observing the completed sundial, you will note that the hour markers, *the pebbles,* are not equidistant. **[40]** *Your spacing of the markers* has demonstrated that shadows move faster in the morning and the evening than during the middle of the day.

Writing Application
Using Phrases in a Newspaper Article

Verbal and Appositive Phrases   As a reporter for the local newspaper, you have just attended your community's annual dog show. Write a short news article on the show. Be sure you use at least three verbal phrases and three appositive phrases.

Prewriting   First, make a list of the top dogs in the show. Give their names, their breeds, their owners, and their personalities. You may wish to gather information about dog breeds from an encyclopedia or other source.

Writing   Newspaper articles usually present the most important information first, so be sure to include the *who, what, when,* and *where* of the dog show in the beginning of the article. Describe how the winners were chosen, and explain why each winner was judged to be the best in its class. You may also want to describe other features of the show, such as the setting, the size and enthusiasm of the crowd, or the owners' preshow grooming of contestants.

Revising   Read your first draft to a friend or family member, and ask for his or her reactions. Determine that you have given adequate information in as clear a manner as possible.

Publishing   Check to make sure that you have used at least three verbal phrases and three appositive phrases. Also, check your spelling, especially of the names of dog breeds. Proofread your article for any errors in grammar, usage, and mechanics. You and your classmates may wish to read your finished articles aloud.

The Clause
Independent Clauses and Subordinate Clauses

Handwritten margin notes:

clauses

• has s/v
* independent/
main
 – stands
alone & is
a complete
thought
• dependent/
subordinate
 – need to be
attached to
independent/
main & does not
express complete
thoughts

Diagnostic Preview

A. Identifying and Classifying Clauses

Identify the italicized clause in each of the following sentences as an *independent clause* or a *subordinate clause*. Then, identify each of the subordinate clauses as an *adjective clause*, an *adverb clause*, or a *noun clause*.

EXAMPLES
1. The New York bridge *that most people recognize* is the Brooklyn Bridge.
   1. subordinate clause—adjective clause
2. Known around the world, *the Brooklyn Bridge may be the most famous bridge in the United States.*
   2. independent clause

1. The Brooklyn Bridge, *which spans the East River between Brooklyn and Manhattan in New York City*, is one of the engineering wonders of the world. *[S/ADJ]*
2. *The bridge was designed and built by John Roebling and Washington Roebling, a father-and-son engineering team* who were pioneers in the use of steel-wire cables. *[S/ADV]*
3. *Although she was not an engineer*, Emily Roebling, Washington's wife, assisted in the efforts to complete the bridge. *[S/ADV]*
4. *What impresses many people* who see the bridge is the strength and beauty of its design. *[S/ADJ]*
5. Massive granite towers *that are supported by concrete-filled shafts* are among its remarkable features.

6. The steel-wire cables give the bridge a graceful appearance *that resembles a spider's web.*

7. The Roeblings discovered *that construction work could be both slow and dangerous.*

8. *Because they were required at times to work underwater in airtight chambers called caissons,* many workers, including the designer Washington Roebling, suffered from caisson disease, or decompression sickness.

9. *Since they were used to working in ships' rigging at great heights,* sailors were hired to string the miles of cable.

10. *John Roebling injured his foot at the work site,* and as a result, he died of tetanus shortly after construction began.

B. Classifying Sentences According to Structure

Classify each of the sentences in the following paragraph as *simple, compound, complex,* or *compound-complex.*

EXAMPLE   [1] Washington and Emily Roebling worked together to complete the project.

    1. simple

[11] After succeeding his father on the project, Washington Roebling was stricken by caisson disease; therefore, he was confined to bed. [12] The Roeblings lived in a house that was near the construction site, and Washington supervised the work through a telescope. [13] He dictated instructions to Emily, and she relayed them to the work crew. [14] Whether the work on the bridge could have continued without her assistance is doubtful. [15] When the bridge was finally completed in 1883, President Chester A. Arthur attended the dedication ceremony. [16] Because of his illness, Washington Roebling was unable to attend the ceremonies. [17] Instead, the President visited Roebling's home to honor the man who had struggled so valiantly to complete the bridge. [18] The bridge took thirteen years to build. [19] At the time of its completion, it was the world's longest suspension bridge. [20] The bridge is now more than a century old, and it still stands as a monument to the artistry, sacrifice, and determination of all the people who planned and built it.

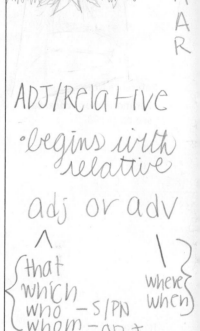

┌HELP─

A subordinate clause that is capitalized and punctuated as if it were a sentence is a **sentence fragment.**

Reference Note

For information about correcting **sentence fragments,** see page 446.

What Is a Clause?

4a. A *clause* is a word group that contains a verb and its subject and that is used as a sentence or as part of a sentence.

Every clause has a subject and a verb, but not all clauses express complete thoughts. Those that do are called *independent clauses.* Those that do not are called *subordinate clauses.*

Independent Clauses

4b. An *independent* (or *main*) *clause* expresses a complete thought and can stand by itself as a sentence.

EXAMPLE
$$\overset{S}{} \overset{V}{}$$
The outfielders missed easy fly balls.

Reference Note

For more about **commas,** see page 298.

Independent clauses that express related ideas can be joined together in a single sentence. Often, the clauses are linked by a comma and one of the coordinating conjunctions (*and, but, or, nor, for, so,* or *yet*).

EXAMPLE
$$\overset{S}{} \overset{V}{} \overset{S}{}$$
The outfielders missed easy fly balls**, and** the infielders
$$\overset{V}{}$$
were throwing wildly.

Related independent clauses can be linked by a semicolon.

EXAMPLE
$$\overset{S}{} \overset{V}{} \overset{S}{}$$
The outfielders missed easy fly balls**;** the infielders
$$\overset{V}{}$$
were throwing wildly.

Reference Note

For more information on using **semicolons to join independent clauses,** see page 322.

A conjunctive adverb or transitional expression followed by a comma can be used after the semicolon to express the relationship between the independent clauses.

EXAMPLES
$$\overset{S}{} \overset{V}{}$$
The outfielders missed easy fly balls**; moreover,** the
$$\overset{S}{} \overset{V}{}$$
infielders were throwing wildly.

$$\overset{S}{} \overset{V}{}$$
The outfielders missed easy fly balls**; in addition,** the
$$\overset{S}{} \overset{V}{}$$
infielders were throwing wildly.

Common Conjunctive Adverbs		
also	however	nevertheless
anyway	instead	otherwise
besides	likewise	still
consequently	meanwhile	then
furthermore	moreover	therefore

Common Transitional Expressions		
as a result	for example	in other words
at any rate	in addition	on the contrary
by the way	in fact	on the other hand

Subordinate Clauses

4c. A *subordinate* (or *dependent*) *clause* does not express a complete thought and cannot stand alone as a sentence.

EXAMPLES   whom we spoke to yesterday

because no students have applied for them

The thought expressed by a subordinate clause becomes part of a complete thought when the clause is combined with an independent clause.

EXAMPLES   The woman **whom we spoke to yesterday** told us about sources of financial aid for college applicants.

Some scholarships are still available **because no students have applied for them.**

Oral Practice   **Identifying Independent and Subordinate Clauses**

Read the following sentences aloud. Then, identify each italicized clause as *independent* or *subordinate*.

EXAMPLE   1. One of the guests *who spoke at the ceremony* was Barbara Jordan.

1. *subordinate*

1. *Whenever I think of Barbara Jordan,* I imagine her as she looks in a picture taken at my mother's college graduation in 1986.

2. According to my mother, *Jordan spoke eloquently about the importance of values in our society.*

3. *Of course, her choice of subject matter surprised no one* since Jordan had long been known as an important ethical force in American politics.

4. *When Jordan began her public service career in 1966,* she became the first African American woman to serve in the Texas legislature.

5. In 1972, she won a seat in the U.S. House of Representatives, *where only one other black woman—Shirley Chisholm—had ever been a member.*

6. However, Jordan was still not widely recognized *until she gave the keynote speech at the 1976 Democratic National Convention.*

7. Seen on television by millions of people, *Jordan immediately gained national attention.*

8. Two years after the speech, Jordan decided *that she would retire from national politics.*

9. After she returned to Texas in 1978, *Jordan taught at the University of Texas at Austin.*

10. From 1991 until her death in 1996, she served on various government committees and used *what she had learned in her many years of public service* to fight corruption in politics.

Complements and Modifiers in Subordinate Clauses

A subordinate clause may contain complements and modifiers.

EXAMPLES   since she told **us the truth** [*Us* is the indirect object of the verb *told,* and *truth* is the direct object of *told. The* modifies *truth.*]

when I am **busy** [*Busy* is a predicate adjective modifying the subject *I.*]

after he had cooked **for us** [*For us* is a prepositional phrase modifying the verb *had cooked.*]

that he **recently** painted [*That* is the direct object of the verb *painted; recently* is an adverb modifying *painted.*]

who they were [*Who* is a predicate nominative identifying the subject *they.*]

Reference Note

For more about the different kinds of **complements,** see page 48. For more about **adjectives** and **adverbs,** see page 212. For more about **prepositional phrases,** see page 65.

> **Exercise 1** **Identifying Subjects, Verbs, and Complements in Subordinate Clauses**

Identify the subject and the verb in the italicized subordinate clause in each of the following sentences. Then, identify each complement in the clause as a *predicate adjective*, a *predicate nominative*, a *direct object*, or an *indirect object*.

EXAMPLE   1. *After he shows us his new boat,* we will go swimming.

       1. *he*—subject; *shows*—verb; *us*—indirect object; *boat*—direct object

1. We couldn't see *who had won the race.*
2. Kelly says *that her new house is beautiful.*
3. *After we passed the test,* we celebrated.
4. They couldn't tell *who the winner was.*
5. The horse *that you rode yesterday* was skittish.
6. She is the celebrity *whom we saw at the restaurant.*
7. Do you know *which country she is touring?*
8. *Because you had not given us the right address,* we missed the party.
9. Look for the mouse *that you heard last night.*
10. *Until Mike lent me this book,* I had never heard of the author Rudolfo A. Anaya.

Uses of Subordinate Clauses

Subordinate clauses can be used as adjectives, adverbs, or nouns.

The Adjective Clause

4d. An *adjective clause* is a subordinate clause that modifies a noun or a pronoun.

An adjective clause tells *what kind* or *which one* and generally follows the word or words it modifies.

EXAMPLES   I am now reading this book, **which is a historical novel about the Irish revolt of 1798.** [The adjective clause modifies the noun *book,* telling what kind of book.]

       A photograph of those **who had participated in the school's Earth Day celebration** appeared on the front page of the local newspaper. [The adjective clause modifies the pronoun *those,* telling which ones.]

HELP

Before doing Exercise 1, you may want to review **complements** in Chapter 2.

STYLE TIP

Although a series of short, simple sentences can be effective, a variety of sentence structures is usually more effective. To change choppy sentences into smoother writing, combine shorter sentences by changing some into subordinate clauses. Also, avoid unnecessary repetition of subjects, verbs, and pronouns.

CHOPPY
    Ted runs every day. Ted is in training. He is training for a marathon.

SMOOTH
    Ted, who is in training for a marathon, runs every day.

In the example above, two of the short sentences are combined into a single subordinate clause.

—HELP—

Generally, an adjective clause that modifies a proper noun, such as *Emil* in the second example, is nonessential and is therefore set off by commas.

Reference Note

See page 302 for more about **essential** and **nonessential clauses**.

NOTE Depending on how it is used, an adjective clause is either *essential* or *nonessential*. An **essential** (or **restrictive**) **clause** contains information necessary to the sentence's meaning. A **nonessential** (or **nonrestrictive**) **clause** contains information that can be omitted without affecting the sentence's basic meaning. An essential clause is not set off by commas; a nonessential clause is set off by commas.

ESSENTIAL The oboe is the only instrument **that I can play well.** [The adjective clause is essential because omitting it would change the basic meaning of the sentence.]

NONESSENTIAL Emil, **who can play many instruments,** taught me how to play the oboe. [The adjective clause is nonessential because omitting it would not affect the basic meaning of the sentence.]

Relative Pronouns

An adjective clause is usually introduced by a *relative pronoun*.

Common Relative Pronouns				
who	whom	whose	which	that

These pronouns are called *relative pronouns* because they are used to relate an adjective clause to the word or word group the clause modifies. That word or word group is called the *antecedent* of the relative pronoun. Each relative pronoun also serves a grammatical function within the adjective clause.

EXAMPLES Isabella Baumfree was an abolitionist **who is most often remembered as Sojourner Truth.** [*Who* relates the adjective clause to the noun *abolitionist*. *Who* also serves as the subject of the verb *is remembered* in the adjective clause.]

The topic **about which he is writing** is controversial. [*Which* relates the adjective clause to the noun *topic*. *Which* also serves as the object of the preposition *about* in the adjective clause.]

She is the person **whom I trust most.** [*Whom* relates the adjective clause to the noun *person*. *Whom* also serves as the direct object of the verb *trust* in the adjective clause.]

Do you know the name of the group **whose recording is number one on the charts**? [*Whose* relates the adjective clause to the noun *group*. *Whose* also serves as a possessive pronoun modifying *recording* in the adjective clause.]

Sometimes the relative pronoun is left out of a sentence. In such a sentence, the pronoun is understood and still serves a grammatical function within the adjective clause.

EXAMPLE   Ms. Chung is the legislator [**that** or **whom**] **we met.** [*That or whom* is understood. The understood relative pronoun relates the adjective clause to *legislator* and serves as the direct object of the verb *met* in the adjective clause.]

Reference Note

For information on using **who** and **whom** correctly, see page 156.

NOTE   *Who* and *whom* refer to persons only; *which* refers to things only; *that* refers to persons or things.

To modify a place or a time, an adjective clause may be introduced by the word *where* or *when*. When used in such a way, these words are called *relative adverbs.*

EXAMPLES   Here is the spot **where we will have lunch.** [*Where* relates the adjective clause to the noun *spot.*]

This is the season **when it rains almost every day.** [*When* relates the adjective clause to the noun *season.*]

Exercise 2   Identifying Adjective Clauses

Identify the adjective clauses in the following sentences, and underline the relative pronoun or relative adverb in each clause. Then, give the word or words to which the relative pronoun or relative adverb relates. If a sentence contains an adjective clause from which the relative pronoun has been omitted, add the relative pronoun in parentheses and underline it.

HELP

Some sentences in Exercise 2 contain more than one adjective clause.

EXAMPLES   1. The topic that Melissa chose for her essay was difficult.

1. *that Melissa chose for her essay—topic*

2. The other topics she had considered were just as difficult.

2. *(that) she had considered—topics*

1. A speech community is a group of people <u>who</u> speak the same language.
2. There are speech communities <u>that contain</u> millions of people and some that have only a few people.
3. The first language you learn is called your native language.
4. People <u>who master a second language</u> are bilingual.
5. Those <u>who conduct business internationally</u> often need to know more than one language.
6. English, French, and Spanish, <u>which many diplomats can speak,</u> are among the six official languages of the United Nations.

7. Russian, Chinese, and Arabic are the other three languages that are used officially at the UN.
8. People for whom language study is important include telephone operators, hotel managers, and police officers.
9. Tourists traveling to countries where they do not know the local languages can find themselves at a disadvantage.
10. French is a language that is widely understood in parts of Europe, Africa, Southeast Asia, and the Middle East.

The Adverb Clause

4e. An *adverb clause* is a subordinate clause that modifies a verb, an adjective, or an adverb.

Reference Note

Introductory adverb clauses are usually set off by **commas**. See page 306.

An adverb clause tells *how, when, where, why, to what extent,* or *under what condition.*

EXAMPLES   Donna sounds **as if she has caught a cold.** [The adverb clause modifies the verb *sounds,* telling how Donna sounds.]

Before we left, we lowered the blinds. [The adverb clause modifies the verb *lowered,* telling when we lowered the blinds.]

You will see our house **where the road curves right.** [The adverb clause modifies the verb *will see,* telling where you will see our house.]

Will you move **so that I can see**? [The adverb clause modifies the verb *will move,* telling why you will move.]

Your stereo is louder **than it should be.** [The adverb clause modifies the adjective *louder,* telling to what extent your stereo is louder.]

Andrew can type faster **than anyone else in his computer class can.** [The adverb clause modifies the adverb *faster,* telling to what extent Andrew can type faster.]

As long as he starts early, he will arrive on time. [The adverb clause modifies the verb *will arrive,* telling under what condition he will arrive on time.]

Subordinating Conjunctions

An adverb clause is introduced by a *subordinating conjunction*—a word that shows the relationship between the adverb clause and the

GRAMMAR

word or words that the clause modifies. Unlike a relative pronoun, which introduces an adjective clause, a subordinating conjunction does not serve a grammatical function in the clause it introduces.

Common Subordinating Conjunctions		
after	even though	unless
although	if	until
as	in order that	when
as if	once	whenever
as long as	provided that	where
as soon as	since	wherever
as though	so that	whether
because	than	while
before	though	why

Reference Note

Some of the wo[rds] this chart can be [used] as **adverbs** (see [ ]) or **prepositions** [ ] page 24).

Exercise 3 Identifying Adverb Clauses and Subordinating Conjunctions

Identify the adverb clause in each of the following sentences, and circle the subordinating conjunction.

EXAMPLE
1. While the others worked inside the house, Ruth, Lou, and I worked in the yard.

1. While the others worked inside the house

1. Because the house had been vacant for so long, the lawn and gardens were overgrown.
2. The grass in the front looked as if it hadn't been cut in months.
3. Ruth began mowing the lawn while Lou and I weeded the flower beds.
4. We decided to borrow some tools because the weeds were extremely thick.
5. We were unable to cut through the heavy undergrowth until we started using gardening shears.
6. Before we pulled out the weeds, we couldn't even see the roses.
7. We piled the debris in a huge mound so that it could be hauled away later.
8. After Ruth had mowed the lawn, she was exhausted.
9. We all stretched out in the shade when we stopped for a rest.
10. Long hours in the sun had made us feel as though the day would never end.

COMPUTER TIP

Because an adverb clause usually does not have a fixed location in a sentence, the writer must choose where to put the clause. The best place for it is usually a matter of personal taste and style, but often the placement is determined by the context.

If you use a computer, you can easily experiment with the placement of adverb clauses in sentences. Print out different versions of the same sentence containing the adverb clause along with the sentences that immediately precede and follow it. Read each version aloud to see how the placement of the clause affects the flow, rhythm, and overall meaning of the passage.

Uses of Subordinate Clauses

Using Adverb Clauses

Complete the following sentences by adding adverb clauses.

EXAMPLE   **1.** _____, I usually go straight home.

          1. When I finish work, I usually go straight home.

  1. _____, the show was canceled.

  2. _____, the telephone rang.

  3. The child was delighted _____.

  4. Constance will work _____.

  5. _____, her dog goes with her.

  6. David and Sandra plan to go biking _____.

  7. Let me know _____.

  8. Cindy is going to the bookstore _____.

  9. I bring my cell phone _____.

  10. _____, Hiroshi is an accomplished pianist.

MEETING THE CHALLENGE

What do you think the future will be like? What events will happen, and what other events will they cause? What conditions will lead to important changes? Write a poem made up of at least five "if . . . then" statements. Your poem will contain at least five subordinate clauses and five independent clauses. Highlight the subordinate clauses in one color and the independent clauses in another color.

Review A   **Identifying Adjective and Adverb Clauses**

Identify the subordinate clauses in the following paragraph. Then, tell whether each is an *adjective clause* or an *adverb clause*.

EXAMPLE   **[1]** Someone who pilots a balloon is an aeronaut.

    1. who pilots a balloon—adjective clause

[1] In 1978, the aeronauts Ben Abruzzo, Max Anderson, and Larry Newman, whose home was Albuquerque, New Mexico, became the first people ever to pilot a balloon across the Atlantic Ocean. [2] Although Abruzzo and Anderson had been forced to land in the ocean in an

earlier attempt in *Double Eagle,* they had not given up. [**3**] Instead, they had acquired a new balloon, which they had named *Double Eagle II.* [**4**] Newman joined them because experience had shown the need for a third crew member. [**5**] On its journey from Maine to France, *Double Eagle II* was airborne for 137 hours, which is a little less than six days. [**6**] Although *Double Eagle II* relied on the wind's force, the balloon didn't just drift across the Atlantic; the aeronauts piloted it. [**7**] Abruzzo, Anderson, and Newman had to understand meteorology so that they could take advantage of favorable winds. [**8**] They also had to regulate their altitude constantly by adjusting their supply of helium and by losing ballast, as the balloonists shown on the previous page are doing. [**9**] When the balloon gained too much altitude, the crew lowered the aircraft by releasing some of the gas. [**10**] If the balloon lost altitude, the crew raised it by discarding ballast.

The Noun Clause

4f. A *noun clause* is a subordinate clause that is used as a noun.

A noun clause may be used as a subject, a predicate nominative, a direct object, an indirect object, or the object of a preposition.

SUBJECT	**What I need** is my own room.
PREDICATE NOMINATIVE	The happiest time in my life was **when we went to Costa Rica for the summer.**
DIRECT OBJECT	She believes **that lost time is never found again.**
INDIRECT OBJECT	We will give **whoever wins the contest** a prize.
OBJECT OF PREPOSITION	She has written an article about **how she was elected to the Senate.**

Common Introductory Words for Noun Clauses		
how	where	whoever
that	whether	whom
what	which	whomever
whatever	whichever	whose
when	who	why

Reference Note

For more about **subjects,** see page 37. For more about **predicate nominatives,** see page 51. For more about **direct** and **indirect objects,** see page 54. For more about **objects of prepositions,** see page 24.

Reference Note

Some of the words in this chart can be used to introduce **adjective clauses** (see page 93) and **adverb clauses** (see page 96).

Sometimes the introductory word serves a grammatical function within the noun clause, and sometimes it does not.

PN   S   V

EXAMPLES   Do you know **what the problem is**? [The introductory word *what* is a predicate nominative of the subject *problem—the problem is what.*]

S   V

I know **that she is worried.** [The introductory word *that* has no grammatical function in the clause.]

In some sentences the word that introduces a noun clause can be omitted.

EXAMPLES   He told us [**that**] **attendance is improving.** [The introductory word *that* is understood.]

The judge mentioned [**that**] **she was born in Guyana.** [The introductory word *that* is understood.]

Reference Note

For information about another kind of noun clause—**the infinitive clause**—see page 79.

—HELP—

Some sentences in Exercise 5 have more than one noun clause.

Exercise 5   Identifying and Classifying Noun Clauses

Identify the noun clauses in the following sentences. Then, tell how each clause is used: as a *subject*, a *predicate nominative*, a *direct object*, an *indirect object*, or an *object of a preposition*.

EXAMPLE   **1.** Mr. Perkins, the band director, announced that we would play at halftime this week.

    1. that we would play at halftime this week—direct object

1. Mr. Perkins did not tell us, however, what we would be playing during the halftime show.

2. What we can never predict is whether he will choose a familiar march or a show tune.

3. He always gives whoever is asked to play each selection a chance to express an opinion about it.

4. He is genuinely interested in what we think of his sometimes unusual choices.

5. A drummer once told Mr. Perkins she did not like most show tunes.

6. How she could say that was a mystery to me.

7. Mr. Perkins told us we would play a medley of marches.

8. What everyone wanted to know immediately was who would play the solos.

9. He understands why that was our first question.

10. The crowd always applauds enthusiastically for whoever plays a solo.

Review B Identifying Adjective, Adverb, and Noun Clauses

Each sentence in the following paragraph contains at least one subordinate clause. Identify each subordinate clause, and tell whether it is an *adjective clause*, an *adverb clause*, or a *noun clause*.

EXAMPLE
[1] What's so special about the Blue Grotto, which the Italians call *Grotta Azzurra*?

1. *which the Italians call* Grotta Azzurra—*adjective clause*

[1] In the photo below, you can see why the color and the hidden location of the Blue Grotto have made it famous. [2] The grotto is a cavern that can be entered only from the sea. [3] Do you know where the Blue Grotto is located? [4] It is on the west side of the Italian island of Capri, which lies at the entrance to the Bay of Naples. [5] Since the only opening to the cavern is approximately three feet high, visitors must lie down in a rowboat to enter the grotto. [6] The sapphire blue of the water inside the spacious, oval cavern is created by light that is refracted through the deep pool. [7] Although the calm, blue water looks inviting, the grotto is no longer a swimming hole. [8] In the past, however, people who lived in the area greatly enjoyed swimming there. [9] Tour guides tell whoever goes there that centuries ago Tiberius, a Roman emperor, used the Blue Grotto as his private swimming pool. [10] Seeing it today, you would agree that it's a pool fit for an emperor.

Sentences Classified According to Structure

Reference Note

Sentences may also be **classified according to purpose.** See page 57.

The *structure* of a sentence is determined by the number and types of clauses it has.

4g. A sentence can be classified, depending on its structure, as *simple, compound, complex,* or *compound-complex.*

(1) A *simple sentence* contains one independent clause and no subordinate clauses.

A simple sentence may contain a compound subject, a compound verb, and any number of phrases.

EXAMPLES

S   S   V

Cora and **Kareem bought** party supplies at the mall. [compound subject]

S   V   V

Later, **they drove** to school and **decorated** the cafeteria for the Ecology Club's annual banquet. [compound verb]

(2) A *compound sentence* contains two or more independent clauses and no subordinate clauses.

Reference Note

See pages 301 and 322 for more information on **punctuating compound sentences.**

A compound sentence is two or more independent clauses joined together by (1) a comma and a coordinating conjunction, (2) a semi-colon, or (3) a semicolon and a conjunctive adverb such as *therefore, however,* or *consequently* followed by a comma.

EXAMPLES

S   V

Cora hung colorful streamers from the ceiling**, and**

S   V

Kareem set party favors on the tables.

S   V   S

After an hour, they took a short break**;** then they

V

went back to work.

S   V

They agreed not to take any more breaks**; otherwise,**

S   V

they would be late getting home.

> **NOTE** Do not mistake a simple sentence with a compound subject or compound verb for a compound sentence.

$$\overset{\text{S}\quad\text{V}}{}$$

SIMPLE
SENTENCE

To pass the time, **they talked** about school and

$$\overset{\text{V}}{}$$

told stories about their families. [compound verb]

COMPOUND
SENTENCE

$$\overset{\text{S}\quad\text{V}}{}$$

To pass the time, **they talked** about school, and

$$\overset{\text{S}\quad\text{V}}{}$$

they told stories about their families.

(3) A *complex sentence* contains one independent clause and at least one subordinate clause.

EXAMPLE

$$\overset{\text{S}\qquad\text{V}\qquad\qquad\text{S}}{}$$

When they had finished their work, they

$$\overset{\text{V}}{}$$

complimented each other on the results.

(4) A *compound-complex* sentence contains two or more independent clauses and at least one subordinate clause.

EXAMPLE

$$\overset{\text{S}\quad\text{V}}{}$$

Cora waited for just the right moment to ask

$$\overset{\text{S}\qquad\qquad\text{V}}{}$$

Kareem to the banquet, and he promptly accepted her

$$\overset{\text{S}\qquad\text{V}}{}$$

invitation, adding that he had been planning to ask her.

Exercise 6 Classifying Sentences According to Structure

Classify each of the sentences in the following paragraph as *simple, compound, complex,* or *compound-complex.*

EXAMPLE
1. The Key Club decided to sponsor a rummage sale.

1. simple

1. Organizing the rummage sale, the Key Club requested donations from everyone at school.

2. The club members accepted whatever was donated, but they welcomed housewares most.

STYLE **TIP**

Paragraphs in which all the sentences have the same structure can be monotonous to read. To keep your readers interested in your ideas, evaluate your writing to see whether you've used a variety of sentence structures. Then, use revising techniques—adding, cutting, replacing, and reordering—to enliven your writing by varying the structure of your sentences.

COMPUTER TIP

A word processor can help you check for varied sentence structure in your writing. Make a copy of your document. By inserting a return or a page break after every period, you can view the sentences in a vertical list and compare the structures of each sentence in a particular paragraph. Make any revisions on the properly formatted copy of your document.

3. The principal donated a vacuum cleaner; the soccer coach contributed a set of dishes; and several of the teachers provided towels and sheets.
4. The club sold almost everything that had been donated, and the members celebrated their success.
5. Afterward, they gave all the profits that they had made from the sale to the city's homeless shelter.
6. The shelter's employees were grateful for the donations.
7. They offered the members of the Key Club the chance to tour the facility.
8. John took photos, and I interviewed both staff members and clients of the shelter.
9. After we had finished our article, we took it to the editor of the school newspaper.
10. The story was published in the next issue, and we received many compliments even though we hadn't expected any praise.

Review C **Writing Sentences with Varied Structures**

Write your own sentences according to the following guidelines.

EXAMPLE   1. Write a simple sentence containing a compound subject.
            1. *My aunt and uncle live nearby.*

1. Write a simple sentence containing a compound verb.
2. Write a compound sentence containing two independent clauses joined by a comma and the conjunction *but*.
3. Write a compound sentence containing two independent clauses joined by a semicolon, a conjunctive adverb, and a comma.
4. Write a complex sentence containing an adjective clause.
5. Write a complex sentence beginning with an adverb clause.
6. Write a complex sentence ending with an adverb clause.
7. Write a complex sentence containing a noun clause used as the direct object.
8. Write a complex sentence containing a noun clause used as the subject.
9. Write a complex sentence containing a noun clause used as the object of a preposition.
10. Write a compound-complex sentence.

Chapter Review

A. Identifying and Classifying Clauses

For each of the following sentences, identify the italicized clause as *independent* or *subordinate*. Tell whether each subordinate clause functions in the sentence as an *adjective clause*, an *adverb clause*, or a *noun clause*.

1. Scientists have recently discovered *that chameleons are not masters of disguise.*

2. *Their changes of color are not attempts at camouflage;* they are responses to changes in light and temperature.

3. Chameleons, *which dislike any contact*, will tolerate it for the purpose of breeding.

4. *When two chameleons cross paths,* they do their best to frighten each other by hissing, snapping, and changing color.

5. Some scientists think *that such encounters control the chameleons' changes in color.*

6. Males occasionally fight, but *most chameleons try to avoid physical confrontation.*

7. Almost all of the species *that make up the chameleon family* live in trees.

8. *Because the chameleon moves slowly,* it would become an easy prey without its natural green and brown coloration.

9. *The chameleon's tongue is sticky and has numerous folds and furrows* that are lined with hooklike cells.

10. The tongue is propelled by a set of muscles *that can extend it as far as one and one-half times the length of the chameleon's body.*

B. Identifying and Classifying Subordinate Clauses

Identify each subordinate clause in the following sentences. Then, tell whether each subordinate clause is an *adjective clause*, an *adverb clause*, or a *noun clause*.

11. Before you buy the sweater, try it on.

12. Chang, whose mother is a dentist, just lost his retainer.

13. Do you know who won the speech contest?

14. The raccoon that scattered our garbage has annoyed us.

15. Don't agree to do the project if you don't like to paint.

16. Lisa said that she would provide food for the trip.

17. Until you pay back the money, I will charge you interest.

18. Reynaldo was thrilled with what you gave him for his birthday.

19. We saw the movie that you recommended.

20. The CD that you borrowed yesterday belongs to my brother.

21. After we have dinner, let's remember to call Grandpa.

22. Do you know what the capital of Nigeria is?

23. Lilliput, which was invented by Jonathan Swift, is the land of tiny people in Swift's *Gulliver's Travels.*

24. Ariana was a bit worried about what you said.

25. The boy who climbed the tree to save the parakeet has endeared himself to everybody.

26. Our parents heard a song that moved them deeply.

27. Have you heard what happened at the intersection this morning?

28. If you don't like camping, don't go on the trip.

29. Tom and Phyllis said they would pay our dog's boarding costs.

30. We know who is responsible for the success of the summer musical.

C. Classifying Sentences According to Structure

Classify each of the following sentences as *simple, compound, complex,* or *compound-complex.*

31. The Bugatti Motor Club hosted an exhibit of old motoring prints.

32. When our team finished the project, we all went out to lunch at the Mumbai Grill, and our friend Mina met us there.

33. The hotel guests were surprised when the alarm went off.

34. Bill gave a speech, and I took notes.

35. Georges Bizet was the French composer who wrote *Carmen,* which is definitely my favorite opera.

36. The store employees decorated the storefront, the manager put on his best suit, and the customers arrived promptly at eight.

37. We students were very proud of our award-winning teachers.

38. The weather inland was unseasonably cold and frosty, but on the coast a mild wind was blowing from the south.

39. Our short film was shown in one of the theaters downtown; despite our dire predictions, it was fairly well received.

40. Under the foundations of many an old building in Rome, especially near the Forum and Colosseum, are even older foundations, some dating back to the late Empire.

Writing Application
Writing an Art Recommendation

Using Subordinate Clauses   The student council has decided to decorate your school hallways with posters of popular artworks. The council has requested recommendations, including brief descriptions, for artworks that students would like to see. Write two paragraphs about two works (one paragraph on each work) that you would like to recommend. Use specific details, and include at least five subordinate clauses.

Prewriting   Review art books to find pictures of two artworks that you like. Think about why you particularly like these works, and jot down your reasons.

Writing   As you write, you may think of additional details and reasons. If you do, consider how they may fit in with the rest of your notes. Add to your rough draft any new information that fits in smoothly.

Revising   Read through your paragraphs to be sure they each have a topic sentence supported by your reasons for recommending each artwork. Check to see that you have used a total of at least five subordinate clauses in the two paragraphs. If you have not, try combining sentences by creating adjective, adverb, or noun clauses.

Publishing   Proofread your paragraphs for any errors in grammar, punctuation, and spelling. Share your recommendations with your classmates. You may want to vote on your five favorite works to determine your class's preferences.

Agreement
Subject and Verb, Pronoun and Antecedent

Diagnostic Preview

A. Identifying Subject-Verb Agreement and Pronoun-Antecedent Agreement

In most of the following sentences, either a verb does not agree with its subject or a pronoun does not agree with its antecedent. For each incorrect verb or pronoun, write the correct form. If a sentence is already correct, write *C*.

EXAMPLES   **1.** Every leaf, flower, and seedpod were glimmering with frost.

   1. was

   2. Were any tickets left at the box office for me?

   2. C

1. There was women, as well as men, who set out on the perilous journey into new territory.
2. The Morenos, I think, have the best chance of winning.
3. The store, the hotel, and the airport is all in a ten-mile radius of the beach.
4. *Bronzeville Boys and Girls* are a collection of poems by Gwendolyn Brooks.

5. Neither of the candidates has prepared their statement.
6. Mr. Ortega, along with other members of his firm, have established a scholarship fund for art students.
7. To apply for the scholarship, a student must submit at least four samples of their work.
8. The test results showed that about 80 percent of the respondents was in the average group.
9. A hostile crowd gathers outside the courtroom to show their disapproval of the verdict.
10. The committee was preparing their speeches for the meeting with the new governor.

B. Identifying Subject-Verb Agreement and Pronoun-Antecedent Agreement

For each sentence in the following paragraph, write the correct form of each incorrect verb or pronoun. If a sentence is already correct, write *C*.

EXAMPLE   **[1]** Aunt Bonnie, along with several other Peace Corps volunteers, are going to Kenya.

     1. *is going*

[11] Neither my brothers nor my dad were surprised to hear that Aunt Bonnie is going to Kenya as a Peace Corps volunteer. [12] First, she and the other members of the Kenya group gathers in Philadelphia for a few days of orientation. [13] Their focus at this point are to meet one another and get acquainted. [14] Then the whole group travels together to Nairobi, Kenya, where everyone will have their last chance for months to enjoy hot running water! [15] After one night in Nairobi, half of them leaves for the town of Naivasha for eleven weeks of cultural sensitivity training. [16] Each of the volunteers get to live with a Kenyan family during this period of training. [17] The close, daily contact will help them learn to converse in Swahili, one of the languages that is spoken in Kenya. [18] Bonnie don't know yet where exactly in Kenya she is going to be posted. [19] She, as well as the other members of her group, expects to be assigned to the area of greatest need. [20] No one in the group has been told their specific job assignment, but Bonnie says she will probably be helping Kenyans develop small businesses.

Agreement of Subject and Verb

5a. **A verb should agree in number with its subject.**

A word that refers to one person, place, thing, or idea is *singular* in number. A word that refers to more than one is *plural* in number.

Singular	video	child	I	thief	herself
Plural	videos	children	we	thieves	themselves

Reference Note

For more about forming the **plurals of nouns,** see page 385.

HELP

Most of the time, nouns ending in *–s* are plural (*aunts, bushes, cities, tacos, friends*); verbs ending in *–s* are generally singular (*gives, takes, does, has, is*). Note, though, that verbs used with the pronouns *I* and *you* do not end in *–s.*

EXAMPLES
I **know** him.

You **understand.**

Exercise 1 Identifying Words as Singular or Plural

Identify each of the following words as either *singular* or *plural.*

EXAMPLES   **1.** uncles

   1. *plural*

   2. leaf

   2. *singular*

1. stories
2. one
3. several
4. applies
5. people
6. mouse
7. genius
8. teeth
9. ability
10. says
11. he
12. has
13. both
14. toy
15. woman
16. pods
17. donates
18. donation
19. key
20. many

(1) Singular subjects take singular verbs.

EXAMPLES   **Earline attends** college. [The singular verb *attends* agrees with the singular subject *Earline*.]

That **boy delivers** newspapers. [The singular verb *delivers* agrees with the singular subject *boy*.]

(2) Plural subjects take plural verbs.

EXAMPLES   **They attend** college. [The plural verb *attend* agrees with the plural subject *They*.]

Those **boys deliver** newspapers. [The plural verb *deliver* agrees with the plural subject *boys*.]

In a verb phrase, the first helping (auxiliary) verb agrees in number with the subject.

Reference Note

For more about **helping verbs,** see page 15.

EXAMPLES   **Earline is attending** college.
   They are attending college.

USAGE

A **boy** in my class **has been delivering** newspapers.

Two **boys** in my class **have been delivering** newspapers.

NOTE A gerund phrase or an infinitive phrase used as a complete subject takes a singular verb. Do not be misled by any particular noun or pronoun in the phrase. The gerund or infinitive serves as a singular simple subject.

EXAMPLES **Working with you and the others has been** a privilege.
[The singular verb *has been* is used because the gerund *Working*, not the pronoun *you* or *others*, is the subject of the verb.]

To finish our science projects is our immediate goal.
[The singular verb *is* is used because the infinitive *To finish*, not the noun *projects*, is the subject of the verb.]

Reference Note

For more about **gerund phrases** and **infinitive phrases,** see page 76 and page 78.

USAGE

Exercise 2 Selecting Verbs That Agree with Their Subjects

Choose the verb in parentheses that agrees with each subject given.

EXAMPLE **1.** bells (*is ringing, are ringing*)
  1. are ringing

1. people (*walks, walk*)
2. you (*is, are*)
3. house (*has stood, have stood*)
4. we (*talks, talk*)
5. Joan (*was, were*)
6. cattle (*is running, are running*)
7. result (*is, are*)
8. they (*believes, believe*)
9. crews (*sails, sail*)
10. women (*seems, seem*)
11. Lauren and Sierra (*laughs, laugh*)
12. everyone (*is, are*)
13. otters (*has swum, have swum*)
14. students (*graduates, graduate*)
15. boulder (*weighs, weigh*)
16. firefighting (*saves, save*)
17. Phoebe (*reads, read*)
18. jets (*flies, fly*)
19. children (*sings, sing*)
20. to whisper (*is, are*)

(3) The number of a subject usually is not determined by a word in a phrase or clause following the subject.

SINGULAR A **book** of poems **is** on the shelf. [The prepositional phrase *of poems* does not affect the number of the subject *book*.]

PLURAL The **dinosaurs** from the Jurassic Period **include** the Seismosaurus. [The prepositional phrase *from the Jurassic Period* does not affect the number of the subject *dinosaurs*.]

Reference Note

For more about **phrases,** see Chapter 3. For more about **clauses,** see Chapter 4.

SINGULAR   The only **mammal** that has wings **is** the bat. [The subordinate clause *that has wings* does not affect the number of the subject *mammal*.]

PLURAL   **Frogs,** which live both on land and in water, **are** amphibians. [The subordinate clause *which live both on land and in water* does not affect the number of the subject *Frogs*.]

NOTE   *Together with, in addition to, as well as,* and *along with* are compound prepositions. Words in phrases beginning with compound prepositions do not affect the number of the subject or verb.

EXAMPLES   His technical **skills,** together with his delightful sense of humor, **have enabled** Enrique to become a successful computer consultant.

His delightful **sense** of humor, together with his technical skills, **has enabled** Enrique to become a successful computer consultant.

(4) A negative construction following the subject does not change the number of the subject.

EXAMPLE   **Carl,** not Juan and I, **is doing** the artwork.

> **Exercise 3**   **Choosing Verbs That Agree with Their Subjects**

Identify the subject in each of the following sentences. Then, choose the verb in parentheses that agrees in number with the subject.

EXAMPLE   1. The price of haircuts (*has, have*) gone up.

     1. *price—has*

1. A heaping basket of turnip greens (*was, were*) sitting on the counter.
2. The cost of two new snow tires (*was, were*) more than I had expected.
3. The community college course on collecting stamps always (*attracts, attract*) many people.
4. The members of the Pak family (*meets, meet*) for a reunion every year.
5. The carpeting you saw in the upstairs and downstairs rooms (*is, are*) going to be replaced.
6. The turquoise stones in this Navajo ring certainly (*is, are*) pretty.
7. One friend of my brothers (*says, say*) that I look a little like his cousin.
8. The package sent by my cousins (*was, were*) smashed in the mail.

9. Not all the singers who tried out for the school choir (*sings, sing*) equally well.

10. Burt, not Anne and Laura, (*has, have*) borrowed the bicycle pump.

Review A **Completing Sentences That Demonstrate Agreement**

Anna Mary Robertson Moses (1860–1961), better known as Grandma Moses, became famous for her paintings of rural America. Add words to the following word groups to complete ten sentences about this Grandma Moses painting, titled *The Barn Dance.* Make sure that all verbs agree with their subjects. Be prepared to identify the subject and verb in each sentence.

EXAMPLE   **1.** barn are

         1. The doors of the barn are wide open.

1. clouds look

2. musician is playing

3. horse is drinking

4. barn dance are enjoying

5. buildings in the distance is

6. green wagon are waving

7. along with laughter and conversation, fills

8. guests have noticed the cloudy

9. who are at this barn dance

10. horses pulls

The Barn Dance by Grandma Moses, 1860–1961, Copyright 1989.
Grandma Moses Properties Co., New York.

USAGE

Agreement of Subject and Verb   **113**

The words *one*, *thing*, and *body* are singular, and so are the indefinite pronouns that contain these words.

EXAMPLES
Was any**one** hurrying?

No**thing has** been clarified.

Every**body welcomes** the good weather.

Indefinite Pronouns

An *indefinite pronoun* refers to a person, a place, a thing, or an idea that may or may not be specifically named.

EXAMPLES Has **anyone** loaded the van?

    Some of the campsites are vacant.

    Please pack **everything** we will need for camping.

    All of the space in the back seat is filled.

5b. **Some indefinite pronouns are singular; others are plural. Certain indefinite pronouns may be either singular or plural, depending on how they are used.**

(1) The following indefinite pronouns are singular: *anybody, anyone, anything, each, either, everybody, everyone, everything, neither, nobody, no one, nothing, one, somebody, someone,* **and** *something.*

EXAMPLES **Neither** of the animals in the pen **has been fed** this morning.

    Somebody is bringing a CD player to the birthday party on Saturday.

    Was everyone on the volleyball team on time for the class picture at noon?

    One of the puppies **has chewed** a hole in your tennis shoe.

NOTE *Either* and *neither* can be used as adjectives and correlative conjunctions as well as indefinite pronouns. When either word is used as an adjective or a correlative conjunction, it cannot be the subject of a sentence. Carefully identify the subject when you are deciding what form of a verb to use.

ADJECTIVE **Neither** animal has been fed. [The verb agrees with the subject *animal. Neither* modifies *animal.*]

CORRELATIVE CONJUNCTION **Neither** the cow nor the pigs have been fed yet. [The verb agrees with the subject that is nearer to it—*pigs. Neither* is part of the correlative conjunction *Neither . . . nor.*]

INDEFINITE PRONOUN **Neither** of the animals **has been fed.** [The verb agrees with the subject *Neither.*]

(2) The following indefinite pronouns are plural: *both, few, many,* and *several.*

EXAMPLES   Have **both** of them **been** informed?

A **few** in the crowd **were** rowdy.

Many of the staff **volunteer** with local charities.

Several of the women **are** pilots.

(3) The following indefinite pronouns may be either singular or plural, depending on how they are used: *all, any, more, most, none,* and *some.*

These pronouns are singular when they refer to singular words and are plural when they refer to plural words.

SINGULAR   **Most** of the job **was finished.** [*Most* refers to the singular noun *job.*]

PLURAL   **Most** of the jobs **were finished.** [*Most* refers to the plural noun *jobs.*]

SINGULAR   **Has any** of the shipment **arrived**? [*Any* refers to the singular noun *shipment.*]

PLURAL   **Have any** of the shipments **arrived**? [*Any* refers to the plural noun *shipments.*]

SINGULAR   **None** of the test **was** difficult. [*None* refers to the singular noun *test.*]

PLURAL   **None** of the tests **were** difficult. [*None* refers to the plural noun *tests.*]

In each of the examples above, the object of the prepositional phrase following the indefinite pronoun provides a clue to the number of the pronoun.

NOTE   In a sentence that does not include a phrase after the subject, you must find the number of the noun to which the pronoun refers. Make sure the verb has the same number as the antecedent.

EXAMPLES   **Most was** interesting. [The pronoun *Most* may be referring to a portion of a book, of a movie, of a conversation, or some other thing.]

Most were interesting. [The pronoun *Most* may be referring to a number of books, photographs, ideas, or other things.]

—HELP—

Many of the words listed in Rule 5b, (1)–(3), can be used either as pronouns or as adjectives.

ADJECTIVES
   One child is there.
   Many children have left.
   Some children remain.

PRONOUNS
   One is there.
   Many have left.
   Some remain.

USAGE

Using Verbs That Agree with Indefinite Pronouns

Read the following sentences aloud, stressing the italicized words.

1. *One* of those cups *is* broken.
2. Choose a bicycle; *either is* ready to go.
3. A *few* of the girls *are* experienced riders.
4. *Each* of the mariachi bands *has* performed one number.
5. *Some* of your mice *were* eating the cheese.
6. *Most* of the milk that I bought *is* gone.
7. *Neither* of these cars *has* a radio.
8. Here are the apples. *None are* ripe.

Exercise 4 **Writing Sentences with Verbs That Agree with Their Subjects**

Rewrite each of the following sentences according to the directions in parentheses. Then, change the number of the verb to agree with the new subject.

EXAMPLE   **1.** Each of these books was written by Margaret Atwood. (Change *Each* to *All*.)

    1. All of these books were written by Margaret Atwood.

  1. Everyone easily understands the rules of this game. (Change *Everyone* to *Most people*.)
  2. Neither of the actresses was nominated. (Change *Neither* to *Both*.)
  3. Has each of your cousins had a turn? (Change *each* to *both*.)
  4. Some of the trees were destroyed. (Change *trees* to *crop*.)
  5. Have any of the apples been harvested? (Change *apples* to *wheat*.)
  6. Nobody has visited that picnic area. (Change *Nobody* to *Many of our neighbors*.)
  7. Each is well trained. (Change *Each* to *Several*.)
  8. One of the tires needs air. (Change *One* to *All*.)
  9. All of the fruit was eaten. (Change *fruit* to *pears*.)
10. One of the puzzle pieces is missing. (Change *One* to *Some*.)

Exercise 5 **Correcting Errors in Subject-Verb Agreement**

The subjects and verbs in some of the sentences on the next page do not agree. If a sentence is incorrect, write the correct form of the verb. If the sentence is already correct, write *C*.

EXAMPLE   **1.** Most of the world's diamonds comes from mines in Africa.

   1. come

1. Several of the forwards on the team was commended by the captain.
2. Neither of the coaches were happy with the decision.
3. Each of us are going to make a large poster for the upcoming election.
4. Some of the frozen yogurt have started to melt.
5. Does both of those games require special gear?
6. Either of Mr. Catalano's assistants have approval and can go.
7. None of the buildings were damaged by the hail.
8. None of the food have been frozen.
9. Neither of the book reports were finished on time.
10. Does anyone want to help me make gefilte fish for the Passover feast?

(Review B) **Selecting Verbs That Agree with Their Subjects**

For each of the following sentences, choose the verb in parentheses that agrees with the subject.

EXAMPLE   **1.** How (*does, do*) astronauts on a space shuttle prepare their meals?

   1. do

1. (*Has, Have*) any of you ever wondered how meals are served to space-shuttle astronauts?
2. Each of the items for the day's menu (*comes, come*) sealed in its own container.
3. To help reduce weight on the spacecraft, many of the foods (*is, are*) dehydrated.
4. At mealtime, someone in the crew (*adds, add*) water to the scrambled eggs, vegetables, and puddings.
5. All of the water mixed with these foods (*is, are*) a byproduct of the fuel cells that provide the space-craft's electricity.
6. Of course, because there is no gravity, not one of the beverages (*is, are*) pourable.
7. If a container is accidentally jolted, any uncovered liquid (*bounces, bounce*) into the air like a ball, as you can see.

USAGE

8. Some of the food (*is, are*) covered in sauce so that surface tension will help to keep the food in dishes.
9. Amazingly, most of the foods (*tastes, taste*) delicious.
10. The menu for the astronauts even (*includes, include*) steaks and strawberries.

Compound Subjects

A *compound subject* consists of two or more subjects that are joined by a conjunction and that have the same verb.

5c. Subjects joined by *and* generally take a plural verb.

EXAMPLES   **Ramón** and **she like** hiking.

Her **brother,** her **uncle,** and her **cousin are** teachers.

Both the **scout** and the **counselor were** helpful guides.

NOTE   Subjects joined by *and* that name only one person, place, thing, or idea take singular verbs. Singular compound nouns containing *and* also take singular verbs.

EXAMPLE   The club's **secretary and treasurer was** Eduardo. [one person]

Country and western has become our favorite kind of music. [one kind of music]

The **bed and breakfast** down the street **is** always reserved weeks in advance. [one place to stay]

5d. Singular subjects joined by *or* or *nor* take a singular verb. Plural subjects joined by *or* or *nor* take a plural verb.

EXAMPLES   **Marcelo** or **Donya knows** the address.

Neither our **phone** nor our **doorbell was working.**

Do the **Wilsons** or the **Campbells live** there?

Neither **cardinals** nor **finches come** to the birdfeeder.

5e. When a singular subject and a plural subject are joined by *or* or *nor,* the verb agrees with the subject nearer the verb.

EXAMPLES   Either **Harry** or his **aunts are planning** the activities for the beach party.

Neither the **potatoes** nor the **roast is** done.

STYLE TIP

You can usually avoid awkward constructions like those shown under Rule 5e by rewording your sentence so that each subject has its own verb.

EXAMPLES

Either **Harry is planning** the activities for the beach party, or his **aunts are.**

The **potatoes are** not done, and neither **is** the **roast.**

USAGE

Oral Practice 2 Using Verbs That Agree with Compound Subjects

Read the following sentences aloud, stressing the italicized words.

1. *Both* Steve *and* Edie *want* to be first-chair violin.
2. You *and* I *are* in the same Spanish class.
3. *Neither* Gretchen *nor* Colleen *knows* the answer.
4. *Neither* Sam *nor* Miguel *likes* sports.
5. *Either* Judy *or* Bob *washes* the dishes tonight.
6. Roger *and* Carla *play* basketball every Saturday.
7. *Are* cats *or* dogs popular pets in the United States?
8. *Both* Marilyn *and* Marge *have* summer jobs.

Exercise 6 Choosing Verbs That Agree with Their Subjects

For each of the following sentences, choose the verb in parentheses that agrees with the subject of the sentence.

EXAMPLE   1. The *pipa* and the *cheng* (*is, are*) the main instruments used in Chinese music.

      1. are

1. Neither my older brother Alexander nor my sister Elizabeth (*has, have*) a car.
2. Marlon and she (*is, are*) the dance champions.
3. Our relatives and yours (*is, are*) hosting a barbecue next Saturday afternoon.
4. Both Kathleen and Jackson (*plays, play*) a good game of tennis.
5. Either the director or the actors (*is, are*) going to have to compromise.
6. Neither the grapes nor the cantaloupe (*was, were*) ripe enough for us to eat.
7. Both Roberto and Caroline (*is, are*) popular camp counselors.
8. Our class or theirs (*is, are*) going to sponsor the spring festival and dance.
9. Either the faucet or the shower head (*leaks, leak*).
10. Either a transistor or a capacitor (*has, have*) burned out in this receiver.

USAGE

Special Problems in Subject-Verb Agreement

Reference Note

For more about **nouns**, see page 3.

5f. Collective nouns may be either singular or plural, depending on their meaning in a sentence.

A *collective noun* is a noun whose singular form names a group.

Commonly Used Collective Nouns			
army	club	group	school
assembly	committee	herd	squad
audience	crowd	jury	staff
band	faculty	majority	swarm
choir	family	number	team
class	flock	public	troop

A collective noun is

- singular when it refers to the group as a unit
- plural when it refers to the individual members or parts of the group

SINGULAR	The **class has met** its substitute teacher. [the class as a unit]
PLURAL	The **class were disagreeing** with one another about the answers. [the class as individuals]

SINGULAR	The **team is** on the field. [the team as a unit]
PLURAL	The **team are working** together. [the team as individuals]

Exercise 7 Writing Sentences with Singular and Plural Collective Nouns

For each of the following collective nouns, write one sentence using the singular and one sentence using the plural.

EXAMPLE   **1.** cast

1. singular—*The cast is having a wrap party.*

   plural—*After the play, the cast are joining their friends and family for a wrap party.*

1. squad   **3.** flock   **5.** group   **7.** troop   **9.** crowd
2. choir   **4.** jury   **6.** band   **8.** committee   **10.** family

USAGE

Review C **Writing Sentences with Verbs That Agree with Their Subjects**

Rewrite the following sentences according to the instructions in parentheses. Change the number of the verb if necessary.

EXAMPLE   1. The faculty are discussing their class schedules with the guidance counselors. (Change *discussing their class schedules* to *in a meeting.*)

    1. *The faculty is in a meeting with the guidance counselors.*

1. Both of the records are in the Top Forty. (Change *Both* to *Neither.*)
2. The choir has been rehearsing with the conductor. (Change *with the conductor* to *in small groups.*)
3. Everybody in the chorus is trying out for the school play. (Change *Everybody* to *No one.*)
4. Neither Carrie nor Jana is in the Pep Club this semester. (Change *Neither . . . nor* to *Both . . . and.*)
5. Gabriel García Márquez and Octavio Paz have won prizes in literature. (Change *and* to *or.*)
6. All of your papers were graded. (Change *All* to *Each.*)
7. Some of the wood burns. (Change *wood* to *logs.*)
8. The delighted team was waving and running around the stadium. (Change *waving and running around the stadium* to *assembling to accept their medals.*)
9. Either my cousins or Adrienne is bringing the pizza. (Reverse the order of the subjects.)
10. Macaroni and cheese always tastes good. (Change *and* to *or.*)
11. The archaeologist and the geologist are lecturing tomorrow. (Change *and* to *or.*)
12. They exercise regularly. (Change *They* to *She.*)
13. Either a banana or grapes are my favorite dessert. (Reverse the order of the subjects.)
14. Each of the flowers was beautiful. (Change *Each* to *All.*)
15. Tamisha and Heather's favorite pastime is jumping rope. (Change *Tamisha and Heather's* to *Tamisha's.*)
16. Neither of the flights is full. (Change *Neither* to *Both.*)
17. Most of the beans were gone. (Change *beans* to *bread.*)
18. The family was in the living room. (Change *in the living room* to *reading their favorite books.*)
19. The man or the woman is going to win. (Change *or* to *and.*)
20. All of us are happy. (Change *All* to *Not one.*)

STYLE **TIP**

When a construction like the ones under Rule 5g seems awkward to you, revise the sentence to avoid using a predicate nominative.

EXAMPLE
I use tomatoes as the main ingredient in salsa.

STYLE **TIP**

Many people consider contractions informal. Therefore, in formal speech and writing, it is generally best to avoid using contractions.

5g. A verb agrees with its subject but not necessarily with a predicate nominative.

	S		PN
EXAMPLES   The main **ingredient** in salsa **is tomatoes.**

              S   PN
           Tomatoes are the main **ingredient** in salsa.

5h. When the subject follows the verb, find the subject and make sure that the verb agrees with it.

In sentences beginning with *Here* or *There* and in questions, the subject generally follows the verb or part of the verb.

EXAMPLES   Here **is** a **set** of keys.

               Here **are** the **keys.**

               Do they know the price?
               Does he know the price?

NOTE   A contraction such as *here's, how's, there's, what's,* or *where's* includes the singular verb *is* or *has.* Use such a contraction only when a singular subject follows it.

INCORRECT   In an article in this magazine, there's several photos of the construction of the memorial to Chief Crazy Horse.

CORRECT   In an article in this magazine, there **are** several **photos** of the construction of the memorial to Chief Crazy Horse.

CORRECT   In this magazine, there**'s** an **article** with several photos of the construction of the memorial to Chief Crazy Horse.

Exercise 8   Proofreading for Subject-Verb Agreement

For each of the following sentences, if the subject and verb do not agree, write the correct form of the verb. If the verb already agrees with the subject, write *C*.

EXAMPLE   **1.** Sore muscles is a symptom of the flu.

          1. are

   1. When's your finals?
   2. One requirement for becoming a pilot are quick reflexes.
   3. Where's the nearest movie theater?
   4. The highlight of the evening were the performances by the dance troupes.
   5. Do the club meet Tuesday, Wednesday, and Thursday?

6. Methods for conserving energy is what the panel will discuss.
7. The most important component in this watch are the batteries.
8. Here's the books you reserved.
9. Maria Theresa's favorite part of the movie was the scenes in New England.
10. There's the keys that you misplaced.

Review D **Identifying Sentences with Subject-Verb Agreement**

For each of the following sentences, if the subject and verb do not agree, write the correct form of the verb. Be ready to explain your correction. If the verb already agrees with the subject, write *C*.

EXAMPLE   1. What's the typical ingredients of the soup called gazpacho?

1. *are*

1. Steven and Maria is the first team to finish.
2. There's the boats I told you about.
3. Both my father and sister wants to see the Dodgers game.
4. Either the twins or Jamie are playing a practical joke.
5. How was the swimming and sailing at the beach?
6. Each of these old photos show your uncle Ahmad wearing a colorful, flowing dashiki.
7. Neither the windows nor the door is locked.
8. Contemporary rock-and-roll are rooted in ancient rhythms.
9. There's several football games on television on Sunday.
10. Where's my socks?

┌**HELP**┐

In the example for Review D, the verb is changed to agree with the plural subject, *ingredients*.

USAGE

5i. **An expression of an amount (a measurement, a percentage, or a fraction, for example) may be singular or plural, depending on how it is used.**

An expression of an amount is

- singular when the amount is thought of as a unit

- plural when the amount is thought of as separate parts

SINGULAR   **Two years is** a long time. [one time]
PLURAL   Two **years** (1995 and 1998) **were** especially rainy. [separate years]

SINGULAR   **Fifteen dollars was** the price. [one price]
PLURAL   Fifteen **dollars were** torn. [separate dollar bills]

A fraction or a percentage is

- singular when it refers to a singular word
- plural when it refers to a plural word

SINGULAR   **Nine tenths** [*or* **Ninety percent**] of the student body **is** present today. [The fraction, or the percentage, refers to the singular noun *student body.*]

PLURAL   **Nine tenths** [*or* **Ninety percent**] of the students **are** present today. [The fraction, or the percentage, refers to the plural word *students.*]

Generally, a measurement (such as length, weight, capacity, or area) is singular.

EXAMPLES   **Nine square feet equals** one square yard.

           Six hundred kilometers is the distance we traveled today.

           Three cups of flour is what the recipe requires.

NOTE   In the expression *the number of, number* takes a singular verb. In the expression *a number of, number* takes a plural verb.

EXAMPLES   **The** number of female athletes **is growing.**

           A number of girls **like** strenuous sports.

5j. When the relative pronoun *that, which,* or *who* is the subject in an adjective clause, the verb in the clause agrees with the word to which the relative pronoun refers.

EXAMPLE   A *corps de ballet* is a group of ballet dancers **that perform** together. [*That* refers to the plural noun *dancers* and therefore requires the plural verb *perform.*]

           The Dutch painter Piet Mondrian, **who was** part of an art movement known as *de Stijl,* was fond of the colors red, yellow, and blue. [*Who* refers to the singular noun *Piet Mondrian* and therefore requires the singular verb *was.*]

NOTE   When preceded by *one of* + a plural word, the relative pronoun takes a plural verb. When preceded by *the only one of* + a plural word, the relative pronoun takes a singular verb.

PLURAL   Melba is **one of those players who** always **try** their best.

SINGULAR   Melba is **the only one of those players who** always **tries** her best.

USAGE

5k. A subject preceded by *every* or *many a(n)* takes a singular verb.

EXAMPLE   **Every** parent and grandparent **is looking** on proudly.

                Many a hopeful performer **has gone** to Broadway in search of fame.

Exercise 9   Proofreading for Subject-Verb Agreement

For each of the following sentences, if the subject and verb do not agree, write the correct form of the verb. If the verb already agrees with the subject, write *C*.

EXAMPLES   **1.** Twenty-four dollars was scattered on the counter.

             1. were

            2. Every one of them have left.

            2. has

1. Many a sophomore and junior are participating.
2. Every takeoff and landing are cleared with the control tower.
3. Two thirds of my research paper have been typed.
4. Emilio has cousins who raise tropical fish.
5. Eight pounds were the baby's weight at birth.
6. Forty-eight percent of the seniors is planning to go to college.
7. Fifteen dollars is all we have raised so far.
8. Egypt is one of the nations that borders the Red Sea.
9. Silvia knows some people who owns a Christmas-tree farm.
10. Pluto is the only one of the planets that cross the orbit of another planet in our solar system.

5l. The contractions *don't* and *doesn't* should agree with their subjects.

Use *don't* (the contraction of *do not*) with the subjects *I* and *you* and with all plural subjects.

EXAMPLES   **I don't** have any paper.

                You don't need special permission.

                The **players don't** seem nervous.

Reference Note

For more information about **contractions,** see page 361.

USAGE

Use *doesn't* (the contraction of *does not*) with all singular subjects except *I* and *you*.

EXAMPLES **Doesn't it** show up in this picture?

The **tire doesn't** have enough air.

Exercise 10 Using *Don't* and *Doesn't* Correctly in Sentences

Choose the correct form (*don't* or *doesn't*) for each of the following sentences.

EXAMPLES 1. _____ Lea speak several languages?
1. *Doesn't*

2. The birds _____ seem bothered by the wind.
2. *don't*

1. The calf _____ look very strong.
2. It _____ look good with that jacket.
3. We _____ play racquetball.
4. _____ these piñatas look colorful?
5. I _____ mind helping out.
6. You _____ have to watch the program.
7. Loretta _____ enjoy cleaning house.
8. A few of the contests _____ award cash prizes.
9. _____ it arrive tomorrow?
10. _____ they tinker with cars?

5m. Some nouns that are plural in form take singular verbs.

The following nouns take singular verbs.

civics	gymnastics	news
economics	linguistics	physics
electronics	mathematics	summons
genetics	molasses	

EXAMPLES **Linguistics is** the science of language.

News of the concert's cancellation **was** disappointing to the band members.

Has mathematics always **been** your best subject?

NOTE Many nouns ending in *–ics,* such as *acoustics, athletics, ethics, politics, statistics,* and *tactics,* may be singular or plural, depending on how they are used. Generally, such a noun takes a singular verb when the noun names a science, system, or skill. The noun takes a plural verb when the noun names qualities, activities, or individual items.

EXAMPLES **Acoustics deals** with the transmission of sound.

The **acoustics** in the new auditorium **are** excellent.

Some nouns that are plural in form but that refer to single items take plural verbs.

binoculars	pants	shears
eyeglasses	pliers	shorts
Olympics	scissors	slacks

EXAMPLES **Are** the **scissors** sharp enough?

The **pliers seem** to be missing.

Your gray **slacks are** in the laundry.

5n. Even when plural in form, the title of a creative work (such as a book, song, movie, or painting) generally takes a singular verb.

EXAMPLES ***Majors and Minors* is** a collection of Paul Laurence Dunbar's poetry. [one book]

***The Gleaners* is** a famous painting by Jean-François Millet. [one work of art]

Four Saints in Three Acts, with music by Virgil Thomson and words by Gertrude Stein, **was** first **produced** in 1934, with an African American cast. [one musical work]

5o. Even when plural in form, the name of a country, a city, or an organization generally takes a singular verb.

EXAMPLES The **Solomon Islands is** in the South Pacific Ocean.

Is Grand Rapids smaller than Detroit?

Carrier Computers is having a sale on laptops.

HELP

If you do not know whether a noun that is plural in form is singular or plural in meaning, look up the word in a dictionary.

COMPUTER TIP

Some word-processing programs can find problems in subject-verb agreement. You can use such a program to search for errors when you proofread your writing. If you are not sure that a usage that the program identifies as an error is truly an error, check this textbook.

USAGE

For each of the following sentences, if the subject and verb do not agree, write the correct form of the verb. If the verb already agrees with the subject, write *C*.

EXAMPLE 1. Where is my favorite khaki shorts?

1. *are*

1. Des Moines are the capital of Iowa.
2. The United Nations have its headquarters in New York City.
3. "Tales from the Vienna Woods" are one of Johann Strauss's most popular waltzes.
4. The Philippines comprise more than seven thousand islands.
5. Statistics are the collection of mathematical data.
6. The United Arab Emirates generate most of its revenue from the sale of oil.
7. Civics are definitely Alejandra's best subject.
8. When he is making alterations, the tailor's scissors usually hang around his neck on a leather band.
9. *Vermilion Lotuses* were among the paintings by Chinese artist Chang Dai-chien exhibited at the Smithsonian Institution.
10. Are the Olympics on television this afternoon?

Review E Choosing Verbs That Agree with Their Subjects

Choose the correct form of the verb given in parentheses in each of the following sentences.

EXAMPLE 1. (*Doesn't, Don't*) the French phrase *joie de vivre* mean "joy of living"?

1. *Doesn't*

1. Nguyen, along with her family, (*has, have*) invited me to the Vietnamese National Day celebration in the park.
2. They (*wasn't, weren't*) interested in learning how to play the accordion.
3. Carlos, not Martha or Jan, (*was, were*) answering all the letters.
4. Many of them (*has, have*) already read the novel.
5. *The Birds* (*was, were*) one of Alfred Hitchcock's great movies.
6. (*Doesn't, Don't*) Chuck intend to join the Air Force when he graduates?

7. Caroline, like most of her classmates, (*wishes, wish*) vacation could last forever.
8. There (*is, are*) some good programs on educational television.
9. Neither of those books by Naguib Mahfouz (*is, are*) on our reading list.
10. The shears (*doesn't, don't*) need sharpening.

Review F   Choosing Verbs That Agree with Their Subjects

For each of the following sentences, choose the correct form of the verb in parentheses.

EXAMPLE   1. The quills of a porcupine (*was, were*) used to make this pair of moccasins.

   1. *were*

1. (*Doesn't, Don't*) these quilled moccasins look as if they are beaded?
2. Quillwork, one of the traditional Plains Indians handicrafts, (*is, are*) an ancient and sophisticated art form.
3. The number of quills that grow on one porcupine (*is, are*) greater than you might think—about thirty thousand!
4. Five inches (*is, are*) the maximum length of these tubular spines.
5. Before being used in quillwork, every porcupine quill (*is, are*) dyed a bright color, softened in water, and flattened in an unusual way.
6. The quillworker, usually a woman, (*squeeze, squeezes*) each quill flat by pulling it between her teeth.
7. Among the Sioux, worn teeth were considered a badge of great honor because items decorated with the colorful quillwork (*was, were*) so important in tribal life.
8. Working the quills into complex geometric patterns (*require, requires*) great skill and coordination.
9. In quill weaving, each of the ribbonlike quills (*is, are*) passed tightly over and under threads of fiber or leather.
10. The finished quillwork (*is, are*) sewn onto clothing, saddlebags, or cradleboards as a decoration.

For each of the following sentences, if the verb and the subject do not agree, supply the correct form of the verb. If the verb and subject already agree, write *C*.

EXAMPLE   1. *Sleeping Musicians* were painted by Rufino Tamayo.

           1. *was painted*

1. Gymnastics help keep me limber.
2. Few objections, besides the one about chartering the bus, was raised.
3. *Six Characters in Search of an Author* is a modern play that raises many interesting questions about art and reality.
4. Some of this land is far too hilly to farm.
5. In Maine, there's many miles of rocky coastline.
6. Four minutes were his time in that race.
7. Performing in front of a thousand people don't seem to bother the cellist Yo-Yo Ma.
8. Two thirds of a cup of milk is needed for this recipe.
9. Every three years my family have a reunion in Mexico, where my grandparents still live.
10. Every student, teacher, and administrator are contributing to the fund-raising drive.

Agreement of Pronoun and Antecedent

The noun or pronoun that a pronoun refers to is called its *antecedent*.

5p. A pronoun should agree in both number and gender with its antecedent.

(1) Use singular pronouns to refer to singular antecedents. Use plural pronouns to refer to plural antecedents.

SINGULAR   **Richard Strauss** composed many operas. *Der Rosenkavalier* is perhaps **his** most famous.

PLURAL   The mountain **climbers** believe that **they** will reach the summit by Friday.

(2) Some singular pronouns indicate *gender*—*masculine, feminine,* or *neuter* (neither masculine nor feminine).

Masculine	he	him	his	himself
Feminine	she	her	hers	herself
Neuter	it	it	its	itself

EXAMPLES   Does **Margaret** like **her** dance class?

Arturo is doing **his** homework.

Because the **car** wouldn't start, **it** had to be towed.

Indefinite Pronouns

5q. Indefinite pronouns agree with their antecedents according to the following rules.

(1) The indefinite pronouns *anybody, anyone, anything, each, either, everybody, everyone, everything, neither, nobody, no one, nothing, one, somebody, someone,* and *something* are singular.

Notice that the use of a phrase or a clause after the indefinite pronoun does not change the number of the antecedent.

EXAMPLES   **Each** of the teams had **its** mascot at the game.

One of the boys left **his** pen behind.

Everybody in the girls' league has paid **her** dues.

When you do not know the gender of the antecedent, use both the masculine and the feminine pronoun forms, connected by *or.*

EXAMPLES   **Someone** left **his or her** pen behind.

Everybody in the club has paid **his or her** dues.

NOTE   When the meaning of *everyone* or *everybody* is clearly plural, it is common in informal speech and writing to use a plural pronoun to refer to it. In formal speech and writing, you should revise the sentence to eliminate the confusion rather than use the wrong pronoun form.

CONFUSING   When everyone arrives, explain the situation to him or her.
 INFORMAL   When everyone arrives, explain the situation to them.
   FORMAL   When **all** the people arrive, explain the situation to **them.**

┌HELP─

Some of the words listed in Rule 5q (1) can also be used as adjectives and as parts of correlative conjunctions.

ADJECTIVE
  Each flea hops.

CORRELATIVE CONJUNCTION
  Either Fido **or** the flea hops.

Reference Note

For more about **adjectives,** see page 10. For more about **correlative conjunctions,** see page 26.

USAGE

Review G

(2) The indefinite pronouns *both, few, many,* and *several* are plural.

EXAMPLES   **Both** of the candidates clearly stated **their** positions on the issue.

Many of the actors already know **their** lines.

(3) The indefinite pronouns *all, any, more, most, none,* and *some* may be singular or plural, depending on how they are used in a sentence.

Each of these pronouns is singular when it refers to a singular word and is plural when it refers to a plural word.

SINGULAR   **Most** of this money belongs to Ms. Hayek. Would you take **it** to her, please? [*It* is used because *Most* refers to the singular noun *money.*]

PLURAL   **Most** of these coins are rare, but I don't know what **they** are worth. [*They* is used because *Most* refers to the plural noun *coins.*]

Exercise 12 **Choosing Pronouns That Agree with Their Antecedents**

For the blanks in the following sentences, choose pronouns that agree with their antecedents.

EXAMPLE   **1.** Everyone on the boys' wrestling team did _____ best at practice today.

          1. *his*

1. Some of the nations successfully defended _____ borders.
2. Neither of the sisters wanted to recite _____ lines.
3. Did any of the visitors forget _____ personal belongings?
4. One of the exhibits had _____ date changed from A.D. 1200 to A.D. 1350.
5. Each of the candidates bought _____ own TV air time.
6. Someone left _____ books behind.
7. Everyone who will need extra time should raise _____ hand.
8. Many of these blossoms were smaller than we had expected _____ to be.
9. If you find a few of the pieces, Sara said she could use _____.
10. Each of the dolphins displays _____ particular characteristics.

Compound Antecedents

5r. Pronouns agree with compound antecedents according to the following rules.

(1) Use a plural pronoun to refer to two or more antecedents joined by *and.*

EXAMPLE   The **guide** and the **ranger** wrapped **their** rain ponchos in **their** saddle rolls.

NOTE   Antecedents joined by *and* that name only one person, place, thing, or idea take singular pronouns.

EXAMPLE   For dinner, I'm preparing **liver and onions.** I think you'll enjoy **it.**

(2) Use a singular pronoun to refer to two or more singular antecedents joined by *or* **or** *nor.*

EXAMPLE   Neither Heidi nor Beth took **her** umbrella with **her.**

Using a pronoun to refer to antecedents of different number may create an unclear or awkward sentence.

UNCLEAR   Neither the parrots nor the macaw has eaten its fruit. [*Its* agrees with the nearest antecedent, *macaw*, but the sentence is unclear. Does it mean that none of the birds have eaten their own fruit, that the parrots have not eaten the macaw's fruit, or that the macaw has not eaten its own fruit?]

Neither the macaw nor the parrots have eaten their fruit. [*Their* agrees with the nearest antecedent, *parrots*, but the sentence is unclear. Does it mean that none of the birds have eaten their own fruit, that the parrots have not eaten their own fruit, or that the macaw has not eaten the parrots' fruit?]

AWKWARD   Neither the macaw nor the parrots have eaten its or their fruit.

It is best to revise sentences to avoid unclear and awkward constructions like the ones above.

REVISED   Neither the macaw nor the parrots have eaten **the** fruit.
            None of the birds have eaten **their** fruit.

> **STYLE   TIP**
>
> Sentences with singular antecedents joined by *or* or *nor* can be misleading or may sound awkward when the antecedents are of different genders. Avoid using such sentences in your writing.
>
> MISLEADING
>   Neither Karen nor Brian took his camera along. [Did Karen not take along Brian's camera, either?]
>
> AWKWARD
>   Neither Karen nor Brian took her or his camera along. [Did Karen and Brian intend to take only one camera along—either hers or his?]
>
> IMPROVED
>   Neither Karen nor Brian took **a** camera along. [The article *a* replaces the confusing pronoun.]
>
> IMPROVED
>   **Karen and Brian** did not take **their** cameras along. [Antecedents joined by *and* require a plural pronoun, which does not indicate gender.]

USAGE

Special Problems in Pronoun-Antecedent Agreement

Reference Note

For a list of commonly used **collective nouns,** see page 120.

5s. A collective noun is singular when the noun refers to the group as a unit and plural when the noun refers to the individual members or parts of the group.

SINGULAR   The **orchestra** was looking forward to performing **its** rendition of Beethoven's *Pastoral Symphony*. [*Its* is used because the orchestra would perform the rendition as a unit.]

PLURAL   The **orchestra** were tuning **their** instruments when the conductor arrived. [*Their* is used because the members of the orchestra were tuning separate instruments.]

5t. An expression of an amount (a measurement, a percentage, or a fraction, for example) may take a singular or plural pronoun, depending on how it is used.

An expression of an amount is

- singular when the amount is thought of as a unit
- plural when the amount is thought of as separate parts

SINGULAR   **Two days** is a long time. **It** could seem like forever. [one time]

PLURAL   **Two days** (Monday and Friday) were especially cold and rainy. **They** were so wet that baseball practice was canceled. [two separate days]

SINGULAR   **Five dollars** was the price. I had **it** in my pocket. [one price]

PLURAL   **Five dollars** were torn. The vending machine would not accept **them.** [separate dollars]

A fraction or a percentage is

- singular when it refers to a singular word
- plural when it refers to a plural word

SINGULAR   **Nine tenths** [or **Ninety percent**] of the colony has returned to **its** usual routine. [The fraction, or the percentage, refers to the singular noun *colony.*]

PLURAL   **Three tenths** [or **Thirty percent**] of the ants have returned to **their** usual routines. [The fraction, or the percentage, refers to the plural word *ants.*]

Generally, a measurement (such as a length, weight, capacity, or area) is singular.

EXAMPLES   **Nine square feet** equals one square yard. **This** is how much material you will need.

Six hundred kilometers is the distance we traveled today. How far is **that** in miles?

5u. Some nouns that are plural in form take singular pronouns.

(1) The following nouns take singular pronouns.

civics	genetics	mathematics	physics
economics	gymnastics	molasses	summons
electronics	linguistics	news	

EXAMPLE   I have good **news.** Would you like to hear **it**?

NOTE Many nouns ending in *–ics,* such as *acoustics, athletics, ethics, politics, statistics,* and *tactics,* may take singular or plural pronouns, depending on how the nouns are used. Generally, when such a noun names a science, system, or skill, the noun takes a singular pronoun. When the noun names qualities, activities, or individual items, the noun takes a plural pronoun.

SINGULAR   The colonel explained **tactics** and how **it** differs from strategy.

PLURAL   The colonel outlined the **tactics,** and the general approved **them.**

Some nouns that are plural in form but that refer to single items take plural pronouns.

binoculars	shears	pants
Olympics	slacks	scissors
pliers	eyeglasses	shorts

EXAMPLE   Marissa is looking for the **scissors.** Do you know where **they** are?

(2) Even when plural in form, the title of a creative work (such as a book, song, movie, or painting) or the name of a country, a city, or an organization generally takes a singular pronoun.

EXAMPLES   Have you read ***Thousand Cranes***? **It** was written by Yasunari Kawabata.

Reference Note
For information on when **to spell out numbers** and **when to use numerals,** see page 389.

HELP
Check a dictionary if you are not sure whether to use a singular or plural pronoun to refer to an antecedent ending in *–ics.*

USAGE

Agreement of Pronoun and Antecedent   **135**

My all-time favorite film is ***Dances with Wolves.*** One of **its** principal characters is played by the Canadian actor Graham Greene.

When we visited the **Philippines,** we spent most of our time on **its** chief island, Luzon.

I grew up near **Hot Springs,** Arkansas. **Its** claim to fame is **its** popular health resort.

Have you gone to **Sir Books–A–Lot**? **It** may have a copy of the book you need.

N O T E The names of some teams, though plural in form, may take singular or plural pronouns. When the name refers to the organization as a unit, use a singular pronoun. When the name refers to the members of the organization, use a plural pronoun.

SINGULAR The **St. Louis Cardinals** won **its** first World Series title in 1926. [*Its* is used because the St. Louis Cardinals won as a unit.]

PLURAL Signing autographs, the **St. Louis Cardinals** thanked **their** fans for supporting **them** throughout the season. [*Their* and *them* are used because the individual players signed autographs and thanked the fans.]

5v. The number of a relative pronoun (such as *that, which,* or *who*) is determined by the number of its antecedent.

SINGULAR Jessica, **who** always takes pride in **her** work, has been appointed editor of the school yearbook. [*Who* is singular because it refers to the singular noun *Jessica. Her* is used to agree with *who.*]

PLURAL All **who** want to volunteer **their** time should sign up. [*Who* is plural because it refers to the plural pronoun *All. Their* is used to agree with *who.*]

(Exercise 13) **Choosing Pronouns That Agree with Their Antecedents**

For the blanks in the following sentences, choose pronouns that agree with their antecedents.

EXAMPLE **1.** I just read *Franny and Zooey;* have you read _____?

    1. it

1. If I don't pack the binoculars now, I'll forget _____.

MEETING THE CHALLENGE

Write a headline and one-page newspaper article describing a sensational event. For example, the article could cover the headline "Giant Squirrels Squash City." Your article should contain at least five examples of correct subject-verb agreement and five examples of correct pronoun-antecedent agreement.

2. I'm looking for someone on the boys' swimming team who has parked _____ car in my space.

3. They have twelve dollars; is _____ enough?

4. Did the team scrimmage with _____ arch-rival?

5. Two thirds of the crew members have already had _____ turns standing watch.

6. The Millers and the Doyles had _____ windows broken by the hail last night.

7. All of the art class buy _____ own paper.

8. I could buy a bag of peanuts for sixty cents if I had _____ in correct change.

9. Either Stu or Mike will lend me _____ fishing gear.

10. The eyeglasses broke when _____ were dropped.

Review H **Making Pronouns Agree with Their Antecedents**

Most of the following sentences contain pronouns that do not agree with their antecedents. If any pronoun does not agree with its antecedent, supply the correct pronoun or pronouns. If all of the pronouns in a sentence agree with their antecedents, write *C*.

EXAMPLE   1. Each of the girls enjoyed themselves.
          1. *herself*

1. All of the students at the Children's Theater summer camp brought his lunch.

2. The leader of the camp and his assistant told the class about their goals for the summer.

3. All of the students will be performing a play written by herself.

4. Both Carla and Jane want the lead role for themselves.

5. Each student will provide his own costumes.

6. The students worked together well to write her play.

7. Owen is one of those students who always knows their lines.

8. Allison and Joyce sang a song they wrote themselves.

9. Franklin and Jacob hit his cues expertly.

10. At the final performance of the play, the members of the audience clapped its hands and cheered.

Review I **Identifying Subject-Verb Agreement and Pronoun-Antecedent Agreement**

Some of the following sentences contain an error in agreement. If a verb or pronoun is wrong, correct it. If the sentence is already correct, write *C*.

EXAMPLE   **1.** The gorilla, as well as many other mammals, are in danger of becoming extinct.

       1. is

1. Both Sid and Nikki like their new neighborhood and their new apartment.
2. Are either of you a member of the African American Cultural Society?
3. The computer camp lasts for five weeks. These are two weeks more than the tennis camp.
4. One of the police officers turned in their badge today.
5. Neither Fernando nor Bruce has brought all of their camping gear.
6. *All Dogs Go to Heaven* are my young nephews' favorite animated feature.
7. Which pair of these Navajo earrings were made by Narciso?
8. Where is the Athletics Department?
9. Just before the parade started, each of the eight men inside the gigantic dragon costume got their final instructions from Mr. Yee.
10. A few in the crowd was murmuring impatiently.
11. Is any of those peanuts left?
12. Either Tiger Woods or Se Ri Pak is Melinda's golf hero.
13. Every one of those stray cattle are going to have to be rounded up.
14. An additional feature of these models are the built-in stereo speakers.
15. Somebody has gone off and left their car running.
16. If anybody calls, tell them I'll be back by six o'clock this evening.
17. Each team has its own colors and symbol.
18. One of the goats were nibbling on a discarded popcorn box.
19. Are there no end to these questions?
20. Here's a pair of gloves for you.

Review J Choosing Verbs That Agree with Their Subjects and Pronouns That Agree with Their Antecedents

For each of the following sentences, choose the correct verb or pronoun given in parentheses.

EXAMPLE   **1.** Not every one of the world's deserts (*is, are*) hot and sandy.

     1. is

1. Neither the manager nor the two salespeople (*was, were*) prepared for the number of customers.
2. Neither of the sets of barbells (*was, were*) easy to lift.
3. Where (*is, are*) the box of nails that came with this bookshelf kit?
4. The class have had (*it's, their*) individual portraits made.
5. The Harlem Globetrotters (*is, are*) surely one of the best-loved basketball teams in the world.
6. There (*is, are*) leftover macaroni and cheese in the refrigerator.
7. If anybody likes a spectacle, (*he or she, they*) will love seeing a drum corps competition.
8. Several members of the audience (*was, were*) waving wildly, hoping that Martin Yan would wave back.
9. Where (*has, have*) the sports section of today's newspaper gone?
10. Anyone who wants to get (*his or her, their*) program autographed by Jimmy Smits had better hurry.

Review K Using Subject-Verb Agreement and Pronoun-Antecedent Agreement Correctly

Revise each of the following sentences according to the directions given in parentheses. Be sure to change other words, especially verbs and pronouns, as necessary.

EXAMPLE   **1.** Both of the boys desperately want to go to the circus. (Change *Both* to *Each*.)

    1. Each of the boys desperately wants to go to the circus.

1. Both of their parents have agreed to the idea. (Change *Both* to *One*.)
2. To pay for the tickets, Jorge has to empty his piggy bank or his secret hiding place of all its money. (Change *his piggy bank or* to *both his piggy bank and*.)
3. Because of the excitement, none of the boys will eat much of their dinner tonight. (Change *none* to *neither*.)

4. Both of the boys want to bring their cameras. (Change *Both* to *One*.)

5. Each of them has earned an enjoyable evening of watching clowns, tigers, and elephants. (Change *Each* to *All*.)

6. Every one of the clowns has his or her own special tricks and stunts. (Change *Every one* to *All*.)

7. None of the people from town want to miss tonight's performance. (Change *None* to *Not one*.)

8. Not all of the families in town have money for tickets. (Change *Not all of the families* to *Not every family*.)

9. All but one of the free tickets to the circus have been picked up. (Change *All but* to *Only*.)

10. Much of the money the circus takes in will be given to the Children's Hospital; it will help pay for a new X-ray machine. (Change *Much of the money* to *Many of the donations*.)

Chapter Review

A. Identifying Subject-Verb Agreement

For each sentence, write the verb in parentheses that agrees with its subject.

1. Either the dog or the cat (*get, gets*) the party leftovers.
2. There (*is, are*) four herbs that almost any gardener can grow: basil, thyme, marjoram, and oregano.
3. All of these old letters (*was, were*) tied with ribbon and stored in a trunk in the attic.
4. Each of them (*is, are*) penned in bold, flowing handwriting.
5. Both Alicia and Isabel (*thinks, think*) that the former owner of the house put the letters in the attic.
6. Neither potatoes nor peanuts (*is, are*) grown on this farm anymore.
7. Two thirds of the electorate (*was, were*) at the polls in the last election.
8. Is it true that *Troilus and Cressida* (*is, are*) by Shakespeare?
9. Here (*is, are*) the latest scores of today's basketball games.
10. Most of the children on the school bus (*was, were*) talking and laughing.
11. Don't you think that five miles (*is, are*) too far to walk tonight?
12. A cool spring near the cottages (*supply, supplies*) them with water.
13. Politics (*is, are*) a popular topic of conversation during an election year.
14. Every man, woman, and child (*was, were*) frightened by the earthquake.
15. Neither of them (*knows, know*) for sure who wrote that message.
16. The jury (*has, have*) returned a verdict.
17. On the supervisors (*rest, rests*) the responsibility for implementing safe procedures.
18. The two songs we played at the Independence Day concert (*was, were*) written by Carly Simon.
19. There (*has, have*) been many visitors on the fairground today.
20. Everybody in the theater (*was, were*) thrilled by the rescue scene.

B. Choosing Pronouns That Agree with Their Antecedents

Provide personal pronouns to complete the following sentences correctly.

21. Either my sister Lavinia or my friend Millicent will let me borrow _____ camping equipment.

22. I looked in the cupboard for the scissors, but I couldn't find _____.

23. Three of the cars had _____ windows broken by thieves last night.

24. Not long ago, I saw *Romeo and Juliet;* have you seen _____ ?

25. I'm looking for Stan and Joel; do you know _____ ?

26. We visited Honduras and spent three days in _____ capital, Tegucigalpa.

27. Mothers Against Drunk Driving has _____ meeting in the conference room tonight.

28. Three quarters of the city's voters cast _____ ballots.

29. I need fifty cents; could you lend _____ to me?

30. The sunglasses had stains on _____ lenses.

C. Identifying Subject-Verb Agreement and Pronoun-Antecedent Agreement

In most of the following sentences, either a verb does not agree with its subject or a pronoun does not agree with its antecedent. Revise each incorrect sentence to correct the error. If a sentence is already correct, write *C.*

31. The meeting got out of hand when the discussion period began because everyone tried to express their opinion at the same time.

32. There on the corner of your desk are the package of books that I returned and that you claimed you never received.

33. Two students from each class is going to the state capital to attend a special conference on education.

34. Each of them are expected to bring back a report on the conference so that classmates can get firsthand information.

35. Since they will be on vacation next month, neither Miguel nor his sister are going to enter the mixed-doubles tennis tournament.

36. The audience expressed their admiration for the dancer's grace and skill by applauding wildly.

37. After the senator had read the proposed amendment, anyone who disagreed with the ruling was allowed to state their reason.

38. This collection of old Italian folk tales demonstrate the wisdom, humor, and creativity of my ancestors.

39. She is one of those competitive people who perform best under pressure.

40. Since neither of you have ever tasted fried plantains, my mother has invited you to eat a Cuban meal at our house tonight.

Writing Application

Using Agreement in a Letter

Pronoun-Antecedent Agreement   Your best friend moved away two months ago. You have just received a postcard from him or her, asking what's been happening recently in your hometown. You answer the postcard by writing a short letter that brings your friend up to date. In your letter, include at least five pronouns that agree with their antecedents.

Prewriting   Make a list of several interesting things to tell your friend. You may write about your real hometown or about one you have made up. Decide on the order in which you will tell about the items on your list. You may want to use time order (telling when things happened) or spatial order (telling where things happened).

Writing   As you write, think about how to make your letter interesting to your friend. Use details that will help him or her picture the town and its people.

Revising   Ask a classmate to read your letter. Are the events you describe interesting? Is it absolutely clear who did what and what belongs to whom? Use your reader's suggestions to revise your letter so that nothing in the letter is confusing.

Publishing   Proofread your letter for any errors in grammar, usage, and mechanics. Be sure that all pronouns agree with their antecedents. The class may wish to post the completed letters on a class bulletin board or Web page.

Using Pronouns Correctly

Nominative, Objective, and Possessive Case; Clear Reference

Diagnostic Preview

A. Proofreading Sentences for Correct Pronoun Forms

Most of the following sentences contain an incorrect pronoun form. Revise each sentence by supplying the correct pronoun form. If a sentence is already correct, write *C.*

EXAMPLE   **1.** She and myself have different tai chi instructors.

        1. She and I have different tai chi instructors.

1. Del is as good at math as her.
2. He's the sportscaster who irritates me with his pretentious talk.
3. Do you remember to who the letter was addressed?
4. Steve showed the photos to Cecilia and I.
5. It can't be them; that's not their car.
6. Ben and you can come with they and me.
7. That geometry theorem was familiar to everyone in the class except him and I.
8. Us band members have to be at school early to practice marching.
9. There was some misunderstanding between he and his brother.
10. In front of the school stood two children, Charlene and he.

B. Proofreading Sentences for Correct Forms and Uses

Most of the following sentences contain at least one incorrect pronoun form or an unclear pronoun reference. Revise each sentence either by supplying the correct pronoun form(s) or by correcting the faulty pronoun reference. If a sentence is already correct, write *C*.

EXAMPLES
1. Dad and me went to the all-star basketball game.
   1. *Dad and I went to the all-star basketball game.*

2. Many people outside the arena wanted to buy our tickets, which didn't surprise us.
   2. *That many people outside the arena wanted to buy our tickets didn't surprise us.*

11. There's nothing like an action-packed all-star basketball game to give Dad and I a thrill!
12. The score was tied when Tate's shot bounced off the rim, and McKinley and Luke rushed for it.
13. As gravity pulled him and Luke toward the floor, McKinley managed to tip the ball to Gambrell.
14. Gambrell saw Davis coming, dribbled behind his own back, and eluded he and Fowler.
15. When Davis and Fowler collided, nobody was more surprised than them.
16. If my team made this, we would win.
17. Gambrell looked for Tran and realized that the blur streaking up the court on the left was him.
18. He had to pass to whomever was open, and Tran was the one.
19. Tran took a shot and missed; four players struggled for the ball, which went in, which meant that Tran and his teammates won!
20. In the whirlwind action during the last couple of seconds, the frantic referee couldn't see whom had fouled who.

Case Forms of Personal Pronouns

Case is the form that a noun or pronoun takes to show its relationship to other words in a sentence. In English, there are three cases: *nominative, objective,* and *possessive.* Nouns have the same form in both the nominative and the objective cases. Nouns usually add an apostrophe and an *s* to form the possessive case.

Personal pronouns have different forms for the different cases.

Case Forms of Personal Pronouns		
Nominative Case		
	Singular	**Plural**
First Person	I	we
Second Person	you	you
Third Person	he, she, it	they
Objective Case		
	Singular	**Plural**
First Person	me	us
Second Person	you	you
Third Person	him, her, it	them
Possessive Case		
	Singular	**Plural**
First Person	my, mine	our, ours
Second Person	your, yours	your, yours
Third Person	his, her, hers, its	their, theirs

NOTE Notice that *you* and *it* have the same form in the nominative and objective cases. All other personal pronouns have different forms for each. Notice also that only third-person singular pronouns indicate gender (masculine, feminine, or neuter).

Exercise 1 Identifying Personal Pronouns in a Paragraph

Each sentence in the following paragraph contains at least one pronoun. Identify each personal pronoun. Then, give its person, number, case, and, if applicable, its gender.

EXAMPLE   1. Jeffrey and I were chatting in front of his locker before the Art Club meeting.

1. *I—first person, singular, nominative case; his—third person, singular, possessive case, masculine*

1. Jeffrey mentioned your interest in African art and Francine's interest in modern art.

USAGE

2. Did you and she know that African masks like the one below left influenced the development of the Modernist movement in art?

3. I've learned that African carvings inspired such twentieth-century artists as Pablo Picasso, who created this painting on the right.

4. The year 1905 was probably when he and his friends first saw African masks exhibited in Paris.

5. Amedeo Modigliani was especially affected by the stark masks, and he and Picasso created many works based on them.

6. Notice that the eyes in Modigliani's carving are very close together and that they and the lips look much like small knobs.

7. I used to think that Modigliani made his faces too long by mistake, but the error was mine.

8. Ms. Keller told me that he was copying the exaggerated shapes of Ivory Coast masks.

9. Picasso and Modigliani were only two of many European artists who got their inspiration from African art.

10. Obviously, we students weren't giving credit where credit was due!

The Nominative Case

Personal pronouns in the nominative case—*I, you, he, she, it, we,* and *they*—are used as subjects of verbs and as predicate nominatives.

6a. A subject of a verb should be in the nominative case.

A *subject of a verb* tells whom or what a sentence or a clause is about.

EXAMPLES   **I** solved the problem. [*I* is the subject of *solved.*]

They know that **we** are going. [*They* is the subject of *know,* and *we* is the subject of *are going.*]

Al and **she** cleaned the house. [*Al and she* is the compound subject of *cleaned.*]

┌HELP──

Personal pronouns in the nominative case may also be used as **appositives.**

Reference Note

For information on **appositives,** see page 81.

Oral Practice 1 Using Pronouns as Subjects

Read each of the following sentences aloud, stressing the italicized words.

1. *She* and *I* gave the dog a bath.
2. Terry and *he* plan to try out for the soccer team.
3. *We* sophomores organized the recycling campaign.
4. James Earl Jones and *she* are excellent role models for young actors.
5. Are *you* and *he* doing the report?
6. Either *we* or *they* may go to the championship finals.
7. The drill team and *we* took the bus.
8. The twins said that *they* go everywhere together.

Exercise 2 Using Personal Pronouns in the Nominative Case to Complete Sentences

Supply a personal pronoun for each blank in the following sentences. Vary your pronouns, but do not use *you* or *it*.

EXAMPLE 1. What part in the play does _____ have?

1. *she*

1. The judge and _____ studied the evidence.
2. Ted and _____ took the wrong train.
3. Linda and _____ are planning a party.
4. _____ are having a science fair.
5. Either Julius or _____ will give you a ride.
6. _____ and _____ have been rivals for years.
7. I'm sure _____ knew about the meeting.
8. Soon _____ and _____ will be graduating.
9. Did you know that _____ and _____ saw a Broadway production of *West Side Story*?
10. _____ and _____ love the Asian dumplings served at restaurants.

Exercise 3 Writing Sentences with Pronouns in the Nominative Case

Use the following subjects in sentences of your own.

EXAMPLE 1. we and they

1. *We and they are meeting after dinner.*

1. we teenagers
2. the other shoppers and I
3. he and his friends
4. Liz, Michelle, and she

5. they and their classmates   8. the children and I

6. she and her mother   9. we boys

7. you and he   10. they and their dogs

6b. **A predicate nominative should be in the nominative case.**

A *predicate nominative* completes the meaning of a linking verb and identifies or refers to the subject of the verb. A personal pronoun used as a predicate nominative generally completes the meaning of a form of the verb *be: am, is, are, was, were, be, been,* or *being.*

EXAMPLES   It was **I** who took the message.

             The winner might be **he.**

             Could the caller have been **she**?

Exercise 4   **Using Pronouns as Predicate Nominatives**

Complete each of the following sentences by supplying the personal pronoun called for in parentheses.

EXAMPLE   1. It was _____ who was the first emperor of China's Yuan dynasty. (*third person, singular, masculine*)

        1. *he*

1. Do you think it was _____? (*third person, singular, feminine*)
2. It must have been _____. (*third person, singular, masculine*)
3. Good friends are _____. (*third person, plural*)
4. The pranksters were _____. (*first person, plural*)
5. It was _____ at the door. (*third person, plural*)
6. It is _____. (*first person, singular*)
7. It may have been _____ on the phone. (*third person, singular, feminine*)
8. The winners should be _____. (*third person, plural*)
9. The best cook here is _____. (*third person, singular, masculine*)
10. The volunteers were _____. (*first person, plural*)

Review A   **Using Pronouns in the Nominative Case Correctly in Sentences**

Supply a personal pronoun for the blank in each of the following sentences. Use a variety of different pronouns, but do not use *you* or *it*. Be ready to explain the reasons for your choices.

EXAMPLE   1. Are you and _____ going to the Fourth of July celebration?

        1. *he*

| TIPS | & | TRICKS |

To help you determine which pronoun form to use as a predicate nominative, try each form as the simple subject of the verb.

EXAMPLE
The two teams in the final round were (*they, them*).

CHOICES
they were or *them were*?

ANSWER
The two teams in the final round were **they.**

USAGE

Reference Note

For information on **predicate nominatives,** see page 51.

| STYLE | TIP |

Expressions such as *It's me, This is her,* and *It was them* are examples of informal usage. Though common in everyday situations, such expressions should be avoided in formal speaking and writing. (The formal versions of the italicized expressions above are *It is I, This is she,* and *It was they.*)

─HELP─

In the example for Review A, the nominative-case pronoun *he* is correct because the pronoun is used as a subject.

1. Everyone applauded when Patty and _____ took a bow.
2. When I saw Dame Kiri Te Kanawa in front of Lincoln Center, I couldn't believe it was _____.
3. Where did Barry and _____ go after school?
4. Jimmy and _____ caught the runaway piglets.
5. The one that you need to see is _____.
6. Skip argued that Lana and _____ made the error.
7. Was it Teresa or _____ who hit the home run?
8. Either David or _____ might be able to do it.
9. My sister and _____ love the South African musical group Ladysmith Black Mambazo.
10. I believe that the Masked Marvel has to be _____.

Review B Using Pronouns in the Nominative Case

For each blank in the following paragraph, supply an appropriate personal pronoun. Do not use *you* or *it*.

EXAMPLE [1] _____ have learned from Mrs. Soto the value of recycling.
1. *We*

[1] _____ who are in Mrs. Soto's class are determined to win this year's "Save the Earth" trophy at our school. The two most enthusiastic people in our class are probably Pilar and [2] _____. I guess that's why Mrs. Soto asked whether [3] _____ and [4] _____ would organize the paper drive. Pilar explained to the class that if Americans recycled only their Sunday newspapers, half a million trees would be saved every Sunday! To illustrate her point, [5] _____ showed this photo. That is [6] _____ standing next to 580 pounds of paper—the amount the average American uses in one year. [7] _____ have gathered some other facts to inspire our classmates to recycle. Our friend Ben said that [8] _____ and his mother heard on the radio that the average American uses 1,500 aluminum drink cans every year. [9] _____ were amazed to learn that the energy saved from recycling just one aluminum can could keep a TV set running for three hours! No matter who wins the trophy, it will definitely be [10] _____ who share the prize of a cleaner, healthier planet.

The Objective Case

Personal pronouns in the objective case—*me, you, him, her, it, us,* and *them*—are used as direct objects, indirect objects, and objects of prepositions.

6c. A direct object should be in the objective case.

A **direct object** tells who or what either receives the action of a transitive verb or shows the result of the action.

EXAMPLES   Coach Johnson has been training **us.**

The coach has turned **them** into the best team in the state.

6d. An indirect object should be in the objective case.

An **indirect object** often appears in sentences containing direct objects. An indirect object tells *to whom* or *to what* or *for whom* or *for what* the action of a transitive verb is done.

EXAMPLES   Serena paid **him** a compliment.

Carlos saved **me** a seat in the first row.

NOTE   Indirect objects do not follow prepositions. A pronoun preceded by a preposition is the object of a preposition.

Exercise 5   Using Pronouns in the Objective Case to Complete Sentences

Supply a personal pronoun for the blank in each of the following sentences. Use a variety of pronouns, but do not use *you* or *it.*

EXAMPLE   **1.** Donya sent Celie and _____ a postcard from Mexico City.
       1. him

1. The old sailor warned _____ about the danger.
2. The city awarded _____ its highest honor for their bravery.
3. You could ask Deborah or _____.
4. The crowd cheered _____ heartily.
5. Make sure that you ask _____ what her telephone number is.
6. The shark in that movie didn't scare _____ at all.
7. How can I recognize _____?
8. We saw Norman and _____ in their horse costume at the party.
9. Did you give Paula and _____ their assignments?
10. I bought my father and _____ identical birthday presents this year.

HELP

Personal pronouns in the objective case may also be used as **appositives.**

Reference Note

For information on **appositives,** see page 81. For more about **direct objects,** see page 54. For information on **transitive verbs,** see page 19. For more about **indirect objects,** see page 55.

HELP

Although more than one answer is possible for some items in Exercise 5, you need to give only one response for each.

USAGE

6 c, d

┌HELP─┐

In Review C,
the expression *Number 1*
indicates a first-person
singular pronoun.

┌ TIPS **&** TRICKS ┐

To help you determine
which pronoun form(s) to
use in compound direct
and indirect objects, try
each form with the verb.

EXAMPLE
The news surprised both
(*they, them*) and (*we, us*).

CHOICES
surprised they or *surprised
them*?

surprised we or *surprised
us*?

ANSWER
The news surprised both
them and **us.**

Review C **Using Pronouns in the Nominative
and Objective Cases**

The cheerleading squad is learning a new pyramid routine. To help
organize the cheerleaders, the coach has assigned each one a number.
In the following sentences, use a correct personal pronoun in place of
each italicized expression.

EXAMPLES   **1.** Coach Welber tells Cara and *Number 5* where to
position themselves.

1. *her*

2. I asked whether *Number 8 and Number 1* can be in the
pyramid next time.

2. *we*

1. The three people forming the base of the pyramid are Harley,
Michael, and *Number 5.*
2. Kimiko is the smallest, so it is *Number 6* who is at the top first.
3. *Number 8 and Number 1* give *Number 6* a boost.
4. After *Number 4* and Emilio have been in the middle row awhile,
Rosie and *Number 1* ask for a turn.
5. Please show Luisa and *Number 6 and Number 3* their new positions.
6. Give Rosie or *Number 1* a signal when you are ready to jump
down, Kimiko.
7. Next time, the ones in the middle row will be Harley and *Number 8.*
8. If anyone can support the person on top well, it's *Number 3.*
9. The winners of the next cheerleading meet will surely be
Numbers 1 through 8.
10. Come here, and I'll tell you and *Number 4* about the next
new formation.

6e. An object of a preposition should be in the objective case.

A noun or pronoun that follows a preposition is called an *object of the preposition.* Together, a preposition, its object, and any modifiers of that object make up a *prepositional phrase.*

EXAMPLES   to **them**   with **him**   for both **her** and **us**

from **me**   next to **us**   between **you** and **me**

Reference Note

For lists of **commonly used prepositions,** see page 24. For more about **prepositional phrases,** see page 65.

(Oral Practice 2) **Using Pronouns as Objects of Prepositions**

Read each of the following sentences aloud, stressing the italicized words.

1. There were calls for Walker and *us.*
2. This message is from Dolores and *her.*
3. With Arnie and *them* were the Malone twins.
4. Margo looked toward Francine and *me.*
5. They gave copies to *him* and *me.*
6. This drawing is by either Hector or *him.*
7. Don't hold this against Cho and *her.*
8. Between Vince and *him* sat an iguana.

(Exercise 6) **Selecting Pronoun Forms for Objects of Prepositions**

Choose the correct pronoun forms in parentheses in the following sentences.

EXAMPLE   1. Have you spoken to (*he, him*) or (*she, her*) recently?

1. *him, her*

1. The referee called fouls on (*them, they*) and (*I, me*).
2. Fishing with Grandpa and (*he, him*) was fun.
3. We didn't want to leave without you and (*she, her*).
4. They assigned the same lab equipment to (*them, they*) and (*we, us*).
5. The duke directed a haughty sneer at the jester and (*he, him*).
6. After Carmen rolled the corn husks around the tamales, she handed them to Arturo and (*me, I*).
7. Everyone but Kevin and (*she, her*) thinks this commentator is the best one on television.
8. Between you and (*me, I*), I'd rather not.
9. The wary skunk circled around (*she, her*) and (*me, I*).
10. Uncle Vic will get the details from you and (*we, us*).

USAGE

TIPS & TRICKS

To help you determine which pronoun form(s) to use in a compound object of a preposition, try each form with the preposition.

EXAMPLE
Gwen wrote to (*she, her*) and (*I, me*).

CHOICES
to *she* or to *her*?

to *I* or to *me*?

ANSWER
Gwen wrote to **her** and **me.**

STYLE TIP

As a matter of courtesy, first-person pronouns are placed at the end of compound constructions.

NOMINATIVE CASE
Dad and **I** went shopping.

OBJECTIVE CASE
Mom met Dad and **me** for lunch.

POSSESSIVE CASE
I surprised them by paying for both their lunches and **mine**.

Exercise 7 Writing Sentences Using Pronouns as Objects of Prepositions

Write sentences of your own, using each of the following prepositions with a compound object. Use a personal pronoun for at least one of the objects in each sentence.

EXAMPLE   1. toward
            1. *The whooping crane stalked toward Mike and me.*

1. against	**3.** for	**5.** except	**7.** without	**9.** by
2. across	**4.** before	**6.** between	**8.** near	**10.** over

Review D Selecting Correct Forms of Pronouns

For the numbered sentences in the following paragraph, choose the correct pronoun forms in parentheses.

EXAMPLE   **[1]** Tina, Susan, and (*I, me*) are best friends.
            1. I

[1] Last fall, Tina talked Susan and (*I, me*) into going on a canoe trip with the Wilderness Club. [2] She warned (*we, us*) that we might get a good dunking before we were through. [3] When we set out, Susan and (*I, me*) could barely steer our canoe. [4] We watched another canoeist and saw how (*she, her*) and her partner maneuvered their craft. [5] Both they and (*we, us*) did well until we hit the rapids or, rather, until the rapids hit (*we, us*). [6] Susan grabbed our sleeping bags, and (*she, her*) and (*I, me*) both scrambled for our ice chest. [7] All of (*we, us*) were drenched, but no quitters were (*we, us*). [8] Tina's warning haunted all of (*we, us*) as (*we, us*) contemplated waterlogged sandwiches, soggy salads, and banana muffins with tadpoles in them. [9] Later, Susan and (*I, me*) discovered that our bedrolls had become portable water beds. [10] After a cold, squishy night, (*I, me*) concluded that wise are (*they, them*) who heed the voice of experience.

The Possessive Case

The personal pronouns in the possessive case—*my, mine, your, yours, his, her, hers, its, our, ours, their,* and *theirs*—are used to show ownership or possession.

6f. The possessive pronouns *mine, yours, his, hers, its, ours,* and *theirs* can be used in the same way that the personal pronouns in the nominative and objective cases are used.

SUBJECT	**Mine** has a flat tire.
PREDICATE NOMINATIVE	This key is **yours.**
DIRECT OBJECT	Mrs. Fong takes **hers** for a walk twice a day.
INDIRECT OBJECT	Most teachers are not assigning **theirs** any homework for the holidays.
OBJECT OF PREPOSITION	Their coach spoke to **ours** about a possible rematch.

6g. The possessive pronouns *my, your, his, her, its, our,* and *their* are used to modify nouns and pronouns.

EXAMPLES　　**My** bicycle has a flat tire. [*My* modifies *bicycle.*]

　　　　　　This is **your** key. [*Your* modifies *key.*]

　　　　　　Mrs. Fong takes **her** dogs for a walk twice a day. [*Her* modifies *dogs.*]

　　　　　　Most teachers are not assigning **their** students any home-work for the holidays. [*Their* modifies *students.*]

　　　　　　Their coach spoke to **our** coach about a possible rematch. [*Their* and *our* each modify *coach.*]

NOTE　Some authorities prefer to call the possessive pronouns *my, your, his, her, its, our,* and *their* adjectives. Follow your teacher's instructions regarding these possessive forms.

6h. A noun or pronoun preceding a gerund generally should be in the possessive case.

A *gerund* is a verb form that ends in *–ing* and functions as a noun. Since a gerund serves as a noun, the noun or pronoun that precedes it should be in the possessive case in order to modify the gerund.

Reference Note

For more on **gerunds** and **present participles,** see pages 74 and 70.

EXAMPLE　　They approved of the **students'** [or **their**] organizing a cleanup campaign.

Do not confuse a gerund with a *present participle,* which is also a verb form that ends in *–ing.* A gerund acts as a noun, whereas a present partici-ple serves as an adjective or as part of a verb phrase. The noun or pronoun preceding a present participle should generally not be in the possessive case.

EXAMPLE　　Every day after school, the principal saw **students** [or **them**] working diligently.

NOTE
Often the form of a noun or pronoun before an *–ing* word depends on the meaning you want to express. If you want to emphasize the *–ing* word, use the possessive form. If you want to emphasize the noun or pronoun preceding the *–ing* word, do not use the possessive form. Notice the difference in emphasis in the following sentences.

EXAMPLES   I can't imagine cousin **Liam's** [or **his**] driving. [emphasis on the gerund *driving*]

I can't imagine cousin **Liam** [or **him**] driving. [emphasis on the noun or pronoun preceding the present participle *driving*]

Special Problems in Pronoun Usage

The Relative Pronouns *Who* and *Whom*

6i. The use of *who* or *whom* in a subordinate clause depends on how the pronoun functions in the clause.

Nominative Case	who, whoever
Objective Case	whom, whomever

Follow these steps to decide whether to use *who* or *whom* in a subordinate clause.

STEP 1   Find the subordinate clause.

STEP 2   Decide how the pronoun is used in the clause—as a subject, predicate nominative, direct object, indirect object, or object of a preposition.

STEP 3   Determine the case of the pronoun according to the rules of standard, formal English.

STEP 4   Select the correct form of the pronoun.

EXAMPLE   Rick is the only student (*who, whom*) earned a perfect score.

STEP 1   The subordinate clause is (*who, whom*) *earned a perfect score.*

STEP 2   In this clause the pronoun is the subject of the verb *earned.*

STEP 3   As a subject the pronoun should be in the nominative case.

STEP 4   The nominative form is *who.*

ANSWER   Rick is the only student **who** earned a perfect score.

STYLE TIP

In informal English, the use of *whom* is becoming less common. However, in formal speech and writing, it is still important to distinguish between *who* and *whom*.

Reference Note

For information on **subordinate clauses,** see page 91.

USAGE

EXAMPLE	Did they say (*who, whom*) the winner is?
STEP 1	The subordinate clause is (*who, whom*) *the winner is.*
STEP 2	In this clause the pronoun is the predicate nominative: *the winner is* (*who, whom*).
STEP 3	As a predicate nominative, the pronoun should be in the nominative case.
STEP 4	The nominative form is *who.*
ANSWER	Did they say **who** the winner is?

EXAMPLE	I saw Sabrina, (*who, whom*) I know from school.
STEP 1	The subordinate clause is (*who, whom*) *I know from school.*
STEP 2	In this clause the pronoun is the direct object of the verb *know: I know* (*who, whom*).
STEP 3	As a direct object, the pronoun should be in the objective case.
STEP 4	The objective form is *whom.*
ANSWER	I saw Sabrina, **whom** I know from school.

COMPUTER TIP

If you use a computer, you can use the search feature of a word-processing program to find each use of *who* or *whom* in a document. Then you can check to make sure that you have used the correct form of the pronoun in each instance.

USAGE

Remember that no words outside the subordinate clause affect the case of a pronoun in the clause. In the first example above, the whole clause *who the winner is* is the direct object of the verb *Did say* in the independent clause. In the subordinate clause, though, *who* is used as a predicate nominative, which takes the nominative case.

NOTE The relative pronoun *whom* is often left out of a subordinate adjective clause but is nevertheless understood.

EXAMPLE The man [whom] we saw on the elevator looked familiar.
[*Whom* is understood to be the direct object of *saw.*]

Exercise 8 **Selecting *Who* or *Whom* to Complete Sentences Correctly**

For each of the following sentences, choose the correct form, *who* or *whom,* in parentheses.

EXAMPLE **1.** (*Who, Whom*) did you speak to yesterday?

  1. Whom

1. The student (*who, whom*) saw the eclipse is here.
2. (*Who, Whom*) did you vote for in the election?
3. Are you the person to (*who, whom*) I give my essay?

4. I don't know (*who, whom*) has my notebook.
5. (*Who, Whom*) is on the telephone?
6. To (*who, whom*) are you speaking?
7. They are the people about (*who, whom*) I was talking.
8. He is not (*who, whom*) won the award.
9. Jonathan saw (*who, whom*) you greeted.
10. I feel sometimes that I don't know (*who, whom*) you are anymore.

Exercise 9 Determining the Use of *Who* and *Whom* in Subordinate Clauses

Identify the subordinate clause containing *who* or *whom* in each of the following sentences. Then, tell how *who* or *whom* is used in the clause—as a *subject, predicate nominative, direct object,* or *object of a preposition.*

EXAMPLES
1. She is someone whom we all admire.
1. *whom we all admire—direct object*

2. He is the person about whom I wrote my report.
2. *about whom I wrote my report—object of a preposition*

1. The people who are born in Puerto Rico live in a commonwealth, with its own Senate, Supreme Court, and Cabinet.
2. In 1969, the governor needed a secretary of labor on whom he could depend.
3. The person whom he appointed would occupy the most difficult and sensitive position in the Cabinet.
4. Do you know who the choice was?
5. The choice fell to Mrs. Julia Rivera De Vincenti, who became the first woman to occupy a Cabinet post in Puerto Rico.
6. De Vincenti, who had completed the requirements for a Ph.D. degree in management and collective bargaining at Cornell University, was a good choice.
7. De Vincenti, who was later appointed to the U.S. Mission to the United Nations, was the first Puerto Rican to serve in that capacity.
8. She addressed the General Assembly and showed that she was a person on whom they could rely.
9. She praised her compatriots, from whom new advances in agriculture had recently come.
10. I'm sure her compatriots appreciated her praise, for De Vincenti was someone who herself was worthy of praise.

Appositives

6j. A pronoun used as an appositive should be in the same case as the word to which it refers.

An *appositive* appears next to another noun or pronoun to identify or describe that noun or pronoun.

EXAMPLES   The late arrivals—**she, he,** and **I**—missed the first act. [The pronouns are in the nominative case because they refer to the subject *arrivals*.]

The co-captains should be the best bowlers, **he** and **she.** [The pronouns are in the nominative case because they refer to the predicate nominative *bowlers*.]

The article you're reading mentions the winners, **her** and **me.** [The pronouns are in the objective case because they refer to the direct object *winners*.]

Ms. Lee gave the debaters, **them** and **us,** name tags. [The pronouns are in the objective case because they refer to the indirect object *debaters*.]

The contestants were narrowed to two finalists, **him** and **her.** [The pronouns are in the objective case because they refer to *finalists*, the object of the preposition *to*.]

The pronoun *we* or *us* is sometimes followed by a noun appositive.

EXAMPLES   **We** sophomores raised the most money for charity. [The pronoun is in the nominative case because it is the subject of the verb *raised*. The appositive *sophomores* identifies *We*.]

The judges awarded **us** members of the marching band a superior rating. [The pronoun is in the objective case because it is the indirect object of the verb *awarded*. The appositive *members* identifies *us*.]

> **Review E**   Selecting Pronouns to Complete Sentences Correctly

Choose the correct pronoun form in parentheses in each of the following sentences. Then, tell whether the pronoun is used as a *subject*, a *predicate nominative*, a *direct object*, an *indirect object*, an *object of a preposition*, or an *appositive*.

EXAMPLE   **1.** Andre is giving Jena and (*I, me*) marimba lessons.

    1. me—indirect object

TIPS & TRICKS

To help you determine which pronoun form(s) to use as an appositive or with an appositive, read the sentence with only the pronoun.

AS AN APPOSITIVE
The coach congratulated the two starting forwards, Angela and (*I, me*).

CHOICES
The coach congratulated I or *The coach congratulated me*?

ANSWER
The coach congratulated the two starting forwards, Angela and **me.**

BEFORE A NOUN APPOSITIVE
(*We, Us*) girls made the playoffs!

CHOICES
We made the playoffs or *Us made the playoffs*?

ANSWER
We girls made the playoffs!

USAGE

Reference Note

For information on **appositives,** see page 81.

1. The two winners, Sean and (*she, her*), received huge green ribbons decorated with shamrocks.
2. Will Meg and (*she, her*) run the concession stand?
3. The coach asked you and (*I, me*) for help with the equipment.
4. Becky and (*she, her*) rode their bikes to the meeting.
5. The lighting crew for the play was Manuel and (*I, me*).
6. They treat very well (*whoever, whomever*) they hire.
7. I think that Denzel Washington and (*he, him*) starred in *Much Ado About Nothing*.
8. They met my cousins—Jennie and (*she, her*)—at the airport.
9. Joe Leaphorn and Jim Chee are the Navajo detectives (*who, whom*) Tony Hillerman writes about in his crime stories.
10. The people who were costumed as pirates are (*they, them*).

Review F **Proofreading for Correct Pronoun Forms**

Most of the sentences in the following paragraph contain at least one pronoun that is used incorrectly. Identify each incorrect pronoun, and write the correct form. If the sentence is already correct, write *C*.

EXAMPLE **[1]** Two of my cousins and me tried to determine how everyone else at the family reunion was related to we cousins.

1. *me—I; we—us*

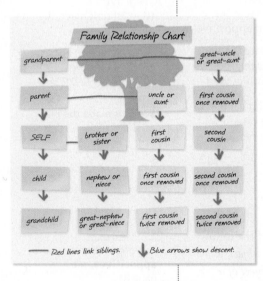

Family Relationship Chart

grandparent → parent → SELF → child → grandchild

great-uncle or great-aunt → uncle or aunt → brother or sister / first cousin → nephew or niece / first cousin once removed / second cousin → great-nephew or great-niece / first cousin twice removed / second cousin twice removed

first cousin once removed → second cousin → second cousin once removed

—— Red lines link siblings. ↓ Blue arrows show descent.

[1] Us cousins were getting so confused at the family reunion that Rochelle, Darla, and me made the Family Relationship Chart shown at left. [2] Before long, the busiest people at the picnic were they and me! [3] Aunts and uncles consulted us to find out who they were related to and just how they were related. [4] It all started when Jules wanted to know the connection between him and Vicky. [5] We figured out that Vicky is the great-granddaughter of Jules's grandmother's brother, so her and Jules are second cousins once removed. [6] Looking at our chart, we could see that Vicky and Jules are in different generations, even though him and her are the same age. [7] All afternoon, curious relatives besieged Rochelle, Darla, and I with many questions. [8] We helped whomever asked us. [9] Grandmother said she was very proud of we girls. [10] Everyone learned something new about our family ties that day and gave the two other girls and I a big round of applause.

Write the correct form of each incorrect pronoun in the following sentences. Write *C* if all of the pronouns in a sentence are in the correct case.

EXAMPLE   **1.** Nelson Mandela, whom shared the Nobel Peace Prize in 1993, was elected president of South Africa in 1994.

    1. *who*

1. Be careful who you tell.

2. May Marie and I cut a few pictures out of this old copy of *Ebony*?

3. My family goes to the dentist who Ms. Calhoun recommended.

4. Coretta said there would be other flag bearers in addition to Hugh and I.

5. At the head of the parade were us Girl Scouts.

6. The treaty gave them and the Ojibwa people the right to harvest wild rice there.

7. Nobody except Josh and him finished the project.

8. Joanne and us found a great beach.

9. Did your father and them reach an agreement about the boundary dispute?

10. We wish we had neighbors that were more like Sylvia and he.

Review H Selecting Pronouns to Complete Sentences

For each of the following sentences, choose the correct pronoun in parentheses. Be prepared to give a reason for your answer.

EXAMPLE   **1.** Jason and (*I, me*) attended the Golden Spurs horse show.

    1. *I*

1. Heather and (*he, him*) live on a blueberry farm.

2. Did the teacher give that assignment to (*whoever, whomever*) was absent yesterday?

3. We wondered (*who, whom*) started the rumor.

4. Do you intercept passes as well as Robin and (*she, her*) do?

5. The supporting players were Dina, Janelle, and (*she, her*).

6. I was standing in line behind Dave and (*he, him*).

7. You and (*I, me*) could write our biographical sketches on General Colin L. Powell, the first African American to serve as secretary of state.

8. The skit was written by Cy and (*he, him*).

MEETING THE CHALLENGE

Write a riddle poem. First, think of a person, place, thing, or idea you want to describe. Then, describe your choice without actually naming it. Include at least two uses each of *who* and *whom* and three pronoun appositives in your poem. Check for correct pronoun usage, and then trade poems with a classmate to see whether you can guess each other's riddle.

USAGE

┌─HELP─

In the example for Review H, the nominative-case pronoun *I* is correct because the pronoun is used as a subject.

9. The electrician warned (*he, him*) and (*I, me*) about the frayed wires.

10. Amy Tan, (*who, whom*) the critics had praised, autographed a copy of her novel for me.

STYLE **TIP**

The words *hisself, theirself,* and *theirselves* are non-standard English. Always use *himself* and *themselves* instead.

Reflexive and Intensive Pronouns

Reflexive and intensive pronouns (sometimes called *compound personal pronouns*) have the same forms.

Reflexive and Intensive Pronouns		
	Singular	Plural
First Person	myself	ourselves
Second Person	yourself	yourselves
Third Person	himself, herself, itself	themselves

A **reflexive pronoun** refers to the subject of a verb and may serve as a direct object, an indirect object, a predicate nominative, or an object of a preposition.

DIRECT OBJECT	Diners at this restaurant serve **themselves.**
INDIRECT OBJECT	I made **myself** a gyro sandwich.
PREDICATE NOMINATIVE	Dale is just not **himself** today.
OBJECT OF PREPOSITION	He suddenly remembered the promise he had made to **himself.**

An **intensive pronoun** has only one function: to emphasize its antecedent.

EXAMPLES Don't you think we can install the computer program **ourselves**?

Only you **yourself** can make that decision.

TIPS & TRICKS

To help you decide whether a pronoun ending in *–self* or *–selves* is reflexive or intensive, use this test: Omit the pronoun from the sentence. You can omit an intensive pronoun, but not a reflexive pronoun, from a sentence without significantly changing the meaning of the sentence.

INTENSIVE
Did you change the oil in the car **yourself**?
[*Yourself* can be omitted: *Did you change the oil in the car?*]

REFLEXIVE
Did you hurt **yourself**?
[*Yourself* is the direct object of *Did hurt* and cannot be omitted without changing the meaning of the sentence.]

NOTE A pronoun ending in *–self* or *–selves* should not be used in place of a personal pronoun.

NONSTANDARD	Sonia and myself sang a duet in the talent show.
STANDARD	Sonia and **I** sang a duet in the talent show.
NONSTANDARD	Chad bought tickets for himself and myself.
STANDARD	Chad bought tickets for himself and **me.**

USAGE

Exercise 10) Using Reflexive and Intensive Pronouns

For each blank in the following sentences, supply a pronoun ending in –*self* or –*selves* that correctly completes the sentence. Then, identify the pronoun as *reflexive* or *intensive*. If neither a reflexive nor an intensive pronoun would be correct, give a personal pronoun.

┌HELP──

Some sentences in Exercise 10 have more than one possible correct answer, but you need to give only one answer for each item.

EXAMPLE   1. Did Jamal make this delicious stew _____ ?

          1. *himself—intensive*

1. Working quickly and efficiently, we volunteers decorated the auditorium all by _____ .
2. Mona's cat cleans _____ right after it eats.
3. Did Julio and _____ have a good time at the concert?
4. Having gotten my braces off, I finally feel like _____ again.
5. The judges _____ could not reach a consensus.
6. How are Eric and _____ supposed to react in this scene?
7. Only time _____ will prove one of us right.
8. Give _____ a big pat on the back.
9. Where do you think they have hidden _____ ?
10. With her fever gone, Carla is _____ today.

Pronouns in Incomplete Constructions

6k. A pronoun following *than* or *as* in an incomplete construction should be in the same case as it would be if the construction were completed.

EXAMPLES   I know Mac better than **he** [knows Mac].
           I know Mac better than [I know] **him**.

           Do you visit Aunt Bessie as often as **we** [visit Aunt Bessie]?
           Do you visit Aunt Bessie as often as [you visit] **us**?

Exercise 11) Selecting Pronouns for Incomplete Constructions

For each of the sentences on the next page, choose the correct form of the pronoun in parentheses. Also, supply in parentheses the missing part of the incomplete construction. Then, give the use of the pronoun in its clause. If the construction may be completed in two different ways, provide both completions and tell how the pronoun in each completion is used.

1. I like Jay Leno better than (*she, her*).

        1. *she (likes Jay Leno)—subject; (I like) her—direct object*

HELP

Not all sentences in Exercise 11 can be completed in more than one way.

 1. We played defense better than (*they, them*).
 2. When our marching band won the state finals, nobody was as pleased as (*I, me*).
 3. Nobody tried harder than (*she, her*).
 4. You are a month younger than (*he, him*).
 5. I know Millie better than (*she, her*).
 6. Did you walk as far in the walkathon as (*I, me*)?
 7. Richard bought more tickets than (*we, us*).
 8. Bianca lives farther away than (*we, us*).
 9. She visited Lisa more often than (*I, me*).
10. Carlos plays classical guitar in the style of Andrés Segovia but, of course, not as well as (*he, him*).

Reference Note

For information on **pronoun-antecedent agreement,** see page 130.

Clear Pronoun Reference

Generally, a pronoun has no definite meaning by itself. Its meaning is clear only when the word or word group it stands for is known. This word or word group is called the ***antecedent*** of the pronoun.

6l. A pronoun should refer clearly to its antecedent.

(1) Avoid an *ambiguous reference,* which occurs when any one of two or more words can be a pronoun's antecedent.

AMBIGUOUS	Marissa called Yolanda while she was at the library last weekend. [Who was at the library, Marissa or Yolanda?]
CLEAR	While Marissa was at the library last weekend, **she** called Yolanda.

or

CLEAR	While Yolanda was at the library last weekend, Marissa called **her.**

AMBIGUOUS	After viewing Roy's paintings and Elton's sculpture, the judges awarded his work the blue ribbon. [Whose work was awarded the blue ribbon?]
CLEAR	The judges awarded Elton the blue ribbon after viewing **his** sculpture and Roy's paintings.

or

CLEAR	The judges awarded Roy the blue ribbon after viewing **his** paintings and Elton's sculpture.

USAGE

(2) Avoid a *general reference*, which is the use of a pronoun that refers to a general idea rather than to a specific antecedent.

Most general reference errors are caused by the misuse of the pronouns *it, this, that, which,* and *such.*

GENERAL	Paul has a job interview after school today. That explains why he is wearing a suit. [*That* has no specific antecedent.]
CLEAR	Paul is wearing a suit because he has a job interview after school today.

or

CLEAR	The reason Paul is wearing a suit is that he has a job interview after school today.

GENERAL	My biology class is going to the coast this week, which should be fun. [*Which* has no specific antecedent.]
CLEAR	My biology class is going to the coast this week. The trip should be fun.

or

CLEAR	Going to the coast with my biology class this week should be fun.

(3) Avoid a *weak reference*, which occurs when a pronoun refers to an antecedent that has been suggested but not expressed.

WEAK	Ryan is multilingual. One of those that he speaks fluently is Mandarin. [The antecedent *languages* is suggested by the use of the pronoun *those* but is not expressed.]
CLEAR	Ryan speaks several languages. One of those that he speaks fluently is Mandarin.

or

CLEAR	Ryan is multilingual. One of the languages that he speaks fluently is Mandarin.

WEAK	Royale writes stories, and she hopes to make it her career. [The antecedent *writing* is suggested by the use of the pronoun *it* but is not expressed.]
CLEAR	Royale writes stories, and she hopes to make writing her career.

(4) Avoid an *indefinite reference,* which is the use of a pronoun that refers to no specific antecedent and that is unnecessary to the meaning of the sentence.

Most indefinite reference errors are caused by the misuse of the pronouns *it, they,* and *you.*

BLONDIE reprinted with special permission of King Features Syndicate, Inc.

USAGE

| INDEFINITE | In the newspaper, it reported that the robbers had been caught. [The pronoun *it* is not necessary to the meaning of the sentence.] |
| CLEAR | The newspaper reported that the robbers had been caught. |

| INDEFINITE | During the Middle Ages in Europe, you very likely would not live past the age of thirty. [The pronoun *you* does not truly refer to the reader and does not have any specific antecedent.] |
| CLEAR | During the Middle Ages in Europe, a person very likely would not live past the age of thirty. |

Exercise 12 Revising Unclear Pronoun References

The following sentences contain unclear pronoun references. Revise each faulty sentence.

EXAMPLE
1. In a brochure recently published by the Environmental Protection Agency (EPA), it promotes precycling to reduce waste.

1. *A brochure recently published by the Environmental Protection Agency (EPA) promotes precycling to reduce waste.*

1. The newest twist in recycling is *precycling*—cutting it off at its source.
2. Last month, after reading the EPA's brochure, my family decided to put its ideas into practice.
3. We now choose products that have less packaging; we carry groceries home in reusable cloth bags instead of paper or plastic ones; and we buy containers that can be refilled, which is easy.
4. Sara asked Mom if she could write to the Mail Preference Service, Direct Marketing Association and ask that our names not be sold to mailing-list companies.
5. That greatly reduced the amount of junk mail we get.
6. When we do have waste products, inventing new ways to use them becomes a challenge in creative thinking; one of them was mine.
7. Now we pack fragile objects in bits of plastic foam and other non-recyclable materials so that they don't get broken in shipping.
8. We use plastic produce bags as sandwich wrappers or as liners for small trash cans, and it works just fine.
9. We also convert cottage cheese cartons and margarine tubs into food-storage containers, and we plan to make a habit of it.
10. In just a few short weeks, we've learned that by remembering the three *r*'s—*reduce, reuse,* and *recycle*—you can help to protect our precious environment.

USAGE

Chapter Review

A. Using Pronouns Correctly in Sentences

For each sentence, choose the correct word in parentheses.

1. Francis said that in a few years he would give his stamp collection to his brother and (*I, me*).
2. Everyone was waiting impatiently to find out (*who, whom*) the new cheerleader would be.
3. My little sister is a much better basketball player than (*I, me*).
4. After the accident, the police questioned (*he, him*).
5. We found that (*she, her*) was the one who called twice last night.
6. At the self-service gas station, drivers must pump gasoline (*theirselves, themselves*).
7. Speaking of Ken Griffey, Jr., (*he, him*) and his dad are the first father and son ever to play professional baseball together on the same team.
8. Seeing a car with an out-of-state license plate in my driveway, I ran inside to see (*who, whom*) was there.
9. That trailer with the silver stripe is (*our, ours*).
10. Do you mind (*me, my*) eating while we walk?

B. Selecting Pronouns to Complete Sentences Correctly

Choose the correct pronoun form in parentheses. Then, tell whether the pronoun is used as a *subject*, a *predicate nominative*, a *direct object*, an *indirect object*, an *object of a preposition*, or an *appositive*.

11. The two Italian drivers, Dario and (*he, him*), came in first and second.
12. The entire cast in the first scene of the second act consisted of Beth and (*I, me*).
13. They met Stuart and (*he, him*) at the railroad station.
14. I thought the best soloists in the band were (*they, them*).
15. Teddy and (*she, her*) arrived with minutes to spare.
16. (*Whoever, Whomever*) wants to learn about good manners should listen to my aunt Rita.

17. The stars of that movie were Robert Duvall and (*he, him*).

18. Edmond Dantès was the wronged prisoner about (*who, whom*) Alexandre Dumas wrote in *The Count of Monte Cristo.*

19. Will Colin and (*he, him*) help us with the painting?

20. Ms. Oliveira asked you and (*I, me*) about staying and helping with the decorations.

21. I asked my mother (*who, whom*) called last night.

22. The pair of ballad singers, Tommy and (*she, her*), left the stage to great applause.

23. The person (*who, whom*) you spoke about will be the next leader of the expedition.

24. We gave Louis and (*he, him*) a ride to school.

25. She is a better swimmer than (*I, me*), but the coach said he needed both of us on the team.

26. I will support (*whoever, whomever*) is selected for president.

27. It is not fair to give (*they, them*) extra responsibilities just because they are more responsible.

28. (*Who, Whom*) is supervising the drama festival this year?

29. To go on the field trip, you need written permission from your parents and (*I, me*).

30. Everyone else finished the test earlier than (*they, them*).

C. Proofreading Sentences for Correct Pronoun Usage

Most of the following sentences contain errors in pronoun usage. Write the correct pronoun form for each error. If a sentence is already correct, write *C.*

31. Us athletes have little time to spend watching television.

32. The one who organized the new filing system was she.

33. Ask Lorna and he about the outcome of the race.

34. Ramona had not decided who she would vote for in the election.

35. Between you and I, that painting is worth much more.

36. We are willing to help whoever is in need.

37. Edna said that you speak Spanish better than her.

38. We can only guess whom it was.

39. The package was sent to Rob and I.

40. The drama coaches are Mr. Rolando and she.

Writing Application
Using Pronouns Correctly in a Letter

Clear Pronoun Reference   Your favorite musical group isn't happy with the director of their latest video. As a result, they are sponsoring a "Be a Music Video Director" contest. To enter, you have to write a letter explaining your idea for a different video of the same song. Tell which singers, dancers, and musicians you would cast in your video. Include at least ten pronouns in your sentences. Be sure that no pronoun has an unclear antecedent.

Prewriting   Start by choosing the song for which you want to make a video. Then, list some ideas for three or four scenes in your video. Next to each scene idea, list the performers you would use in that scene and describe the action. In addition to actual people, you may want to have cartoon characters or other animated figures in your video.

Writing   As you write sentences about your music video, make the sequence of events clear. Make the spatial relationships clear, too, telling where the cast members are in relation to each other.

Revising   Check the rough draft of your letter to be sure that your explanation is clear. If you have included too many performers or too many details, eliminate the least interesting ones.

Publishing   Read your letter, looking for inexact uses of the pronouns *it*, *this*, *that*, and *which*. If your sentences contain inexact pronoun references, revise those sentences. Proofread your letter to correct errors in grammar, punctuation, and spelling. Your class may wish to vote on the best music video idea in each of several categories, such as rock, country, and rap.

7

Using Verbs Correctly
Principal Parts, Tense, Voice, Mood

Diagnostic Preview

A. Writing the Past and Past Participle Forms of Irregular Verbs

For each of the following sentences, write the correct form (past or past participle) of the italicized verb.

EXAMPLES
1. *know*   I have _____ Zoe since we were in kindergarten together.

1. *known*

2. *swim*   Has Samuel ever _____ out to the rocky island in the middle of the lake?

2. *swum*

1. *ride*   Jeffrey and Lee have _____ their bikes fifty miles today.
2. *write* I read the letters Grandpa _____ to Grandma in 1960.
3. *take*   Dad, I know that you've _____ us to two concerts this year, but please take us to just one more.
4. *fall*   All that winter day the snow _____, blanketing everything.
5. *see*   Rebecca soon _____ why the old house had sold so cheaply.
6. *drink* The gerbil has _____ most of its water.
7. *begin* As darkness fell and the children still had not returned, I _____ to worry.
8. *bring* Margot has _____ popcorn and apples for the party.

9. *speak*   At the assembly yesterday, Sergeant Lewis _____ about responsible driving.

10. *give*   The Nez Perce had _____ the starving fur traders food and helped them repair their canoes.

B. Revising Sentences to Correct Problems in Verb Tense and Voice

Rewrite the following sentences, replacing verbs that are in the wrong tense or that are in an awkward voice. If a sentence is already correct, write *C*.

EXAMPLES   **[1]** Genna gave her report on Captain James Cook and shows us some maps and pictures of the areas he had explored.

1. *Genna gave her report on Captain James Cook and showed us some maps and pictures of the areas he had explored.*

[2] We were surprised to learn how many places were explored by him.

2. *We were surprised to learn how many places he had explored.*

[11] Captain Cook, one of the greatest explorers of all time, sailed large areas of the Pacific Ocean and makes accurate maps of the region. [12] Cook joins the navy as a seaman in 1755, and many promotions were received by him before he became the master of a ship in 1757. [13] Because of his knowledge of geography, astronomy, and mathematics, he is selected to lead a scientific expedition to the Pacific. [14] The purpose of Cook's expedition is to observe the passage of Venus between Earth and the sun, a very rare occurrence. [15] On the voyage, Cook wins a battle against scurvy, a serious disease caused by lack of vitamin C. [16] Raw cabbage, which contained vitamin C, was eaten by the sailors to prevent the disease. [17] By the time the voyage is over, the ship traveled around Cape Horn to Tahiti in the Pacific Ocean. [18] After he observes the passage of Venus, Cook sails off to explore the east coast of New Zealand, which was claimed by him for England. [19] The Hawaiian Islands were later explored by Cook on his final voyage to the Pacific and were named the Sandwich Islands by him. [20] In a dispute over a canoe, Cook was killed by island inhabitants, and in accordance with naval tradition, he was buried at sea in 1779.

C. Determining Correct Uses of *Lie* and *Lay*, *Sit* and *Set*, and *Rise* and *Raise*

If a verb form in one of the following sentences is incorrect, write the correct form. If a sentence is already correct, write *C*.

EXAMPLE   **1.** Has Matt already risen the flag?

         1. raised

21. You can sit the wastebasket in the corner.
22. Everyone rose when the judge entered the courtroom, and then everyone sat when she sat.
23. The mysterious shape suddenly raised from the shadows.
24. I like to lay out under the stars and just think.
25. The servant had lain out the emperor's robes of yellow, the color that only members of Chinese royalty were permitted to wear.

The Principal Parts of Verbs

Verbs have four basic forms called ***principal parts.*** All of a verb's other forms come from its principal parts.

7a. The four principal parts of a verb are the ***base form,*** the ***present participle,*** the ***past,*** and the ***past participle.***

NOTE   Some authorities refer to the base form as the *infinitive.* Follow your teacher's instructions when labeling this verb form.

┌HELP───

The words *is* and *have* are included in the chart to the right because helping verbs are used with the present participle and past participle to form some tenses.

Reference Note

For more about using **helping verbs,** see page 15.

Base Form	Present Participle	Past	Past Participle
believe	[is] believing	believed	[have] believed
walk	[is] walking	walked	[have] walked
teach	[is] teaching	taught	[have] taught
run	[is] running	ran	[have] run
do	[is] doing	did	[have] done
be	[is] being	was, were	[have] been
cost	[is] costing	cost	[have] cost

NOTE Sometimes a past participle is used with a form of *be,* as in *was chosen, are known, is being seen.* This use of the verb is called the **passive voice.**

EXAMPLES A complete list of rules **is given** to all the contestants two weeks before the competition.

If a book is due on a Sunday, no fines **are charged** if the book **is returned** by the following Monday.

Reference Note
For more about **passive-voice verbs,** see page 199.

Regular Verbs

7b. A *regular verb* generally forms its past and past participle by adding *–d* or *–ed* to the base form.

Base Form	Present Participle	Past	Past Participle
receive	[is] receiving	received	[have] received
blame	[is] blaming	blamed	[have] blamed
work	[is] working	worked	[have] worked

One common error in the use of the past and the past participle forms of a regular verb is leaving off the *–d* or *–ed* ending.

NONSTANDARD	They use to live in Waco, Texas.
STANDARD	They **used** to live in Waco, Texas.

NONSTANDARD	Are you suppose to meet with them tomorrow?
STANDARD	Are you **supposed** to meet with them tomorrow?

NONSTANDARD	She ask me to go to the dance.
STANDARD	She **asked** me to go to the dance.

Reference Note
For a discussion of **standard** and **nonstandard usage,** see page 236.

NOTE Most regular verbs that end in *e* drop the *e* before adding *–ing.* Some regular verbs double the final consonant before adding *–ing* or *–ed.*

EXAMPLES snore snoring snored

nap napping napped

Reference Note
For guidelines on spelling verbs when **adding *–d, –ed,* or *–ing,*** see page 382.

USAGE

7
a, b

A few regular verbs have alternative past and past participle forms ending in *t*.

┌HELP─

The regular verbs *deal* and *mean* always form the past and the past participle by adding *t*: dealt, (have) dealt; meant, (have) meant.

Base Form	Present Participle	Past	Past Participle
burn	[is] burning	burned *or* burnt	[have] burned *or* burnt
leap	[is] leaping	leaped *or* leapt	[have] leaped *or* leapt
dream	[is] dreaming	dreamed *or* dreamt	[have] dreamed *or* dreamt

Exercise 1 Using the Past Form of Regular Verbs

Give the correct past form of each verb in parentheses.

EXAMPLE   1. With a mighty heave, the elephant (*push*) the log out of the river.

1. *pushed*

1. Charlene (*answer*) all the questions correctly.
2. When Greg was in Ireland, he (*kiss*) the Blarney stone.
3. As I walked by, they (*smile*).
4. Melissa (*pull*) the wagon, which was full of rag dolls.
5. Denise (*watch*) the wildlife through her binoculars.
6. Spence and James (*play*) the trombone and the clarinet at the concert last night.
7. Mother Teresa (*help*) many people.
8. After receiving the postcard, Eduardo (*laugh*).
9. Last Saturday, my friends (*dance*) the polka at our school's international festival.
10. Tracy (*paint*) a powerful self-portrait that will appear in next month's exhibit.

Irregular Verbs

7c. An **irregular verb** forms its past and past participle in some way other than by adding *–d* or *–ed* to the base form.

An irregular verb forms its past and past participle in one of the following ways: (1) changing consonants, (2) changing vowels, (3) changing vowels *and* consonants, or (4) making no change.

	Base Form	Past	Past Participle
Consonant Change	bend	bent	[have] bent
	send	sent	[have] sent
Vowel Change	sing	sang	[have] sung
Vowel and Consonant Change	catch	caught	[have] caught
	go	went	[have] gone
	fly	flew	[have] flown
No Change	set	set	[have] set

Principal Parts of Common Irregular Verbs

Base Form	Present Participle	Past	Past Participle
become	[is] becoming	became	[have] become
begin	[is] beginning	began	[have] begun
blow	[is] blowing	blew	[have] blown
break	[is] breaking	broke	[have] broken
bring	[is] bringing	brought	[have] brought
build	[is] building	built	[have] built
burn	[is] burning	burned *or* burnt	[have] burned *or* burnt
burst	[is] bursting	burst	[have] burst
buy	[is] buying	bought	[have] bought
catch	[is] catching	caught	[have] caught
choose	[is] choosing	chose	[have] chosen
come	[is] coming	came	[have] come
cost	[is] costing	cost	[have] cost
cut	[is] cutting	cut	[have] cut
dive	[is] diving	dove *or* dived	[have] dived
do	[is] doing	did	[have] done
draw	[is] drawing	drew	[have] drawn
drink	[is] drinking	drank	[have] drunk
drive	[is] driving	drove	[have] driven

USAGE

┌HELP─

Since most English verbs are regular, people sometimes try to make irregular verbs follow the regular pattern. However, such verb forms as *throwed, knowed, shrinked,* and *choosed* are considered nonstandard.

If you are not sure whether a verb is regular or irregular, look it up in a dictionary. Entries for irregular verbs list the principal parts. If an entry for a verb does not list the principal parts, the verb is a regular verb.

(continued)

(continued)

Principal Parts of Common Irregular Verbs

Base Form	Present Participle	Past	Past Participle
eat	[is] eating	ate	[have] eaten
fall	[is] falling	fell	[have] fallen
feel	[is] feeling	felt	[have] felt
fight	[is] fighting	fought	[have] fought
find	[is] finding	found	[have] found
fly	[is] flying	flew	[have] flown
forgive	[is] forgiving	forgave	[have] forgiven
freeze	[is] freezing	froze	[have] frozen
get	[is] getting	got	[have] got or gotten
give	[is] giving	gave	[have] given
go	[is] going	went	[have] gone
grow	[is] growing	grew	[have] grown
have	[is] having	had	[have] had
hear	[is] hearing	heard	[have] heard
hide	[is] hiding	hid	[have] hidden or hid
hit	[is] hitting	hit	[have] hit
know	[is] knowing	knew	[have] known
lead	[is] leading	led	[have] led
leave	[is] leaving	left	[have] left
let	[is] letting	let	[have] let
light	[is] lighting	lighted or lit	[have] lighted or lit
lose	[is] losing	lost	[have] lost
make	[is] making	made	[have] made
pay	[is] paying	paid	[have] paid
put	[is] putting	put	[have] put
read	[is] reading	read	[have] read
ride	[is] riding	rode	[have] ridden
ring	[is] ringing	rang	[have] rung
run	[is] running	ran	[have] run
say	[is] saying	said	[have] said

─HELP─

Some verbs have two correct past or past participle forms. However, these forms are not always interchangeable.

EXAMPLES
He **shone** the candle into the cellar. [*Shined* would also be correct.]

I **shined** my shoes. [*Shone* would be incorrect in this usage.]

If you are unsure about which past participle to use, check an up-to-date dictionary.

USAGE

Principal Parts of Common Irregular Verbs

Base Form	Present Participle	Past	Past Participle
see	[is] seeing	saw	[have] seen
seek	[is] seeking	sought	[have] sought
sell	[is] selling	sold	[have] sold
send	[is] sending	sent	[have] sent
sing	[is] singing	sang	[have] sung
sink	[is] sinking	sank *or* sunk	[have] sunk
sleep	[is] sleeping	slept	[have] slept
speak	[is] speaking	spoke	[have] spoken
spend	[is] spending	spent	[have] spent
stand	[is] standing	stood	[have] stood
steal	[is] stealing	stole	[have] stolen
swim	[is] swimming	swam	[have] swum
take	[is] taking	took	[have] taken
teach	[is] teaching	taught	[have] taught
tear	[is] tearing	tore	[have] torn
tell	[is] telling	told	[have] told
think	[is] thinking	thought	[have] thought
throw	[is] throwing	threw	[have] thrown
wear	[is] wearing	wore	[have] worn
win	[is] winning	won	[have] won
write	[is] writing	wrote	[have] written

Oral Practice 1 **Using Regular and Irregular Verbs**

Read each sentence aloud, stressing each italicized verb.

1. Keisha *is braiding* Tiffany's hair in cornrows.
2. Bob *read* the want ads today, just as he *has read* them all week.
3. Mom, I *am bringing* you breakfast, but I *have eaten* your toast!
4. Warren *drew* the designs for the posters.
5. Paloma Picasso, the jewelry designer, *has chosen* an artistic career different from her famous father's.
6. Carrie *went* to Penn State; Hector *is going* to Boston College.
7. Someone *ate* the spaghetti, but nobody *has touched* the baked beans.
8. If you *have* never *seen* a meteor shower, *run* outside right now!

USAGE

USAGE

Exercise 2 Using the Past and Past Participle Forms of Irregular Verbs

Give the correct form (past or past participle) of the verb given before each of the following sentences.

EXAMPLE   **1.** *write*   Diego has _____ a report on Pueblo culture.

         1. *written*

1. *sing*   The rain fell after we had _____ the national anthem.
2. *begin*   I had already _____ my homework.
3. *freeze*   The subzero winds nearly _____ the Pawnee hunters as they tracked the herd of bison.
4. *fly*   Last summer we _____ in a lighter-than-air balloon.
5. *see*   During our visit to Hawaii, we _____ a group of performers do a traditional hula dance.
6. *take*   My sister has _____ that course.
7. *fall*   By the time Rolando finished carving the little figure, hundreds of tiny wood shavings had _____ to the floor.
8. *throw*   The horse had _____ its shoe.
9. *break*   We hoped we hadn't _____ the machine.
10. *speak*   Harley's grandmother _____ to our class about her trip to the Olympics.

Exercise 3 Using the Past and Past Participle Forms of Irregular Verbs

Give the correct form (past or past participle) of each italicized verb in the following paragraph.

EXAMPLE   Have you **[1]** (*see*) any of the artwork by Henry Ossawa Tanner?

         1. seen

We recently **[1]** (*see*) paintings by the African American artist Henry Ossawa Tanner. Tanner had **[2]** (*choose*) his lifelong career in art by the time he was thirteen years old. While walking in a park one day, he and his father had **[3]** (*come*) upon a landscape artist at work. Years later, Tanner **[4]** (*write*), "It was this simple event that . . . set me on fire." Young Henry **[5]** (*bring*) such eagerness to his work that, before long, he **[6]** (*teach*) himself to draw well enough to be admitted to one of the finest art schools in the country. His paintings were beautiful but did not sell well, so Tanner **[7]** (*go*) abroad. He **[8]** (*fall*) in love with the city of Paris and lived and worked there for the rest of his life, winning many important painting awards. Shown here is his best-known work, *The Banjo Lesson*, which he painted in Paris from sketches he had **[9]** (*draw*) years earlier in North Carolina. In 1969, long after Tanner's death, a touring exhibit finally **[10]** (*give*) Americans a look at the work of this gifted artist.

Henry Ossawa Tanner, *The Banjo Lesson* (1893). Hampton University Museum, Hampton, VA.

Exercise 4 **Choosing the Past and Past Participle Forms of Irregular Verbs**

Choose the correct verb form in parentheses in each of the following sentences.

EXAMPLE　**1.** Frieda has (*gave, given*) much thought to pursuing a career in engineering.

　1. given

1. We (*did, done*) everything we could to help him.
2. Who has (*drank, drunk*) all the orange juice?
3. Someone has already (*tore, torn*) out the coupon.
4. I wish you had (*spoke, spoken*) to me about it sooner.
5. I dived off the board and (*swam, swum*) the length of the pool.
6. You must have (*rung, rang*) the doorbell while I was outside.
7. Nancy had never (*ate, eaten*) a tamale before.
8. Lois (*blowed, blew*) up the balloon.
9. Suddenly the balloon (*burst, bursted*).
10. We (*drove, driven*) to the train station in a hurry.

Six Troublesome Verbs

Lie and *Lay*

The verb *lie* means "to rest," "to recline," or "to be in a place." *Lie* does not take a direct object. The verb *lay* means "to put (something) in place." *Lay* generally takes a direct object.

Principal Parts of *Lie* and *Lay*			
Base Form	Present Participle	Past	Past Participle
lie	[is] lying	lay	[have] lain
lay	[is] laying	laid	[have] laid

EXAMPLES Please **lie** down. [no direct object]

The packages **are lying** here. [no direct object]

The key **lay** on the shelf. [no direct object]

The old papers **had lain** on the desk for months. [no direct object]

Please **lay** the tools down. [*Tools* is the direct object.]

I **am laying** your packages here. [*Packages* is the direct object.]

The boy **laid** the key on the shelf. [*Key* is the direct object.]

He **had laid** the old papers on the desk. [*Papers* is the direct object.]

Oral Practice 2 **Using the Forms of *Lie* and *Lay* in Sentences**

Read each of the following sentences aloud, stressing the italicized verb.

1. The mason *is laying* the tiles on the patio.
2. A light haze *lay* over the hills.
3. The cat *laid* its toy on the doorsill.
4. Someone's books *are lying* in the hall.
5. She *had lain* down for a nap.
6. Where *could* I *have laid* the recipe?
7. *Lay* the material on the counter.
8. You *could lie* down and relax.

USAGE

Exercise 5 Choosing the Forms of *Lie* and *Lay*

Choose the correct verb form in parentheses in each of the following sentences.

EXAMPLE 1. The sheet music is (*lying, laying*) on the piano.

1. *lying*

1. Do not (*lay, lie*) the socks there.
2. Eduardo (*lay, laid*) in the sleeping bag and waited for sleep.
3. The pasture (*lies, lays*) in the valley.
4. A sheet (*lay, laid*) over the rug to catch paint spatters.
5. The clothing had (*lain, laid*) on the floor all week.
6. Katy had (*lay, laid*) the book down.
7. Mrs. Nakamoto was (*lying, laying*) out everything necessary for the tea ceremony.
8. The theories developed by Albert Einstein have (*lay, laid*) the groundwork for many other scientific discoveries.
9. The cat has been (*lying, laying*) on my coat.
10. (*Lying, Laying*) the tip by my plate, I rose to leave the restaurant.

Exercise 6 Using the Forms of *Lie* and *Lay*

If a verb in the following sentences is incorrect, write the correct form. If the verb is already correct, write *C*.

EXAMPLES 1. On the bed laid the child's favorite doll.

1. *lay*

2. Julia had lain rose petals along the stage.

2. *laid*

1. The towels laying in the corner all need to be washed.
2. Yesterday, all we did was lie around and play CDs.
3. The runner crossed the finish line and laid down in the grass.
4. The fox had laid in the thicket until the hunters had passed.
5. After I had tripped, I sat there feeling embarrassed, my groceries laying all around me.
6. He was lying under the car, tinkering with the muffler.
7. The workers had lain down their tools and gone to lunch.
8. My gym bag was laying right where I had left it.
9. In his speech, Cesar Chavez lay the responsibility for social change on the shoulders of all citizens.
10. She sighed and lay down the phone receiver.

TIPS & TRICKS

To decide whether to use *lie* or *lay,* ask yourself the following questions:

QUESTION 1
What do I mean? (Is the meaning "to be in a place," or is it "to put in a place"?)

QUESTION 2
What time does the verb express?

QUESTION 3
Which principal part shows this time?

EXAMPLE
Feeling very drowsy, I (*lay, laid*) on the couch.

QUESTION 1
Here the meaning is "to be in a place." Therefore, the verb should be a form of *lie.*

QUESTION 2
The time is past.

QUESTION 3
The past form of *lie* is *lay.*

ANSWER
Feeling very drowsy, I **lay** on the couch.

USAGE

Exercise 7 Proofreading for the Correct Forms of *Lie* and *Lay*

In each of the following sentences, a form of *lie* or *lay* is used. If the wrong form is used, write the correct form. If a sentence is already correct, write *C*.

EXAMPLES
1. Oscar rarely spends the weekends laying on the couch.
    1. *lying*

2. He had planned to spend his Saturday lying new tile in the kitchen.
    2. *laying*

1. Several boxes of fired-clay tiles laid on the floor of the garage.
2. Before he started, he lay out all his materials and carefully read the directions on the container of adhesive.
3. At first, he made good progress and had lain sixteen rows of tile by lunch time.
4. Then he ate a sandwich and laid down on the sofa for a few minutes.
5. When he returned to the kitchen, Oscar found that his dog, Stanley, was laying where the next row of tiles was supposed to go.
6. Oscar had forgotten that Stanley liked to lay in that particular place on the kitchen floor.
7. In fact, Stanley had lain there for his morning nap ever since he was a puppy.
8. Oscar got a juicy meat scrap out of the refrigerator and laid it on the floor just beyond Stanley's snoring nose.
9. The wily Stanley had been laying in wait and, in a flash, grabbed the meat.
10. To Oscar's dismay, Stanley resumed his nap with a satisfied sigh, and Oscar learned that the worker isn't the only one who can lay down on the job!

USAGE

Sit and Set

The verb *sit* means "to rest in a seated, upright position" or "to be in a place." *Sit* seldom takes a direct object. The verb *set* means "to put (something) in a place." *Set* generally takes a direct object. Notice that the past and the past participle of *set* are the same as the base form.

Principal Parts of *Sit* and *Set*			
Base Form	Present Participle	Past	Past Participle
sit	[is] sitting	sat	[have] sat
set	[is] setting	set	[have] set

EXAMPLES

You **may sit** here. [no direct object]

Where **are** Diana and Vince **sitting**? [no direct object]

The guest speaker **sat** between Eduardo and me. [no direct object]

His bicycle **has sat** in our driveway for a week. [no direct object]

You **may set** your books here. [*Books* is the direct object.]

Where **are** Diana and Vince **setting** the computer desk? [*Desk* is the direct object.]

The guest speaker **set** his briefcase between Eduardo and me. [*Briefcase* is the direct object.]

He **had set** his bicycle in our driveway last week. [*Bicycle* is the direct object.]

Oral Practice 3 Using the Correct Forms of *Sit* and *Set* in Sentences

Read each of the following sentences aloud, stressing the italicized verb.

1. *Set* the groceries on the counter.
2. The travelers *set* out early to avoid the midday heat.
3. Would you please *set* the chairs under the tree in the front yard?
4. The bird *sat* on the wire.
5. During Hanukkah, we always *set* the menorah in a place of honor.
6. We *had sat* in the lobby for an hour.
7. They *have been sitting* on the porch.
8. Rosa Parks made history when she chose to *sit* rather than to give up her seat to a white passenger.

STYLE TIP

You may know that the word *set* has more meanings than the one given here. Check in a dictionary to see if the meaning you intend requires an object.

EXAMPLE

The sun **sets** in the west. [Here, *sets* does not take an object.]

USAGE

Exercise 8 Selecting the Correct Forms of *Sit* and *Set*

Choose the correct verb form in parentheses in each of the following sentences.

EXAMPLE 1. He (*sat, set*) on the park bench and read the newspaper.

1. sat

1. A few of us were (*sitting, setting*) at our desks.
2. He had (*sat, set*) in the rocker since dusk.
3. He (*sat, set*) the package on the doorstep.
4. Ida was (*sitting, setting*) out the chips and dip for the guests.
5. We had been (*sitting, setting*) on a freshly painted bench.
6. They (*sat, set*) the seedlings in the window boxes.
7. He had (*sit, set*) his retainer on his lunch tray.
8. (*Sit, Set*) this Pueblo pottery in the display case.
9. I could (*sit, set*) and watch the birds all day.
10. We patiently (*sat, set*) and waited for the travelers to arrive.

Exercise 9 Writing the Forms of *Sit* and *Set*

For each numbered blank in the following paragraph, write the correct form of *sit* or *set*.

EXAMPLE Before [1] _____ down to rest, Meriwether Lewis and William Clark decided that the group should climb to the top of the bluff.

1. *sitting*

To gain a view of the surrounding land, Lewis and Clark's group climbed to an outcropping of gray rocks that [1] _____ atop the bluff. It was late afternoon, and the Shoshone guide Sacagawea [2] _____ her pack down beside the rocks and [3] _____ down in their shade to rest. Lewis saw her from where he was [4] _____ nearby and approached with a friendly "May I [5] _____ here with you?" Several other members of the expedition saw them [6] _____ together and wondered what they were discussing. In fact, Lewis was asking her in what direction she thought the party should [7] _____ out in the morning. Gazing westward from the bluff, Sacagawea saw that she was in familiar territory and soon [8] _____ her mind on heading down the mountainside toward the northwest. By the time the sun had [9] _____, Lewis agreed that the route she had chosen would be the easiest to follow. A wise leader, he realized that he had never [10] _____ foot in these lands, while she had passed this way before.

The Granger Collection, New York.

Review A   **Choosing the Correct Forms of *Lie* and *Lay* and *Sit* and *Set***

Choose the correct verb form in parentheses in each of the following sentences.

EXAMPLE   **1.** She (*set, sat*) at the computer, reading her e-mail.

        1. sat

1. (*Setting, Sitting*) on the table was a pair of scissors.

2. Please (*sit, set*) the carton down carefully.

3. Sakura folded her kimono and (*lay, laid*) down to sleep.

4. (*Sit, Set*) all the way back in your seat.

5. The dirty dishes had (*laid, lain*) in the sink for hours.

6. Yesterday, Tom (*lay, laid*) the blame for his lateness on his clock.

7. The cat always (*sits, sets*) on the couch.

8. If only we could have (*laid, lain*) our hands on the treasure!

9. The tickets to the Wynton Marsalis concert were (*lying, laying*) right where I had left them.

10. King Tut's tomb (*lay, laid*) undisturbed for centuries.

11. Have you ever (*sat, set*) around with nothing to do?

12. She (*sat, set*) down at her desk with her checkbook and calculator in front of her.

13. Santa Anna, (*setting, sitting*) on his horse, ordered his troops to attack the Alamo.

14. The beached rowboat (*lay, laid*) on its side.

15. She (*sat, set*) looking toward the horizon.

16. Laura had just (*sat, set*) down when the phone rang.

17. Julie (*lay, laid*) her handbag on the counter.

18. Pieces of the jigsaw puzzle were (*lying, laying*) on the floor.

19. Jack was (*setting, sitting*) outside on the top step.

20. Were you (*lying, laying*) down for a while before dinner?

Rise and *Raise*

The verb *rise* means "to go up" or "to get up." *Rise* does not take a direct object. The verb *raise* means "to lift" or "to cause (something) to rise." *Raise* generally takes a direct object.

Principal Parts of *Rise* and *Raise*			
Base Form	**Present Participle**	**Past**	**Past Participle**
rise	[is] rising	rose	[have] risen
raise	[is] raising	raised	[have] raised

EXAMPLES I usually **rise** at 6:00 A.M. [no direct object]

She **is rising** uncertainly. [no direct object]

The banner **rose** in the gust of wind. [no direct object]

Has the price of gasoline **risen**? [no direct object]

I usually **raise** the blinds at 6:00 A.M. [*Blinds* is the direct object.]

She **is raising** her hand uncertainly. [*Hand* is the direct object.]

The gust of wind **raised** the banner. [*Banner* is the direct object.]

The gas station **has raised** the price of gasoline. [*Price* is the direct object.]

Oral Practice 4 **Using the Forms of *Rise* and *Raise***

Read each of the following sentences aloud, stressing the italicized verb.

1. *Has* the moon *risen* yet?

2. The builders *raised* the roof of the new house at noon.

3. The temperature *rose* as the sun climbed higher.

4. Listening to "I Have a Dream," a speech by Dr. Martin Luther King, Jr., always *raises* my spirits.
5. Trails of mist *were rising* from the lake.
6. How much *did* the river *rise* during the flood?
7. The butterfly *rose* from the leaf and flitted away.
8. My baby sister *was raising* her head to look around.

Exercise 10 Using the Correct Forms of *Rise* and *Raise*

For the blank in each of the following sentences, write the correct form of *rise* or *raise*.

EXAMPLE   1. Does the orderly ـــــ the flag every morning?

             1. *raise*

1. ـــــ the cards higher, please.
2. The gigantic Kodiak bear is ـــــ on its hind legs to look around.
3. The tide ـــــ and falls because of the moon.
4. Carlos and Pilar ـــــ the piñata above the heads of the children.
5. Up toward the clouds ـــــ the jet.
6. Many American Indian peoples have traditionally ـــــ corn as a staple food crop.
7. Prices have ـــــ in the last few years.
8. The traffic officer had ـــــ his hand to signal us.
9. My sister and I had ـ_____ before the sun came up this morning.
10. Robert Kennedy ـ_____ to fame in the 1960s.

Review B Using the Correct Forms of *Lie* and *Lay,* *Sit* and *Set,* and *Rise* and *Raise*

If a verb in one of the following sentences is incorrect, write the correct form. If a sentence is already correct, write *C.*

EXAMPLE   1. The baby starlings were setting in the nest.

             1. *sitting*

1. Set the eggs down carefully.
2. The frog was setting on the lily pad and croaking loudly.
3. The judge studied the papers and then lay them beside her gavel.
4. The cattle were lying in the shade by the stream.
5. Do you think the temperature will raise much higher?
6. Wanda sat out the equipment for the experiment.
7. Why don't you lie those things down?

8. Instead of laying down, you should be getting some type of strenuous exercise.

9. The raccoon raised up on its hind legs.

10. Set down for a while and relax.

Tense

7d. The *tense* of a verb indicates the time of the action or the state of being expressed by the verb.

Verbs in English have six tenses: *present, past, future, present perfect, past perfect,* and *future perfect.* These tenses are formed from the four principal parts of verbs. The following time line shows how the six tenses are related to one another.

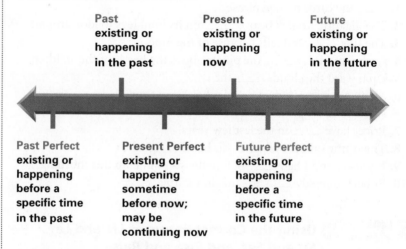

Past
existing or
happening
in the past

Present
existing or
happening
now

Future
existing or
happening
in the future

Past Perfect
existing or
happening
before a
specific time
in the past

Present Perfect
existing or
happening
sometime
before now;
may be
continuing now

Future Perfect
existing or
happening
before a
specific time
in the future

Verb Conjugation

Listing all of the forms of a verb according to tense is called *conjugating* a verb. The following charts show all six tenses of a regular verb (*talk*) and of an irregular verb (*give*).

Principal Parts of the Regular Verb *Talk*			
Base Form	**Present Participle**	**Past**	**Past Participle**
talk	[is] talking	talked	[have] talked

Conjugation of the Regular Verb *Talk*

Present Tense

Singular	*Plural*
I talk	we talk
you talk	you talk
he, she, *or* it talks	they talk

Past Tense

Singular	*Plural*
I talked	we talked
you talked	you talked
he, she, *or* it talked	they talked

Future Tense

Singular	*Plural*
I will (shall) talk	we will (shall) talk
you will (shall) talk	you will (shall) talk
he, she, *or* it will (shall) talk	they will (shall) talk

Present Perfect Tense

Singular	*Plural*
I have talked	we have talked
you have talked	you have talked
he, she, *or* it has talked	they have talked

Past Perfect Tense

Singular	*Plural*
I had talked	we had talked
you had talked	you had talked
he, she, *or* it had talked	they had talked

Future Perfect Tense

Singular	*Plural*
I will (shall) have talked	we will (shall) have talked
you will (shall) have talked	you will (shall) have talked
he, she, *or* it will (shall) have talked	they will (shall) have talked

STYLE TIP

Traditionally, the helping verbs *shall* and *will* were used differently. Now, however, *shall* can be used almost interchangeably with *will.*

Reference Note

For information on **using shall and will,** see page 198.

Each tense has another form, called the *progressive form,* which is used to express continuing action or state of being. The progressive form consists of the appropriate tense of the verb *be* and the present participle of a verb.

Present Progressive	am, are, is talking
Past Progressive	was, were talking
Future Progressive	will (shall) be talking
Present Perfect Progressive	has, have been talking
Past Perfect Progressive	had been talking
Future Perfect Progressive	will (shall) have been talking

Only the present and the past tenses have another form, called the *emphatic form,* which is used to show emphasis. In the present tense, the emphatic form consists of the helping verb *do* or *does* and the base form of the verb. In the past tense, the emphatic form consists of the verb *did* and the base form of a verb.

Present Emphatic	do, does talk
Past Emphatic	did talk

NOTE The emphatic form is also used in questions and negative statements. These uses do not place any special emphasis on the verbs.

QUESTION Why **do** snakes **shed** their skins?

NEGATIVE
STATEMENT If Uncle Pedro **does**n't **arrive** soon, we should call Aunt Lu.

Principal Parts of the Irregular Verb *Give*

Base Form	Present Participle	Past	Past Participle
give	[is] giving	gave	[have] given

Conjugation of the Irregular Verb *Give*

Present Tense

Singular	*Plural*
I give	we give
you give	you give
he, she, *or* it gives	they give

Present Progressive: *am, are, is giving*

Present Emphatic: *do, does give*

USAGE

Conjugation of the Irregular Verb *Give*

Past Tense

Singular	*Plural*
I gave	we gave
you gave	you gave
he, she, *or* it gave	they gave

Past Progressive: *was, were giving*
Past Emphatic: *did give*

Future Tense

Singular	*Plural*
I will (shall) give	we will (shall) give
you will (shall) give	you will (shall) give
he, she, *or* it will (shall) give	they will (shall) give

Future Progressive: *will (shall) be giving*

Present Perfect Tense

Singular	*Plural*
I have given	we have given
you have given	you have given
he, she, *or* it has given	they have given

Present Perfect Progressive: *has, have been giving*

Past Perfect Tense

Singular	*Plural*
I had given	we had given
you had given	you had given
he, she, *or* it had given	they had given

Past Perfect Progressive: *had been giving*

Future Perfect Tense

Singular	*Plural*
I will (shall) have given	we will (shall) have given
you will (shall) have given	you will (shall) have given
he, she, *or* it will (shall) have given	they will (shall) have given

Future Perfect Progressive: *will (shall) have been giving*

┌─HELP─

The conjugation of the verb *give* in the chart at left is in the active voice. Many verbs can be in either the active voice or the passive voice.

Reference Note

For a discussion of the uses of the **active voice** and the **passive voice,** see page 199. For the **conjugation of *give* in the passive voice,** see page 200.

USAGE

USAGE

The Uses of the Tenses

7e. Each of the six tenses has its own uses.

(1) The *present tense* expresses an action or a state of being that is occurring now, at the present time.

EXAMPLES   Sonja **owns** a calculator. [present]

                 Larry **is** in the Chess Club. [present]

                 We **are rehearsing** the play. [present progressive]

                 I **do appreciate** your helping me. [present emphatic]

The present tense is also used

- to show customary or habitual action or state of being

EXAMPLE   He **runs** two miles a day.

- to state a general truth—something that is always true

EXAMPLE   The equator **divides** the earth's surface into the Northern and Southern Hemispheres.

- to summarize the plot or subject matter of a literary work (such use is called *literary present*)

EXAMPLE   In Act III of *The Tragedy of Julius Caesar*, the conspirators **assassinate** the Roman leader.

- to make a historical event seem current (such use is called *historical present*)

EXAMPLE   During the unstable years following the 1910 Mexican Revolution, Emiliano Zapata and his army **occupy** Mexico City three different times.

- to express future time

EXAMPLE   We **travel** abroad next month.

(2) The *past tense* expresses an action or a state of being that occurred in the past and did not continue into the present.

EXAMPLES   I **ran** toward the door. [past]

                 Tomás **was** the club's president last year. [past]

                 The boys **were playing** football. [past progressive]

                 We certainly **did enjoy** your performance. [past emphatic]

(3) The *future tense* expresses an action or a state of being that will occur. The future tense is usually formed with the helping verb *will* or *shall* and the base form of a verb.

EXAMPLES   I **will travel** this fall. [future]

I **shall leave** soon. [future]

Gia and I **will be** there at seven o'clock. [future]

Will you **be waiting** for us? [future progressive]

A future action or state of being may also be expressed by using

- the present tense of *be* followed by *going to* and the base form of a verb

EXAMPLE   **Are** you **going to drive** her to the airport?

- the present tense of *be* followed by *about to* and the base form of the verb

EXAMPLE   They **are about to begin** the ceremony.

- the present tense of a verb with a word or word group that expresses future time

EXAMPLE   I **take** my driving test **next Friday.**

(4) The *present perfect tense* expresses an action or a state of being that occurred at an indefinite time in the past. The present perfect tense is usually formed with the helping verb *have* or *has* and the past participle of a verb.

EXAMPLES   She **has visited** Chicago. [present perfect]

They **have been** to the office. [present perfect]

The present perfect tense may also be used to express an action or a state of being that began in the past and that continues into the present.

EXAMPLES   She **has worked** there several years. [present perfect]

I **have been taking** guitar lessons for nearly six months. [present perfect progressive]

NOTE Use the past tense, not the present perfect tense, to express a specific time in the past.

EXAMPLE   We **saw** [*not* have seen] the movie last night.

(5) The *past perfect tense* expresses an action or a state of being that ended before another past action or state of being occurred. The past perfect tense is usually formed with the helping verb *had* and the past participle of the verb.

EXAMPLES   After Mary Anne **had revised** her essay, she handed it in. [past perfect]

Mr. Hahn told us that he **had been** a Peace Corps volunteer in Somalia. [past perfect]

The frustrated chemist finally realized that she **had been overlooking** an important step in the experiment. [past perfect progressive]

(6) The *future perfect tense* expresses an action or a state of being that will end before another future action or state of being. The future perfect tense is usually formed with the helping verbs *shall have* or *will have* and the past participle of a verb.

EXAMPLES   By the time you receive this postcard, **I will have returned** home. [future perfect]

Before then, you and he **will have become** U.S. citizens by naturalization. [future perfect]

At the end of this year, I **will have been attending** school for ten years. [future perfect progressive]

Exercise 11 Identifying the Tenses of Verbs

Identify the tenses of the verbs in each of the following pairs of sentences. Also tell whether the verbs are in progressive or emphatic form. Be prepared to explain the difference in meaning between the sentences in each pair.

EXAMPLE   **1.** My sister took piano lessons for two years.
        My sister has been taking piano lessons for two years.

    1. took—past; has been taking—present perfect progressive

1. I will start the assignment this afternoon.
   I will have started the assignment by this afternoon.

2. What happened here?
   What has been happening here?

3. She lived in Cleveland for four years.
   She has lived in Cleveland for four years.

┌─**HELP**─

In Exercise 11, the use of the past and present perfect verb tenses gives the example sentences different meanings.

My sister took piano lessons for two years. [The past tense *took* indicates that the piano lessons occurred in the past and did not continue into the present.]

My sister has been taking piano lessons for two years. [The progressive form of the present perfect tense *has been taking* indicates that the piano lessons began in the past and are continuing into the present.]

4. I do have an after-school job.

I did have an after-school job.

5. Some students were practicing karate during their lunch break.

Some students have been practicing karate during their lunch break.

Exercise 12 **Using the Different Tenses of Verbs**

Change the tense of the verb in each of the following sentences by following the directions given in the parentheses.

EXAMPLE   **1.** Have you done your homework? (Change to *past emphatic.*)

1. *Did you do your homework?*

1. Otto lived here for a year. (Change to *future perfect.*)
2. I leave for school at 7:00 A.M. (Change to *future.*)
3. Have you read Thomas Sowell's excellent how-to book *Choosing a College*? (Change to *present perfect progressive.*)
4. Will you go? (Change to *past emphatic.*)
5. Were they at the party? (Change to *past perfect.*)
6. Were you there? (Change to *present perfect.*)
7. The soloist sings well. (Change to *present emphatic.*)
8. The bus arrives on time. (Change to *future.*)
9. By then, Cammi had returned. (Change to *future perfect.*)
10. The klezmer band will play for an hour without a break. (Change to *future perfect progressive.*)

Consistency of Tense

7f. Do not change needlessly from one tense to another.

(1) When describing events that occur at the same time, use verbs in the same tense.

EXAMPLES   Roy **looked** through his binoculars and **saw** a large bear as it **raced** back to the woods. [All of the verbs are in the past tense.]

Roy **looks** through his binoculars and **sees** a large bear as it **races** back to the woods. [All of the verbs are in the present tense.]

(2) When describing events that occur at different times, use verbs in different tenses to show the sequence of events.

Yesterday, Donald **told** us that his brother **works** part time at the animal shelter. [The past tense *told* is correct because the action of telling occurred at a specific time in the past. The present tense *works* is correct because the action of working occurs now.]

Sela's family **lives** next door but **will be moving** to Salinas, California, next month. [The present tense *lives* is correct because the action of living occurs now. The future tense *will be moving* is correct because the action of moving will be occurring in the future.]

┌─HELP─
Some sentences
in Exercise 13 contain more
than one error.

Exercise 13 Proofreading for Consistency of Tense

Most of the sentences in the following passage contain at least one error in the use of tenses. Revise the incorrect sentences to correct each error. If a sentence is already correct, write *C*.

EXAMPLE [1] The American Revolution began in 1775 and ends in 1783.

1. *The American Revolution began in 1775 and ended in 1783.*

[1] The painting below depicts the outcome of one of the most important battles of the American Revolution, a battle that took place in September and October 1777 at Saratoga, New York. [2] The leader of the British troops, General John Burgoyne, had set up camp near Saratoga and is planning to march south to Albany. [3] Burgoyne's

The Granger Collection, New York.

USAGE

army has been weakened by a recent attack from an American militia, which had ambushed some of his troops at Bennington, Vermont. [4] Although the march to Albany is dangerous, Burgoyne decided to take the risk because he feels bound by orders from London.

[5] Meanwhile, also near Saratoga, the American troops under General Horatio Gates gather reinforcements and supplies. [6] The American forces outnumbered their British enemies by a margin of nearly two to one. [7] The Americans are much better equipped than the British, whose provisions are badly depleted.

[8] In spite of these disadvantages, the British launch an attack on the Americans on September 19, 1777. [9] After four hours of fierce fighting, the Americans, led by General Gates or General Benedict Arnold (who later became an infamous traitor to the American cause), withdraw. [10] The British, however, have suffered serious losses, including many officers. [11] Burgoyne urgently sends messages to the British command in New York and asked for new orders. [12] He never received a response, possibly because the messages are intercepted. [13] Burgoyne's tactics became desperate. [14] He boldly leads a fresh attack against the Americans on October 7. [15] This time, however, his troops endure even worse casualties, and the next day Burgoyne prepares to retreat.

[16] The Americans surround Burgoyne's army before it could leave Saratoga. [17] As the painting shows, Burgoyne had surrendered to Benedict Arnold. [18] The Convention of Saratoga, under which Burgoyne gave up his entire force of six thousand troops, is signed on October 17. [19] Saratoga becomes a turning point in the American Revolution. [20] Six years later, in 1783, the British signed a peace treaty with the Americans, and the American Revolution ended.

Modals

7g. A *modal* is a helping (or auxiliary) verb that is joined with a main verb or an infinitive to express an attitude toward the action or state of being of the main verb.

The helping verbs *can, could, may, might, must, ought, shall, should, will,* and *would* are used as modals.

(1) The modal *can* or *could* is used to express ability.

EXAMPLES   **Can** you **speak** French?

I could have gone, but I was too tired.

Reference Note

For more about **helping (auxiliary) verbs** and **main verbs,** see page 15.

USAGE

(2) The modal *may* is used to express permission or possibility.

EXAMPLES   You **may leave** the table. [permission]

It seems that her truck's struts **may be** defective. [possibility]

(3) The modal *might*, like *may*, is used to express possibility. Often, the possibility expressed by *might* is less likely than the possibility expressed by *may*.

EXAMPLE   My brother said he **might be** home late.

(4) The modal *must* is used most often to express a requirement. Sometimes, *must* is used to express an explanation.

EXAMPLES   The hippopotamus **must spend** most of its time in the water, or its skin will become dry. [requirement]

He **must have been caught** in traffic. [explanation]

(5) The modal *ought* is used to express an obligation or a likelihood.

EXAMPLES   Does Ms. Garza think that she **ought to promote** Mr. Whitman? [obligation]

The tornado **ought to be gone** soon. [likelihood]

(6) The modal *will* or *shall* is used to express future time.

EXAMPLES   When **will** (or **shall**) we **leave** for lunch?

Tim **will take** a look at your car.

(7) The modal *should* is used to express a recommendation, an obligation, or a possibility.

EXAMPLES   Mom **should go** to the doctor for her sprain. [recommendation]

Students **should hand in** their homework on time. [obligation]

Should you **have** any complaints about the service, please do not hesitate to let us know. [possibility]

(8) The modal *would* is used to express the conditional form of a verb.

A conditional verb form usually appears in an independent clause that is joined with an "if" clause. The "if" clause explains *under what condition(s)* the action or state of being of the conditional verb takes place.

STYLE   TIP

In the past, careful writers and speakers of English made a distinction between the modals *shall* and *will*. Nowadays, however, writers and speakers tend to use *will* in most cases. Only in certain situations do they typically use *shall*.

EXAMPLE
Shall we dance?

USAGE

EXAMPLE   If the economy had been better, the president **would have won** reelection. [conditional]

Would is also used to express future time in a subordinate clause when the main verb in the independent clause is in the past tense.

EXAMPLE   They promised us that they **would bring** the music. [subordinate clause]

Additionally, *would* is used to express an action that was repeated in the past, an invitation or offer, or a polite request.

EXAMPLES   Every day I **would get up** early and **go** for a walk. [repeated past action]

               Would you **like** some of this pie? [offer]

               Would you please **tell** me the time? [polite request]

Exercise 14   Writing Appropriate Modals

For each of the following sentences, supply an appropriate modal.

EXAMPLE   **1.** If we are all agreed, I _____ write the final document.

               1. *will*

1. I _____ have forgotten to answer that question.
2. No, Jeff, you _____ not let your hamster out of its cage.
3. "I _____ try to finish by tomorrow," Maria said.
4. The weather report said it _____ snow, or it _____ not.
5. All participants _____ return the permission slips by Friday.
6. Colleen _____ almost reach the light bulb.
7. After reviewing the entries, the panel _____ announce its decision.
8. Even with the manual, I simply _____ not figure out this program.
9. Frank _____ be happy to help, if you ask him nicely.
10. As soon as you finish your part of the report, Sharon _____ write the conclusion.

Active Voice and Passive Voice

Voice is the form a transitive verb takes to indicate whether the subject of the verb performs or receives the action.

7h. When the subject of a verb performs the action, the verb is in the *active voice*. When the subject of a verb receives the action, the verb is in the *passive voice*.

Reference Note

For further discussion of **transitive verbs,** see page 19. For more information about **direct objects,** see page 54.

S T Y L E   T I P

Choosing between the active voice and the passive voice is a matter of style, not correctness. Be aware, however, that using the passive voice can sometimes produce an awkward or weak effect.

AWKWARD PASSIVE
The yardwork will be finished tomorrow by me.

ACTIVE
I **will finish** the yardwork tomorrow.

USAGE

As the following examples show,

- a verb in the active voice has a direct object, which tells who or what receives the action; a verb in the passive voice does not have a direct object.
- a verb in the passive voice may or may not be followed by a prepositional phrase that begins with *by* and tells who or what performs the action.

	S	V	DO

ACTIVE VOICE   The blazing fire **destroyed** the outside walls. [The subject *fire* performs the action; the direct object *walls* receives the action.]

	S	V

PASSIVE VOICE   The outside walls **were destroyed** by the blazing fire. [The subject *walls* receives the action; *fire,* the object of the preposition *by,* performs the action.]

	S	V

PASSIVE VOICE   The outside walls **were destroyed.** [The subject *walls* receives the action; the performer of the action is not given.]

	S	V	DO

ACTIVE VOICE   She **grows** corn on her farm. [The subject *She* performs the action; the direct object *corn* receives the action.]

	S	V

PASSIVE VOICE   Corn **is grown** on her farm. [The subject *Corn* receives the action; the performer of the action is not given.]

As shown above, a verb in the passive voice is always a verb phrase that consists of a form of the verb *be* and the past participle of a verb. The following chart shows the conjugation of the verb *give* in the passive voice.

Conjugation of the Irregular Verb *Give* in the Passive Voice	
Present Tense	
Singular	*Plural*
I am given	we are given
you are given	you are given
he, she, *or* it is given	they are given

Reference Note

For the **conjugation** of the **verb *give* in the active voice,** see the chart on page 190.

Conjugation of the Irregular Verb *Give* in the Passive Voice	
Past Tense	
Singular	*Plural*
I was given	we were given
you were given	you were given
he, she, *or* it was given	they were given
Future Tense	
Singular	*Plural*
I will (shall) be given	we will (shall) be given
you will (shall) be given	you will (shall) be given
he, she, *or* it will (shall) be given	they will (shall) be given
Present Perfect Tense	
Singular	*Plural*
I have been given	we have been given
you have been given	you have been given
he, she, *or* it has been given	they have been given
Past Perfect Tense	
Singular	*Plural*
I had been given	we had been given
you had been given	you had been given
he, she, *or* it had been given	they had been given
Future Perfect Tense	
Singular	*Plural*
I will (shall) have been given	we will (shall) have been given
you will (shall) have been given	you will (shall) have been given
he, she, *or* it will (shall) have been given	they will (shall) have been given

USAGE

─HELP─

Because the use of *be* or *been* with *being* is awkward, in the passive voice the progressive form is generally used only in the present tense and past tense.

EXAMPLES
My favorite teacher **is being given** an award.
[present progressive, passive voice]

My favorite teacher **was being given** an award.
[past progressive, passive voice]

USAGE

Using the Passive Voice

7i. The passive voice should be used sparingly.

Use the passive voice

- when you want to emphasize the receiver of the action

EXAMPLE   The mayor **was reelected** by a landslide.

- when you do not know, or do not want to reveal, the performer of the action

EXAMPLE   Vicious rumors **have been spread** about the politician.

Exercise 15 **Identifying Verbs in the Active and Passive Voices**

Identify the verb in each of the following sentences as *active* or *passive*. If the verb is in the passive voice, revise the sentence so that the verb is in the active voice.

EXAMPLE   1. We were shown by our art teacher some prints of Lucia Wilcox's artwork.

1. *passive—Our art teacher showed us some prints of Lucia Wilcox's artwork.*

1. The paintings of Lucia Wilcox are admired by many artists around the world.
2. Her blindness during her last years made her final works particularly interesting.
3. She was befriended and taught by Raoul Dufy, Fernand Léger, Robert Motherwell, and Jackson Pollock.
4. Her paintings have been shown often in gallery exhibits around the world.
5. She lost her eyesight suddenly, though not unexpectedly.
6. Her blindness was caused by a tumor near the optic nerve.
7. According to Wilcox, after losing her vision, she had better sight than anyone else.
8. Her vision and her mind were described by her as free of "static" and "distractions."
9. Because of her blindness, her style and subject matter were altered from energetic silhouettes to larger canvases in lush colors.
10. Her style was imitated by many well-known artists.

Exercise 16 Using the Passive Voice

Rewrite any of the following sentences that contain awkward passive-voice constructions. If you think a sentence is best the way it is, write *C* and be prepared to explain your answer.

EXAMPLE   **1.** My car was serviced by Tom, my favorite mechanic.

   1. Tom, my favorite mechanic, serviced my car.

1. According to the editorial, the city's surplus money was wasted by inefficient politicians.

2. My home was damaged by a tornado recently.

3. The right-rear tire must have been punctured by a nail in the driveway.

4. The bridge was damaged by rushing water.

5. The classroom computer was stolen over the weekend.

6. While I was away visiting my cousins in Nebraska, my cat was fed by my neighbor.

7. My sleep was interrupted by loud, bass-heavy music from our neighbors' party.

8. The president's failure to be reelected was caused by sudden economic downturn.

9. The farmer's crops were destroyed by drought back in the 1980s.

10. The book was read by them.

┌─H E L P─
In the example for Exercise 16, the performer of the action is known, and there is no reason to emphasize the receiver of the action. The passive voice is unnecessary and awkward.

USAGE

Review C Choosing the Correct Forms of Verbs

Choose the correct verb form in parentheses in each of the following sentences.

EXAMPLE   **1.** Has the club (*risen, raised*) its membership dues?

   1. raised

1. Little Billy was (*lying, laying*) in wait for us.

2. He had accidentally (*thrown, throwed*) his homework away.

3. The spilled laundry (*laid, lay*) in a wet heap.

4. We ate until we almost (*burst, bursted*).

5. The kitten (*drank, drunk*) from the dog's bowl.

6. Haven't you ever (*swam, swum*) in a lake before?

7. When Chief Dan George walked to the podium, cheers (*rang, rung*) out.

8. Have you ever (*rode, ridden*) a roller coaster?

9. I knew I should have (*brought, brung*) my camera.

10. Uh-oh, this phone was (*broke, broken*) during the move.

Mood

7j. *Mood* is the form a verb takes to indicate the attitude of the person using the verb.

(1) The *indicative mood* is used to express a fact, an opinion, or a question.

EXAMPLES   Jose Saramago **is** the Portuguese writer who **won** the Nobel Prize in literature in 1998. [fact]

They **think** we **are** next in line. [opinion]

Can you **name** the first three presidents of the United States? [question]

(2) The *imperative mood* is used to express a direct command or request.

EXAMPLES   **Close** that window! [direct command]

Please **read** that paper aloud. [request]

(3) The *subjunctive mood* is used to express a suggestion, a necessity, a condition contrary to fact, or a wish.

EXAMPLES   Her parents recommend that Alison **try** cooking as a career. [suggestion]

It is essential that we **be** at the airport on time. [necessity]

If I **were** you, I would call them immediately. [condition contrary to fact]

I wish you **were** here. [wish]

Exercise 17   Identifying Mood Forms of Verbs

Identify the mood of the italicized verb in each of the following sentences as *indicative*, *imperative*, or *subjunctive*.

EXAMPLE   1. It is necessary that we *review* the safety instructions.

1. *subjunctive*

1. What *is* Pearl's favorite book?
2. *Look* at my uncle's photos of Kenya.
3. It is required that we *take* a science class next year.
4. Mr. McEwan *toured* the Aran Islands last summer.
5. I suggest that you *put* on a life jacket before water-skiing.

USAGE

6. I *think* Rosalinda's stereo will be perfect for the party.
7. Soon-hee wishes the camping trip *were* next Saturday.
8. *Try* out for the leading role, Eric.
9. Sri Lanka *is* off the southern coast of India.
10. My friend David teases me as though he *were* my brother.

Review D   Choosing the Correct Forms of Irregular Verbs

Supply the correct form of each italicized verb in the following paragraph.

EXAMPLE   I liked this picture as soon as I [1] (*see*) it.

   1. *saw*

   Have you ever [1] (*see*) this fascinating picture of an impossible structure? It is called <u>Waterfall</u>, and it was [2] (*draw*) by the Dutch artist M. C. Escher. He [3] (*take*) the basic idea for this artwork from the optical illusion shown below. As you can see, a two-story waterfall has [4] (*set*) a miller's wheel in motion. Then, after the water has [5] (*leave*) the wheel, it zigzags through a channel until it [6] (*come*) to the top of the waterfall again. Wait, though—has the water [7] (*go*) uphill on its way back to the top of the waterfall? No, obviously the stream has [8] (*run*) away from the fall on the same level as the bottom of the fall. Then how can the water now be back at the top where it [9] (*begin*)? Escher never answered that question, but he once wrote that if the miller simply [10] (*throw*) in a bucket of water now and then to replace water that had evaporated, he would have a "perpetual motion" machine!

© Roger Penrose

Mood   **205**

Chapter Review

A. Writing the Past or Past Participle Form of Verbs

Write the correct past or past participle form of the italicized verb in parentheses in each of the following sentences.

1. Although Emily Dickinson (*write*) poetry most of her life, very little of her work was published until after her death.
2. When he saw that the animals had (*drink*) all the water, he gave them more.
3. Regarding weeds as unwanted intruders, she pulled them from the ground and (*throw*) them over the fence.
4. The water was cold and daylight was fading, so he (*swim*) only a short distance before turning back to shore.
5. The dew (*freeze*) during the night, covering each twig and blade of grass with a crisp, silvery coating.
6. After my brother had given his new puppy a bath, he (*seem*) to be wetter than the dog.
7. She (*speak*) in such a low, hushed voice that the people in the audience had to strain to hear her remarks.
8. Frightened by the traffic, the deer (*run*) back into the forest.
9. At the front of the parade was an officer who (*ride*) a prancing black horse.
10. When the church bell (*ring*) on Tuesday evening, the villagers became alarmed.

B. Revising Verb Tense or Voice

Revise the following paragraph, correcting verbs that are in the wrong tense or that use passive voice awkwardly. If a sentence is already correct, write *C*.

[11] Miguel de Cervantes was born in 1547 in Alcalá de Henares, near Madrid, Spain. [12] Unlike most other writers of his time, he does not attend a university. [13] Cervantes is acquiring a somewhat different form of education by serving as a soldier and being captured by pirates. [14] He is held captive by the pirates for five years until his

family ransoms him. [15] Little was written by him until he is in his late thirties. [16] In 1605, at the age of fifty-eight, Cervantes is publishing the first part of his masterwork, *Don Quixote;* then he wrote nothing significant for eight years. [17] In 1615, the second part of *Don Quixote* was published. [18] Cervantes' life has been continuing to have ups and downs, and a series of government jobs prevent him from writing full time. [19] However, in the last three years of his life, many fine works were written by him. [20] Cervantes has lived a fascinating life, and world literature is richer because of it.

C. Determining Correct Use of *Lie* and *Lay, Sit* and *Set,* and *Rise* and *Raise* in Sentences

Most of the following sentences contain at least one error in the use of *lie* or *lay, sit* or *set,* or *rise* or *raise.* Identify each incorrect verb, and write the correct form. If a sentence is already correct, write *C.*

21. We left our lawn furniture setting on the patio.
22. Grandpa decided to sit the plates on the sideboard.
23. They lain the bricks next to where we set out the logs.
24. When the dough has raised for thirty minutes, turn it onto the floured board.
25. The sun has set and the moon is rising.
26. When people in the United States are rising from bed in the morning, people in China are laying down to sleep.
27. As the enemy patrol passed by, the parachutists laid quietly in the undergrowth.
28. Cadet Rojas rose the flag to the sound of reveille on the bugle.
29. I feel a little dizzy; I think I'll lay down for a while.
30. The architect raised to go find the blueprints.

D. Using the Different Tenses of Verbs

Change the tense of the verb in each of the following sentences by following the directions given in parentheses.

31. Pamela sat at her desk for an hour. (Change to *future perfect.*)
32. The lead actor changes costumes quickly. (Change to *present emphatic.*)

33. Have you watched the TV miniseries on Thomas Jefferson? (Change to *present perfect progressive.*)

34. Sean will speak for half an hour. (Change to *future perfect progressive.*)

35. Were you at the inauguration? (Change to *past perfect.*)

36. Were we ever informed? (Change to *present perfect.*)

37. Dad leaves for the office at 7:30 A.M. (Change to *future.*)

38. The plane arrives on time. (Change to *future.*)

39. By then, the Holts had checked in at the hotel. (Change to *future perfect.*)

40. They are talking to the police. (Change to *past emphatic.*)

E. Choosing the Correct Forms of Verbs

Write the correct form of each italicized verb in the following sentences. In some instances you will need to add *have, has,* or *had.*

41. The bed is unmade; he must (*lie*) down for a while before he went out.

42. During yesterday's storm, flying debris (*break*) most of the windows and littered the floors.

43. The car isn't in the garage; they must (*take*) it.

44. I was feeling very tired when I got home, so I (*lie*) down right away.

45. Hot and dusty from their long walk up the sloping road, the men seized the water jugs and (*drink*) every drop.

46. Several people (*rise*) to protest, but the presiding officer silenced their complaints at once.

47. That sweater didn't fit when I tried it on this morning; it must (*shrink*) in the wash yesterday.

48. After heavy rains had continued day after day, the water (*burst*) through the dam and flooded the fields.

49. So far, she (*take*) every opportunity to promote the plan.

50. After they (*ride*) several miles in silence, the leader suddenly started singing.

Writing Application
Using Verb Tense in an Essay

Establishing Time of Action   It's Cultural Appreciation Week at your school. Your teacher has asked you to write a short essay about your own cultural or ethnic group. In your essay, you should explore several ways in which people of your heritage have enriched life in your community. Use correct verb tenses to describe some of the contributions these people have made in the past, some activities they are currently involved in, and what you think they might offer in the future. Use at least five different verb tenses in your essay.

Prewriting   Brainstorm a list of your ethnic or cultural group's outstanding leaders, scholars, athletes, and artists, as well as activities, events, clubs, and community service projects. Select three or four of the group's main contributions to mention in your essay. Many people can claim more than one ethnic or cultural heritage. If you can, you may want to write about the group you know the best or the one in which you are most interested.

Writing   While you are writing your first draft, try to add details that show the uniqueness of your cultural heritage. Consider how you can use verb tenses to make the sequence of events in your essay clear.

Revising   Read through your essay to be sure that you have included at least one contribution from each different time period: the past, the present, and (speculatively) the future. Check to see that you have used at least five different tenses.

Publishing   Make sure that you have formed all verbs correctly, paying special attention to irregular verbs. Proofread your essay for any errors in grammar, usage, and mechanics. You might create a bulletin board display of all the essays your classmates have written; or your class may wish to prepare a cultural-appreciation presentation for another class or for the whole school. If one is available, you may also want to post your essay on a class Web site.

Using Modifiers Correctly
Forms, Comparison, and Placement

Diagnostic Preview

A. Revising Sentences to Correct Errors in the Use and Placement of Modifiers

Most of the following sentences contain an error in the use or placement of modifiers. Revise each incorrect sentence to correct the faulty modifier. If a sentence is already correct, write *C*.

EXAMPLE   1. The planets that are most farthest from the sun are Neptune and Pluto.

          1. *The planets that are farthest from the sun are Neptune and Pluto.*

1. While building a fire in front of the hogan, Manaba's dog began to tug at the hem of her doeskin dress.
2. The greenhouse effect may be causing more higher temperatures worldwide.
3. Adrianne knows more about chemistry than anybody in her class.
4. Hank worked rather hasty so he could catch up with Nina.

5. Marian felt bad, but she knew things could be worser.
6. Millie can sing as well as Scott, but of the two, he's the best dancer.
7. By playing carefully, the game was won.
8. Steady and confident, a keen sense of balance enables Mohawk ironworkers to help build tall bridges and buildings.
9. Although Helen would be better in the leading role, Wenona will probably get the part because she is more reliable.
10. Because one carton of chemicals smelled badly, it was examined before being used in the laboratory.

B. Revising a Paragraph to Correct Errors in the Use and Placement of Modifiers

Most of the sentences in the following paragraph contain an error in the use or placement of modifiers. Revise each incorrect sentence. You may need to add or rearrange words for clarity. If a sentence is already correct, write *C*.

EXAMPLE **[1]** My aunt Penny had enclosed a ticket in my birthday card for Bobby McFerrin's concert.

1. *My aunt Penny had enclosed in my birthday card a ticket for Bobby McFerrin's concert.*

[11] Hailed by many critics as one of today's greatest male vocalists, my aunt Penny took me to see Bobby McFerrin. [12] Waiting for the concert to start, the auditorium was filled with eager fans. [13] Wondering where the band was, I kept my eyes on the empty stage. [14] When it was time for the show to start, a slender, barefoot man walked out from the wings, carrying a cordless microphone dressed only in blue jeans. [15] Assuming he was a stagehand, he began to sing, and then I realized that this was Bobby McFerrin! [16] Instantly, the complex rhythm of the music fascinated the audience that he made up as he went along. [17] I suddenly understood why one of his popularest albums is called *Spontaneous Inventions*! [18] Alone in the spotlight with only his voice and no band at all, two thousand people sat spellbound until he took his final bow. [19] All his life, Bobby McFerrin has enjoyed listening to and performing jazz, pop, rock, soul, African, and classical music. [20] Bobby's parents are both classical musicians, and he thanks them for giving him a rich musical environment on the back of every album he makes.

What Is a Modifier?

A *modifier* is a word or word group that makes the meaning of another word or word group more specific. The two kinds of modifiers are *adjectives* and *adverbs*.

One-Word Modifiers

Adjectives make the meanings of nouns and pronouns more specific.

Reference Note

For more information on **adjectives,** see page 10.

ADJECTIVES   Etta has a **mischievous** smile. [The adjective *mischievous* makes the meaning of the noun *smile* more specific.]

Only he answered the letter. [The adjective *Only* makes the meaning of the pronoun *he* more specific.]

Isn't his dog **well-behaved**? [The compound adjective *well-behaved* makes the meaning of the noun *dog* more specific.]

Adverbs make the meanings of verbs, adjectives, and other adverbs more specific.

Reference Note

For information on **adverbs,** see page 20.

ADVERBS   Etta smiled **mischievously.** [The adverb *mischievously* makes the meaning of the verb *smiled* more specific.]

The tree is **quite** healthy. [The adverb *quite* makes the meaning of the adjective *healthy* more specific.]

The car went **surprisingly** fast. [The adverb *surprisingly* makes the meaning of the adverb *fast* more specific.]

Reference Note

For information on **subjects and predicates,** see page 37. For information on **predicate adjectives,** see page 52.

8a. If a word in the predicate modifies the subject of the verb, use the adjective form. If the word modifies the verb, use the adverb form.

ADJECTIVE   The cantor's voice was **beautiful.** [*Beautiful* modifies *voice.*]
ADVERB   The cantor sang **beautifully.** [*Beautifully* modifies *sang.*]

ADJECTIVE   The corn grew **tall.** [*Tall* modifies *corn.*]
ADVERB   The corn grew **quickly.** [*Quickly* modifies *grew.*]

USAGE

Adjective or Adverb?

While many adverbs end in *–ly,* others do not. Furthermore, not all words with the *–ly* ending are adverbs. Some adjectives also end in *–ly.* Therefore, you cannot tell whether a word is an adjective or an adverb simply by looking for the *–ly* ending.

Adverbs Not Ending in *–ly*	
call **soon**	remain **here**
not concerned	let **loose**
arrive **home**	**very** tall

Adjectives Ending in *–ly*	
elderly dachshund	**holy** place
curly lettuce	**silly** remark
only time	**timely** event

Some words can be used as both adjectives and adverbs. To decide whether a word is an adjective or an adverb, determine how the word is used in the sentence.

Adjectives	Adverbs
She is an **only** child.	She has **only** one brother.
That fighter is a **fast** plane.	The plane goes **fast**.
He caught the **last** boat.	They left **last**.

Exercise 1 Identifying Adjectives and Adverbs and the Words They Modify

Identify the adjectives and adverbs in the paragraph on the following page, and give the words they modify.

EXAMPLE   [1] First, get a craft knife and some stiff black paper.

1. *First—adverb—get; craft—adjective—knife; some—adjective—paper; stiff—adjective—paper; black—adjective—paper*

┌─HELP─
Include only one-word modifiers in your answers to Exercise 1. Also, do not include the articles *a, an,* and *the.*

[1] In many cultures, cutting paper to make pictures is a traditional art. [2] For example, Mexican artisans use a small, very sharp knife to cut designs in pieces of colored paper. [3] As the oddly shaped scraps fall away, an image is slowly revealed. [4] Planning the work is a challenge because each part of the picture must connect somehow to the border or to another part of the design. [5] As you can see in these designs, the artist sometimes leaves a background pattern of stripes or lines to support the main subject. [6] The knife must not be even slightly dull, or the artist might accidentally tear one of the tiny paper bridges! [7] The work is very intricate. [8] Artisans must be meticulous. [9] Visualizing the finished product before actually completing it is a necessary skill. [10] Sharpening the knives that are used is an important skill, too.

Phrases Used as Modifiers

Like one-word modifiers, phrases can also be used as adjectives and adverbs.

EXAMPLES
It is time **for departure.** [The prepositional phrase *for departure* acts as an adjective that modifies the noun *time.*]

Bringing tears to our eyes, the comedian told some of her best jokes. [The participial phrase *Bringing tears to our eyes* acts as an adjective that modifies the noun *comedian.*]

Dr. Makowski is the one **to ask next.** [The infinitive phrase *to ask next* acts as an adjective that modifies the pronoun *one.*]

Tina is becoming fluent **in Italian.** [The prepositional phrase *in Italian* acts as an adverb that modifies the adjective *fluent.*]

Speak **with clarity in debates.** [The prepositional phrases *with clarity* and *in debates* act as adverbs that modify the verb *Speak.*]

The truck driver swerved just quickly enough **to avoid a collision.** [The infinitive phrase *to avoid a collision* acts as an adverb that modifies the adverb *enough.*]

Reference Note

For information about **different kinds of phrases,** see page 65.

USAGE

Clauses Used as Modifiers

Like words and phrases, clauses can also be used as adjectives and adverbs.

EXAMPLES   Raphael is the painter **that I like best.** [The adjective clause *that I like best* modifies the noun *painter*.]

         Before my great-grandfather left Russia, he sat in his kitchen one last time. [The adverb clause *Before my great-grandfather left Russia* modifies the verb *sat*.]

Reference Note

For information on **clauses,** see page 90.

Eight Troublesome Modifiers

Bad and *Badly*

Bad is an adjective. In most uses, *badly* is an adverb.

ADJECTIVE   Fido was **bad.**
ADVERB   Fido behaved **badly.**

    Remember that a word that modifies the subject of a verb should be in adjective form.

NONSTANDARD   The cheese smelled badly.
STANDARD   The cheese smelled **bad.** [*Bad* modifies *cheese*.]

> NOTE   In informal situations, *bad* or *badly* is acceptable after *feel*.
>
> INFORMAL   She feels **badly** about the mistake.
> FORMAL   She feels **bad** about the mistake.

Reference Note

For information on **using standard English,** see page 236.

Good and *Well*

Good is an adjective. It should not be used to modify a verb.

NONSTANDARD   She sings good.
STANDARD   She sings **well.**
STANDARD   Her singing sounds **good.** [*Good* is an adjective that modifies the noun *singing*.]

Well may be used either as an adjective or as an adverb. As an adjective, *well* has two meanings: "in good health" and "satisfactory."

EXAMPLES   Trish is **well.** [Trish is in good health.]

         All is **well.** [All is satisfactory.]

USAGE

As an adverb, *well* means "capably."

EXAMPLE   Pedro did **well** in the music competition.

Slow and *Slowly*

In informal situations, *slow* is used as both an adjective and an adverb.

EXAMPLES   We took a **slow** boat to China. [*Slow* is an adjective modifying *boat*.]

                Please go **slow.** [*Slow* is an adverb modifying *go*.]

Slowly is always an adverb. In formal uses, you should use *slowly* rather than *slow*.

EXAMPLES   The train **slowly** came to a stop.

                Drive **slowly** on slippery roads.

Real and *Really*

Real is an adjective meaning "actual" or "genuine." *Really* is an adverb meaning "actually" or "truly."

EXAMPLES   Tom is a **real** mountain climber. [*Real* is an adjective modifying *climber*.]

                The flood victims **really** need assistance. [*Really* is an adverb modifying *need*.]

Although in everyday situations *real* is commonly used as an adverb meaning "very," avoid using it as an adverb in formal speaking and writing.

INFORMAL   He kicked **real** well in the game.
  FORMAL   He kicked **really** well in the game.

| STYLE   TIP |

Really is overused in everyday speech. When possible, use a more descriptive adverb in place of *really*.

> **Oral Practice**   **Choosing Correct Adjective and Adverb Forms**

In the following sentences, choose the modifier that is correct according to the rules of formal, standard English. Then, read aloud each sentence, including the modifer you have chosen.

EXAMPLE   **1.** Each of the gymnasts performed (*real, really*) well.

          1. really

1. I can't hear you (*good, well*) when the water is running.
2. The opening paragraph is written (*good, well*).
3. The situation looks (*bad, badly*).

USAGE

4. Why does ketchup come out of the bottle so (*slow, slowly*)?
5. She certainly plays the marimba (*good, well*).
6. Can you dance (*real, really*) well?
7. These shoes don't fit (*bad, badly*) at all.
8. Our coach said that we should do the exercise (*slow, slowly*).
9. Did you do (*good, well*) on the last algebra test?
10. The chef at the corner cafe cooks (*real, really*) spicy food.

Exercise 2 Using Adjective and Adverb Forms Correctly

Each of the following sentences contains at least one italicized adjective or adverb. If the italicized word is incorrect according to the rules of formal, standard English, give the correct word. If the sentence is already correct, write *C*.

EXAMPLE   1. Soon after my brother Skipper opened his new shop, he grew *real* concerned about its future.

        1. *really*

1. My brother opened Skipper's Skate City last April 1, and as the graph below shows, the shop did not do *well* at first.
2. Skipper wondered whether business had started *slow* because he wasn't advertising enough or because his display window wasn't drawing in people.
3. He'd see people walking *slow* past the shop and pointing at the gear on display, but hardly anyone stopped.

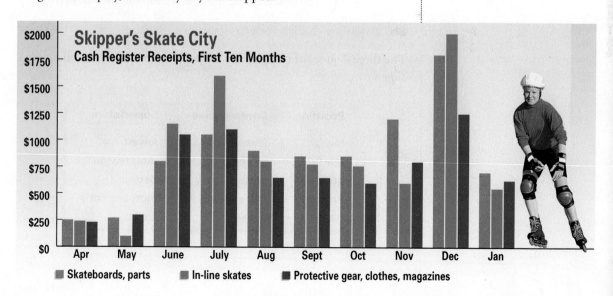

Skipper's Skate City
Cash Register Receipts, First Ten Months

■ Skateboards, parts   ■ In-line skates   ■ Protective gear, clothes, magazines

Eight Troublesome Modifiers   **217**

4. By the end of May, Skipper thought about giving up because he was doing so *bad*.
5. He would have felt *real* bad about failing, especially because Dad had lent him money to open the shop.
6. Then school let out, and within days, business was going *good*.
7. In-line skates and skateboards started selling *real* well; in fact, by the end of summer, Skipper was able to pay Dad back.
8. When school started, skateboards kept selling *good,* but total sales fell somewhat.
9. Skipper's receipts looked rather *badly* during the fall, but thanks to Christmas and Hanukkah, all went *good* in December.
10. By then, Skipper was a veteran of seasonal business cycles; he wasn't fazed when January's receipts weren't as *well* as those of other months.

Comparison of Modifiers

Modifiers—adjectives and adverbs—may be used to make comparisons.

ADJECTIVES   Juan is nearly as **tall** as I.
Robert is **taller** than I.
Of all the players, Antoine is the **tallest.**

ADVERBS   No other land animal can run as **fast** as the cheetah.
The cheetah can run **faster** than any other land animal.
Of all land animals, the cheetah can run the **fastest.**

8b. Modifiers change form to show comparison.

The three degrees of comparison are *positive, comparative,* and *superlative.*

Positive	Comparative	Superlative
low	lower	lowest
fearful	more fearful	most fearful
good	better	best
promptly	more promptly	most promptly
badly	worse	worst

Regular Comparison

(1) Most one-syllable modifiers form the comparative degree by adding *–er* and the superlative degree by adding *–est.*

Positive	Comparative	Superlative
thin	thin**ner**	thin**nest**
safe	saf**er**	saf**est**
dry	dri**er**	dri**est**
fast	fast**er**	fast**est**
soon	soon**er**	soon**est**

(2) Two-syllable modifiers may form the comparative degree by adding *–er* and the superlative degree by adding *–est*, or they may form the comparative degree by using *more* and the superlative degree by using *most.*

Positive	Comparative	Superlative
lovely	lovel**ier**	lovel**iest**
tricky	tricki**er**	tricki**est**
awkward	**more** awkward	**most** awkward
firmly	**more** firmly	**most** firmly
rapid	**more** rapid	**most** rapid

(3) Modifiers that have three or more syllables form the comparative degree by using *more* and the superlative degree by using *most.*

Positive	Comparative	Superlative
enthusiastic	**more** enthusiastic	**most** enthusiastic
fortunate	**more** fortunate	**most** fortunate
predictably	**more** predictably	**most** predictably
effectively	**more** effectively	**most** effectively
significantly	**more** significantly	**most** significantly

USAGE

STYLE TIP

Many two-syllable modifiers may correctly form the comparative and superlative degrees by either adding *–er* and *–est* or using *more* and *most.*

If adding *–er* or *–est* makes a word sound awkward, use *more* or *most* instead.

AWKWARD
  specialer

BETTER
  more special

HELP

A dictionary will tell you when a word forms its comparative or superlative form in some way other than by adding *–er* or *–est* or *more* or *most.* Look in a dictionary if you are not sure whether a word has irregular comparative or superlative forms or whether you need to change the spelling of a word before adding *–er* or *–est.*

(4) To show a decrease in the qualities they express, modifiers form the comparative degree by using *less* and the superlative degree by using *least*.

Positive	Comparative	Superlative
calm	**less** calm	**least** calm
frequent	**less** frequent	**least** frequent
helpful	**less** helpful	**least** helpful
slowly	**less** slowly	**least** slowly
courageously	**less** courageously	**least** courageously

Irregular Comparison

The comparative and superlative degrees of some modifiers are irregular in form.

Positive	Comparative	Superlative
bad	worse	worst
badly	worse	worst
ill	worse	worst
good	better	best
well	better	best
little	less	least
many	more	most
much	more	most
far	farther	farthest
	or further	*or* furthest

TIPS & TRICKS

The word *little* also has regular comparative and superlative forms: *littler, littlest.* These forms are used to describe physical size (the *littlest* toad). The forms *less* and *least* are used to describe an amount (*less* money).

NOTE Do not add *–er, –est* or *more, most* to irregularly compared forms. For example, use *worse*, not *worser* or *more worse*.

Exercise 3 **Writing the Comparative and Superlative Forms of Modifiers**

Write the comparative and superlative forms of each of the following modifiers.

EXAMPLE   1. skillful

1. *more (less) skillful; most (least) skillful*

1. loudly
2. bad
3. humid
4. efficiently
5. silly
6. good
7. likely
8. well
9. fundamental
10. clearly

11. dark
12. wild
13. deep
14. heavy
15. pretty
16. healthy
17. attractive
18. intelligent
19. eccentric
20. friendly

Use of Comparative and Superlative Forms

8c. Use the comparative degree when comparing two things. Use the superlative degree when comparing more than two.

COMPARATIVE   Omaha is **larger** than Lincoln.
Roberto is a **better** typist than I am.
Which of these two shirts is **less expensive**?

SUPERLATIVE   Omaha is the **largest** city in Nebraska.
Roberto is the **best** typist in the class.
Which of these four shirts is **least expensive?**

8d. Include the word *other* or *else* when comparing one member of a group with the rest of the group.

ILLOGICAL   Rhode Island is smaller than any state in the Union. [Rhode Island is a state in the Union. Logically, Rhode Island cannot be smaller than itself.]

LOGICAL   Rhode Island is smaller than any **other** state in the Union.

ILLOGICAL   Stan is taller than anyone in his class. [Stan is a member of his class. Logically, Stan cannot be taller than himself.]

LOGICAL   Stan is taller than anyone **else** in his class.

8e. Avoid using double comparisons.

A **double comparison** is incorrect because it contains both *–er* and *more (less)* or both *–est* and *most (least)*.

STYLE   TIP

In informal situations, the superlative degree is commonly used to compare two things.

EXAMPLES
May the best team [of two] win.

Put your best foot forward.

In formal speaking and writing, however, the comparative degree should be used when two things are being compared.

Reference Note

For a discussion of **standard** and **nonstandard English,** see page 236.

| NONSTANDARD | The second movie was more funnier than the first one. |
| STANDARD | The second movie was **funnier** than the first one. |

NONSTANDARD	What is the most deadliest snake?
STANDARD	What is the **deadliest** snake?
STANDARD	What is the **most deadly** snake?

| NONSTANDARD | Pancho is the least dullest debater. |
| STANDARD | Pancho is the **least dull** debater. |

8f. Be sure your comparisons are clear.

When making comparisons, indicate clearly what items are being compared.

UNCLEAR	The climate of Arizona is drier than South Carolina. [The sentence incorrectly compares a climate to a state.]
CLEAR	The climate of Arizona is drier than **the climate** of South Carolina.
CLEAR	The climate of Arizona is drier than **that** of South Carolina.

| UNCLEAR | Fresh vegetables at a farmers' market are sometimes lower in price than a grocery. [The sentence incorrectly compares vegetables to a grocery.] |
| CLEAR | Fresh vegetables at a farmers' market are sometimes lower in price than **those at** a grocery. |

Reference Note

For information on **irregular comparisons,** see page 220.

State both parts of a comparison completely if there is any chance of misunderstanding.

UNCLEAR	We know her better than Dena.
CLEAR	We know her better than **we know** Dena.
CLEAR	We know her better than Dena **does.**

Exercise 4 Using Modifiers Correctly

Most of the following sentences contain an error in the use of modifiers. Identify each error, and then write the correct form. If a sentence is already correct, write *C*.

EXAMPLE 1. Of the Ganges and Amazon rivers, which is more longer?

　　　　 1. *more longer—longer*

1. Laurie is more friendlier than she used to be.
2. Which of the four seasons do you like better?
3. I never saw a leader more stronger than Chief Billie of the Seminoles.

4. Margaret Mead was one of the world's most famous anthropologists.

5. Of the two colleges that I am considering, Spelman College in Atlanta looks more interesting.

6. Anika arrived earlier than anyone in her family.

7. Muscles in the leg are stronger than the arm.

8. Denver's elevation is higher than that of any major city in the United States.

9. I wrote to Sally more often than Carlos.

10. This year's drought was much worse than last year.

Review A   Correcting Errors in the Use of Modifiers

Each of the sentences in the following paragraph contains at least one error in the use of adjectives and adverbs. Find each error, and supply the necessary correction.

EXAMPLE   **[1]** Of the four pots shown on this page, which do you think is the more delicate one?

    1. *more delicate—most delicate*

[1] Among ceramic artists of the Southwest, perhaps the most famousest are the four women who made these coiled pots, using techniques handed down for more than 2,000 years. [2] Lucy Lewis's Acoma pottery is more delicate than any Southwest pottery. [3] Lewis used the most whitest clay. [4] Because this clay is scarce, the walls of her pots are the thinner of them all. [5] Maria Martinez's San Ildefonso pottery is more thicker and heavier than Lewis. [6] Of all the Southwest pottery styles, Martinez's black-on-black pottery may be the most best known. [7] No color is used, but the background areas of the black pot are burnished slowly with a small smooth stone until they become quite a bit more shinier than the main design. [8] Many of Margaret Tafoya's Santa Clara pots are also solid black, but of these two kinds of black pottery, the Santa Clara pots are the heaviest. [9] The bold, colorful Hopi pots of Fannie Nampeyo may be the more impressive achievement of all, because Nampeyo's family had to re-create the technique by studying shards of ancient pots found in 1895. [10] The pottery by these four women is beautifuller than many other artists.

Dangling Modifiers

| S T Y L E | T I P |

A dangling modifier may occur when a sentence is in the passive voice. Rewriting sentences in the active voice not only eliminates many dangling modifiers but also makes your writing more interesting and lively. If you frequently find dangling modifiers in your writing, concentrate on staying in the active voice.

PASSIVE VOICE
Reaching as high as I could, the ball was caught just before it reached the fence. [*Reaching as high as I could* is a dangling modifier.]

ACTIVE VOICE
Reaching as high as I could, I caught the ball just before it reached the fence. [*Reaching as high as I could* modifies *I*.]

8g. Avoid using dangling modifiers.

A modifying word, phrase, or clause that does not clearly and sensibly modify a word or word group in a sentence is a ***dangling modifier.*** To correct a dangling modifier, add or replace words to make the meaning clear and logical.

DANGLING	Frustrated, all of the scientists' data were reexamined. [Were the scientists' data frustrated?]
CLEAR	Frustrated, the **scientists** reexamined all of their data.
DANGLING	Looking back over my shoulder, the team went into a huddle. [Was the team looking back over my shoulder?]
CLEAR	Looking back over my shoulder, **I** saw the team going into a huddle.
DANGLING	Riding to the store, my front bicycle tire went flat. [Was the bicycle tire riding to the store?]
CLEAR	While **I** was riding to the store, my front bicycle tire went flat.
DANGLING	To qualify for the Olympics, many trial heats must be won. [Do trial heats qualify for the Olympics?]
CLEAR	To qualify for the Olympics, a **runner** must win many trial heats.

or

Before a runner may qualify for the Olympics, **he or she** must win many trial heats.

When a modifying participial or infinitive phrase comes at the beginning of a sentence, as in the examples above, the phrase is followed by a comma. Immediately after that comma should come the word or word group that the phrase modifies.

> **NOTE** A sentence may appear to have a dangling modifier when *you* is the understood subject. In such cases, the modifier is not dangling; it is modifying the understood subject.
>
> EXAMPLE   To assemble the bookcase, (you) read the instructions.

Reference Note
For information on the **understood subject,** see page 45.

Exercise 5   Correcting Dangling Modifiers

The following sentences contain dangling modifiers. Revise each sentence so that its meaning is clear and correct.

USAGE

EXAMPLE   **1.** Running through the park, the lake looked cool and inviting.

1. *Running through the park, I thought the lake looked cool and inviting.*

or

As I ran through the park, I thought the lake looked cool and inviting.

1. Hurrying through the last fifty pages, the book was fascinating.
2. Being a novice basketball player, my dribbling needs work.
3. When leaving the train, the station is on the right.
4. Exhausted by the hard work, a long nap sounded good.
5. Driving through the Rockies, the landscape was magnificent.
6. Having overslept, my exam results were poor.
7. Although excited, sleep came easily.
8. As a new student, it was difficult at first to find my way around.
9. To repair an appliance, experience is helpful.
10. Looking at recent consumer surveys, more Americans are working at home.

┌HELP─

Although two revisions for the example in Exercise 5 are shown, you need to give only one for each item.

Misplaced Modifiers

8h. Avoid using misplaced modifiers.

A word, phrase, or clause that seems to modify the wrong word or word group in a sentence is a ***misplaced modifier.*** Place modifying words, phrases, and clauses as near as possible to the words they modify.

MEETING THE CHALLENGE

Write a short story containing misplaced modifers that cause upheaval in the lives of the characters. Then, revise the story, correcting the misplaced modifers and thus restoring peace to the characters.

Misplaced One-Word Modifiers

MISPLACED   Alone, thoughts of returning soon to earth comforted the astronaut living in the space station. [Were the thoughts alone?]

CLEAR   Thoughts of returning soon to earth comforted the astronaut living **alone** in the space station.

MISPLACED   Exhausted, a good night's rest was what the hikers needed. [Was a good night's rest exhausted?]

CLEAR   A good night's rest was what the **exhausted** hikers needed.

Be sure to place modifiers correctly to state clearly the meaning you intend.

EXAMPLES **Only** on Saturdays, my brother and I watch cartoons for an hour. [My brother and I watch on Saturdays, not on any other days.]

On Saturdays, my **only** brother and I watch cartoons for an hour. [I have no other brothers.]

On Saturdays, my brother and I watch **only** cartoons for an hour. [My brother and I watch nothing but cartoons.]

On Saturdays, my brother and I watch cartoons for **only** an hour. [My brother and I watch for no more than an hour.]

NOTE One-word modifiers such as *almost, even, hardly, just, merely, nearly, not,* and *only* generally should be placed directly before the words they modify.

MISPLACED According to the club's minutes, all of the members were not at the meeting on Friday.

CLEAR According to the club's minutes, **not** all of the members were at the meeting on Friday.

MISPLACED Before 12:00 P.M., the restaurant only serves breakfast.

CLEAR Before 12:00 P.M., the restaurant serves **only** breakfast.

Misplaced Phrase Modifiers

Adjective phrases, adverb phrases, and verbal phrases should be placed near the words they modify.

MISPLACED I'm lucky because I feel that I can always talk about my problems with my dad. [Does *with my dad* modify *talk* or *problems*?]

CLEAR I'm lucky because I feel that I can always talk **with my dad** about my problems.

MISPLACED Early Spanish explorers encountered a hostile environment searching for gold in the Americas. [Does *searching for gold in the Americas* modify *explorers* or *environment*?]

CLEAR **Searching for gold in the Americas,** early Spanish explorers encountered a hostile environment.

Reference Note

For a discussion of the different kinds of **phrases,** see Chapter 3. For information on **using commas to set off modifying phrases,** see page 302.

MISPLACED	You will need a crescent wrench to assemble the bookshelf.
	[Does *to assemble the bookshelf* modify *You* or *wrench*?]
CLEAR	**To assemble the bookshelf,** you will need a crescent wrench.

Exercise 6   Revising Sentences by Correcting Misplaced One-Word and Phrase Modifiers

The following sentences contain misplaced one-word and phrase modifiers. Revise each sentence so that its meaning is clear and correct.

EXAMPLE
1. Our cat was waiting on the front porch for us to come home patiently.

1. *Our cat was waiting patiently on the front porch for us to come home.*

1. Rosa Parks calmly refused to move to the back of the bus with quiet dignity.
2. I found a huge boulder taking a shortcut through the woods.
3. On one of his fruit trees, Mr. Tate noticed some caterpillars.
4. Our ancestors hunted deer, bison, and other large animals with weapons made of wood and stone.
5. Flying over the bridge, Missie spotted a blue heron.
6. We noticed several signs advertising the new theme park riding down the highway.
7. We could see corn growing from our car window.
8. Barking wildly and straining at the chain, the letter carrier was forced to retreat from the dog.
9. The softball team almost practices every afternoon.
10. He recounted an incident about a nuclear chain reaction during his chemistry lecture.
11. Pierre saw a Great Dane cycling through the park.
12. Tired from their hiking, we offered shelter to the backpackers.
13. Stress has almost caused all of his hair to turn gray.
14. She had a raincoat over her arm with a blue lining.
15. The two women hurried before the bus's departure to get a snack from the vending machine.
16. I have nearly read all of his books.
17. The boy ate all the yogurt with red sneakers.
18. Jan watched a deer sitting in a chair on the porch.
19. They listened to the symphony standing in the mezzanine of the auditorium.
20. Running, the course seemed very long to the athlete.

Reference Note

For a discussion of the different kinds of **clauses,** see Chapter 4. For information on **using commas to set off modifying clauses,** see page 302.

Misplaced Clause Modifiers

Adjective and adverb clauses should be placed near the words they modify.

MISPLACED	Each player on the team will receive a trophy that wins the tournament.
CLEAR	Each player on the team **that wins the tournament** will receive a trophy.

MISPLACED	The bowl slipped off the table, which was full of gravy, and broke.
CLEAR	The bowl, **which was full of gravy,** slipped off the table and broke.

MISPLACED	The spelunkers saw many bats hanging upside down from their roosts while they were exploring the cave.
CLEAR	**While they were exploring the cave,** the spelunkers saw many bats hanging upside down from their roosts.

MISPLACED	Kirstie couldn't attend the farewell party for her nephew who was moving to El Paso because she was ill.
CLEAR	**Because she was ill,** Kirstie couldn't attend the farewell party for her nephew who was moving to El Paso.

COMPUTER TIP

A spell-checker can easily find nonstandard forms such as *baddest, expensiver,* and *mostest.* However, you will need to examine placement of modifiers yourself.

Exercise 7 **Revising Sentences by Correcting Misplaced Clause Modifiers**

The following sentences contain misplaced clause modifiers. Revise each sentence so that its meaning is clear and correct.

EXAMPLE   1. Because he has allergies, Dr. Crane gives our pet beagle a shot once a month.

1. *Because our pet beagle has allergies, Dr. Crane gives him a shot once a month.*

1. I gave some of the baseball cards to my cousin that I had acquired over the years.
2. The plane landed safely on the runway that had the engine trouble.
3. That picture was hanging on the wall, which we bought in Canada.
4. They took the backpack to the manager's office, which appeared to be lost.
5. Jan showed the rooms to her visitors that she had painted.
6. That is a good plan for meeting the deadline next Friday that you have proposed.

7. She sang a song titled "On the Shore" at the talent show, which she had written herself.
8. I adopted a kitten at the animal shelter that needed a home.
9. I served dinner to a friend that I cooked myself.
10. The plate fell on the floor that was full of baked beans.

Review B **Correcting Dangling and Misplaced Modifiers**

The following sentences contain dangling and misplaced modifiers. Revise each sentence so that its meaning is clear and correct.

EXAMPLE   1. Hurrying, my books slipped out of my hands and fell down the stairs.

     1. *As I was hurrying, my books slipped out of my hands and fell down the stairs.*

1. Caught in the net, escape was impossible.
2. Looking through the telescope, the moon seemed enormous.
3. While out running, his mouth got dry.
4. The ocean came into view going around the bend.
5. Doing a few tap-dance steps, the wooden floor got scratched.
6. Built on a steep hillside overlooking the sea, we found the ocean view breathtaking.
7. I mentioned the book to my sister Roseanne that I recently read.
8. After finishing the housework, the room almost sparkled.
9. To make manicotti, pasta is stuffed with ricotta cheese.
10. Glenda sang a song about finding true love in a high, clear voice.
11. Looking at her passport, there was no visa stamp.
12. Running up and down the bungalow walls, she saw dozens of mice.
13. While standing in front of the fun-house mirror, her reflection was tall and thin.
14. Painted, we thought the house looked much better.
15. Singing in the shower, the hot water ran out.
16. Reaching for the telephone, the books toppled and fell to the floor.
17. Lauren told the interviewer about the time she performed for the president when she was interviewed.
18. While driving to work, the radio broke.
19. Songbirds have been coming to the birdfeeders, which migrate this time of year.
20. Sitting in the freezer, she saw two kinds of frozen yogurt.

┌**HELP**─

In Review C,
you may need to rearrange
or add words to make the
meaning clear.

Review C **Correcting Errors in the Use of Modifiers**

Most of the sentences in the following paragraph contain at least one error in the use of modifiers. Revise each sentence according to the rules of standard, formal English. If a sentence is already correct, write *C*.

EXAMPLE **[1]** Egyptian priests inscribed a decree on a black stone honoring Ptolemy V, a king of Egypt (203–181 B.C.).

1. *Egyptian priests inscribed on a black stone a decree honoring Ptolemy V, a king of Egypt (203–181 B.C.).*

[1] Much about life in ancient Egypt before the 1800s was unknown because nobody could read Egyptian hieroglyphics. [2] Then, this black stone found in the Nile Delta gave Egyptology the most publicity than it had ever had before. [3] Found in 1799 near a village called Rosetta, archaeologists called the slab the Rosetta Stone. [4] The slab was inscribed with three bands across its polished surface of writing, each in a different language: hieroglyphics on the top, another unknown language in the middle, and Greek on the bottom. [5] Scholars could read the Greek writing, which stated that each of the three bands contained the same decree in honor of Ptolemy V. [6] Full of excitement, it was hoped by archaeologists that they could use the Greek part to decipher the hieroglyphics. [7] Progress in translating the individual hieroglyphics, however, went real slowly. [8] It had been thought that each of the symbols stood for a whole word until this time.

[9] However, a French scholar working on the Rosetta Stone named Jean François Champollion wondered why it took more hieroglyphic symbols than Greek words to write the same message. [10] He correctly guessed that certain symbols stand for parts of words, and after working hard for twenty years, many of the signs were proved to stand for sounds.

Chapter Review

A. Correcting Errors in the Use of the Comparative and Superlative Forms

Each of the following sentences contains an error in the use of modifiers. Identify each error, and then write the correct form.

1. I was more hungrier than I thought, so I ate three plums.
2. He was the more able and intelligent of the three job applicants.
3. Was Hitler notoriouser than Stalin?
4. John, Richard's twin brother, was the oldest by three minutes.
5. After Diego had started lifting weights, he bragged that he was stronger than anyone in town.
6. People who live along this road complain because it is the worse road in the entire township.
7. Both Floyd and his brother are landscape designers who are in demand throughout the state, but Floyd is best known in this area.
8. After the band practiced, it sounded more better.
9. When I had a choice of strawberry or vanilla, I took vanilla because I liked it best.
10. Looking across the water at sunset, you can see the beautifullest view you can imagine.

B. Revising Sentences by Correcting Dangling and Misplaced Modifiers

┌HELP─

In Part B of the Chapter Review, you may have to add or delete some words. Be sure to use commas where they are needed to set off the introductory and interrupting modifiers.

Each of the following sentences contains a dangling or misplaced modifier. Write each sentence, arranging the words so that the meaning is logical and clear.

11. Yipping and running in circles, they saw that the dogs could herd the sheep into the pen.
12. The winners marched off the platform carrying trophies.
13. A police officer warned students who drive too fast about accidents during the defensive-driving class.
14. After escaping from slavery, the importance of education was often stressed by Frederick Douglass.
15. We went to visit my grandmother, who used to be a history teacher at my school yesterday.

USAGE

16. Climbing the stairs, his glasses fell off.

17. Maria took a close-up photograph of a lion with a telephoto lens.

18. Nesting in a tree outside my window, I see a small bird.

19. A young woman knocked on the door wearing a suit and hat.

20. Walking in the sunshine, it felt warm to us.

C. Revising Sentences by Correcting Unclear Comparisons and Incorrect, Misplaced, and Dangling Modifiers

Each of the following sentences contains an unclear comparison, an incorrect form of a modifier, a misplaced modifier, or a dangling modifier. Write each sentence, correcting the error.

21. Seeing that no damage had been done, their cars drove away in opposite directions.

22. Working long hours and taking few vacations, the success that he had longed for came to him after many years.

23. The temperature in Houston is higher than Chicago.

24. Looking through a telescope, the Cliffs of Dover came into view.

25. The branches of the tree hung over the fence that we planted.

26. Walking very careful over the uneven cobblestones, the elderly woman made her way from one end of the lane to the other.

27. The gift was more costlier than I had expected it to be.

28. The glass fell onto the floor, that was full of cranberry juice.

29. Balking, I quickly grew frustrated with the mule.

30. Michael hoped that his time on the sprint was faster than Patrick.

Writing Application

Using Comparison in a Consumer Guide

Comparative and Superlative Degrees   You and your sister Charlotte plan to buy a piece of audio equipment together. You have found a magazine article comparing several brands and showing the information in a big table. However, because Charlotte is visually impaired, the table can't help her decide. She asks you to narrow the choices to four brands, and then to write and record on audiotape a short comparison of their prices and features.

Prewriting   Find a magazine article that contains a table comparing different kinds of audio equipment. Study the table, and list the features that you think would be most important. Then, choose four products that seem acceptable, and jot down some comparisons.

Writing   As you write your first draft, carefully select comparative and superlative modifiers so that your explanation is not confusing. Tell why you would eliminate certain models from consideration. Include each of the degrees of comparison: positive, comparative, and superlative.

Revising   Ask a classmate to evaluate the clarity of your comparison. Add or revise details of the comparison to eliminate confusion.

Publishing   Using your textbook, check to be sure that you have used adjectives and adverbs correctly. Proofread your comparison for any errors in grammar, usage, and punctuation. You and your classmates may want to collect the paragraphs and bind them in a booklet titled *An Audio Equipment Consumer Guide*.

A Glossary of Usage
Common Usage Problems

Diagnostic Preview

A. Revising Errors in Usage

In each of the following sets of word groups, one word group contains an error in the use of standard, formal English. Identify the word group that contains an error, and then write the word group correctly.

EXAMPLE   **1. a.** Her speech implies that a change is needed.
       b. Leave me have some oranges, too.
       c. This house is somewhat larger than our old one.

       1. b. Let me have some oranges, too.

1. a. wasn't no reason
   b. words had no effect
   c. can hardly wait

2. a. families that emigrated to New Zealand
   b. sail as far as the channel marker
   c. made allusions to classical literature

3. a. being that he was alone
   b. when the people accepted new ways
   c. the woman who was elected

4. a. what kind of frog
   b. overtime besides the regular work
   c. an hypnotic speaker

5. **a.** saw on TV that our team had won
   b. Lee Haney proudly excepted his Mr. Olympia trophy.
   c. the house beside the highway

6. **a.** that he is doing alright
   b. Let him have his own way.
   c. Leave the door open when you go.

7. **a.** Teach your dog this trick.
   b. I'm feeling kind of ill.
   c. might have been too late

8. **a.** Simira is taller than her sister.
   b. Dough will rise in a warm place.
   c. We read where the damage was extensive.

9. **a.** Try to be on time.
   b. They walked a long way.
   c. Them stairs are dangerous and need repairs.

10. **a.** The bag burst, spilling the rice.
    b. The Polynesian alphabet has less characters than the English alphabet does.
    c. Take those books off that shelf.

B. Proofreading Paragraphs to Correct Usage Errors

Revise each of the sentences in the following paragraphs to correct the error in the use of standard, formal English.

EXAMPLE   **[1]** The last time I visited my aunt and uncle in Florida, they told me about a interesting town.

      1. *The last time I visited my aunt and uncle in Florida, they told me about an interesting town.*

[11] After the Civil War ended, Joseph E. Clarke decided that African Americans had ought to start a town of their own. [12] He wanted to build such a town, but no one would sell or donate land for this kind of an endeavor. [13] However, Joseph Clarke was a man who had great determination, and he wasn't hardly going to give up hope. [14] Finally, in 1877, with money what was donated by a New York philanthropist and with land offered by a Floridian named Josiah Eaton, Clarke obtained the first twelve acres of what would become Eatonville, Florida.

[15] Eatonville, located just beside Orlando, is recognized as the oldest incorporated African American town anywheres in the United

States. [16] This here community has always been populated and governed entirely by black people. [17] The African Americans which flocked to Eatonville built homes, churches, and schools, and they cultivated gardens and orange groves. [18] The residents didn't lose no time in establishing a library, a post office, and a newspaper. [19] Today, after more than a hundred years of self-government, the citizens of Eatonville continue to feel the affects of Joseph Clarke's courage and vision. [20] With its light industry, new businesses, and booming real estate development, Eatonville enjoys economic growth, just like the rest of central Florida does.

About the Glossary

This chapter provides a compact glossary of common problems in English usage. A *glossary* is an alphabetical list of special terms or expressions with definitions, explanations, and examples. You will notice that some examples in this glossary are labeled *nonstandard, standard, formal,* or *informal.*

The label *nonstandard* identifies usage that is suitable only in the most casual speaking situations and in writing that attempts to re-create casual speech. *Standard* English is language that is grammatically correct and appropriate in formal and informal situations. *Formal* identifies standard usage that is appropriate in serious speaking and writing situations (such as in speeches and in compositions for school). The label *informal* indicates standard usage common in conversation and in everyday writing such as personal letters. In doing the exercises in this chapter, be sure to use only standard English.

Formal	Informal
angry	steamed
unpleasant	yucky
agreeable	cool
very impressive	totally awesome
accelerate	step on it

a, an   Each of these words, called an **indefinite article,** refers to a member of a general group. Use *a* before words beginning with a consonant sound; use *an* before words beginning with a vowel sound.

Reference Note

For a list of **words often confused,** see page 391. Use the **index** at the back of the book to find information about other usage problems.

HELP

The word *diction* is often used to refer to word choice. Your choice of words affects the tone and clarity of what you say and write. When you know which usages are formal, informal, standard, and nonstandard, you can choose diction that is appropriate to any audience.

Reference Note

For more information about **articles,** see page 10.

USAGE

EXAMPLES   In ancient Greece and Rome, **a** person would go to see **an** oracle to consult the gods.

Did Jimmy Lee have to buy **a** uniform for his new job? [*A* is used before *uniform* because *uniform* begins with a consonant sound.]

Several of the tourists searched for **a** hotel for more than **an** hour. [*A* is used before *hotel* because *hotel* begins with a consonant sound. *An* is used before *hour* because *hour* begins with a vowel sound.]

accept, except   *Accept* is a verb that means "to receive." *Except* may be either a verb or a preposition. As a verb, *except* means "to leave out." As a preposition, *except* means "excluding."

EXAMPLES   Gary did not **accept** the bribe.

Students who were absent last week will be **excepted** from the group of students taking today's test.

Everybody **except** me knew the answer.

affect, effect   *Affect* is generally used as a verb meaning "to influence." *Effect* used as a verb means "to accomplish" or "to bring about." Used as a noun, *effect* means "the result of some action."

EXAMPLES   Working part time did not seem to **affect** his study habits.

Did the medicine **effect** a cure?

Coach Cortez said that the weather had little **effect** on the teams' performances.

ain't   *Ain't* is nonstandard. Avoid using *ain't* in formal speaking and in all writing other than dialogue.

EXAMPLES   These **aren't** [not *ain't*] my shoes.

Chris **isn't** [not *ain't*] going to the concert.

all ready, already   See page 391.

all right   *All right* means "satisfactory"; "unhurt, safe"; "correct"; or, when used in reply to a question or to introduce a remark, "yes." Although the spelling *alright* is sometimes used, it has not become accepted as standard usage.

EXAMPLES   The storm is over, and everyone is **all right.**

All right, I'll call you later.

Reference Note

For more about **verbs,** see page 15. For more about **prepositions,** see page 24.

USAGE

all the farther, all the faster   These expressions are used informally in some parts of the United States. In formal situations, use *as far as* and *as fast as.*

INFORMAL   This is all the farther we can go.

FORMAL   This is **as far as** we can go.

allusion, illusion   An *allusion* is an indirect reference to something. An *illusion* is a mistaken idea or a misleading appearance.

EXAMPLES   The poem's title is an **allusion** to a Hopi folk tale.

The documentary shattered viewers' **illusions** about migrant workers.

The magician was a master of **illusion.**

a lot   Write the expression *a lot* as two words. *A lot* is often used informally as a noun meaning "a large number or amount" or as an adverb meaning "a great deal" or "very much."

INFORMAL   A lot of critics have praised the film.

FORMAL   **A large number** of critics have praised the film.

INFORMAL   Our guests arrived a lot earlier than we had expected.

FORMAL   Our guests arrived **much** earlier than we had expected.

among   See **between, among.**

and etc.   *Etc.* is the abbreviation of the Latin words *et cetera,* meaning "and others" or "and so forth." Therefore, *and* should not be used before *etc.*

EXAMPLE   I earn money by baby-sitting, running errands, mowing lawns, **etc.** [not *and etc.*]

anyways, anywheres, everywheres, nowheres, somewheres   Use these words without an *s* at the end.

EXAMPLE   **Anywhere** [not *Anywheres*] you travel, you see the same hotel chains.

as   See **like, as, as if, as though.**

as if, as though   See **like, as, as if, as though.**

at   Do not use *at* after *where.*

NONSTANDARD   Where did you see them at?

STANDARD   Where did you see them?

STYLE   TIP

The expression *a lot* is overused. Try replacing *a lot* with a more descriptive, specific word or phrase.

EXAMPLES
mountains of homework

four subjects' worth of homework

STYLE   TIP

Like other abbreviations, *etc.* is rarely appropriate in formal writing and speaking.

USAGE

a while, awhile   The noun *while*, often preceded by the article *a*, means "a period of time." *Awhile* is an adverb meaning "for a short period of time."

EXAMPLES   I haven't heard from my pen pal for **a while.**

I usually read **awhile** before going to bed.

bad, badly   See page 215.

barely   See **The Double Negative** (page 254).

because   In formal situations, do not use the construction *reason . . . because.* Instead use *reason . . . that.*

INFORMAL   The reason we are holding the fund-raiser is because we want to buy new band uniforms.

FORMAL   The **reason** we are holding the fund-raiser is **that** we want to buy new band uniforms.

The sentence may also be revised without the use of *the reason.*

FORMAL   We are holding the fund-raiser because we want to buy new band uniforms.

being as, being that   Use *because* or *since* instead of these expressions.

NONSTANDARD   Being as her grades were so good, she got a scholarship.
STANDARD   **Because** her grades were so good, she got a scholarship.

NONSTANDARD   Being that he was late, he had to stand.
STANDARD   **Since** he was late, he had to stand.

beside, besides   *Beside* is a preposition meaning "by the side of." *Besides* as a preposition means "in addition to." As an adverb, *besides* means "moreover."

EXAMPLES   He glanced at the person **beside** him.

Did anybody **besides** you see what happened?

I liked the sweater; **besides,** I needed a new one.

between, among   Use *between* when referring to two things at a time, even if they are part of a larger group.

EXAMPLES   A strong bond exists **between** the twins.

I paused **between** chapters. [Although there are more than two chapters, I paused only between any two of them.]

Reference Note

For more about **nouns,** see page 3. For more about **adverbs,** see page 20.

USAGE

COMPUTER TIP

The spellchecker on a computer will catch misspelled words such as *anywheres* and *nowheres*. The grammar checker may catch errors such as double negatives. However, in the case of words often confused, such as *than* and *then* and *between* and *among*, you will need to check your work yourself for correct usage.

Use *among* when referring to all members of a group rather than to separate individuals in the group.

EXAMPLES   We distributed the pamphlets **among** the crowd.

There was some disagreement **among** the editorial staff.

borrow, lend, loan   The verb *borrow* means "to take [something] temporarily." The verb *lend* means "to give [something] temporarily."

EXAMPLES   May I **borrow** your binoculars?

I'll be glad to **lend** you my binoculars.

Loan, a noun in formal English, is sometimes used in place of the verb *lend* in informal situations.

INFORMAL   Will you **loan** me your umbrella?
FORMAL   Will you **lend** me your umbrella?

bring, take   *Bring* means "to come carrying something." *Take* means "to go away carrying something." Think of *bring* as related to *come* and *take* as related to *go.*

EXAMPLES   **Bring** your radio when you come over tomorrow.

Don't forget to **take** your coat when you go.

bust, busted   Avoid using these words as verbs. Instead, use a form of *break* or *burst* or *catch* or *arrest.*

EXAMPLES   I **broke** [not *busted*] the switch on the stereo.

The water main **burst** [not *busted*].

Did the police **arrest** [not *bust*] the suspects?

but, only   See **The Double Negative** (page 254).

Exercise 1   Identifying Standard Usage

For each of the following sentences, choose the correct word from the pair given in parentheses.

EXAMPLE   **1.** They stood there for (*a while, awhile*), gazing at the clear night sky.

    1. *a while*

1. The tasks were divided evenly (*among, between*) the two scouts.
2. The audience was deeply (*affected, effected*) by Simon Estes's powerful baritone voice.

3. We were afraid the bull had (*busted, broken*) loose.

4. No one (*accept, except*) the sophomores will attend.

5. Please (*bring, take*) these papers when you leave.

6. Penicillin has had a profound (*affect, effect*) on modern medicine.

7. I couldn't find the cat (*anywhere, anywheres*).

8. Uncle Joe said that the crosslike rays radiating from the moon were an (*allusion, illusion*) caused by the screen door.

9. (*Beside, Besides*) Julie and Zack, who else has signed up for Saturday's 10K walk?

10. In his remarks about Dr. Martin Luther King, Jr., the speaker made an (*allusion, illusion*) to Gandhi, whose nonviolent protests paved the way for the civil rights movement in the United States.

Exercise 2 **Proofreading to Correct Usage Errors**

Revise each of the following sentences by correcting the error or errors in usage. If a sentence is already correct, write *C*.

EXAMPLE   1. Where was Frank Matsura's photography studio at?

    1. *Where was Frank Matsura's photography studio?*

1. In 1903, this young Japanese artist, Frank Matsura, arrived somewhere in the backwoods settlement of Conconully, Washington.

2. This was all the farther he would go, for he lived in or near this rough frontier settlement for the remaining ten years of his life.

3. When he came to town, Matsura was wearing a elegant formal suit and was carrying bulky camera equipment he had taken with him.

4. Back in Seattle, Matsura had excepted a job in Conconully as a helper and laundryman at the Elliott Hotel.

5. Soon he was living in a tiny room behind the kitchen and performing his menial job with alot of energy and cheer.

6. When he was off duty, he carried his camera everywheres he went, photographing the area's people, scenery, events, and etc.

7. After a while, he settled in nearby Okanogan and opened a small studio.

8. Being as Matsura was a warm, extroverted person, he made many friends between settlers and American Indians alike.

9. Oddly, though, he never told anyone about his past, even after he had lived there a while.

10. To this day, nobody knows who he really was, where he was born at, or why he chose to live and die so far from his home.

can, may   Use *can* to express ability. Use *may* to express possibility.

EXAMPLES   Do you think you **can** repair this camera?

Ethan has said that he **may** run for class president.

To express permission in formal situations, use *may,* not *can.*

INFORMAL   Can I sit here?

FORMAL   **May** I sit here?

can't hardly, can't scarcely   See **The Double Negative** (page 254).

could of   Do not use *of* in place of *have* after verbs such as *could, should, would, might, must,* and *ought.*

EXAMPLE   Muriel **could have** [not *could of*] gone with us.

discover, invent   *Discover* means "to find, see, or learn about something that already exists." *Invent* means "to be the first to make or do something."

EXAMPLES   Luis W. Alvarez **discovered** many subatomic particles.

Sarah Boone **invented** the ironing board.

Reference Note

For more information about **contractions,** see page 361.

don't, doesn't   *Don't* is the contraction of *do not. Doesn't* is the contraction of *does not.* Use *doesn't,* not *don't,* with singular subjects except *I* and *you.*

EXAMPLES   It **doesn't** [not *don't*] matter to me.

The poem **doesn't** [not *don't*] rhyme.

effect   See **affect, effect.**

emigrate, immigrate   *Emigrate* means "to leave a country to settle elsewhere." *Immigrate* means "to come into a country to settle there."

EXAMPLES   My great-grandfather **emigrated** from Mexico.

Much of Australia's population is composed of people who **immigrated** there in recent centuries.

everywheres See **anyways,** etc.

except See **accept, except.**

fewer, less *Fewer* is used with plural nouns. It tells "how many." *Less* is used with singular nouns. It tells "how much."

EXAMPLES There are **fewer** whales than there once were.

We should have bought **less** meat and more vegetables.

good, well See page 215.

had of Do not use *had of* for *had.*

EXAMPLE If I **had** [not *had of*] only known that you wanted to read Mary Shelley's *Frankenstein*, I would have lent you my copy.

had ought, hadn't ought Do not use *had* or *hadn't* with *ought.*

NONSTANDARD	You hadn't ought to say such things.
STANDARD	You **ought** not to say such things.
STANDARD	You **shouldn't** say such things.

NONSTANDARD	They had ought to have left earlier.
STANDARD	They **ought** to have left earlier.
STANDARD	They **should** have left earlier.

hardly See **The Double Negative** (page 254).

he, she, it, they Do not use a pronoun along with its antecedent as the subject of a verb. Such an error is called the *double subject.*

NONSTANDARD	My father he works downtown.
STANDARD	My **father works** downtown.

hisself, theirself, theirselves These words are nonstandard. Use *himself* instead of *hisself,* and use *themselves* instead of *theirself* or *theirselves.*

EXAMPLES My uncle considers **himself** [not *hisself*] an average golfer.

The members of the Ecology Club should be very proud of **themselves** [not *theirself* or *theirselves*].

hopefully *Hopefully* is an adverb meaning "in a hopeful manner." In formal situations, avoid using *hopefully* for an expression such as *I hope* or *it is hoped.*

HELP

Use *fewer* with things that can be counted. Use *less* with things that cannot be counted.

EXAMPLE
Theresa has (*fewer, less*) CDs than Tracey does.

ASK
Can you count CDs? [yes]

ANSWER
Theresa has **fewer** CDs than Tracey does.

USAGE

Reference Note

For more information about **pronouns,** see page 6.

INFORMAL	Hopefully, the new tennis courts will be open next month.
FORMAL	**I hope** the new tennis courts will be open next month.
FORMAL	We listened **hopefully** as the coach gave an update about the new tennis courts.

illusion   See **allusion, illusion.**

immigrate   See **emigrate, immigrate.**

imply, infer   *Imply* means "to suggest." *Infer* means "to interpret" or "to draw as a conclusion."

EXAMPLES	In her speech, the candidate **implied** that she is for tax reform.
	From the candidate's speech, I **inferred** that she is for tax reform.

invent   See **discover, invent.**

it's, its   See page 394.

Exercise 3   Identifying Standard Usage

For each of the following sentences, choose the correct word from the pair given in parentheses.

EXAMPLE	**1.** (*Gary Soto, Gary Soto he*) is my favorite writer.
	1. *Gary Soto*

1. Did he say that he had painted the mural (*himself, hisself*)?
2. From his letter, I (*implied, inferred*) he would be away all summer.
3. He (*don't, doesn't*) always say what he means.
4. (*Emigration, Immigration*) to Alaska was spurred by the gold rush.
5. The heat has affected the growing season; we'll harvest (*fewer, less*) olives this year.
6. You could (*have, of*) borrowed some paper and a pencil from me.
7. As beasts of burden, dogs served the Comanches (*good, well*), often pulling a travois laden with more than forty pounds of baggage.
8. Mary Beth Stearns (*discovered, invented*) a technique for studying electrons.
9. Many French Canadians (*emigrated, immigrated*) from Quebec to work in the industries of New England.
10. Audrey must (*have, of*) taken my jacket by mistake.

Revise the following sentences to correct each error in the use of standard, formal English. If a sentence is already correct, write *C*.

EXAMPLE   **1.** Hopefully, the ambigrams shown here will motivate you to create similar designs.

   1. *I hope the ambigrams shown here will motivate you to create similar designs.*

1. A scientist, philosopher, and writer, Douglas R. Hofstadter he enjoys creating symmetrical designs from written words.
2. He and a friend discovered a new pastime; the resulting designs are called ambigrams.
3. Not every word lends itself to this method, but you might be surprised at how many words can be made into ambigrams.
4. As you might of known already, a *palindrome* is a word or expression that has the same letters in the same sequence both forward and backward—for example, *toot* or *Madam, I'm Adam.*
5. I don't mean to infer, though, that an ambigram has to be a palindrome—an ambigram simply has to look symmetrical.
6. Usually, ambigrams they can't be formed unless you tinker with the letter shapes and connect them in new ways.
7. You had ought to start with a word that has six letters or fewer.
8. For some good ideas, you may want to look below at the ambigrams for the words *Jamal, Steve, Chris, Felix, Wendy, Mexico,* and *dance.*
9. Don't forget that you can mix cursive, printed, capital, and lowercase letters to create affects like the ones in these ambigrams.
10. If you become stumped, you might find that you could of succeeded by adding some decorative flourishes.

kind of, sort of   In formal situations, avoid using either of these expressions for the adverb *rather* or *somewhat*.

INFORMAL   The waves were sort of rough.

 FORMAL   The waves were **rather** [or *somewhat*] rough.

kind of a(n), sort of a(n)   In formal situations, omit the *a* or *an*.

EXAMPLE   This bolt takes a special **kind of** [not *kind of a*] nut.

kinds, sorts, types   With the singular form of each of these words, use *this* or *that*. With the plural form, use *these* or *those*.

EXAMPLE   I know more about **that kind** of music than about any of **those** other **kinds.**

learn, teach   *Learn* means "to gain knowledge." *Teach* means "to provide with knowledge."

EXAMPLES   She **learned** how to saddle a horse.

The stable owner **taught** her how.

leave, let   *Leave* means "to go away." *Let* means "to allow" or "to permit." Avoid using *leave* for *let*.

EXAMPLES   We had to **leave** early to catch the plane.

Let [not *Leave*] them go first.

We **let** [not *left*] the trapped bird go free.

less   See **fewer, less.**

lie, lay   See page 180.

like, as, as if, as though   In formal situations, do not use the preposition *like* for the conjunction *as, as if,* or *as though* to introduce a subordinate clause.

INFORMAL   This animal sheds its skin like a snake does.

 FORMAL   This animal sheds its skin **as** a snake does.

INFORMAL   This looks like it might be the right place.

 FORMAL   This looks **as if** [or *as though*] it might be the right place.

Reference Note

For more information about **subordinate clauses,** see Chapter 4. For more about **conjunctions,** see page 26.

might of, must of   See **could of.**

neither, never, no, nobody, no one, not (–n't), nothing, nowhere   See **The Double Negative** (page 254).

nowheres   See **anyways,** etc.

a number of, the number of   *A number of* is generally plural and *the number of* is generally singular. Make sure that the verb agrees with the subject.

EXAMPLES   **A number of** job positions **are** open.

The number of job positions **is** limited.

of   See **could of.**

of   Do not use the preposition *of* after other prepositions such as *inside, off,* and *outside.*

EXAMPLES   The diver jumped **off** [not *off of*] the board.

Outside [not *Outside of*] the building was a patio.

off, off of   Do not use *off* or *off of* in place of *from.*

NONSTANDARD   Here's the money I borrowed off of you.

STANDARD   Here's the money I borrowed **from** you.

only   See **The Double Negative** (page 254).

ought to of   See **could of.**

Exercise 5   **Identifying Standard Usage**

For each of the following sentences, choose from the choices given in parentheses the word or expression that is correct according to the rules of standard, formal English.

EXAMPLE   1.   Who (*learned, taught*) you how to play mah-jongg?

1.   *taught*

1. The total length of the Great Wall of China is about 4,000 miles, if branches (*off, off of*) the main wall are included.
2. Carlos was (*outside, outside of*) the house.
3. We went to the hardware store for a special (*kind of, kind of a*) wrench.
4. Rachel Carson's books (*learned, taught*) me to care about ecology.
5. (*Leave, Let*) us listen without any interruptions.
6. How many pamphlets did you get (*from, off of*) the sales representative?
7. Why did she feel (*like, as if*) she'd said something wrong?
8. T. J. said the number of unclaimed prizes (*was, were*) surprising.

9. Why didn't the U.S. government (*leave, let*) the Cherokee people stay in their Southeast homelands?
10. They didn't want to take the boat out because the waves looked (*kind of, rather*) choppy.

┌HELP┐
Some sentences in Exercise 6 contain more than one error.

Exercise 6 Proofreading to Correct Usage Errors

Revise each of the following sentences by correcting the error or errors in the use of formal, standard English. If a sentence is already correct, write *C*.

EXAMPLE 1. My mother once tried to learn me how to do fancy needlework.

1. *My mother once tried to teach me how to do fancy needlework.*

1. Until recent times, most young girls learned to do fancy needlework.
2. Beginning when a girl was kind of young, her mother or another woman would learn her many embroidery stitches.
3. Then, at the age of nine or ten, the girl would be given the task of making a sampler like the one shown here, using every kind of a stitch she knew.
4. Usually, the girl's parents wouldn't leave her be idle.
5. She had to work on the sampler every day like her life depended on it!
6. When the sampler was finished, it didn't lie inside of a drawer.

7. Instead, it was left on display to show that the girl was industrious and well educated in homemaking skills.
8. Many people think these sort of sampler must have been popular in America and nowhere else.
9. However, a number of countries in Europe, Asia, and Africa have prized this kind of a needlework exercise for centuries.
10. Today, American girls aren't judged by their stitchery like they once were, and some never learn anything about needlework.

reason . . . because   See **because.**

rise, raise   See page 186.

scarcely   See **The Double Negative** (page 254).

she   See **he, she, it, they.**

should of   See **could of.**

sit, set   See page 183.

some, somewhat   In formal situations, avoid using *some* as an adverb meaning "to some extent." Use *somewhat.*

INFORMAL   This medicine should help your cough some.

FORMAL   This medicine should help your cough **somewhat.**

somewheres   See **anyways,** etc.

sort of   See **kind of, sort of.**

sort of a   See **kind of a(n), sort of a(n).**

sorts   See **kinds, sorts, types.**

suppose to, supposed to   To express an intention or plan, use the verb form *supposed* before an infinitive.

EXAMPLE   We were **supposed to** [not *suppose to*] meet Wendy at eight o'clock.

Reference Note

For more information about **infinitives,** see page 77.

take, bring   See **bring, take.**

teach   See **learn, teach.**

than, then   *Than* is a subordinating conjunction used in comparisons. *Then* is an adverb meaning "at that time" or "next."

EXAMPLES   She is younger **than** you are.

I swept the floor; **then** I emptied the trash.

Reference Note

For more information about **subordinating conjunctions,** see page 96.

USAGE

that   See **who, which, that.**

their, there, they're   See page 397.

theirself, theirselves   See **hisself, theirself, theirselves.**

them   Do not use *them* as an adjective. Use *those* instead.

EXAMPLE   It's one of **those** [not *them*] fancy show dogs.

they   See **he, she, it, they.**

this here, that there   Avoid using *here* or *there* after *this* or *that.*

EXAMPLE   Let's rent **this** [not *this here*] movie instead of **that** [not *that there*] one.

try and, try to   Use *try to*, not *try and.*

EXAMPLE   When you're at bat, you must **try to** [not *try and*] relax.

types   See **kinds, sorts, types.**

unless   See **without, unless.**

use to, used to   Do not leave off the *d* when you write *used to.*

EXAMPLE   Alicia **used to** [not *use to*] take tae kwon do lessons.

way, ways   Use *way*, not *ways*, when referring to a distance.

EXAMPLE   She lives quite a **way** [not *ways*] from here.

well   See page 215.

Reference Note

For more information about **adjective clauses,** see page 93.

what   Do not use *what* in place of *that* to introduce an adjective clause.

EXAMPLE   This is the book **that** [not *what*] I told you about.

when, where   Do not use *when* or *where* incorrectly to begin a definition.

NONSTANDARD   *SRO* is when tickets for all the seats have been sold, leaving standing room only.

STANDARD   *SRO* means that tickets for all the seats have been sold, leaving standing room only.

STANDARD   *SRO* is the abbreviation for *standing room only;* it means that tickets for all the seats have been sold.

where   Do not use *where* for *that.*

EXAMPLE   I read **that** [not *where*] the word *bayou* comes from the Choctaw word *bayuk*, meaning "small stream."

where . . . at   See **at.**

who, which, that   *Who* refers to people only. *Which* refers to things only. *That* refers to either people or things.

EXAMPLES   Carlotta, **who** is a sophomore, won the gold medal.

Her medal, **which** is actually gold-plated, is quite heavy.

Carlotta is the runner **that** [or *who*] won the gold medal.

This medal is not the first one **that** she has won.

who, whom   See page 156.

who's, whose   See page 398.

without, unless   Do not use the preposition *without* in place of the conjunction *unless* to introduce a subordinate clause.

EXAMPLE   I can't use the car **unless** [not *without*] I ask Mom.

would of   See **could of.**

your, you're   See page 398.

MEETING THE CHALLENGE

Write a review of a book or short story you have recently read. Your analysis should include the correct use of at least five entries in the Glossary of Usage as well as the title of the work and its author. Proofread your review, checking for correct grammar, spelling, and punctuation.

USAGE

> **Exercise 7**   **Revising Errors in Usage**

Revise each of the following sentences to correct the error in usage.

EXAMPLE   **1.** I am use to the noise.

   1. I am used to the noise.

1. A solar eclipse is when the moon comes between the earth and the sun and blocks the light.
2. The workers which put up that new office building certainly finished it quickly.
3. Ronald E. McNair was aboard the space shuttle what exploded in January 1986.
4. Was the senator suppose to arrive this morning?
5. A run-on sentence is where two sentences are erroneously joined as a single sentence.
6. As soon as the rain lets up some, we'll leave.
7. Them mosquitoes can drive a person nearly crazy.
8. The receiver carried the ball a long ways down the field before he was tackled.
9. I think I read in the paper where Amy Tan has a new novel coming out next month.
10. I'm tired of trying to cut the grass with this here old lawn mower, which should be in an antique exhibit.

Review A   Identifying Standard Usage

For each of the following sentences, choose the correct word or word group from the choices given in parentheses.

EXAMPLE   1. If it (*don't, doesn't*) rain tonight, we'll start harvesting the crop tomorrow.

1. *doesn't*

1. Thanks to modern medicine, there are (*fewer, less*) cases of tetanus and diphtheria nowadays.
2. I tried to (*learn, teach*) my dog to do tricks, but he just sat and stared at me.
3. I see (*where, that*) pandas are an endangered species.
4. Cape Porpoise is (*somewhere, somewheres*) near Portsmouth.
5. Priscilla wrote a longer paper (*than, then*) Tammy did.
6. To make American Indian fry bread, you need flour, baking powder, salt, (*and etc., etc.*)
7. We (*hadn't ought, ought not*) to decide until we are certain of all the facts.
8. Amy couldn't see the screen (*without, unless*) I took off my hat.
9. Someone must (*of, have*) left the door unlocked.
10. Lewis Latimer (*discovered, invented*) an improved filament for the earliest electric light bulbs.

Review B   Identifying Standard Usage

For each of the following sentences, choose from the choices given in parentheses the word or word group that is correct according to the rules of formal, standard English.

EXAMPLE   1. The rear-view mirror fell (*off, off of*) Ted's bike.

1. *off*

1. Bradley has written a number of hit songs, and he (*don't, doesn't*) look (*as if, like*) he's ever going to stop.
2. (*Inside, Inside of*) the box was (*a, an*) heap of glittering gems.
3. May I (*imply, infer*) from your yawns that you are bored?
4. My great-grandmother (*emigrated, immigrated*) from Italy when she was a young woman.
5. (*Beside, Besides*) speaking Spanish, Vera can speak a little Portuguese.
6. Linda (*doesn't, don't*) enjoy doing (*those, that*) sort of exercise.
7. Ahead of us on the desert, a lake seemed to sparkle, but it was only an (*allusion, illusion*).

8. This prolonged water shortage will (*affect, effect*) the whole state (*accept, except*) for two counties.

9. I don't think my parents will (*leave, let*) me borrow the car in this kind of weather.

10. Because of the indiscriminate slaughter, each year there were (*fewer, less*) bison.

11. When Wilmer is very tired, he (*don't, doesn't*) talk much.

12. The disagreement (*between, among*) the two friends caused a number of problems.

13. When he goes to the next potluck dinner, he will (*bring, take*) potato salad.

14. We saw several puffins, eight sea lions, a humpback whale, and (*a, an*) eagle while we were on a daylong Alaskan cruise.

15. I felt as if I (*could have, could of*) run forever.

16. The mayor (*which, who*) used to wear running clothes has been reelected.

17. (*Them, Those*) Asian currencies are rising rapidly in value.

18. Rick wanted to (*try and, try to*) complete a painting each week.

19. The weary explorers traveled quite a (*way, ways*) during their three-week journey.

20. Did you read (*where, that*) the food bank is in need of donations?

Review C ▸ Proofreading a Paragraph to Correct Usage Errors

Revise each of the sentences in the following paragraph by correcting the error or errors in the use of formal, standard English. If a sentence is already correct, write *C.*

EXAMPLE **[1]** Sequoyah was the person which devised the Cherokee alphabet.

1. *Sequoyah was the person who devised the Cherokee alphabet.*

[1] Imagine single-handedly discovering a system for writing a language that had never before been written! [2] In about 1809, the Cherokee scholar Sequoyah became aware of "talking leaves," the written pages that were used by white people to communicate with one another. [3] Being that Sequoyah he felt that the ability to write had greatly helped white people, he decided he had ought to create a similar system for his people. [4] Instead of making up an alphabet like the one used in English, he chose to create this here syllabary. [5] Each

The Granger Collection, New York

character in Sequoyah's syllabary stands for one of the eighty-five syllables what are used in speaking Cherokee. [6] Sequoyah copied some letters from a English book, but in his system they have different meanings. [7] During the twelve years that it took Sequoyah to complete his writing system, he was ridiculed by many Cherokees who thought his efforts were kind of foolish. [8] However, after the syllabary was finished and accepted by most Cherokees, they realized they should not of scoffed. [9] After a while, thousands learned how to read and write, and soon books and newspapers were being printed in Cherokee. [10] Sequoyah was honored by his people for learning them to read and write, and his writing method is still used today.

The Double Negative

A *double negative* is the use of two or more negative words to express a single negative idea. Before the 1700s, two or more negatives were often used in the same sentence for emphasis. In English, this usage is no longer considered correct, and a double negative is regarded as non-standard. Avoid using double negatives in your writing and speaking.

Common Negative Words			
barely	neither	none	nowhere
but (meaning "only")	never	no one	only
	no	not (–n't)	scarcely
hardly	nobody	nothing	

NONSTANDARD	Jade wasn't but a child then.
STANDARD	Jade **was but** a child then.

NONSTANDARD	We hadn't scarcely enough time to finish the test.
STANDARD	We **had scarcely** enough time to finish the test.

NONSTANDARD	There isn't no reason to be nervous.
STANDARD	There **is no** reason to be nervous.
STANDARD	There **isn't any** reason to be nervous.

NONSTANDARD	We searched for clues but didn't find none.
STANDARD	We searched for clues but **found none.**
STANDARD	We searched for clues but **didn't find any.**

NONSTANDARD	I didn't hear nothing.
STANDARD	I **heard nothing.**
STANDARD	I **didn't hear anything.**

HAGAR THE HORRIBLE reprinted with special permission of King Features Syndicate, Inc.

Exercise 8 — Revising Sentences That Contain Double Negatives

Each of the following sentences contains too many negative words. Revise each sentence. Be careful not to change the intended meaning.

EXAMPLE
1. Theo wanted some ancient Greek coins, but the coin dealer didn't have none.

1. *Theo wanted some ancient Greek coins, but the coin dealer had none.*

or

Theo wanted some ancient Greek coins, but the coin dealer didn't have any.

┌HELP─

The sentences in Exercise 8 may be correctly revised in more than one way. You need to give only one revision for each.

1. The boy hadn't never been in an airplane.
2. After a lazy summer, Pat can't hardly jog a mile.
3. She was sleeping so soundly she didn't hear nothing.
4. Angela looked for Easter eggs but she didn't see none.
5. Lee Ann has not never been to the Grand Canyon.
6. Char did not want no part of the childish plan.
7. Isn't there no milk left at the store?
8. The stranded motorist doesn't have no spare tire.
9. No one has never walked on the planet Mars.
10. There isn't scarcely any hope for that team to win.

Revise each of the following sentences, correcting the error or errors in the use of formal, standard English. Practice saying aloud the corrected sentences.

EXAMPLE

1. Now a museum, the Imperial Palace (also called the Forbidden City) use to be the home of China's royal family.

1. *Now a museum, the Imperial Palace (also called the Forbidden City) used to be the home of China's royal family.*

1. They don't have hardly any chance to score before the buzzer sounds; the situation looks sort of hopeless to me.
2. You ought to have seen how beautiful Santa Fe was at Christmas, with nearly every house surrounded by flickering *farolitos*—paper-bag lanterns that have candles inside of them.
3. I might of gone to the concert if I had of heard about it earlier.
4. Pam and her sister Stacey look so much alike that you can't hardly see the differences among them.
5. My cousins didn't hardly know how to swim, but they wouldn't of missed going to the lake.
6. Them reference books in the library are kept in some kind of a special section.
7. This here is the car what I told you about.
8. Hadn't you ought to try and help them?
9. Many of the American Indian leaders which visited Washington, D.C., in the late 1800s proudly wore their traditional clothing rather than dress like their white hosts did.
10. I wonder where them fishing poles are at.
11. We don't live in that there neighborhood no more.
12. We might of gone on the tour, but we wouldn't of had no camera to take pictures.
13. A foot fault in tennis is when the server steps over the base line before hitting the ball.
14. Since there wasn't scarcely any rainfall last spring, there are less mosquitoes this summer.
15. When the play was over, the audience seemed sort of subdued.
16. Shing searched for rice noodles in the grocery store but didn't find none.
17. I saw on the news where many manufacturers will install an improved security system in their new cars.

18. Miss Kim she likes to give those kind of surprise quizzes.
19. Let's try and finish early so we can relax some.
20. In the early 1500s, Ponce de León searched for the Fountain of Youth somewhere on the island of Bimini.

Nonsexist Language

Nonsexist language is language that applies to people in general, both male and female. For example, the nonsexist terms *humanity, human beings,* and *people* can substitute for the gender-specific term *mankind.*

In the past, many skills and occupations were generally closed to either men or women. Words like *seamstress, stewardess,* and *mailman* reflect those limitations. Since most jobs can now be held by both men and women, language is adjusting to reflect this change.

When you are referring generally to people, use nonsexist expressions rather than gender-specific ones. Following are some widely used nonsexist terms that you can use to replace gender-specific ones.

Gender-Specific	Nonsexist
businessman	executive, businessperson
chairman	chairperson, chair
common man	ordinary person
congressman	representative
deliveryman	delivery person
fireman	firefighter
foreman	supervisor
housewife	homemaker
mailman	mail carrier
male nurse	nurse
man-made	synthetic, manufactured
mankind	humanity
manpower	workers, human resources
May the best man win!	May the best person win!
policeman	police officer
salesman	salesperson, salesclerk
seamstress	needleworker
steward, stewardess	flight attendant
weatherman	meteorologist

USAGE

If the antecedent of a pronoun may be either masculine or feminine, use both masculine and feminine pronouns to refer to it.

EXAMPLES **Anyone** who wants to be considered should present **his or her** application to the office.

Any applicant may bring a résumé with **him or her** to the office.

Often, you can avoid the awkward *his or her* construction (or the alternative *his/her*) by substituting an article (*a, an,* or *the*) for the construction. Another solution is to reword the sentence, using the plural forms of both the pronoun and its antecedent.

EXAMPLES Any interested **applicant** may submit **a** proposal.

All interested **applicants** may submit **their** proposals.

Oral Practice   Using Nonsexist Language

Read each of the following sentences aloud. Then, revise the sentences, replacing gender-specific terms and awkward expressions, and read the revised sentences aloud.

EXAMPLE   1. The factory is advertising for a night watchman.

1. *The factory is advertising for a security guard.*

1. The weathermen predict sunny skies for the rest of the week.
2. The new chairman is in the office.
3. She was a published authoress and an admired public figure.
4. The male nurse in Grandma's ward was helpful and kind.
5. One of Suzi's ambitions is to become a congressman.
6. We wanted to find the address, so we looked for a mailman.
7. That environmental research will benefit all mankind.
8. Senator Dupont's political platform was full of references to the common man.
9. The career of fireman is a noble one.
10. Aboard that airline, the stewardesses wear red.

PEANUTS reprinted by permission of United Feature Synndicate, Inc.

Chapter Review

A. Revising Expressions by Correcting Errors in Usage

In each of the following sets of word groups, one word group contains an error in usage. Rewrite this word group correctly, using standard, formal usage.

1. a. anywheres you travel
   b. as fast as sound travels
   c. to learn Greek cooking from him

2. a. affect the outcome
   b. the candidate implied in his speech
   c. among his two opponents

3. a. made illusions to the Bible
   b. fewer participants in the contest
   c. asked what kind of car that is

4. a. family that emigrated from Germany
   b. should of gone yesterday
   c. discovered another planet

5. a. to try and win the game
   b. feeling all right
   c. that kind of car

6. a. letting the dog out
   b. an effect of cold weather
   c. books, pencils, papers, and etc.

7. a. ate everything accept the peas and dessert
   b. older than you
   c. bringing your records when you come over

8. a. I heard nothing.
   b. Lisa can hardly tell the difference.
   c. That cat ain't Samantha, is it?

9. a. picture that fell off the wall
   b. that kind of a dog
   c. larger than he is

USAGE

10. **a.** sitting beside the tree
    b. going a little ways
    c. not reality but illusion

11. **a.** whose coat doesn't fit well
    b. that fewer people learned to read back then
    c. inside of the cabinet

12. **a.** car looking like it had been wrecked
    b. chair that was blue
    c. water jug that burst

13. **a.** She effected an improvement.
    b. This is a problem that must be resolved.
    c. Less students joined the club this year.

14. **a.** Take the package to the mail room.
    b. Apples fell off of the tree.
    c. That will scarcely be enough food for all of them.

15. **a.** invented a better safety device
    b. if no one beside my aunt knows
    c. if you're feeling all right

16. **a.** Funds were allotted among six counties.
    b. Where is my hammer at?
    c. This is as far as the fence extends.

17. **a.** We are going nowhere, Mary Sue.
    b. Doesn't he know the way?
    c. He knows more then he reveals.

18. **a.** We were gone for a hour.
    b. Try to learn this poem.
    c. Leave the green grapes on the vine.

19. **a.** I have saved alot of money.
    b. Please stay awhile, John.
    c. One of the glasses broke.

20. **a.** It was an illusion caused by light on the surface.
    b. Their report implies a need for funds.
    c. That dog he limps.

21. **a.** no exception to this rule
    b. being that she is the oldest
    c. taking a torque wrench to Robin's garage

22. **a.** The reason he left is that he's upset.
    b. The crust looked like it had been burned.
    c. They ought to study before the test.

23. **a.** when the ice busted a pipe
    b. so he can lend me a dollar
    c. emigrate from their birthplace

24. **a.** and leave me have my turn
    b. the mechanic who worked on our car
    c. somewhat cold for swimming

25. **a.** haven't only three days of vacation
    b. the effects of smoking
    c. learned that the winner had been announced

26. **a.** Davenport, Iowa, was as far as we could go on a tank of gas.
    b. Name the river between the cities.
    c. Davy will learn the children good manners.

27. **a.** should have taken more time
    b. everywheres you go
    c. Uncle Mark and Aunt Zita taught themselves how to repair a computer.

28. **a.** A number of different kinds of birds nest there.
    b. I'm reporting on the invention of the internal-combustion engine.
    c. By calling me by my last name, the teacher infers disapproval.

29. **a.** outside of the assembly hall
    b. as if he had seen a ghost
    c. asking how much he borrowed from you

30. **a.** In the morning we let the raccoon go.
    b. Engine knock is when a car engine makes a pinging sound because of low-octane fuel.
    c. Kathryn is supposed to work late.

B. Proofreading a Paragraph to Correct Usage Errors

Revise the paragraph on the following page by rewriting each sentence to correct the error or errors in the use of formal, standard English. If a sentence is already correct, write *C*.

[31] I can't hardly believe what this book says about King Arthur. [32] It says that there wasn't no real King Arthur who ruled England during the Middle Ages. [33] Arthur was actually a powerful chieftain around A.D. 500, at the outset of the so-called Dark Ages. [34] The book infers that the legend of a noble king who introduced chivalry into England is the work of storytellers. [35] Most of the illusions to the Round Table are based on a fifteenth-century work called *Le Morte Darthur* by Sir Thomas Malory. [36] Some of the legends say that Arthur excepted more than a thousand knights for membership at the Round Table. [37] Although there might of been some truth to these legends, Malory's version says there were two hundred fifty knights who earned the right to sit at the Round Table; others say twelve. [38] Some of the most famous contests were among Modred, a wicked man, and Sir Lancelot, a brave defender of honor. [39] When Arthur lay dying, he was taken away to the magical isle of Avalon. [40] The story doesn't go no further, but it implies that Arthur will return someday to inspire noble deeds.

C. Identifying Standard Usage

For each of the following sentences, choose from the choices given in parentheses the word or word group that is correct according to the rules of standard, formal English.

41. With a little effort you (*could have, could of*) written a better report.
42. Shane's answer to my question was (*kind of, rather*) vague.
43. For the band trip I must remember to take my uniform, music, instrument, (*etc., and etc.*)
44. We wanted to go (*everywhere, everywheres*) on our one-week vacation.
45. It looked (*like, as if*) the fire had started in the hayloft.
46. Our team (*had ought, ought*) to win the championship.
47. (*This, This here*) store is having sales in all of its departments.
48. We can't go swimming (*without, unless*) we clean our rooms first.
49. Where should we (*meet, meet at*)?
50. I heard (*where, that*) the mayor would not run for reelection.

USAGE

Writing Application

Creating a Flier

Using Formal, Standard English   Create a flier for an organization that will soon be providing a public service in your community. The organization you choose might provide health, recreation, or housing services, or it might do something else. In a one-page flier, describe the organization's goals and achievements and explain some of the services it offers. Include at least five examples of standard usage covered in this chapter, and underline each example.

Prewriting   Begin by listing services that your community needs, and note what kinds of organizations supply these services. You may write about a real service group, such as the American Heart Association, or you may wish to write about a fictitious group. Also, list some of the positive effects the group will likely have on your community. Organize your notes so that you can present your information in several coherent paragraphs.

Writing   As you write your first draft, you may think of points you would like to add or changes you would like to make in the presentation of your information. If so, look back over your prewriting notes and determine where your additions and changes will best fit.

Revising   Give your flier to a classmate to read, and use your partner's comments on the clarity of your writing to help you make any necessary revisions.

Publishing   Check your flier for errors in grammar, spelling, and usage. With your teacher's permission, you could post your flier on the class bulletin board or Web page.

Capitalization
Standard Uses of Capitalization

Diagnostic Preview

A. Capitalizing Sentences Correctly

For each of the following sentences, correctly write the words that should be capitalized.

EXAMPLE   **1.** Renée searched everywhere in freeport, maine, until she found a gift at l. l. bean for her grandparents.

     1. Freeport; Maine; L. L. Bean

1. Our september trip to ireland included a stay in kilkee, a coastal village.

2. At the end of class, ms. kwan said that friday's geology II exam will include questions about the appalachian mountains.

3. We should change our dollars to pesos before we board the flight to santiago, chile.

4. The thanksgiving day parade traveled from martin luther king, jr., boulevard to fifty-first street.

5. During their trip to colorado, the barreras hiked up pikes peak.

6. The title of her new television special is *one in a million.*

7. Both ernest hemingway and walt disney once worked for the *kansas city star.*

8. Every easter sunday, grandma penny sings "we praise thee, o god, our redeemer, creator," which was translated from german.

9. One of the cities of the incas, machu picchu, lay hidden among the andes mountains in southern peru and was never discovered by spanish conquerors.

10. In 1982, the colombian writer gabriel garcía márquez was awarded the nobel prize in literature.

11. The winner of the first kentucky derby, the annual race at churchill downs in louisville, was a horse named aristides.

12. In 1983, sally ride became the first american woman in space when the space shuttle *challenger* was launched from cape canaveral.

13. Frederick douglass was the first african american member of the department of justice's u.s. marshals service.

14. If Beth improves her grades in english and history II, her parents will let her apply for a job at the walgreens drugstore on forty-third street.

15. Our debate team argued in favor of pro-american economic policies as the best way to foster democracy in the developing countries of africa, asia, and south america.

B. Capitalizing a Paragraph Correctly

For each sentence in the following paragraph, correctly write the words that should be capitalized.

EXAMPLE   **[1]** Last summer we visited my uncle carlos, who lives in new york city.

    1. *Carlos; New York City*

[16] One of new york city's most popular tourist attractions is the empire state building. [17] The building, at fifth avenue and thirty-fourth street, attracts 2,500,000 visitors a year. [18] Among them are troops of boy scouts and girl scouts, who camp out on the eighty-sixth floor. [19] The building was financed by john jakob raskob, the founder of general motors. [20] It opened in 1931, during the great depression. [21] At the time, it was the tallest building on earth (1,250 feet), but it's since been overshadowed by chicago's sears tower (1,450 feet) and buildings in other countries. [22] The observatory on the one hundred second floor accounts for much of the empire state building's continuing appeal; when the weather is clear, the observatory provides a view of five states: new york, new jersey, connecticut, pennsylvania, and massachusetts. [23] On may 1, 2006, publicists threw a party to mark the building's seventy-fifth birthday. [24] The building also had a starring role in the 1933 movie *king kong*, which was remade in 2005. [25] Another event is the mass wedding on valentine's day on the 80th floor.

Using Capital Letters Correctly

┌HELP┐
In your reading, you will notice variation in the use of capitalization. Most writers, however, follow the rules presented in this chapter. In your own writing, following these rules will help you communicate clearly with the widest possible audience.

Reference Note

For more about using **capital letters in quotations,** see page 341.

10a. Capitalize the first word in every sentence.

EXAMPLES   **T**he Second Seminole War lasted nearly eight years.

After the war many Seminoles remained in the Everglades and never officially made peace with the U.S. government.

The first word of a quoted sentence should begin with a capital letter, whether or not the quotation begins your sentence.

EXAMPLE   In *Walden,* Henry David Thoreau writes, "**I**f you have built castles in the air, your work need not be lost; that is where they should be."

When quoting only part of a sentence, capitalize the first word of the quotation if (1) the person you are quoting capitalized it or (2) it is the first word of your sentence.

EXAMPLES   What is suggested by the metaphor "**c**astles in the air"?

"**C**astles in the air" is a metaphor that suggests one's dreams, goals, or ambitions.

(NOTE)   Capitalize the first word of a sentence fragment used in dialogue.

EXAMPLE   When he was asked whether he had read *Walden,* Mario answered, "**O**nly part of it."

|STYLE   TIP|

Some poets do not capitalize lines of poetry. When you quote from a writer's work, use capital letters as the writer uses them.

Traditionally, the first word in a line of poetry is capitalized.

EXAMPLES   **S**torm, blow me from here
With your fiercest wind
Let me float across the sky
'**T**ill I can rest again.

Maya Angelou, "Woman Work"

10b. Capitalize the pronoun *I* and the interjection *O.*

The interjection *O,* usually used only for invocations, is followed by the name of the person or thing being addressed. Do not confuse *O* with the common interjection *oh,* which is capitalized only when it begins a sentence or is part of a title.

EXAMPLES   The first line **I** read in the poem was "Hear us, **O** Zeus."

I finished the race, but **oh,** was **I** exhausted.

MECHANICS

NOTE *Oh,* unlike *O,* is followed by a mark of punctuation, usually a comma or an exclamation point.

10c. Capitalize the first word in both the salutation and the closing of a letter.

EXAMPLES   **D**ear Mr. Velazquez: **M**y dear Jennifer,

              Sincerely yours,   **Y**ours truly,

10d. Capitalize proper nouns and proper adjectives.

A *common noun* names one of a group of persons, places, things, or ideas. A *proper noun* names a particular person, place, thing, or idea. A *proper adjective* is formed from a proper noun.

A common noun is capitalized when it

- begins a sentence

      or

- begins a direct quotation

      or

- is part of a title

Common Nouns	Proper Nouns	Proper Adjectives
a **w**riter	**D**ickens	**D**ickensian character
a **r**eligion	**B**uddhism	**B**uddhist monk
a **c**ountry	**F**rance	**F**rench bread
a **q**ueen	**V**ictoria	**V**ictorian era
a **p**lanet	**V**enus	**V**enusian terrain
a **r**egion	the **M**idwest	**M**idwestern values

In a compound proper noun, articles, coordinating conjunctions, and short prepositions (those with fewer than five letters) are not capitalized.

EXAMPLES   Prince **o**f Wales

              National Association **f**or **t**he Advancement **o**f Colored People

              Girl Scouts **o**f **t**he United States **o**f America

---

Reference Note

For information on **commas and colons in salutations,** see pages 313 and 328.

MEETING THE CHALLENGE

Choose a country. Then, write a paragraph giving a short biographical sketch of a current or former leader of that country. In your paragraph, correctly use and capitalize at least five proper nouns and five proper adjectives.

Reference Note

For more information about **common nouns** and **proper nouns,** see page 4. For more about **proper adjectives,** see page 13.

MECHANICS

NOTE Proper nouns and proper adjectives may lose their capitals after long use.

EXAMPLES **d**iesel   **b**ologna   **b**raille   **w**att

When you are not sure whether to capitalize a word, check a dictionary to see in which uses (if any) it is capitalized.

COMPUTER TIP

The range of correct spellings of personal names can foil even the best spell-checking software. One way to avoid this problem is to customize your spell-checker. If your software allows, add to it frequently used names that you have difficulty spelling or capitalizing correctly.

(1) Capitalize the names of persons and animals.

Persons	**N**olan **R**yan	**L**atrice **K**antor	**H. H. M**unro
	William the **C**onqueror	**D**r. **E**ileen **C**ruz **B**ill **G**ates	**J**erome **W**ilson, **J**r.
Animals	**L**assie **B**abe	**S**ocks **R**over	**W**hite **F**ang **F**luff

NOTE Some names contain more than one capital letter. Usage varies in the capitalization of *van, von, du, de la,* and other parts of multiword names. When possible, verify the spelling of a name with the person with that name, or check in a reference source.

EXAMPLES **D**e **L**a **C**ruz   **M**c**E**nroe   **R**ed **C**loud   **V**an **D**ongen

de **l**a **M**are   **O'S**hea   **W**ells-**B**arnett   **v**an **G**ogh

Reference Note

For information about **capitalizing abbreviations** such as *Dr.* and *Jr.,* see page 284.

(2) Capitalize initials in names and abbreviations that come before or after names.

EXAMPLES **J. D.** Rockefeller   Louis **J.** Halle   **D**r. Suzi Cohen

Tom Taliaferro, **M.D.**   **S**r. Garcia   **M**s. Bradford

Exercise 1 **Proofreading Paragraphs for Correct Capitalization**

Most of the sentences in the following paragraphs contain errors in capitalization. Write the correct form of each incorrect word. If the capitalization of a sentence is already correct, write *C*.

EXAMPLE   **[1]** These pictures capture only a few of the many sides of Gordon parks, renowned Photographer, film director, writer, and composer.

1. *Parks; photographer*

[**1**] A self-taught photographer, gordon Parks grew up in Fort Scott, Kansas. [**2**] after winning a rosenwald Fellowship for a series of pictures about life in Chicago's Slums, He got his first full-time photography job with the Farm Security Administration in Washington, D.C. [**3**] In 1949, he joined the staff of *Life* magazine. [**4**] During his nearly twenty years with *Life,* Parks covered assignments ranging from Junior High School science conventions to Paris Fashion Shows. [**5**] He also wrote many of the essays that accompanied his photographs, as well as two Volumes of autobiography, *A Choice of Weapons* and *Voices in the Mirror.*

[**6**] turning to a career in the movie industry in 1968, Parks moved to Hollywood, where his son Gordon Parks, jr., took this photograph of him preparing to direct a scene from the film version of *The Learning Tree.* [**7**] Parks also wrote the film's screenplay and, working at the grand piano in his Hollywood apartment, its musical score. [**8**] His success with the film led to other writing and directing projects, including *Leadbelly,* the story of the blues musician Huddie ledbetter.

[**9**] In September 1997, an exhibition of his photography opened at the Corcoran Gallery in Washington, D.C. [**10**] Some of his best-known projects have included *Voices in the Mirror* and the words and music for *Martin,* a classical Ballet honoring the late dr. martin luther king, jr.

(3) Capitalize geographical names.

Type of Name	Examples	
Countries	the **N**etherlands **G**hana	**A**rgentina **S**witzerland
Towns, Cities	**C**hicago **S**tratford-on-**A**von **S**an **D**iego	**L**aredo **B**erlin **St**. **P**etersburg
Counties, Townships, Parishes, Provinces	**O**range **C**ounty **F**ranklin **T**ownship **E**ast **B**aton **R**ouge **P**arish	**C**addo **P**arish **Y**orkshire **C**ape of **G**ood **H**ope **P**rovince
States	**O**regon **N**ew **Y**ork	**T**exas **S**outh **C**arolina
Regions	the **M**iddle **E**ast the **W**est the **N**ortheast	**G**reat **P**lains **Y**ukon **S**un **B**elt

NOTE Words such as *south, east,* and *northwest* are not capitalized when they indicate direction.

EXAMPLES   **w**est of the bridge   heading **n**orth

Type of Name	Examples	
Continents	**S**outh **A**merica **A**sia	**E**urope **A**frica
Islands	**G**alveston **I**sland the **L**esser **A**ntilles	the **I**sle of **W**ight **K**ey **W**est
Mountains	**A**llegheny **M**ountains **S**ierra **M**adre	**M**ount **St**. **H**elens **P**ikes **P**eak
Other Geographical Names	**S**henandoah **V**alley **B**ryce **C**anyon **C**ape **H**atteras	**K**alahari **D**esert **T**impanogos **C**ave **S**inai **P**eninsula

Type of Name	Examples	
Bodies of Water	Atlantic Ocean Red Sea Persian Gulf	Suwanee River Rio Grande Lake of the Ozarks

Parks, Forests	Redwood State Park
	North Tongass
	    National Forest
		Bernheim Forest
		Stone Mountain
		    Memorial Park

Roads, Highways, Streets	Route 41 Interstate 10 Sunshine State Parkway	Central Avenue South Fiftieth Street Pleasant Hill Road

NOTE The second word in a hyphenated street number begins with a lowercase letter.

EXAMPLE   Fifty-third Street

A word such as *city, island, river,* or *street* is generally not capitalized unless it is part of a proper noun.

Proper Nouns	Common Nouns
traffic in Mexico City	traffic in a large city
visiting Captiva Island	visiting a barrier island
bridging the Ohio River	bridging the river
across Delancey Street	across a congested street

Oral Practice   Using Correct Capitalization

Read the following word groups aloud. Then, say which words in each word group should be capitalized. If a word group is already correct, say "correct."

EXAMPLE   1. atop granite peak
             1. *atop Granite Peak*

1. zion national park
2. gulf of tonkin
3. explored Mount ararat
4. hiking trails in a state park
5. at moon lake
6. a house on starve island
7. beside the ohio river
8. in lancaster county

STYLE   TIP

Since *rio* is Spanish for "river," *Rio Grande River* is redundant. Use only *Rio Grande.*

Other terms to watch for are

- *sierra,* Spanish for "mountain range" [Use only *Sierra Nevada,* not *Sierra Nevada Mountains.*]
- *yama,* Japanese for "mountain" [Use only *Fuji-yama* or *Mount Fuji,* not *Mount Fuji-yama.*]
- *sahara,* Arabic for "desert" [Use only *Sahara,* not *Sahara Desert.*]
- *gobi,* Mongolian for "desert" [Use only *Gobi,* not *Gobi Desert.*]

MECHANICS

9. mekong delta
10. across baffin bay
11. ventura boulevard
12. the tides in the bay
13. new york skyline
14. forty-fifth street

15. near the isle of wight
16. the west side of the river
17. population of the north
18. near dundee mountain
19. coffee from brazil
20. coast of australia

Exercise 2 Proofreading a Paragraph for Correct Capitalization

Capitalize the words that should begin with a capital letter in the following paragraph. Do not include the words already capitalized. If a sentence is already correct, write *C*.

EXAMPLE **[1]** Until last year I'd never been farther from lawrenceburg, tennessee, than pulaski, which is only seventeen miles east.

1. *Lawrenceburg; Tennessee; Pulaski*

[1] Naturally, I was excited when our choir decided to have an international arts and crafts fair to raise money for a trip to washington, d.c. [2] Colleen O'Roark suggested that the fair feature crafts and food from countries in europe, africa, and asia. [3] Juana Santiago, whose family is from venezuela, pointed out that we should also include items from central america and south america. [4] Julian Moore, who is from Monrovia, said he'd bring a display of Liberian baskets. [5] Karen Cohen offered items from quebec, one of our neighbors to the north. [6] Maxine Hirano, who was born in tokyo, japan, promised to demonstrate paper folding. [7] Some of us met later at Paula Bowen's house, on the northeast corner of columbus street and

hickory lane, to choose items to represent the united states. [8] We selected American Indian artifacts from the southwest, country crafts from the appalachian mountains, and shell gifts from the states along the gulf of mexico. [9] Erin McCall, whose family moved to lexington avenue from phoenix, arizona, volunteered to bring rocks that she had bought at a gift shop in petrified forest national park. [10] When the fair was over, we had raised enough money to include on our trip to the nation's capital a tour of mammoth cave national park in kentucky.

(4) Capitalize the names of organizations, teams, institutions, and government bodies.

Type of Name	Examples
Organizations	American Medical Association National Honor Society League of Women Voters Organization of American States
Teams	Eastside Jets Harlem Globetrotters New York Rangers Portsmouth Chess Masters
Institutions	Good Samaritan Hospital Ridgemont High School Stanford University
Government Bodies	Department of the Interior Tampa City Council the Nuclear Regulatory Commission

NOTE Do not capitalize words such as *democratic, republican,* and *socialist* when they refer to principles or forms of government. Capitalize these words only when they refer to specific political parties.

EXAMPLES Voting is part of the **d**emocratic process.

Was George W. Bush the **R**epublican nominee?

(5) Capitalize the names of businesses and brand names of business products.

Type of Name	Examples	
Businesses	Thrifty Dry Cleaners Sears, Roebuck and Co.	First National Bank Fields Department Store
Business Products	Schwinn Mesa GMC Jimmy	Callaway Big Bertha Apple Macintosh

| STYLE TIP |

The word *party* in the name of a political party may be capitalized or not; either way is correct.

EXAMPLE
Republican **P**arty
or
Republican **p**arty

Within a piece of writing, be consistent about using a capital or lowercase letter to begin the word *party*.

MECHANICS

NOTE A common noun that follows a brand name and identifies the type of product is not capitalized.

EXAMPLES Schwinn **b**icycle, Callaway **g**olf **c**lub, Apple **c**omputer

(6) Capitalize the names of buildings and other structures.

┌HELP─
Do not capita-
lize words like *hotel,*
theater, college, or *high*
school unless they are part
of a proper name.

EXAMPLES
a local **h**igh **s**chool

Jackson **H**igh **S**chool

Type of Name	Examples	
Buildings and Other Structures	Detroit Westin Hotel	Mosque of Omar
	Fox Theater	Buckingham Palace
	Colosseum	San Roque Dam
	Washington Mutual Tower	Queens-Midtown Tunnel
	Natchez Trace Parkway Bridge	Metropolitan Museum

(7) Capitalize the names of monuments, memorials, and awards.

Type of Name	Examples
Monuments, Memorials, and Awards	Dinosaur National Monument
	Korean War Veterans Memorial
	Effigy Mounds National Monument
	Nobel Prize
	Perry's Victory and International Peace Memorial
	Heisman Trophy

Do not capitalize a word such as *building, monument,* or *award* unless it is part of a proper noun.

(8) Capitalize the names of historical events and periods, special events, and holidays and other calendar items.

Type of Name	Examples	
Historical Events and Periods	the Battle of Gettysburg	the Dark Ages
	the Yalta Conference	Great Depression
	Children's Crusade	the Stone Age

Type of Name	Examples	
Special Events	the **B**oston **M**arathon the **N**ational **M**inority **J**ob **E**xpo	the **A**ll-**S**tar **G**ame the **I**owa **S**tate **F**air **S**pecial **O**lympics
Holidays and Other Calendar Items	**V**alentine's **D**ay **E**arth **D**ay **C**inco de **M**ayo	**F**riday **M**arch **K**wanzaa

NOTE Do not capitalize the name of a season unless the season is being personified or is part of a proper name.

EXAMPLES We looked forward to **s**pring after the long **w**inter.

Autumn in her russet garb followed green **S**ummer.

Are you going to the **W**inter Wonderland Dance?

Exercise 3 Identifying and Correcting Errors in Capitalization

Correct the capitalization errors in each of the following sentences by capitalizing letters as needed.

EXAMPLE 1. Some Norse folk tales originated in the Dark ages.

1. *Ages*

1. Dr. Fields applied to his local branch of the American medical association.
2. Gary works in the afternoons at Ridgeway discount appliance mart.
3. The house of Representatives passed the bills, but they died in the senate.
4. One of Lena's ancestors was at the battle of the Argonne.
5. Did you say you were planning to run in the Boston marathon?
6. Thanksgiving day always falls on the fourth Thursday in november.
7. When it was completed in 1973, the Sears tower in Chicago was the tallest building in the world.
8. Aaron couldn't decide whether to cheer for his hometown team, the Wisconsin badgers, or his new favorite, the Texas longhorns.
9. Her ambition is to win a pulitzer Prize someday.
10. The library's new Apple macintosh is scheduled to be delivered next week.

STYLE **TIP**

The words *black* and *white* may or may not be capitalized when they refer to races. Either way is correct. Within a piece of writing, be consistent in using capital or lowercase letters to begin those words.

STYLE **TIP**

Some writers capitalize all pronouns that refer to a specific deity. Other writers capitalize such pronouns only to prevent confusion.

EXAMPLE
Job wondered why the Lord allowed **H**is servant to suffer. [Capitalizing *His* makes it clear that the pronoun refers to *the Lord* and not to *Job*.]

Reference Note

For information on using italics with **names of ships, trains, aircraft, and spacecraft,** see page 339.

(9) Capitalize the names of nationalities, races, and peoples.

Type of Name	Examples		
Nationalities, Races, and Peoples	**I**talian **A**frican **N**avajo	**C**anadian **J**ewish **M**icronesian	**C**aucasian **H**ispanic **I**ndo-**I**ranian

(10) Capitalize the names of religions and their followers, holy days and celebrations, sacred writings, and specific deities.

Type of Name	Examples	
Religions and Followers	**J**udaism **B**uddhism **C**hristianity	**M**uslim **C**onfucian **M**ormon
Holy Days and Celebrations	**A**sh **W**ednesday **R**amadan **Y**om **K**ippur	**H**anukkah **C**hristmas **E**ve **P**entecost
Holy Writings	the **B**ible the **T**almud the **K**oran	**R**ig-**V**eda **E**xodus **D**ead **S**ea **S**crolls
Specific Deities	**A**llah **G**od	**V**ishnu the **H**oly **S**pirit

NOTE The words *god* and *goddess* are not capitalized when they refer to the deities of ancient mythology. The names of specific mythological deities are capitalized, however.

EXAMPLE   The Roman **g**oddess of grain was **C**eres.

(11) Capitalize the names of ships, trains, aircraft, and spacecraft.

Type of Name	Examples	
Ships, Trains, Aircraft, and Spacecraft	*Queen **M**ary* *R.M.S. **T**itanic* *Lake **S**hore Limited* *Electra*	*Spirit of **S**t. Louis* *Orient **E**xpress* *Enterprise* *Atlantis*

NOTE The names of the make and model of a vehicle also are capitalized.

EXAMPLES   **M**itsubishi **E**clipse [car]

Kris **K**raft [boat]

(12) Capitalize the names of planets, stars, constellations, and other heavenly bodies.

EXAMPLES   **P**luto [planet]   **P**ollux [star]

Andromeda Galaxy [galaxy]   **U**rsa **M**ajor [constellation]

Great **N**ebula [nebula]   **T**itan [moon]

NOTE The word *earth* is not capitalized unless it is used along with the name of another heavenly body that is capitalized. The words *sun* and *moon* are generally not capitalized.

EXAMPLES   Unlike **E**arth, neither **M**ercury nor **V**enus has a **m**oon.

The **s**un is a star.

The **m**oon is the **e**arth's only natural satellite.

10e. Do not capitalize the names of school subjects, except course names followed by a number and the names of language classes.

Type of Name	Examples		
School Subjects	**a**lgebra	**c**hemistry	**m**usic
	Algebra II	**C**hemistry I	**M**usic 101
	Latin	German	**M**andarin
	English	**S**panish	**D**utch

NOTE Do not capitalize the class name *freshman, sophomore, junior,* or *senior* unless it is part of a proper noun.

EXAMPLES   A number of **s**ophomores attended this spring's **J**unior **P**rom.

The **S**ophomore **S**ingers performed for the **f**reshmen.

TIPS & TRICKS

Generally, a singular noun identified by a number or letter is capitalized.

EXAMPLES
Room 13   Figure C
Chapter 21   Example D
Channel 32   **S**uite 4A

However, the word *page* is usually not capitalized, nor is a plural noun followed by two or more numbers or letters.

EXAMPLE
Look at **c**harts A and B on **p**age 273.

MECHANICS

Using Capital Letters Correctly   **277**

Identify the words that should be capitalized in each of the following sentences. Do not include words that are already capitalized.

EXAMPLE 1. The spanish explorer juan ponce de león landed in florida in 1513.

  1. *Spanish; Juan Ponce de León; Florida*

1. The area now known as florida was originally inhabited by native american peoples, including the apalachees, the creeks, and the seminoles.

2. The state is bounded on the north by alabama and georgia, on the east by the atlantic ocean, on the south by the straits of florida and the gulf of mexico, and on the west by alabama and the gulf of mexico.

3. The spanish founded st. augustine, the state's first permanent european settlement, in 1565, making it the oldest colonial city in the united states.

4. When spain ceded florida to the united states in 1821, the u.s. government demanded that the native peoples move west.

5. The strength and dignity of the seminole leader osceola, who led his people in the fight to retain their lands, are evident in this 1838 painting by george catlin.

6. Most of the seminoles eventually moved to present-day oklahoma, but a few hundred fled to the everglades, a huge wilderness area in southern florida that now includes everglades national park.

7. Founded in 1886, eatonville, florida, is the oldest incorporated african american town in the united states.

8. After the cuban revolution in the late 1950s, and again in the early 1980s, many cubans fled to miami.

9. Miami has also served as a major point of entry for haitian refugees who have braved the atlantic ocean in search of a better life.

10. Among the asians who have settled in the state are refugees from vietnam, many of whom make their living fishing along the northern coast of florida.

Osceola by George Catlin. Courtesy of the Department of Library Services. American Museum of National History.

Proofreading Paragraphs for Correct Capitalization

Identify the words that should be capitalized in each sentence in the following paragraphs. Do not include words that are already capitalized.

EXAMPLES **[1]** Trivia games test your knowledge of subjects as diverse as american inventors, the korean war, and popular music.

1. *American, Korean War*

[2] my parents have played trivia games against my brother and me since we moved to cleveland four years ago.

2. *My, Cleveland*

[1] Last saturday, may 18, my brother Ted and i finally won our first trivia match against our parents. [2] Some of the courses Ted is taking this semester are history, political science, and french; mine include world literature I and geography II. [3] We surged into the lead when our parents couldn't remember that the first united states satellite, *explorer I,* followed the soviet union's *sputnik I* into space. [4] From my geography class, I remembered that mount McKinley is the highest point and death valley is the lowest point on the north american continent.

[5] Our parents rallied for the lead by knowing that the boy on the cracker jack® box is named jack and that his dog's name is bingo. [6] Then Ted came up with the fact that the steel framework of the statue of liberty was designed by the frenchman alexandre gustave eiffel, who also designed the eiffel tower in paris. [7] None of us knew that john wilkes booth was only twenty-six years old when he shot abraham lincoln at ford's theater on good friday in 1865. [8] Mom, who has always been a loyal democrat, knew that *engine 1401*—the southern railways locomotive that carried franklin d. roosevelt's body from warm springs, georgia, to washington, D.C.—can now be seen in the smithsonian institution.

[9] Ted and I lost several points because I didn't know that kleenex® tissues were first used as gas-mask filters during world war I. [10] However, Ted won the game for us by remembering that the white house was called the executive mansion before it was burned by the british during the war of 1812.

Reference Note

For more information about **capitalizing and punctuating abbreviations,** see page 284.

see page 284.

| S T Y L E | | T I P |

For special emphasis or clarity, writers sometimes capitalize a title used alone or following a person's name.

EXAMPLES
The **G**overnor firmly stated her opinion on the issue.

Her predecessor called the new **P**rincipal **C**hief "the best person for the job."

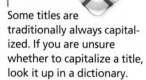

┌HELP──

Some titles are traditionally always capitalized. If you are unsure whether to capitalize a title, look it up in a dictionary.

10f. Capitalize titles.

(1) Capitalize a person's title when the title comes before the person's name.

Type of Name	Examples	
Titles	**G**eneral Powell	**D**r. Sakamoto
	President Kennedy	**M**arshal Foch
	Queen Margrethe	**A**rchbishop Tutu

Generally, a title used alone or following a person's name is not capitalized, especially if the title is preceded by *a* or *the.*

EXAMPLES In 1991, Boris Yeltsin became the first freely elected **p**resident of the Russian Federation.

Who was the U.S. **p**resident during World War II?

Christine Todd Whitman served as **g**overnor of New Jersey in the 1990s.

A title used alone in direct address is generally capitalized.

EXAMPLES Well, **M**ayor, will you please test the microphone?

Do you intend to visit the disaster area, **G**overnor?

Please be seated, **S**ir [*or* sir].

(2) Capitalize a word showing family relationship when the word is used before or in place of a person's name, unless the word follows a possessive noun or pronoun.

EXAMPLES **A**unt Edith   **U**ncle Fred   **G**randmother Bechtel

my **a**unt Edith   your **u**ncle Fred   Maria's **g**randmother

(3) Capitalize the first and last words and all other important words in titles and subtitles.

Unimportant words in a title include

- articles: *a, an, the*
- coordinating conjunctions: *and, but, for, nor, or, so,* and *yet*
- short prepositions (fewer than five letters): *of, to, in, for, from, with*

NOTE Capitalize an article (*a, an,* or *the*) at the beginning of a title or subtitle only if it is the first word of the official title or subtitle.

EXAMPLES Last summer, Joan read *The Outsiders* and *Harriet Beecher Stowe: A Life.*

Joan reads both *The Atlantic Monthly* and **t**he *Rocky Mountain News.*

Type of Title	Examples
Books	*Songs of the Tewa* *Silent Dancing: A Partial Remembrance of Puerto Rican Childhood*
Chapters and Other Parts of Books	"The Philippines: Its Land and Resources" "Index of Literary Skills: A Writer's Guide"
Periodicals	*U.S. News & World Report* *Chicago Sun-Times*
Poems	"Love Without Love" "I Like to See It Lap the Miles"
Short Stories	"The Man to Send Rain Clouds" "The Woman Who Had No Eye for Small Details"
Plays	*A Raisin in the Sun* *Sunday in the Park with George*
Historical Documents	Treaty of Versailles Articles of Confederation
Movies	*Antz* *Ever After* *The Parent Trap* *The Prince of Egypt*
Radio and TV Programs	*War of the Worlds* *Face the Nation* *Hercules: The Legendary Journeys*
Works of Art	*Crossing the Brook* *Two Mexican Women and Child*

(continued)

┌ **HELP** ─

The official title of a book is found on its title page. The official title of a newspaper or other periodical is found on its masthead, which usually appears on the editorial page or the table of contents.

Reference Note

For information about which **titles** should be **italicized** and which should be in **quotation marks,** see pages 338 and 345.

Type of Title	Examples	
Musical Works	"Blue Moon" *Amahl and the Night Visitors*	
Albums and CDs	*Echoes of Time and the River* *In Memory of a Summer Day*	
Videos and Video Games	*Pocahontas II: Journey to a New World* *Fast Break*	
Comic Strips	*Calvin and Hobbes* *Cathy*	*Dilbert* *Jump Start*

Review C Correcting Capitalization Errors

Most of the following sentences contain errors in capitalization. Write the correct form of each word that contains an error. If the capitalization of a sentence is already correct, write *C*.

EXAMPLE
1. In 1995, a. leon higgenbotham, the jurist and civil rights advocate, was awarded the presidential medal of freedom.

1. *A. Leon Higgenbotham, Presidential Medal, Freedom*

1. At the hirshhorn museum in washington, d.c., Millicent and James saw one of georgia o'keeffe's finest paintings, *cow's skull: red, white and blue.*

2. In *people* magazine, Kim read about bill cosby's earlier television series *the cosby show.*

3. When I visited grandma Sánchez at white sparrow Hospital, I read to her from jimmy santiago baca's *martín & meditations on the south valley.*

4. In 1908, mary baker eddy founded the *christian science monitor.*

5. My cousin Judy's favorite statue is *indian hunter* by paul manship.

6. I enjoyed reading annie dillard's *pilgrim at tinker creek,* particularly the chapter "the horns of the altar."

7. The prize-winning journalist carl t. rowan was the first african american to serve on the National Security council.

8. The president addressed the american people in a television news broadcast after he had met with the president of France.

9. Well, Governor, will Mayor Johnson and the county commissioners attend the groundbreaking ceremony for the new hospital?

10. Jane White, the president of the latin club, showed us a videotape of *julius caesar*.

Review D **Proofreading Paragraphs for Correct Capitalization**

The sentences in the following paragraphs contain errors in capitalization. Write the correct form of each incorrect word.

EXAMPLE **[1]** The energetic personality of montana's former state senator from the Fiftieth District is obvious in the Painting by Christopher Magadini below.

1. *Montana's, painting*

[1] Bill Yellowtail, jr., the first member of the crow people to serve in the Montana State Senate, represented an area hit hard by drought and a decline in the demand for beef. [2] Yellowtail, a democrat, ran for office to help save the Area's remaining small family farms and ranches. [3] A Rancher himself, he raises cattle in the Lodge Grass valley in Southeastern Montana with his Mother, his brother, and his sister.

[4] Yellowtail supplements his income from ranching by outfitting fly-fishing trips on the Bighorn river. [5] In addition, he works as a Tour Guide on the Crow reservation and at the Custer battlefield national monument. [6] He has also served as a consultant for the Montana-wyoming Agriculture-Tourist Project, which is helping ranchers develop tourism as an industry; as a member of the Board of Directors of the Nature Conservancy; and as the director of the Environmental protection agency.

[7] After graduating from Lodge Grass high school at the head of his class, Yellowtail attended dartmouth College in hanover, New Hampshire. [8] Although Dartmouth was founded to educate american Indians, Yellowtail was the first american indian to enroll there in twenty years. [9] At first he was unprepared academically, but by the time he Graduated in 1971, he was on the dean's list. [10] Regarding his major subject, Geography, Yellowtail said, "the relationship between humanity and the environment is little understood; it's a Discipline we very much need today."

Abbreviations

10g. Generally, abbreviations are capitalized if the words that they stand for are capitalized.

An *abbreviation* is a shortened form of a word or word group.

EXAMPLE   The **G**en. Science I [General Science I] classes will be going to the planetarium on **F**ri. [Friday], **D**ec. [December] 15.

Abbreviations of most proper nouns and of titles used along with proper nouns are capitalized.

(1) Capitalize abbreviations that come before or after names of persons, such as *Mr., Mrs., Ms., Dr., Gen., Ph.D., Jr.,* and *Sr.*

EXAMPLES   **M**s. Christina O'Reilly   **G**en. Marcus Whitman

John H. Glenn, **J**r.   Sharon Roberts, **Ph.D.**

(2) Capitalize abbreviations of geographical names.

EXAMPLES   **M**t. **S**t. **H**elens   Madera **C**o.   **T**ex.

Ozark **M**ts.   Bahama **I**s.   **F**la.

> **NOTE**   A two-letter state code without periods is used when the abbreviation is followed by a ZIP Code. Each letter of the abbreviation is capitalized.
>
> EXAMPLE   Atlanta, **GA** 30328-1647

(3) In addresses, capitalize abbreviations such as *St., Ave., Dr., Rd., P.O., Rm.,* and *Apt.*

EXAMPLES   531 Guadalupe **A**ve.   **P.O.** Box 1628

2414 Grand **S**t.   33 Hillside **D**r., **A**pt. 17A

Witte Hall, **R**m. 1018   658 Culver **C**t.

(4) Capitalize abbreviations of the names of organizations, government bodies, and businesses.

EXAMPLES   American Dental **A**ssn.   **U.S. D**ept. of Transportation

Motorola, **I**nc.   Digital Equipment **C**orp.

Reference Note

For information on **punctuating abbreviations** that come before or after names in sentences, see page 294.

STYLE   TIP

Only a few abbreviations are appropriate in the regular text of a formal paper written for a general audience. In tables, notes, and bibliographies, abbreviations are used more freely in order to save space.

MECHANICS

Some proper nouns are often abbreviated to a series of capital letters without periods.

National Aeronautics and Space Administration	**NASA**
Federal Communications Commission	**FCC**
General Motors	**GM**
Brigham Young University	**BYU**
Public Broadcasting Service	**PBS**

Some common nouns, too, are abbreviated to a series of capital letters without periods.

STYLE TIP

As you can see in the examples to the left, many common abbreviations are capitalized though the spelled-out words are not.

personal computer	**PC**	television	**TV**
chief executive officer	**CEO**	vice president	**VP**
central processing unit	**CPU**	deoxyribonucleic acid	**DNA**
frequency modulation	**FM**	videocassette recorder	**VCR**

However, the abbreviations of most common nouns, with or without periods, are not capitalized.

pages	**pp.**	pound	**lb**
lines	**ll**	tablespoon	**tbsp**
transitive verb	**vt.**	centimeter	**cm**
abbreviation	**abbr.**	kilogram	**kg**
inch(es)	**in.**	miles per hour	**mph**

NOTE The abbreviations of most units of measurement do not include periods. To prevent confusion with the word *in,* however, writers should include a period in the abbreviation of *inch* or *inches* (*in.*).

Exercise 4 Correctly Capitalizing Abbreviations

For the following word groups, correct any errors in the capitalization of abbreviations. If a word group is already correct, write *C.*

EXAMPLE **1.** to get his teeth cleaned by dr. Larson

        1. Dr.

1. 330 Farley rd.
2. two sources written by Herbert Hunter, ph.d.
3. 2904 Spring st., apt. 1501
4. that Widgets, inc., is hiring summer help

HELP

If you are not sure how to capitalize or punctuate an abbreviation, look it up in a dictionary.

MECHANICS

5. because ms. Lynch will be the interim ceo
6. visiting Tulsa, okla.; Wichita, kans.; and Omaha, neb.
7. the guest speaker maj. Felicia Payne
8. writing your research paper on a PC
9. ability to lift 50 lbs
10. sending entries to p.o. box 1770, San Antonio, Tx 78297-1770
11. the educational tape from Nasa that is stuck in the vcr
12. said mr. Wills wrote a book about st. Augustine
13. to contact dr. Tuomala by writing to rm. 302, 1403 Washtenaw ave., Ann Arbor, mi 48014-3177
14. reaching a speed of 250 MPH
15. the CPU in your new computer
16. a convention in ft. Worth, Texas
17. 1 Tbsp of oregano
18. Brian Donovan, Jr.
19. the film school at ucla
20. the u.s. dept. of the Treasury

PEANUTS reprinted by permission of United Feature Syndicate, Inc.

Chapter Review

A. Using Capitalization Correctly

For each of the following sentences, identify the word or words containing an error in capitalization and correct each error. If a sentence is already correct, write *C*.

1. This year my easiest classes are geometry, spanish, and American history.
2. Mexico city is built on the site of tenochtitlán, the aztec capital.
3. We rent DVDs from the Grand Media company.
4. Colorado is located West of the Great Plains.
5. Lansing, Michigan, is in Ingham county.
6. She lives at 321 Maple boulevard, which is south of here.
7. My RCA Stereo is ten years old and still works well.
8. Maggie entered her poodle in the San Marcos Dog club's show.
9. They live half a block north of Twenty-first Street.
10. Our neighbors are alumni of Howard university in Washington, d.c.
11. Last Spring my stepsister Lisa joined the National Audubon society.
12. While we were in San Juan, puerto rico, we toured El Morro Castle.
13. The club members celebrated Bastille Day by having dinner at a French restaurant.
14. Has Ms. Davis written to the U.S. department of Agriculture for information on soybean cultivation in the Midwest?
15. Mars was the Roman God of war.
16. We're holding a car wash next Saturday to raise money for the Habans high school fall festival.
17. The Islands that make up the west indies separate the Atlantic ocean from the gulf of mexico and the Caribbean sea.
18. Would you like to be the first student to ride in a Spaceship to another planet?
19. The post–Civil war period known as reconstruction officially ended in 1877.
20. Erica wants to be secretary of the Shutterbug Club.

MECHANICS

B. Capitalizing Words in a Paragraph Correctly

For each sentence in the following paragraph, write correctly the words that should be capitalized or made lowercase. If a sentence is already correct, write *C*.

[**21**] Cartoons and Caricatures have been popular since at least the Eighteenth Century. [**22**] George cruikshank and William hogarth were two of the most famous cartoonists in england in the 1700s and 1800s. [**23**] In the early 1840s, the famous British satirical magazine *punch* was established. [**24**] *punch*, a weekly, ran a feature called *"punch's* cartoons," which became very popular. [**25**] However, the person who is sometimes considered the originator of modern cartooning was the french artist Honoré Daumier (1808–1879), who was once briefly imprisoned for creating a vicious caricature of king Louis-Philippe. [**26**] In the United States, Thomas nast gained Fame in 1874 by introducing the elephant into his cartoons as the symbol of the Republican party. [**27**] Nast also made the Donkey the symbol of the democratic party. [**28**] In the early twentieth century, other well-known american cartoonists included Charles Addams, peter arno, and James thurber. [**29**] More recently, Gary Larson, Scott Adams, and Garry Trudeau have been among the best-known U.S. cartoonists. [**30**] The next time you pick up the Comics page in your favorite paper, spare a thought for all the History behind those cartoons!

C. Using Capitalization Correctly

For each of the following items, write the entire word group, correcting the words that should be capitalized or made lowercase. If a word group is already correct, write *C*.

31. Forty-Second Street

32. cars from germany

33. interstate 35

34. hernandez high school

35. the Metropolitan museum of modern art

36. Thomas Jefferson State Park

37. african american artist

38. the *titanic*

39. andromeda galaxy

40. American History 101

D. Correcting Sentences by Capitalizing Words

Most of the following sentences contain errors in capitalization. Write the correct form of each word that contains an error. If the capitalization of a sentence is already correct, write *C*.

41. Mom and dad subscribe to *Newsweek* and *U.S. news & world report*.

42. Lucy enjoyed reading Mark Twain's *The Innocents Abroad* and has been asking for other Twain titles.

43. The speed of 100 MPH is roughly equivalent to 160 KPH (kilometers per hour).

44. Ramon is registered to take english, math II, and German.

45. Everyone was happy that Monday, columbus day, was a Holiday.

Writing Application
Writing a Guidebook

Using Capital Letters   You have been asked to write a guidebook for visitors to your town. Write an informative booklet that helps visitors take a brief walking or driving tour through your town. Be sure to capitalize the proper nouns you use.

Prewriting   List the sights you will include in your guidebook. (If you live in a large city, you may need to limit the tour to only one part of the city or to the city's main sights.) For information on the town's history, you may want to check the local library.

Writing   As you write your first draft, try to anticipate questions tourists may ask. You may want to make a map of your tour with the various sights labeled.

Revising   Have you included enough information about each sight, and is the information correct? Add, delete, change, or rearrange details as necessary to make your guidebook clearer and more interesting.

Publishing   Proofread your work carefully for errors in grammar, usage, and mechanics. Pay special attention to the correct use of capital letters. After sharing your guidebook with your classmates, you and they may want to compile a larger guidebook to give to students new to your city.

Punctuation
End Marks and Commas

Diagnostic Preview

A. Correcting Sentences by Adding Periods, Question Marks, Exclamation Points, and Commas

Rewrite the following sentences, adding periods, question marks, exclamation points, and commas where they are needed.

EXAMPLE   **1.** When is the bus coming or has it already left

          1. When is the bus coming, or has it already left?

1. On June 1 2000 I wrote to the Wisconsin Department of Development at 123 Washington Ave. Madison WI 53702-0645

2. Federico Peña the mayor of Denver Colorado from 1983 to 1991 was born in Laredo Texas in 1947.

3. Wow Bill what a great save you made on the last play of last night's game

4. Water transports nutrients throughout the body aids in digestion and helps regulate body temperature

5. I M Pei who was born in China has designed many buildings in the United States for example City Hall in Dallas Texas and the Government Center in Boston Massachusetts

6. The chief crops grown in Trinidad an island in the Caribbean are sugar coffee cocoa citrus fruits and bananas

7. Did you know that Diné College located in Tsaile Arizona was founded in 1968

8. If I finish my report if I do the laundry and if I promise to be home by eleven may I go to the concert

9. After I stayed up very late I was exhausted of course yet I couldn't fall asleep right away

10. Along with the letters and magazines in our mailbox last Wednesday we found a large heavy package addressed to Phyllis M Saunders M D

B. Correcting Paragraphs by Adding Periods, Question Marks, Exclamation Points, and Commas

Rewrite each sentence in the following paragraphs, adding periods, question marks, exclamation points, and commas where they are needed.

EXAMPLE
[1] As soon as I got home I called my best friend Stephanie to tell her about my vacation

1. *As soon as I got home, I called my best friend, Stephanie, to tell her about my vacation.*

[11] Stephanie have you ever visited Cody Wyoming [12] Well if you do visit be sure to stop by the Buffalo Bill Historical Center [13] Opened in 1927 in memory of William "Buffalo Bill" Cody an army scout who later had his own Wild West show the center is actually four museums in one [14] The Buffalo Bill Museum the Whitney Gallery of Western Art the Cody Firearms Museum and the Plains Indian Museum are all under one roof.

[15] All of the museums are interesting but the best one I believe is the Plains Indian Museum which has artifacts from American Indian cowhands settlers and roving artists [16] Of all the treasures in the museum's collections the highlight is an exhibit on Tatanka Iyotake better known as Sitting Bull the mighty Sioux warrior holy man chief and statesman [17] The exhibit includes a dozen drawings that Sitting Bull who was born about 1831 and died in 1890 made while he was a prisoner at Fort Randall an army post in the Dakota Territory [18] Depicting some of his many battlefield conquests the drawings reveal his talent for design and composition

[19] Other displays show weapons clothing and accessories of the Cheyenne Shoshone Crow Arapaho Blackfoot and Gros Ventre peoples [20] What a journey back through time the museum offers

End Marks

An *end mark*—a period, a question mark, or an exclamation point—is used to indicate the purpose of a sentence. A period is also used at the end of many abbreviations.

Reference Note

For more information on **classifying sentences according to purpose,** see page 57.

S T Y L E   T I P

In dialogue, a declarative or an interrogative sentence that expresses strong emotion may be followed by an exclamation point instead of a period or a question mark.

EXAMPLES
There you are!

Why are you always late!

11a. A statement (a declarative sentence) is followed by a period.

EXAMPLES   Barb needed a ride home.

Margaret Walker's poems celebrate the trials and triumphs of African Americans.

11b. A direct question (an interrogative sentence) is followed by a question mark.

EXAMPLES   What score did you get on the road test?

Weren't you nervous?

A direct question should be followed by a question mark even if the word order is like that of a declarative sentence.

EXAMPLES   You got what score on the road test?

You weren't nervous?

NOTE   Be sure to distinguish between a declarative sentence that contains an indirect question and an interrogative sentence, which asks a direct question.

INDIRECT QUESTION   She asked me who nominated him for class president. [declarative sentence]

DIRECT QUESTION   Who nominated him for class president? [interrogative sentence]

11c. An exclamation (an exclamatory sentence or a strong interjection) is followed by an exclamation point.

EXAMPLES   What an exciting game that was! [exclamatory sentence]

Oh, no! Not again! [strong interjection]

A mild interjection is generally followed by a comma.

EXAMPLES   Well, what do you think I should do?

Oh, I suppose that would be acceptable.

NOTE Instead of an exclamation point or a comma, another mark of punctuation—a period, a question mark, or a dash, for example—may be used after an interjection, depending on the meaning of the sentence.

EXAMPLES   "Hmm. That's a difficult question," responded Alina.

"Well? What's the answer?" Roberto inquired.

"Oh—no, that's not right," Salvador said, changing his mind.

11d. **A request or command (an imperative sentence) is followed by either a period or an exclamation point.**

Generally, a request or a mild command is followed by a period; a strong command is followed by an exclamation point.

EXAMPLES   Open the door, please. [request]

Open the door. [mild command]

Open the door right now! [strong command]

Exercise 1   Using End Marks

Rewrite the following sentences, adding or replacing end marks as needed. If a sentence is already correct, write *C*.

EXAMPLE   1. Ouch Please be more careful, Sarah

      1. *Ouch! Please be more careful, Sarah.*

1. Did you know that Teresa is moving to Hammond
2. Yikes A rattlesnake.
3. Alexander the Great was born more than two thousand years ago.
4. I read an article about chuckwallas?
5. "Wow. Great shot?"
6. Can you tell me the way to Prater Park!
7. Generally, the green chile is spicier than the red
8. St. Stephen's Cathedral is certainly a beautiful sight?
9. Did you know that Paul McCartney is actually Sir Paul.
10. Gloria wakes up early every day to go for a walk
11. Irene asked whether the student named most likely to succeed was Phil Assad?
12. Will you be able to meet us at the Bristol Hotel!
13. The master of ceremonies was Joel Bourgeois
14. The author Laura Ingalls Wilder was born in Wisconsin
15. When did the Harts move to San Marcos

Reference Note

For more information about **dashes,** see page 368. For more about **interjections,** see page 27.

STYLE   TIP

In dialogue, sometimes a command or request is expressed as if it were a question. The meaning, however, may be imperative, in which case a period or exclamation point is used.

EXAMPLES

May I have your full attention, please.

Will you pay attention!

STYLE   TIP

Sometimes (most often in dialogue), a writer will use more than one end mark to express (1) intense emotion or (2) a combination of emotions.

EXAMPLES

"I will never—and I mean never—ride a roller coaster again!!" Barbara exclaimed. [intense emotion]

"You said what?!" Alejandro shouted. [combination of curiosity and surprise]

Although acceptable in informal or creative writing, the use of double end punctuation should be avoided in formal writing.

MECHANICS

16. Have you ever heard the music of Theseus Flatow.

17. Ask Tonya whether Kennedy is one of her favorite presidents.

18. How exciting the first moonwalk must have been.

19. Did you know that some of the world's most venomous snakes are found in Australia!

20. Boy I'd love to be a veterinarian.

Abbreviations

An *abbreviation* is a shortened form of a word or phrase.

11e. **Many abbreviations are followed by a period.**

Personal Names

Abbreviate given names only if the person is most commonly known by the abbreviated form of the name.

EXAMPLES Louis **J.** Halle John **F.** Kennedy **W.E.B.** DuBois

     Ida **B.** Wells **M.F.K.** Fisher **M. C.** Escher

┌HELP─
Leave a space between two initials, but not between three or more.

EXAMPLES
P. D. James
J.R.R. Tolkien

Titles

You may abbreviate social titles whether used before the full name or before the last name alone.

EXAMPLES **Mr.** Xavier Jackson **Mrs.** Laval

     Dr. Beth Higgins **Sr.** (Señor) Guzman

You may abbreviate civil and military titles used before full names or before initials and last names. Spell them out before last names alone.

EXAMPLES **Sen.** John Glenn **Senator** Glenn

     Gen. Colin Powell **General** Powell

Abbreviate titles and academic degrees that follow proper names.

EXAMPLES Harry Connick, **Jr.** John **H.** Watson, **M.D.**

If a statement ends with an abbreviation, do not use an additional period as an end mark. However, do use a question mark or an exclamation point if one is needed.

EXAMPLES This is Patrick Lewis, Jr.

     Do you know Patrick Lewis, Jr.?

MECHANICS

NOTE Do not include the titles *Mr., Mrs., Ms.,* or *Dr.* when you use a professional title or degree after a name.

EXAMPLE **Dr.** Peter Neibergall *or* Peter Neibergall, **M.D.** [not *Dr. Peter Neibergall, M.D.*]

Agencies and Organizations

An ***acronym*** is a word formed from the first (or first few) letters of a series of words. Acronyms are written without periods. The abbreviations for many agencies and organizations are written as acronyms.

AMA, American Medical Association	USN, United States Navy
CIA, Central Intelligence Agency	UN, United Nations

After spelling out the first use of the names of agencies and organizations, abbreviate these names and other things commonly known by their acronyms.

EXAMPLE After the fall of the Berlin Wall in 1989, most Eastern European nations applied to join the **North Atlantic Treaty Organization,** their former enemy. Poland, Hungary, and the Czech Republic subsequently joined **NATO** in 1999.

Geographical Terms

In regular text, spell out names of states and other political units whether they stand alone or follow other geographical terms. Abbreviate them in tables, notes, and bibliographies.

TEXT Frank McCourt spent his early years in Brooklyn, New York, and Limerick, Ireland.

On our vacation to Canada, we visited Québec City, the capital of the Province of Québec.

TABLE
London, U.K.	Dublin, Ire.
Québec City, P.Q.	Oxnard, Calif.

FOOTNOTE ³The Public Library in New Castle, Del., has an entire collection of early Thomaston manuscripts.

BIBLIOGRAPHY *The Great Law of Peace and the Constitution of the*
ENTRY *United States of America.* Akwesasne, **N.Y.**: Tree of Peace, 1988.

STYLE TIP

Only a few abbreviations are appropriate in the regular text of a formal paper written for a general audience. In tables, notes, and bibliographies, abbreviations are used more freely in order to save space.

HELP

Look up an abbreviation in a dictionary if you are unsure whether it requires periods.

STYLE TIP

A few acronyms, such as *radar, laser,* and *sonar,* are now considered common nouns. They do not need to be spelled out on first use and are no longer capitalized. When you are unsure whether an acronym should be capitalized, look it up in an up-to-date dictionary.

STYLE TIP

Include the traditional abbreviation for the District of Columbia, *D.C.,* with the city name, *Washington,* to distinguish it from the state of Washington.

MECHANICS

In regular text, spell out every word in an address. Some words should be abbreviated in envelope addresses and may be abbreviated in tables and notes.

> **NOTE** Two-letter state abbreviations without periods are used only when the ZIP Code is included.
>
> EXAMPLE   Stilwell, **KS** 66085-8808

Time

Abbreviate the two most frequently used era designations, *A.D.* and *B.C.* The abbreviation *A.D.* stands for the Latin phrase *anno Domini*, which means "in the year of the Lord." It is used with dates in the Christian era. When used with a specific year number, *A.D.* precedes the number. When used with the name of a century, it follows the name. The abbreviation *B.C.*, which stands for "before Christ," is used for dates before the Christian era. It follows either a specific year number or the name of a century.

EXAMPLES   In **A.D.** 1452, the Ottoman Turks invaded Constantinople.

By the end of the first century **A.D.**, the Romans had conquered much of Europe.

Cleopatra was a Greek-speaking queen of Egypt in the first century **B.C.**

In regular text, spell out the names of months and days whether they appear alone or in dates. Both types of names may be abbreviated in tables, notes, and bibliographies.

TEXT   Our next meeting will take place on the last **Tuesday** in **October.**

TABLE   Tues. afternoon
Oct. 13, 2002

FOOTNOTE   "These authors first met on **Jan.** 16, 1887.

BIBLIOGRAPHY   Ibata, David. "Information Highway to the Future,"
ENTRY   *Chicago Tribune,* 17 **Nov.** 1992, final **ed.**, **sec.** 1:8.

Abbreviate the designations for the two halves of the day measured by clock time. The abbreviation *A.M.* stands for the Latin phrase *ante meridiem*, meaning "before noon." The abbreviation *P.M.* stands for

COMPUTER TIP

Publishers usually print time abbreviations as small capitals, like this: A.M. Your word processor may offer small capitals as a style option. If it does not, or if you are writing by hand, you may use either upper-case or lowercase letters for time abbreviations, as long as you are consistent in each piece of writing.

─HELP─

In your reading, you may come across the abbreviations *C.E.* and *B.C.E.* These abbreviations stand for *Common Era* and *Before Common Era.* They are used instead of *A.D.* and *B.C.,* respectively, and are used after the date.

EXAMPLES
752 **C.E.**

3000 **B.C.E.**

MECHANICS

post meridiem, meaning "after noon." Both abbreviations follow the numerals designating the specific time.

EXAMPLES   Andrew works five days a week from 8:00 **A.M.** until 5:00 **P.M.**

Units of Measurement

In regular text, spell out the names of units of measurement, whether they stand alone or follow a spelled-out number or a numeral. Such names may be abbreviated in tables and notes when they follow a numeral. Most such abbreviations are written without periods. However, do use a period after the abbreviation for *inch* (*in.*) to prevent confusion with the word *in.*

TEXT   The speed limit here is sixty **miles per hour** [not *mph*].
            The dorm room measured twenty **feet** [not *ft*] by fourteen.

TABLE

1 **tbsp** vinegar	75°**F**
6 **ft** 6 **in.**	5 **oz** cumin

Exercise 2 **Using Abbreviations**

Rewrite the following sentences, correcting errors in the use of abbreviations in formal writing.

EXAMPLE   1. I was born in Miami, FL.
             1. I was born in Miami, Florida.

1. A. Lincoln was president of the United States from 1861 to 1865 and led the Union during the Civil War.
2. The flight for Santiago departs today at 4:30 P.M. in the afternoon.
3. Charlemagne ruled as emperor of the Romans until 814 A.D.
4. Duluth, MN, and Superior, WI, are two principal United States ports on Lake Superior.
5. The parcel was addressed to Mrs. Clare on Newcome Street in Ashburton Falls, MA.
6. Alexander the Great was born in Macedonia in B.C. 356.
7. The final speaker of the evening was Lt. Holden.
8. Please chew with your mouth closed, J. R..
9. Did that happen in 47 B.C?
10. The dogs were tired, as they had been playing since 6:00 A.M. in the morning.

STYLE   TIP

Do not use *A.M.* or *P.M.* with numbers spelled out as words or as substitutes for the words *morning, afternoon,* or *evening.*

EXAMPLE

The festival will begin at 8:00 **P.M.** (or **eight o'clock in the evening**) Saturday [not *eight P.M. Saturday*].

Also, do not use the words *morning, afternoon,* or *evening* with numerals followed by *A.M.* or *P.M.*

EXAMPLE

The next train for Greenwich leaves at **1:30 P.M.** (or **one-thirty in the afternoon**) [not *1:30 P.M. in the afternoon*].

Review A Using Periods, Question Marks, and Exclamation Points

Insert periods, question marks, and exclamation points correctly in the following sentences. Use each type of end mark—period, question mark, and exclamation point—at least once.

EXAMPLE   1. Oh boy, it was a good thing we were friends?

           1. *Oh boy, it was a good thing we were friends!*

1. Hey, Jo, my cousin Liz and I went hiking near Denver, Colorado
2. We carried our backpacks and slept in tents along the way
3. Each afternoon, we would make a cup of cocoa
4. Halfway through our trip, I wondered where the other box of instant cocoa was
5. Liz appeared puzzled
6. Which of us was responsible for packing all the food items
7. She thought I was, and I thought she was
8. Luckily, we have always gotten along well
9. At the end of the trip, Liz reached into her pack to get a jacket
10. Instead of a jacket, there was the other box of cocoa

Commas

Items in a Series

11f. Use commas to separate items in a series.

EXAMPLES   The camp counselor distributed baseballs, bats, volleyballs, tennis rackets, and bandages. [words in a series]

            We have a government of the people, by the people, and for the people. [phrases in a series]

            I know I will pass the test if I take good notes, if I study hard, and if I get a good night's sleep. [clauses in a series]

When the last two items in a series are joined by *and, or,* or *nor,* the comma before the conjunction is sometimes omitted when the comma is not needed to make the meaning of the sentence clear.

CLEAR WITHOUT COMMA   The entertainers sang, danced and juggled.

NOT CLEAR WITHOUT COMMA	John, Sue and Marian went fishing. [Did John go fishing, or is he being addressed?]
CLEAR WITH COMMA	John, Sue, and Marian went fishing.

NOTE Words customarily used in pairs—such as *macaroni and cheese* and *law and order*—are set off as one item in a series.

EXAMPLE   We could order a sandwich, macaroni and cheese, or soup.

If all the items in a series are joined by *and, or,* or *nor,* do not use commas to separate them.

EXAMPLES   We ran **and** walked **and** even limped to the finish line.

He said that neither poverty **nor** discrimination **nor** discouragement prevented Derek Walcott from becoming an accomplished writer.

Independent clauses in a series are generally separated by semicolons. Short independent clauses, however, may be separated by commas.

EXAMPLES   We swam laps in the cool, refreshing pool; after that, we jogged around the lake; and we exercised with free weights, stationary bicycles, and rowing machines.

We swam, we jogged, and we exercised.

11g. Use commas to separate two or more adjectives preceding a noun.

EXAMPLE   I've had a long, hectic, tiring day.

When the last adjective in a series is thought of as part of the noun, the comma before the adjective is omitted.

EXAMPLES   I mailed the package at the main post office. [Together, *post* and *office* name a place.]

For lunch we had smooth, creamy broccoli soup. [Together, *broccoli* and *soup* name a thing.]

You can use two tests to determine whether an adjective and a noun form a unit.

TEST 1:   Insert the word *and* between the adjectives preceding the noun. If *and* fits sensibly between them, use a comma. In the first example above, *and* cannot be logically inserted: *main and post office*. In the second example, *and* sounds sensible between the first two adjectives (*smooth and creamy*) but not between the second and third adjectives (*creamy and broccoli*).

┌─ S T Y L E   ✏   T I P ─┐

For clarity, some writers prefer always to use the comma before the conjunction in a series. Follow your teacher's instructions on this point.

Reference Note

For more about using **semicolons,** see page 322.

MECHANICS

Reference Note

A word such as *post office* is called a **compound noun.** For more about **compound nouns,** see page 4.

TEST 2: Change the order of the adjectives. If the order of the adjectives can be reversed sensibly, use a comma. *Creamy, smooth broccoli soup* makes sense, but *broccoli creamy soup* and *post main office* do not.

NOTE If a word modifies one of the adjectives preceding the noun, the word is an adverb, not an adjective, and therefore should not be followed by a comma.

EXAMPLE Which of these neckties looks best with this **light** green shirt? [*Light* modifies the adjective *green,* not the noun *shirt.*]

Exercise 3 Correcting Sentences by Adding Commas

For each of the following sentences, write each word that should be followed by a comma, and then add the comma. If a sentence is already correct, write *C.*

EXAMPLE 1. The king wore a thick warm luxurious robe.
1. *thick, warm,*

1. One terrible summer when we were little, I had mumps you had measles and he had chickenpox.
2. The river overflowed again and filled our basement and drenched our neighbor's carpet.
3. Coriander cumin and saffron are three spices that are widely used in traditional Mexican cooking.
4. I took a flashlight a sleeping bag extra tennis shoes a rod and reel and a parka on our camping trip.
5. Magic Johnson Michael Jordan Larry Bird and Julius Erving have each received a Most Valuable Player award at least once for their achievements on the basketball court.
6. At the gymnastics meet, Les performed on the parallel bars the rings and the high bar.
7. With a quick powerful leap, the stunt double bounded over the burning balcony.
8. We looked in the sink on the floor and on Kim's clothing for her missing contact lens.
9. Have you read any of the novels by Jane Austen or the Brontë sisters or Virginia Woolf?
10. A little blond child in faded bluejeans emerged from the shrubbery to stare at the mail carrier.

Independent Clauses

11h. Use a comma before *and, but, for, nor, or, so,* or *yet* when the conjunction joins independent clauses.

EXAMPLES   Patrick brought the sandwiches**, and** Cindy brought the potato salad.

We got there on time**, but** Jeff and María were late.

> **NOTE** Always use a comma before *yet, so,* or *for* joining independent clauses. The comma is sometimes left out before *and, but, or,* or *nor* if the independent clauses are very short and the sentence will not be misunderstood without it.
>
> EXAMPLES   He was apprehensive**, yet** he was also excited.
>
> The bears failed to catch any salmon**, so** they went away.
>
> I applied for the job **and** I got it.

Do not confuse a compound sentence with a simple sentence that has a compound verb. Generally, a comma does not precede the conjunction joining the parts of a compound verb.

Reference Note

For more about **simple sentences and compound sentences,** see page 102. For more about **compound subjects and compound verbs,** see page 45.

COMPOUND SENTENCE	Han brought charcoal and lighter fluid**, but** she forgot matches. [two independent clauses]
SIMPLE SENTENCE	Han brought charcoal and lighter fluid **but** forgot matches. [one independent clause with a compound verb]

If the independent clauses contain commas, a semicolon may be required to separate them.

EXAMPLE   One of the cats had brown**,** black**,** and yellow spots**;** and the other**,** younger one was pure black.

Reference Note

For more about **semicolons,** see page 322.

Exercise 4 Correcting Sentences by Adding Commas

For each of the following sentences, write the word that should be followed by a comma, and add the comma after it. If a sentence is already correct, write *C*.

EXAMPLE   **1.** Uncle Phil carefully steered the boat through the narrow channel and Lynn began baiting the hooks.

    1. *channel,*

1. All students must arrive on time for no one will be admitted late.

2. The movie review complimented all the performers but the leading actress received the strongest praise.
3. A few rowdy spectators tried to grab the star so the bodyguards formed a ring around him.
4. The Japanese actors in Kabuki plays do not speak but they pantomime lines chanted by narrators on the stage.
5. Some people today work fewer hours than their grandparents did yet for many there never seem to be enough hours in a day.
6. The cost of living is rising for consumers pay higher prices than they did last year for gasoline and other products.
7. Our guide led and we followed closely.
8. Two groups of Hopi disagreed about how to run the town of Oraibi; they settled the matter with a tug of war and the losers moved away and founded the town of Hotevilla.
9. She did not like the story in the science fiction magazine nor did she enjoy the illustrations.
10. High school graduates may go on to college or may begin working immediately.

Nonessential Clauses and Phrases

11i. Use commas to set off nonessential subordinate clauses and nonessential participial phrases.

A **nonessential** (or **nonrestrictive**) subordinate clause or participial phrase contains information that is not necessary to the basic meaning of the sentence.

NONESSENTIAL CLAUSES	Emilia Ortiz, **who lives across the street from me,** won a scholarship to Stanford University.
	The capital of Massachusetts is Boston, **which is sometimes called the Athens of America.**
NONESSENTIAL PHRASES	Kelly, **waiting outside the stage door,** got the band leader's autograph.
	Born in Detroit, Robert Hayden was educated at the University of Michigan and later became a distinguished professor there.

The nonessential clause or phrase in each of the preceding examples can be left out without changing the main idea of the sentence.

TIPS & TRICKS

Generally, a subordinate clause or a participial phrase that modifies a proper noun is nonessential.

MECHANICS

EXAMPLES   Emilia Ortiz won a scholarship to Stanford University.

The capital of Massachusetts is Boston.

Kelly got the band leader's autograph.

Robert Hayden was educated at the University of Michigan and later became a distinguished professor there.

An *essential* (or *restrictive*) *subordinate clause* or *participial phrase* is not set off by commas because it contains information that is necessary to the meaning of the sentence.

ESSENTIAL CLAUSES	The sophomores **who made the Honor Roll** were listed in the school newspaper.
	Library books **that are lost or damaged** must be replaced.
ESSENTIAL PHRASES	Students **planning to try out for a role in the play** should sign up no later than Friday afternoon.
	Two poems **written by Lorna Dee Cervantes** are included in our literature book.

Notice how leaving out the essential clause or phrase affects the main idea of each of the examples above.

EXAMPLES   The sophomores were listed in the school newspaper. [Which sophomores?]

Library books must be replaced. [Which library books?]

Students should sign up no later than Friday afternoon. [Which students?]

Two poems are included in our literature book. [Which two poems?]

Some subordinate clauses and participial phrases may be either essential or nonessential. The presence or absence of commas tells the reader how the clause or phrase relates to the main idea of the sentence.

| NONESSENTIAL CLAUSE | Marla's sister**,** **who attends Stanford University,** sent her a sweatshirt. [Marla has only one sister. That sister sent the sweatshirt.] |
| ESSENTIAL CLAUSE | Marla's sister **who attends Stanford University** sent her a sweatshirt. [Marla has more than one sister. The one attending Stanford University sent the sweatshirt.] |

TIPS & **TRICKS**

Generally, a subordinate clause or a participial phrase that tells *which one(s)* of two or more is essential. Also, a subordinate clause beginning with *that* and modifying a noun or pronoun is generally essential.

Reference Note

For more about **subordinate clauses,** see page 91. For more about **participial phrases,** see page 71.

MECHANICS

NONESSENTIAL PHRASE	My former lab partner**, now living in Chicago,** visited me last week. [I have only one former lab partner. That person visited me last week.]
ESSENTIAL PHRASE	My former lab partner **now living in Chicago** visited me last week. [I have more than one former lab partner. The one living in Chicago visited me last week.]

Exercise 5 Correcting Sentences by Adding Commas

For each of the following sentences, write each word that should be followed by a comma and add the comma after it. If a sentence is already correct, write *C*.

EXAMPLE 1. Gigantic supermarkets which offer a stunning variety of goods and services developed from much smaller stores that first opened in the nineteenth century.

   1. *supermarkets, services,*

1. The stores that became the world's first self-serve supermarkets were designed by Clarence Saunders who was an innovative entrepreneur.
2. Saunders who lived in Memphis, Tennessee named his stores Piggly Wiggly.
3. Some say that he got the idea for the name when he saw a fat pig wiggling under a fence.

4. The first Piggly Wiggly store which opened in 1916 had only one long aisle.

5. Customers shopping there saw all the products before they came to the exit.

6. Noticing that people often had difficulty finding products Albert Gerrard opened his own grocery store.

7. All of the items that were for sale were arranged alphabetically.

8. The name that Gerrard selected for his store was Alpha-Beta.

9. George Hartford who founded the Great Atlantic & Pacific Tea Company in 1859 nicknamed his stores A&P.

10. Developed by Michael Cullen the model for today's huge supermarkets opened in an abandoned garage in New York in 1930.

Introductory Elements

11j. Use a comma after certain introductory elements.

(1) Use a comma to set off a mild exclamation such as *well, oh,* or *why* at the beginning of a sentence. Other introductory words such as *yes* and *no* are also set off by commas.

EXAMPLES   **Sure,** I'll go with you.

           Oh, look at that car!

           No, I haven't taken the exam yet.

(2) Use a comma after an introductory participle or participial phrase.

EXAMPLES   **Shivering,** the couple hurried into the warm lobby of the movie theater.

           Calling for a timeout, the referee blew his whistle and signaled.

           Exhausted after a three-mile swim, Diana emerged from the water.

Reference Note

For more information about correcting **misplaced and dangling modifiers,** see page 224.

NOTE When writing an introductory participial phrase, make sure that it modifies the subject in the sentence; otherwise, the phrase is a misplaced or dangling modifier.

MISPLACED	Swimming in the huge aquarium, visitors of all ages were fascinated by the rare species of tropical fish. [Were visitors swimming in the aquarium?]
REVISED	Swimming in the huge aquarium, the rare species of tropical fish fascinated visitors of all ages.
REVISED	Visitors of all ages were fascinated by the rare species of tropical fish swimming in the huge aquarium.
DANGLING	Looking through the magazine, a recipe for *fattoush,* a delicious Syrian bread salad, caught Chris's attention. [Was a recipe looking through the magazine?]
REVISED	Looking through the magazine, Chris spotted a recipe for *fattoush,* a delicious Syrian bread salad.

Reference Note

For more information about **prepositional phrases,** see page 65.

(3) Use a comma after an introductory prepositional phrase if the phrase is long or if two or more phrases appear together.

EXAMPLES   **During the long bus ride home,** we sang songs and told stories to amuse ourselves.

By the light of the harvest moon in September, we went on an old-fashioned hayride.

Reference Note

For more information about **parenthetical expressions,** see pages 311 and 368.

A single, short introductory prepositional phrase is not followed by a comma unless the sentence is awkward to read without one or unless the phrase is parenthetical.

EXAMPLES   In the book the writer develops a clever plot. [The sentence is clear without the comma.]

In the book, review pages 236–290. [Without the comma, *book review* could be read as a compound noun.]

In the book review, the critic praised the writer's clever plot. [Without the comma, *review* could be read as a verb.]

By the way, do you have a copy of the book? [The phrase is parenthetical.]

(4) Use a comma after an introductory adverb clause.

An introductory adverb clause may appear at the beginning of a sentence or before any independent clause in the sentence.

EXAMPLES   **When you've gone to this school for a while,** you'll know your way around, too.

The first game of the season is Friday; **after we claim our first victory,** we'll celebrate at Darcy's Deli.

NOTE   Generally, an adverb clause that comes at the end of a sentence is not preceded by a comma.

EXAMPLE   Wolfgang Amadeus Mozart composed his first opera **when he was twelve years old.**

Exercise 6) Correcting Sentences with Introductory Elements by Adding Commas

For each of the following sentences, write the word that should be followed by a comma and add the comma after it. If a sentence is already correct, write *C*.

EXAMPLE   1. Trying to reduce the amount of fat in their diets many Americans are eating less meat.

1. *diets,*

1. Yes for many people around the world, meat is not a daily food staple.
2. Serving as a main source of nutrition whole grains such as corn, oats, wheat, and rice feed millions.
3. In Mexico a favorite nutritious dish is a corn tortilla with beans.
4. Because the soybean is high in protein it has been a principal crop in Asian countries for more than five thousand years.
5. If you'd like more variety in your diet you may want to substitute unrefined whole grains for meat occasionally.
6. Offering healthful alternatives to meat whole grains contain nutrients such as vitamins, proteins, amino acids, and starches.
7. In the process of making spoilage-resistant products some food manufacturers refine whole grains.
8. Refined for commercial use the grains lose most of their food value because the nutritious outer hulls are stripped away.
9. If you take time in the supermarket you should be able to find whole grains.
10. Since many cookbooks now include recipes for grain dishes you can learn to use grains in many tasty snacks and meals.

MECHANICS

Review B Using Commas in a Paragraph

For the following sentences, write each word that should be followed by a comma. Then, add a comma after each word.

EXAMPLES
[1] Throughout the ages around the world people have used weapons for hunting for fighting, and for defending themselves from wild animals.

1. *world, hunting,*

[2] According to archaeologists weapons were among the earliest tools.

2. *archaeologists,*

[1] Many weapons that were produced in early times were similar in appearance function and design. [2] The English word *weapon* is related to the Old English *wæpen* the Dutch *wapen* the German *Waffe* and an earlier common root. [3] Sticks stones and natural poisons such as the toxic sweat of these Central and South American frogs were probably the first weapons. [4] Among those varieties of weapons the stick thrown by hand became one of the most heavily specialized. [5] As you can see the dart the arrow the spear the lance and the javelin were all developed from the stick thrown by hand. [6] Another kind of weapon, the sling, was used all over the world for it was easy to make and not too difficult to master. [7] According to the Biblical account, when the Hebrew king David was just a boy he killed the Philistine giant Goliath with a simple hand-made sling. [8] An unusual weapon similar to the sling is the bola which is a cord with heavy weights of stone or wood or metal at the ends. [9] In some parts of South America gauchos still use bolas which can entangle cattle without inflicting pain injury or death. [10] Over the centuries these simple weapons have been developed into highly sophisticated and deadly artillery such as the missiles used in modern warfare.

MEETING THE CHALLENGE

Write a one-page short story about any subject you like. In your short story include five sentences that use introductory phrases or clauses. Be sure to punctuate sentences correctly.

Interrupters

11k. Use commas to set off an expression that interrupts a sentence.

(1) Use commas to set off nonessential appositives and nonessential appositive phrases.

An *appositive* is a noun or pronoun placed beside another noun or pronoun to identify or describe it. An *appositive phrase* consists of an appositive and its modifiers.

EXAMPLES   A former senator from Kansas, **Nancy Landon Kassebaum,** was the principal speaker. [appositive]

Do you know him, **the boy wearing the blue shirt**? [appositive phrase]

A *nonessential* (or *nonrestrictive*) *appositive* or *appositive phrase* adds information that is unnecessary to the basic meaning of the sentence. In other words, the meaning of the sentence is clear and complete with or without the appositive or appositive phrase.

EXAMPLES   Have you read *At Home in India*, **a book by Cynthia Bowles**?

On July 20, 1969, Neil Armstrong, **one of the three astronauts on the Apollo 11 mission,** became the first person to walk on the moon.

Notice that the meaning of each of the examples above remains clear and complete without the appositive phrase.

EXAMPLES   Have you read *At Home in India*?

On July 20, 1969, Neil Armstrong became the first person to walk on the moon.

An *essential* (or *restrictive*) *appositive* or *appositive phrase* is not set off by commas because it adds information that makes the noun or pronoun it identifies or explains more specific. In other words, if you were to omit an essential appositive or appositive phrase, you would leave out key information or would change the intended meaning of the sentence.

EXAMPLES   My friend **James** helped me.

Speaking of movies, have you seen the animated film ***The Prince of Egypt***?

MECHANICS

┌ **TIPS** & **TRICKS** ┐

Generally, an appositive or appositive phrase that tells *which one(s)* of two or more is essential.

Reference Note

For more information about **appositives** and **appositive phrases,** see page 309.

Notice how omitting the appositive from each of the preceding examples changes the meaning of the sentence.

EXAMPLES   **My friend helped me.** [Which friend?]

Speaking of movies, have you seen the animated film? [Which animated film?]

> Exercise 7   **Correcting Sentences with Appositives and Appositive Phrases by Adding Commas**

Correctly punctuate the appositives and appositive phrases in the following sentences. If a sentence is already correct, write *C*.

EXAMPLE   1. Leonardo da Vinci an Italian Renaissance artist is perhaps best remembered for painting *Mona Lisa*.

1. *Leonardo da Vinci, an Italian Renaissance artist, is perhaps best remembered for painting* Mona Lisa.

1. Between 1500 and 1506, Leonardo da Vinci a brilliant man created several major works.
2. My favorite painting *Mona Lisa* was painted then.
3. Leonardo's painting *Mona Lisa* is a prized possession of the Louvre in Paris.
4. The painting a portrait of a young Florentine woman is slightly cracked as a result of temperature changes.
5. The *Mona Lisa* an ideal type of portrait revolutionized portrait painting.
6. Leonardo's work influenced the young painter Raphael.
7. Raphael's painting *The Grand Duke's Madonna* was done in the style of *Mona Lisa*.
8. In 1911 an Italian house painter Vincenzo Perugia stole the *Mona Lisa* from its frame.
9. For two years members of the Paris police some of the world's cleverest detectives were baffled by the crime.
10. Since its recovery, the painting one of the most valuable portraits in the world has been closely guarded.

Mona Lisa by Leonardo da Vinci.

(2) Use commas to set off words used in direct address.

EXAMPLES   **David,** please close the door.

Did you call me, **Mother**?

Yes, **Mr. Ramos,** I turned in my paper.

Reference Note

For information on **words of direct address,** see page 45.

MECHANICS

(3) Use commas to set off parenthetical expressions.

A *parenthetical expression* is a side remark that adds information or shows a relationship between ideas.

Common Parenthetical Expressions		
after all	however	nevertheless
at any rate	I believe	of course
consequently	in fact	on the contrary
for example	in the first place	on the other hand
for instance	meanwhile	that is
generally speaking	moreover	therefore

EXAMPLES   **In fact,** Emily Dickinson is my favorite poet.

You are, **I hope,** planning to arrive on time.

Sometimes such expressions are not used parenthetically and are not set off by commas.

PARENTHETICAL   Long-distance calls are a bargain, **at any rate**.
[meaning "in any case"]

NOT PARENTHETICAL   Long-distance calls are a bargain **at any rate**.
[meaning "at any cost"]

NOTE   A contrasting expression introduced by *not* is parenthetical and should be set off by commas.

EXAMPLE   Emily Brontë, **not her sister Charlotte,** wrote *Wuthering Heights.*

Review C **Correcting Paragraphs by Adding Commas**

For the following paragraphs, write each word that should be followed by a comma and add the comma after it.

EXAMPLE   **[1]** The artist Faith Ringgold painstakingly hand-letters her beautiful unique story quilts.

    1. *beautiful,*

[1] Continuing the ancient tradition of quilting Ringgold combines printed dyed and pieced fabric with acrylic paintings or photo etchings. [2] By placing the tradition in a new context the artist gives it new meaning.

Reference Note

Parentheses and **dashes** are sometimes used to set off parenthetical expressions. See page 368.

COMPUTER TIP

If you use a computer, you may want to create a file of the parenthetical expressions listed on this page. Refer to this file as you proofread your writing, and be sure that you have punctuated these expressions correctly. If your word-processing software has a search function, use the function to speed up your proofreading. The computer will search for and highlight each occurrence of whatever expression you select.

MECHANICS

Faith Ringgold, *Double Dutch on the Golden Gate Bridge* (1988). Acrylic, canvas, painted, dyed, pieced fabric (68½″ × 68″). © 1988 Faith Ringgold Inc. Private Collection.

[3] Ringgold whose earlier works include landscapes murals masks and soft sculptures began making story quilts in 1980. [4] Titled *Echoes of Harlem* the first one was a collaboration between the artist and her mother the dress designer Willi Posey who learned quilting from her own grandmother who had learned it from her own mother a slave.

[5] Most of Ringgold's story quilts are designed to be viewed as parts of a series not as separate pieces and many include portions of a narrative linking the works in the series. [6] The work pictured here *Double Dutch on the Golden Gate Bridge* has no accompanying text and is from the *Woman on a Bridge* series which includes five works. [7] Capturing the excitement of a childhood game it depicts a pastime cherished by generations of African Americans. [8] The work speaks however to more than a single culture and appeals to all people who recognize in it joyful moments from their childhoods.

[9] Ringgold still lives and works in Harlem the section of New York City where she was born. [10] Did you know Amy that one of her story quilts sold for $40,000 and is in the permanent collection of the city's Guggenheim Museum a major gallery of modern art?

Conventional Uses of Commas

11l. Use commas in certain conventional situations.

(1) Use commas to separate items in dates and addresses.

EXAMPLES On Saturday, June 21, 1999, Robert moved to Miami Beach, Florida, with his parents.

His new address is 814 Georgia Avenue, Miami Beach, FL 33139-0814.

Notice that a comma generally separates the last item in a date or an address from the words that follow it.

Do not use commas to set off the following items.

- the month from the day

EXAMPLE   My brother's birthday is **October 22.**

- the month from the year when the day is given before the month

EXAMPLE   Was the date of your graduation **20 May 2000**?

- the month from the year when no day is given

EXAMPLE   The hottest month on record here is **August 1996.**

- a house number from a street name

EXAMPLE   Ms. Lee lives at **531 Winchester Street.**

- a state abbreviation from a ZIP Code

EXAMPLE   Is the last part of your new address Richmond,
           VA 23235-4766?

- items preceded by prepositions

EXAMPLE   The McCaslins moved to 419 Cedar Avenue **in** Chicago **on**
           September 10 **of** 1998.

(2) Use a comma after the salutation of a personal letter and after the closing of any letter.

EXAMPLES   Dear Marcus,   Dear Aunt Meg,

           Affectionately yours,   Sincerely yours,

NOTE   Use a colon after the salutation of a business letter.

EXAMPLES   Dear Dr. Cho:

           To whom it may concern:

Reference Note

For more about **colons,**
see page 327.

(3) Use a comma to set off an abbreviation, such as *Jr., Sr.,* **or** *M.D.,* **that follows a person's name.**

Notice that when words follow a person's title, a comma appears both before and after the title.

EXAMPLES   Elena Moreno, **M.D.**

           Russell E. Davis, **Jr.,** has been elected mayor.

Unnecessary Commas

11m. Do not use unnecessary commas.

Too many commas can be as confusing as too few. Do not use a comma unless a rule requires one or unless the meaning would be unclear without it.

CONFUSING   On Friday, after school, my friend, Rita, and I played bad-minton at her house until her dog, Ruffles, a frisky, golden retriever, joined us and ran off with the shuttlecock, clenched in its teeth.

CLEAR   On Friday after school, my friend Rita and I played bad-minton at her house until her dog Ruffles, a frisky golden retriever, joined us and ran off with the shuttlecock clenched in its teeth.

Exercise 8   Correcting Sentences by Adding Commas

For the following sentences, write each word that should be followed by a comma and add the comma after it.

EXAMPLE   **1.** On our way to Birmingham Alabama we stayed overnight in Chattanooga Tennessee.

   1. Birmingham, Alabama, Chattanooga,

1. On August 1 1999 we moved from Eureka California to 220 Tuxford Place Thousand Oaks California.
2. We left Tampa Florida on Monday June 15 and arrived in Albuquerque New Mexico on June 17.
3. The hotel on Gulfport Road was destroyed by fire on Tuesday March 13 1984.
4. My brother received a letter that began, "Dear John There's something I've been meaning to tell you."
5. We interviewed Franklin R. Thomas M.D. at his emergency clinic on Wilson Road.
6. In two weeks Christa and Jerry will travel hundreds of miles to participate in a triathlon.
7. The party will take place October 9 at 2480 Hastings Road in Birmingham Alabama.
8. Raphael X. Gideon Sr. is our new police chief.
9. Marcia traveled to Tyler Texas and Orlando Florida last month.
10. Dr. Martin Luther King Jr. was born on January 15 1929.

Oral Practice Proofreading a Letter for Correct Comma Usage

Read aloud the following letter. Then, tell where commas should be added or deleted.

EXAMPLE **[1]** Uncle Victor lives in a small white house.

1. *small,*

[**1**] August 26 2009

[**2**] Dear Amy

[**3**] I received your letter, and wanted to send a quick reply answering your questions. [**4**] Uncle Victor does in fact have a new address; he and Aunt Margo moved to a faraway, beautiful land of sunshine. [**5**] Their new address is 1300 Fairwood Drive San Diego CA 99069. [**6**] They moved last month and Uncle Victor started his new job last Wednesday, morning. [**7**] They plan to be back in town to tie up loose ends by selling their house picking up their dogs and visiting with friends on Friday September 4. [**8**] I will have a few friends over for dinner that night, and hope you can come. [**9**] I will by the way be cooking my famous Greek dinner.

[**10**] Affectionately yours

Roy

Review D Revising Paragraphs by Adding Commas

For the sentences in the following paragraphs, write each word that should be followed by a comma and add the comma after it. If a sentence is already correct, write *C*.

EXAMPLE **[1]** In their study of the culture of the ancient Greeks the drama students read about the three playwrights Aeschylus Sophocles, and Aristophanes.

1. *Greeks, Aeschylus,*

┌HELP─

Some of the sentences in Review D need more than one comma.

[1] As early as the sixth century B.C. plays were performed in Athens Greece in the amphitheater pictured below the Theater of Dionysus. [2] The Theater of Dionysus is located on the south slope of the Acropolis an elevated fortified section of Athens. [3] The plays presented in ancient Greece marked the beginning of drama in the Western world. [4] In fact the English word *theater* comes from the Greek word *theatron* which means "a place for seeing."

[5] Wearing masks to show which characters they were portraying the actors in ancient dramas often played several different roles. [6] In addition all roles including those of female characters were performed by men.

[7] Although records show that Greek playwrights wrote hundreds of tragedies fewer than thirty-five of these plays survive. [8] The earliest Greek dramatist Aeschylus wrote the *Oresteia* a powerful story of murder revenge and divine mercy. [9] Sophocles often regarded as the greatest dramatist of all time is credited with writing more than one hundred plays. [10] Among the surviving works of Aristophanes whom the ancient Greeks considered the greatest comic playwright are the three satires *The Clouds The Wasps* and *The Frogs.*

Chapter Review

A. Using End Marks

Add or replace end marks in the following sentences, as needed.

1. Have you heard of the Bengali writer Rabindranath Tagore
2. Wow Look at that sunset
3. Last week I saw the cartoon version of *Alice in Wonderland*?
4. The first speaker was the Reverend James Elliot
5. Will you be in town next Friday!
6. Will you turn the radio down a little!
7. When was the impressive Swedish golfer Eric Estlund born.
8. "Oh, no" exclaimed Paul in dismay.
9. Musical backup was provided by the Hill Trio
10. What an absolutely marvelous exercise.

B. Correcting Sentences by Adding Punctuation

Add periods, question marks, exclamation points, and commas where they are needed in the following sentences. If a sentence is already punctuated correctly, write *C*.

11. Although scholars aren't certain about who was the first European printer to use movable type Johann Gutenberg is usually credited
12. The students who have signed up for the field trip may leave at noon but all the others must attend classes
13. Gloria did you notice where I left my bowling ball
14. Miriam Colón who was born in Puerto Rico founded the Puerto Rican Traveling Theatre
15. Was the Great Pyramid in Egypt built sometime between 2600 and 2500 B.C.?
16. Vendors sold T-shirts, buttons caps and pennants to the sports fans outside the stadium
17. Listening to the orchestra play "The Star-Spangled Banner" I realized that I'm proud to be American
18. The hikers munched on sunflower seeds and quenched their thirst with ice-cold refreshing spring water
19. Isn't their address 1042 Cleveland Avenue Enid OK 73703

MECHANICS

20. Marian Anderson a contralto was the first African American to become a permanent member of the Metropolitan Opera Company

21. Wow That's amazing

22. We rushed to the airport stood in line bought our tickets and then heard that the flight had been delayed for three hours

23. Norm has had quite a run of bad luck yet he still says tomorrow will be a better day for he prides himself on being an optimist

24. That Ming vase wrapped in cotton and packed in a crate was delivered to the museum earlier today

25. If we're late for practice again however Ms Stubbs will drop us from the team

26. How lucky I was

27. At the beginning of the eighteenth century Chikamatsu Monzaemon wrote the first Japanese tragedies to focus on the lives of common ordinary people

28. Nowadays the Sioux generally speaking make their living as farmers and ranchers

29. Jan Matzeliger an inventor in Lynn Massachusetts revolutionized the shoe industry in 1883 with his machine that joined the top of a shoe to its sole

30. These five students should report to the auditorium after lunch: Victoria Berlanga Jeff McKinley Mary Alice Shaw Kathryn Rogers and Henry Boylan Miles Jr

C. Correcting Paragraphs by Adding Punctuation

For each sentence in the following paragraph, add periods, question marks, exclamation points, and commas where they are needed.

[31] Going to visit Uncle Ricky is one of my greatest pleasures for he owns and operates a semitrailer [32] His big rig an eighteen-wheeler affectionately named "Pug" is used to haul produce from coast to coast [33] One of Uncle Ricky's craziest experiences was the time he left Boston and drove to 2842 Beltline Drive Logan Virginia to deliver a load of oranges grapefruit and lemons [34] When he arrived at the address he was dumbfounded [35] As a matter of fact

the address turned out to be that of a citrus orchard **[36]** Obviously, the orchard had been producing Logan's finest fruit for years **[37]** Climbing back on board "Pug" Uncle Ricky checked his shipping order **[38]** He realized with dismay that he should have delivered the shipment to Logan Vermont instead of Logan Virginia **[39]** Fortunately it was a clear run up a couple of interstates for "Pug" and Uncle Ricky delivered his fruit only half a day late **[40]** Now he chuckles about it and says wryly, "Well I did wonder how I had managed to arrive a whole day early"

Writing Application
Using Commas in Instructions

Using Commas Correctly   Create an educational board game or computer game, and write instructions explaining how to play it. Include information from at least one of your school subjects, such as math, science, or history. Use commas to make your instructions as clear as possible.

Prewriting   Choose a subject area that interests you. Then, decide what the object of the game will be. Jot down notes about the number of players, the kinds of supplies or equipment needed, and other rules of the game. Give your game a catchy title, and then arrange the instructions in an order that will be easy for players to follow.

Writing   Keep in mind that your instructions will be the players' only source of information. Try to anticipate their questions, and aim for a conversational tone, as if you were explaining the game in person.

Revising   Ask some of your friends to play the game. As you watch, note any problems they have with understanding the instructions. Then, add, delete, replace, or rearrange information to make the instructions easier to understand.

Publishing   Proofread your instructions, paying special attention to your use of end marks and commas. Use a computer to make a clean printout, or photocopy a neatly handwritten copy. You might offer copies of your game to your school's media center or to a community service organization.

12 Punctuation
Semicolons and Colons

Diagnostic Preview

Correcting Sentences by Adding Semicolons and Colons

For each of the following sentences, write the word or numeral that precedes each punctuation error. Then, add the semicolon or colon needed.

EXAMPLE   1. Please bring the following items books, pencils, and newspapers.

　　　　　　　1. *items:*

1. My aunt Pam loves to play backgammon and chess however, she rarely has time because she works at two jobs.
2. In 1904, Mary McLeod Bethune founded a school for girls in Daytona Beach, Florida that school is now Bethune-Cookman College.
3. Psalm 23 1–6 is one of the best-known passages in the Bible.
4. According to one book that I have read, *The Real McCoy The Life of an African-American Inventor,* an oil can used in railroad mainte-nance gave rise to the popular expression "the real McCoy."
5. If I had a million dollars, I would visit London, England Cairo, Egypt Buenos Aires, Argentina and Tokyo, Japan.
6. We have to write reports for gym class on one of the following athletes Jesse Owens, Sonja Henie, Jim Thorpe, Althea Gibson, or Babe Didrikson Zaharias.

7. Our neighbor's cocker spaniel barked all night long as a result, I did not sleep well.

8. Candace will have to take Sandra's place in tonight's performance unfortunately, Sandra sprained her ankle and cannot walk.

9. I have ridden bicycles, horses, and motorcycles and I have traveled in trains, buses, and planes.

10. Asia has both the highest and the lowest points on the earth's surface Mount Everest, the highest, soars 29,028 feet the Dead Sea, a salt lake, lies 1,300 feet below sea level.

11. Instructed to be prompt, we arrived at school at 7 15 A.M., but the doors were locked consequently, we had to wait until 7 30 A.M. to enter the building.

12. Indira Gandhi, who served for many years as the prime minister of India, grew up in the world of civic life, politics, and government for her father, Jawaharlal Nehru, was the first prime minister of India, from 1947 to 1964.

13. My friends Ruth and Cindy disagree about the role of fate in life Ruth believes that people can control their own destiny, but Cindy insists that people are simply pawns of fate.

14. I don't like to prepare outlines nevertheless, the highest grade I ever received was for a report that I wrote from an outline.

15. Mr. Kowalski has always regretted that he did not learn to speak Polish when he was a child now he is taking a conversational Polish class at the college.

16. The computer software business is an enormous, growing industry in fact, people can buy software that does everything from balancing budgets to plotting biorhythm charts.

17. Every morning Lonnie rises at 5 00, jogs until 5 30, showers, eats breakfast by 6 15, and catches the 6 35 bus.

18. Red Cloud, a leader of the Oglala Sioux, was a military genius he successfully defended Sioux lands against settlers who wanted to build a trail from Laramie, Wyoming, to Virginia City, Montana.

19. Gates of the Arctic National Park, which is located in northern Alaska, is well known for its large populations of certain animals caribou, grizzly bears, moose, and wolves.

20. If you want to send fragile items through the mail, the post office recommends that you do the following pack them in fiberboard containers use foam, plastic, or padding to cushion them and then seal the package carefully, reinforcing it with filament tape.

Semicolons

12a. Use a semicolon between independent clauses that are closely related in thought and that are not joined by *and, but, for, nor, or, so,* or *yet.*

EXAMPLES   Everyone else in my family excels in a particular sport; I seem to be the only exception.

        The river is rising rapidly; it is expected to crest by noon.

12b. Use a semicolon between independent clauses joined by a conjunctive adverb or a transitional expression.

EXAMPLES   Leonor is planning to become an engineer; **however,** she is also interested in graphic design.

        Only two people registered for the pottery lessons; **as a result,** the class was canceled.

Notice in the examples above that the conjunctive adverb and the transitional expression are each followed by a comma.

Commonly Used Conjunctive Adverbs

accordingly	furthermore	meanwhile	otherwise
also	however	moreover	still
besides	indeed	nevertheless	then
consequently	instead	next	therefore

Commonly Used Transitional Expressions

as a result	for instance	in fact	in spite of
for example	in conclusion	in other words	that is

NOTE When a conjunctive adverb or a transitional expression appears within one of the clauses instead of between the clauses, it is usually set off by commas. The two clauses may still be separated by a semicolon.

EXAMPLES   Ralph Ellison is best known for his 1952 novel, *Invisible Man;* he also, **however,** wrote short stories and essays.

        Not all birds migrate south for the winter; cardinals, **for instance,** can stay in northern climates year round.

Reference Note

For information on using a **comma** to **separate independent clauses that are joined by a coordinating conjunction,** see page 301.

Reference Note

For information about **conjunctive adverbs,** see page 90.

S T Y L E   T I P

Use a semicolon to join independent clauses only if the ideas in the clauses are closely related.

INCORRECT
Greg likes Italian food; Marla prefers going to the beach.

CORRECT
Greg likes Italian food; Marla prefers Chinese food.

MECHANICS

Using conjunctive adverbs and transitional expressions can help you clearly show relationships between ideas. Notice in the examples below how these expressions clarify the relationship between the ideas expressed in the clauses.

EXAMPLES   The class has finished the nonfiction unit**;** **therefore,** we will begin the poetry unit on Monday. [Two ideas have a cause-and-effect relationship.]

The poems will be discussed in class**;** **meanwhile,** we will be working on our research papers on our own time. [Two ideas have a time relationship.]

Most students are studying poets from the distant past**;** I**,** **however,** am researching the poetic devices of a modern songwriter. [Two ideas have a contradictory relationship.]

Exercise 1 **Correcting Sentences by Adding Commas and Semicolons**

For the following sentences, write each word that should be followed by a semicolon or a comma. Add the needed punctuation mark after the word.

EXAMPLE   1. The clever carving shown here was handmade in Mexico today carvings like this are sold all over the world.

1. *Mexico;*

1. The carvings come from the Oaxaca (pronounced wä•hä´•kä) Valley in fact 90 percent of the two hundred families who make them live in just three villages.
2. Carving has been a tradition among Oaxacans for hundreds of years only recently however have the artists sold their works outside the valley.
3. In many families, the fathers and older sons do the actual carving meanwhile the other family members sand and paint the figures.
4. The artists find inspiration for their creations in everyday life for example religion and nature are rich sources of ideas.
5. Even those carvers whose works have won worldwide acclaim have chosen to continue living in the valley their ties to their families and communities are very strong.

MECHANICS

6. Art in Mexico is varied and distinctive and it exhibits a strong Spanish influence.

7. The Zapotec and Mixtec peoples of Puebla and Oaxaca have a long history of artistic craftsmanship the Mixtec were considered master goldsmiths.

8. The Mixtec built a tremendous pyramid in Cholula it was the largest pyramid of the ancient world.

9. During the thirteenth century, stone was a favorite medium of these peoples they also used bone, gold, jade, and wood.

10. Much of the art from southern Central America was destroyed during the years of the Spanish conquest but several historical manuscripts survive today.

| STYLE   TIP |

Use a semicolon between clauses joined by a coordinating conjunction only when a semicolon is needed to prevent misreading, as in the examples of confusing sentences given to the right. If a sentence is clear without a semicolon, don't add one just because the clauses contain commas.

EXAMPLE
Lana, you are the best musician I know, and you're a great dancer, too. [clear without a semicolon]

12c. **You may need to use a semicolon (rather than a comma) before a coordinating conjunction to join independent clauses that contain commas.**

CONFUSING   June sat with Tony, Pat, and me, and Josh sat with Flora, Zack, and Geraldo.

CLEAR   June sat with Tony, Pat, and me; and Josh sat with Flora, Zack, and Geraldo.

CONFUSING   Searching for the house key, I found a dime, a nickel, and a penny, and John, my brother, found his lost watch.

CLEAR   Searching for the house key, I found a dime, a nickel, and a penny; and John, my brother, found his lost watch.

12d. **Use a semicolon between items in a series if the items contain commas.**

EXAMPLES   In 2000, the three largest metropolitan areas in the United States were New York, New York; Los Angeles, California; and Chicago, Illinois.

You may turn in your book reports on Thursday, September 14; Friday, September 15; Monday, September 18; or Tuesday, September 19.

Exercise 2 **Correcting Sentences by Adding Semicolons**

For the following sentences, write each word that should be followed by a semicolon. Add the needed punctuation mark after the word. If a sentence is already correct, write *C*.

MECHANICS

EXAMPLE   **1.** The winners of the regional science fair were Anya
            Garcia, who came in first, Jeff Ford, who came in second,
            and Alberto Robinson, who came in third.

        1. *first; second;*

1. The president of the student council has appointed the following
   members to chair committees: Anna Maria Chen, fundraising, Ben
   Cohen, volunteer services, and Donna Massad, event planning.
2. Fortunately, Candace remembered the address, or we would have
   been quite late, Roseanne.
3. Eli went to the matinee with Jae, Kerry, and Sung; but Josh, Taylor,
   and I preferred to go hiking.
4. After his concert in New York, my uncle Vittorio will come to visit
   on Thursday, March 25, Friday, March 26, or Saturday, March 27.
5. Would you prefer to live in Boston, Massachusetts, San Francisco,
   California, or Seattle, Washington?
6. Performers in the show were Tony Fernandez, trumpet and
   trombone, Donna Lee Bryant, clarinet and saxophone, and Danica
   Ward, drums and steel guitar.
7. I bought my sister several gifts, including a book, a skirt, and a
   tennis racket, but, unfortunately, I couldn't find a present for my
   mother, who wants an antique desk.
8. We admired the atrium's flowering vines, rock formations, and
   fountains, and then we stepped out into the courtyard, followed
   the flagstone path, and crossed the bridge over the goldfish pond.
9. To prepare for the performance we must set the stage, check the
   lights, and test the sound system; then, the dancers will take their
   places, the audience will be seated, and the curtain will rise.
10. On our backpacking trip to Eastern Europe, we hope to visit
    Prague, Czech Republic, Budapest, Hungary, Bucharest, Romania,
    and Krakow, Poland.

Review A   **Correcting Sentences by Adding Commas
and Semicolons**

For the following sentences, write each word that should be followed
by a semicolon or a comma. Add the needed punctuation mark after
each word. If a sentence is already correct, write *C*.

EXAMPLE   **1.** The diagram on the next page shows the typical seating
            plan of a symphony orchestra a conductor occupies the
            podium.

        1. *orchestra;*

HELP

Some sentences
in Review A may
need more than one
punctuation mark.

1. All of the instruments in a symphony orchestra are divided into classes based on how they produce sound many musicians can play several instruments within a class.
2. The four classes are strings, woodwinds, brass, and percussion.
3. Some of the stringed instruments are played with a bow some are plucked with the fingers or with a pick still others are operated by means of a keyboard.
4. Woodwinds, which were once made mainly of wood, include the flute, the clarinet, and the saxophone but other materials, such as metal or plastic, are often used nowadays.
5. Most brass instruments, such as the trumpet, tuba, and cornet, have valves that regulate the pitch but the trombone, my favorite instrument, has a sliding section for this purpose.
6. Kettledrums, or timpani, are percussion instruments that can be tuned to a specific pitch most other kinds of drums, the cymbals, and the triangle however cannot be tuned.
7. A conductor's job is to coordinate the sounds produced by these different instruments however this task is only one of a conductor's responsibilities.
8. Conductors must study the theory of music for years furthermore they must be skilled at playing at least one instrument.
9. Many people think a conductor just establishes the tempo of the music they do not realize that he or she also selects the music, interprets the composer's meaning, and brings out the best performance in each musician.
10. The goal of many conductors is to lead a major orchestra such as one of those in London, England Mexico City, Mexico Boston, Massachusetts or Chicago, Illinois.

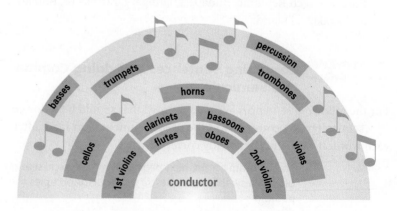

Colons

12e. Use a colon to mean "note what follows."

(1) Use a colon before a list of items, especially after expressions such as *the following* and *as follows.*

EXAMPLES   In Washington, D.C., we visited four important national sites**:** the White House, the Washington Monument, the Vietnam Veterans Memorial, and the Lincoln Memorial.

The only tools allowed in the examination area are **as follows:** pencils, compasses, rulers, and protractors.

During summer vacation, Juanita read biographies of **the following** people**:** John Ross and Annie Wauneka.

NOTE Do not use a colon between a verb and its complements or between a preposition and its objects.

INCORRECT   At the new amusement park we rode: the roller coaster, the Ferris wheel, the bumper cars, and the water slide.

CORRECT   At the new amusement park we rode the roller coaster, the Ferris wheel, the bumper cars, and the water slide.
[The list serves as the direct object of the verb *rode.*]

INCORRECT   Our family has lived in: California, Arizona, and Texas.

CORRECT   Our family has lived in California, Arizona, and Texas.
[The list serves as the object of the preposition *in.*]

(2) Use a colon before a long, formal statement or quotation.

EXAMPLE   Thomas Paine's first pamphlet in the series *The American Crisis* starts with these famous words**:**

These are the times that try men's souls. The summer soldier and the sunshine patriot will, in this crisis, shrink from the service of their country; but he that stands it *now* deserves the love and thanks of man and woman.

12f. Use a colon before a statement that explains or clarifies a preceding statement.

EXAMPLES   He deserves a raise**:** He completed the project on schedule and under budget.

Preston slapped his forehead**:** He had forgotten to put oregano in the sauce.

HELP

When a list of words, phrases, or subordinate clauses follows a colon, the first word of the list is generally lowercase.

EXAMPLE
When you walk into class, you need to have the following with you: **y**our textbook, a pen and a pencil, writing paper, and a good attitude.

Reference Note

For information on **complements,** see page 48. For information on **objects of prepositions,** see page 65.

Reference Note

For information on using **long quotations,** see page 345.

HELP

When an independent clause follows a colon, the first word of the clause begins with a capital letter.

EXAMPLE
The current debate is still best summed up by Mark Twain: "**It** is better to support schools than jails."

MECHANICS

12g. Use a colon in certain conventional situations.

(1) Use a colon between the hour and the minute.

EXAMPLES   6**:**15 P.M.   9**:**55 tomorrow morning

(2) Use a colon between chapter and verse in Biblical references.

EXAMPLES   Psalm 8**:**9   I Corinthians 13**:**1–13

(3) Use a colon between a title and a subtitle.

EXAMPLES   *I Like Jazz***:** *The Essence of Billie Holiday* [recording]

*Tilting Knights***:** *King Richard and Saladin* [painting]

(4) Use a colon after the salutation of a business letter.

EXAMPLES   Dear Ms. Weinberg**:**   Dear Sir or Madam**:**

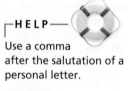

┌─HELP──
Use a comma after the salutation of a personal letter.

EXAMPLE
  Dear Suzanne**,**

Oral Practice   **Correcting Sentences by Adding Colons**

Read aloud the following sentences. Then, say each word or numeral that should be followed by a colon. If a sentence is already correct, say "correct."

EXAMPLE   1. I began my acceptance speech as follows "Fellow students, thank you for your votes!"

    1. *follows:*

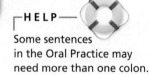

┌─HELP──
Some sentences in the Oral Practice may need more than one colon.

1. My little sister's favorite book is *The Great Kapok Tree A Tale of the Amazon Rain Forest* by Lynn Cherry.
2. Sometimes the paper comes at 7 15 A.M., but other times it doesn't hit the driveway until 8 00.
3. My niece has several items embossed with that logo a poster, a nightgown, a notebook, and a clock.
4. In William Shakespeare's play *The Tragedy of Julius Caesar,* Caesar has this to say of courage "Cowards die many times before their deaths, /The valiant taste of death but once."
5. Sherry's favorite artists are Jacob Lawrence, Romare Bearden, and Margaret Burroughs.
6. I think the story of Moses and Pharaoh's daughter is told in Exodus 2 5–10.
7. The directions were as follows Cover with plastic wrap, place in microwave oven, and cook for at least ten minutes.
8. I prefer my bicycle to a car for three reasons I don't have to pay for gasoline, I don't need insurance, and I don't waste time looking for a place to park.

9. In Cuba, which is a Spanish-speaking country, most of the people are of Spanish, African, or Spanish-African descent.
10. We should buy a house Our taxes would be lower, and we'd have more space.

COMPUTER TIP

Some software programs can evaluate your writing for common errors in the use of semicolons and colons. Such programs can help you as you proofread your drafts. Remember, however, that software cannot find every error. You will still need to proofread your writing carefully.

Review B **Proofreading Sentences for Correct Use of Semicolons and Colons**

Each of the following sentences contains at least one error in the use of semicolons or colons. For each error, write the word or numeral that precedes the missing or incorrect punctuation and add the correct punctuation.

EXAMPLE   1. The electricity was out for three days, the phones were not working for a week.

    1. *days;*

1. I made a list so that I would remember everything we needed toothpaste, milk, wax paper, and cat food.
2. The entrance exam was finished, however, I would remain nervous until the results came back.
3. The carpet was green, black, and brown, so red, orange, and pink have been ruled out for the wall color.
4. The awards went to John, who read from *Evangeline,* Ann, who read from *The Bridge,* and Garrett, who read from *The Waste Land.*
5. The vacuum hose was brittle and cracked therefore, taping it was not going to be enough.
6. The bus to the game will be leaving at precisely 3 45.
7. Lupe was going to title her essay "Mary Had a Little Lamb; The Social and Personal Benefits of Pet Ownership."
8. The three-person teams will be as follows, Takara, Lani, and Nick, Jessica, Vince, and Tyrone, and Peter, Dolores, and Ruben.
9. Jeremy had this Mark Twain quote taped to his folder, "Man is the only animal that blushes. Or needs to."
10. Sue Ann thought she had all the homework she could handle: on the other hand, she still had two more classes in the afternoon.

MEETING THE CHALLENGE

Think of a task that you perform with ease but that someone else may find confusing, such as baking bread or operating a digital camera. Then, write a paragraph listing the steps needed to complete the task. Correctly use at least two examples of semicolons and colons in your instructions.

MECHANICS

Review C **Correcting a Business Letter by Adding Semicolons and Colons**

For the numbered word groups in the letter excerpt on the following page, write each word that should be followed by a semicolon or a colon. Place the needed punctuation mark after each word.

[1] Hampton University was founded in 1868 it was originally named Hampton Normal and Agricultural Institute.

1. *1868;*

[1] Dear Sir or Madam

[2] The media coordinator at Central High School suggested that I write to you she explained that Hampton has an extensive collection of materials on African American history. **[3]** For my history class I am preparing an oral report on the March on Washington of August 28, 1963, and if possible, I would like to display pictures of the march.

[4] I am particularly interested in pictures of the following speakers Floyd McKissick, John Lewis, Roy Wilkins, and Dr. Martin Luther King, Jr. **[5]** I would also like pictures showing the size and diversity of the crowd for example, a shot of the marchers filling the area around the Reflecting Pool between the Lincoln Memorial and the Washington Monument would be especially effective. **[6]** Either prints or slides will be useful however, I would prefer slides if they are available.

[7] My grandfather, who took part in the march, vividly remembers these words of Dr. King "Let us not seek to satisfy our thirst for freedom by drinking from the cup of bitterness and hatred." **[8]** Grandpa took several rolls of film that day unfortunately, the pictures were lost in a fire a few years ago.

[9] Please send me information on ordering copies of suitable pictures a stamped, self-addressed envelope is enclosed. **[10]** Thank you for your help I appreciate your attention to my request.

Sincerely,

Jesse Fletcher

Jesse Fletcher

MECHANICS

Chapter Review

A. Correcting Sentences by Using Semicolons and Colons

Most of the following sentences have a comma or no punctuation mark where a semicolon or a colon should be used. Write the word or numeral preceding each error; then, add the needed punctuation mark. If a sentence is already correct, write *C*.

1. American Indians inhabited North America long before any Europeans however, many Native Americans weren't recognized as citizens of the United States until 1924.

2. The planning committee meeting is scheduled for 3 15 this afternoon please don't be late.

3. The following committees will report at that time budget, membership, awards, and programs.

4. Every morning after I get up, I read a Bible verse this morning I read John 14 27.

5. We left some food out for the stray dog it looked so forlorn huddled in the doorway.

6. Our modern literature class has read these poems "Incident," by Countee Cullen, "The Love Song of J. Alfred Prufrock," by T. S. Eliot, and "Ars Poetica," by Archibald MacLeish.

7. When she transferred to Barton Academy, Millie joined several clubs, helped in planning the Spring Carnival, and worked at a food bank for the needy nevertheless, it took her months to make some new friends.

8. While campaigning to become mayor of San Antonio, Maria Antonietta Berriozabal summed up her point of view in these words: "Our greatest resource is our people. We have to deal with business interests and human needs simultaneously."

9. Conrad Aiken was a correspondent for *The New Yorker* and also wrote essays and short stories he is best known, however, for his narrative and philosophical poetry.

10. The Bering Strait links the Arctic Ocean with the Bering Sea both the strait and the sea are named for Vitus Bering, a Danish explorer of the eighteenth century.

11. The late S. I. Hayakawa once made this statement "It is not true that we have only one life to live; if we can read, we can live as many more lives and as many kinds of lives as we wish."

12. The winners in the Douglas Fun Run last Saturday morning were Otis Williams, a sophomore, Janice Hicks, a senior, and Rodrigo Campas, a junior.

13. They opposed every motion that came before the council meeting in addition, they said they would circulate petitions if any of the proposals passed.

14. At first the children were afraid, believing that they were lost only after their teacher reassured them that she knew the way did they settle down.

15. This design will be applied to the following types of machines commercial, manufacturing, military, and agricultural.

16. Uncle Ed became manager of Zaharias Cars and Trucks, Inc., he is a former Formula One racing driver.

17. In addition to her coming-of-age short stories, Doris Lessing, who grew up in Rhodesia (now Zimbabwe), has written several books, one of which is *African Laughter Four Visits to Zimbabwe.*

18. In the past twelve years, Justin has lived in Tucson, Arizona, Dallas, Texas, Shreveport, Louisiana, and Tulsa, Oklahoma.

19. For the golf tournament, seasoned players were paired with players new to the game consequently, the experienced players were frustrated and the novices were confused.

20. When Hernando Cortes invaded Mexico in 1519, he burned his ships as a result, his troops were unable to desert, and there was little point in mutiny.

B. Correcting Sentences by Adding Colons

Correct the following sentences by writing each word or numeral that should be followed by a colon and then adding the colon. If a sentence is already correct, write *C.*

21. For the first time he could remember, the 6 52 train to Grand Central was late.

22. At his retirement dinner, Mr. Gonzalo had this to say "It was a long and rewarding career, but I'm glad it's over."

23. Dr. Duran's favorite dishes are spiced pork, Spanish rice, fried zucchini, and julienned King Edward potatoes.

24. In his office, Mr. McMurdo has various mementos of the war a German helmet, a recruiting poster, a bullet casing, a model of a tank, and a signed photograph of General Bradley.

25. In Rome, they visited three famous attractions St. Peter's Church, the Colosseum, and the Spanish Steps.

26. On the car ferry, signs were posted with the following directions Roll Up Your Windows, Turn Off Your Engine, No Smoking, and Stay in Your Car.

27. I live in the mountains for two reasons, The air is clean, and there aren't too many people.

28. Exodus 20 3 contains the following famous quote "Thou shalt have no other gods before me."

29. There are three countries I'd like to visit above all France, Japan, and Greece.

30. Ms. Lozano assigned us to write an essay on one of the following American leaders Franklin D. Roosevelt, Abraham Lincoln, or Susan B. Anthony.

C. Correcting Sentences by Adding Semicolons and Colons

For each of the following sentences, write the word or numeral preceding each punctuation error; then, write the missing semicolon or colon. If a sentence is already correct, write *C*.

HELP—

Some items in Part C contain more than one punctuation error.

31. The Bible reading for last Sunday included John 3 1–21 and Romans 12 1–2.

32. Mr. Jackson's plane arrived twenty minutes late because of the dense fog, consequently, he missed the flight to Denver.

33. I have finally narrowed my choices for a housewarming gift a self-cleaning iron, a blender, some place mats and napkins, or casserole dishes.

34. You should start saving your money: Open a savings account, invest in stocks or bonds, or buy a certificate of deposit.

35. The following clubs will have their yearbook pictures taken at 2 15, the Pep Club, the Photography Club, and the Modern Dance Club.

36. At the airfield we saw two signs To the North Pole and To the South Pole.

37. Aunt Patty and my cousin Josh will be leaving with us fortunately, Mom and Dad should be able to join us later, after all.

38. Sandra, Dan, Grace, and Pete voted for Latrice and Kris, Bertha and the Hobbs twins chose Jerry and Cass.

39. You need to get the following supplies at the store orange juice, laundry detergent, bread, and dog food.

40. The hideous painting had been taken down in its place someone had put up a poster.

41. Maria says she wants to go to a college in the Northeast however, she still has two years to decide.

42. Mrs. Patel's favorite colors are green, beige, and turquoise.

43. I quote from the introduction "The main purpose of this book is to educate, not to entertain."

44. She had two main objections to the film It was too long, and she could hardly understand a word the actors said.

45. Three days a week Mom is up by 6 30, but on the other days she sleeps until 7 15 or so.

46. Marquand's survey included the three most critical locations Mount Jefferson, Gurney Point, and Fort Rollerton.

47. Dr. Burkhardt loudly requested sesame oil, flour, vinegar, and caraway seeds.

48. Mario had forgotten his clarinet he was, therefore, prevented from practicing with the others.

49. Mr. Cahill assumed that everyone in the room had read his book he referred to it several times during his talk.

50. The membership of the international committee was as follows Japan, two, Italy, five, Mexico, three, France, five, Germany, four, United States, five.

Writing Application

Punctuating a Business Letter

Using Semicolons and Colons   You have just won the grand prize in Blue Star Airlines' Fly-by-Night Sweepstakes. For one week, you can travel free to anywhere Blue Star flies in the United States—just so long as your flights depart between 8:00 P.M. and 4:00 A.M. You can remain in one location for the whole week, or you can travel to as many places as you like. To use your prize, you must give Blue Star Airlines a detailed itinerary of your trip before you plan to take it. Write a letter, giving the information needed. Use semicolons and colons to make your information easy to understand.

Prewriting   First, decide where you would most like to go. (If you plan to include more than one destination, remember that the trip is to last only one week from start to finish.) Then, arrange the information in a clearly understandable order.

Writing   As you write your first draft, remember that the accuracy and completeness of your letter will affect how well the trip is planned and, therefore, how much you enjoy your trip.

Revising   Put yourself in the ticket agent's place as you evaluate the letter. Have you included all the necessary information? Have you arranged the details in a clearly understandable order?

Publishing   Make sure that you use the correct form for a business letter. Proofread your letter carefully, paying special attention to your use of semicolons and colons. Also, be sure that you correctly spell the names of your destinations. With your teacher's permission, post the completed letter on a class bulletin board or Web page.

Punctuation

Italics, Quotation Marks, and Ellipsis Points

Diagnostic Preview

Correcting Sentences by Adding Italics (Underlining), Quotation Marks, and Ellipsis Points

Add or correct italics (underlining), quotation marks, and ellipsis points where they are needed in the following sentences. If a sentence is already correct, write *C*.

EXAMPLE   **1.** Have you read the Mayan folk tale The Hummingbird King? asked Soledad.

        1. "Have you read the Mayan folk tale 'The Hummingbird King'?" asked Soledad.

1. Why did you buy another sleeping bag? she asked.

2. In his speech, Chief Joseph of the Nez Perce said that he would never fight again.

3. The dance company is performing Swan Lake, a ballet composed by Tchaikovsky.

4. Anita asked, Why did he say, I won't go to the game?

5. The Boston Cooking School Cookbook, now known as The Fannie Farmer Cookbook, was first published in 1891.

6. The first word my baby brother said was bird.

7. There's an article in this issue of Newsweek that I'd like you to read, said Joan.

8. Orson Welles wrote and directed the movie Citizen Kane.

9. Her street address has four 4's in it, said Rose. Did you know that?

10. Susan drove one hundred miles, he replied, to see you and your family on your birthday.

11. My sister is the editor of Reverie, the Jefferson High School literary journal.

12. Please write to me, Joyce requested. I want to keep in touch with you during your travels.

13. In my report on Dee Brown's book Bury My Heart at Wounded Knee, I almost forgot to cite the New Republic magazine as the source of one of the quotations I used.

14. As we ran down the street, Charles shouted, Faster! Faster!

15. Sally said, John just whispered, I'll be at the game tonight.

16. Mrs. Rivera said that our history assignment is to read the next chapter: Great Ideals in the Constitution.

17. Did you read the article The Costs of College Today?

18. My aunt asked, What did your friend mean when he said that you look rad in your new glasses?

19. The Novelist is in a collection of W. H. Auden's shorter poems.

20. You often use the French expression au revoir, said Hannah.

21. The editorial concluded with the statement "The end result . . . . . . will be a total breakdown of communications."

22. "I'll bring a cooler for the sandwiches," Jason said.

23. Isn't the song One Headlight on The Wallflowers' second album, Bringing Down the Horse?

24. Jaime said, "We need to get that finished before . . well, at least before the shop closes."

25. Maria is reading The Hobbit again; this will be the third time she's read the book.

Italics

Italics are printed letters that lean to the right, *like this*. When you are writing or typing, indicate italics by underlining. If your composition were printed, the typesetter would set the underlined words in italics. For instance, if you were to type

```
All sophomores in our school read The Good
Earth by Pearl Buck.
```

the sentence would be printed like this:

All sophomores in our school read *The Good Earth* by Pearl Buck.

COMPUTER TIP

Most word-processing software and printers are capable of producing italic type.

Reference Note

For information about **capitalizing titles,** see page 280.

┌ T I P S & T R I C K S ┐

Generally, the title of an entire work (book, magazine, TV series) is italicized, and the title of a part (chapter, article, episode) is enclosed in quotation marks.

Reference Note

For examples of **titles that are not italicized but are enclosed in quotation marks,** see page 345.

┌HELP┐

Long musical works include operas, symphonies, ballets, oratorios, and concertos.

13a. Use italics (underlining) for titles and subtitles of books, plays, long poems, periodicals, works of art, movies, TV series, and long musical works and recordings.

Type of Title	Examples	
Books	*The Bean Trees*	*Summer Sisters*
Plays	*Hedda Gabler*	*Twelfth Night*
Long Poems	*Sundiata: An Epic of Old Mali*	*Evangeline*
Periodicals	*Kansas City Times*	*Sports Illustrated*
Works of Art	*Three Musicians*	*Hercules and Antaeus*
Movies	*The Wizard of Oz*	*Jaws*
TV Series	*Sesame Street*	*Nova*
Long Musical Works and Recordings	*The Maid of Orleans* *The Magic Flute*	*The Nutcracker* *The Four Seasons*

NOTE   A long poem is one that is long enough to be published as a separate volume. Such poems are usually divided into titled or numbered sections, such as cantos, parts, or books. The titles of these sections should be enclosed in quotation marks.

EXAMPLE   Alejandro's report is on **"**What the Thunder Said,**"** the fifth stanza of T. S. Eliot's poem ***The Waste Land.***

The articles *a, an,* and *the* written before a title are italicized (and capitalized) only when they are part of the official title. If you are not sure whether to include an article in a title, you can check the title page of a book or the masthead or table of contents of a periodical for the official title.

EXAMPLES   Charles Dickens's book ***A*** *Christmas Carol* is a holiday favorite.

The article in ***The*** *Wall Street Journal* mentioned that among his other accomplishments, Frederick Douglass founded **the** *North Star,* a newspaper he published for seventeen years.

13b. Use italics (underlining) for the names of ships, trains, aircraft, and spacecraft.

Type of Name	Examples
Ships	*Lusitania*
Trains	*Orient-Express*
Aircraft	*Memphis Belle*
Spacecraft	*Pioneer 11*

13c. Use italics (underlining) for words, letters, symbols, and numerals referred to as such and for foreign words that have not been adopted into English.

EXAMPLES   The first **o** in **zoology** is pronounced with a long **o** sound.

In math, what does the **%** mean?

Sometimes his **3**'s look just like his **8**'s.

Montana's state motto is **Oro y Plata,** the Spanish phrase for "gold and silver."

NOTE   English has borrowed many words and expressions from other languages. Some of these words and expressions have become part of the English vocabulary and are no longer italicized.

EXAMPLES   hors d'oeuvre (French)   quesadilla (Spanish)

moccasin (Algonquian)   tae kwon do (Korean)

If you are not sure whether to italicize a word of foreign origin, look it up in a recent dictionary.

MECHANICS

STYLE TIP

Generally, do not use italics for the title of your own paper. However, if your title contains a title that belongs in italics, you will need to use italics for that part of the title.

EXAMPLES
The Universal Appeal of the Works of Barbara Kingsolver [contains no title that belongs in italics]

The Biblical Allusions in *Jane Eyre* [contains a book title, which belongs in italics]

Be creative when giving your paper a title. Avoid using the title of another work as the complete title of your own work.

Oral Practice   **Correcting Sentences by Adding Italics (Underlining)**

Read aloud the following sentences. Then, say which words or word groups should be italicized in each sentence.

EXAMPLE   1. In 1988, Toni Morrison won the Pulitzer Prize for her novel Beloved.

1. *Beloved*

1. Does the Vietnamese word chiao mean the same thing as the Italian word ciao?

2. The first full-length animated film, Snow White and the Seven Dwarfs, used two million drawings.

3. Among the items that the Pilgrims brought with them on the Mayflower were apple seeds.

4. James Earle Fraser, best known for his painting End of the Trail, designed the U.S. buffalo nickel.

5. In the eighteenth century, Edward Gibbon wrote the influential book History of the Decline and Fall of the Roman Empire.

6. In Voyage to the Bottom of the Sea, an old TV series, the submarine Seaview was commanded by Admiral Nelson.

7. Daktari is Swahili for the English word doctor.

8. The first U.S. space shuttle was named Columbia.

9. Richard Sears met Alvah Roebuck through an ad in the Chicago Daily News.

10. The three M's referred to in the company name 3M stand for Minnesota Mining and Manufacturing.

STYLE · TIP

Writers sometimes use italics (underlining) for emphasis, especially in written dialogue. The italic type shows how the sentence is supposed to be spoken. Read the following sentences aloud. Notice that by italicizing different words, the writer can change the meaning of a sentence.

EXAMPLES
"Are you going to buy the *green* shirt?" asked Ellen. [Will you buy the green shirt, not the blue one?]

"Are you going to buy the green *shirt*?" asked Ellen. [Will you buy the green shirt, not the green pants?]

"Are *you* going to buy the green shirt?" asked Ellen. [Will you, not your brother, buy it?]

Italicizing (underlining) words for emphasis is a handy technique that should not be overused. It can quickly lose its impact.

Exercise 1 Correcting Sentences by Adding Italics (Underlining)

Identify all the words and word groups that should be italicized in the following sentences.

EXAMPLE 1. Have you read The Wonderful Adventures of Nils by Selma Lagerlöf?

1. *The Wonderful Adventures of Nils*

1. I just finished reading Ellen Gilchrist's book The Courts of Love.

2. Kay enjoyed the movie Bringing Up Baby.

3. Occasionally, my cousins like to watch reruns of The Brady Bunch on television.

4. Antigone is a play by Sophocles.

5. Every morning while eating a bagel, she reads The New York Times.

6. My oldest brother's favorite painting is The Potato Eaters by Vincent van Gogh.

7. Europe's first transcontinental express train was the Orient-Express.

8. Charles Lindbergh flew across the Atlantic Ocean in the airplane Spirit of Saint Louis.

9. A poster of Salvador Dali's painting The Persistence of Memory hangs in our school library.

10. I subscribe to several magazines, including Escape and Entertainment Weekly.

MECHANICS

Quotation Marks

13d. Use quotation marks to enclose a **_direct quotation_**—a person's exact words.

> DIRECT
> QUOTATION   Joan said, "My legs are sore from jogging."

Remember to place quotation marks at both the beginning and the end of a direct quotation.

> INCORRECT   "I'm taking the road test tomorrow, said Reed.
> CORRECT   "I'm taking the road test tomorrow," said Reed.

Do not use quotation marks to enclose an **_indirect quotation_**—a rewording of a person's exact words.

> INDIRECT
> QUOTATION   Joan said that her legs were sore from jogging.
>   [a rewording of Joan's exact words]

(1) A directly quoted sentence begins with a capital letter.

EXAMPLE   Bianca asked, "When do we get our uniforms?"

Captitalize a directly quoted remark, even if the remark is not a complete sentence.

EXAMPLE   Mr. Lozano answered, "On Friday, of course."

> NOTE   If a direct quotation is obviously a fragment of the original quotation, it may begin with a lowercase letter.
>
> EXAMPLE   Christine promised to be here "as soon as possible."

(2) When an interrupting expression divides a quoted sentence into two parts, the second part begins with a lowercase letter.

EXAMPLES   "I hope," said Diego, "that it doesn't rain during the fiesta."

"I'm not sure," remarked Annette, "whether I'll be able to attend the meeting."

If the second part of a quotation is a complete sentence, a period (not a comma) follows the interrupting expression, and the second part begins with a capital letter.

EXAMPLE   "The date has been set," said Greg. "We can't change it."

MECHANICS

┌─ **HELP** ─

An expression identifying the speaker is not part of a direct quotation and should not appear inside the quotation marks.

INCORRECT
"Where, I inquired, have I seen you before?"

CORRECT
"Where," I inquired, "have I seen you before?"

When a direct quotation of two or more sentences by the same speaker is not divided, only one set of quotation marks is used.

INCORRECT   Tamisha suggested, "Let's donate the profits from the car wash to Project Day Care." "It provides help for many low-income working parents in this area."

CORRECT   Tamisha suggested, "Let's donate the profits from the car wash to Project Day Care. It provides help for many low-income working parents in this area."

(3) **A direct quotation can be set off from the rest of the sentence by a comma, a question mark, or an exclamation point, but not by a period.**

EXAMPLES   "Remember that your research reports are due Monday," Mrs. Castañeda announced.

"On what date does the Ides of March fall?" Elwyn asked.

"That's easy! It's March 15!" Dot exclaimed.

(4) **When used with quotation marks, other marks of punctuation are placed according to the following rules:**

- Commas and periods are placed inside the closing quotation marks.

EXAMPLE   "The concert tickets are sold out," Mary said, "and I had really hoped to go."

- Colons and semicolons are placed outside the closing quotation marks.

EXAMPLES   The following students have been named "most likely to succeed": Corey Brown and Sally Ling.

Paka quoted a Cameroonian proverb, "By trying often, the monkey learns to jump from the tree"; it reminded me of the expression "If at first you don't succeed, try, try again."

- A question mark or an exclamation point is placed inside the closing quotation marks if the quotation itself is a question or an exclamation. Otherwise, a question mark or exclamation point is placed outside the closing quotation marks.

EXAMPLES   "What time is the game tomorrow?" Maria asked.

Why did you shout, "It doesn't matter"?

While I was at bat, Vicky kept shouting, "Hit it over the fence!"

Don't say "I'd rather not"!

> **NOTE** When both the sentence and the quotation at the end of the sentence are questions (or exclamations), only one question mark (or exclamation point) is used. It is placed inside the closing quotation marks.
>
> EXAMPLE   Who asked "What time is it?"

Exercise 2 **Writing Sentences with Direct and Indirect Quotations**

Add quotation marks where they are needed in the following sentences. If a sentence is already correct, write *C*.

EXAMPLE   **1.** When I saw this ad in the paper, I said to Grandmother Hsu, *T'ai chi* is Chinese, isn't it?

   1. When I saw this ad in the paper, I said to Grandmother Hsu, "T'ai chi is Chinese, isn't it?"

1. She seemed pleased that I'd asked and replied, Yes, it's short for *t'ai chi ch'uan.*
2. She explained that t'ai chi ch'uan was developed in ancient China as a system of self-defense and as an aid to meditation.
3. The ad says that it's for health and relaxation, I said.
4. Yes, she agreed, it's that, too; it improves coordination and flexibility. In fact, in China, people of all ages practice it.
5. You see, she went on, its postures and movements are all based on those of animals such as monkeys, birds, and snakes.
6. Snakes! I exclaimed.
7. Why do you twist your face so? Grandmother asked. If you observe a snake closely, you'll see how gracefully it moves.
8. That's true, I admitted.
9. Maybe, I said, thinking aloud, I'll check out this grand opening.
10. Imagine my surprise when Grandmother replied with a wide smile, I'll see you there. I'm one of the instructors.

ANNOUNCING

The Grand Opening of

Pathway T'ai Chi Studio
for health and relaxation

604 49th St.
Sunday, November 10
1:00 P.M.–5:00 P.M.

Complimentary refreshments will be served.
All Ages Welcome

13e. When you write dialogue (a conversation), begin a new paragraph every time the speaker changes, and enclose each speaker's words in quotation marks.

EXAMPLE

A man of Merv, well known as the home of complicated thinkers, ran shouting one night through the city's streets. "Thief, Thief!" he cried.

The people surrounded him, and when he was a little calmer, asked: "Where was the thief?"

"In my house."

"Did you see him?"

"No."

"Was anything missing?"

"No."

"How do you know there was a thief then?"

"I was lying in bed when I remembered that thieves break into houses without a sound, and move very quietly. I could hear nothing, so I knew that there was a thief in the house, you fool!"

Niamat Khan, "The Thief"

NOTE A long passage quoted from a book or another printed source is usually set off from the rest of the text. The entire passage is usually indented and double-spaced. When a quoted passage has been set off in one of these ways, no quotation marks are necessary unless the passage contains dialogue.

EXAMPLE

```
In his speech after his last battle
against the whites, the Sauk chief
Black Hawk displayed pride and honor
in the face of defeat:
          The bullets flew like birds
          in the air, and whizzed by our
          ears like the wind through the
          trees in winter. My warriors
          fell around me; it began to
          look dismal. I saw my evil day
          at hand. The sun rose dim on us
          in the morning, and at night
          it sank in a dark cloud, and
          looked like a ball of fire.
          That was the last sun that
          shone on Black Hawk.
```

13f. When a quoted passage consists of more than one paragraph, put quotation marks at the beginning of each paragraph and at the end of the entire passage. Do not put quotation marks after any paragraph but the last.

EXAMPLE   "Now, this car is one of our hottest sellers. It has bucket seats, a CD player, and alloy wheels.

   "It's also one of the safest cars on the road because of its heavy suspension and antilock brake system. It gets good gas mileage, too.

   "All in all, I think this would be the perfect car for you."

13g. Use quotation marks to enclose titles (including subtitles) of short works such as short stories, poems, essays, articles, songs, episodes of TV series, and chapters and other parts of books and periodicals.

Type of Title	Examples
Short Stories	"The Unicorn in the Garden" "The Gift of the Magi"
Poems	"Fire and Ice" "I Am of the Earth"
Essays	"Choice: A Tribute to Dr. Martin Luther King, Jr." "Marco Polo: Journey to China"
Articles	"The Ghost Dance" "Searching for Freedom"
Songs	"What's Going On" "I Will Remember You"
Episodes of TV Series	"Jerry's High School Reunion"
Chapters and Other Parts of Books, Periodicals	"Twentieth-Century Playwrights" "In Search of a New Frontier"

13h. Use single quotation marks to enclose a quotation or title within a quotation.

EXAMPLES   Ron said, "Dad yelled, 'No way!'"

   Val asked, "Did you like my rendition of 'America the Beautiful'?"

Reference Note

For examples of **titles that are italicized, not enclosed in quotation marks,** see page 338.

—HELP—

The titles of long poems are italicized.

STYLE   TIP

Generally, do not use quotation marks for the title of your own paper. However, if your title contains a title that belongs in quotation marks, you will need to use quotation marks for that part of your title.

EXAMPLES
Aesop: A Master Storyteller [contains no title that belongs in quotation marks]

Cassie in "Song of the Trees": A Character Analysis [contains a short-story title, which belongs in quotation marks]

MECHANICS

MEETING THE CHALLENGE

Create a concept for a new TV show. Choose a format (such as sitcom, drama, or game show) and develop the setting and characters. Then, write a description of the show's concept and brief summaries of the content of the first three episodes. Be sure to correctly punctuate and capitalize the series and episode titles.

13i. Use quotation marks to enclose slang words, technical terms, and unusual uses of words.

EXAMPLES   My oldest brother said my new shoes are **"**da bomb.**"**

My mother **"**dogged**"** me about finishing my homework.

Fire burns oxygen quickly; my chemistry teacher says flame is a **"**gas-guzzler.**"**

Review A   **Correcting Sentences by Adding Italics (Underlining) or Quotation Marks**

For each of the following sentences, correctly write all the words that should be italicized (underlined) or enclosed in quotation marks.

EXAMPLE   1.   He read aloud The Tell-Tale Heart from The Collected Stories of Edgar Allan Poe.

   1.   "The Tell-Tale Heart"; The Collected Stories of Edgar Allan Poe

1. Mr. Croce used the word denouement when he was discussing Rudolfo Anaya's novel Bless Me, Ultima.
2. By next Thursday I have to read the following works: The Medicine Bag, a short story by Virginia Driving Hawk Sneve; Crown of Shadows, a play by Rodolfo Usigli; and Daisy Bates: First Lady of Little Rock, an article by Lerone Bennett, Jr.
3. Have you read the newspaper article El Niño, Global Weather Disaster? asked Ewan.
4. While we were working on our essays, Karen asked me how many m's are in the word accommodate.
5. Oswald Rivera's novel Fire and Rain is about the Vietnam War.
6. Kim said her report, titled The Wit of Oscar Wilde, includes quotes from the short story titled The Happy Prince as well as the play The Importance of Being Earnest.
7. We had risotto alla milanese for dinner.
8. Mr. Guerra explained that the short story Luke Baldwin's Vow deals with conflicts in values.
9. Wouldn't Words to Live By be an excellent title for our song? Tomás asked.
10. She crossed the t with such a flourish that she obscured the letters above it.

Review B **Correcting Sentences by Adding Italics (Underlining) and Quotation Marks**

Rewrite the following dialogue, and add italics (underlining), quotation marks, and paragraph breaks and indentions where they are needed.

EXAMPLE **[1]** Look at this intriguing painting, said Marshall.

1. *"Look at this intriguing painting,"* said Marshall.

[1] He told us that he'd found the painting in Mexican American Artists, a book by Jacinto Quirate; the painting is in the chapter called The Third Decade.

[2] The painting is by the man in the photograph below, Emilio Aguirre, he explained, who titled it Alpha 1.

[3] What do you see when you look at it? he asked.

[4] You can't miss the Y on the left and the T on the right, he said.

[5] He went on, Can you make out the profile of a person sitting on the ground to the left of the T?

[6] Laura said, Yes, the head is an O; but I objected, saying that it looked more like a Q to me.

[7] I guess you're right, she said. Anyway, the G outlines the front of the body.

[8] Ben asked, Is the little b on the big O supposed to be the person's glasses? Also, he added, isn't that an M in the background, behind the T?

[9] Look at this! exclaimed Marlene. If you turn the painting ninety degrees to the left, the body looks like a question mark.

[10] Can you see why we all agreed when she said, Intriguing really is the word for Alpha 1?

Ellipsis Points

13j. Use ellipsis points (. . .) to mark omissions from quoted material.

ORIGINAL   The room overlooking the square had an ornate stone balcony with a view of the chateau. That building was an early-Renaissance confection of towers and turrets, partly encircled by the old city walls. I remember that next to the chateau was the town hall, a handsome, square Second Empire structure. A stand of plane trees and a parking lot full of cars adjoined the main gate. Beyond the city walls lay the yellow mustard fields rolling into the hazy distance.

(1) When you omit words from the middle of a sentence, use three spaced ellipsis points.

EXAMPLE   "The room overlooking the square had **. . .** a view of the chateau."

NOTE   Be sure to include a space before the first ellipsis point and after the last one.

⌐HELP─

Notice that in the example under Rule 13j(2), the word *next* is capitalized, even though it was not capitalized in the original. *Next* is capitalized in the example because it is being used as the first word of the sentence. The capital *N* is in brackets to show that the capital was added by the person quoting the material—that *next* was lowercased in the original.

(2) When you omit words from the beginning of a sentence within a quoted passage, keep the previous sentence's end punctuation and follow it with the points of ellipsis.

EXAMPLE   "That building was an early-Renaissance confection of towers and turrets, partly encircled by the old city walls**. . . .** [N]ext to the chateau was the town hall, a handsome, square Second Empire structure."

(3) When you omit words at the end of a sentence within a quoted passage, keep the sentence's end punctuation and follow it with the points of ellipsis.

EXAMPLE   "That building was an early-Renaissance confection of towers and turrets**. . . .** I remember that next to the chateau was the town hall, a handsome, square Second Empire structure."

(4) When you omit one or more complete sentences from within a quoted passage, keep the previous sentence's end punctuation and follow it with the points of ellipsis.

EXAMPLE   "That building was an early-Renaissance confection of towers and turrets, partly encircled by the old city walls**. . . .** Beyond the city walls lay the yellow mustard fields rolling into the hazy distance."

To show that one or more lines of poetry have been omitted, use an entire line of spaced periods.

COMPLETE   Loveliest of trees, the cherry now
POEM   Is hung with bloom along the bough,
And stands about the woodland ride
Wearing white for Eastertide.

Now, of my threescore years and ten,
Twenty will not come again,
And take from seventy springs a score,
It only leaves me fifty more.

And since to look at things in bloom
Fifty springs are little room,
About the woodlands I will go
To see the cherry hung with snow.

A. E. Housman, "Loveliest of Trees"

POEM WITH   Loveliest of trees, the cherry now
OMISSION   Is hung with bloom along the bough,
And stands about the woodland ride
Wearing white for Eastertide.

. . . .

And since to look at things in bloom
Fifty springs are little room,
About the woodlands I will go
To see the cherry hung with snow.

Notice that the line of periods here marks the omission of four lines of poetry. Also, notice that the line of ellipses is as long as the preceding line of poetry.

13k. Use three ellipsis points (. . .) to indicate a pause in written dialogue.

EXAMPLE   "Yes, but ● ● ● oh well, all right," she said.

┌HELP─
Do not begin a quoted passage with points of ellipsis.

INCORRECT
". . . That building was an early-Renaissance confection of towers and turrets, partly encircled by the old city walls."

CORRECT
"That building was an early-Renaissance con- fection of towers and turrets, partly encircled by the old city walls."

Omit the underscored parts of the following passages. Use ellipsis points and end marks to punctuate each omission correctly.

EXAMPLE   1. The old twin-gabled house, which my aunt had intended to sell, was struck by lightning.

1. The old twin-gabled house . . . was struck by lightning.

1. Santa Fe is one of the most popular vacation destinations in the United States. Why is a small city in the mountains of northern New Mexico, more than an hour's drive from the nearest airport, such a top tourist draw? The climate is superb, the cuisine is outstanding, and the combination of cultures is unique.

2. Senator McRory, a key figure in state politics for most of his fifty-four years, has decided to run for governor in the next election.

3. According to the newspaper article, "Master Gardener Yamamoto won the top award in the international bonsai competition, the first such event of the season. He plans to use the money to build an addition to his nursery."

4. A mature bull elephant, huge yet graceful, charged toward the water hole and scared the lions away.

5. The path curves onward and up,
Shining like a scimitar's blade
In the early morning rain,
Guiding us to higher things.

6. Ambition and duty are the twin motives of the character of Teng in this movie, as they frequently are in the lives of real people.

7. The new airport, which will greatly increase the city's commercial and cultural ties to the outside world, will open next May.

8. "This novel is well-written but is quite unsatisfactory as a thriller. Its young author is known and deservedly respected for his realistic short stories set along the coast of Oregon and northern California, but he has much to learn before he can master the subtleties of plot and atmosphere," the book review said.

9. Mr. Sánchez arrived early from his long journey and promised he would show us his slides as soon as he had fully recovered the use of his voice.

10. "Was it true? Was it even possible? A complete reversal, her decision seems to contradict everything I know about her character," May thought aloud.

Chapter Review

A. Correcting Sentences by Adding Italics (Underlining) and Quotation Marks

Write each letter, word, title, or word group that should be italicized (underlined) or in quotation marks. Then, supply the needed underlining or quotation marks.

1. Carlos Chavez, a Mexican composer and conductor, wrote the Sinfonìa de Antígona in 1933.
2. We have subscribed to the Orlando Sentinel for two years.
3. Are you going to help me, he asked, or shall I look for someone else?
4. Michael Crichton wrote the book Jurassic Park, which was made into a movie by Steven Spielberg.
5. Grandma's favorite expression is Mind your p's and q's!
6. Carla served a delicious Mediterranean appetizer called pulpo; when I asked her what it was, she told me it was octopus.
7. For our homework assignment we have to define ionization, electrolyte, quark, and neutrino.
8. During the Civil War, the Merrimack, on the Confederate side, and the Monitor, on the Union side, fought to a draw in the first battle between ironclad ships.
9. I never should have agreed to be on that committee, wailed Ellie. When I asked Mary to help, she said, Not on your life! Now I'm stuck doing all the work!
10. Where have you been, Ron? asked Leroy. The bus is leaving.
11. These students are Elwood High's finest scholars, the principal said, announcing the following scholarship winners: Daphne Johnson, Michael Lewis, Ruben Perez, and Winnie Chung.
12. One of my favorite TV shows, Disaster Chronicles, ran an episode called Volcanoes in Italy.
13. Sam, who's from Boston, drops the r's from the ends of words.
14. Politicians still quote Abraham Lincoln's expression government of the people, by the people, for the people.
15. We discussed Ann Bank's magazine article Rafting with Kids.
16. Indians Today, the Real and the Unreal is the opening chapter in Vine Deloria's book Custer Died for Your Sins.

17. My mother has never liked the term baby boomer.
18. Many articles about Emily Dickinson's poems contain the term paradox.
19. When the players came onto the field, the fans shouted, Go for it!
20. Have you seen Louise Nevelson's sculpture Young Shadows?

B. Correcting Sentences by Adding Italics (Underlining)

Write all the words and word groups that should be italicized in the following sentences.

21. Have you seen the movie A Bug's Life?
22. One of Claude Monet's first paintings was called Impression: Sunrise.
23. One of Bernard Shaw's best-known plays is Pygmalion, on which the musical My Fair Lady was based.
24. My cousins Suzi and Désirée, happy to be on vacation, took the train California Zephyr to Los Angeles last summer.
25. One of Dad's favorite TV programs is Frontline.
26. I read an article in Sports Illustrated while I waited.
27. One of the fastest locomotives of its time was the Flying Scotsman, built in Britain in 1923.
28. Was Enola Gay the plane that dropped the atomic bomb on Hiroshima?
29. A Clergyman's Daughter is a novel by George Orwell.
30. Last night we all watched Star Trek: The Next Generation; one of my favorite episodes was showing.

C. Using Ellipsis Points Correctly

Omit the underscored parts of the following passages. Use ellipsis points and end marks to punctuate each omission correctly.

31. Our cousin Carlos, one of his college's star baseball players, is going to training camp in Arizona this spring.
32. The man was tall, in his mid-thirties, with a full mustache and short brown hair. His hair was combed straight back. He spoke with what I thought was a slight Midwestern accent.

33. Here, take my hand and follow me
    <u>Thou eager one, dreamer of dreams,</u>
    <u>Singer of life's oldest song,</u>
    And together we will find the golden crown.

34. Dr. Bustamante, <u>a widely admired personality in the Chilean emigrant community,</u> is almost certain to be chosen as deputy mayor.

35. The film <u>is atmospheric and well acted, but it</u> is too long by at least half an hour.

Writing Application
Writing an Interior Dialogue

Using Punctuation   You are scheduled to give an oral report on a short story of your own choosing. Write an interior dialogue recording your thoughts as you decide which of two stories to use. Use the marks of punctuation covered in this chapter in your interior dialogue.

Prewriting   List the titles of several short stories you have read. Then, choose the two about which you feel most strongly. Next, determine how you will distinguish between your different points of view as you decide which story to choose. For example, you could use your first name for one side, your middle name for another, and other names for as many different points of view as you have.

Writing   Write down your thoughts as you consider the pros and cons of using the two stories, presenting each thought in a correctly punctuated dialogue spoken from each point of view. Keep writing until you reach a decision. Try to keep track of where you are in the decision-making process.

Revising   Read over your dialogue and check whether your diction (word choice) and sentence structure sound authentic to you. Can you tell at all times to which story you're referring? Is it clear which one you decided to report on, and why?

Publishing   Check your dialogue for errors in grammar, spelling, and punctuation. Then, you and your classmates could record your dialogues on audiotape or act them out for one another in person or on videotape.

Punctuation

Apostrophes, Hyphens, Dashes, Parentheses, Brackets

Diagnostic Preview

A. Correcting Sentences by Using Apostrophes and Hyphens

For each of the following sentences, write the word or words that should have an apostrophe or a hyphen, and add the appropriate punctuation mark. If a sentence is already correct, write *C*.

EXAMPLE   **1.** Michaels stamp collection contains thirty two rare stamps.

　　　　　1. Michael's

　　　　　thirty-two

1. Because of the sudden blizzard, the armies supplies were cut off.

2. Its frustrating when the car wont start because its battery is dead.

3. After hours of discussion, we decided that we need a two thirds majority to pass new rules in the student council.

4. Even though Li moved here from Korea just last year and is still learning English, shes making As in most of her classes.

5. If you go to the game on Saturday, whos going to watch the children at home?

6. Miranda had the flu this past week, and now she has five days worth of homework to do this weekend.

7. Rodney interviewed the treasurer elect of the honor society for the "Personality Profile" column in the school newspaper.

8. James Berry, who was born in Jamaica, wrote the well received collection of short stories *A Thief in the Village and Other Stories.*

9. You should know that my aunts favorite expression is "Never let the sun set on your anger."

10. My cousin Murray has worked at a resort in New Yorks Catskill Mountains for twenty one years.

11. The store clerk said she would refund our deposit if we return the tape recorder by five oclock.

12. The alarm clock hasnt worked since the morning I knocked it off the shelf.

13. Let's plan to go camping in mid October; the leaves will be turn ing gold and red, the weather will be cool but not cold, and I'll have a new tent by then.

14. You have such a wonderful singing voice that I'm sure youll get a part in the childrens summer theater production.

15. Dont be alarmed, Brian; the red +s on your history paper indicate correct answers.

B. Correcting Sentences by Using Dashes, Parentheses, and Brackets

Rewrite the following sentences, adding dashes, parentheses, and brackets where they are needed.

EXAMPLE   1. The books on that table they are all nonfiction are on sale today.

1. *The books on that table—they are all nonfiction—are on sale today.*

16. The discovery of gold at Sutter's Mill brought floods of people settlers, miners, prospectors, and merchants to California in their covered wagons.

17. The old white house on Tenth Street it was once a governor's mansion is a landmark in our town.

18. Answer the ten questions on this English quiz be careful; they're tricky! and then write a couplet or a limerick for extra credit.

19. John Steinbeck 1902–1968 won the Nobel Prize in literature in 1962.

20. According to O'Neal, Satchmo (the great jazz musician Louis Armstrong 1900–1971) profoundly influenced American music.

┌HELP
Although some of the sentences in Part B of the Diagnostic Preview may be correctly revised in more than one way, you need to give only one revision for each sentence.

MECHANICS

Apostrophes

Possessive Case

The possessive case of a noun or a pronoun shows ownership or possession.

EXAMPLES **Jorge's** calculator has a solar battery.

Where did you buy **yours**?

Pam's aunt is a plumber.

The birds had fed **their** young.

Nouns in the Possessive Case

14a. To form the possessive of most singular nouns, add an apostrophe and an *s*.

EXAMPLES Barbara**'s** house   one boy**'s** uniform

a week**'s** salary   that stereo**'s** speakers

When forming the possessive of a singular noun ending in an *s* or a *z* sound, add only an apostrophe if

- the noun has more than one syllable

       and

- the addition of *s* would make the noun awkward to pronounce

EXAMPLES Odysseus**'** adventures   for goodness**'** sake

Buenos Aires**'** citizens   the species**'** characteristics

Xerxes**'** army   each of that TV series**'** characters

If a singular noun ending in an *s* or a *z* sound does not satisfy both of these conditions, add an apostrophe and an *s*.

EXAMPLES Carlos**'s** bicycle   a bus**'s** tires

Charles Dickens**'s** novels   my boss**'s** orders

14b. To form the possessive case of a plural noun ending in *s*, add only the apostrophe.

EXAMPLES cats**'** owners   cities**'** problems

coaches**'** records   princesses**'** duties

The few plural nouns that do not end in *s* form the possessive case by adding an apostrophe and an *s*.

EXAMPLES   geese**'s** migration   children**'s** stories

> NOTE In most cases, you should not use an apostrophe to form the plural of a noun.
>
> INCORRECT   The four horse's pulled the wagon.
>   CORRECT   The four **horses** pulled the wagon.

Reference Note

For more examples of **plural nouns that do not end in s,** see page 386.

Reference Note

For information on using an apostrophe and an *s* to form the **plurals of letters, numerals, symbols, and words referred to as words,** see pages 364 and 387.

Exercise 1 Writing the Possessive Forms of Nouns

Make four columns headed *Singular, Singular Possessive, Plural,* and *Plural Possessive.* Write those forms of each of the following nouns.

EXAMPLE	Singular	Singular Possessive	Plural	Plural Possessive
1.	temple	temple's	temples	temples'

1. governor	11. stereo
2. secretary	12. president
3. bird	13. bear
4. spacecraft	14. photograph
5. woman	15. grandmother
6. picture	16. jacket
7. pencil	17. dress
8. class	18. novel
9. chief	19. cup
10. mouse	20. lapse

┌HELP─

If you do not know how to spell a plural form, look up the word in a dictionary.

Pronouns in the Possessive Case

14c. Do not use an apostrophe with possessive personal pronouns or with the possessive pronoun *whose.*

Possessive Personal Pronouns	
Singular	**Plural**
my, mine	our, ours
your, yours	your, yours
his, her, hers, its	their, theirs

MECHANICS

Reference Note

Do not confuse the possessive personal pronouns **your, their, theirs, its,** and **whose** with the contractions **you're, they're, there's, it's,** and **who's.** See page 362.

Reference Note

See page 9 for a list of **indefinite pronouns.**

My, your, his, her, its, our, and *their* are generally used before nouns. *Mine, yours, his, hers, ours,* and *theirs* are used as subjects, complements, or objects of prepositions. Note that *his* may be used either way.

EXAMPLES

This is **my** desk.	This desk is **mine.**
I borrowed **your** pencil.	I borrowed a pencil of **yours.**
His work is excellent.	**His** is the best work.

14d. To form the possessive of an indefinite pronoun, add an apostrophe and an *s.*

EXAMPLES   anyone**'s** choice   either**'s** idea

NOTE   The correct possessive forms of *someone else* and *each other* are *someone else's* and *each other's.*

Compounds in the Possessive Case

14e. Form the possessive of only the last word in a compound noun, such as the name of an organization or a business, and in a word group showing joint possession.

Compound Nouns	Urban League**'s** office Acosta and Rivera**'s** law firm sister-in-law**'s** office
Joint Possession	Bob and Jim**'s** canoe my aunt and uncle**'s** photograph

When a possessive pronoun is part of a word group showing joint possession, each noun in the word group is also possessive in form.

EXAMPLE   Sean**'s** and **her** conversation

NOTE   The possessive of an **acronym** (a word formed from the first—or first few—letters of a series of words) or of an **initialism** (an abbreviation pronounced letter by letter) is formed by adding an apostrophe and an *s.*

ACRONYM   NATO**'s** member nations

INITIALISM   NBC**'s** new television program

14f. Form the possessive of each noun in a word group that expresses individual possession of similar items.

EXAMPLES   Michael**'s** and Lila**'s** wallets

             Denise**'s** and Mark**'s** books

┌─ S T Y L E ╱ T I P ─┐

To avoid forming a possessive that sounds awkward,
use a phrase beginning
with *of* or *for* instead.

AWKWARD
  the Samuel H. Scripps
  American Dance Festival
  Award's winner

IMPROVED
  the winner **of** the Samuel
  H. Scripps American
  Dance Festival Award

Exercise 2   Using Apostrophes Correctly

Rewrite the following word groups, adding and deleting apostrophes where needed. If a word group is already correct, write *C*.

EXAMPLE   1. the cameras lens

            1. *the camera's lens*

1. one of your's	11. a Jazz Festivals end
2. Anns and my project	12. anyone elses pizza
3. their tennis shoes	13. Jims and Debs parents
4. my father-in-laws boat	14. the UNs general assembly
5. each others books	15. my loaves of bread
6. Joe and Roys room	16. Sallys and his' horses
7. Lynns and Mikes shoes	17. any of their's
8. someones art	18. neithers hope
9. whose feats	19. Jeremiahs and Josephs toys
10. PBSs' fundraiser	20. Ross' and Reeds team

Review A   Correcting Paragraphs by Adding Apostrophes

For the sentences in the following paragraphs, write each word that should be in the possessive case, and add the missing apostrophe.

EXAMPLE   **[1]** Last weekend I took my friends suggestion to join a pottery class at our citys art center.

           1. *friend's; city's*

[1] The art centers catalogue offers a variety of classes. [2] The instructors credentials really make it hard to choose which class I want to take. [3] The painting teachers class description sounds really interesting. [4] My paintings usually look like childrens fingerpaintings, so I could probably benefit from some instruction! [5] I checked on the art stores prices on supplies in case I decide to take the class.

[6] My friends mother makes pottery, and she is quite talented.
[7] The Joneses lovely planters on their front porch were made by her.
[8] My friends persuasion and the catalogues description really helped
me make up my mind. [9] After seeing her mothers lovely creations, I
visited Bob and Ruths craft store to buy clay and supplies. [10] I am
also looking forward to learning how to use the centers kiln and glaze.

Review B Proofreading for Errors in Possessive Forms

Most of the following sentences contain an incorrect possessive form.
For each error, give the correct form of the word. If a sentence is
already correct, write *C*.

EXAMPLE　　**1.** The island nation of the Philippines shows signs of both
　　　　　　　　Spains and the United States occupations.

　　　　　　1. Spain's; United States'

1. The countrys national languages are Pilipino and English, but its
people also speak Spanish and various regional languages.
2. Did you know that the yo-yos earliest use was as a weapon in the
Philippine jungles?
3. My mothers boss was visiting the Philippines when Joseph Estrada
became president in 1998.
4. President Estrada's previous career was that of film actor.
5. Tina's and Phil's plan to visit the Philippines was postponed when
their baby was born.
6. The Philippines capital and largest city is Manila, which is on the
big island of Luzon.
7. Both Kim and Marta's lunches came with delicious Filipino custard.
8. It's anyones guess how many islands actually make up the
Philippines, though there are certainly more than seven thousand islands.

9. The Spanish monarch who's soldiers named the Philippines was King Philip II.
10. Childrens pastimes in the Philippines include kite flying and swimming.

Contractions

14g. Use an apostrophe to show where letters, words, or numerals have been omitted in a contraction.

A *contraction* is a shortened form of a word, a group of words, or a numeral. The apostrophes in contractions show where letters, words, or numerals have been left out.

14
g

Common Contractions	
who is . . . . who's	she will . . . . . she'll
there is . . . . there's	I am. . . . . I'm
could have . . . . . could've	you are . . . . . you're
1999 . . . . '99	we had. . . . . . we'd
of the clock . . . . o'clock	she has . . . . . . she's
let us . . . . let's	Lisa is . . . . Lisa's
I would . . . . I'd	they are . . . . . they're

Generally, the adverb *not* can be shortened to *n't* and added to a verb without any change in the spelling of the verb.

EXAMPLES
is not . . . . isn't	were not . . . . weren't
are not . . . . aren't	has not . . . . hasn't
does not . . . . doesn't	have not . . . . haven't
do not . . . . don't	had not . . . . hadn't
did not . . . . didn't	would not . . . . . . wouldn't
was not . . . . wasn't	should not . . . . . shouldn't

EXCEPTIONS cannot . . . . **can't**   will not . . . . **won't**

MECHANICS

STYLE TIP
Many people consider contractions informal. Therefore, it is generally best to avoid using them in formal writing and speech.

Do not confuse contractions with possessive pronouns.

Contractions	Possessive Pronouns
Who's [Who is] next? **Who's** [Who has] helped you?	**Whose** turn is next?
It's [It is] purring. **It's** [It has] been asleep.	Listen to **its** purr.
You're [You are] late.	**Your** report is late.
There's [There is] a mule. **They're** [They are] healthy pets.	That mule is **theirs.** **Their** pets are healthy.

Oral Practice   **Using Contractions**

Read aloud each of the following sentences, filling in the blank with an appropriate contraction.

EXAMPLE   1. We tried to call Beth and Jennifer, but they _____ answer their phone.

1. *didn't*

1. _____ he going to the awards ceremony?
2. I fed the fish, but they _____ eating.
3. Marla has two cats, and _____ beautiful.
4. _____ bring me her notes tonight so I can study them.
5. _____ go to a movie.
6. Mom said _____ one apple in the basket.
7. He is sick, so he _____ coming with us.
8. I _____ believe the summer is already over.
9. You _____ read a scary book when you're home alone.
10. I _____ gotten the mail yet.

Exercise 3   **Recognizing the Correct Uses of Contractions and Possessives**

Choose the correct word in parentheses in each of the following sentences.

EXAMPLE   1. (*It's, Its*) never too late to learn something new.

1. *It's*

1. (*You're, Your*) sure that (*you're, your*) allowed to bring (*you're, your*) book to the exam?

2. (*Whose, Who's*) idea was it to visit the National Civil Rights Museum in Memphis during (*you're, your*) trip?

3. (*They're, Their*) trying to sell (*they're, their*) house.

4. (*It's, Its*) the best one of (*it's, its*) kind.

5. Do you know (*who's, whose*) responsible for (*they're, their*) confusion?

6. I hope the dog can find (*it's, its*) way (*they're, there*).

7. (*It's, Its*) Philip (*who's, whose*) always late.

8. Although (*it's, its*) been snowing all day, they're still planning to go.

9. (*Who's, Whose*) the designer of (*they're, their*) float in Galveston's Mardi Gras parade?

10. I know (*you're, your*) upset with the plan, but (*it's, its*) the only way to solve the problem.

Review C **Correcting Sentences by Adding Apostrophes**

Identify each word that needs an apostrophe in the following sentences. Then, correctly write the word.

EXAMPLE   **1.** Werent you the one who said you didnt like eggplant?

    1. Weren't; didn't

1. Whos going to be at Leon and Joshs party?

2. Lets hide and see whether theyll look for us.

3. I cant find the calamata olives and the feta cheese for the Greek salad.

4. Is the doctors appointment at nine oclock?

5. Cleve doesnt have time to mow both David's and Rays lawns.

6. The parents faces brightened as their children crossed the stage.

7. Were lucky that that dogs howls didn't awaken them.

8. Im trying to follow Pauls map to Jeans house.

9. Its extremely cold; therefore, I dont think you should go skiing.

10. Elise couldnt remember the characteristics of the tiger in the Chinese zodiac.

11. After track practice, hes going to record his best times.

12. It doesnt matter to me, but shes adamant about making her point.

13. We dont know whos batting next.

14. Im going to the dance with my best friend.

15. The Salvation Armys office is organizing the benefit concert.

16. Nothings going to stop them from playing volleyball after school.

17. You must stir the ingredients until theyre well blended.

18. After spending two weeks in Italy, Mary didnt want to come home.

19. Mom, please hang Teds jacket next to yours.

20. Youre responsible for counting the money.

Plurals

14h. Use an apostrophe and an *s* to form the plurals of numerals, symbols, all lowercase letters, some uppercase letters, and some words referred to as words.

EXAMPLES   Most of your cursive *u*'**s** and *U*'**s** are the same size.

Mr. Carr suggested that I replace some of the *so*'**s** in my paper with other words.

These *2*'**s** look like *7*'**s.**

It appears that the author has confused @'**s** and &'**s.**

Note that in the first example, the plurals of *u* and *U* could be misread as *us* and *Us* if the apostrophes were omitted. In the second example, the plural of *so* could be misread as the acronym *sos* if the apostrophe were omitted.

Reference Note

For more on forming the **plurals of numerals, symbols, letters, and words referred to as words,** see page 387.

STYLE TIP

Many writers add only an *s* to some of the kinds of plurals listed in Rule 14h. However, using both an apostrophe and *s* is not wrong and may be necessary to make your meaning clear. Therefore, it is a good idea always to include the apostrophe.

Be sure to use apostrophes consistently.

EXAMPLE

Are those *I*'**s** or *L*'**s**? [Without an apostrophe, the plural of *I* would spell the word *Is*. Since an apostrophe and *s* are used to form the plural of one letter, an apostrophe and *s* are used with the other letter for consistency.]

Review D **Correcting Sentences by Adding Apostrophes**

For each of the following sentences, write all the items needing apostrophes, and add the apostrophes.

EXAMPLE   **1.** You may agree with the school boards decision, but I dont.

1. *school board's; don't*

1. Are these &s or 8s?
2. You forgot that there are two *as* at the beginning of *aardvark*.
3. My stepsister graduated from high school in 97 and graduated from college in 01.
4. Lewis Carrolls novel *Alices Adventures in Wonderland* was originally called *Alices Adventures Underground*.
5. Whos going to change the babies diapers?
6. After school were going to visit his sister; shes in St. Marys Hospital.
7. Did you write *os* or *0s* in the margin?
8. Its been six weeks since I checked the cars oil and its tires.
9. Your story would be better if youd remove about ten *verys*.
10. She learned the Hawaiian alphabets twelve letters, but Max didnt.

MECHANICS

Hyphens

Word Division

14i. Use a hyphen to divide a word at the end of a line.

EXAMPLE   How long had the new museum been under con-
            struction before it was opened?

    When dividing a word at the end of a line, keep in mind the
following rules:

(1) Do not divide a one-syllable word.

INCORRECT   After a long journey the Spanish explorers reach-
             ed their destination.
CORRECT   After a long journey the Spanish explorers reached
             their destination.
CORRECT   After a long journey the Spanish explorers
             reached their destination.

(2) Divide a word only between syllables.

INCORRECT   The fans stood and cheered while the band was pla-
             ying the victory song.
CORRECT   The fans stood and cheered while the band was play-
             ing the victory song.

(3) Divide an already hyphenated word only at the hyphen.

INCORRECT   My stepsister Melissa plans to take a course in self-de-
             fense.
CORRECT   My stepsister Melissa plans to take a course in self-
             defense.
INCORRECT   Ms. Malamud always seems to have such a hap-
             py-go-lucky attitude.
CORRECT   Ms. Malamud always seems to have such a happy-
             go-lucky attitude.
CORRECT   Ms. Malamud always seems to have such a happy-go-
             lucky attitude.

(4) Do not divide a word so that one letter stands alone.

INCORRECT   In the gloomy twilight, we had caught a momentar-
             y glimpse of them.
CORRECT   In the gloomy twilight, we had caught a momen-
             tary glimpse of them.

─HELP─

If you are not
entirely sure about the
syllabication of a word—
that is, the division of a
word into syllables—look
up the word in a dictionary.
Many dictionaries show
how to break words into
syllables.

TIPS & TRICKS

Generally, a word containing double consonants may
be divided between the
double consonants.

EXAMPLES
  cor-rect   begin-ning

Generally, a word with a
prefix or suffix made up of
more than one letter may
be divided between the
prefix and the base word
(root) or between the base
word and the suffix.

EXAMPLES
  semi-circle   pro-mote
  peace-ful   sign-ing

MECHANICS

Exercise 4 Using Hyphens to Divide Words at the Ends of Lines

Write each of the following words, adding hyphens in each place where you could divide the word at the end of a line. If a word should not be divided, write *no hyphen*. If you are unsure where to divide a word, look in a dictionary that shows syllable breaks.

EXAMPLE   **1.** harmonious

1. *har-mo-ni-ous*

1. Olympic
2. algebra
3. toast
4. pemmican
5. drummer
6. alert
7. someone
8. Honduras
9. reservation
10. ditch
11. circle
12. traveling
13. kudzu
14. satisfaction
15. donation
16. mansion
17. topography
18. greet
19. self-esteem
20. Johnny-come-lately

Compound Words

Some compound words are written as one word (*blueberry*); some are hyphenated (*blue-collar*); and some are written as two or more words (*blue jay, Blue Ridge Mountains*).

Whenever you are not sure about the spelling of a compound word, look up the word in an up-to-date dictionary.

14j. Use a hyphen with compound numbers from *twenty-one* to *ninety-nine* and with fractions used as modifiers.

EXAMPLES   **twenty-seven** students

a **two-thirds** majority [but *two thirds of the class*]

14k. Use a hyphen with the prefixes *all–, ex–, great–,* and *self–;* with the suffixes *–elect* and *–free;* and with all prefixes before a proper noun or proper adjective.

EXAMPLES   **all-**purpose   detergent-**free**

ex-president   **anti-**Stalinist

great-grandmother   **mid-**December

self-control   **non-**Francophile

secretary-**elect**   **pro-**American

| STYLE   TIP |

The prefix *half* often requires a hyphen, as in *half-life, half-moon,* and *half-truth.* However, sometimes *half* is used without a hyphen, either as part of a single word (*halftone, halfway, halfback*) or as a separate word (*half shell, half pint, half note*). If you are not sure how to spell a compound containing *half*, look up the word in a dictionary.

14l. Hyphenate a compound adjective when it precedes the noun it modifies.

EXAMPLES   a **well-organized** trip [but *a trip that was well organized*]

           an **after-school** job

Do not use a hyphen if one of the modifiers is an adverb ending in *ly*.

EXAMPLE   a **perfectly good** answer

NOTE   Some compound adjectives are always hyphenated, whether they precede or follow the nouns they modify.

EXAMPLES   a **down-to-earth** person

           a person who is **down-to-earth**

      If you have any doubt about whether a compound adjective is hyphenated, look up the word in an up-to-date dictionary.

Exercise 5   **Hyphenating Words Correctly**

For each of the following sentences, write and hyphenate the compound words that should be hyphenated.

EXAMPLE   1. The host of that late night show interviewed an expert on Italy's pre Renaissance years.

       1. *late-night; pre-Renaissance*

1. Ex students were not allowed at the festively decorated prom party.
2. His self confidence faded when he forgot his well planned speech.
3. Twenty five students said they had never heard of the well traveled Overland Trail to California.
4. Three fourths of the class voted, and the proposal was defeated by a seven tenths majority.
5. Our governor elect was once an all American football player.
6. In our debate on the United Nations, the pro UN side defeated the anti UN side.
7. General Colin Powell, who is a former resident of the Bronx, spoke quite eloquently about the importance of self determination.
8. Christopher's test scores ranked in the eighty eighth percentile.
9. You must turn in your reports by mid November.
10. My uncle's recipe for halftime nachos calls for fat free cheese and spicy salsa.

MEETING THE CHALLENGE

Why do we need to use hyphens? Discuss this question in a short essay in which you *break* five hyphen rules or subrules from this chapter. Then, list the five rules or subrules that your essay violated.

MECHANICS

Dashes

Sometimes a word, phrase, or sentence is used parenthetically; that is, it breaks into the main thought of a sentence. Most parenthetical elements are set off by commas or by parentheses.

EXAMPLES   Felipe, **however,** had a better idea.

Her suggestion **(that we serve fruit and cheese instead of junk food)** was approved unanimously.

Sometimes, though, such elements call for a sharper separation from the rest of the sentence. In such cases, dashes are used.

14m. Use a dash to indicate the beginning and the end of an abrupt break in thought or speech or to indicate an unfinished thought.

EXAMPLES   The party—I'm sorry I forgot to tell you—was not changed to next week.

"What I meant was—" Vonda began as the doorbell rang.

14n. Use a dash to mean *namely, that is,* or *in other words,* or to otherwise introduce an explanation. Also, use a dash after the explanation if the sentence continues.

EXAMPLES   Our family owns two vehicles—a station wagon and a pickup truck. [*namely*]

The weather was unseasonably warm—in the low eighties—for February. [*that is*]

NOTE   Either a dash or a colon is acceptable in the first example for 14n.

Parentheses

14o. Use parentheses to enclose informative or explanatory material of minor importance.

EXAMPLES   The Temple of the Magician **(**I never thought I'd actually see it**)** rose majestically against the purple sky of Uxmal, in the Mexican Yucatán.

Eleanor Roosevelt **(**1884–1962**)** helped draft the Universal Declaration of Human Rights.

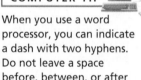

COMPUTER TIP

When you use a word processor, you can indicate a dash with two hyphens. Do not leave a space before, between, or after the hyphens. When you write by hand, use an unbroken line about as long as two hyphens.

STYLE   TIP

Dates in parentheses after a person's name indicate the years of that person's birth and death. If the person is still alive, put the closing parenthesis immediately after the dash.

EXAMPLE
George Lucas (1944–) was born in Modesto, California.

Be sure that the material enclosed in parentheses can be omitted without affecting the intended meaning or basic structure of the sentence.

INCORRECT	When my six-year-old cousin said ("It's the first inning"), the rest of us watching the football game started laughing.
CORRECT	When my six-year-old cousin said, **"It's the first inning,"** the rest of us watching the football game started laughing.

INCORRECT	I sent the package on October 12 (that was ten days ago via express mail.)
CORRECT	I sent the package on October 12 **(that was ten days ago)** via express mail.

A sentence enclosed in parentheses may fall within another sentence or may stand by itself.

(1) A parenthetical sentence that falls within another sentence

- does not begin with a capital letter unless it begins with a word that should be capitalized

- does not end with a period but may end with a question mark or exclamation point

EXAMPLES   When we reached Shaker Heights **(it's just outside Cleveland),** we met our cousins for dinner.

The John Hancock Tower **(isn't it in Boston?)** was designed by I. M. Pei.

NOTE   Generally, when parenthetical material falls within a sentence, punctuation does not precede the opening parenthesis but may follow the closing parenthesis.

INCORRECT	Reading the novel by Samuel Clemens, (better known as Mark Twain) I learned much about American society in the nineteenth century.
CORRECT	Reading the novel by Samuel Clemens (better known as Mark Twain), I learned much about American society in the nineteenth century. [The comma following the closing parenthesis is used to set off the introductory participial phrase.]

(2) A parenthetical sentence that stands by itself

- begins with a capital letter

- ends with a period, a question mark, or an exclamation point

STYLE   TIP

Too many parenthetical expressions in a piece of writing can distract the reader from the main idea. Keep your meaning clear by limiting the number of parenthetical expressions you use.

MECHANICS

EXAMPLES   On the scoring sheet, mark your answers with a lead pencil. **(Do not use ink.)**

In 1996 he won another gold medal for the high dive. **(That was his ninth!)**

Follow these guidelines for determining when to use commas, dashes, and parentheses to enclose parenthetical material:

1. Remember that only material that can be omitted without changing the basic meaning or structure of the sentence is considered parenthetical.
2. Use commas to set off parenthetical material that is closely related to the rest of the sentence.

EXAMPLE   We rehearsed for the show, a wonderful musical comedy.

3. Use a dash to indicate the beginning and the end of an abrupt change in thought or to indicate an unfinished thought.

EXAMPLE   We rehearsed for the show—which many called the musical event of the year!

4. Use parentheses to indicate that the parenthetical material is of minor importance.

EXAMPLE   We rehearsed for the show (at least those of us who could remember our lines did).

5. Don't overuse parenthetical material, or you may confuse your readers.

COMPUTER TIP

With the search-and-replace function of a word-processing program, you can check your writing for the incorrect or inappropriate uses of apostrophes, hyphens, dashes, and parentheses. Take full advantage of such a program when you are proofreading your work.

Brackets

14p. Use brackets to enclose an explanation or added information within quoted or parenthetical material.

EXAMPLES   The secretary of state, in her speech, said: "Diplomatic efforts seek to establish talks between the two nations **[North and South Korea]**." [The words are enclosed in brackets to show that they have been inserted into the quotation and are not the speaker's words.]

The faltering performance of the Russian economy in recent years has caused fluctuations in the world's financial markets. (See page 15 **[Graph 1A]** for a chronology.)

Exercise 6 Correcting Sentences by Using Dashes, Parentheses, and Brackets

Rewrite the following sentences, adding dashes, parentheses, and brackets where they are needed. If a sentence is already correct, write *C*.

EXAMPLE   **1.** Garth Brooks and Shania Twain I have every one of their albums have won many awards.

     1. Garth Brooks and Shania Twain (I have every one of their albums) have won many awards.

1. "Yankee Doodle" it was the unofficial United States anthem at the time was played after the signing of the Treaty of Ghent.
2. While standing at the top of Pikes Peak, Katherine Lee Bates wrote the words to the song "America the Beautiful."
3. Lauryn Hill I love her songs! gave a concert here, and it sold out.
4. There were three original members of the Sons of the Pioneers Roy Rogers his real name was Leonard Slye, Bob Nolan, and Tim Spencer.
5. Linda Ronstadt has recorded many kinds of music, including rock, songs from the 1930's and 1940's, and Mexican tunes.
6. The Beatles used several names Foreverly Brothers, the Cavemen, the Moondogs, and the Quarrymen before they became the Beatles.
7. Last night's concert was about average the songs were good, but the singers were uninspired.
8. Cathy said, "I will listen to one of your CDs Mozart's *Requiem*, perhaps if you will listen to one of Lenny Kravitz's CDs."
9. Bob Dylan (1941– born Robert Allen Zimmerman) wrote "Blowin' in the Wind."
10. That singer's version of "The Star-Spangled Banner" have you heard it? wouldn't Francis Scott Key be pleased? was very inspiring.

┌─HELP─

Some sentences in Exercise 6 have more than one possible answer. You need to give only one answer for each sentence.

Review E Proofreading for Errors in Punctuation

Each of the following sentences contains at least one error in punctuation. Correct the errors by adding apostrophes, hyphens, dashes, parentheses, and brackets where they are needed.

EXAMPLE   **1.** Dont you ever wonder I frequently do about who invented different kinds of machines and tools?

     1. Don't you ever wonder—I frequently do—about who invented different kinds of machines and tools?

or

     Don't you ever wonder (I frequently do) about who invented different kinds of machines and tools?

┌─HELP─

Although two possible answers are given for the example in Review E, you need to give only one answer for each sentence.

1. Both Trishs and Roberts reports the ones required for social studies were about the shoe industry.
2. Trish said that she chose the subject because at least seventy five percent of the world's students wear shoes.
3. I thought the other report the one Robert gave on the invention of the lasting machine was more interesting, though.
4. Robert wrote, "The lasting machine (its parts are numbered in the patent drawing provided see the picture below) changed the shoe industrys future."
5. The machines inventor the distinguished looking young man pictured below was Jan Matzeliger.
6. He came to the United States from Dutch Guiana now Suriname before 1880 and found work as a shoemakers apprentice.
7. Matzeliger wasnt happy with how much of the workers time was spent putting shoes together.
8. Within ten years time he perfected a machine that shaped leather for the upper shoe and attached it to the sole.
9. Matzeligers patent for this much needed machine was granted in 1883.
10. The United Shoe Manufacturing Companys decision to buy the machine ultimately gave that company control of the United States shoe market.

The Granger Collection, New York.

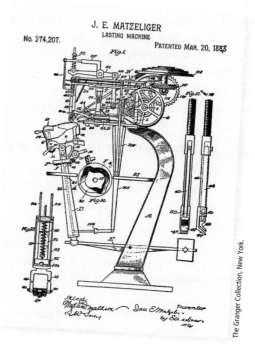

J. E. MATZELIGER
LASTING MACHINE
No. 274,207.
PATENTED MAR. 20, 1883

The Granger Collection, New York.

Chapter Review

A. Using Apostrophes and Hyphens Correctly

Add or delete apostrophes and hyphens as necessary in the following sentences.

┌HELP┐
Some sentences in the Chapter Review contain more than one error.

1. The towns record on supporting youth projects has been good.
2. The wet, muddy boots were lined up outside the door to the house.
3. Only fifty three people went to our ballet recital, and thirty of them were our relatives.
4. Everyones favorite performer was certainly the man in the turtleneck.
5. Christophers writing is hard to read because his *a*s look like *o*s.
6. The womens basketball team, which is coached by an ex Laker, has run up quite an impressive string of victories.
7. Sampson and Smiths French Bakery, which displays its pastries in the window, is around the corner from my house.
8. Mr. Millers watercolors dont appeal to me, but they were given the jurys highest award.
9. Approximately twenty out of twenty five students agree that self esteem is among the most important personal qualities.
10. To verify safety standards, we have compared twenty-seven sport utility vehicles.
11. Theres someone at the door, and were already late for school!
12. Hes used too many *therefore*s in his sentences to get an A on his composition.
13. There are three *5*s and four *8*s missing from your answer's.
14. My sister-in-laws job is selling childrens sportswear.
15. The Jameses address contains four *7*s.

B. Using Dashes, Brackets, and Parentheses Correctly

Add dashes, brackets, and parentheses where they are needed in each of the following sentences. Do not add commas or colons.

16. My cousins like many of Charley Pride's songs his "Crystal Chandeliers" is their favorite.

17. This report contains information about agriculture in those three South American countries Brazil, Argentina, and Colombia see Graph 3A on pp. 24–25.

18. I read the wrong chapter for my homework a disastrous mistake!

19. Mary Ellen Jefferson, a former district attorney, will speak at Thursday's assembly I'll have to miss gym class and will address the topic of student rights.

20. Bessie Coleman I read an article about her was the first licensed African American pilot.

C. Writing the Possessive Forms of Nouns

Write the singular possessive and plural possessive form of each of the following nouns.

21. house	**25.** cow	**28.** goose
22. computer	**26.** president	**29.** wife
23. uncle	**27.** trellis	**30.** theory
24. coach		

D. Proofreading a Paragraph for Errors in Punctuation

Each sentence in the following paragraph contains at least one error in punctuation. Correct the errors by adding or deleting apostrophes, hyphens, dashes, and parentheses.

[31] The kangaroo, possibly Australias most famous indigenous animal, is a marsupial, a kind of mammal. [32] Marsupial's offspring are born extremely undeveloped. [33] A newborn joey a baby kangaroo measures only about one inch long. [34] A kangaroos pouch the pocket like opening in the mother's belly where the joey completes its development is one of the animal kingdoms' most unusual features. [35] With their huge hind feet, long tails, and small, deer like heads, kangaroos are among the worlds' most distinctive creatures. [36] Kangaroos and wallabies their smaller cousins both belong to an animal family called macropods the name means "big foot" in Latin which includes other animals such as the so called hare wallaby, the bettong, and the potoroo. [37] Kangaroo's life spans vary from six to eight years, on average. [38] They have few enemies and are protected by Australias no poaching laws. [39] Theyre fast, too; large specimens top speed is as

high as 30 miles per hour. **[40]** So closely are they bound up with Australias identity that the symbol of Qantas, the national airline, is yes, you guessed it a leaping "roo."

Writing Application
Punctuating a Poem

Using Dashes   You have decided to enter a local poetry contest for high school students. All the poems must reflect students' ideas about current events. For the contest, write a poem that uses at least four dashes.

Prewriting   Start by making a list of current events that interest you. Then, choose a subject from your list, and freewrite about it. List as many sensory details as you can to describe your subject. Then, start grouping the details to create a loose structure for your poem.

Writing   Use your freewriting notes to write your first draft. As you form your ideas into lines of poetry, choose words and punctuation carefully, paying attention to both the images and the rhythms they create.

Revising   Read your poem silently to be sure that it says what you want it to say. Add, cut, or rearrange details to express your ideas more effectively. Then, read your poem aloud and listen to the rhythm of the words you have used. Make any changes that you feel will improve the rhythm, keeping in mind that you must include at least four dashes in the poem.

Publishing   Be sure to check the spelling and punctuation in your poem. If you have typed your poem or are using a word processor, check to see that the spacing around hyphens and dashes is correct. If your class has a Web page, you may want to collect your poems and publish them on the Internet.

Spelling
Improving Your Spelling

Diagnostic Preview

Correcting Misspelled and Misused Words and Numerals

Proofread the following sentences, and correctly write any misspelled or misused words or numerals.

EXAMPLE   **1.** Our parents will be dineing out tonight.

　　　　　1. dining

　1. When I went to the barn, the cows and calfs were eating hay.
　2. Do you know weather Mars was a Roman diety?
　3. I don't know whether the relay team won 1st or 2nd place.
　4. Our Thanksgiving meal consists of turkey, stuffing, beans, cranberries, and potatos.
　5. The principle's name is Mr. Goodson.
　6. The child carried the turtle carefuly across the road.
　7. Jill didn't mispell any words on the test.
　8. The basketball team missed the bus, so they had to forfiet the game.
　9. If I've told you once, I've told you 1,000 times: Don't exaggerate!
　10. We decieved Janice so that she would not know we were throwing a surprise birthday party for her.
　11. The affects of this weather system were completly unexpected.
　12. I felt that the emergency team was quite couragous.
　13. The director said two hundred seventeen people applied for the job.
　14. If you excede the speed limit, you might get a ticket.

15. I was grateful to be offerred the lead in the play.
16. My parents' dog, an enormous Great Dane, is always getting into mischeif.
17. Arguement is useless in this situation.
18. A Japanese animated cartoon will preceed the action movie.
19. Ed wants to write playes for a living.
20. Lauren ate 6 pieces of kiwi fruit.

Good Spelling Habits

15a. To learn the spelling of a word, pronounce it, study it, and write it.

(1) Pronounce words carefully.

EXAMPLES   **athl**etic [not *athaletic*]

              escape [not *excape*]

              heigh**t** [not *heighth*]

(2) Spell by syllables.

A *syllable* is a word part that can be pronounced as one uninterrupted sound.

EXAMPLES   pul • sate [two syllables]

              bul • le • tin [three syllables]

              en • vi • ron • ment [four syllables]

(3) Use a dictionary.

Do not guess about correct spelling. Look up any words you do not know how to spell. In the dictionary, you can often find other, related words that may help you remember the correct spelling. For example, you may find *denomination* easier to spell after you see its kinship with the words *nominate* and *denominator*.

(4) Proofread for careless spelling errors.

Always proofread what you have written so that you can eliminate careless spelling errors, such as typos (*thier* for *their*), missing letters (*temperture* for *temperature*), and the misuse of words that sound similar (*principal* for *principle*).

┌HELP─

If you are not sure about the correct pronunciation of a word, look it up in a current dictionary. The pronunciation of the word will usually be given in parentheses after the main entry. Use the pronunciation key in the dictionary to help you pronounce the word correctly.

MECHANICS

COMPUTER TIP

Spellcheckers can help you proofread your writing. Even the best spellcheckers are not foolproof, however. Some accept British spellings, obsolete words, archaic spellings, and words that are spelled correctly but are used incorrectly (such as *affect* for *effect*). Always double-check your writing to make sure that your spelling is error-free.

(5) Keep a spelling notebook.

Divide each page into four columns:

COLUMN 1   Correctly write any word you find troublesome.

COLUMN 2   Write the word again, dividing it into syllables and marking the stressed syllable(s). (You may need to use a dictionary.)

COLUMN 3   Write the word again, circling the difficult part(s).

COLUMN 4   Write down any comments that might help you remember the correct spelling.

Correct Spelling	Syllables and Accents	Trouble Spot	Comments
February	Feb'·ru·ar·y	Feb(ru)ary	Pronounce correctly.
disapproval	dis'·ap·prov·al	di(sa)pprov(al)	Study Rules 15e and 15g.

Spelling Rules

ie and *ei*

15b. Write *ie* when the sound is long *e*, except after *c*.

EXAMPLES   ch**ie**f, bel**ie**ve, n**ie**ce, ach**ie**ve, perc**ei**ve, rec**ei**pt

EXCEPTIONS   **ei**ther, l**ei**sure, n**ei**ther, prot**ei**n

15c. Write *ei* when the sound is not long *e*.

EXAMPLES   forf**ei**t, fr**ei**ght, h**ei**ght, n**ei**ghbor, v**ei**l, w**ei**gh

EXCEPTIONS   anc**ie**nt, misch**ie**f, pat**ie**nce

–cede, –ceed, and *–sede*

15d. The only English word ending in *–sede* is *supersede*. The only words ending in *–ceed* are *exceed, proceed,* and *succeed.* Most other words with this sound end in *–cede.*

EXAMPLES   con**cede**, pre**cede**, re**cede**, ac**cede**

TIPS & TRICKS

Remember this rhyme:
i before *e*
except after *c*
or when sounded like *a*
as in *neighbor* and *weigh*.

┌HELP──

Rules 15b and 15c apply only when the *i* and the *e* are in the same syllable.

EXAMPLES
sci • ence   de • i • ty

Exercise 1 Proofreading Sentences to Correct Spelling Errors

Proofread each of the following sentences, and correctly write the misspelled word or words.

┌HELP┐

None of the proper nouns in Exercise 1 are misspelled.

EXAMPLE   1. Niether my neice nor I have tried bungee jumping.

         1. *Neither, niece*

1. During the 1920s, one craze superceded another, each one weirder than the one that preceeded it.
2. Pictured at right is fifteen-year-old Avon Foreman, who acheived fame in Baltimore for his bizarre liesure-time activity.
3. In 1929, he spent ten days, ten hours, ten minutes, and ten seconds perched atop a hickory sapling, at a hieght of eighteen feet.
4. Freinds and neighbors crowded around to give encouragement.
5. He even succeded in attracting the attention of the mayor, William F. Broening, who wrote to him that his "grit and stamina . . . show that the old pioneer spirit of early America is being kept alive by the youth of today."
6. The mayor beleived that Avon was indeed someone to look up to, evidently.
7. People continue to participate in and succede at a number of curious endeavors.
8. There are attempts to cross Antarctica using only dog sleds, leaps from great hieghts, and contests to see how many people will fit into a small car.
9. It seems that humans will always try to acheive unusual goals.
10. Undoubtedly, many people have recieved great entertainment from these occasionally ridiculous activities.

Adding Prefixes

A *prefix* is one or more letters or syllables added to the beginning of a word to create a new word that has a different meaning.

15e. When adding a prefix, do not change the spelling of the original word.

EXAMPLES   mis + spell = mis**spell**   dis + advantage = dis**advantage**

            un + likely = un**likely**   il + legible = il**legible**

MECHANICS

Adding Suffixes

A *suffix* is one or more letters or syllables added to the end of a word to create a new word with a different meaning.

15f. When adding the suffix *–ly* or *–ness*, do not change the spelling of the original word.

EXAMPLES   nice + ly = **nice**ly   mean + ness = **mean**ness

                   usual + ly = **usual**ly   same + ness = **same**ness

Words ending in *y* usually change the *y* to *i* before *–ness* and *–ly*:

EXAMPLES   empty—empt**i**ness; easy—eas**i**ly

However, most one-syllable adjectives ending in *y* follow Rule 15f:

EXAMPLES   shy—**shy**ly; dry—**dry**ness

True, due, and *whole* drop the final *e* before *–ly*:

EXAMPLES   true—**tru**ly; due—**du**ly; whole—**whol**ly

Exercise 2   Spelling Words with Prefixes and Suffixes

Write each of the following words, adding the prefix or suffix given.

EXAMPLE   **1.** il + legible

                1. illegible

1. heavy + ness	**11.** ordinary + ly
2. dis + satisfied	**12.** im + mature
3. il + legal	**13.** sudden + ness
4. un + nerve	**14.** special + ly
5. sincere + ly	**15.** over + rate
6. whole + ly	**16.** il + logical
7. mis + understood	**17.** un + flattering
8. ready + ness	**18.** dis + illusion
9. un + likely	**19.** stubborn + ness
10. happy + ly	**20.** shy + ness

15g. Drop the final silent *e* before adding a suffix beginning with a vowel.

EXAMPLES   dine + ing = **din**ing   safe + er = **saf**er

                  use + able = **us**able   nice + est = **nic**est

EXCEPTIONS   Keep the final silent *e*

- in a word ending in *ce* or *ge* before a suffix beginning with *a* or *o*

  service + able = **service**able

  advantage + ous = **advantage**ous

- in *dye* and in *singe* before *–ing:* **dye**ing and **singe**ing [to avoid confusion with *dying* and *singing*]

- in *mile* before *–age:* **mile**age

15h. Keep the final silent *e* before adding a suffix beginning with a consonant.

EXAMPLES   use + ful = **use**ful   care + less = **care**less

pave + ment = **pave**ment   live + ly = **live**ly

hope + ful = **hope**ful   large + ly = **large**ly

EXCEPTIONS   true + ly = **tru**ly   nine + th = **nin**th

argue + ment = **argu**ment   awe + ful = **aw**ful

Oral Practice   **Spelling Words with Suffixes**

Spell aloud each of the following words, adding the suffix given.

EXAMPLES   **1.** amuse + ing

1. *amusing*

2. care + ful

2. *careful*

1. courage + ous
2. nine + ty
3. advance + ing
4. hope + less
5. approve + al
6. note + able
7. ride + ing
8. outrage + ous
9. dye + ing
10. true + ly

15i. For words ending in *y* preceded by a consonant, change the *y* to *i* before adding any suffix that does not begin with *i*.

EXAMPLES   lively + ness = **liveli**ness   rely + ed = **reli**ed

bury + al = **buri**al   funny + er = **funni**er

hasty + est = **hasti**est   study + ing = **study**ing

HELP

Some one-syllable words do not follow Rule 15i.

EXAMPLES
dry—**dry**ness
shy—**shy**ly

15j. For words ending in *y* preceded by a vowel, keep the *y* when adding a suffix.

EXAMPLES   enjoy + able = **enjoy**able   play + ful = **play**ful

survey + or = **survey**or   delay + ing = **delay**ing

EXCEPTIONS   lay—**lai**d   pay—**pai**d   say—**sai**d   day—**dai**ly

Exercise 3   **Spelling Words with Suffixes**

Write each of the following words, adding the suffix given.

EXAMPLES   **1.** ready + ly

1. *readily*

2. relay + ing

2. *relaying*

1. happy + est
2. marry + ing
3. relay + ed
4. shiny + er
5. obey + ed

6. spy + ing
7. employ + ing
8. try + ed
9. day + ly
10. busy + ly

15k. Double the final consonant before adding a suffix that begins with a vowel if the word (1) has only one syllable or has the accent on the final syllable and (2) ends in a single consonant preceded by a single vowel.

EXAMPLES   drop + ed = dro**pped**   run + er = ru**nner**

begin + ing = begi**nning**   regret + able = regre**ttable**

EXCEPTIONS   For words ending in *w* or *x*, do not double the final consonant.

few + er = **few**er   throw + ing = **throw**ing

fax + es = **fax**es   perplex + ed = **perplex**ed

When a word satisfies both conditions but the addition of the suffix causes the accent to shift, do not double the final consonant.

EXAMPLES   confer + ence = **confer**ence

prefer + able = **prefer**able

EXCEPTIONS   excel—exce**llent**, exce**llence**, exce**llency**

┌HELP──

The final consonant of some words may or may not be doubled. Either spelling is acceptable.

EXAMPLES
travel + ed = trave**led**
or trave**lled**

cancel + ing = cance**ling**
or cance**lling**

Exercise 4 Spelling Words with Suffixes

Write each of the following words, adding the suffix given.

EXAMPLE   **1.** slip + ed

    1. slipped

1. sad + er   **11.** excel + ence
2. propel + er   **12.** run + ing
3. shovel + ing   **13.** wax + ed
4. refer + al   **14.** droop + ed
5. repel + ent   **15.** drop + ing
6. confer + ed   **16.** accept + ance
7. suffer + ance   **17.** refer + ence
8. hop + ing   **18.** beep + ing
9. shop + ed   **19.** endow + ing
10. remit + ance   **20.** mow + er

© John Caldwell 1986.

Review A Proofreading a Paragraph to Correct Spelling Errors

Proofread the following paragraph, correcting each misspelled word.

EXAMPLE   **[1]** In what battle were the Shawnee cheif Tecumseh, his brother, and thier followers defeatted by William Henry Harrison?

    1. chief; their; defeated

┌HELP─

No proper
nouns in Review A
are misspelled.

George Catlin, *The Open Door, Known as the Prophet, Brother of Tecumseh*. National Museum of American Art, Washington, DC/ Art Resource, New York.

[1] The Shawnee war chief Tecumseh was commited to the goal of uniting American Indians. [2] He believed that unification was the only way to prevent white settlers from siezing the land on which his people lived. [3] Opposed to treaties that forced Native Americans to forfiet their land, Tecumseh believed that the land was owned by no one. [4] After much hard work, he succeded in convincing some midwestern American Indian peoples to join together. [5] With his brother, known as the Shawnee Prophet, Tecumseh urged his people to preserve their traditional ways of liveing and not to surrender the land. [6] Tecumseh and the Shawnee Prophet, at left, led thier followers in building Prophetstown at the location indicated on the map of Indiana below. [7] In 1811, while Tecumseh was delivering a speech in a neighboring village, the governor of the Indiana Territory, William Henry Harrison, and his forces easly attacked Prophetstown. [8] Against Tecumseh's wishes, the Shawnee Prophet and his followers proceeded to counterattack and finally had to consede defeat in the Battle of Tippecanoe. [9] Overun by Harrison, Tecumseh's people scattered, leaving the town in ruins and bringing to an end twenty years of Tecumseh's work. [10] Tecumseh had planed to start over, but his death in 1813 at the Battle of the Thames ended all hopes of uniting the various Native American nations.

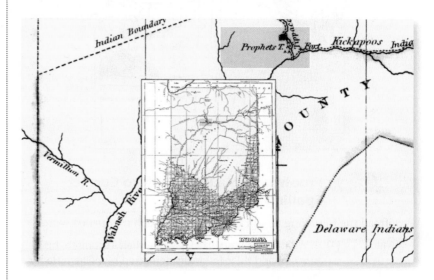

Forming Plurals of Nouns

15l. The singular form of a noun names one person, place, thing, or idea. The plural form names more than one. Remembering the following rules will help you spell the plural forms of nouns.

(1) For most nouns, add *s*.

SINGULAR	dog	kite	pencil	video	club	McGregor
PLURAL	dog**s**	kite**s**	pencil**s**	video**s**	club**s**	McGregor**s**

(2) For nouns ending in *s, x, z, ch*, or *sh*, add *es*.

SINGULAR	glass	suffix	waltz	trench	bush	Gomez
PLURAL	glass**es**	suffix**es**	waltz**es**	trench**es**	bush**es**	Gomez**es**

(3) For nouns ending in *y* preceded by a vowel, add *s*.

SINGULAR	alloy	turkey	essay	attorney	decoy	Sunday
PLURAL	alloy**s**	turkey**s**	essay**s**	attorney**s**	decoy**s**	Sunday**s**

(4) For nouns ending in *y* preceded by a consonant, change the *y* to *i* and add *es*.

SINGULAR	city	enemy	spy	penny	country
PLURAL	cit**ies**	enem**ies**	sp**ies**	penn**ies**	countr**ies**

> NOTE For most proper nouns ending in *y* preceded by a consonant, add *s*.
>
> EXAMPLES   Murphy—Murphy**s**
> Brody—Brody**s**

(5) For some nouns ending in *f* or *fe*, add *s*. For others, change the *f* or *fe* to *v* and add *es*.

SINGULAR	belief	roof	fife	wolf	knife	leaf
PLURAL	belief**s**	roof**s**	fife**s**	wol**ves**	kni**ves**	lea**ves**

(6) For nouns ending in *o* preceded by a vowel, add *s*.

SINGULAR	patio	rodeo	ratio	barrio	kangaroo	Valerio
PLURAL	patio**s**	rodeo**s**	ratio**s**	barrio**s**	kangaroo**s**	Valerio**s**

(7) For most nouns ending in *o* preceded by a consonant, add *es*.

SINGULAR	tomato	potato	hero	echo	torpedo
PLURAL	tomato**es**	potato**es**	hero**es**	echo**es**	torpedo**es**

┌HELP─

Some one-syllable words ending in *z* double the final consonant when forming plurals.

EXAMPLES
quiz   fez
quiz**zes**   fez**zes**

┌HELP─

For most proper nouns ending in *f* or *fe*, add *s*.

EXAMPLES
van Cleef—van Cleef**s**
Radcliffe—Radcliffe**s**

┌TIPS & TRICKS┐

Noticing how the plural is pronounced will help you remember whether to change the *f* or *fe* to *v*.

MECHANICS

For some common nouns ending in *o* preceded by a consonant (especially those referring to music) and for proper nouns, add *s*.

SINGULAR	taco	dojo	soprano	allegro	Sato
PLURAL	taco**s**	dojo**s**	soprano**s**	allegro**s**	Sato**s**

> **NOTE** For some nouns ending in *o* preceded by a consonant, you may add either *s* or *es*.
>
> | SINGULAR | cargo | mosquito | motto | zero |
> |---|---|---|---|---|
> | PLURAL | cargo**s** | mosquito**s** | motto**s** | zero**s** |
> | | *or* | *or* | *or* | *or* |
> | | cargo**es** | mosquito**es** | motto**es** | zero**es** |

(8) The plurals of a few nouns are formed irregularly.

SINGULAR	child	ox	woman	tooth	mouse	foot
PLURAL	child**ren**	ox**en**	wom**e**n	t**ee**th	m**i**ce	f**ee**t

(9) For a few nouns, the singular and the plural forms are the same.

SINGULAR AND PLURAL	Chinese	scissors	salmon
	sheep	aircraft	binoculars

Compound Nouns

(10) For most compound nouns, form the plural of only the last word of the compound.

SINGULAR	bookkeeper	stepchild	two-year-old	grand jury
PLURAL	bookkeeper**s**	stepchild**ren**	two-year-old**s**	grand jur**ies**

(11) For many compound nouns in which one of the words is modified by the other word or words, form the plural of the word modified.

SINGULAR	editor in chief	son-in-law	chief of staff	runner-up
PLURAL	editor**s** in chief	son**s**-in-law	chief**s** of staff	runner**s**-up

> **NOTE** Some compound nouns have two acceptable plural forms.
>
> | SINGULAR | surgeon general | court-martial |
> |---|---|---|
> | PLURAL | surgeon**s** general | court**s**-martial |
> | | *or* | *or* |
> | | surgeon general**s** | court-martial**s** |

Words Borrowed from Other Languages

(12) For some nouns borrowed from other languages, plurals are formed as in the original languages.

Singular	Plural
alumnus [male]	alumni [male]
alumna [female]	alumnae [female]
phenomenon	phenomena
parenthesis	parentheses
datum	data

NOTE A few nouns borrowed from other languages have two acceptable plural forms. For each of the following nouns, the plural form preferred in English is given first.

SINGULAR	formula	index	cactus	seraph
PLURAL	formulas	indexes	cactuses	seraphs
	or	or	or	or
	formulae	indices	cacti	seraphim

    If you are ever in doubt about which spelling to use, remember that a dictionary generally lists the preferred spelling first.

Numerals, Letters, Symbols, and Words Used as Words

(13) To form the plurals of numerals, most capital letters, symbols, and most words referred to as words, add an *s* or both an apostrophe and an *s.*

SINGULAR	8	1700	T	&	and
PLURAL	8s	1700s	Ts	&s	ands
	or	or	or	or	or
	8's	1700's	T's	&'s	and's

EXAMPLES   His *7s* [or *7's*] look like *Ts* [or *T's*].

                    Do not write *&s* [or *&'s*] for *ands* [or *and's*].

                    Phillis Wheatley wrote during the 1700s [or 1700's].

HELP

Whenever you are unsure how to form the plural of a word, look up the word in a dictionary.

MECHANICS

To prevent confusion, add both an apostrophe and an *s* to form the plurals of all lowercase letters, certain capital letters, and some words referred to as words.

EXAMPLES   The word *accommodate* has two *a*'s, two *c*'s, two *o*'s, and two *m*'s.

His essay is filled with *I*'s. [Without an apostrophe, the plural of the pronoun *I* could be confused with the word *Is*.]

Make sure that each one of your *her*'s has a clear antecedent. [Without an apostrophe, the plural of the word *her* could be confused with the possessive pronoun *hers*.]

Exercise 5   Spelling the Plurals of Nouns

Write the plural form of each of the following nouns.

EXAMPLES   **1.** piano
             1. *pianos*

             2. curriculum
             2. *curricula*

1. girl	**11.** cafeteria
2. valley	**12.** dormitory
3. sky	**13.** goose
4. coach	**14.** parenthesis
5. Japanese	**15.** diary
6. sister-in-law	**16.** blizzard
7. solo	**17.** patio
8. self	**18.** deer
9. notebook	**19.** abolitionist
10. stereo	**20.** 1900

Review B   Applying Spelling Rules

Use Rules 15b–15l to explain the spellings of the following words.

EXAMPLE   **1.** boxes
            1. *Add es to form the plural of a noun ending in x.*

1. crises	**6.** misstep
2. deceive	**7.** meanness
3. proceed	**8.** noticeable
4. placement	**9.** referred
5. sopranos	**10.** countries

Writing Numbers

15m. Spell out a number that begins a sentence.

EXAMPLE　　**Two thousand** students attend Shawnee High School, I believe.

If a number appears awkward when spelled out, revise the sentence so that it does not begin with the number.

EXAMPLE　　I believe the number of students who attend Shawnee High School is **2,103.**

15n. Spell out a *cardinal number*—a number that states how many—that can be expressed in one or two words. Otherwise, use numerals.

EXAMPLES　　**fourteen** dogs　　**thirty-one** days　　**one thousand** votes

　　　　　　514 dogs　　　　**331** days　　　　**2,670** votes

Generally, do not spell out some numbers and use numerals for others in the same context. If numerals are required for any of the numbers, be consistent by using numerals for all of the numbers.

INCONSISTENT　　In the election, Lou Ann received ninety votes, and Darla received 103.

CONSISTENT　　In the election, Lou Ann received **90** votes, and Darla received **103.**

However, to distinguish between numbers that appear beside each other but that count different things, spell out one number and use numerals for the other.

EXAMPLE　　They bought **two 25**-pound bags of dog food.

15o. Spell out an *ordinal number*—a number that expresses order.

EXAMPLE　　My brother placed **third** [not *3rd*] in the **first** [not *1st*] race.

15p. Use numerals to express numbers in conventional situations.

Conventional situations include

- identification numbers

EXAMPLES　　Room **16**　　pages **359–407**　　Chapter **3**

　　　　　　Channel **32**　　Interstate **10**　　Rule **26k**

S T Y L E	T I P

For large round numbers, you may use words only, numerals only, or a combination of words and numerals.

EXAMPLES
eight million dollars
or
$8 million

32,800,000,000
or
32.8 billion

Reference Note

Compound cardinal numbers from twenty-one to ninety-nine are hyphenated. For more about **hyphenated numbers,** see page 366.

MECHANICS

┌HELP─

Compound ordinal numbers from twenty-first to ninety-ninth are hyphenated.

STYLE | **TIP**

In sentences, spell out the names of units of measurement (such as *pounds* and *feet*) whether they stand alone or follow numerals or spelled-out numbers. In charts and tables, however, you may use the abbreviations for units of measurement (such as *lb* and *ft*) when they follow numerals.

Similarly, spell out the words for symbols (such as *degrees* for ° and *percent* for %). In charts and tables, however, you may use the symbols when they follow numerals.

STYLE | **TIP**

Do not use *A.M.* or *P.M.* with a spelled-out number or as a substitute for the words *morning, afternoon,* and *evening.*

INCORRECT
The concert begins at eight P.M.

CORRECT
The concert begins at **8:00 P.M.** (or **eight o'clock in the evening**).

- measurements/statistics

EXAMPLES   **68** degrees   **4½** feet   **14.5** pounds

               20 percent   **16** years old   score of **32** to **18**

- addresses

EXAMPLES   **18** Kresge Way   Charlotte, NC **28243-0018**

- dates

EXAMPLES   May **5, 2000**   **44** B.C.   A.D. **893**

- times of day

EXAMPLES   **6:30** A.M.   **11:15** P.M.

NOTE   Spell out a number used with *o'clock.*

    EXAMPLE   **five o'clock** in the morning

Review C   **Proofreading a Paragraph to Correct Spelling Errors**

Proofread the following paragraph, correcting the misspelled or misused words or expressions.

EXAMPLE   **[1]** 5 days ago, all of the members of my family except one joined my grandparentes in a lovly celebration of their wedding anniversary.

       1.   *Five; grandparents; lovely*

     [1] Last Saturday my mom's parents, Grandma and Grandpa Reyes, celebrated their fortyeth anniversary by repeating their wedding vows in a beautiful ceremony at St. Teresa's Church. **[2]** Since I have my learnner's permit now and it was light out when we went to the church, Mom let me drive. **[3]** My aunts and uncles on Mom's side of the family were there with their husbands and wifes. **[4]** In addition, all of my cousins except Ernesto, whom I had been especially hopeing to see, attended the ceremony. **[5]** Unfortunately, the flights from Denver, where Ernesto goes to college, had been canceled because it had snowed heavyly there the night before. **[6]** Although I missed Ernesto, I enjoyed visiting with many of the 85 friends and family members who had come to the celebration. **[7]** Grandma and Grandpa had insisted that anniversary gifts were unecessary, but this time they were overruled. **[8]** You could tell that they were truely stunned when they opened the gift from their children. [9] Mom and her sisters and brothers had chiped in to buy them plane tickets to Mexico City, where they were born. [10] Everyone had such a good time that we have already started planing for Grandma and Grandpa's 50th anniversary.

Words Often Confused

You can prevent many spelling errors by learning the difference between the words grouped together in this section. Some of them are confusing because they are *homonyms*—that is, they are pronounced alike. Others are confusing because they are spelled the same or nearly the same.

Reference Note

In the Glossary of Usage, Chapter 9, you can find many other words that are often confused or misused. You can also look the words up in a dictionary.

MECHANICS

affect	[verb] *to influence* How did that sad movie *affect* you?
effect	[verb] *to accomplish, to bring about;* [noun] *a consequence; a result* Head Start centers can *effect* an improvement in the lives of many children. What *effect* did the rain have on the crops?
all ready	[adjective] *all prepared* We were *all ready* to leave.
already	[adverb] *previously* We had *already* painted the sets.
all right	[adjective] *satisfactory;* [adverb] *satisfactorily* The match was difficult, but your playing was *all right.* I think I did *all right,* too. [This is the only acceptable spelling. Although the spelling *alright* is in some dictionaries, it has not become standard usage.]
all together	[adjective] *in the same place;* [adverb] *at the same time* The players were *all together* in the gym. Sing *all together,* now.
altogether	[adverb] *entirely* I am not *altogether* convinced.
altar	[noun] *a table or stand at which religious rites are performed* When you reach the *altar,* you must kneel.
alter	[verb] *to change* When did you *alter* the schedule?

(continued)

(continued)

brake	[verb] *to slow down or to stop;* [noun] *a device used to slow down or to stop* She tried to *brake* the bicycle with the hand *brake*.
break	[verb] *to cause to come apart, to fracture;* [noun] *a fracture* I did not *break* my wrist; I sprained it. The doctor said it is not a *break*, but a sprain.
capital	[noun] *center of government; money or property used in business;* [adjective] *punishable by death; of major importance; excellent; uppercase* What is the *capital* of Zimbabwe? You need *capital* to start a business. Do you support *capital* punishment? Begin every sentence with a *capital* letter.
capitol	[noun] *a building where a legislature meets* We could see the *capitol* from our hotel.
choose	[verb, rhymes with *shoes*] *to select* We *choose* partners today.
chose	[verb, past form of *choose*, rhymes with *nose*] *selected* Each of us *chose* a partner yesterday.
coarse	[adjective] *rough, crude* Burlap is a *coarse* fabric.
course	[noun] *a part of a meal; a series of studies; a playing field; a path of action;* [also used after *of* to mean *naturally* or *certainly*] She skipped the first *course* at dinner. The speech *course* helped my diction. A new golf *course* opened last week. What *course* will resolve the conflict? Of *course*, you are always welcome.
complement	[noun] *that which makes whole or complete;* [verb] *to make whole or complete* Without a *complement,* the sentence is incomplete. That scarf *complements* your outfit nicely.
compliment	[noun] *praise, a courteous act or statement;* [verb] *to express praise or respect* He received many *compliments* on his cooking. I *complimented* her on her success.

MECHANICS

TIPS & TRICKS

Here is an easy way to remember the difference between *capital* and *capitol*. There is a d**o**me on the capit**o**l building.

TIPS & TRICKS

Here is an easy way to remember the difference between *complement* and *compliment*. A compl**e**-ment is something that compl**e**tes.

consul	[noun] *a person appointed by a government to serve its citizens in a foreign country* The United States *consul* in Tokyo met with a group of tourists.
council	[noun] *a group called together to accomplish a job* Members of the *council* voted on the resolution.
counsel	[noun] *advice;* [verb] *to advise* Sue followed her aunt's *counsel.* Sue's aunt *counseled* her to take judo lessons.
councilor	[noun] *a member of a council* The majority of the *councilors* voted for the resolution.
counselor	[noun] *an advisor* Ask your guidance *counselor.*
desert	[noun, pronounced des′ • ert] *a dry region* The caravan crossed the *desert* at night.
desert	[verb, pronounced de • sert′] *to leave or abandon* They did not *desert* the sinking ship.
dessert	[noun, pronounced des • sert′] *the final, sweet course of a meal* For *dessert* we had fresh fruit.

Exercise 6 **Distinguishing Between Words Often Confused**

From the choices in parentheses, select the correct word or word group for each of the following sentences.

EXAMPLE   **1.** Is the Kalahari (*Desert, Dessert*) in Africa?

    1. Desert

1. They were (*all together, altogether*) in favor of the party.
2. The illness has had a strange (*affect, effect*) on everyone.
3. My cousin knows the (*capitol, capital*) city of every state.
4. Have you had your car's (*brakes, breaks*) inspected?
5. The British (*council, consul*) (*counciled, counseled*) the reporter to leave the country.
6. After all his worry, everything turned out (*all right, alright*).
7. Christopher said that the two new players for the guard position will (*compliment, complement*) our basketball team.
8. The actors were (*all ready, already*) for the audition.
9. My uncle will serve either flan or sopapillas for (*desert, dessert*).
10. Did you (*choose, chose*) that topic for your essay?

formally	[adverb] *in a proper or dignified manner, according to strict rules* Do you plan to dress *formally* for the party?
formerly	[adverb] *previously, in the past* This lake was *formerly* a valley.
hear	[verb] *to receive sounds through the ears* Please speak up; I can't *hear* you.
here	[adverb] *at this place* Let's sit *here*.
its	[possessive form of *it*] *belonging to it* The town has not raised *its* tax rate in years.
it's	[contraction of *it is* or *it has*] *It's* cold, and *it's* started to snow.
lead	[verb, rhymes with *need*] *to go first; to guide* Who will *lead* the Juneteenth parade?
led	[verb, past form of *lead*] He *led* us five miles out of the way.
lead	[noun, rhymes with *red*] *graphite in a pencil; a heavy metal* A pencil *lead* is not made of the metal *lead*.
loose	[adjective, rhymes with *goose*] *free; not close together; not firmly fastened* I forgot to lock the gate, and now the pigs are *loose*. Put all your *loose* papers in a folder. My little brother has two *loose* teeth.
lose	[verb, rhymes with *snooze*] *to suffer loss of* Don't *lose* your tickets.
miner	[noun] *a worker in a mine* The trapped *miners* were finally rescued.
minor	[noun] *a person under legal age;* [adjective] *less important* The curfew applies only to *minors*. He suffered *minor* injuries in the accident.
moral	[adjective] *good, virtuous;* [noun] *a lesson of conduct* We admire a *moral* person. The story's *moral* is "Look before you leap."
morale	[noun] *mental condition, spirit* After three defeats, the team's *morale* was low.

RUBES by Leigh Rubin. By permission of Leigh Rubin and Creators Syndicate.

Miner surgery.

passed	[verb, past form of *pass*] *went by, beyond, over, or through* The tortoise *passed* the hare and won the race.
past	[noun] *time gone by;* [adjective] *of a former time;* [preposition] *beyond* Sitting Bull told many stories about the *past.* Adele read the minutes of the *past* meeting. The dog walked right *past* the cat.
peace	[noun] *calmness (as opposed to strife or war)* All hoped that the treaty would bring *peace.*
piece	[noun] *a part of something* We found the missing *piece* of the puzzle.

┌TIPS & TRICKS┐

Here is a way to remember the difference between *peace* and *piece*. You eat a pi**e**ce of pi**e**.

Exercise 7 **Distinguishing Between Words Often Confused**

From the choices in parentheses, select the correct word for each of the following sentences.

EXAMPLE
1. Marcy would like a (*peace, piece*) of pumpkin bread.
   1. *piece*

1. Where did you (*here, hear*) that Kiowa legend?
2. If you (*lose, loose*) the directions, we will never get there.
3. The mail from home improved the troops' (*moral, morale*).
4. The estate is being held in trust until the heir is no longer a (*minor, miner*).
5. My horse (*lead, led*) the parade.
6. In only a few minutes, the guest speaker will be (*hear, here*).
7. After he went on a diet, his clothes were too (*lose, loose*).
8. (*Formerly, Formally*), that cellist performed with the Boston Pops.
9. (*It's, Its*) not every day that her parents let her use the car.
10. On the tour, we (*past, passed*) the homes of many celebrities.

Review D **Proofreading an Article for Errors in the Use of Words Often Confused**

Proofread the article on the next page, correcting each incorrectly used word. If all words in a sentence are already used correctly, write *C.*

EXAMPLE
[1] The state legislature was not in session when the NHS members toured the capital.
   1. *capitol*

┌HELP┐

Some sentences in Review D contain more than one error.

MECHANICS

NHS MEMBERS MEET GOVERNOR
by Cornelia Charnes, Staff Writer

[1] One of the advantages of living in the state capitol is having the opportunity to see state government up close. [2] Last Friday, twenty-seven members of our school's National Honor Society chapter toured the nearby capital building. [3] Tour guide Floyd Welty, who lead the group, outlined the workings of the government's three branches and pointed out many of the building's architectural features. [4] The students ate lunch in the underground cafeteria and even got to meet Governor (formally State Senator) Iola Jones.

[5] The group met Governor Jones just as they were already to leave the building. [6] Said student Botan Park, "Governor Jones shook hands with each of us and complimented us on being honor students. [7] Even though we're still miners, she told us, 'I want to here from you whenever you have a concern with my administration's policies.'"

[8] "Of course," added student Elena Cruz, "its her first term as governor, and we will be eligible to vote when she comes up for reelection."

[9] The group's sponsor, guidance councilor Diego Vargas, said, "I have been taking groups there for the passed ten years, but I have never met a governor before. [10] Meeting Governor Jones had a big effect on the students and on me."

personal	[adjective] *individual, private* The store manager gave us her *personal* attention.
personnel	[noun] *a group of people employed in the same work or service* The management added *personnel* to handle the increased workload.
principal	[noun] *the head of a school;* [adjective] *main or most important* The *principal* of our school is Mr. Osaka. The *principal* export of Brazil is coffee.
principle	[noun] *a rule of conduct; a fact or a general truth* Her *principles* are very high. Dr. Martin Luther King, Jr., supported the *principle* of nonviolence.
quiet	[adjective] *silent, still* The library is a *quiet* place to study.
quite	[adverb] *completely, rather, very* Are you *quite* sure this is the right path?

TIPS & TRICKS

Here is an easy way to remember the difference between *principal* and *principle*. The princi**pal** is your **pal.**

shone	[verb, past form of *shine*] *gave off light* The stars *shone* brightly last night.
shown	[verb, past participle form of *show*] *put or brought into view* The slides were *shown* after dinner.
stationary	[adjective] *in a fixed position* Are these desks movable or *stationary*?
stationery	[noun] *writing paper* Colored *stationery* is not appropriate for business letters.
than	[conjunction, used for comparisons] She arrived earlier *than* I did.
then	[adverb] *at that time; next* I didn't know you *then.* We swam for an hour; *then* we ate.
their	[possessive of *they*] *belonging to them* *Their* apartment has a view of the river.
there	[adverb] *at that place;* [also used as an expletive to begin a sentence] I have not been *there* in a long time. *There* is too much pepper in my soup.
they're	[contraction of *they are*] *They're* reading a book by Virginia Driving Hawk Sneve.

TIPS & TRICKS

Here is an easy way to remember the difference between *stationary* and *stationery.* You write a lett**er** on station**er**y.

Reference Note

For information on **possessive pronouns,** see page 154. For information on **adverbs,** see page 20. For information on **forming contractions,** see page 361.

MECHANICS

Exercise 8 **Distinguishing Between Words Often Confused**

From the choices in parentheses, select the correct word for each of the following sentences.

EXAMPLE **1.** We stayed in San Juan longer (*than, then*) we had planned.

 1. than

1. I am learning some of the (*principals, principles*) of physics.
2. The gold ring (*shone, shown*) with a warm glow.
3. He acts much older (*than, then*) he is.
4. The bookstore is having a big sale on (*stationery, stationary*).
5. You ask too many (*personnel, personal*) questions.
6. Soon after the strange uproar, all became (*quite, quiet*) again.
7. The *pad thai* they serve here is (*quite, quiet*) good.

MEETING THE CHALLENGE

Write a song, jingle, or chant to teach the differences between words often confused. You may set your words to a familiar or original tune, or you may wish to create a rhythmic beat. Cover at least four Words Often Confused entries, and check your work for correct spelling.

MECHANICS

8. Several Pueblo artists are displaying (*there, their, they're*) work.

9. If you see the (*principle, principal*) in the hall, tell her she's wanted in the main office.

10. (*Their, They're, There*) parents may not let them go.

to	[preposition; also part of the infinitive form of a verb] Please return these books *to* the library.
	He began *to* whistle.
too	[adverb] *also; more than enough* Rubén Blades is a musician and an attorney, *too*.
	You are *too* young to drive.
two	[adjective] *the sum of one + one;* [noun] *the number between one and three* I will graduate in *two* years.
	Two of my friends and I have great tickets for the Yo-Yo Ma concert.
waist	[noun] *the midsection of the body* At the Japanese restaurant, the server wore an obi around her *waist*.
waste	[noun] *a needless expense; unused material;* [verb] *to use foolishly* Waiting in line was a *waste* of time.
	Waste not; want not.
weather	[noun] *conditions outdoors* As the meteorologist predicted, the *weather* has been perfect all week.
whether	[conjunction; indicates alternative or doubt] They don't know *whether* or not they will go to the concert next weekend.
who's	[contraction of *who is* or *who has*] *Who's* there?
	Who's been coaching them?
whose	[possessive form of *who*] *belonging to whom* *Whose* book is this?
your	[possessive form of *you*] *belonging to you* *Your* coat is in the closet.
you're	[contraction of *you are*] *You're* always on time.

Exercise 9 **Distinguishing Between Words Often Confused**

From the choices in parentheses, select the correct word for each of the following sentences.

EXAMPLE
   1. Are you planning (*to, too, two*) go (*to, too, two*) the dance, (*to, too, two*)?

   1. to; to; too

1. Around his (*waste, waist*) he wore a handmade leather belt.
2. (*You're, Your*) mother made a delicious Korean dinner of *bulgogi.*
3. There was (*too, to, two*) much traffic on the interstate for us (*too, to, two*) enjoy the ride.
4. (*Whose, Who's*) going to use that ticket now?
5. It really doesn't matter (*whose, who's*) fault it is this time.
6. You, (*to, two, too*), can be a better speller if you try.
7. (*Weather, Whether*) or not it rains, we will be there.
8. Don't you agree that this is fine (*whether, weather*) for a softball game, Ivory?
9. (*Your, You're*) sure Ms. Thompson wanted to see me?
10. I don't know (*whose, who's*) taller, Hakeem Olajuwon or Reggie Miller.

Exercise 10 **Proofreading a Paragraph to Correct Errors in the Use of Words Often Confused**

Proofread the following paragraph, correcting errors in the use of words often confused.

EXAMPLE
   [1] Who's face is on this postage stamp?

   1. Whose

[1] The face on the postage stamp shown at the right is that of Benjamin Banneker, considered too be the first African American man of science. [2] First issued on February 15, 1980, this stamp honors a man who's contributions in the areas of mathematics and astronomy are impressive. [3] Banneker grew up on a farm in Maryland in the 1700s, a time when life was particularly difficult for African American people weather they were slaves or not. [4] Although free, Banneker, to, faced prejudice and discrimination. [5] However, a neighbor who was interested in science gave some astronomy equipment too Banneker.

The Granger Collection, New York.

[6] Banneker waisted no time in using it to determine when the sun and moon rose and set, when the brightest stars set, and when eclipses occurred. [7] All of this information was very helpful to a variety of people, including sailors who needed to chart courses and farmers who needed to know the whether. [8] Banneker compiled his data into an almanac, and after to or three attempts, he succeeded in getting his almanacs published each year for several years. [9] These popular books received widespread attention, and Benjamin Banneker became a symbol of what African Americans could do when their lives were not waisted in slavery. [10] If your someone who collects commemorative postage stamps, you will likely want this one, which celebrates the achievements of this gifted scientist.

Review E · Proofreading an Essay to Correct Errors in Spelling and in the Use of Words Often Confused

┌HELP┐
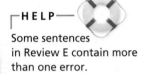
Some sentences in Review E contain more than one error.

Proofread the following paragraphs, correcting errors in spelling and in the use of words often confused. If all the words in a sentence are correct, write *C*.

EXAMPLE [1] When you take the road test for your driver's license, I hope that you're expereince will be better then mine was.

1. *your; experience; than*

[1] One of my most embarrassing moments occured the day I took the road test too get my driver's license. [2] Since one of the branches of the Motor Vehicle Department is near my dad's office, I met Dad their after school. [3] He tryed to calm me down by telling me that the world would not end if I did not pass the first time. [4] Still, my hands were shakeing noticably when I got behind the wheel.

[5] The examiner, Mrs. Ferro, was very patient. [6] She assured me that the coarse was "a peice of cake" and that she would not ask me to do anything ilegal to try to trick me. [7] She said I would be fine if I just proceded steadly and did not overeact to her instructions.

[8] Everything went surprisingly well until we reached the end of the course and Mrs. Ferro told me to stop the car and turn off the ignition. [9] I stopped, alright; I accidentaly slamed on the breaks so hard that we both went lurching forward against our seat belts. [10] Luckily, niether of us sustainned any injurys, and I succeeded in passing the test, despite mistakeing the end of the course for a cliff.

Chapter Review

A. Proofreading Sentences to Correct Spelling Errors

Proofread the following sentences, and correctly write the misspelled words. If a sentence is already correct, write *C*.

1. The new model with two sliding doors will supercede the old model with only one.

2. We had to wait for a long time at the level crossing for the frieght train to pass.

3. The restaurants of New Orleans are known for their atmosphere and fine dineing.

4. On the long drive through the Australian outback, we saw several kangaroos hoping alongside the road.

5. When nations are enemys, they send spys to gather information about one another.

6. Last Saturday we felt tired, so we decided to stay home and rent a couple of videoes.

7. Timothy Grant is actually one of my brother-in-laws; the other is Sammy Dunn.

8. Dot your *i*'s and cross your *t*'s, as my aunt Edna always used to say.

9. Do we put those figures inside brackets, or should we use parenthesises?

10. 245 people signed the petition.

11. The great French writer Voltaire lived during the 1700s.

12. The best-looking horses at the ranch were a pair of three-years-old.

13. Is this word mispelled?

14. People should be considerate of each other and not display meaness or hostility.

15. The first impression of the cathedral interior was one of great, echoing emptyness.

16. As Mr. Spock would say, their decision was ilogical.

17. Dad impulsively sent away for a set of Japanese steak knifes.

18. On the sewing table there were a sewing kit, a bolt of cloth, and Mom's and Grandma's scissorses.

19. When he writes, his eights look like threes.

20. My brother Walter wieghs 180 pounds and stands six feet tall.

B. Proofreading a Paragraph to Correct Spelling Errors

Proofread the following paragraph, and correctly write the misspelled words. If a sentence is already correct, write *C.*

[**21**] If I had to chose my favorite animal, it might be the Florida manatee, or sea cow. [**22**] Of coarse, I like dogs, cats, and elephants, but I have heard that manatees are extremly gentle and pateint. [**23**] I also read somewhere that manatees are more closely related to elephants than to seals or whales. [**24**] Normaly, manatees live near the shore in swamps or near the banks of canals. [**25**] A hungry sea cow can eat two hundred pounds of grass. [**26**] Unlike many other animals, manatees never run out of teath. [**27**] Manatees are very useful in clearing vegetation from the canals, so there often protected by law. [**28**] However, boat propelers often injure the animals. [**29**] Also, manatees and there cousins the dugongs have been hunted, especialy as sources of meat and oil. [**30**] Weather these beautyful creatures manage to survive as a species depends largely on us humans.

C. Distinguishing Between Words Often Confused

For each of the following sentences, write the correct word or words in parentheses.

31. That organization is growing; it is (*there, they're, their*) belief that society should devote more resources to the poor.

32. The sky is (*quite, quiet*) clear this evening, so we should be able to see the constellations.

33. The tiger slowly made (*its, it's*) way through the underbrush and then disappeared from view.

34. The gardener gave me a (*personal, personnel*) tour of the center's famous rose garden.

35. "Don't (*waste, waist*) your money on that CD; the songs are terrible," Luis warned us.

36. The mayor welcomed the new Swedish (*council, consul, counsel*) and her staff at a special reception.

37. I'm not sure what is meant by a (*capitol, capital*) offense.

38. The stock market crash in 1929 (*affected, effected*) the economy.

39. Do you know if the movie will be (*shone, shown*) at the children's film series?

40. Working conditions for coal (*minors, miners*) in the United States improved significantly during the twentieth century.

41. (*Your, You're*) coat is lying on the sofa.

42. We went out after dinner, but there were (*two, to, too*) many people in the street, so we came home.

43. What is the (*capitol, capital*) of Portugal?

44. Put on the emergency (*brake, break*) when you park on a hill.

45. Sometimes it's hard to know the (*moral, morale*) thing to do, but we must try.

46. She was so considerate that we (*complimented, complemented*) her on her kindness.

47. Striding off into the fields, Archie (*led, lead*) his troupe toward the mountains.

48. It was remarkable to watch the space shuttle land at great speed and for it to be completely (*stationery, stationary*) minutes later.

49. Uncle Ruben never eats junk food; he worries about his (*waste, waist*).

50. When you apply for a job, your application is forwarded to the (*personal, personnel*) department.

Writing Application

Using Correct Spelling in an Application Letter

Spelling Words   Imagine the best job you could have. Then, write the letter of application that will get you that job. The letter should be short—no longer than two paragraphs—and should be as clear as possible. In your letter use ten words from the spelling lists on the following pages.

Prewriting   Start by making a list of five jobs that might interest you. Do some research in specialist publications or on the Internet to find the major requirements of your dream job so that you can use professional terms authoritatively in your letter. Once you have drawn up a list of dream jobs, choose one job and freewrite about it. Write down as many details as you can to describe the job, its responsibilities, and where you see the job taking you in the future.

Writing Use your freewriting notes to write the first draft of your letter. Explain how your training and experience make you suited for this particular job.

Revising Ask a classmate to read your letter and offer feedback. Rearrange or cut details to make the letter more effective.

Publishing Proofread your letter for any errors in grammar, usage, and mechanics. Be sure that all words are spelled correctly. With your teacher's approval, you might suggest a contest among your classmates to determine which students get their dream jobs. Post the completed letters on the class bulletin board or Web page, and follow up with the announcement of the successful applicants.

100 Commonly Misspelled Words

ache	could	happiness	raise	tonight
again	country	having	read	too
always	dear	hear	ready	trouble
among	doctor	here	said	truly
answered	does	hoarse	says	Tuesday
any	don't	hour	scene	two
been	done	instead	seems	very
beginning	early	knew	separate	wear
believe	easy	know	shoes	Wednesday
break	enemy	laid	similar	week
built	enough	loose	since	where
business	every	lose	straight	whether
busy	existence	making	sugar	which
buy	February	meant	sure	whole
can't	finally	minute	tear	women
chief	forty	none	their	won't
choose	friend	often	there	would
color	grammar	once	though	write
coming	guess	piece	through	writing
cough	half	probably	tired	wrote

300 Spelling Words

absence	agriculture	athlete	civilization
absorption	amateur	bankruptcy	cocoon
abundant	ambassador	basically	commencement
acceptable	analysis	beneficial	commissioner
accidentally	analyze	benefited	committed
accommodation	angel	bicycle	comparative
accompaniment	annual	breathe	comparison
accurate	apparatus	brilliant	competition
accustomed	appearance	bulletin	conceivable
achievement	application		confidential
acquaintance	appropriate	calendar	confirmation
actuality	approximately	category	conscientious
adequately	arousing	changeable	consciousness
administration	arrangement	characteristic	consequently
adolescent	ascend	chemistry	considerable
aggressive	association	circumstance	consistency

continuous
controlled
controversial
cordially
corps
correspondence
criticize
curiosity
curriculum

definition
delegate
denied
develop
difference
disastrous
disciple
dissatisfied
distinction
distinguished
dividend
dominant
dormitory

earnest
easily
ecstasy
eighth
eliminate
embroidery
endeavor
enormous
equipment
especially
essential
estimation
etiquette
exaggeration
examination
exceedingly
exceptional
excitable
executive
exercise
exhaustion

exhibition
expense
experience
extension
extraordinary

fallacy
fantasies
favorably
fiery
financial
foreigner
forfeit
fragile
fulfill
fundamentally

gasoline
gentleman
grammatically
grateful
guidance
gymnasium

handkerchief
heroic
hindrance
humorist
hygiene
hypocrisy

illustrate
imitation
immense
inability
incidentally
indispensable
influential
innocence
inquiry
institute
intellect
interference
interpretation
interruption
interval

irrelevant
irresistible
island

jealousy
journal

laborious
liability
lightning
likelihood
liveliest
locally
luxury
magnificence
maintenance
maneuver
mansion
martyr
maturity
medical
merchandise
merit
miniature
mischievous
missile
misspelled
monotony
mortgage
municipal

narrative
naturally
neighbor
noticeable
nuisance

obstacle
occasionally
occupy
odor
offensive
omitted
opinion
opposition
optimism

ordinary
organization
ornament

pageant
pamphlet
parachute
parallel
pastime
peaceable
peasant
peril
permanent
persistent
perspiration
pertain
phase
picnic
pigeon
playwright
pleasant
poison
politician
positively
possibility
practically
practice
precede
precisely
predominant
preferred
prejudice
preliminary
preparation
primitive
priority
prisoner
procedure
proceedings
procession
prominent
proposition
prosperous
prove

psychology
publicity
purposes

qualities
quantities
questionnaire

readily
reference
referring
regard
register
rehearsal
religious
remembrance
representative
requirement
resistance

resolution
responsibility
restaurant
ridiculous

satisfactorily
security
senator
sensibility
sheer
sheriff
significance
simile
situated
solution
sophomore
souvenir
specific
specimen

spiritual
strenuous
stretch
substantial
subtle
successful
sufficient
summarize
superintendent
suppress
surgeon
suspense
syllable
symbol
symphony

technique
temperature
tendency

tournament
traffic
twelfth
tying
tyranny

unanimous
undoubtedly
unforgettable
unpleasant
unusually

vacancies
varies
vengeance
villain

Correcting Common Errors

Key Language Skills Review

This chapter reviews key skills and concepts that pose special problems for writers.

- **Sentence Fragments and Run-on Sentences**
- **Subject-Verb and Pronoun-Antecedent Agreement**
- **Pronoun Usage**
- **Verb Forms**
- **Comparison of Modifiers**
- **Misplaced and Dangling Modifiers**
- **Standard Usage**
- **Capitalization**
- **Punctuation**
- **Spelling**

Most of the exercises in this chapter follow the same format as the exercises found throughout the grammar, usage, and mechanics sections of this book. You will notice, however, that two sets of review exercises are presented in standardized test formats. These exercises are designed to provide you with practice not only in solving usage and mechanics problems but also in dealing with these kinds of problems on standardized tests.

┌─**H E L P**─

Remember that all of the exercises in this chapter are testing your knowledge of the rules of standard, formal English. These are the rules you should use in your schoolwork.

Reference Note

For more about **standard** and **nonstandard English** and **formal** and **informal English,** see page 236.

Exercise 1 Identifying Sentences and Sentence Fragments

Identify each of the following word groups as either a *sentence fragment* or a *sentence*.

EXAMPLE   **1.** Running along the bank of the shallow creek.

        1. sentence fragment

1. Science Technology Associates creating multimedia science products.
2. Claudia needs a new ink cartridge for her printer.
3. A new art exhibit from January 1 until March 15.
4. When he went to the new restaurant, Marchel ordered chicken satay.
5. A line of cars miles long.
6. The tadpoles under the log when the rain began.
7. We played checkers first; then we played chess.
8. Because there is an expiration date.
9. The rocks on the beach were very smooth.
10. Otters swimming and playing in the river.

Reference Note

For information about **sentence fragments,** see page 35.

Exercise 2 Identifying Sentences and Run-on Sentences

Identify each of the following word groups as either a *run-on sentence* or a *sentence*.

EXAMPLE   **1.** On Saturday I went to the park to walk my dog and play soccer with my friends, they were visiting from out of town for the weekend.

        1. run-on sentence

1. All of my friends went to the concert last Saturday, I couldn't go.
2. The triathletes swam, biked, and ran, I bet they slept well that night.
3. The villagers work together when it is time to harvest the crops.
4. After the storm, the porch was covered with leaves and sticks.
5. It was a hot summer day, Joshua played in the pool.
6. Our next-door neighbor rang the doorbell our dog barked.
7. If we don't hurry, we'll be late for the play, we won't be allowed to enter until the first intermission.
8. Vincent van Gogh, who is famous for paintings such as *Starry Night,* was born in the Netherlands.
9. Tom realized he had no pen he asked Bob if he could borrow one.
10. After falling asleep on the sofa, the children were carried to bed by their parents.

Reference Note

For information about **run-on sentences,** see page 454.

COMMON ERRORS

Reference Note

For information about **sentence fragments,** see page 35.

Exercise 3   Identifying Sentences and Correcting Sentence Fragments

Most of the following word groups are sentence fragments. If a word group is a sentence fragment, write it correctly, making it a complete sentence. You may need to change the punctuation and capitalization. If the word group is already a complete sentence, write *S*.

EXAMPLE   1. When we left the soccer field.

        1. It was still morning when we left the soccer field.

1. Fixed the smoke detector in the hall.
2. A new picture taken for his passport.
3. Born in Cleveland, Ohio, in the autumn of 1991.
4. Ruth tried out her new in-line skates today.
5. Playing basketball with friends from the neighborhood.
6. Wasn't that an exciting and pleasant surprise?
7. Because that high school has a new athletic program for students with disabilities.
8. The new movie about dinosaurs on Tuesday.
9. By the time the clowns arrived, the party was almost over.
10. Is a good role model?

Reference Note

For information about **run-on sentences,** see page 454.

Exercise 4   Correcting Run-on Sentences

Correctly write each of the following run-on sentences.

EXAMPLE   1. Thunder roared and rumbled lightning flashed across the dark skies.

        1. Thunder roared and rumbled, and lightning flashed across the dark skies.

                or

        Thunder roared and rumbled; lightning flashed across the dark skies.

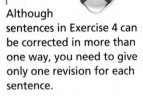

HELP

Although sentences in Exercise 4 can be corrected in more than one way, you need to give only one revision for each sentence.

1. David Diaz has captured many honors for his artwork he won the 1995 Caldecott Medal for the picture book *Smoky Night.*
2. Jeremy wants to ask Iris to the dance, he doesn't know if she already has a date.
3. Rabindranath Tagore wrote the national anthems of two countries, India and Bangladesh, I wonder if anyone else has written two national anthems.
4. The math problems in the homework assignment were easy there were too many of them.

5. Five golfers from Madison High School were chosen for the tournament, this will be the first tournament for three of them.
6. Radio waves travel at the speed of light they can go through many solid objects, including the walls of most buildings.
7. My mother supports the incumbent candidate for treasurer my father will vote for the challenger.
8. Socrates was not afraid to die, he faced his own death sentence with bravery and self-assurance.
9. The largest province in Canada is Quebec, the capital of the province is Quebec City.
10. Lena wanted to learn how to stencil, she enrolled in a stenciling course at the library.

<hr>

Exercise 5 **Correcting Sentence Fragments and Run-on Sentences**

Each of the following word groups is a sentence fragment, a run-on sentence, or a complete sentence. First, identify each by writing *F* for a sentence fragment, *R* for a run-on sentence, or *S* for a complete sentence. Then, correct each sentence fragment or run-on sentence.

Reference Note

For information about **sentence fragments,** see page 35. For information on **run-on sentences,** see page 454.

EXAMPLE   1. Nearly all cultures having traditional folk dances.
　　　　　　1. *F—Nearly all cultures have traditional folk dances.*

1. Most folk dances start as celebrations or religious rituals, such dances are often passed down from generation to generation.
2. Certain dances to bring good fortune to the dancers.
3. Some communities developed dances that they believed cured diseases, for instance, the tarantella developed in Italy as a ritual antidote for the bite of the tarantula.
4. Other dances celebrating birth, marriage, harvests, success in battle, and even death.
5. Over time, most folk dances change.
6. That some dances originally having religious or ritual significance have come to be danced purely for recreation.
7. Anyone who knows the origins of "Ring-Around-the-Rosy"?
8. In the United States, the square dance may be the most popular kind of folk dance clogging is common, too.
9. The do-si-do is a movement in square dancing in which two dancers start out facing one another, circle each other back-to-back, and then return to a facing position.
10. The term *do-si-do* from *dos à dos,* which, I believe, is French for "back-to-back."

Reference Note

For information about **subject-verb agreement,** see page 110.

Reference Note

For information about **subject-verb agreement,** see page 110.

Exercise 6 Identifying Verbs That Agree with Their Subjects

For each of the following sentences, choose the form of the verb in parentheses that agrees with the subject.

EXAMPLE   **1.** The cultural heritage of New Mexico's cities (*is, are*) reflected in their architecture, food, and customs.

          1. *is*

1. Many of the people who visit New Mexico (*spend, spends*) time in Albuquerque.

2. The architecture of the buildings (*represent, represents*) various periods in the city's history.

3. (*Has, Have*) anyone here ever read about or seen Albuquerque's Old Town?

4. One of the books Ana read (*identify, identifies*) Old Town as the site of the city's original settlement, founded by Spanish settlers in 1706.

5. Arts, crafts, and food now (*fill, fills*) the shops around the Old Town Plaza.

6. Amy's family (*has, have*) its annual reunion in Albuquerque.

7. Near Albuquerque (*is, are*) a number of American Indian reservations.

8. The pictures we took of the Rio Grande gorge (*give, gives*) you an idea of what the landscape is like in central New Mexico.

9. Neither Juan nor his parents (*was, were*) aware that near Albuquerque are mountains that often have snow on them.

10. Just to the east of the city (*is, are*) the Sandia Mountains.

Exercise 7 Proofreading Sentences for Correct Subject-Verb Agreement

Most of the following sentences contain errors in subject-verb agreement. If a verb does not agree with its subject, write that subject and the correct form of the verb. If a sentence is already correct, write *C.*

EXAMPLE   **1.** Each of them repeat the chorus after the soloist finishes.

          1. *Each repeats*

1. Someone I know drop in every time I try to finish my work.

2. News of his accomplishments have spread in recent years.

3. Here's the articles about Buck Ramsey that Han said she would lend you.
4. Has everybody signed up for a service project?
5. The picture of Nanci, Lyle, and Michelle are on the bulletin board.
6. St. Elmo's fire, which has been seen around the masts of ships, the propellers and wingtips of planes, and even the horns of cattle, is an odd glow that sometimes accompanies a steady electric discharge.
7. Under some rocks in the woods were a small box.
8. Tornadoes that occur in the Northern Hemisphere whirls in a counterclockwise direction.
9. The herd of cattle belong to Ms. Tallerud.
10. Singing and playing the guitar is also among Jan's talents.

Exercise 8 **Selecting Pronouns That Agree with Their Antecedents**

For each blank in the following sentences, select a pronoun that agrees with its antecedent.

Reference Note

For information about **pronoun-antecedent agreement,** see page 130.

EXAMPLE   1. One of the boys left _____ report card in the gym today.

              1. *his*

1. Each member of the women's soccer team had played _____ best during the game.
2. All of the students in my biology class have planted _____ seeds along the school's front entrance.
3. Nicholas or Benjamin will demonstrate _____ favorite drawing technique in class today.
4. Mr. Williams told us that anyone who wants to go on the field trip should turn in _____ permission slip on Monday.
5. Each of the novels has _____ own significance in the trilogy.
6. If someone wants to use the computer in the library, _____ should do so this afternoon.
7. Neither Karen nor Susan has finished researching _____ topic.
8. Any one of the passengers could have left _____ jacket on the train.
9. If Ricky and Joe are ready at 7:45 A.M., _____ will be able to ride the bus to school.
10. If we're going to go hiking, everyone should bring _____ own lunch and wear a comfortable pair of shoes.

COMMON ERRORS

Reference Note

For information about **pronoun-antecedent agreement,** see page 130.

Exercise 9 Proofreading Sentences for Correct Pronoun-Antecedent Agreement

Most of the following sentences contain pronouns that do not agree with their antecedents. If a sentence contains an error, rewrite the sentence to correct the error. If a sentence is already correct, write *C*.

EXAMPLE
1. Almost everybody I know has their favorite comic strips.

1. *Almost everybody I know has his or her favorite comic strips.*

1. Sara, one of my friends in the fourth-period art class, raised their hand and asked Mrs. Seymour about the history of comic strips.

2. Mrs. Seymour asked everyone to bring a sketchpad, their drawing pencils, and the Sunday comics to class the following day so that we could begin designing a class comic strip.

3. I can't remember whether it was Sara or Gillian who showed me a copy of the *Calvin and Hobbes* collection titled *Scientific Progress Goes "Boink,"* which they had bought at the mall.

4. The vivid colors and elaborate artistry of a comic strip like *Prince Valiant* or *Calvin and Hobbes* often help make them a popular Sunday strip.

5. Today, about 100 million people in the United States spend some of his or her time each day reading comics.

6. Juan and Robert offered to show the class their collections of adventure comics from the 1940s; each of them will give his presentation on Thursday.

7. Are you familiar with Linus and Lucy Van Pelt and his or her friends Charlie Brown and Snoopy?

8. In 1894, Joseph Pulitzer, one of the most famous newspaper publishers in the United States, introduced the first newspaper comic strip in their paper, *New York World.*

9. The magazine-style comic book first appeared in the 1930s; they usually feature serialized stories about the same group of characters.

10. If anyone wants to learn more about the history of comics, they could research the topic at a library.

Identifying Correct Forms of Pronouns

Choose the correct pronoun in parentheses in each of the following sentences.

EXAMPLE   **1.** Jesse and (*I, me*) will compete at the track meet.

       1. *I*

1. The police officer gave (*them, they*) tickets for speeding in a school zone.
2. The state's best hockey coach is (*he, him*).
3. The soloists in tonight's choir concert will be accompanied on piano by (*she, her*) and Paul.
4. Mr. Fishburn wondered (*who, whom*) had left a gift on his front doorstep.
5. The next president of the debate team will likely be (*she, her*).
6. Yes, the university has offered (*us, we*) scholarships.
7. Three volunteers, Hester, Kim, and (*I, me*), will help paint the mural in the gym.
8. Mrs. Murphy paid my sister and (*I, me*) ten dollars to shovel snow from her driveway.
9. "Are you going with Christy and (*him, he*) to tomorrow's soccer game?" Janet asked.
10. Carl Lewis and Michael Johnson are the two athletes (*who, whom*) I watched most closely during the 1996 Olympics.

Proofreading Sentences for Correct Forms of Pronouns

Identify each incorrect pronoun in the following sentences, and write the correct form. If a sentence is already correct, write *C*.

EXAMPLE   **1.** The new neighbors thought that we and them should have a picnic.

       1. *them—they*

1. Are you going to ride with him or I?
2. Us girls are tutoring students this summer.
3. The new exchange students are here; do you know them?
4. The most talented artist in our class is her.
5. When I was raising money for charity, the executives who I contacted were very generous.
6. My father and me plan to drive to New York this summer.

Reference Note

For information about **using pronouns correctly,** see page 144.

Reference Note

For information about **using pronouns correctly,** see page 144.

COMMON ERRORS

7. Did the teacher give them an assignment different from the one she gave us?

8. The boy thanked she and Paula for buying some of his lemonade.

9. It would be nice if they would bring our friends and we a pitcher of water.

10. He is the author who everyone adores.

Reference Note

For information about **inexact pronoun reference,** see page 164.

Exercise 12 Rewriting Sentences to Correct Inexact Pronoun References

Rewrite each of the following sentences to correct the inexact pronoun reference.

EXAMPLE   1. Domingo first read about Tomás Rivera when he was in the school library.

1. *When Domingo was in the school library, he read about Tomás Rivera for the first time.*

1. In the catalog, they tell about Tomás Rivera's novel, which is titled *. . . y no se lo tragó la tierra.*

2. As a boy, Rivera worked as a migrant field hand. That may partly explain why he wrote so vividly about migrant workers in his book.

3. Rivera worked long hours in the fields, and it interrupted his formal education.

4. In the novel, it focuses on a Mexican American family of migrant workers.

5. The family follows crops and the work they provide; it means that they have to move often.

6. Rivera's novel is about the migrant workers' search for justice, and it is inspiring.

7. After reading a novel by Tomás Rivera and short stories by Reuben Sánchez, I decided to read more of his works.

8. Mandy talked to Adrianne about the conflicts in Rivera's novel after she had read it.

9. In the biography of Rivera, it states that in his later life he became the first Mexican American chancellor in the University of California system.

10. After he said that the film *And the Earth Did Not Swallow Him* was based on Rivera's novel, Todd went with Rajiv to the library to check out the video.

For each of the following sentences, provide the correct past or past participle form of the verb in italics.

Reference Note

For information about **using verbs correctly,** see page 170.

EXAMPLE   1. *write*   Joyce Carol Thomas _____ *Brown Honey in Broomwheat Tea.*

1. *wrote*

1. *become*   During the Cenozoic era, South America and North America _____ linked by a land bridge.
2. *speak*   I had _____ to Jim before he left.
3. *bring*   Geraldine has _____ me her new copy of *A Gathering of Flowers: Stories About Being Young in America.*
4. *give*   Yesterday, Teresa _____ flowers to her grandmother.
5. *know*   We _____ that the first czar of Russia was known as Ivan the Terrible.
6. *hear*   Jonas had _____ that the picnic was postponed.
7. *choose*   I wonder what subject Celeste _____ for her world history presentation last week.
8. *drive*   My aunt Judy has _____ me to my ballet lessons every week this year.
9. *teach*   Who _____ Jorge to play the clarinet?
10. *ride*   I once _____ a bus across Oklahoma.
11. *break*   Two hundred million years ago, the land mass known as Pangaea _____ apart.
12. *forget*   Danny _____ to leave the front door unlocked so that I could get in.
13. *sing*   Sandra _____ a ballad, which she dedicated to her mother and grandmother.
14. *fall*   When I stepped on the patch of ice, I almost _____.
15. *leave*   They _____ hours ago.
16. *begin*   The Paleozoic era _____ 540 million years ago.
17. *think*   Conrad _____ he had money in his checking account, but he didn't.
18. *do*   How many times _____ you have to work that math problem before you got it right?
19. *freeze*   When Chris and Michael were hiking in Colorado, their water _____ overnight.
20. *go*   Last year, her family _____ to Asia.

COMMON ERRORS

Reference Note

For information about **verb forms,** see page 190.

Reference Note

For information on **verb tenses,** see page 188.

Exercise 14 Proofreading Sentences for Correct Verb Forms

Identify each incorrect verb form in the following sentences, and write the correct form. If a sentence is already correct, write *C.*

EXAMPLE   **1.** From the 1920s through the 1940s, people in the United States listened to radio programs and gone to the movies more than they do now.

           1. *gone—went*

1. The popularity of TV programs brung about the end of many radio shows.

2. It has not took very long for television to become one of the most popular forms of entertainment in the United States.

3. I use to think television had always been around, but the first regular TV broadcasts in the United States weren't until 1939.

4. Demonstrations of televisions drawed big crowds at the New York World's Fair in 1939.

5. In 1941, when the United States begun fighting in World War II, television broadcasting was suspended, but it resumed in 1945.

6. The sales of television sets soared after World War II, and by 1951, telecasts reached viewers from coast to coast.

7. Color programs weren't showed until 1953.

8. Of course, I've seen old black-and-white TV programs.

9. I also have heared some of the old radio shows from before the days of television.

10. Have you ever thought about how television has changed the way people in the United States spend their leisure time?

Exercise 15 Using the Different Tenses of Verbs in Sentences

Change the tense of the verb in each of the following sentences according to the directions given after the sentence.

EXAMPLE   **1.** Ingrid studied French for two years. (Change *studied* to a present perfect form.)

           1. *Ingrid has studied French for two years.*

1. Will's brother will graduate from college in the spring. (Change *will graduate* to a future perfect form.)

2. Adrian purchased new glasses before he went on vacation. (Change *purchased* to a past perfect form.)

3. Have you read any of Naomi Shihab Nye's poems? (Change *Have read* to a present perfect progressive form.)

4. The twins will play the same kind of instrument at the talent show. (Change *Will play* to a past emphatic form.)

5. The acrobats are performing this evening. (Change *are performing* to a present perfect form.)

6. Will you work in your uncle's blacksmith shop this summer? (Change *Will work* to a past progressive form.)

7. Bianca and Charles asked whether the building has an emergency evacuation plan. (Change *asked* to a future form.)

8. The new amusement park gives discounts to groups every day of the week. (Change *gives* to a past perfect form.)

9. Scott had hoped to take the driving test on Tuesday. (Change *had hoped* to a present emphatic form.)

10. The jugglers demonstrated their talent all afternoon. (Change *demonstrated* to a future form.)

Exercise 16 Revising a Paragraph to Make the Tenses of the Verbs Consistent

Read the following paragraph, and decide whether to rewrite it in the present or past tense. Then, rewrite it, changing the verb forms to correct any unnecessary changes in tense.

EXAMPLE　　[1] The children were eager to hear a story, so I begin to tell them the Navajo legend of Eagle Boy.

1. *The children are eager to hear a story, so I begin to tell them the Navajo legend of Eagle Boy.*

or

The children were eager to hear a story, so I began to tell them the Navajo legend of Eagle Boy.

[1] A young Navajo boy who lives with his parents often dreamed of eagles flying overhead. [2] One day, Father Eagle flew down to the boy, caught hold of his shirt, and carries him to a nest high on a cliff. [3] Father and Mother Eagle feed the boy cornmeal and then took him to the eagle people at the top of the sky. [4] Eventually, the boy goes to the home of Eagle Chief, who told him to remain there. [5] After Eagle Chief leaves, the boy became curious about an animal that he sees outside. [6] When the boy opens the door slightly to look more closely, Big Wind blew it completely open, pulling the boy outside, where the trickster Coyote is waiting. [7] The boy was soon tricked into touching Coyote's fur and turns into a coyote himself. [8] When Eagle Chief

Reference Note

For information about **consistent verb tense,** see page 195.

HELP

Although the example in Exercise 16 gives two possible revisions, you need to give only one revision for each sentence.

COMMON ERRORS

returns, he restored the boy. [9] Afterward, Eagle Chief names him Eagle Boy and gave him an eagle feather. [10] Eagle Boy then returns home to his parents, and he eventually became a great medicine man.

Exercise 17 Proofreading for Correct Comparative and Superlative Forms

Most of the following sentences contain errors in the use of comparative and superlative forms of modifiers. If a modifier is incorrect, give the correct form. If a sentence is already correct, write *C*.

EXAMPLE   1. The second time I made lasagna, I prepared it most quickly.

            1. *more quickly*

1. I planted lantana and petunias next to each other; the lantana grew best because it could withstand heat and drought.
2. The more exciting field trip of any this year is scheduled for this fall.
3. I wonder which of the two mountain peaks is tallest.
4. Of the club's many members, he is less likely to run for president because he is so shy.
5. The more suspenseful chapter in the novel told of a violent storm that damaged the sails of the pirate ship and drove the ship off course.
6. Which is most fun for you, painting with watercolors or sketching?
7. Watching the two dogs dig in the ground, Carl laughed as the more younger one retrieved a small toy.
8. The colorfulest sunset I ever saw in Montana was near Billings.
9. Outside the theater, we all agreed that the movie was the least satisfying sequel that we had ever seen.
10. Of all the mailboxes in the neighborhood, ours is the more unusual.

Exercise 18 Proofreading Sentences for Correct Use of Modifiers and Comparisons

Revise the following sentences to correct each error in the use of modifiers and comparisons.

EXAMPLE   1. In most areas, daisies are more easier to grow than orchids.

            1. *In most areas, daisies are easier to grow than orchids.*

1. Termites work in the dark and are less likelier to be seen than many other insects.
2. Raphael types faster than any student in his class.

3. Fortunately, no one was injured bad when the boats collided.
4. Although elephants are the largest land mammals, blue whales are the most largest mammals of all.
5. My friend Tim is more creative than anyone in his school.
6. The lion is more bigger than the lioness.
7. Aunt Gloria is more resilient than anyone I know.
8. I don't see good without my glasses.
9. The trekkers walked careful up the hill.
10. Kilimanjaro is the more magnificent mountain of any in Africa.

Exercise 19 Correcting Misplaced Modifiers

Each of the following sentences contains a misplaced modifier. Rewrite each sentence to correct the placement of the modifier.

EXAMPLE
    1. Flying in close formation, the crowd watched the squadron of small biplanes overhead.

    1. *The crowd watched the squadron of small biplanes flying in close formation overhead.*

1. Gathered into a heap, Nathan looked at the stalks of sugar cane.
2. I have always enjoyed listening to stories about my mother's childhood with my sister.
3. We watched the sun rise from our front porch.
4. Frank listened to music climbing the mountain.
5. We watched a film about how comets are formed in science class.
6. I saw a deer going to check the mail.
7. About six inches long, the *Tyrannosaurus rex* had sharp teeth.
8. They noticed a turtle on a log wading across the river.
9. We learned that the bridge had once collapsed as we rode over it.
10. Mr. Spinoza saw many earthworms planting his garden.

Exercise 20 Correcting Dangling Modifiers

Each of the following sentences contains a dangling modifier. Rewrite each sentence so that the modifier clearly and sensibly modifies a word in the sentence.

EXAMPLE
    1. Looking through the binoculars, the bird was brightly colored.

    1. *Looking through the binoculars, I saw that the bird was brightly colored.*

1. While practicing the piano, the music fell off the music rack.

Reference Note

For information about **misplaced modifiers,** see page 225.

Reference Note

For information about **dangling modifiers,** see page 224.

Grammar and Usage **421**

2. The people below looked like ants, peering down from the top of the Empire State Building.

3. Unable to complete the assignment on time, Bob's report had to be turned in late.

4. Perched on a high stool by the kitchen counter, the potatoes were easy to peel.

5. After stretching to warm up, the running shoes were tightly laced on my feet.

6. My telephone rang right after walking in the front door.

7. Determined to reach the finish line, the marathon seemed endless.

8. Looking overgrown and scraggly, the McKinneys decided to spend the weekend doing yardwork.

9. Studying fossil oysters found in Kansas, it was hypothesized that a shallow sea once covered at least part of that state.

10. All alone, the dark woods were mysterious and silent.

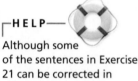

┌─HELP──
Although some of the sentences in Exercise 21 can be corrected in more than one way, you need to give only one revision for each sentence.

Reference Note

┌ For information about **double negatives,** see page 254. For information about **common usage errors,** see page 234.

Exercise 21 **Correcting Double Negatives and Other Errors in Usage**

Eliminate the double negatives and other errors in formal, standard usage in the following sentences.

EXAMPLE   1. Karen should of brought her delicious chow mein to the potluck dinner yesterday.

1. *Karen should have brought her delicious chow mein to the potluck dinner yesterday.*

1. I went to the beach yesterday to look for driftwood and shells but couldn't find none.

2. Just try and imagine a city without vehicles of any sort!

3. I would rather go to the county park on this beautiful afternoon then stay indoors.

4. Our track team practiced until we weren't able to run no more.

5. The engine sounds like it is ready to fall out of the old truck.

6. We didn't want to see neither of the movies that were showing at the theater.

7. At breakfast this morning, my little brother found a small toy inside of that box of cereal.

8. Joel drove a long ways across town just to trade one football card.

9. Unfortunately, my science experiment didn't work as good as I thought it would.

10. This long stretch of highway has hardly no curves in it.

Exercise 22 Correcting Errors in Usage

Identify and correct each error in the use of formal, standard English in the following sentences.

Reference Note

For information about **common usage errors,** see page 234.

EXAMPLE   1. Young people with inventive minds had ought to be encouraged!

     1. *had ought—ought*

1. People from five to nineteen years old have discovered some new and important products and processes.
2. As a teenager, young Jerrald Spencer use to take apart electronic appliances just to see how they worked.
3. In 1977, at the age of fifteen, Spencer created his first marketed invention, a kind of an electronic toy.
4. That there toy led to a whole series of specialty toys sold in major department stores.
5. In 1895, the teenager Cathy Evans invented an unique process known as "tufting" for decorating bedspreads.
6. Her invention had a tremendous affect on the carpet industry; in fact, most carpet made today involves the process she developed.
7. In 1922, eighteen-year-old Ralph Samuelson decided to try and use snow skis to ski on water.
8. He didn't think that skiing on water would be much harder then skiing on snow.
9. Like he thought, after many tries his skis worked!
10. If you want to be an inventor, you won't succeed without you try.

Exercise 23 Proofreading Sentences to Correct Errors in Usage

Each of the following sentences contains an error in the use of formal, standard English. Identify each error. Then, write the correct usage.

Reference Note

For information about **common usage errors,** see page 234.

EXAMPLE   1. The tour guide last summer learned us much about the Lincoln Memorial.

     1. *learned—taught*

1. This memorial, who was dedicated in 1922, is a popular attraction in Washington, D.C.
2. No less than 150 million people have visited the monument.
3. I was kind of amazed to hear that the memorial was built on what used to be marshland.
4. The architect Henry Bacon he designed the memorial.

5. I implied from our guide's talk that the Parthenon in Greece inspired Bacon's design.
6. It is not an allusion that the massive columns of both the Parthenon and the Lincoln Memorial tilt slightly inward.
7. The architects designed the columns this way because rows of truly straight columns give buildings the affect of bulging at the top.
8. I read where Daniel Chester French interviewed Lincoln's son Robert before sculpting the memorial's statue of Lincoln.
9. The spectacular 175-ton statue was carved in sections by the Piccirilli brothers, whose family had immigrated from Italy and settled in the United States.
10. The Gettysburg Address is inscribed on a wall inside of the memorial's hall.

Grammar and Usage Test: Section 1

DIRECTIONS In the following sentences, either part or all of each sentence is underlined. Using the rules of formal, standard English, choose the answer that most clearly expresses the meaning of the sentence. If there is no error, choose A. Indicate your response by shading in the appropriate oval on your answer sheet.

EXAMPLE 1. Has everyone <u>chosen a topic for their</u> essay?

(**A**) chosen a topic for their

(**B**) chose a topic for their

(**C**) choosed a topic for their

(**D**) chosen a topic for his or her

(**E**) chosen a topic for his and her

ANSWER 1. A B C D E

1. In the 1936 Olympic Games, <u>I read that Jesse Owens won four gold medals.</u>

(**A**) In the 1936 Olympic Games, I read that Jesse Owens won four gold medals.

(**B**) In the 1936 Olympic Games, I read that four gold medals were won by Jesse Owens.

(**C**) I read where Jesse Owens won four gold medals in the 1936 Olympic Games.

(**D**) I read in the 1936 Olympic Games that Jesse Owens won four gold medals.

(**E**) I read that Jesse Owens won four gold medals in the 1936 Olympic Games.

2. In some sports, a "goose egg" is <u>when a player has a score of zero.</u>

(**A**) when a player has a score of zero

(**B**) where a player has a score of zero

(**C**) a score of zero

(**D**) scoring a zero

(**E**) that a player has a score of zero

3. <u>I can't hardly remember a time when the temperature was lower than it is today.</u>

(**A**) I can't hardly remember a time when the temperature was lower than it is today.

(**B**) I can't hardly remember a time when the temperature was lower then it is today.

(**C**) I can hardly remember a time when the temperature was more lower than it is today.

(**D**) I can hardly remember a time when the temperature was lower then it is today.

(**E**) I can hardly remember a time when the temperature was lower than it is today.

4. This evening <u>less people will be driving</u> cars to the parade because there is less space available for parking.

  (A) less people will be driving

  (B) fewer people will be driving

  (C) less people will have been driving

  (D) fewer people will have been driving

  (E) fewer people driven

5. The first tennis match was <u>between she and I.</u>

  (A) between she and I

  (B) between her and I

  (C) between her and me

  (D) between she and me

  (E) among her and me

6. <u>While running to the bus stop this morning, some books fell out of my backpack.</u>

  (A) While running to the bus stop this morning, some books fell out of my backpack.

  (B) While running this morning, some books fell out of my backpack at the bus stop.

  (C) While I was running to the bus stop this morning, some books fell out of my backpack.

  (D) Some books fell out of my backpack while running to the bus stop this morning.

  (E) I was running to the bus stop this morning while some of my books fell out of my backpack.

7. Raymond knows how to repair lawn mowers, <u>and he plans to make it his summer job</u>.

  (A) and he plans to make it his summer job

  (B) and he plans to make that his summer job

  (C) and that is his plan for a summer job

  (D) and he plans to make repairing lawn mowers his summer job

  (E) which is his plan for a summer job

8. Creole dishes, the origins of which can be traced to Spanish, African, and Caribbean cooking.

(A) Creole dishes, the origins of which can be traced to Spanish, African, and Caribbean cooking.

(B) The origins of Creole dishes, which can be traced to Spanish, African, and Caribbean cooking.

(C) Tracing the origins of Creole dishes to Spanish, African, and Caribbean cooking.

(D) Spanish, African, and Caribbean cooking, which are the origins of Creole dishes.

(E) The origins of Creole dishes can be traced to Spanish, African, and Caribbean cooking.

9. The coach doesn't think that him and I have practiced free throws enough today.

(A) doesn't think that him and I

(B) don't think that him and me

(C) doesn't think that he and I

(D) don't think that he and me

(E) doesn't think that him and me

10. Some of the people who are standing in line have all ready bought their tickets.

(A) who are standing in line have all ready

(B) who are standing in line have already

(C) whom are standing in line have all ready

(D) whom are standing in line have already

(E) which are standing in line have already

THE GRIZZWELLS reprinted by permission of Newspaper Enterprise Association, Inc.

Grammar and Usage Test: Section 2

DIRECTIONS   Read the paragraph below. For each numbered blank, select the word or group of words on the next page that best completes the sentence. Indicate your response by shading in the appropriate oval on your answer sheet.

EXAMPLE   __(1)__ you ever heard of sick building syndrome?

    1. **(A)** Has

         (B) Have

         (C) Did

         (D) Were

         (E) Hasn't

ANSWER   1.   Ⓐ **Ⓑ** Ⓒ Ⓓ Ⓔ

In the early 1980s, a number of health problems suffered by office workers __(1)__ for the first time as symptoms of a single ailment called sick building syndrome. In addition to fatigue and eye irritation, __(2)__ symptoms included headaches, sore throats, colds, and flu. Studies indicate that sick building syndrome, __(3)__ has been responsible for a 30 percent rise in absenteeism in some businesses, can cause as much as a 40 percent drop in productivity. The problems resulting from this syndrome __(4)__ are caused by such indoor pollutants as formaldehyde, benzene, and trichloroethylene. These substances, which are found in furniture, insulation, and paint, __(5)__ trapped in climate-controlled buildings. Even though these pollutants are so widespread, the situation __(6)__ hopeless. Research originally conducted to help astronauts __(7)__ to a simple, effective solution—houseplants. Microorganisms in the roots of a potted plant __(8)__ with the plant to remove harmful substances from the air. The __(9)__ plants include chrysanthemums, which remove benzene, and spider plants, which remove formaldehyde. In addition, both peace lilies and English ivy __(10)__ trichloroethylene.

1. **(A)** identified
   (B) was identified
   (C) were identified
   (D) being identified
   (E) was being identified

2. **(A)** these
   (B) them
   (C) these here
   (D) these kind of
   (E) them kind of

3. **(A)** they
   (B) which
   (C) who
   (D) what
   (E) it

4. **(A)** more likely
   (B) more likelier
   (C) likelier
   (D) most likely
   (E) most likeliest

5. **(A)** becomes
   (B) becomed
   (C) becoming
   (D) become
   (E) is becoming

6. **(A)** is in no way
   (B) is not in no way
   (C) aren't in no way
   (D) it isn't hardly
   (E) isn't hardly

7. **(A)** have led
   (B) has led
   (C) has lead
   (D) leads
   (E) have lead

8. **(A)** they interact
   (B) it interacts
   (C) interact
   (D) interacts
   (E) is interacting

9. **(A)** most useful
   (B) usefullest
   (C) most usefullest
   (D) more usefuller
   (E) usefuller

10. **(A)** removes
    (B) they remove
    (C) removed
    (D) were removing
    (E) remove

Reference Note

For information about **capitalization**, see page 264.

Each of the following word groups contains at least one error in capitalization. Correct the errors either by changing capital letters to lowercase letters or by changing lowercase letters to capital letters. Some capital letters are already correctly used.

EXAMPLE   1. Robert Burns's poem "a red, red rose"

           1. *Robert Burns's poem "A Red, Red Rose"*

1. my aunt elizabeth
2. growing up in the midwest
3. *the middle passage* by V. S. Naipaul
4. kansas city royals
5. west of sixty-fifth street
6. winter in denver
7. grandma's brother
8. senator Ann Greene
9. latin, art, and geometry II
10. a buddhist temple
11. the battle Of vicksburg
12. dr. l. f. livingstone
13. the book *a room with a view*
14. American indian pictographs
15. french-Speaking countries
16. a xerox® photocopier
17. Father's day
18. A vietnamese festival
19. orbiting mars or earth
20. Grand teton national park
21. the archaeology of greece and sparta
22. a jewish synagogue
23. toni Morrison's book *jazz*
24. 7926 broadway boulevard
25. William Shakespeare's play *twelfth night*

Exercise 25 Correcting Errors in Capitalization

Reference Note

For information about **capitalization**, see page 264.

Each of the following sentences contains errors in capitalization. Correct the errors either by changing capital letters to lowercase letters or by changing lowercase letters to capital letters. Some capital letters are already used correctly.

EXAMPLE   1. oren lyons's formal title is faith keeper of the turtle clan.

            1. *Oren Lyons's formal title is Faith Keeper of the Turtle Clan.*

1. i recently read about oren lyons, an Influential onondaga chief.
2. he is an american indian leader featured in *The Encyclopedia Of Native America,* which is a reference we use in our American History class.
3. the onondaga are an iroquois people.
4. before assuming this important position, mr. lyons was a successful commercial artist in new york city.
5. the iroquois tradition of having faith keepers dates back to hundreds of years before the pilgrims landed at plymouth rock.
6. mr. lyons edits a publication called *daybreak,* which is dedicated to the seventh generation to come.
7. as faith keeper, mr. lyons is responsible for making decisions that will ensure that the earth is habitable for another seven generations.
8. He also has many other responsibilities, including speaking before the united nations.
9. mr. lyons, other members of the iroquois league, and a group of lakota sioux addressed the united nations in geneva, switzerland.
10. Faith keepers work to uphold the traditions of their people as well as the principles of Democracy, community, and reverence for the Natural World.

Exercise 26 Proofreading Sentences for the Correct Use of Commas

Each of the following sentences needs at least one comma. Write the word or numeral that comes before each missing comma, and add the comma.

Reference Note

For information about **using commas,** see page 298.

EXAMPLE   1. After separating the clear glass from the colored glass we collected paper for recycling.

            1. *colored glass,*

1. Orb weavers are spiders that create beautiful complicated round webs.
2. We had planned to climb the mountain but the trail was closed because mountain lions had been sighted in the area.
3. Cheeky the neighbor's dog that chewed up my athletic shoes is now kept in his own yard.
4. Oh when will I stop worrying about things that will never happen?

5. Italy in my opinion is the most beautiful country in the world.
6. On July 20 1969 the *Apollo 2* lunar module landed on the moon.
7. I wasn't chosen for the track team but I am trying out for soccer next week.
8. The American painter Charles Russell who is famous for his scenes of life in the West is my favorite artist.
9. The Perseid meteor shower which occurs annually appears to originate in the constellation Perseus.
10. Tired of waiting for the movie to start the audience began to murmur and fidget.

Exercise 27 Using Commas Correctly

Each of the following sentences needs at least one comma. Write the word or numeral that comes before each missing comma, and add the comma.

Reference Note

For information about **using commas,** see page 298.

EXAMPLE 1. Tony have you ever heard of Dr. Percy L. Julian?

1. *Tony,*

1. Julian born in Montgomery Alabama in 1899 grew up to become a renowned scientist.
2. After studying at DePauw University he graduated with highest honors; in fact he received a Phi Beta Kappa key and delivered the valedictory address.
3. Julian went on to Harvard where he earned a master's degree and then traveled to Austria to earn a Ph.D. at the University of Vienna.
4. As Ahmed says Dr. Julian must have been a brilliant man.
5. Dr. Julian taught at Howard University and West Virginia University but his fame began after he went to work as a research chemist for Glidden a paint company in Chicago Illinois.
6. During World War II Dr. Julian created a firefighting foam which by the way was made from soybean protein.
7. He received the 1947 Spingarn Medal which is the NAACP's highest award.
8. Interested in finding other uses for soybeans Dr. Julian established Julian Laboratories and its subsidiaries.
9. Over the course of his lifetime he developed an inexpensive cortisone for arthritis sufferers drugs to relieve glaucoma drugs to help victims of rheumatic fever and many other helpful medicines.
10. Dr. Julian died in 1975 but his impressive achievements live on.

Using Semicolons and Colons Correctly

The following sentences need semicolons and colons. Write the word or numeral preceding and the word or numeral following the needed punctuation, and add the proper punctuation. In some instances you will need to replace commas with either semicolons or colons.

Reference Note

For information about **semicolons and colons,** see Chapter 12.

EXAMPLE

1. My brother likes to read adventure novels I prefer autobiographies of sports figures.

1. *novels; I*

1. We both signed up for field hockey, however, the heavy snow has prevented practice all month.
2. In art class Juanna, Elaine, and Jim used acrylics and Todd, Tonya, and Jasper used oils.
3. We missed the 4 15 bus and had to wait for the 5 30 one.
4. The movie she recommended was *Geronimo An American Legend.*
5. From this airport there are direct flights to Frankfurt, Germany, Rome, Italy, London, England, and Paris, France.
6. Our choir is singing a song based on Psalm 19 14.
7. Our neighborhood has fiestas for various holidays for example, we have a piñata party on Cinco de Mayo each year.
8. I walk to school each day with Darla, Gene, and Greg and Sven, Petra, and Arnold join us on the walk home.
9. I have several postcards that my stepsister sent me from towns with unusual names, for instance, here are ones from Cut and Shoot, Texas, and Truth or Consequences, New Mexico.
10. The Ecology Club has adopted the following projects this semester setting out recycling bins, planting trees in the schoolyard, and adopting two miles of highway to keep clean.

Exercise 29 **Punctuating Dialogue**

Add paragraph indentions and insert quotation marks and other punctuation where needed in the dialogue on the following page.

Reference Note

For information about **punctuating dialogue,** see page 341.

EXAMPLES

[1] Hey, Sarah, I hear you've become a vegetarian Colin said. Won't you get tired of eating just vegetables?

1. *"Hey, Sarah, I hear you've become a vegetarian," Colin said. "Won't you get tired of eating just vegetables?"*

[2] You've got some things to learn about vegetarians! Sarah said.

2. *"You've got some things to learn about vegetarians!" Sarah said.*

COMMON ERRORS

[1] Well, teach me Colin said. What is a vegetarian?

[2] You know that a vegetarian is a person who doesn't eat meat Sarah said but you don't know what a vegetarian does eat.

[3] Your mistake is one that many people make. They think that a vegetarian eats only vegetables, but vegetarians eat quite a variety of foods.

[4] Colin replied Okay, what else do vegetarians eat?

[5] Well, Sarah answered I eat whatever I want that isn't meat, and I try to eat healthful foods. I eat vegetables, of course, but also grains, breads, pastas, beans, nuts, soups, cereals, and fruit.

[6] Do you eat eggs and dairy products?

[7] Yes, Sarah replied I do, but some vegetarians don't. For instance, I sometimes eat quiche, cheese and vegetable enchiladas, and bowls of cereal with milk.

[8] Colin said, I guess you aren't having any trouble finding things to eat. I'm wondering, though, why you decided to become a vegetarian.

[9] I just wanted to feel better. Studies show that being a vegetarian is very healthful Sarah said.

[10] Colin said I remember learning that a diet without any animal products is cholesterol-free. You'll have to tell me about other health benefits of vegetarianism.

Exercise 30 Punctuating and Capitalizing Quotations and Titles

For each of the following sentences, insert quotation marks and other marks of punctuation where needed, and change lowercase letters to capital letters as necessary.

EXAMPLE   1. Should the U.S. flag be flown at the same level as or higher than a state flag asked Earl

1. *"Should the U.S. flag be flown at the same level as or higher than a state flag?" asked Earl.*

1. Megan's note says, The electrician at the repair shop said that our stereo would be ready by 5:00 P.M.

2. Physical therapy Karen said is really strengthening my brother's legs.

3. Leiningen Versus the Ants, by Carl Stephenson, is a frightening short story Bob said.

4. That's right, Victoria he replied You will want to plant the azaleas in partial sunlight.

Reference Note

For information about **punctuating quotations and titles,** see page 341.

COMMON ERRORS

5. Sean asked why did Paul yell Get off the porch! at the dog?
6. The following graduates have been named "most likely to succeed: Alexandra, Michael, and Jim.
7. When she hit her finger with the hammer while repairing the roof, Hannah yelled that does it!
8. What I asked the doctor is the patella?
9. The song Long Distance Call was one of the hits of the Chicago blues singer Muddy Waters.
10. No! Paula exclaimed I didn't say to use the green paint!

Exercise 31 **Using Apostrophes Correctly**

Revise the following word groups, adding apostrophes where they are needed. If a word group is already correct, write *C*.

Reference Note
For information on **apostrophes,** see page 356.

EXAMPLE   1. giving to United Ways fund
                    1. *giving to United Way's fund*

1. somebodys hat
2. Are these Kims poems?
3. Judys and his show
4. ten oclock
5. both planes engines
6. The box was theirs.
7. How many *as* are in *aardvark*?
8. womens sizes
9. Anya and Tonis team
10. hadnt finished
11. that canoes hull
12. no one elses parents
13. Its memory capacity is huge.
14. that clubs newsletter
15. Mr. Harriss Irish setter
16. neithers fault
17. Howards and Marilyns tests
18. because Im sleepy
19. whose ring
20. Its going to rain.

Exercise 32 **Using Punctuation Correctly**

The following sentences contain errors in the use of end marks, commas, semicolons, colons, quotation marks, apostrophes, and hyphens. Rewrite each sentence correctly.

EXAMPLE   1. When Mr Andrews finished painting the hall we asked him to paint the front porch
                    1. *When Mr. Andrews finished painting the hall, we asked him to paint the front porch.*

1. While she was in Hades Persephone ate the seed's of a pomegranate, in Greek mythology this fruit symbolizes marriage.
2. Someones father works on Royal Street but I cant remember whose.

3. The cities that I have most enjoyed visiting are the following New Orleans Louisiana Seattle Washington and Philadelphia Pennsylvania

4. Yes I have been to Guadalajara said Liza but not recently however I would like to go there again soon.

5. Twenty nine crows are cackling in the front yard and the noise is driving me crazy exclaimed Cathy.

6. Werent you nervous when the lizards snakes and scorpions started crawling around the two actors legs

7. Davids and Marys houses are both near the new shopping center which was completed in mid February.

8. You can give those posters to Margaret, Zack, and Greta and Phillip, Craig, and Matthew will give theirs to me.

9. Bobby yelled The dogs dish is gone said Susan

10. That beautiful well known song is Over the Rainbow its my sister-in-laws favorite song.

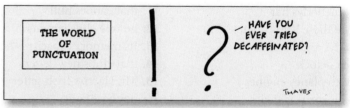

FRANK & ERNEST reprinted by permission of Newspaper Enterprise Association, Inc.

Reference Note

For information about **spelling rules,** see page 378.

Exercise 33 Correcting Spelling Errors

Each of the following sentences contains spelling errors. Correctly write each misspelled word.

EXAMPLE　　1. We forfieted the free vacation and enjoied our leisure time at home.

　　　　　　　1. *forfeited, enjoyed*

1. The dog reacted in a wierd way, stareing straight ahead.

2. The pityful wailing of the kitten helped us find it.

3. We traveled on the route maped out for us and proceded at a steady pace.

4. They finally conceeded that the new system would cost a 3rd less to run than the old one did.

5. When the paper we collected for recycling was wieghed, we were gratifyed to learn that the amount exceeded one ton.

6. Cleanlyness of the work space is especialy important when food is being handled.
7. 40 people signed up for the dance classes to learn waltzs, polkas, and line dances.
8. All the puppys at the animal shelter were cute, but the 1st one they showed us was the one we adopted.
9. My cousin drives 30 miles each way to her job at a wildlife park, where she takes care of the lions, tigers, and wolfs.
10. Both of the monkies are likely to throw tomatos.

Exercise 34 Choosing Between Words Often Confused

From each pair of words in parentheses, choose the word or word group that correctly completes the sentence.

EXAMPLE   1. (*You're, Your*) endangering the pedestrians by skating too fast.

    1. *You're*

1. When I applied for work at the restaurant, I spoke with the (*personal, personnel*) manager.
2. It is important to check the (*breaks, brakes*) on any vehicle before you start driving.
3. We had (*already, all ready*) opened the windows in the art room before Ms. Wong asked us.
4. What theme should we (*choose, chose*) for the prom?
5. Eleanor and Lupita said we could use (*they're, their*) binoculars when we go on the Audubon Society field trip.
6. What (*effect, affect*) will all the rain have on the mown hay?
7. The elephant returned to (*its, it's*) enclosure at feeding time.
8. What did the members of the (*counsel, council*) decide?
9. The (*lose, loose*) wing nut created a rattle in the trunk.
10. Use very fine, not (*course, coarse*), sandpaper for the finishing work on wood furniture or toys.

Reference Note

For information about **words often confused,** see page 391.

Mechanics Test: Section 1

DIRECTIONS Each of the following sentences contains an underlined word or word group. Choose the answer that shows the correct capitalization, punctuation, and spelling of the underlined part. If there is no error, choose answer E (Correct as is). Indicate your response by shading in the appropriate oval on your answer sheet.

EXAMPLE 1. Please post these announcements for the Columbus winter Carnival.

    (A) the Columbus Winter Carnival

    (B) the columbus winter carnival

    (C) The Columbus Winter carnival

    (D) the Columbus Winter carnival

    (E) Correct as is

ANSWER 1.

1. "Can you tell us the moral of the fable, Josh"? asked Ms. Chen.

    (A) moral of the fable, Josh?"   **(D)** moral of the fable, Josh?,"

    (B) morale of the fable, Josh?   **(E)** Correct as is

    (C) moral of the fable," Josh?

2. We'll need streamers balloons and confetti to decorate for the baby shower.

    (A) Well, need streamers, balloons,   **(D)** We'll need streamers balloons,

    (B) We'll need streamers, balloons,   **(E)** Correct as is

    (C) We'll need: streamers, balloons,

3. The words of Dr. Martin Luther King, Jr., are engraved on the Civil Rights Memorial.

    (A) Dr Martin Luther King, Jr.,   **(D)** Dr. Martin Luther King, jr.,

    (B) Dr. Martin Luther King Jr.,   **(E)** Correct as is

    (C) Dr. Martin Luther King, Jr,

4. "Did Coach really say, 'Run another mile?'" gasped Carla.

    (A) mile?"   **(D)** mile,'"

    (B) mile,"   **(E)** Correct as is

    (C) mile'?"

5. Choose a free subscription to one of these <u>magazines *Time*</u>, *Newsweek, Scientific American,* or *Harper's.*
   (A) magazines *Time*
   (B) magazines; *Time,*
   (C) magazines: "Time,"
   (D) magazines: *Time,*
   (E) Correct as is

6. The <u>men's and womens</u> shoe departments and the housewares department are having sales now.
   (A) mens and women's
   (B) men's and women's
   (C) mens' and womens'
   (D) mens and womens
   (E) Correct as is

7. The bus driver <u>said "that we should be quiet."</u>
   (A) said, "That we should be quiet."
   (B) said "That we should be quiet."
   (C) said, that we should be quiet.
   (D) said that we should be quiet.
   (E) Correct as is

8. I've visited three state <u>capitals: Boise, Idaho, Tallahassee, Florida;</u> and Montpelier, Vermont.
   (A) capitals: Boise, Idaho, Tallahassee, Florida,
   (B) capitols: Boise, Idaho; Tallahassee, Florida;
   (C) capitols: Boise; Idaho; Tallahassee; Florida;
   (D) capitals: Boise, Idaho; Tallahassee, Florida;
   (E) Correct as is

9. <u>The weather will not effect their plans</u> for this weekend.
   (A) The weather will not affect their plans
   (B) The whether will not affect their plans
   (C) The weather will not affect they're plans
   (D) The weather will not effect they're plans
   (E) Correct as is

10. <u>Its not John whose</u> left his papers in the library.
    (A) Its not John who's
    (B) It's not John whose
    (C) Its' not John who's
    (D) It's not John who's
    (E) Correct as is

Mechanics Test: Section 2

DIRECTIONS   Each numbered item below contains an underlined word group. Choose the answer that shows the correct capitalization, punctuation, and spelling of the underlined part. If there is no error, choose answer E (Correct as is). Indicate your response by shading in the appropriate oval on your answer sheet.

EXAMPLE   **[1]** February 9 2009

           (A) Febuary 9 2009

           (B) Febuary 9, 2009

           (C) February 9th 2009

           (D) February 9, 2009

           (E) Correct as is

ANSWER   1.   Ⓐ   Ⓑ   Ⓒ   ⬤D   Ⓔ

---

    327 Hickory Lane

[1] Ankeny Iowa 50021

    February 9, 2009

[2] Susan Washington DVM
    49-A Johnson Circle
    Des Moines, IA 51219

[3] Dear Dr. Washington:

Thank you for **[4]** agreing to lead the discussion at our club's next meeting. We members of **[5]** Future Farmers of America know how important the practice of veterinary medicine is to agriculture. **[6]** 39 students have already signed up to attend. As I mentioned on the phone last **[7]** week, our meeting will take place in Healy Lecture hall. We will begin at **[8]** 3:00 P.M, and if things go as planned, I will introduce you soon thereafter. We look forward to hearing **[9]** your views on veterinary medicine, and hope that you will stay for refreshments after the meeting.

[10] yours sincerely,

Michael Yoder
President, FFA
Ankeny High School

1. **(A)** Ankeny, Ia. 50021
   (B) Ankeny, IA 50021
   (C) Ankeny IA, 50021
   (D) Ankeny I.A., 50021
   (E) Correct as is

2. **(A)** Susan Washington DVM.
   (B) Susan Washington; DVM
   (C) Susan Washington, DVM
   (D) Susan Washington: DVM
   (E) Correct as is

3. **(A)** Dear Dr Washington:
   (B) Dear Dr. Washington,
   (C) Dear dr. Washington,
   (D) Dear Dr. Washington;
   (E) Correct as is

4. **(A)** agreing to led
   (B) agreeing, to lead
   (C) agreeing to lead
   (D) agreeing too lead
   (E) Correct as is

5. **(A)** Future Farmers Of America
   (B) future farmers of america
   (C) future farmers of America
   (D) future Farmers of America
   (E) Correct as is

6. **(A)** Thirty nine students
   (B) Thirty-nine students
   (C) Thirty-nine student's
   (D) Thirty-nine students'
   (E) Correct as is

7. **(A)** week: our meeting will take place in Healy lecture hall
   (B) week: our meeting will take place in Healy Lecture Hall
   (C) week, our meeting will take place in Healy lecture hall
   (D) week, our meeting will take place in Healy Lecture Hall
   (E) Correct as is

8. **(A)** 3:00 P M and if things go as planned,
   (B) 3:00 P M., and if things go as planed,
   (C) 3:00 P.M. and if things go as planned,
   (D) 3:00 P.M., and if things go as planned,
   (E) Correct as is

9. **(A)** your'e views on veterinary medicine, and
   (B) you're views on veterinary medicine; and
   (C) your views on veterinary medicine and
   (D) your views on veterinary medicine: and
   (E) Correct as is

10. **(A)** Yours sincerely,
    (B) Yours Sincerely
    (C) Your's sincerely,
    (D) Yours sincerely:
    (E) Correct as is

Sentences

GO TO: go.hrw.com

Writing Complete Sentences

Diagnostic Preview

A. Identifying Sentences and Sentence Fragments

Identify each of the following word groups as a *sentence* or a *sentence fragment*.

EXAMPLE   1. Despite my best intentions and without my
             knowledge.

             1. *sentence fragment*

 1. Getting to know the new neighbors who moved in next door last month.
 2. Whenever my family gathers during the holidays.
 3. The cats, stretching and yawning, woke from a long afternoon nap in the sunny windowsill.
 4. To take a shower, put on clean clothes, and eat a warm meal.
 5. The child listens to the story.
 6. The visitors, who were from Wales, watched the football game intently.
 7. Who was an old friend of my father from his army unit.
 8. Then, in the middle of the night, a loud thump.
 9. Near the gate behind the garage, a single rosebush blooms.
10. Broke into a hundred pieces, despite his best efforts to catch the vase.

B. Revising Sentence Fragments

Rewrite each of the following sentence fragments to create a complete sentence.

EXAMPLE   **1.** Diving and swooping in the swift breeze.

              1. The box kite was diving and swooping in the swift breeze.

11. The big, tortoise-shell cat that chased the squirrel into the willow tree in the backyard.

12. To explore the ocean floor.

13. Relaxing quietly on the front porch on a warm summer evening.

14. A familiar or catchy melody, an interesting rhythm, and clever words.

15. A wall built of enormous hand-cut stones.

C. Identifying and Revising Run-on Sentences

Identify each of the following word groups as a *sentence* or a *run-on sentence.* Then, revise each run-on sentence to make it one or more complete sentences.

EXAMPLE   **1.** Our school's newspaper has won many awards, one of my articles won a prize last year.

              1. run-on sentence—Our school's newspaper has won many awards. One of my articles won a prize last year.

16. Last week, our school sponsored a journalism conference, most of the schools in the area sent representatives.

17. Student newspapers were displayed, and student editors and reporters participated in workshops and discussions.

18. Many schools sent their yearbook staffs, several schools sent student editors of literary magazines as well.

19. An exhibit of photographs taken by students attracted attention, some of the photographers are obviously very talented.

20. Professional journalists came to the conference to offer advice and encouragement.

21. The editor of the daily newspaper was the guest speaker she talked about careers in journalism and publishing.

22. After the editor's speech, the students attended hour-long workshops on a variety of topics then it was time for lunch.

23. In the afternoon, participants went to additional workshops, followed by discussion groups.

24. The workshops on sports reporting, photography, and publication design were especially popular extra chairs had to be added to the rooms for those workshops.

25. By the end of the day, all the participants were tired, but everyone agreed that the conference had been successful.

Sentence Fragments

A **sentence fragment** is a group of words that is only a part of a sentence. Like a fragment of a painting or photograph, a sentence fragment is confusing because it fails to give the whole picture. To communicate clearly, whether at school or in the workplace, you must write complete sentences.

To be complete, a **sentence** must (1) have a subject, (2) have a verb, and (3) express a complete thought. If any of these requirements is not met, the group of words is a fragment rather than a complete sentence.

FRAGMENT	Is a large, hairy spider. [The subject is missing. *What* is a large, hairy spider?]
SENTENCE	The tarantula is a large, hairy spider.
FRAGMENT	Some tarantulas of South America to a body length of 3 1/2 inches. [The verb is missing. *What* do some tarantulas do to a body length of 3 1/2 inches?]
SENTENCE	Some tarantulas of South America can grow to a body length of 3 1/2 inches.
FRAGMENT	Although tarantulas of the United States are feared. [The word group has a subject and a verb, but it does not express a complete thought.]
SENTENCE	Although tarantulas of the United States are feared, their bite is only as dangerous as a bee sting.

Fragments usually occur when you are writing in a hurry or when you are a little careless. For example, you might create a fragment by leaving out an important word or two. Also, you might chop off part of a sentence by putting in a period too soon.

To find out if what you have written is a fragment, you can use the following simple three-part test.

| COMPUTER TIP

Use a grammar checker to find sentence fragments and run-on sentences. These tools are not fool-proof, however, so you should always proofread your own work carefully.

1. Does the word group have a subject?

2. Does the word group have a verb?

3. Does the word group express a complete thought?

If even one of your answers is no, then you have a fragment.

NOTE By itself, a sentence fragment does not express a complete thought. However, a fragment can be used for effect in writing if it is clearly related to a sentence that comes before or after it. Read the following groups of words.

> The snowcapped mountains. The lush valley. The still lake.

By themselves, these fragments do not make sense because we do not know to what they relate. Now, read the fragments along with a sentence placed before them.

> When he reached the peak, the hiker stopped to take in the beauty. The snowcapped mountains. The lush valley. The still lake.

As you can see, the sentence gives the fragments meaning. It provides a context in which the fragments make sense.

Experienced writers sometimes use sentence fragments for effect. In most of your formal writing, however, you should avoid using fragments. As you gain more experience as a writer, you may feel comfortable enough to experiment in your informal writing. Still, it is important to master complete sentences first.

MEETING THE CHALLENGE

Good writers are careful to avoid unintentional sentence fragments, but some writers may use fragments to achieve particular effects. Search a few sources (such as newspaper and magazine articles or chapters from fiction and nonfiction works) for sentence fragments, and keep a log of the fragments you find. Then, review the fragments you have collected and write a brief paragraph in which you consider this question: What function do fragments serve in writing?

Oral Practice **Identifying Sentence Fragments**

Read aloud each word group on the next page. Then, using the three-part test, identify what, if anything, is missing. Say whether the group of words is missing a subject or a verb or whether the group of words has both a subject and a verb but does not express a complete thought. Say *correct* if the words form a complete sentence.

EXAMPLE   **1.** There are three species of blood-eating (vampire) bats.

1. correct

1. Vampire bats only in the tropics of Central and South America.
2. Most horror tales about vampire bats are not true.
3. Vampire bats very small mammals.
4. Although they do bite other animals.
5. That they do not drain their victims of blood.
6. Their small teeth are as sharp as needles.
7. While animals are sleeping.
8. But can be dangerous.
9. Some vampire bats carriers of rabies.
10. The greatest danger to victims is infection.

"What was it like back in the days when people talked and wrote in complete sentences?"

BERRY'S WORLD reprinted by permission of Newspaper Enterprise Association, Inc.

Phrase Fragments

A **phrase** is a group of related words that does not contain both a verb and its subject. Because it does not have all the basic parts of a sentence, a phrase by itself is a fragment. Three kinds of phrases are often mistaken for sentences: *verbal phrases, appositive phrases,* and *prepositional phrases.*

Verbal Phrases

A **verbal** is a word that is formed from a verb but is used as another part of speech. Because verbs and verbals are look-alikes, it is sometimes hard to tell the difference between them. That is why **verbal phrases** (phrases that contain verbals) are easily mistaken for sentences—they can appear to have verbs in them when they really don't.

Watch for verbals in phrases. Some verbals have endings such as *–ing, –d,* or *–ed.* Another kind of verbal often has the word *to* in front of it (*to run, to look*). A verbal phrase alone does not express a complete thought.

FRAGMENT	Our class interested in deserts.
SENTENCE	Our class was interested in deserts.

FRAGMENT	Found in hot and cold climates.
SENTENCE	Found in hot and cold climates, deserts are created when the earth's surface receives little or no rain.

FRAGMENT	Learning about the Gobi.
SENTENCE	Learning about the Gobi made me interested in studying deserts.

Reference Note

For more on **verbal phrases,** such as **participial phrases, gerund phrases,** and **infinitive phrases,** see Chapter 3.

FRAGMENT	To find information about deserts.
SENTENCE	We went to the library to find information about deserts.

NOTE When a verbal phrase modifies, or describes, another word in a sentence, it is usually best to place the phrase as close as possible to the word it modifies. However, some verbal phrases make sense either at the beginning or at the end of the sentence.

Appositive Phrases

An *appositive* is a noun or pronoun that identifies or describes a nearby word in the sentence. An *appositive phrase* consists of an appositive and its modifiers. Because an appositive phrase does not express a complete thought, it cannot stand alone as a complete sentence.

FRAGMENT	A strange rock formation.
SENTENCE	Devils Tower, a strange rock formation, has sage moss and grass on its flat top.

Prepositional Phrases

A *prepositional phrase* is a group of words that contains a preposition, a noun or pronoun called the object of the preposition, and any modifiers of the object.

FRAGMENT	Of volcanic rock.
SENTENCE	Devils Tower is an 865-foot-tall tower of volcanic rock.

Revising Phrase Fragments

Using the photograph on this page to help spark your imagination, create a sentence from each of the following phrase fragments. You may (1) add the fragment to a complete sentence or (2) develop the fragment into a complete sentence by adding a subject, a verb, or both.

EXAMPLE   **1.** moving slowly and deliberately on the surface of Mars

      1. Moving slowly and deliberately on the surface of Mars, the space vehicle Sojourner *looked like a large bug.*

or

      The space vehicle Sojourner *was moving slowly and deliberately on the surface of Mars.*

1. in outer space

2. through asteroid fields

3. to discover the unknown

4. sampling rocks and soil

5. excited and surprised

6. a remote-controlled vehicle

7. fueled by scientists' imaginations

8. on the planet's horizon

9. shattered by asteroids

10. to probe the surface of Mars

Reference Note

For more on **independent and subordinate clauses,** see pages 90 and 91.

Subordinate Clause Fragments

A *clause* is a group of words that contains a verb and its subject. One kind of clause, an *independent clause,* expresses a complete thought and can stand alone as a sentence. For example, the independent clause *I missed the bus* is a complete sentence. However, another kind of clause, the *subordinate clause,* does not express a complete thought and cannot stand alone as a sentence. A subordinate clause fragment is easy to identify because it suggests a question that it does not answer.

FRAGMENT   When flocks of scarlet ibises come to roost in the mangrove trees of the Caroni Swamp. [*What* happens when the ibises roost in the mangrove trees?]

SENTENCE   When flocks of scarlet ibises come to roost in the mangrove trees of the Caroni Swamp, the trees seem to blossom in bright red.

FRAGMENT   Which is the national bird of Trinidad. [Note that this group of words would be a complete sentence if it ended with a question mark. However, as a statement, it does not express a complete thought. It does not tell *which* is the national bird of Trinidad.]

SENTENCE   The scarlet ibis, which is the national bird of Trinidad, begins its flight at sunset.

FRAGMENT   That the government established. [*What* did the government establish?]

SENTENCE   Part of the Caroni Swamp is a bird sanctuary that the government established.

NOTE A subordinate clause telling *why, where, when,* or *how* is an adverb clause and generally may be placed before or after the independent clause. When you combine sentences by inserting an adverb clause, try the clause in both positions to see which reads better to you.

EXAMPLES   **Because it wanted to protect the beautiful bird,** the government of Trinidad established the Caroni Bird Sanctuary.

or

The government of Trinidad established the Caroni Bird Sanctuary **because it wanted to protect the beautiful bird.**

When the adverb clause comes first, remember to separate it from the independent clause with a comma.

Exercise 2   Revising Subordinate Clause Fragments

Use what you have learned about subordinate clause fragments to correct the following paragraph. First, find the clause fragments. Then, revise the paragraph by combining the subordinate clauses with independent clauses. (There may be more than one way to combine clauses.) Change the punctuation and capitalization as necessary.

EXAMPLE   1. Called the "President of the Underground Railroad," Levi Coffin was an American abolitionist. Who sheltered thousands of runaway slaves on their northern flight to freedom.

1. *Called the "President of the Underground Railroad," Levi Coffin was an American abolitionist who sheltered thousands of runaway slaves on their northern flight to freedom.*

Before and during the Civil War, the Underground Railroad helped hundreds of slaves escape to the North. The Underground Railroad was not literally a railroad, but a secret system of travel. Which moved the slaves from one house to another. Until they reached the North and freedom. "Conductors" on the Underground Railroad would plan the slaves' journey to the next "station." One conductor on the Underground Railroad was Harriet Tubman. Who was born a slave in 1821. After she escaped from the South in 1849. She dedicated herself to helping other slaves escape. Because Harriet Tubman was brave. More than three hundred people were able to reach freedom.

Exercise 3 **Using Subordinate Clauses in Sentences**

Use your skills and your imagination to make a complete sentence from each of the following subordinate clauses. To make a complete sentence, add an independent clause at the beginning or end of the subordinate clause. Add capitalization and punctuation wherever necessary.

EXAMPLE   1. because she is a versatile performer

1. *Because she is a versatile performer, that actor has had a long, successful career on stage, in films, and on television.*

1. who inspires me
2. when I rented the movie
3. because I enjoy her acting
4. if the performance is good
5. that wins the award
6. whose singing is wonderful
7. once I controlled my excitement
8. as if she were dancing on air
9. although I never saw her in person
10. which she portrayed with great skill

NOTE You have seen that it is easy to mistake phrases and subordinate clauses for complete sentences. It is also easy to mistake a series of items for a complete sentence. In the following example, the series of items in the second word group is a fragment. It may make sense along with the sentence that comes before it, but it cannot stand on its own because it does not express a complete thought.

FRAGMENT   My brother enjoys different types of science. Biology, chemistry, and astronomy.

To correct the series fragment, you can (1) make it into a complete sentence or (2) link it to the previous sentence with a colon.

SENTENCE   My brother enjoys different types of science. **He enjoys** biology, chemistry, and astronomy.

or

My brother enjoys different types of science: biology, chemistry, and astronomy.

Exercise 4 Identifying and Revising Fragments

The writer of the following paragraph is explaining why she wants to be an oceanographer. However, the sentence fragments in the paragraph make the meaning unclear. Make the paragraph clearer by finding and revising the fragments. To correct each fragment, you can (1) link it to an independent clause or (2) develop it into a complete sentence.

EXAMPLE   Though I love beaches and their waters. I don't get to explore them as much as I would like.

Though I love beaches and their waters, I don't get to explore them as much as I would like.

Whenever I am at the beach. I think about the vast world that exists beneath the ocean's surface. Though the marine life is interesting. The ocean floor is what really interests me. The deepest known spot in the Pacific Ocean is the Mariana Trench. Which is the deepest known spot in any ocean. It lies 36,198 feet below sea level. In 1960, the bathyscaph *Trieste* dove to a record depth in the trench. Plunging 35,810

feet. The Atlantic Ocean is the shallowest
ocean. With an average depth of 11,700
feet. The deepest known spot in the
Atlantic Ocean is the Milwaukee Depth. It
lies 27,493 feet below the surface. In the
Puerto Rico Trench. These trenches exceed
the average depth of the ocean floor.
Reaching deep into the earth's surface.

Run-on Sentences

A **run-on sentence** is two or more complete sentences that are written
as one sentence. Because run-on sentences do not show where one idea
ends and another begins, they can confuse readers. There are two kinds
of run-on sentences: the *fused sentence* and the *comma splice.*

In a **fused sentence,** the writer has joined two or more sentences
with no punctuation between them.

RUN-ON	Measurements originally were related to the sizes of people's hands, arms, and feet an inch was once defined as the width of a thumb.
CORRECT	Measurements originally were related to the sizes of people's hands, arms, and feet**. A**n inch was once defined as the width of a thumb.

In a **comma splice,** the writer has joined two or more sentences
with only a comma to separate them.

RUN-ON	A foot was the length of a person's foot, a yard was the distance from a person's nose to the end of his or her thumb when an arm was outstretched.
CORRECT	A foot was the length of a person's foot**. A** yard was the distance from a person's nose to the end of his or her thumb when an arm was outstretched.

Revising Run-on Sentences

There are several ways to revise a run-on sentence. As shown in the
previous examples, you can always make two separate sentences.
However, you can also make a compound sentence if the independent
clauses in the run-on are closely related.

TIPS & **TRICKS**

To identify run-on sentences, try reading your writing aloud. A natural, distinct pause in your voice usually means that you have come to the end of a thought. If your voice pauses, but your sentence keeps going, you may have a run-on.

Another way to spot run-ons is to look for subjects and verbs. This strategy will help you see where one complete thought ends and another one begins.

Reference Note

For more on **forming compound sentences,** see page 470.

1. You can make a compound sentence by adding a comma and a
coordinating conjunction (*and, but, for, nor, or, so,* or *yet*).

RUN-ON   In photography, an aperture controls the amount of light
exposing the film a shutter controls how long the film is
exposed to the light.

REVISED   In photography, an aperture controls the amount of light
exposing the film**, and** a shutter controls how long the film is
exposed to the light.

2. You can make a compound sentence by adding a semicolon.

RUN-ON   A slower shutter speed allows more light to expose the film a
faster shutter speed allows less light to expose the film.

REVISED   A slower shutter speed allows more light to expose the film**;** a
faster shutter speed allows less light to expose the film.

3. You can make a compound sentence by adding a semicolon and a
conjunctive adverb—a word such as *therefore, instead, meanwhile,
still, also, nevertheless,* or *however.* A conjunctive adverb should be
followed by a comma.

RUN-ON   Cameras have been greatly improved over time, controlling
exposure with the aperture and shutter has remained the same.

REVISED   Cameras have been greatly improved over time**; nevertheless,**
controlling exposure with the aperture and shutter has
remained the same.

Reference Note

For a list of **conjunctive adverbs,** see page 322.

Exercise 5 Revising by Correcting Run-ons

The following items are confusing because they are run-on sentences.
Using the method of revision indicated in parentheses, correct each
run-on sentence.

EXAMPLE

1. Do you know where Cambodia is located, its capital city is Phnom Penh. (Make into two sentences.)

1. *Do you know where Cambodia is located? Its capital city is Phnom Penh.*

1. Cambodia is a Southeast Asian country it is bordered by Thailand, Laos, and Vietnam. (Make into two sentences.)

2. Most of the people living in Cambodia belong to the Khmer ethnic group, people belonging to other ethnic groups also live there. (Use a semicolon and a conjunctive adverb.)

3. Cambodia has a famous river called the Mekong it also has a large lake called Tonle Sap. (Use a comma and a coordinating conjunction.)

4. Like many other Asian countries, Cambodia has a climate that is good for growing rice, no one should be surprised to find out that rice is the country's principal crop. (Use a semicolon and a conjunctive adverb.)

5. More than 200,000 people from other countries visit Cambodia each year most of them are tourists. (Make into two sentences.)

6. In the northwestern part of Cambodia, there is an area known as Angkor it is now a popular site for visitors to the country. (Use a semicolon.)

7. In fact, Angkor is the most popular tourist destination in Cambodia many people visit the country just to see it. (Use a semicolon.)

8. Some of the structures in Angkor are more than eight hundred years old they are world renowned for their beautifully carved details. (Make into two sentences.)

9. Angkor Wat, the most famous monument at Angkor, was originally built as a temple it also served as an astronomical observatory. (Use a comma and a coordinating conjunction.)

10. Another monument, called Angkor Thom, features a structure called the Bayon two hundred stone faces decorate its surface. (Use a semicolon.)

Review A Correcting Fragments and Run-on Sentences

Most of the following items contain fragments or run-on sentences. Correct the fragments and run-on sentences in any of the ways you have learned. If an item is correct, write *C*. Change the punctuation and capitalization wherever necessary.

EXAMPLE
1. A forest a complex ecological system in which trees are the main life-form.

1. *A forest is a complex ecological system in which trees are the main life-form.*

1. Many kinds of forests in the world, including tropical rain forests, temperate forests, and evergreen forests.
2. In rain forests, trees form a dense canopy. Which shuts out much of the sunlight.
3. After falling to the warm, damp forest floor, leaves decay and release nutrients.
4. Animals need forests in order to live forests provide places to live and sources of nourishment.
5. The carefully balanced food chain in forests nourishing all forest creatures.
6. Although some countries that cut down rain forests institute programs to help maintain the forest as a resource.
7. Some forests have been damaged by acid rain, a product of air pollution mixing with rain to develop sulfuric acid.
8. Forests perform several vital functions for other living things, among them are cleaning carbon dioxide from the air and preventing soil erosion.
9. People clearing forests for thousands of years, but deforestation has increased as the earth's population has increased.
10. In order to help save forests, governments have set aside national parks and replaced felled trees with new ones.

Review B Revising Fragments and Run-on Sentences

When you read the following paragraphs, you will notice several sentence fragments and run-on sentences. Revise the paragraphs to make all of the sentences correct and complete. Change the punctuation and capitalization wherever necessary.

EXAMPLE
1. Do you know someone? Who has performed a heroic act.

1. *Do you know someone who has performed a heroic act?*

Heroes come in all shapes and sizes. Women and men, adults and children. However, one hero looked quite different from what you might imagine. Living in Czechoslovakia after World War II and named Antis. This hero was a German shepherd dog.

Shortly before World War II, Antis was adopted by a man named Jan Bozdech. Bozdech served in the British Air Force during the war, afterwards, he returned to his homeland, Czechoslovakia. Because the Soviet Union controlled his country. Bozdech eventually decided to escape to Austria with his dog. During the journey, Antis alerted his master to the presence of police and border patrols, when Bozdech almost drowned trying to cross a fast-flowing river in the dark, Antis grabbed his master's jacket and pulled him to safety.

Near the end of their journey to freedom. A border guard began to walk toward Bozdech. Who was sleeping. Antis diverted the guard's attention by leaping around and distracting him. The guard did not find Bozdech, he and his faithful dog made it to safety.

Chapter Review

A. Identifying Sentences, Sentence Fragments, and Run-on Sentences

Identify each of the following word groups as a *sentence*, a *sentence fragment*, or a *run-on sentence*. If a word group is a sentence fragment, rewrite it to make a complete sentence. If a word group is a run-on sentence, rewrite it to make it one or more complete sentences.

1. The unrelenting heat and high humidity made sleep difficult.
2. Tossing and turning all night long.
3. The air was still, not even a small breeze rustled the dry leaves.
4. About four o'clock in the morning, a distant crack of thunder.
5. The first big raindrops quickly disappeared into the thirsty ground.
6. Then, as the clouds gathered overhead and the wind grew stronger.
7. The trees, whipped by the wind and the slashing rain, bowed and swayed, lightning lit the sky.
8. An hour after dawn, when the sunlight poured in through the windows, she looked outside.
9. Washed clean by the storm, the air almost seemed to sparkle, she pushed the window up and took a deep breath.
10. A welcome relief after weeks of intense heat.

B. Revising Run-on Sentences

Rewrite each run-on sentence to form clear, complete sentences. For some of the items, the method you should use to revise the run-on is given in parentheses.

11. At the art museum, we saw many beautiful paintings, I enjoyed the sculpture galleries more. (Use a comma and a coordinating conjunction.)
12. Last summer he took swimming lessons, now he feels much more confident in the water.
13. Where were you born, I was born in Nashville, Tennessee?
14. No one likes to make mistakes, we can all learn from our mistakes. (Use a semicolon, a conjunctive adverb, and a comma.)

15. Anita learned to knit from her grandmother, her grandmother knows how to spin and weave, too. (Make two sentences.)

16. You could meet us at the basketball court, we could pick you up at your house.

17. I need to improve my keyboarding skills, I've decided to practice for an hour every day after school. (Use a semicolon, a conjunctive adverb, and a comma.)

18. Ricky can't find his house key, he thinks he might have left it on the table at home.

19. We didn't go to the beach yesterday the water was too cold. (Use a comma and a coordinating conjunction.)

20. I will make the salad, you can set the table and pour the drinks.

C. Revising Sentence Fragments and Run-on Sentences

The following paragraphs contain sentence fragments and run-on sentences. Revise the paragraphs, making each sentence clear and complete. You will have to add words and change the punctuation and capitalization in some sentences.

In 1911, Hiram Bingham, a history teacher at Yale University, set out to find the "lost city of the Incas," the city, Vilcabamba, was the last stronghold of the Incas during their sixteenth-century revolt against the Spaniards. Late in July, led by a local resident named Melchor Arteaga. Bingham's group reached the ruins of Machu Picchu, hidden between two mountain peaks. High above the Urubamba River valley.

Later research has shown that Machu Picchu was probably not the Incas' "lost city," Espíritu Pampa, a larger ruin that was excavated in the 1960s, is more likely to have been Vilcabamba, Bingham's discovery was spectacular. The conquering Spaniards apparently never discovered Machu Picchu, the site is not mentioned in the chronicles of the conquest of the Incas.

Machu Picchu was probably occupied from the middle of the fifteenth century. To the beginning or middle of the sixteenth century. Machu Picchu may have been a palace complex of an Inca ruler. Or a fortress, no one is sure. Later exploration in the area indicates that it was part of a network. Fortresses, inns, and signal towers that lined the Inca foot highway.

Three sides of the complex were surrounded by terraced fields, some of those terraces were still being farmed when Bingham arrived in 1911. The terraces were once watered by an aqueduct system, some researchers believe the site may have been abandoned because of lack of water. Thousands of steps and footholds connect the buildings, plazas, and terraces. Some of the buildings and other stone structures at Machu Picchu well preserved.

Today Machu Picchu attracts many visitors. From all over the world. Some tourists arrive by narrow-gauge railroad and a winding road, others hike up to the ruins on the Inca highway. The climb takes three to six days. Up thousands of stone steps, over retaining walls, and through ancient tunnels, at elevations between 8,500 and 13,780 feet.

Although Bingham didn't find the "lost city of the Incas." His explorations and discoveries sparked further exploration of South American archaeological sites. As for Bingham himself, he turned to politics. Serving Connecticut as lieutenant governor and governor, and later becoming a United States senator.

Writing Effective Sentences

Diagnostic Preview

A. Combining Sentences

Combine the sentences in the following items by inserting words or phrases from one sentence into the other sentence or by forming compound subjects or compound verbs.

EXAMPLE   **1.** The lambs ran into the pen. The lambs were bleating for their mothers.

     1. Bleating for their mothers, the lambs ran into the pen.

1. I enjoy visiting the art museum. I usually visit it on weekends.

2. After the soup had been simmering for an hour, Ramona tasted it. She added a little salt and pepper.

3. He was shouting and waving his arms. He got the lifeguard's attention.

4. Mom went to the hardware store this afternoon. She bought more paint.

5. The math test is on Tuesday. The history test is also on Tuesday. The tests will be rescheduled for students who are going on the field trip.

6. The vine was filled with tomatoes. The tomatoes were perfectly ripe and red.

7. The water from the broken pipe covered the basement floor. The water did not do much damage.

8. Eric's birthday is next weekend. Milli's birthday is next weekend, too.
9. The film broke during the most exciting part of the silent movie. We were all disappointed when the film broke.
10. He handed her the telephone message from her parents. The message was important.

B. Combining Sentences by Forming Compound and Complex Sentences

Combine the sentences in the following items by forming compound or complex sentences.

EXAMPLE   **1.** We finally reached our campsite. We sat down to rest and had a drink of water.

     1. After we finally reached our campsite, we sat down to rest and had a drink of water.

11. We couldn't rest long. The sun was setting, and we still had to set up our camp.
12. Rick unpacked the tent. I prepared dinner.
13. We brought our own fuel. No one is allowed to build an open fire in this area.
14. We ate a simple supper. We cleaned up carefully and unrolled our sleeping bags.
15. Everyone was tired. We wanted to stay up and look at the stars.

C. Revising a Paragraph to Improve Sentence Style

Revise the following paragraph to improve the writing style by varying sentence beginnings and structures, correcting nonparallel structures, and revising stringy or wordy sentences.

EXAMPLE   **1.** On Saturday next weekend at two o'clock in the afternoon, my family will host a birthday party to celebrate eight decades of my grandfather's being alive.

     1. Next Saturday afternoon at two o'clock, my family will host my grandfather's eightieth birthday party.

```
Everyone from the family has been invited,
and more than fifty relatives who are mem-
bers of my family have accepted the invi-
tation as of this point in time. Some
family members live in the approximate
```

vicinity of our house, and they will be
bringing dishes of food to eat for the
party, and some family members will be
traveling long distances for this party.
The people who will be traveling long distances to come to the party have made
arrangements to stay at a nearby motel
because our house is too small to accommodate everyone who will be coming for the
eightieth-birthday party. We are happy
that so many relatives are joining us and
to celebrate Grandfather's birthday.

Combining Sentences

Whether you are writing a school essay, a work memo, or a personal
letter, your goal is to communicate your ideas. Therefore, you want
your writing to be clear, effective, and interesting. Short sentences can
be effective, but too many of them make writing sound choppy. For
example, notice how the many short sentences in the following paragraph make it boring to read.

> A geyser is a spring. A geyser shoots
> hot water into the air with great force.
> Some geysers erupt continually. Some gey-
> sers remain inactive for long periods.
> The water seeps into the earth's surface
> through cracks. The water expands into
> steam when it reaches extremely hot rocks.

Sentence combining is a way to improve choppy writing. Below
and on the next page, you can see how the paragraph about geysers can
be improved by combining the short sentences into longer, smoother
sentences.

Notice that even though the sentences are longer, the revised paragraph is shorter and more precise. That is because sentence combining
has helped to eliminate repeated words and ideas.

> A geyser is a spring that shoots hot
> water into the air with great force. Some

geysers erupt continually, while some remain
inactive for long periods. The water seeps
into the earth's surface through cracks and
expands into steam when it reaches extremely
hot rocks.

Inserting Words

You can combine short sentences by taking a key word from one
sentence and inserting it into another sentence. When you do this, you
may have to delete one or more words. You may also have to change
the form of the word you insert.

Using the Same Form	
ORIGINAL	Andrew Lloyd-Webber composed the music for several Broadway musicals. The musicals were popular.
COMBINED	Andrew Lloyd-Webber composed the music for several **popular** Broadway musicals.

Changing the Form	
ORIGINAL	Andrew Lloyd-Webber is best known for his melodic scores. The scores flow.
COMBINED	Andrew Lloyd-Webber is best known for his **flowing** melodic scores.

NOTE When you change the form of a word before inserting it into a sentence, you often add an ending that makes the word an adjective or an
adverb. The endings you will use most frequently are *–ed, –ful, –ing,* and *–ly.*

Exercise 1 Combining Sentences by Inserting Words

On the next page are ten sets of sentences about the many uses of common plants. Combine each set into one sentence by inserting the italicized word(s) from the second sentence into the first sentence. The
directions in parentheses will tell you how to change the form of a
word if it is necessary to do so.

EXAMPLE   1. You can find books that describe the uses of herbs. These
books describe the *many* uses that herbs have.

1. *You can find books that describe the many uses of herbs.*

1. Plants have always been valued for their properties. These properties are *medicinal.*
2. Digitalis, a medicine for heart failure, is extracted from the foxglove plant. Digitalis is *an effective* medicine.
3. The recipes for many old-fashioned herbal remedies have been lost. The loss of these recipes is *unfortunate.* (Add *–ly.*)
4. Some herbal remedies have been passed down through many generations of families. The families *trust* these remedies. (Add *–ed.*)
5. Plants are still used to make products such as shampoos and hair dyes. These products are *beauty* products.
6. The ancient Egyptians used dill in healing. This healing was *herbal.*
7. Research shows that dill helps relax the muscles of the digestive tract. These muscles are the *smooth* muscles.
8. Another herb, echinacea, was adopted by plains settlers as a remedy for stings and snakebites. This was a *folk* remedy.
9. Many recent European studies show that echinacea has remarkable properties. These properties can *heal.* (Add *–ing.*)
10. Did you know that cinnamon was used by the ancient Chinese as a treatment for digestive problems? The cinnamon was a *powder.* (Add *–ed.*)

Oral Practice **Combining Sentences by Inserting Words**

In Exercise 1, the key words were italicized for you. Now it is up to you to decide which words to insert. Read each set of sentences aloud. Then, combine the sentences and say your new sentence aloud. There may be more than one way to combine each set of sentences; choose the combination you think is best. Change the forms of words wherever necessary.

EXAMPLE   1. Standing more than 150 feet tall, the Statue of Liberty is a stop for tourists. The stop is popular.

   1. *Standing more than 150 feet tall, the Statue of Liberty is a popular stop for tourists.*

1. The Statue of Liberty, a copper sculpture on Liberty Island, towers over a bay. The bay is Upper New York Bay.
2. In 1884, France gave the statue to the United States as a gift of friendship. The statue is massive.
3. The people of France donated the money to construct the statue. Their donation was generous.
4. The United States financed the construction of the statue's pedestal. The pedestal is made of concrete.

5. French sculptor Frédéric Auguste Bartholdi tried to complete the statue in time for the centennial celebration of the Declaration of Independence. He was not successful.

6. Alexandre Gustave Eiffel assisted Bartholdi with the design. The design was for the framework.

7. Eiffel constructed the Eiffel Tower in Paris. Eiffel constructed the tower later.

8. To ship the statue across the Atlantic Ocean, workers divided the statue into sections. There were 350 sections.

9. The statue's crown has a deck with twenty-five windows. The crown has an observation deck.

10. In 1986, a restoration of the Statue of Liberty was completed. The restoration was extensive.

Inserting Phrases

You can also combine closely related sentences by reducing one sentence to a phrase and inserting it into the other sentence. When it is inserted, the phrase gives additional information about an idea expressed in the sentence.

Reference Note

For more on **the different kinds of phrases,** see Chapter 3.

Prepositional Phrases

A *prepositional phrase* contains a preposition, its object, and any modifiers of the object. Usually, you can move a prepositional phrase from one sentence into another without changing the phrase in any way.

ORIGINAL   Great Salt Lake is an inland body of saltwater. The lake is in northwestern Utah.

REVISED   Great Salt Lake is an inland body of saltwater **in northwestern Utah.**

Participial Phrases

A *participle* is a word that is formed from a verb and that can be used as an adjective. A participle usually ends in –*ing* or –*ed*. A *participial phrase* contains a participle and any modifiers or complements the participle has. The whole participial phrase acts as an adjective in a sentence.

Sometimes you can combine sentences by reducing one sentence to a participial phrase. When you insert the participial phrase into the other sentence, place it close to the noun or pronoun it modifies. Otherwise, you may confuse your reader.

ORIGINAL	Juanita Platero describes the conflict between old and new ideas. She does this as she writes about Navajo culture.
REVISED	**Writing about Navajo culture,** Juanita Platero describes the conflict between old and new ideas.

Appositive Phrases

An *appositive phrase* is made up of an appositive and its modifiers. It identifies or describes a noun or pronoun in a sentence. Sometimes you can change one sentence into an appositive phrase and insert it into another sentence. Like a participial phrase, an appositive phrase should be placed directly before or after the noun or pronoun it modifies. The phrase should be separated from the rest of the sentence by a comma (or two commas if you place the phrase in the middle of the sentence).

ORIGINAL	Neil Armstrong is best known for his historic first steps on the moon. Neil Armstrong is a former U.S. astronaut.
REVISED	Neil Armstrong, **a former U.S. astronaut,** is best known for his historic first steps on the moon.

Exercise 2 **Combining Sentences by Inserting Phrases**

Insert phrases to combine each of the following pairs of sentences into one sentence. (There may be more than one way to combine each pair.) For some of the sentence pairs, the hints in parentheses will tell you when to change the forms of words and when to add commas. To help you get started, the words you need to insert are italicized in the first five sentence pairs.

EXAMPLE
1. Migrant farmworkers move from region to region. They *follow the seasonal crop harvests.* (Change *follow* to *following,* and add a comma.)

1. *Following the seasonal crop harvests, migrant farmworkers move from region to region.*

1. Migrant laborers move constantly. They *search for work.* (Change *search* to *searching,* and add a comma.)
2. Many live in extreme poverty. They live *without adequate food, shelter, and medical care.*
3. Many migrant laborers are unable to find other kinds of work. They *lack education.* (Change *lack* to *lacking,* and add a comma.)
4. Cesar Chavez championed the rights of migrant farmworkers. He was *a labor union organizer.* (Add two commas.)

5. Chavez was born in Arizona. He was born *on a farm.*
6. His family became migrant workers. They became migrant workers after losing their farm.
7. Chavez helped make the voices of farmworkers heard. He organized grape pickers in the 1960s. (Change *organized* to *organizing,* and add a comma.)
8. He established a union. It was called the National Farm Workers Association.
9. Chavez organized strikes and boycotts. He was committed to nonviolent protest. (Add a comma.)
10. He helped to improve working conditions for migrant laborers. He did this through his organizing efforts.

Compound Subjects and Compound Verbs

You can also combine sentences by using compound subjects and compound verbs. Look for sentences that have the same subject or the same verb. Then, use coordinating conjunctions (such as *and, but, nor, or,* and *yet*) to make a compound subject, a compound verb, or both.

ORIGINAL   Jaguars are large, spotted cats. Leopards also are large, spotted cats.

REVISED   **Jaguars and leopards** are large, spotted cats. [compound subject with the same verb]

ORIGINAL   Jaguars live in the Americas. Jaguars hunt in the Americas.
REVISED   Jaguars **live and hunt** in the Americas. [compound verb with the same subject]

ORIGINAL   Jaguars hunt and attack other animals. Leopards hunt and attack other animals. These cats rarely attack humans.

REVISED   **Jaguars and leopards hunt and attack** other animals **but** rarely **attack** humans. [compound subject and compound verb]

NOTE   When you combine sentences by using compound subjects and compound verbs, make sure your subjects and verbs agree in number.

ORIGINAL   Asia is home to the leopard. Africa is home to the leopard.
REVISED   Asia and Africa **are** home to the leopard.

STYLE   TIP

So is often overworked in writing. Think twice before using it.

Reference Note

For more on **subject-verb agreement,** see page 110.

Combining Sentences by Using Compound Subjects and Compound Verbs

Combine each pair of short, choppy sentences into one sentence by using a compound subject, a compound verb, or both.

EXAMPLE　　1. Frogs are small animals that lack tails. Toads are small animals that lack tails.

　　　　　　1. *Frogs and toads are small animals that lack tails.*

1. Most frogs have long, powerful hind legs. Most frogs can leap almost twenty times their body length.
2. Some frogs live in trees. These frogs have special pads on their fingers and toes that help them cling to tree trunks.
3. Many frogs have poison glands. Most toads have poison glands.
4. The poison spreads over the frog's skin. The poison helps protect the frog.
5. Frogs usually shed their skin several times a year. Frogs often eat their old skin.
6. Frogs catch prey with their sticky tongues. Toads catch prey with their sticky tongues.
7. Compared to frogs, toads have wider bodies. Toads have shorter, weaker back legs than frogs.
8. Toads breed in water. Toads spend most of their life on land.
9. The skin of most toads is dry. The skin of most toads has warts.
10. Toads dislike sunlight and heat. Toads are active at night.

Creating a Compound Sentence

If the thoughts in two sentences are related to one another and are equal in importance, you can combine the sentences to form a *compound sentence.* A compound sentence is two or more independent clauses joined by

- a comma and a coordinating conjunction

or

- a semicolon

or

- a semicolon, a conjunctive adverb, and a comma

Reference Note

For a list of **common conjunctive adverbs,** see page 322.

ORIGINAL　Veins carry blood to the heart. Arteries carry blood away from the heart.

REVISED　Veins carry blood to the heart**, but** arteries carry blood away from the heart. [comma and coordinating conjunction]

or

Veins carry blood to the heart; arteries carry blood away from the heart. [semicolon]

or

Veins carry blood to the heart; **however,** arteries carry blood away from the heart. [semicolon, conjunctive adverb, and comma]

Exercise 4 Combining Sentences into Compound Sentences

Using the three given methods, combine each of the following pairs of sentences into a compound sentence. Try to use each method at least once. Be sure to use the correct punctuation.

EXAMPLE   1. My cousin and I visited Panama last year. We toured the Panama Canal.

1. *My cousin and I visited Panama last year, and we toured the Panama Canal.*

1. In 1881, a French company began building a canal through the Isthmus of Panama. The United States took over construction of the canal in 1903.
2. Workers then labored for ten years to complete the canal. One of the toughest obstacles was disease.
3. The Panama Canal connects the Atlantic and Pacific Oceans. It allows ships sailing between the east and west coasts of the United States to shorten their trips by nearly eight thousand nautical miles.
4. The Panama Canal is a valuable engineering achievement. It has three sets of locks, water-filled chambers which raise and lower ships, that allow the oceans to connect.
5. The canal is about 50 miles long. Because of its winding course, ships exit only 25 miles east or west of their entrance point.
6. Ships need fifteen to twenty hours to get through the canal. Canal pilots guide them through the locks.
7. Some people think the canal runs due east to west across the isthmus. They are wrong.
8. From the Atlantic entrance, the canal goes south to Gatún Lake. It turns east after that.
9. Two routes for the canal were considered. The route through Panama was chosen.

┌HELP┐

Using a
subordinate clause to
convey information of
lesser importance is called
subordination.

10. The United States controlled the Panama Canal Zone after 1914. On January 1, 2000, the Republic of Panama assumed complete control of the canal.

Creating a Complex Sentence

If two sentences are unequal in importance, you can combine them into a **complex sentence.** Just turn the less important idea into a subordinate clause, and attach it to the other sentence (the independent clause).

Adjective Clauses

Reference Note

For more on **independent** and **subordinate clauses,** see pages 90 and 91.

You can make a sentence into an adjective clause by replacing its subject with *who, whom, whose, which,* or *that.* Then you can use the adjective clause to give information about a noun or pronoun in another clause.

ORIGINAL   Christopher Columbus noted the unusual quantity of floating seaweed. He crossed the Sargasso Sea.

REVISED   Christopher Columbus, **who crossed the Sargasso Sea,** noted the unusual quantity of floating seaweed.

ORIGINAL   The Sargasso Sea is a strange, still area. It is part of the Atlantic Ocean.

REVISED   The Sargasso Sea is a strange, still area **that is part of the Atlantic Ocean.**

NOTE   If an adjective clause is not essential to the meaning of the sentence, set it off with commas. If it is essential to the meaning, no commas are necessary.

NONESSENTIAL   This fireplace, **which my brother built,** is a replica of one in Williamsburg, Virginia.

ESSENTIAL   The fireplace **that my brother built** is a replica of one in Williamsburg, Virginia.

Adverb Clauses

Reference Note

For a list of **common subordinating conjunctions,** see page 97.

You can also combine sentences by turning one sentence into an adverb clause. The adverb clause modifies a verb, an adjective, or another adverb in another clause.

To make a sentence into an adverb clause, add a subordinating conjunction (*although, after, because, if, when, while*) at the beginning.

The conjunction shows the relationship between the ideas in the adverb clause and the ideas in the independent clause. If the adverb clause comes first, set it off from the independent clause with a comma.

ORIGINAL   Sailing ships were sometimes trapped in the Sargasso Sea. There wasn't enough wind to sail.

REVISED   Sailing ships were sometimes trapped in the Sargasso Sea **when there wasn't enough wind to sail.**

ORIGINAL   Sailors used to fear the Sargasso Sea. They heard strange tales about it.

REVISED   **Because they heard strange tales about it,** sailors used to fear the Sargasso Sea.

Noun Clauses

You can make a sentence into a noun clause by adding a word like *that, how, what, whatever, who,* or *whoever.* Then you can insert the clause into another clause. When you combine the sentences, you may need to change or delete some words.

ORIGINAL   Someone will arrive first. That person will get the best seat.

REVISED   **Whoever arrives first** will get the best seat.

ORIGINAL   The players were informed. The game had been forfeited.

REVISED   The players were informed **that the game had been forfeited.**

Exercise 5 Combining Sentences into a Complex Sentence

Here are ten pairs of sentences about Napoleon I. Combine each pair by turning the second sentence into a subordinate clause and inserting it into the first sentence. For the first six pairs, you are given hints about how to create the subordinate clauses. For the last four, you will have to use your own judgment. You may have to add or delete some words in the sentences. Add commas where necessary.

EXAMPLE   1. In my history class I am learning about Napoleon I. He was a military genius.

1. *In my history class I am learning about Napoleon I, who was a military genius.*

1. Napoleon I conquered much of Europe. He crowned himself emperor of France in 1804. (Use *who.*)
2. In 1769, Napoleon was born on the French island of Corsica. The island had been purchased from Italy the year before. (Use *which.*)

HELP

Before you begin Exercise 5, review the words that can be used to introduce subordinate clauses. These words are included in the explanations on pages 472 and 473.

3. Napoleon gained control of the French government in 1799. The French people had lost faith in the five-member Directory. (Use *because*.)

4. Napoleon married Marie Louise, daughter of the emperor of Austria, in 1810. France's principal enemy by 1796 was Austria. (Use *although*.)

5. After Paris was captured in 1814, Napoleon was exiled to the small island of Elba. Napoleon gave up the throne. (Use *who*.)

6. Troops praised Napoleon as their emperor on his march back to Paris. The troops had been sent to arrest Napoleon. (Use *that*.)

7. French troops and combined forces from several countries soon clashed in Belgium, although Napoleon had assured his enemies of something. He would not make war.

8. Napoleon was defeated on June 18, 1815, at the Battle of Waterloo. He had won many military battles.

9. Napoleon was captured by a British battleship. At the time, Napoleon was trying to escape to the United States.

10. Napoleon was exiled to the British island of St. Helena in the Atlantic Ocean. Napoleon was considered a threat to peace.

Review A Revising Sentences by Combining

Using all the sentence-combining skills you have learned, revise and rewrite each of the following sets of sentences into one sentence. You may combine by inserting words or phrases, by creating compounds, or by creating complex sentences. You may have to add or delete some words. Add punctuation where necessary.

EXAMPLE
1. I have always been fascinated with espionage. Eventually, I want to work for the CIA.

1. *I have always been fascinated with espionage and eventually want to work for the CIA.*

1. Espionage is the secret collection of intelligence information. The history of espionage goes back over two thousand years.

2. Around 500 B.C., Sun Tzu wrote a book giving instructions on organizing an espionage system. Sun Tzu was a Chinese military theorist.

3. In the nineteenth century, Joseph Fouché, duc d'Otrante, worked to create a network of police agents and spies. Fouché was the French minister of police.

4. In World War I, one of the most famous German spies was Mata Hari. She posed as an Indian dancer in Paris.

5. World War II saw an enormous growth in worldwide espionage. Countries needed quick, accurate information about their enemies.

6. One of the most remarkable intelligence operations in World War II was Operation Double Cross. In Operation Double Cross, almost all the German spies in Great Britain were captured. These German spies were turned into double agents.

7. Japan's most successful espionage led to the attack on the U.S. naval base at Pearl Harbor. This attack was a surprise, and it happened in World War II.

8. Today in the United States, the Central Intelligence Agency gathers secret information. This information is about national security. The Central Intelligence Agency is also called the CIA.

9. The Federal Bureau of Investigation is responsible for counter-espionage within the United States. The FBI was formed in 1908.

10. It is difficult to know the exact number of espionage agents in the world today. Espionage agents work to keep information about themselves hidden.

MEETING THE CHALLENGE

One key to writing well is knowing when to combine sentences and when not to. Experiment with "over-combining": Find a paragraph or passage at least five to ten sentences long, and combine the whole passage into a single sentence. Then, share your work with your classmates. Who has the longest combined sentence? With your teacher's permission, read the longest one aloud to see whether the class can follow it.

Review B **Revising a Paragraph by Combining Sentences**

Using all the sentence-combining skills you have learned, revise and rewrite the following paragraph. Use your judgment about which sentences to combine and how to combine them. Try for smooth, varied sentences that are easy to understand, but do not change the original meaning of the paragraph.

EXAMPLE
1. The prairie dog is a burrowing mammal. The prairie dog lives on the grassy plains of North America.

1. *The prairie dog, a burrowing mammal, lives on the grassy plains of North America.*

```
    Prairie dogs are very sociable. They
live in communities called towns. The towns
can be large. The towns consist of numerous
burrows. The word dog is part of this ani-
mal's name. The prairie dog is actually a
rodent. It gets its name from the sound it
makes. The sound is similar to a dog's
bark. Livestock might step into the burrows
that prairie dogs make. Some ranchers fear
this. However, horses usually do not step
into prairie dog burrows. Cows do not usu-
ally step into prairie dog burrows.
```

Improving Sentence Style

In the first part of this chapter, you learned how to reduce choppiness in your writing by combining sentences. Now you will learn more ways to polish your sentence style and make your writing more effective.

Using Parallel Structure

┌ TIPS & TRICKS ┐

Begin to look for parallel structure in sentences when you combine words, phrases, and clauses by using the coordinating conjunction *and*.

When you join several equal or related ideas in a sentence, it is important that you express these ideas in a similar way. You can do this by balancing the structure of your sentence parts. For example, you should balance an adjective with an adjective, a phrase with a phrase, and a clause with a clause. This kind of balance in writing is called *parallel structure.*

NOT PARALLEL	He learned three things: shooting, passing, and how to dribble. [two gerunds and a phrase]
PARALLEL	He learned three things: **shooting, passing,** and **dribbling.** [three gerunds]
NOT PARALLEL	A good coach must learn to communicate with players, to organize a schedule, and adversity. [two phrases and a noun]
PARALLEL	A good coach must learn **to communicate with players, to organize a schedule,** and **to handle adversity.** [three phrases]
NOT PARALLEL	My sister decided that she would study coaching techniques and to work with the youth basketball league. [a clause and a phrase]
PARALLEL	My sister decided **that she would study coaching techniques** and **that she would work with the youth basketball league.** [two clauses]

Exercise 6   Revising Sentences to Create Parallelism

Some of the following sentences are out of balance. Bring balance to them by using parallel structure. You may have to delete or add some words. If a sentence is already correct, write *C.*

EXAMPLE   **1.** I traveled to Europe last summer, and I visited Greece and was exploring Athens.

1. *I traveled to Europe last summer, and I visited Greece and explored Athens.*

1. Athens, the capital of Greece, is known for its ancient ruins, busy lifestyle, and enjoying fine Greek food.
2. Because it is nearly three thousand years old and its rich history, Athens attracts many visitors.
3. Athens attracts artists and historians and is attractive to tourists.
4. People often drive very fast in Athens and scare the pedestrians.
5. I like seeing the sights in Athens to learn about its history.

6. In Athens I shopped in markets, was wandering about ruins, and visited museums.
7. The National Archaeological Museum holds ancient Greek jewelry, pottery, and sculpture.
8. During the Golden Age, which lasted from 477 to 431 B.C., the statesman Pericles increased Athens's influence in Greece and was reforming its government.
9. Women in ancient Athens were not allowed to vote or holding office.
10. For centuries, the sons of rich Roman families came to Athens to study philosophy and learning culture.

Revising Stringy Sentences

What is a *stringy sentence*? Read this one:

```
    I was going on a fishing trip with my
uncle, and I knew I would need a lot of
luck, and I always fish in the same spot that
my uncle does, but he always catches more
than I do, but this time I brought all of my
fishing lures so that I would be prepared.
```

The **stringy sentence** above has too many independent clauses strung together with coordinating conjunctions like *and* or *but*. Because the ideas are all treated equally, it is difficult to see how they are related to one another. To fix a stringy sentence, you can

- **break the sentence into two or more shorter sentences**
- **turn some of the independent clauses into subordinate clauses or phrases**

Now read the following sentences aloud and hear the difference. Notice how the writer has broken up the stringy sentence into three shorter sentences and turned an independent clause into a subordinate clause.

```
I was going on a fishing trip with my
uncle, and I knew I would need a lot of
luck. Although I always fish in the same spot
that my uncle does, he always catches more
than I do. This time I brought all of my
fishing lures so that I would be prepared.
```

There are usually several ways to revise a stringy sentence. The most important thing is to make the meaning clear for your reader.

Exercise 7 Revising Stringy Sentences

Revise each of the following stringy sentences. For some items, you can break the stringy sentence into two or more shorter sentences. For others, you will have to turn an independent clause into a subordinate clause or a phrase to show the relationship between the ideas. Change the punctuation wherever necessary.

EXAMPLE   **1.** I enjoy listening to music, and I like all kinds of music, but I especially like Broadway show tunes.

    1. I enjoy listening to all kinds of music, but I especially like Broadway show tunes.

1. Music is used for entertainment, relaxation, and self-expression, and it is used in every culture, and it is a very important part of our lives.
2. Music is an ancient art, and people learned to make flutes around 10,000 B.C., and they began to write music around 2500 B.C.
3. Today, much popular music is electronically produced, and many musicians play electric guitars and synthesizers, and some even play electric violins.
4. Different countries have different kinds of music, but some kinds of music are internationally popular, and those kinds include rock music and rap music.
5. Rock music first became popular in the 1950s, and it was inspired by blues and jazz music, but its sound was different from anything people had ever heard before.
6. Musical comedies, or musicals, are plays, and they tell stories through dialogue, songs, and dance, and they have been popular in the United States since the nineteenth century.

7. The influences on the modern musical include vaudeville, minstrel shows, and burlesques, and they all had singing and dancing, but they didn't have unifying plots.

8. My favorite musical is called *West Side Story,* and it is based on William Shakespeare's play *The Tragedy of Romeo and Juliet,* and it features two groups, the Sharks and the Jets.

9. Many musicals debut in New York City on Broadway, and some of the successful musicals tour around the United States and tour other countries as well.

10. Julie Andrews starred on Broadway as the lead character in *My Fair Lady,* even though Audrey Hepburn starred in the film version, and Julie Andrews also starred in the films *The Sound of Music* and *Mary Poppins.*

Revising Wordy Sentences

Read the following sentence.

> Anticipating that tomorrow's forthcoming examination may be perplexing, I have made the astute conclusion that we should diligently scrutinize our scholarly tomes at the decline of day.

When you read sentences like this, you probably wonder what language the writer is using. How much easier and clearer it is to say "The test tomorrow may be hard, so let's study tonight." Here are three tips for creating sentences that are not too wordy.

- **Do not use more words than you need.**

- **Do not use fancy, difficult words where plain, simple ones will do.**

- **Do not repeat words or ideas unless it is absolutely necessary to do so for clarity.**

| WORDY | Our sofa has a lot of weight to it. |
| IMPROVED | Our sofa is heavy. |

| WORDY | First and foremost, you will basically need to be sure to be in contact with the program coordinator. |
| IMPROVED | First, you will need to contact the program coordinator. |

WORDY The reason I am undertaking the task of photographing the exteriors of these abandoned buildings is that I have an interest in architecture.

IMPROVED I am taking pictures of these abandoned buildings because I am interested in architecture.

WORDY Greg speaks Spanish well, and his Spanish is clear and fluent.

IMPROVED Greg speaks clear, fluent Spanish.

Exercise 8 Revising Wordy Sentences

Some of the following sentences are wordy. For each sentence, ask the following questions: Does it have unnecessary words? Does it have fancy words that can be replaced with simple ones? Does it repeat ideas? If you answer yes to any question, revise the sentence to reduce the wordiness. If a sentence doesn't need improvement, write *C*.

EXAMPLE 1. Many numerous caves exist in my home state, which is Texas.

     1. *Numerous caves exist in my home state, Texas.*

1. Caves are dark, damp areas that don't have any light.
2. Many caves have beautiful, icicle-like mineral formations called speleothems.
3. Luray Caverns, which is a cave system that is situated in the area of northern Virginia, is famous for its colorful speleothems.
4. Lascaux Cave, a famous cave in southwestern France, has many ancient, prehistoric wall paintings.
5. Cavefish are small, cave-dwelling fish that are not equipped with optical organs.
6. Lots and lots of caves are still existing in their natural, untouched state.
7. Caving is a popular spare-time recreational activity, but it can be fraught with danger.
8. Cavers use sturdy, strong ropes to help them climb underground cliffs in caves.
9. Troglodytes are various animal species that live in caves and have colorless skin with no color.
10. Someday in the upcoming future I plan to go caving to see all the wondrous sights.

Beyond Sentence Style

Previously in this chapter, you learned how to combine sentences smoothly and how to make sentences clear and balanced. Now you will learn how sentences work together in the larger structure of the *paragraph.*

Varying Sentence Beginnings

You would probably get bored if you ate the same food at every meal. Variety is as important in your writing as it is in your diet. The basic subject-verb sentence pattern is fine sometimes, but if it is all you ever use, your writing will be monotonous.

Read the following paragraph. Notice that while the paragraph is correct, it is boring because every sentence follows the same subject-verb pattern.

```
    The pool was nearly empty on an early
weekend morning. Dedicated swimmers swam
multiple laps. A few sunbathers and parents
with small children sat on the grass at the
edge of the pool and watched. The day grew
hotter, and the sun rose higher. The pool
became more crowded. The pool was soon
filled with young people. They laughed as
they played games and splashed each other.
```

Now read a revised version of the paragraph. Notice how the varied sentence beginnings break the monotony of the subject-verb pattern.

```
    On an early weekend morning, the pool
was nearly empty. Dedicated swimmers swam
multiple laps. A few sunbathers and parents
with small children sat on the grass at the
edge of the pool and watched. As the day
grew hotter and the sun rose higher, the
pool became more crowded. Soon the pool was
filled with young people. Laughing, they
played games and splashed each other.
```

Instead of starting all your sentences with subjects, try opening sentences in a variety of ways. Begin with single-word modifiers, with phrases, and with subordinate clauses. Remember to add commas as necessary after introductory words, phrases, or clauses.

┌HELP┐

One effective
way to vary sentences is to
insert an adverb ending in
–ly at the beginning of a
sentence.

EXAMPLE
  Slowly the noise filled
  the room.

Varying Sentence Beginnings		
Single-Word Modifiers	**Grotesquely,** Dr. Frankenstein's monster began to rise from the table. [adverb]	
	Frightened, Dr. Frankenstein jumped back. [participle]	
	Cackling, Igor ran from the room. [participle]	
Phrases	**With little hope,** Sam entered the writing contest. [prepositional phrase]	
	Excited by his success, Sam accepted the award. [participial phrase]	
Subordinate Clauses	**Because Manuel was tall,** people expected him to play basketball.	
	Although Manuel wasn't interested in play-ing basketball, he always went to the games.	

Exercise 9 **Varying Sentence Beginnings**

Using what you have learned about varying sentence beginnings, revise each of the following sentences. The hint in parentheses will tell you whether to begin with a phrase, a clause, or a single-word modifier.

EXAMPLE   1. Astronomy is one of the oldest of the sciences, and it still intrigues scientists today. (phrase)

1. *Still intriguing scientists today, astronomy is one of the oldest of the sciences.*

1. Maps of the heavens were first drawn on stone or parchment, and they were created by the ancient Chinese. (phrase)
2. Early humans started watching the sun, moon, and stars when they learned that understanding the heavens could help their harvests. (subordinate clause)
3. Astronomers work with large radio and optical telescopes and space probes today. (single-word modifier)
4. The moon lacks wind, atmosphere, and weather and would be an ideal location for an observatory. (phrase)
5. The early Egyptians planned their festivals and events by studying the heavens, but the ancient Greeks were the first to study the sky scientifically. (subordinate clause)
6. Galileo supported Ptolemy's idea that the sun was the center of the universe and was threatened with punishment. (phrase)

7. William Herschel discovered the planet Uranus by using a home-made telescope. (phrase)
8. Astronomers have been able to predict the paths of planets because Newton proved that gravity rules the universe. (subordinate clause)
9. The Hubble Space Telescope was placed in orbit in 1990. (phrase)
10. The Hubble Space Telescope's vision was initially blurry, but it was repaired in 1993 by astronauts. (single-word modifier)

Varying Sentence Structure

You have learned to create different kinds of sentences by combining sentences and varying sentence beginnings. Now you can use this skill to create a better writing style. For varied, interesting paragraphs, it sometimes is not enough just to create sentences of different lengths. You also need to use a variety of sentence structures. That means using a mix of simple, compound, and complex (and sometimes even compound-complex) sentences in your writing.

Read the following short paragraph, which is made up of only simple sentences.

> My sister went to college. She was nervous at first. She was determined to be a success. She worked hard every day. She graduated at the top of her class. I was proud of her. We celebrated after the ceremonies. We ate a big meal. My mother took pictures of the whole family.

Now read the revised version of the paragraph. The writer has included a variety of sentence structures to break the monotony of the first version.

> Although she was nervous at first, my sister went to college. Because she was determined to be a success and because she worked hard, she graduated at the top of her class. I was proud of her. We celebrated after the ceremonies as we ate a big meal, and my mother took pictures of the whole family.

Notice how including subordinate clauses improved some sentences and made the paragraph clearer. Besides adding variety, subordinate clauses help show how the ideas in a sentence are related.

Reference Note

For more on **types of sentence structures,** see page 102.

NOTE Be sure you understand the type of relationship each subordinating conjunction expresses.

CONTRAST   *although, even though, though,* and *while*

REASON   *as, because, considering that, if, since,* and *so that*

TIME   *after, as, as long as, as soon as, before, when,* and *while*

Exercise 10 Revising a Paragraph to Create a Variety of Sentence Structures

Using what you have learned about combining sentences and varying structure, revise the following paragraph to make it smoother and more varied. A combination of different kinds of sentences will make the paragraph much more fun to read.

EXAMPLE   **1.** I had eaten breakfast a few hours ago. I was starving.

   1. *Although I had eaten breakfast a few hours ago, I was starving.*

```
    My friends and I had lunch. We ate at a
food court on the second floor of a mall.
The food court has food from different
countries. About twenty restaurants are
there. Lin had soup and salad. I had a bur-
rito. It was delicious. Joe and Debbie
split a pizza. Then we walked around and
looked at the people. We all imagined what
they were thinking. There was a fashion
show on the main floor. Debbie and I admired
the clothes. Lin and Joe liked estimating
the costs of the outfits. We looked at a
display of new cars. We talked about the
kinds of cars we would like to have.
```

Review C Writing a Paragraph Using a Variety of Sentence Structures

You are the director of a music video for a new song called "The Edge of Dreams." Write a paragraph explaining which singers, dancers, and musicians (real or fictional) you will cast in your video. Capture your reader's attention by using a variety of interesting sentence structures. Avoid wordy and stringy sentences, and be sure to check for parallel structure as you revise.

Chapter Review

A. Combining Sentences

Combine the following sentences by inserting words or phrases, forming compound subjects or compound verbs, or forming compound or complex sentences.

1. He left a piece of information out of his report. The piece of information was crucial.
2. Carmela will receive an award from the mayor tomorrow. Carmela is the student who wrote the winning essay.
3. After searching for hours, I found my keys. I found my keys in between the couch cushions.
4. We went to the pool. We put on sunscreen.
5. Mary Ann has history during first period. Her friend Anita also has history during first period. Mary Ann and Anita don't have any other classes together.
6. The goose chased the dog across the farmyard. The goose was honking and flapping its wings.
7. The basic moves in chess are easy to learn. Mastering the game takes concentration and practice.
8. Mike will clean his room. He'll clean his room after he walks the dog.
9. The librarian carefully unpacked the boxes. The librarian shelved the new books.
10. The sound of coyotes howling woke us up during the night. It was an eerie, lonesome sound.

B. Revising Stringy or Wordy Sentences and Unparallel Structures

Rewrite the following sentences, revising stringy or wordy sentences and correcting unparallel sentence structures. Some of the items may have more than one style problem.

11. During the course of the afternoon, the heat from the star at the center of our solar system grew more intolerable and unbearable.
12. When Kurt visits London, he plans to visit the Tower of London, ride on the subways, and on eating fish and chips.

13. The dressmaker measured the length of the dress, and then she pinned up the hem, and before she did the final stitching, she asked the customer to try on the dress again.

14. Owing to my inability to control my financial excesses, I seem to be without sufficient funds to buy lunch at the present time.

15. The trees in our backyard provide a lot of shade for the house because they have leafy branches that overhang the house.

16. Mary always does better in Spanish than I do, even though I study and practice my vocabulary every night, but Mary must study even more, or maybe she has a special talent for languages.

17. My parents decided that they would not book a Caribbean cruise and to go to the Bahamas instead.

18. My father's means of transportation that is powered by an internal combustion engine has been, without regard to the fact that it is a new vehicle, in the repair facility no fewer than ten times since the point of time at which he purchased it.

19. I always baby-sit my neighbor's two children, and the family pays me well to baby-sit, and I usually enjoy taking care of the children, but last Friday night, they were both really fussy, and none of us had very much fun.

20. To get enough sleep, eat nutritious food, and exercising every day are the keys to good health.

C. Revising a Paragraph to Improve Sentence Style

Revise the following paragraph, using a variety of sentence beginnings and sentence structures to improve the style of the writing.

> Kristin learned to make bread from her grandfather. Her grandfather bakes bread at least twice every week. Kristin always liked the smell of baking bread at her grandfather's house. Kristin watched her grandfather at first. Her grandfather dissolves the yeast in some lukewarm water and adds a pinch of sugar. He wants the yeast to bubble and foam. That way he knows the yeast will make the bread rise. Kristin and her grandfather added the

yeast mixture to the flour and other ingredients. They stirred until the ingredients were well mixed. Kristin's grandfather showed her how to knead the dough next. Kneading dough is hard work. Kristin kneaded for almost ten minutes. Kristin worked until the dough was smooth and elastic. She divided the dough into three balls, covered them, and put them in a warm place to rise. The dough was ready in about an hour. Kristin punched each ball of dough hard. All the air came out, and the dough collapsed. Then Kristin formed the dough into loaves and put them into loaf pans. She left the dough to rise again for another hour. She baked the bread in the preheated oven.

Sentence Diagramming

The Sentence Diagram

A *sentence diagram* is a picture of how the parts of a sentence fit together and how the words in a sentence are related.

Subjects and Verbs

Reference Note

For more information about **subjects** and **verbs,** see page 37.

Every sentence diagram begins with a horizontal line intersected by a short vertical line, which divides the subject from the verb.

EXAMPLE   **Alice Walker wrote** *The Color Purple.*

Alice Walker	wrote

Understood Subjects

Reference Note

For more information about **understood subjects,** see page 45.

EXAMPLE   Answer the phone, please.

(you)	Answer

Nouns of Direct Address

Reference Note

For more information about **nouns of direct address,** see page 45.

EXAMPLE   Pass me the picante sauce, **Gina.**

Gina

(you)	Pass

Compound Subjects

EXAMPLE   **Arturo** and **Patsy** are dancing the conga.

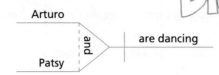

Reference Note

For more information about **compound subjects,** see page 45.

Compound Verbs

EXAMPLE   Roger **swims** and **dives.**

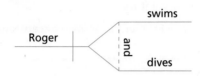

Reference Note

For more information about **compound verbs,** see page 46.

Compound Subjects and Compound Verbs

EXAMPLE   **Kittens** and **puppies can play** together and **become** friends.

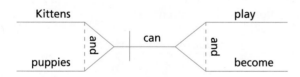

When the parts of a compound subject or a compound predicate are joined by a correlative conjunction, diagram the sentence this way:

EXAMPLE   **Both** Norma **and** Lisa will **not only** perform **but also** teach.

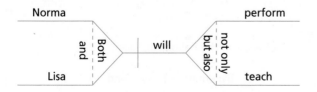

Reference Note

For more information about **correlative conjunctions,** see page 26.

SENTENCES

Modifiers

Reference Note

For more information about **adjectives,** see page 10. For more about **adverbs,** see page 20.

Adjectives and Adverbs

Adjectives and adverbs are written on slanting lines beneath the words they modify.

EXAMPLE   **The blue** car **quickly** swerved **left.**

```
          car  |  swerved
    The    blue    quickly    left
```

An adverb that modifies an adjective or an adverb is placed on a line connected to the word it modifies.

EXAMPLE   The Neville Brothers performed **exceptionally** well.

```
    Neville Brothers  |  performed
            The              well
                          exceptionally
```

Reference Note

For more about questions and sentences beginning with **Here** and **There,** see page 44.

Here, There, and *Where* as Modifiers

EXAMPLES   **Here** come the astronauts!

```
    astronauts  |  come
          the        Here
```

There goes the new Mohawk leader.

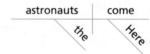

```
                    leader  |  goes
        the   new   Mohawk       There
```

Where will the balloonists land?

```
    balloonists  |  will land
          the          Where
```

NOTE Sometimes *There* begins a sentence but does not modify the verb. When used in this way, *There* is called an *expletive* and is diagrammed on a line by itself.

EXAMPLE   **There** are seven stars in the Pleiades.

Subject Complements

A subject complement is placed after the verb on the same horizontal line as the simple subject and the verb. A line *slanting toward the subject* separates the subject complement from the verb.

Reference Note

For more information about **subject complements,** see page 51.

Predicate Nominatives

EXAMPLE   Some dogs are good **companions.**

Predicate Adjectives

EXAMPLE   That cockatiel is **friendly.**

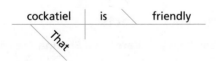

Compound Subject Complements

EXAMPLE   Martin Yan is both a **chef** and a **comedian.**

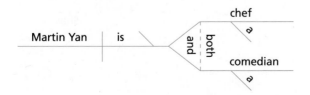

Objects

Reference Note

For more information about **direct objects,** see page 54.

Direct Objects

A direct object is placed after the verb on the same horizontal line as the simple subject and the verb. A *vertical* line separates the direct object from the verb.

EXAMPLE   Cathy led the **band.**

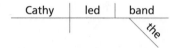

Compound Direct Objects

EXAMPLE   We heard **cheers** and **whistles.**

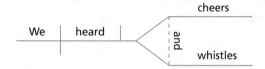

Reference Note

For more information about **indirect objects,** see page 55.

Indirect Objects

An indirect object is diagrammed on a horizontal line beneath the verb.

EXAMPLE   They gave **her** a present.

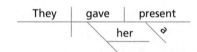

Compound Indirect Objects

EXAMPLE   Mr. Stephens lent **Karen** and **Shanna** *The Fire Next Time.*

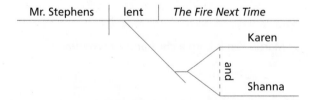

SENTENCES

Phrases

Prepositional Phrases

The preposition is placed on a slanting line leading down from the word that the phrase modifies. The object of the preposition is placed on a horizontal line connected to the slanting line.

Reference Note

For more information about **prepositional phrases,** see page 65.

EXAMPLES   The steep slopes **of the mountains** are covered **with forests.** [adjective phrase modifying the subject; adverb phrase modifying the verb]

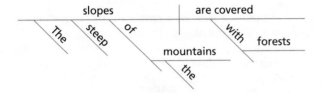

They sailed late **in the fall.** [adverb phrase modifying an adverb]

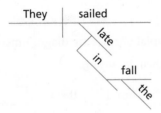

Nina read this Chinese folk tale to **Aaron** and **Joey.** [compound object of preposition]

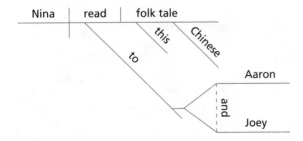

SENTENCES

Down the valley and **across the plain** wanders the river.
[two phrases modifying the same word]

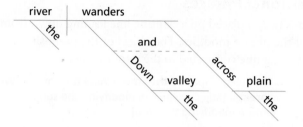

The princess lived **in a castle on the mountain.** [phrase modifying the object of another preposition]

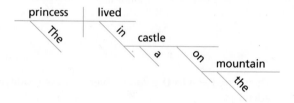

Reference Note

For more information about **participles** and **participial phrases,** see page 70.

Participles and Participial Phrases

Participles and participial phrases are diagrammed as follows.

EXAMPLES   I heard them **laughing.**

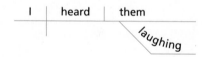

Waving her hat, Sara flagged the train **speeding down the track.**

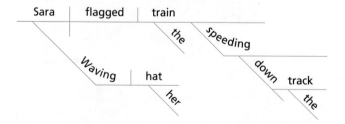

Notice above that the participle *Waving* has a direct object (*hat*), which is diagrammed in the same way that a direct object of a main verb is.

Gerunds and Gerund Phrases

Gerunds and gerund phrases are diagrammed as follows.

EXAMPLES   **Waiting** is not easy. [gerund used as subject]

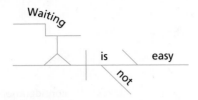

    Waiting patiently for hours is often a sure means of **observing wild animals.** [gerund phrases used as subject and as object of a preposition]

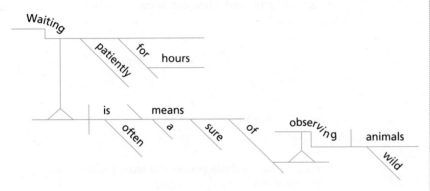

Notice above that the gerund *observing* has a direct object (*animals*).

Reference Note

For more information about **gerunds** and **gerund phrases,** see page 74.

Infinitives and Infinitive Phrases

Infinitives and infinitive phrases used as modifiers are diagrammed in the same way as prepositional phrases.

EXAMPLE   He plays **to win.** [infinitive used as adverb]

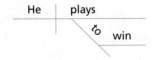

Reference Note

For more information about **infinitives** and **infinitive phrases,** see page 77.

SENTENCES

Infinitives and infinitive phrases used as nouns are diagrammed as follows.

EXAMPLES **To choose the right career** takes careful consideration. [infinitive phrase used as subject]

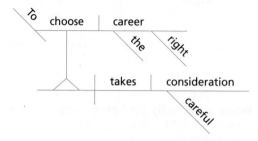

She is hoping **to visit Morocco soon.** [infinitive phrase used as direct object]

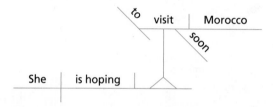

My brother watched **me prune the tree.** [infinitive clause with subject, *me*, and with *to* omitted]

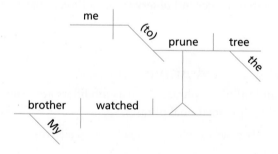

Appositives and Appositive Phrases

Place the appositive in parentheses after the word it identifies or describes.

Reference Note

For more information about **appositives** and **appositive phrases,** see page 81.

SENTENCES

EXAMPLES   My cousin **Bryan** is a carpenter.

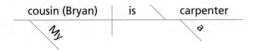

Mohammed Tahir comes from Yemen, **a country near
Saudi Arabia.**

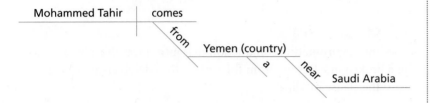

Subordinate Clauses

Adjective Clauses

An adjective clause is joined to the word it modifies by a broken line
leading from the modified word to the relative pronoun.

EXAMPLES   The coat **that I wanted** was too expensive.

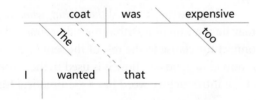

The box, **which contained the treasure,** was missing.

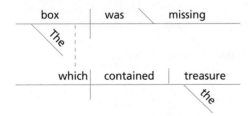

Reference Note

For more information
about **adjective clauses,**
see page 93.

SENTENCES

EXAMPLE   She is the woman **from whom we bought the used car.**

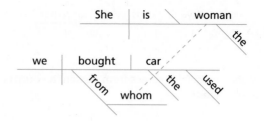

Adverb Clauses

Reference Note

For more information about **adverb clauses,** see page 96.

Place the subordinating conjunction that introduces the adverb clause on a broken line leading from the verb in the adverb clause to the word the clause modifies.

EXAMPLE   **Before a hurricane strikes,** ample warning is given.

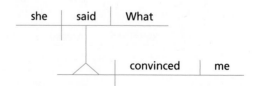

Noun Clauses

Reference Note

For more information about **noun clauses,** see page 99.

Noun clauses often begin with the word *that, what, who,* or *which.* These words may have a function within the subordinate clause or may simply connect the clause to the rest of the sentence. How a noun clause is diagrammed depends on how it is used in the sentence and whether or not the introductory word has a grammatical function in the noun clause.

EXAMPLE   **What she said** convinced me. [The noun clause is used as the subject of the independent clause. *What* functions as the direct object in the noun clause.]

EXAMPLE We know **that you won the prize.** [The noun clause is the direct object of the independent clause. *That* has no grammatical function in the noun clause.]

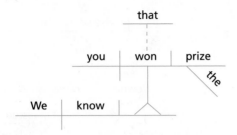

If the introductory word is omitted from the noun clause in the preceding sentence, the sentence is diagrammed like this.

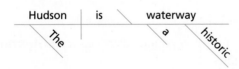

Sentences Classified According to Structure

Simple Sentences

EXAMPLES The Hudson is a historic waterway. [one independent clause]

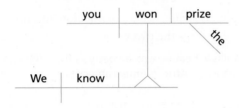

Denise hit a home run. [one independent clause]

Reference Note

For more information about **simple sentences,** see page 102.

Reference Note

For more information about **compound sentences,** see page 102.

Compound Sentences

EXAMPLE   A strange dog chased us, but the owner came to our rescue.
[two independent clauses]

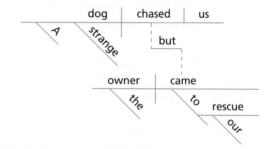

If the compound sentence has a semicolon and no conjunction, a straight broken line joins the two verbs.

EXAMPLE   Phillis Wheatley wrote poetry in the 1700s; she was the first published African American poet.

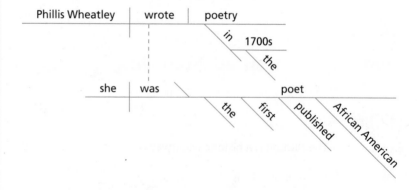

Notice above that the compound adjective *African American* is written on one slanted line.

If the clauses of a compound sentence are joined by a semicolon and a conjunctive adverb (such as *consequently, therefore, nevertheless, however, moreover,* or *otherwise*), place the conjunctive adverb on a slanting line below the verb it modifies.

Reference Note

For more information about **conjunctive adverbs,** see page 90.

EXAMPLE   Dylan works part time after school; **consequently,** he can afford to buy a new bike.

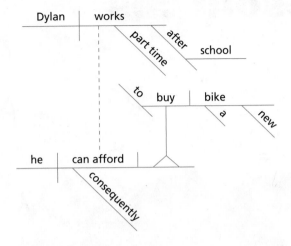

Complex Sentences

EXAMPLE   As night fell, the storm grew worse. [one independent clause and one subordinate clause]

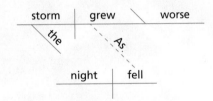

Reference Note

For more information about **complex sentences,** see page 103.

Compound-Complex Sentences

EXAMPLE   The room that Carrie painted had been white, but she changed the color. [two independent clauses and one subordinate clause]

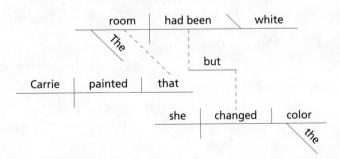

Reference Note

For more information about **compound-complex sentences,** see page 103.

PART 3

Resources

GO TO: go.hrw.com

Manuscript Form

Why Is Manuscript Form Important?

What is manuscript form, and why should you care about it? *Manuscript form* refers to the overall appearance of a document. A legible, professional-looking manuscript gives the impression that the writer cares not only about what he or she has to say but also about what the reader thinks. A manuscript that is an illegible jumble, on the other hand, gives the impression that the writer is careless, is not thinking clearly, or does not respect the reader.

Such impressions affect our lives every day. For example, a busy employer faced with the task of evaluating multiple job résumés may simply discard the sloppy ones without ever reading them. If we value what we write and want others to understand and value it too, then we should present our ideas in the best form possible. To help you present your ideas as effectively as possible, this section of the book covers basic guidelines for preparing and presenting manuscripts and provides a sample research paper as a model.

General Guidelines for Preparing Manuscripts

The following guidelines are general style rules to use in formal, nonfiction writing. Such writing includes papers and reports for school, letters of application for jobs or colleges, letters to the editor, and press releases for clubs and other organizations.

Content and Organization

1. Begin the paper with an introductory paragraph that contains a thesis sentence.

2. Develop and support your thesis in body paragraphs.

3. Follow the principles of unity and coherence. That is, develop one and only one big idea (your thesis), and make sure that your paragraphs and sentences flow smoothly without any gaps in the sequence of ideas.

4. Place charts, graphs, tables, and illustrations close to the text they illustrate. Label and number each one.

5. Follow the conventions of standard grammar, usage, capitalization, punctuation, and spelling.

6. Include a conclusion.

Appearance

1. Submit manuscript that is legible. Type or print out your paper using black ink; or when your teacher permits handwriting, write neatly using blue or black ink. (Other colors are harder to read.) If the printer or typewriter you are using is printing words that are faint and hard to read, change the ink cartridge or the ribbon.

2. Keep all pages neat and clean. If you discover errors and if you are working on a word processor, you can easily correct the errors and print out a fresh copy. If you write your paper by hand or on a typewriter, you generally may make a few corrections with correction tape and insert the revisions neatly. To replace a letter, word, or phrase, neatly cross out what you want to replace. Then, insert a caret mark (^) below the line, and write the inserted item above the line.

EXAMPLE

The ~~daily~~ ^weekly^ broadcasts continued all that summer.

Paper and Font

1. Use quality 8½ × 11 inch paper.
2. Use only one side of the paper.
3. When using a word processor, use an easy-to-read font size. Size twelve is standard.
4. Use a standard font, such as Times New Roman, that does not call attention to itself. Flowery, highly stylized fonts are hard to read. They look unprofessional, and they dis-

tract the reader from the ideas you are trying to convey.

Plagiarism

Do not plagiarize. Plagiarism is the unacknowledged borrowing of someone else's words or ideas and the submission of those words or ideas as one's own. Honest writers document all borrowings, whether those borrowings are quoted or merely paraphrased.

Back-up files

When you are ready to submit your work, be sure to save a copy—a printout, a photocopy, or an electronic file—for yourself.

Academic Manuscript Style

In school you will write some very formal papers—research reports or term papers, for example. For such assignments, you will need to follow not only general manuscript guidelines but also some very specific guidelines especially for academic manuscripts.

The academic manuscript style summarized on the following pages follows the style recommended by the Modern Language Association in the *MLA Handbook for Writers of Research Papers*. Two other popular manuscript styles are the format recommended by the American Psychological Association, known as APA style, and the one published in *The Chicago Manual of Style*. Style manuals are updated from time to time, so be sure you are using the most current version. When formatting papers for school, be sure to follow your teachers' instructions on which manuscript style to use.

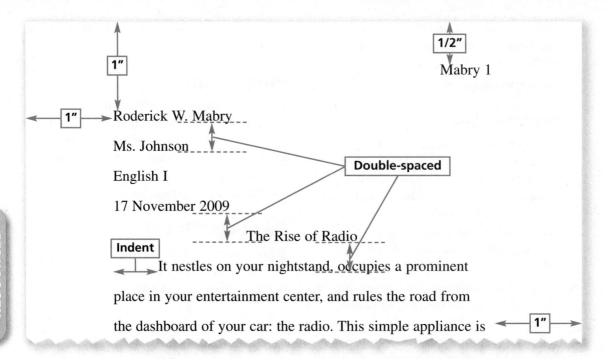

1/2"

Mabry 1

1"

1"

Roderick W. Mabry

Ms. Johnson

English I

17 November 2009

Double-spaced

The Rise of Radio

Indent

It nestles on your nightstand, occupies a prominent

place in your entertainment center, and rules the road from

the dashboard of your car: the radio. This simple appliance is

1"

Title Page, Margins, and Spacing

1. Leave one-inch margins on the top, sides, and bottom of each page.
2. Starting with the first page, number all your pages in the upper right-hand corner. Precede each page number with your last name. Computer software can help you create this "header."
3. Place your heading—your name, your teacher's name, your class, and the date—in the upper left-hand corner of the first page. (If your teacher requires a separate cover sheet, follow his or her instructions.)
4. Double-space between the header and the heading. Double-space the lines in the heading. Double-space between the heading and your title. (This rule does not apply if your teacher requires a cover sheet.)
5. Center the title, and capitalize the appropriate letters in it.

6. Double-space between the title and the body of the paper.
7. Do not underline or use quotation marks to enclose your own title at the head of your own paper. If you use someone else's title within your title, use quotation marks or underlining, as appropriate, with the other person's title only.

EXAMPLE

An Analysis of Symbolism in Yeats' "The Second Coming"

8. When typing or word-processing, always double-space the lines. (In a handwritten paper, skip every other ruled line unless your teacher instructs you otherwise.)
9. Do not use more than a double-space, even between paragraphs.
10. Indent the beginning of each paragraph one-half inch (five spaces).

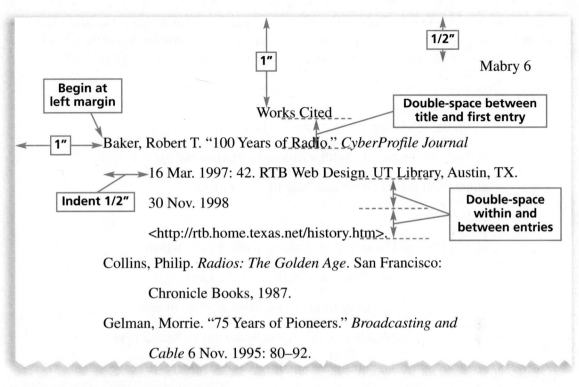

1/2"

1"

Begin at left margin

Works Cited

Double-space between title and first entry

1"

Baker, Robert T. "100 Years of Radio." *CyberProfile Journal*

16 Mar. 1997: 42. RTB Web Design. UT Library, Austin, TX.

Indent 1/2"

30 Nov. 1998

Double-space within and between entries

<http://rtb.home.texas.net/history.htm>.

Collins, Philip. *Radios: The Golden Age*. San Francisco:

Chronicle Books, 1987.

Gelman, Morrie. "75 Years of Pioneers." *Broadcasting and*

Cable 6 Nov. 1995: 80–92.

Documenting Sources

Works Cited Page

1. In a research paper or any other paper that incorporates information from other sources, add a works cited page at the end.
2. Continue numbering the pages of your paper through the works cited page.
3. The entries on the works cited page should be in alphabetical order, according to the last name of the author. For works with no author, the entry should be alphabetized according to the first main word in the title.
4. Do not number the sources on your works cited page.

Documentation in the Body of the Essay

1. Use parenthetical citations within the body of your paper to acknowledge any paraphrased idea or quotation that you have borrowed from someone else. The parenthetical citation refers to specific source documentation on the works cited page. Place the parenthetical citations at the **end** of the material that you borrowed from some other source.

EXAMPLE

Newspapers worried that radio would drive them out of business (Henderson 90).

2. If the citation appears at the end of a sentence, the citation comes before the closing period, as shown above. If the citation appears at the end of a dependent clause or after the first half of a compound sentence, the citation comes before the sentence comma.

EXAMPLE

Newspapers worried that radio would drive them out of business (Henderson 90), but it did not.

RESOURCES

3. For quotations of five or more lines, indent all of the lines one inch (about ten spaces) from the left margin. Do not use quotation marks to enclose indented quotations. Also, place end punctuation at the end of the quoted material, not after the closing parenthesis.

In the following passage, we see how effectively the author sets the mood. With a little imagination, we can almost feel the moist air and hear the murmured conversations.

←— 1″ —→ The streetlights along Toole Street, which meandered downhill from the Language Academy to the town, were already lit and twinkled mistily through the trees. Standing at the gates were small groups of students, clustered together according to nationality. As Myles passed by, he could not help overhearing intense conversations in Spanish, German, and Japanese; all of his students had momentarily abandoned English in the urgency of deciding where to go for the weekend and how to get there. (Boylan 58)

Model Research Paper

The following final draft of a research paper closely follows the guidelines for MLA style given on the preceding pages. (Note: The pages of the model paper are smaller than 8½ × 11, and the margins of the paper are less than one inch wide to allow room for annotations.)

Mabry 1

Roderick W. Mabry

Ms. Johnson

English I

17 November 2009

The Rise of Radio

It nestles on your nightstand, occupies a prominent place in your entertainment center, and rules the road from the dashboard of your car: the radio. This simple appliance is so common that most people take it for granted, yet radio is a relatively new invention. In fact, the first commercial radio station, KDKA in Pittsburgh, did not go on the air until 1920 (Stark 120). Before long, however, the new medium dramatically affected the nation's entertainment, information delivery, and economy.

The invention of radio was made possible by a number of earlier developments. German physicist Heinrich Hertz, drawing on established mathematical principles, discovered the existence of radio waves in 1887. Eight years later, in Italy,

(continued)

HEADING

your name

your teacher's name

your class

date

THESIS SENTENCE: tells focus of the paper

TOPIC SENTENCE: tells focus of the paragraph and is a subtopic of the thesis

RESOURCES

Mabry 2

Guglielmo Marconi successfully completed the first wireless transmission of Morse code signals. An American invention helped move radio closer to reality: Lee De Forest's 1907 Audion, which made it possible to transmit sounds, not just signals. A full decade before KDKA debuted, De Forest broadcast a live performance by famed Italian tenor Enrico Caruso from New York City's Metropolitan Opera House (Yenne 77).

Few people were equipped to hear that landmark broadcast, however, because radio was still very much a do-it-yourself project; most people built their own receivers. In 1921, one such "tinkerer," twenty-eight-year-old Franklin Malcolm Doolittle of New Haven, Connecticut, even used his homemade transmitter to broadcast the Yale-Princeton football game from his home (Gelman 80). The first commercially produced receivers became available in 1920, when a Pittsburgh department store began offering sets for ten dollars. The response was so enthusiastic that Westinghouse began mass producing the appliances (Baker).

When radio found its way into the majority of American households, it brought the nation together in an unprecedented

FIRST REFERENCE: Full name of inventor is used.

SECOND REFERENCE: last name only

This parenthetical citation indicates that paraphrased information in the paragraph comes from Yenne, page 77. *Yenne* refers to *Yenne, Bill* on the works cited page.

In the Baker citation, no page number is listed because this information comes from an unpaginated online source.

way. Radio reached into "once dreary homes, reducing the

 isolation of the hinterlands and leveling class distinctions"

(Henderson 44). At first radio programming simply duplicated

existing forms of entertainment: singers, musicians, comedians,

lecturers. Coping with technical difficulties left little time for

creating new types of shows. Later, as the technical problems

were resolved, programmers began adapting existing formats

and experimenting with new types of shows, including variety

shows, serials, game shows, and amateur hours ("Radio as a

Medium of Communication" 212). As programming expanded,

radio truly became, in researcher Amy Henderson's words, "a

theater of the mind" (144).

　　　　The introduction of radio also radically altered the way

people learned about events in the outside world. For the first

time in history, everyone could receive the same information

simultaneously. As sociologists Robert and Helen Lynd, writing

in the 1920s, noted, "With but little equipment one can call the

life of the rest of the world from the air . . ." (qtd. in Monk 173).

Live coverage gave news events an immediacy far greater than

newspapers or newsreels could provide. In fact, most people

> When parenthetical documenta-tion follows closing quotation marks at the end of a sentence, the period should be placed after the parentheses.

> These parentheses contain only the page number because the author is named in the text.

> This citation tells us that the quotation from Robert and Helen Lynd was found in a book edited by Linda R. Monk.

RESOURCES

(continued)

Mabry 4

first learned of such historic events as the 1941 Japanese attack on Pearl Harbor from the radio (Stark 120).

> Equally important was radio's impact on the economy. The first, and most noticeable, effect was to add a new consumer product to people's wish lists. Most early sets were strictly functional—"a box, some wire, and headphones" (Baker). Once the initial demand was satisfied, however, manufacturers began stimulating repeat sales by offering new models each year, with the goal of placing a "radio in every room" (Collins 10).

The demand for sets was a boon to manufacturers, but it struck fear into some other segments of the economy. Newspapers worried that radio would drive them out of business (Henderson 90). Similarly, members of the traditional entertainment industry feared that the new technology would cut into the sales of tickets and recordings (Stark 120).

Surprisingly, advertisers were slow to realize the opportunities radio offered. At first, most business people assumed that profits would come solely from the sale of sets and replacement parts. In addition, paid advertising was considered

Note again how strong topic sentences control the content of the paragraph and develop a subtopic of the thesis sentence.

The parenthetical citation for Henderson is placed directly at the end of the paraphrase.

improper for what was initially viewed as a "new, pure instrument of democracy" (Weiner). Instead, early programs were underwritten by "sponsors," with companies receiving only a brief, discreet acknowledgment in return for their support. Eventually, however, this approach gave way to the direct advertising that is familiar today (Weiner).

Reviewing the rise of radio makes clear how instrumental the medium was in shaping the nation's entertainment, information delivery, and economy. Today, with the advent of television and the Internet, radio is no longer the primary source of news and entertainment for most people, nor is its impact on the economy as far-reaching. Still, each day millions of listeners wake, work, and play to the rhythms of radio, and many would be lost without it. The radio may have been muted, but it has not been unplugged.

Mabry ends his paper with a concluding paragraph that is entirely his own statement. First, he restates the thesis in the form of a conclusion. Then, he places the history of the radio in its modern context.

(continued)

RESOURCES

(continued)

Center and capitalize *Works Cited,* but do not put it in quotation marks or underline it.

Entries are alphabetized according to the last name of the author.

Carefully punctuate all entries.

Indent second and subsequent lines of entries five spaces.

If no author is listed, alphabetize according to the first main word in the title.

The online address (URL) is enclosed by these signs: < >.

Works Cited

Baker, Robert T. "100 Years of Radio." *CyberProfile Journal* 16

Mar. 1997: 42. RTB Web Design. UT Library, Austin, TX.

30 Nov. 1998 <http://rtb. home. texas.net/history.htm>.

Collins, Philip. *Radios: The Golden Age.* San Francisco:

Chronicle Books, 1987.

Gelman, Morrie. "75 Years of Pioneers." *Broadcasting and*

Cable 6 Nov. 1995: 80–92.

Henderson, Amy. *On the Air.* Washington: Smithsonian

Inst., 1988.

Monk, Linda R., ed. *Ordinary Americans.* Alexandria, VA:

Close Up, 1994.

"Radio as a Medium of Communication." *The Encyclopedia*

Americana. International ed. 1998.

Stark, Phyllis. "On the Air." *Billboard* 1 Nov. 1994: 120–124.

Weiner, Neil. "Stories from Early Radio." *Background Briefing.*

14 Apr. 1996. 28 Mar. 1999 <http://www.background

briefing.com/radio.html>.

Yenne, Bill. *100 Events That Shaped World History.* San

Francisco: Bluewood, 1993.

RESOURCES

The History of English

Origins and Uses

The oldest English-language documents still in existence were first written about 1,300 years ago, but the English language was spoken long before that. Over the centuries, English has evolved into the very different but equally rich and expressive language that it is today. The history of this development is a story of people, places, and times.

Beginnings of English

Many of the world's languages come from an ancient language called **Proto-Indo-European.** There are no records of this parent language, but it was probably spoken by peoples who lived in southeast Europe or Asia Minor six or seven thousand years ago. Tribes of these people slowly migrated throughout Europe and as far east as India. As they wandered in different directions, each tribe developed its own **dialect,** or distinct version of the language. The dialects eventually developed into separate languages. English, French, German, Italian, and Spanish are just a few of the languages that eventually developed through many stages from Proto-Indo-European. The kinship is obvious in the similarities of many words. The word *north* is an example.

EXAMPLE

ENGLISH: *north*

FRENCH: *nord*

GERMAN: *norden*

ITALIAN: *nord*

SPANISH: *norte*

Old English

Around A.D. 450, three Germanic tribes from northern Europe—the Angles, Saxons, and Jutes—began to invade, conquer, and settle parts of Britain. They took over land that had been settled centuries earlier by the Celts and later conquered, settled, then abandoned by the Romans. The separate dialects of the Germanic language the Angles, Saxons, and Jutes spoke eventually blended into one language, which was called *Englisc.* Today this language is referred to as **Old English.** Many Old English words have come down to us only slightly altered. Here are some examples.

EXAMPLES

Old English	Modern English
etan	eat
drincan	drink
daeg	day
niht	night

The structure of Old English, however, was very different from English today. Old English relied on word endings, or **inflections,** to indicate a word's gender, number, case, and person. For example, the noun *hund* ("hound" or "dog") was written *hund, hundes, hunde, hundas, hunda,* or *hundum,* depending on its use in a sentence. In contrast, Modern English relies on a word's position in a sentence to show the word's role in that sentence.

As Old English speakers came into contact with speakers of other languages, particularly Latin-speaking missionaries and Norse invaders, new words, or **loanwords,** entered the language. As English speakers learned Latin, they borrowed words such as *school, altar, candle,* and *paper* and made them part of English. Similarly, as Nordic Vikings settled in Britain, Norse words such as *skalpr (scalp), skrap (scrap),* *skith (ski),* and *sky* became part of the English language. In fact, most English words that begin with *sc* or *sk* are of Norse origin.

Middle English

In 1066, the Normans from France seized control of England. For the next 150–200 years, French was used for almost all written communication. It was the language of government, business, law, and literature in England. The common people of England, however, still spoke English—a form gradually changing into the language now called **Middle English.**

Why did the English language not die out under French rule? Several factors weighed in favor of English. For one thing, the English-speaking people—the common people, such as farmers, herders, servants, and craftspeople—outnumbered their French-speaking rulers. For another, the French rulers in England gradually lost contact with their French culture and language. As a result, three hundred years after the French invasion, English was once again the language of government, business, literature, and law in England. By this time, however, its grammar was becoming simpler as many of the complicated word endings disappeared. Both the grammar and structure were more like the English spoken today, as you can see from the following passage by the fourteenth-century poet Geoffrey Chaucer.

Bifel that in that sesoun on a day
In Southwerk at the Tabard, as I lay
Redy to wenden on my pilgrymage
To Caunterbury with ful devout corage,

Modern English

By 1500, almost everyone in England spoke English. However, because speakers and writers in different parts of England used different versions of the language, they often had trouble understanding each other. Gradually, the version spoken in London—the center of English culture, business, and trade—became the most widely used. When William Caxton brought the first printing press to London in 1476, he printed books in the London dialect. As printed books began to spread across England, spelling and grammar began to be "fixed" in print, and London English became the standard throughout England. The availability of cheap books meant that more people were reading and using the new standardized language. Handbooks of proper English usage, spelling, and pronunciation were soon published, along with the first dictionaries.

Although it had been standardized, the English language did not stop growing. As the Renaissance revived interest in classical languages, thousands of Greek and Latin words entered English. At the same time, English expanded into an international language. From the sixteenth century to the nineteenth century, English merchants, explorers, and settlers spread English to other parts of the globe. They also learned new words from other languages, enriching English with imports such as the following:

EXAMPLES

AFRICAN: marimba
DUTCH: cruise
HINDI: jungle
SPANISH: fiesta
TURKISH: yogurt

American English

Immigration to the American colonies in the late seventeenth and early eighteenth centuries brought about a new version of the language—*American English.* Over time, English colonists in America invented new words and changed the pronunciations and uses of some old words. They also borrowed words, such as *squash,* from American Indian languages. By 1776, the version of English spoken in America was distinct enough from that spoken in England to be called American English.

Like the United States itself, American English represents a variety of cultures and peoples. American Indians, Africans, and immigrants from countries around the world have enriched the language with words from their native tongues. Here are some examples.

EXAMPLES

AFRICAN: gumbo, okra
AMERICAN INDIAN: coyote, toboggan
CHINESE: yen, chop suey
GERMAN: kindergarten, frankfurter
SPANISH: canyon, patio

English in the Twenty-First Century

English has become the most widely used language in the world. It is an official language in more than eighty-seven nations and territories. About one third of the world's population speaks English. Diplomats frequently use it to communicate, and it is the world language of science, technology, aviation, and international trade. As people around the world contribute to the language, the word count continues to grow; the last count was over 600,000 words.

Varieties of American English

American English is a rich and flexible language that offers many choices. To speak and write effectively—at home, at school, and on the job—you need to know what the varieties of American English are and how to choose among them.

Dialects of American English

Like all languages, American English has many distinct versions, called *dialects*. Each dialect has unique features of grammar, vocabulary, and pronunciation.

Ethnic Dialects   An *ethnic dialect* is often used by people who share the same cultural heritage. Because Americans come from many different cultures, American English encompasses many different ethnic dialects, including, among others, Irish English, Yiddish English, and the Hispanic English of people from Puerto Rico, Cuba, Mexico, and Latin America. African American Vernacular English, one of the largest ethnic dialects, has elements of African languages and the dialect of the American South.

Regional Dialects   The United States has four major regional dialects: the *Northern,* the *Midland,* the *Southern,* and the *Western.* The pronunciations of words often vary from one dialect to another. For example, some Southerners pronounce the words *ten* and *tin* the same way—as "tin." Some Midlanders and Southerners add an *r* sound to words, so that *wash* sounds like "warsh."

Similarly, regional dialects differ in vocabulary and grammar. For example, someone from New England might call a soft drink *tonic,* while people in other parts of the country might call it *soda* or *pop.* Someone from the South might say "sick *at* my stomach," while someone from the North might say "sick *to* my stomach."

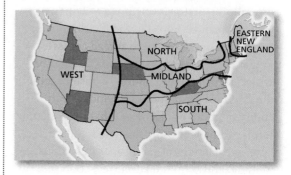

Standard American English

No variety of English is better or more correct than another. However, *standard American English* is the variety of English that is more widely used and accepted than any other in the United States. Because it is commonly understood, it allows people from different regions and cultures to communicate with one another clearly. It is the variety of English you read and hear most often in books and magazines and on radio, television, and the Internet. People are expected to use standard English in most school and business situations. This textbook presents rules and guidelines for using standard American English. To distinguish between standard American English and other varieties, this book uses the labels *standard* and *nonstandard.* Nonstandard language is not "wrong" language—it is language that is inappropriate in situations where standard English is expected.

Standard English—Formal to Informal

Your use of standard English can be formal, informal, or anywhere in between. Which type you choose for communication will depend on many factors, including the occasion and purpose for which you are writing or speaking and your intended audience. The following chart shows some of the appropriate uses of formal and informal standard English.

Uses of Formal and Informal Standard English

Formal

Speaking formal classroom presentations, banquets, dedication ceremonies, and interviews

Writing serious papers and reports, tests, business letters, and job or college applications

Informal

Speaking everyday conversations, group discussions, informal speeches and telephone conversations

Writing personal letters, many types of classroom writing, and many newspaper and magazine articles

Standard English gives you the freedom to say the same things in many different ways. For example, in a formal setting you might say, "I'm pleased to meet you." On a less formal occasion you might choose to say, "Hi, how are you?" or "How's it going?" The differences between formal and informal English are mainly in sentence structure, word choice, and tone.

Features of Formal and Informal Standard English

Formal

Sentence Structure longer and more complex

Word Choice more precise and refined, sometimes technical or scientific

Tone serious and dignified

Informal

Sentence Structure shorter and simpler

Word Choice simple and ordinary, often includes contractions, colloquialisms, and slang

Tone conversational

Colloquialisms   The word *colloquial* comes from a Latin word that means "conversation." *Colloquialisms* are the informal words and phrases of conversational language. They bring flavor and color to everyday speech and a friendly tone to writing. Many colloquialisms are figures of speech.

EXAMPLES   She told me to quit **making such a racket.**

Since quitting her high-paying job, Pat has been **living hand-to-mouth.**

Slang   *Slang* is highly informal English consisting of made-up words or old words used in new ways. It is often used by specific groups of people, such as students, musicians, or military personnel.

EXAMPLES   **bad:** good, excellent

make like: imitate

scarf down: eat greedily

Although some slang words become accepted parts of the language, most have a relatively short life span.

Test Smarts
Taking Standardized Tests in Grammar, Usage, and Mechanics

Becoming "Test-Smart"

Standardized achievement tests, like other tests, measure your skills in specific areas. Standardized achievement tests also compare your performance to the performance of other students at your age or grade level. Some language arts standardized tests measure your skill in using correct capitalization, punctuation, sentence structure, and spelling. Such tests sometimes also measure your ability to evaluate sentence style.

The most important part of preparing for any test, including standardized tests, is learning the content on which you will be tested. To do this, you must

- listen in class
- complete homework assignments
- study to master the concepts and skills presented by your teacher

In addition, you also need to use effective strategies for taking a standardized test. The following pages will teach you how to become test-smart.

General Strategies for Taking Tests

1. **Understand how the test is scored.** If no points will be taken off for wrong answers, plan to answer every question. If wrong answers count against you, plan to answer only questions you know the answer to or questions you can answer with an educated guess.

2. **Stay focused.** Expect to be a little nervous, but focus your attention on doing the best job possible. Try not to be distracted with thoughts that aren't about the test questions.

3. **Get an overview.** Quickly skim the entire test to get an idea of how long the test is and what is on it.

4. **Pace yourself.** Based on your overview, figure out how much time to allow for each section of the test. If time limits are stated for each section, decide how much time to allow for each item. Pace yourself, and check every five to ten minutes to see if you need to work faster. Try to leave a few minutes at the end of the testing period to check your work.

5. **Read all instructions.** Read the instructions for each part of the test carefully. Also, answer the sample questions to be sure you understand how to answer the test questions.

6. **Read all answer choices.** Carefully read *all* of the possible answers before you choose an answer. Note how each possible answer differs from the others. You may want to make an *x* next to each answer choice that you rule out.

7. **Make educated guesses.** If you do not know the answer to a question, see if you can rule out one or more answers and make an educated guess. Don't spend too much time on any one item, though. If you want to think longer about a difficult item, make a light pencil mark next to the item number. You can go back to that question later.

8. **Mark your answers.** Mark the answer sheet carefully and completely. If you plan to go back to an item later, be sure to skip that number on the answer sheet.

9. **Check your work.** If you have time at the end of the test, go back to check your answers. This is also the time to try to answer any questions you skipped. Make sure your marks are complete, and erase any stray marks on the answer sheet.

Strategies for Answering Grammar, Usage, and Mechanics Questions

The questions in standardized tests can take different forms, but the most common form is the multiple-choice question. Here are some strategies for answering that kind of test question.

Correcting parts of sentences

One kind of question contains a sentence with an underlined part. The answer choices show several revised versions of that part. Your job is to decide which revised version makes the sentence correct or whether the underlined part is already correct. First, look at each answer carefully. Immediately rule out any answer in which you notice a grammatical error. If you are still unsure of the correct answer, try approaching the question in one of these two ways.

- **Think how you would rewrite the underlined part.** Look at the answer choices for one that matches your revision. Carefully read each possible answer before you make your final choice. Often, only tiny differences exist between the answers, and you want to choose the *best* answer.

- **Look carefully at the underlined part and at each answer choice, looking for one particular type of error, such as an error in capitalization or spelling.** The best way to look for a particular error is to compare the answer choices to see how they differ both from each other and from the underlined part of the question. For example, if there are differences in capitalization, look at each choice for capitalization errors.

After ruling out incorrect answers, choose the answer with no errors. If there are errors in each of the choices but no errors in the underlined part, your answer will be the "no error" or "correct as is" choice.

EXAMPLE

Directions: Choose the answer that is the **best** revision of the underlined words.

1. My neighbor is painting his <u>house and my brother helped him.</u>

   A. house; and my brother is helping him.

   B. house, and my brother had helped him.

   C. house, and my brother is helping him.

   D. Correct as is

Explanation: In the example above, the possible answers contain differences in punctuation and in verb tense. Therefore, you should check each possible answer for errors in punctuation and verb tense.

   A. You can rule out this choice because it has incorrect punctuation.

   B. This choice creates inconsistent verb tenses, so you can rule out this answer.

   C. This choice has correct punctuation and creates consistent verb tenses.

   D. You can rule out this choice because the original sentence lacks correct punctuation between the clauses and has inconsistent verb tenses.

Answer: Choice C is the only one that contains no errors, so the oval for that answer choice is darkened.

Correcting whole sentences
This type of question is similar to the kind of question previously described. However, here you are looking for mistakes in the entire sentence instead of just an underlined part. The strategies for approaching this type of question are the same as for the other kind of sentence-correction questions. If you don't see the correct answer right away, compare the answer choices to see how they differ. When you find differences, check

each choice for errors relating to that difference. Rule out choices with errors. Repeat the process until you find the correct answer.

EXAMPLE

Directions: Choose the answer that is the **best** revision of the following sentences.

1. After Brad mowed the lawn, he swept the sidewalk and driveway, then he took a shower. And washed his hair.

   A. After Brad mowed the lawn, he swept the sidewalk and driveway. Then he took a shower and washed his hair.

   B. After Brad mowed the lawn, he swept the sidewalk and driveway. Then he took a shower, and washed his hair.

   C. After Brad mowed the lawn. He swept the sidewalk and driveway; then he took a shower and washed his hair.

   D. Correct as is

Explanation: The original word groups and answer choices have differences in sentence structure and punctuation, so you should check each answer choice for errors in sentence structure and punctuation.

   A. This choice contains two complete sentences and correct punctuation.

   B. This choice contains two complete sentences and incorrect punctuation.

   C. This choice begins with a sentence fragment, so you can rule it out.

   D. You can rule out this choice because the original version contains a sentence fragment.

Answer: Choice A is the only one that contains no errors, so the oval for that answer choice is darkened.

Identifying kinds of errors
This type of question has at least one underlined part. Your job is to determine which part, if any,

contains an error. Sometimes, you also may have to decide what type of error (capitalization, punctuation, or spelling) exists. The strategy is the same whether the question has one or several underlined parts. Try to identify an error, and check the answer choices for that type of error. If the original version is correct as written, choose "no error" or "correct as is."

EXAMPLE

Directions: Read the following sentences and decide which type of error, if any, is in the underlined part.

1. Marcia, Jim, and Leroy are participating in <u>Saturday's charity marathon. they</u> are hoping to raise one hundred dollars for the new children's museum.

    A. Spelling error

    B. Capitalization error

    C. Punctuation error

    D. Correct as is

Explanation: If you cannot tell right away what kind of error (if any) is in the original version, go through each answer choice in turn.

   A. All the words are spelled correctly.

   B. The sentences contain a capitalization error. The second sentence incorrectly begins with a lowercase letter.

   C. The sentences are punctuated correctly.

   D. The sentences contain a capitalization error, so you can rule out this choice.

Answer: Because the passage contains a capitalization error, the oval for answer choice B is darkened.

Revising sentence structure

Errors covered by this kind of question include sentence fragments, run-on sentences, repetitive wording, misplaced modifiers, and awkward construction. If you don't immediately spot the error, examine the question and each answer choice for specific types of errors, one type at a time. If you cannot find an error in the original version and if all of the other answer choices have errors, then choose "no error" or "correct as is."

EXAMPLE

Directions: Read the following word groups. If there is an error in sentence structure, choose the answer that best revises the word groups.

1. Mary Lou arranged the mozzarella cheese and fresh tomatoes. On a platter covered with lettuce leaves.

    A. Mary Lou arranged the mozzarella cheese and fresh tomatoes on a platter covered with lettuce leaves.

    B. Mary Lou arranged the mozzarella cheese and fresh tomatoes, on a platter covered with lettuce leaves.

    C. Mary Lou arranged the mozzarella cheese and fresh tomatoes; on a platter covered with lettuce leaves.

    D. Correct as is

Explanation: The original word groups and answer choices have differences in sentence structure and punctuation.

   A. This choice is correctly punctuated and contains a correct, complete sentence.

   B. This choice contains an incorrect comma, so you can rule it out.

   C. This choice contains an incorrect semicolon, so you can rule it out.

   D. The original word groups contain a sentence fragment, so D cannot be correct.

Answer: Choice A is the only one that contains no errors, so the oval for that answer choice is darkened.

Questions about sentence style

These questions are often not about grammar, usage, or mechanics but about content and organization. They may ask about tone, purpose, topic sentences, supporting sentences, audience, sentence combining, appropriateness of content, or transitions. The questions may ask you which is the *best* way to revise the passage, or they may ask you to identify the *main* purpose of the passage. When you see words such as *best*, *main*, and *most likely* or *least likely*, you are not being asked to correct errors; you are being asked to make a judgment about style or meaning.

If the question asks for a particular kind of revision (for example, "What *transition* is needed between sentence 4 and sentence 5?"), analyze each answer choice to see how well it makes that particular revision. Many questions ask for a general revision (for example, "Which is the *best* way to revise the last sentence?"). In such situations, check each answer choice and rule out any choices that have mistakes in grammar, usage, or mechanics. Then, read each choice and use what you have learned in class to judge whether the revision improves the original sentence. If you are combining sentences, be sure to choose the answer that includes all important information, that demonstrates good style, *and* that is grammatically correct.

EXAMPLE

Directions: Choose the answer that shows the **best** way to combine the following sentences.

1. Jacques Cousteau was a filmmaker and author. Jacques Cousteau explored the ocean as a diver and marine scientist.
   A. Jacques Cousteau was a filmmaker and author; Jacques Cousteau explored the ocean as a marine scientist.
   B. Jacques Cousteau was a filmmaker and author, he explored the ocean as a diver and marine scientist.
   C. Jacques Cousteau was a filmmaker and author who explored the ocean as a diver and marine scientist.
   D. Jacques Cousteau was a filmmaker, author, diver, and scientist.

Explanation:

   A. Answer choice A is grammatically correct but unnecessarily repeats the subject *Jacques Cousteau* and leaves out some information.
   B. Choice B is a run-on sentence, so it cannot be the correct answer.
   C. Choice C is grammatically correct, and it demonstrates effective sentence combining.
   D. Choice D is grammatically correct but leaves out some information.

Answer: Because answer choice C shows the best way to combine the sentences, the oval for choice C is darkened.

Fill-in-the-blanks

This type of question tests your ability to fill in blanks in sentences, giving answers that are logical and grammatically correct. A question of this kind might ask you to choose a verb in the appropriate tense. A different question might require a combination of adverbs (*first, next*) to show how parts of the sentence relate. Another question might require a vocabulary word to complete the sentence.

To approach a sentence-completion question, first look for clue words in the sentence. *But*, *however*, and *though* indicate a contrast; *therefore* and *as a result* indicate cause and effect. Using sentence clues, rule out obviously incorrect answer choices. Then, try filling in the blanks with the remaining choices to determine which answer choice makes the most sense. Finally, check to be sure your choice is grammatically correct.

EXAMPLE

Directions: Choose the words that **best** complete the sentence.

1. When Jack _____ the dog, the dog _____ water everywhere.

   A. washes, splashed

   B. washed, will be splashing

   C. will have washed, has splashed

   D. washed, splashed

Explanation:

   A. The verb tenses (present and past) are inconsistent.

   B. The verb tenses (past and future) are inconsistent.

   C. The verb tenses (future perfect and present perfect) are inconsistent.

   D. The verb tenses (past and past) are consistent.

Answer: The oval for choice D is darkened.

Using Your Test Smarts

Remember: Success on standardized tests comes partly from knowing strategies for taking such tests—from being test-smart. Knowing these strategies can help you approach standardized achievement tests more confidently. Do your best to learn your classroom subjects, take practice tests if they are available, and use the strategies outlined in this section. Good luck!

RESOURCES

Grammar at a Glance

┌HELP─

Grammar at a Glance is an alphabetical list of special terms and expressions with examples and references to further information. When you encounter a grammar or usage problem in the revising or proofreading stage of your writing, look for help in this section first. You may find all you need to know right here. If you need more information, **Grammar at a Glance** will show you where in the book to turn for a more complete explanation. If you do not find what you are looking for in **Grammar at a Glance,** turn to the index.

abbreviation An abbreviation is a shortened form of a word or a phrase.

- **capitalization of** (See page 284.)

TITLES USED WITH NAMES	**M**r.	**R**ev.	**J**r.	**E**sq.
KINDS OF ORGANIZATIONS	**C**o.	**I**nc.	**A**dmin.	**C**orp.
PARTS OF ADDRESSES	**B**lvd.	**R**d.	**P**kwy.	**P.O. B**ox
NAMES OF STATES	[without ZIP Codes]		**K**y.	**O**kla.
			Calif.	**S.C.**
	[with ZIP Codes]		**KY**	**OK**
			CA	**SC**
TIMES	**A.M.**	**P.M.**	**B.C.**	**A.D.**

- **punctuation of** (See page 294.)

WITH PERIODS	(See preceding examples.)
WITHOUT PERIODS	RN IOU EPA UNICEF
	DC (D.C. without ZIP Code)
	mg oz yd mph km
	[Exception: in.]

action verb An action verb expresses physical or mental activity. (See page 16.)

EXAMPLE   David **drove** from Vicksburg to Austin.

active voice Active voice is the voice a verb is in when it expresses an action done by its subject. (See page 199. See also **voice.**)

EXAMPLE   Ann **nailed** the planks together.

adjective An adjective modifies a noun or a pronoun. (See page 10.)

EXAMPLE   **An old** oak cast its **huge** shadow across **the front** yard.

adjective clause An adjective clause is a subordinate clause that modifies a noun or a pronoun. (See page 93.)

EXAMPLE   The poetry **that my aunt wrote** remains unpublished.

adjective phrase A prepositional phrase that modifies a noun or a pronoun is called an adjective phrase. (See page 66.)

EXAMPLE   Most **of the school** will be taking part in the fair.

adverb An adverb modifies a verb, an adjective, or another adverb. (See page 20.)

EXAMPLE   Is there **really** enough time for the play?

adverb clause An adverb clause is a subordinate clause that modifies a verb, an adjective, or an adverb. (See page 96.)

EXAMPLE   **Before I went home,** I thanked my hosts.

adverb phrase A prepositional phrase that modifies a verb, an adjective, or an adverb is called an adverb phrase. (See page 67.)

EXAMPLE   Sean and Henry stayed **after school** to help Ms. Gallogly **with the decorations.**

agreement Agreement is the correspondence, or match, between grammatical forms. Grammatical forms agree when they have the same number and gender.

■ **of pronouns and antecedents** (See page 130.)

SINGULAR   The teacher asked **Daniel** to name **his** favorite books, songs, and movies.

PLURAL   The teacher asked the **students** to name **their** favorite books, songs, and movies.

SINGULAR   I think Geraldo can name **each** of the countries and **its** capital city.

PLURAL   I think Geraldo can name **all** of the countries and **their** capital cities.

SINGULAR   Neither **Sue** nor **Christie** has **her** driver's license.

PLURAL   Both **Sue** and **Christie** have **their** driver's licenses.

■ **of subjects and verbs** (See page 110.)

SINGULAR   The **choreographer wants** to change some of the movements of the ballet.

SINGULAR   The **choreographer,** as well as the dancers, **wants** to change some of the movements of the ballet.

PLURAL   The **dancers want** to change some of the movements of the ballet.

PLURAL   The **dancers,** as well as the choreographer, **want** to change some of the movements of the ballet.

SINGULAR   **Each** of these beagle puppies **is** four weeks old.

PLURAL   **All** of these beagle puppies **are** four weeks old.

SINGULAR   **Either Paul or Sonia** usually **goes** fishing with me.

PLURAL   **Both Paul and Sonia** usually **go** fishing with me.

SINGULAR   Here **is** the **list** of sources I used to write my essay on the origins of jazz.

PLURAL   Here **are** the **sources** I used to write my essay on the origins of jazz.

SINGULAR   **Six days is** the length of time the astronauts will spend in space.

PLURAL   **Six days** of the school year **are reserved** for parent-teacher conferences.

SINGULAR   *The Adventures of Tom Sawyer* **includes** a hilarious scene in which Tom pretends to be sick.

PLURAL   Tom's **adventures include** some wild times.

SINGULAR   The principal **ingredient** in the Russian soup borscht **is** beets.

PLURAL   **Beets are** the principal ingredient in the Russian soup borscht.

SINGULAR   "For My People" is one poem **that was written** by Margaret Walker.

PLURAL   "For My People" is one of the poems **that were written** by Margaret Walker.

SINGULAR   "For My People" is the only one of the poems **that was written** by Margaret Walker.

ambiguous reference Ambiguous reference occurs when a pronoun incorrectly refers to either of two antecedents. (See page 164.)

AMBIGUOUS	One of the chief differences between the Seismosaurus and the Tyrannosaurus rex is that it did not eat meat. [Which dinosaur did not eat meat?]
CLEAR	One of the chief differences between the Seismosaurus and the Tyrannosaurus rex is that the Seismosaurus did not eat meat.

antecedent An antecedent is the word or words that a pronoun stands for. (See page 130.)

EXAMPLE **Jim** and **Mimi** spent **their** summer traveling through New Mexico. [*Jim* and *Mimi* are the antecedents of *their.*]

apostrophe

- **to form contractions** (See page 361. See also **contraction.**)
  EXAMPLES aren't   we'll   o'clock   '02

- **to form plurals of letters, numerals, symbols, and words used as words** (See page 364.)

EXAMPLES	*v*'s and *w*'s	*A*'s, *I*'s, and *U*'s
	1700's	PC's
	$'s and ¢'s	replacing *so*'s with *therefore*'s

- **to show possession** (See page 356.)
  EXAMPLES the student's test score

  the students' test scores

  children's tickets

  somebody's gloves

  Mother's and Aunt Shashona's story quilts

  Philip and Nguyen's duet

  one week's [*or* seven days'] vacation

appositive An appositive is a noun or a pronoun placed beside another noun or pronoun to identify or describe it. (See page 81.)

EXAMPLE The Oscar-winning actor **Tom Hanks** was featured on that program.

appositive phrase An appositive phrase consists of an appositive and its modifiers. (See page 81.)

EXAMPLE   Mr. Trevelyan, **our new English teacher,** is from Maine.

article The articles, *a*, *an*, and *the*, are the most frequently used adjectives. (See page 10.)

EXAMPLE   **A** new car dealership rejuvenated **an** abandoned shopping center in **the** suburbs.

bad, badly (See page 215.)

NONSTANDARD   This salad dressing smells badly.
STANDARD   This salad dressing smells **bad.**

base form The base form, or infinitive, is one of the four principal parts of a verb. (See page 172.)

EXAMPLE   Dad is helping Stephanie **ride** her bike.

brackets (See page 370.)

EXAMPLES   The Ashanti proverb "What is bad luck for one man is good luck for another" reminds me of an expression I've often heard at rummage sales: "One man's trash **[**bad luck**]** is another man's treasure **[**good luck**]**."

The *Iliad* and the *Odyssey* (both attributed to Homer **[**some historians question this authorship**]**) are epic poems about events before, during, and after the Trojan War.

capitalization

- **of abbreviations and acronyms** (See page 284. See also **abbreviation.**)

- **of first words** (See page 266.)

EXAMPLES   **S**mall wooden dolls called kachinas represent spirits and ancestors revered by the Hopi.

Mr. Anaka told us, "**T**he publication of Rachel Carson's book *Silent Spring* in 1962 helped to launch our nation's environmental movement."

Dear Dr. Yamaguchi:

Best regards,

- **of proper nouns and proper adjectives** (See page 267.)

Proper Noun	Common Noun
Dr. Martin Luther King, Jr.	minister
Prince Henry the Navigator	explorer
Antarctica	continent
Sierra Leone	country
Los Alamos County	county
New Brunswick Province	province
Marquesas Islands	islands
Lake Tanganyika	body of water
Mount Rainier	mountain
Pacific Rim National Park	park
Shoshone National Forest	forest
Ajanta Caves	cave
Great Salt Lake Desert	desert
Northeast	region
Fifty-sixth Street	street
Republican Party (or party)	political party
Battle of Seven Pines	historical event
Dark Ages	historical period
Cinco de Mayo	holiday
January, April, August, November	calendar items
Kiowa Apache	people
Christianity	religion
Muslim	religious follower
God (but the god Poseidon)	deity
Sukkot, or Feast of Tabernacles	holy days
Upanishads	sacred writing
Great Sand Dunes National Monument	monument
Wells Fargo Center	building
National Book Critics Circle Award	award
Saturn	planet
Polaris, or the North Star	star
Leo Minor, or the Lesser Lion	constellation
Empress of Ireland	ship
Challenger	spacecraft
Punjabi	language

■ **of titles** (See page 280.)

EXAMPLES   **G**overnor Robert La Follette [preceding a name]

Robert La Follette, the former **g**overnor of Wisconsin [following a name]

Welcome, **G**overnor. [direct address]

Uncle Benjamin [*but* my **u**ncle Benjamin]

The People Could Fly: American Black Folktales [book]

Waterlilies in a Pond [work of art]

"**M**any **R**ivers to **C**ross" [song]

"**A V**isit to **G**randmother" [short story]

"**T**he **S**ky **I**s **J**ust **B**eyond the **R**oof" [poem]

Organic Gardening [magazine]

Shoe [comic strip]

case of pronouns Case is the form a pronoun takes to show how it is used in a sentence. (See page 145.)

NOMINATIVE   My friend Justin and **I** are organizing a pet-sitting service.

The only sophomores on the school's debate team are Tyrone and **she.**

In my opinion, both gymnasts, Lori and **she,** deserved the first-place medal.

We student-council officers met with the principal to discuss the schedule of activities for Career Night.

Khufu was the Egyptian king **who** built the Great Pyramid at Giza.

Have you already heard **who** the winner is?

Do you think we should pay you more than **they**? [The pronoun is the subject of the incomplete adverb clause "than they pay you."]

OBJECTIVE   The friendly park attendant directed **us** to the manatee aquarium.

Uncle Theo sent **me** his recipe for moussaka.

The chess match between Lucia and **him** was exciting.

A technical foul has been charged against both basketball players, Melinda and **her.**

Our art teacher showed **us** students some of the origami figures she had made.

Their supervisor wants **them** to learn to use different word-processing programs.

Michael Jordan, **whom** many consider the greatest basketball player of all time, retired from the sport in 2003.

"To **whom** do you wish to speak?" asked the secretary.

Do you think we should pay you as much as **them**? [The pronoun is the direct object of the verb *pay* in the incomplete adverb clause "as much as we pay them."]

POSSESSIVE   **Your** stereo sounds better than **mine** does.

My parents don't approve of **my** watching television.

clause A clause is a group of words that contains a verb and its subject and that is used as part of a sentence. (See page 90.)

EXAMPLE   While I sliced the onions [subordinate clause], Marcia peeled the avocado [independent clause].

colon (See page 327.)

■ **before lists**

EXAMPLES   In a heptathlon, athletes compete in the following events**:** the 100-meter hurdles, the shot put, the high jump, the 200-meter dash, the long jump, the javelin throw, and the 800-meter run.

The United States government is divided into three branches**:** executive, judicial, and legislative.

■ **in conventional situations**

EXAMPLES   3**:**30 P.M.

Genesis 22**:**1–18

*Lincoln at Gettysburg***:** *The Words That Remade America*

Dear Mrs. Wu**:**

comma (See page 298.)

■ **in a series**

EXAMPLE   The principal ingredients of the traditional Navajo dish called *posole* are meat**,** hominy**,** and chili.

■ **in compound sentences**

EXAMPLE   In our production of *Julius Caesar,* Saul portrayed the title character**,** and I played Brutus.

■ **with nonessential phrases and clauses**

EXAMPLES The roving vehicle *Sojourner*, deployed during the Mars *Pathfinder* mission in 1997, provided scientists valuable data about the planet Mars. [nonessential phrase]

Scott Joplin, who helped make ragtime music popular in the early 1900s, composed the ragtime opera *Treemonisha.* [nonessential clause]

■ **with introductory elements**

EXAMPLES On his way to school this morning, Harold stopped at the post office to mail the invitations to his bar mitzvah.

After we had read the poems by Gwendolyn Brooks, our teacher asked us to find examples of simile, metaphor, and personification.

■ **with interrupters**

EXAMPLES That, in my opinion, is a most amusing comic strip.

Citrus fruits, such as oranges and lemons, are good sources of vitamin C.

■ **in conventional situations**

EXAMPLES On Friday, April 10, 2009, Mavis and I flew to Seattle, Washington, to attend a week-long computer seminar.

She sent the job application to 345 Chestnut Street, Oshkosh, WI 54901-0345, on 15 May 2009.

comma splice A comma splice is a run-on sentence in which sentences have been joined with only a comma between them. (See page 454.) (See also **fused sentence, run-on sentence.**)

COMMA SPLICE Usually the earth's moon is full only once each month, however, about every thirty-two months the moon is full twice in the same month, the second full moon is called a blue moon.

REVISED Usually the earth's moon is full only once each month. However, about every thirty-two months the moon is full twice in the same month; the second full moon is called a blue moon.

REVISED Usually the earth's moon is full only once each month. However, about every thirty-two months the moon is full twice in the same month. The second full moon is called a blue moon.

comparison of modifiers (See page 218.)

■ **comparison of adjectives and adverbs**

Positive	Comparative	Superlative
young	young**er**	young**est**
tasty	tast**ier**	tast**iest**
persuasive	**more** persuasive	**most** persuasive
gracefully	**less** gracefully	**least** gracefully
good/well	**better**	**best**

■ **comparing two**

EXAMPLES   Of the giant sequoia and the bristlecone pine, which species is **older**?

Which of these two computer models processes data **more quickly**?

I read that the diamond is **harder** than **any other** natural substance known.

■ **comparing more than two**

EXAMPLES   Extending 6,529 feet (1,990 meters), the Akashi Kaikyo Bridge in Japan is one of the **longest** suspension bridges in the world.

Of all of us in the room, Jorge reacted **most calmly** to the news.

complement A complement is a word or word group that completes the meaning of a verb. (See page 48. See also **direct object, indirect object, predicate adjective,** and **predicate nominative.**)

EXAMPLES   Have you given **Dale** that **book**?

This book is a **favorite,** but that one is even **better.**

complex sentence A complex sentence has one independent clause and at least one subordinate clause. (See page 103.)

EXAMPLES   My neighbor Ms. Tanaka, who is a freelance photojournalist, is planning a trip to the Australian outback.

As Ms. Tanaka and I talked about her plans for her trip to the outback, she showed me photographs of her South American trip, which included a visit to the Galápagos Islands.

compound-complex sentence A compound-complex sentence has two or more independent clauses and at least one subordinate clause. (See page 103.)

EXAMPLES   Hattie Caraway was the wife of the United States senator Thaddeus Caraway, and when he died in 1931, she was asked to serve out his term.

           After she had completed her husband's term, Hattie Caraway ran for the Senate seat in the election of 1932 and won; as a result, she became the first woman elected to the United States Senate.

compound sentence A compound sentence has two or more independent clauses but no subordinate clauses. (See page 102.)

EXAMPLES   In his spare time, Joshua enjoys painting; he especially likes to paint with watercolors.

           The bat has wings and can fly, but it is not a bird; it is a mammal.

conjunction A conjunction joins words or groups of words. (See page 26.)

EXAMPLE   **Both** Andrea **and** Walter were hoping to win **or** at least qualify for the contest, **but** they soon withdrew their names **because** so many people were ahead of them **and** it was late in the year.

contraction A contraction is a shortened form of a word, a numeral, or a group of words. Apostrophes in contractions indicate where letters or numerals have been omitted. (See page 361. See also **apostrophe.**)

EXAMPLES

I've [I have]	here's [here is or here has]
who's [who is or who has]	they're [they are]
couldn't [could not]	it's [it is or it has]
can't [cannot]	don't [do not]
'50–'51 school year [1950–1951]	o'clock [of the clock]

dangling modifier A dangling modifier is a modifying word, phrase, or clause that does not clearly and sensibly modify a word or word group in a sentence. (See page 224.)

| DANGLING | Leading us through the art museum, interesting anecdotes about the artists' lives were told. [Who is leading us through the art museum?] |
| REVISED | Leading us through the art museum, **the tour guide** told interesting anecdotes about the artists' lives. |

dash (See page 368.)

| EXAMPLE | Thousands of fans—23,764, to be exact—attended the championship game. |

declarative sentence A declarative sentence makes a statement and is followed by a period. (See page 57.)

| EXAMPLE | Ben Nevis is the highest mountain in Scotland and is higher than any other peak in Great Britain**.** |

direct object A direct object is a word or word group that receives the action of the verb or shows the result of the action. A direct object answers the question *Whom?* or *What?* after a transitive verb. (See page 54.)

| EXAMPLE | Tom painted the **mural** on the school wall. |

double comparison A double comparison is the nonstandard use of two comparative forms (usually *more* and *–er*) or two superlative forms (usually *most* and *–est*) to express comparison. In standard usage, the single comparative or superlative form is correct. (See page 221.)

| NONSTANDARD | Of the eight puppies, Triton is the most largest. |
| STANDARD | Of the eight puppies, Triton is the **largest.** |

double negative A double negative is the nonstandard use of two or more negative words to express a single negative idea. (See page 254.)

NONSTANDARD	Despite the inclement weather, the pilot didn't have no difficulty landing the plane.
STANDARD	Despite the inclement weather, the pilot **didn't have any** difficulty landing the plane.
STANDARD	Despite the inclement weather, the pilot **had no** difficulty landing the plane.

double subject A double subject occurs when an unnecessary pronoun is used after the subject of a sentence. (See page 243.)

| NONSTANDARD | Most of the businesses in town they close by 6:00 P.M. |
| STANDARD | Most of the businesses in town close by 6:00 P.M. |

end marks (See page 292.)

■ **with sentences**

EXAMPLES   For dessert, Grandmother served warm sopaipillas with honey**.** [declarative sentence]

Is the cedar waxwing, or cedarbird, indigenous to this area**?** [interrogative sentence]

Wow**!** [interjection] What a clever trick that was**!** [exclamatory sentence]

Please help your brother with his homework**.** [imperative sentence]

■ **with abbreviations** (See **abbreviation.**)

EXAMPLES   During spring break, we went to Washington, D.C**.**

When did you go to Washington, D.C.**?**

essential clause/essential phrase An essential, or restrictive, clause or phrase is necessary to the meaning of a sentence and is not set off by commas. (See page 303.)

EXAMPLES   The woman **who helped us** is standing there. [clause]

The woman **standing there** helped us. [phrase]

exclamation point (See **end marks.**)

exclamatory sentence An exclamatory sentence expresses strong feeling and is followed by an exclamation point. (See page 57.)

EXAMPLE   What a magnificent sight that is**!**

fragment (See **sentence fragment.**)

fused sentence A fused sentence is a run-on sentence in which sentences have been joined together with no punctuation between them. (See page 454.) (See also **comma splice, run-on sentence.**)

FUSED   A tanka is a five-line poem that consists of thirty-one syllables the first and third lines contain five syllables each the other lines have seven each.

REVISED	A tanka is a five-line poem that consists of thirty-one syllables; the first and third lines contain five syllables each, **and** the other lines have seven each.

general reference A general reference is the incorrect use of a pro-noun to refer to a general idea rather than to a specific noun. (See page 165.)

GENERAL	Misuko revised and proofread her rough draft on the French Revolution. That took her about three hours. [To what does *That* refer?]
REVISED	Revising and proofreading her rough draft on the French Revolution took Misuko about three hours.

gerund A gerund is a verb form ending in *–ing* that is used as a noun. (See page 74.)

EXAMPLES	**Painting** landscapes is Uncle Arthur's favorite hobby.
	Some people say the best exercise is **swimming.**

gerund phrase A gerund phrase consists of a gerund and its modi-fiers and complements. (See page 76.)

EXAMPLE	By **leaving early,** Erica hoped to arrive before the others.

good, well (See page 215.)

EXAMPLES	Even a **good** bowler will occasionally roll a gutter ball.
	I wish I could bowl as **well** [not *good*] as you.

hyphen (See page 365.)

■ **for division of words**

EXAMPLE	The words *hiss, sizzle, buzz,* and *roar* are good exam-ples of the poetic device called onomatopoeia.

■ **in compound numbers**

EXAMPLE	The ratification of the Twenty-sixth Amendment in 1971 lowered the voting age from twenty-one to eighteen.

■ **with prefixes and suffixes**

EXAMPLES	In mid-December, the citizens of Mexico celebrate the Nine Days of Posada.
	The guest speaker will be ex-Mayor Franklin Jackson.

imperative sentence An imperative sentence gives a command or makes a request and is followed by either a period or an exclamation point. (See page 57.)

EXAMPLES   Please dry the dishes, Juan. [request]

                Sit down! [command]

incomplete construction An incomplete construction is a clause from which words have been omitted. (See page 163.)

EXAMPLE   The study shows that we performed better **than they** [did].

indefinite reference An indefinite reference is the incorrect use of the pronoun *you, it,* or *they* to refer to no particular person or thing. (See page 165.)

INDEFINITE   In the newspaper, it says that the governor is planning to run for president.

REVISED   The newspaper says that the governor is planning to run for president.

independent clause An independent clause (also called a *main clause*) expresses a complete thought and can stand by itself as a sentence. (See page 90.)

EXAMPLE   After we had finished class, **Mr. Smith took us to the park.**

indirect object An indirect object is a noun, pronoun, or word group that often appears in sentences containing direct objects. An indirect object tells *to whom* or *to what* (or *for whom* or *for what*) the action of a transitive verb is done. Indirect objects generally precede direct objects. (See page 55.)

EXAMPLE   Pedro gave the **twins** a snack, and now they're ready to play all day.

infinitive An infinitive is a verb form, usually preceded by *to,* that is used as a noun, an adjective, or an adverb. (See page 77.)

EXAMPLE   Her dearest wish was **to participate** in the rafting trip.

infinitive phrase An infinitive phrase consists of an infinitive and its modifiers and complements. (See page 78.)

RESOURCES

EXAMPLE **To welcome our new neighbors,** we formed the committee called Feel at Home.

interjection An interjection expresses emotion and has no grammatical relation to the rest of the sentence. (See page 27.)

EXAMPLE **Well,** how long do we have to wait?

interrogative sentence An interrogative sentence asks a question and is followed by a question mark. (See page 57.)

EXAMPLE Would you like to come to Dr. Seymour's farewell dinner**?**

intransitive verb An intransitive verb is a verb that does not take an object. (See page 19.)

EXAMPLE The Shadwells **are sleeping.**

irregular verb An irregular verb is a verb that forms its past and past participle in some way other than by adding –d or –ed to the base form. (See page 174. See also **regular verb.**)

Base Form	Present Participle	Past	Past Participle
be	[is] being	was, were	[have] been
cast	[is] casting	cast	[have] cast
fall	[is] falling	fell	[have] fallen
find	[is] finding	found	[have] found
hit	[is] hitting	hit	[have] hit
make	[is] making	made	[have] made
ring	[is] ringing	rang	[have] rung
shake	[is] shaking	shook	[have] shaken
speak	[is] speaking	spoke	[have] spoken
think	[is] thinking	thought	[have] thought

italics (See page 337.)

■ **for titles**   *The Once and Future King* [book]

Popular Science [periodical]

Gamera: The Guardian of the Universe [movie]

Perseus with the Head of Medusa [work of art]

Tales from the Vienna Woods [long musical composition]

■ **for words, letters, and symbols used as such and for foreign words**

EXAMPLES   Using the spellchecker, I discovered that I had transposed the letters *e* and *a* every time I had typed the word *research.*

Using the spellchecker, I discovered that I had transposed the letters *e* and *a* every time I had typed the word **research.**

The story ends with **Requiescat in pace,** the Latin phrase that means "Rest in peace."

its, it's (See page 394.)

EXAMPLES   **Its** [Mexico's] highest point is the volcanic mountain Citlaltépetl.

It's [It is] more than 18,000 feet high.

It's [It has] been a long time since the volcano has erupted.

lie, lay (See page 180.)

EXAMPLES   Weary from their hike, the scouts **lay** down and rested awhile. [past tense of *lie*]

Weary from their hike, the scouts **laid** their backpacks down and rested awhile. [past tense of *lay*]

linking verb A linking verb connects the subject with a word that identifies or describes the subject. (See page 16.)

EXAMPLE   Italy **became** a republic in 1946.

misplaced modifier A misplaced modifier is a word, phrase, or clause that seems to modify the wrong word or words in a sentence. (See page 225.)

MISPLACED   The 4-H clubs throughout the United States, supported by the Department of Agriculture, strive to improve the head, heart, hands, and health of each of their members. [Is the United States supported by the Department of Agriculture?]

REVISED   **Supported by the Department of Agriculture,** the 4-H clubs throughout the United States strive to improve the head, heart, hands, and health of each of their members.

modifier A modifier is a word or word group that makes the meaning of another word or word group more specific. (See page 212.)

EXAMPLE   Gustav Mahler, **a major Austrian** composer **of the early twentieth century, often** used **the** idioms **of popular music in his compositions.**

nonessential clause/nonessential phrase A nonessential, or nonrestrictive, clause or phrase adds information not necessary to the main idea in the sentence and is generally set off by commas. (See page 302.)

EXAMPLES   The church on the corner, **in which the Reverend de Santis once preached,** is being renovated. [nonessential clause]

              The top, **spinning wildly,** bounced down the steps. [nonessential phrase]

noun A noun names a person, place, thing, or idea. (See page 3.)

EXAMPLES   **Billie Holiday** sang beautifully.

              We are vacationing in **Vermont.**

              Please hand me the **scissors.**

              Intelligence is difficult to measure.

noun clause A noun clause is a subordinate clause used as a noun. (See page 99.)

EXAMPLE   Tell me **what you did during the summer.**

number Number is the form a word takes to indicate whether the word is singular or plural. (See page 110.)

SINGULAR	tree	she	child	man
PLURAL	trees	they	children	men

object of a preposition An object of a preposition is the noun or pronoun that completes a prepositional phrase. (See page 24.)

EXAMPLE   One of the old **trees** was struck by **lightning.** [*Of the old trees* and *by lightning* are prepositional phrases.]

parallel structure Parallel structure is the use of the same grammatical forms or structures to balance related ideas in a sentence. (See page 476.)

NONPARALLEL	The main duties of the receptionist are to greet callers, to take messages, and providing information.
PARALLEL	The main duties of the receptionist are **to greet** callers, **to take** messages, and **to provide** information.
PARALLEL	The main duties of the receptionist are **greeting** callers, **taking** messages, and **providing** information.

parentheses (See page 368.)

EXAMPLES	The route traveled by the pony express riders **(**see the map on page 152**)** was dangerous.
	The route traveled by the pony express riders was dangerous. **(**See the map on page 152.**)**

participial phrase A participial phrase consists of a participle and any complements and modifiers it has. (See page 71.)

EXAMPLE	**Considered famous for its resorts,** the Yucatán is also a center of Mayan culture.

participle A participle is a verb form that can be used as an adjective. (See page 70.)

EXAMPLE	I prefer to live in the South, where there are no **freezing** winters.

passive voice The passive voice is the voice a verb is in when it expresses an action done to its subject. (See page 199. See also **voice.**)

EXAMPLE	Mr. Boylan's novel **has been translated** into German.

period (See **end marks.**)

phrase A phrase is a group of related words that does not contain a verb and its subject and that is used as a single part of speech. (See page 65.)

EXAMPLE	Stacy, **Aunt Maeve's golden retriever,** probably **will place** first **in the sporting-dog category.** [*Aunt Maeve's golden retriever* is an appositive phrase. *Will place* is a verb phrase. *In the sporting-dog category* is a prepositional phrase.]

predicate The predicate is the part of a sentence that says something about the subject. (See page 39.)

EXAMPLE   She **wants to be a commercial airline pilot.**

predicate adjective A predicate adjective is an adjective that completes the meaning of a linking verb and that modifies the subject of the verb. (See page 52.)

EXAMPLE   Despite the heat, Bob and Beth appeared **fresh** and **alert.**

predicate nominative A predicate nominative is a noun or pronoun that completes the meaning of a linking verb and identifies or refers to the subject of the verb. (See page 51.)

EXAMPLE   The president of the company is **Francis McGuire, Ph.D.**

prefix A prefix is a word part that is added before a base word or root. (See page 379.)

EXAMPLES   un + fair = **un**fair   re + usable = **re**usable

mis + pronounce =   dis + qualified =
  mispronounce   **dis**qualified

mid + February = **mid**-February   ex + judge = **ex**-judge

preposition A preposition shows the relationship of a noun or a pronoun to some other word in a sentence. (See page 24.)

EXAMPLE   That novel **by** Joseph Conrad is **about** spies **in** nineteenth-century Geneva.

prepositional phrase A prepositional phrase includes a preposition, a noun or pronoun called the object of the preposition, and any modifiers of that object. (See page 24.)

EXAMPLE   **Before breakfast,** I like to watch the sun rise **over the rooftops.**

pronoun A pronoun is used in place of one or more nouns or pronouns. (See page 6.)

EXAMPLES   Paul and **I** wrote to Abigail and expressed **our** pleasure at **her** engagement.

All of the team members prepared **themselves** for the relay.

Who gave **you this**?

question mark (See **end marks.**)

quotation marks (See page 341.)

- **for direct quotations**

  EXAMPLE   "In class tomorrow," said Mr. McDermott, "we will begin studying the decline of the Mayan civilization."

- **with other marks of punctuation** (See also preceding example.)

  EXAMPLES   "In what country will the next Summer Olympics be held?" asked Katrina.

  Which poem by Dorothy Parker begins with the line "A single flow'r he sent me, since we met"?

  The teacher asked, "Who are the protagonist and the antagonist of Larry Woiwode's short story 'The Beginning of Grief'?"

- **for titles**

  EXAMPLES   "Tuesday Siesta" [short story]

  "My Mother Pieced Quilts" [short poem]

  "Wind Beneath My Wings" [song]

regular verb A regular verb is a verb that forms its past and past participle by adding *–d* or *–ed* to the base form. (See page 173. See also **irregular verb.**)

Base Form	Present Participle	Past	Past Participle
ask	[is] asking	asked	[have] asked
deceive	[is] deceiving	deceived	[have] deceived
drown	[is] drowning	drowned	[have] drowned
risk	[is] risking	risked	[have] risked
suppose	[is] supposing	supposed	[have] supposed
use	[is] using	used	[have] used

rise, raise (See page 186.)

EXAMPLES   Huge billows of smoke **rose** from the top of the mountain. [past tense of *rise*]

            They **raised** the window blinds to let in the light and warmth of the sun. [past tense of *raise*]

run-on sentence

A run-on sentence is two or more complete sentences run together as one. (See page 454. See also **comma splice** and **fused sentence.**)

RUN-ON   Troy Menzies is a guitar player my father knew back in the 1960s and 1970s, they went to high school together.

REVISED   Troy Menzies is a guitar player my father knew back in the 1960s and 1970s. They went to high school together.

REVISED   Troy Menzies is a guitar player my father knew back in the 1960s and 1970s; they went to high school together.

semicolon (See page 322.)

■ **in compound sentences with no conjunctions**

EXAMPLE   Norman Rockwell was a prolific artist; he is perhaps best remembered for his cover illustrations for the *Saturday Evening Post.*

■ **in compound sentences with conjunctive adverbs or transitional expressions**

EXAMPLE   Many animals, such as frogs and alligators, are amphibious; **that is,** they can live both on land and in water.

■ **between a series of items when the items contain commas**

EXAMPLE   In the famous Hindu epic *Ramayana,* the main characters are Prince Rama; Sita, his loyal wife; Lakshmana, his devoted brother; and Ravan, the ruler of the demons.

sentence

A sentence is a group of words that contains a subject and a verb and expresses a complete thought. (See page 35.)

EXAMPLE   The swans glided low over the water before landing.

sentence fragment

A sentence fragment is a group of words that is punctuated as if it were a complete sentence but that does not contain both a subject and a verb or that does not express a complete thought. (See pages 35 and 446.)

FRAGMENT	The samisen, a stringed instrument used in Japanese music.
SENTENCE	The samisen, a stringed instrument used in Japanese music, resembles a guitar.

FRAGMENT	Saying goodbye to our cousins.
SENTENCE	Outside, Mother was saying goodbye to our cousins.

simple sentence A simple sentence has one independent clause and no subordinate clauses. (See page 102.)

EXAMPLES   Chief Ta-sunko-witko (Crazy Horse) led the Sioux and Cheyenne forces to victory at the Battle of the Little Bighorn.

Did Mike and Dana go with you to the Cherry Blossom Festival?

sit, set (See page 183.)

EXAMPLES   **Sitting** in his favorite chair, Grandfather told us a story about a talking camel named Yak-yak.

Setting a bowl of popcorn in front of us, Grandfather began telling a story about a talking camel named Yak-yak.

slow, slowly (See page 216.)

EXAMPLES   The traffic was so **slow** on the highway that we decided to take a back road.

The traffic moved so **slowly** on the highway that we decided to take a back road.

stringy sentence A stringy sentence is a sentence that has too many independent clauses. Usually, the clauses are strung together with coordinating conjunctions like *and* or *but*. (See page 477.)

STRINGY   The Greek hero Perseus went in search of the monster Medusa, and guiding the hero on his quest were the goddess Athena and the god Hermes, and in an effort to protect Perseus, Athena provided him with a mirrored shield.

REVISED   The Greek hero Perseus went in search of the monster Medusa. Guiding the hero on his quest were the goddess Athena and the god Hermes. In an effort to protect Perseus, Athena provided him with a mirrored shield.

subject The subject tells whom or what a sentence is about. (See page 37.)

EXAMPLES   **Doves** have always nested under the eaves of that old house.

             Where have **Harry and Lucas** gone?

subject complement A subject complement is a word or word group that completes the meaning of a linking verb and identifies or modifies the subject. (See page 51. See also **predicate adjective** and **predicate nominative.**)

EXAMPLES   Yellow is my least favorite **color.**

             Purple seems **richer.**

subjunctive mood The subjunctive mood is used to express a suggestion, a necessity, a condition contrary to fact, or a wish. (See page 204.)

EXAMPLES   Some of us recommended that Amy **be asked** to serve as the spokesperson for our group.

             If I **were** you, I would deposit the money in a savings account.

subordinate clause A subordinate clause (also called a *dependent clause*) does not express a complete thought and cannot stand alone as a sentence. (See page 91. See also **adjective clause, adverb clause,** and **noun clause.**)

EXAMPLES   The one **that I like** is on order.

             As soon as we get there, we will call you.

             Do you know **what you want**?

suffix A suffix is a word part that is added after a base word or root. (See page 380.)

EXAMPLES

usual + ly = usual**ly**	heavy + ly = heavi**ly**
gentle + ness = gentle**ness**	employ + er = employ**er**
admire + able = admir**able**	replace + able = replace**able**
trap + ing = trapp**ing**	farm + ing = farm**ing**

tense of verbs The tense of verbs indicates the time of the action or state of being expressed by the verb. (See page 188.)

EXAMPLES   He and I **ride** the same bus to school. [present]

She **rode** a horse for the first time last weekend. [past]

Judy **will ride** with the Washingtons to next week's game. [future]

David **has ridden** in the parade for the last three years. [present perfect]

Kelley **had** always **ridden** to school with Dawn, but Dawn moved to another city. [past perfect]

By the time the carnival ends, I **will have ridden** on every ride. [future perfect]

transitive verb A transitive verb is an action verb that takes an object. (See page 19.)

EXAMPLE   Finally, Roderick **took** the step and **bought** the car.

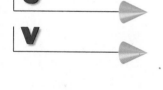

underlining (See **italics.**)

verb A verb expresses an action or a state of being. (See page 15.)

EXAMPLES   He **carved** the figurine and **put** it on the windowsill.

They **are** very funny.

verbal A verbal is a form of a verb used as an adjective, an adverb, or a noun. (See page 70. See also **participle, gerund,** and **infinitive.**)

EXAMPLES   **Thrilled,** I said yes immediately. [participle]

I enjoy **playing** volleyball. [gerund]

The host asked us **to sit.** [infinitive]

verbal phrase A verbal phrase consists of a verbal and any modifiers and complements it has. (See page 70. See also **participial phrase, gerund phrase,** and **infinitive phrase.**)

EXAMPLE   Several large chicken hawks, **wheeling high in the sky,** were no threat to us.

RESOURCES

verb phrase A verb phrase consists of a main verb and at least one helping verb. (See page 39.)

EXAMPLES   **Had** he **met** her before?

Tony and Suzanne **are gardening.**

voice Voice is the form a transitive verb takes to indicate whether the subject of the verb performs or receives the action. (See page 199.)

ACTIVE VOICE   Laotzu **founded** the Chinese philosophy of Taoism in the sixth century B.C.

PASSIVE VOICE   The Chinese philosophy Taoism **was founded** by Laotzu in the sixth century B.C.

weak reference A weak reference is the incorrect use of a pronoun to refer to an antecedent that has not been expressed. (See page 165.)

WEAK   Joan of Arc was a fearless soldier, and it inspired the French troops whom she led into battle. [To what does *it* refer?]

REVISED   Joan of Arc was a fearless soldier, and **her courage** inspired the French troops whom she led into battle.

well (See *good, well.*)

who, whom (See page 156.)

EXAMPLES   Ms. Guitterez, **who** teaches courses in accounting and computer science, has been voted Teacher of the Year.

Ms. Guitterez, **whom** the student body has voted Teacher of the Year, teaches courses in accounting and computer science.

wordiness Wordiness is the use of more words than necessary or the use of fancy words where simple ones will do. (See page 479.)

WORDY   Sandra Cisneros, who is the author who wrote the book titled *The House on Mango Street,* which is a collection of short stories, was born in the city of Chicago in Illinois in the year 1954.

REVISED   Sandra Cisneros, the author of the short-story collection *The House on Mango Street,* was born in Chicago, Illinois, in 1954.

Infinitive phrases
definition of, 78, 540
diagramming and, 495–96
Inflections, 516
Informal English, definition of, 236
Informal speaking
superlative degree and, 221
Inside, 247
Instructions, 319
Intensive pronouns, definition of, 8, 162
Interjections
definition of, 27, 541
punctuation of, 28, 292–93
Interrogative pronouns, 8
Interrogative sentences
definition of, 57, 541
punctuation of, 57, 58, 292
Intervening phrases
subject-verb agreement and, 111
In-text citation, 507-8, 509–14
Intransitive verbs, 19, 541
Introductory elements, punctuation of, 305–307
Invent, discover, 242
Irregular verbs, 174–77, 541
Italics (underlining)
for foreign words, 339
for ships, trains, aircraft, etc., 339
of titles and subtitles, 338, 541–42
used for emphasis, 340
of words, letters, symbols, and numerals, 339, 542
Items in series
colons and, 327
commas and, 298–300, 533
semicolons and, 324
as sentence fragment, 453
Its, it's, 394, 542

Khan, Niamat, 344
Kind of a(n), sort of a(n), 246
Kind of, sort of, 246
Kinds, sorts, types, 246
Know, **principal parts of,** 176

Language. *See also* English language.
nonsexist language, 257–58
Language skills, review of, 408–41
Lay, **principal parts of,** 180
Lay, lie, 180, 542

Lead, **principal parts of,** 176
Lead, led, 394
Leap, **principal parts of,** 174
Learn, teach, 246
Least, less, 220
Leave, let, 246
Leave, **principal parts of,** 176
Legibility, 504–5
Lend, borrow, loan, 240
Less, fewer, 243
Let, **principal parts of,** 176
Letters. *See* Business letters.
Lie, **principal parts of,** 180
Lie, lay, 180, 542
Light, **principal parts of,** 176
Like, as, as if, as though, 246
Linking verbs
definition of, 17, 542
as intransitive, 19
list of, 17
subject complements and, 51
Literary present tense, 192
Loan, borrow, lend, 240
Loanwords, 339, 387, 515
Loose, lose, 394
Lose, **principal parts of,** 176
–ly
parts of speech of words ending in *–ly,* 20
–ly, –ness, 380

M

Main clauses. *See* Independent clauses.
Make, **principal parts of,** 176
Manuscript Form, 504–14
Many a, every, 125
Margins, 506, 509–14
May, 198
May, can, 242
Middle English, 516
Might, 198
Might of, 242
Miner, minor, 394
Misplaced modifiers, 225–28, 542
Modals
definition of, 15, 197
uses of, 197–99
Modern English, 517. *See also* English language.
Modifiers. *See also* Adjective(s); Adverb(s).
bad, badly, 215
clauses used as, 215, 228
comparative degree of, 218–22, 535
comparison of, 218–22, 535
dangling modifiers, 224, 536–37
definition of, 212, 543

Quotations. *See also* Direct quotations.
    capitalization of, 266
    colons and, 327
    direct quotations, 341–43
    direct quotations, use of, 341–43, 344–45, 507–8, 509–14
    indirect quotations, 341
    long quotations set off from text, 344
    punctuation of, 341–43, 546
    within quotations, 345

Raise, **principal parts of,** 186
Raise, rise, 186, 547
Read, **principal parts of,** 176
Reading aloud, to find run-on sentences, 454
Real, really, 216
Receive, **principal parts of,** 173
Reference
    ambiguous pronoun reference, 164
    clear pronoun reference, 164–66
    general pronoun reference, 165
    indefinite pronoun reference, 165–66
    weak pronoun reference, 165
Reflexive pronouns, definition of, 7, 162
Regional dialects, 518
Regular comparison of modifiers, 219–20
Regular verbs, 173–74, 546
Relative adverbs, adjective clauses and, 95
Relative pronouns
    adjective clauses and, 94–95
    list of, 8, 94
    number and, 124, 136
    understood relative pronouns, 95
Restrictive appositives, 309–10
Restrictive clauses, phrases. *See* Essential clauses, phrases.
Ride, **principal parts of,** 176
Ring, **principal parts of,** 176
Rise, **principal parts of,** 186
Rise, raise, 186, 547
Run, **principal parts of,** 172, 176
Run-on sentences
    comma splices and, 454, 534
    definition of, 454, 547
    fused sentences and, 454
    revision of, 454–55

Say, **principal parts of,** 176
Scarcely, 254

Second-person pronouns, 7, 146
–sede, –cede, **and** *–ceed,* 378
See, **principal parts of,** 177
Seek, **principal parts of,** 177
Self– (prefix), 366
Sell, **principal parts of,** 177
Semicolons
    compound sentences and, 322–24, 455, 547
    conjunctive adverbs and, 322–23, 455, 547
    independent clauses and, 90, 299, 322–24
    for items in series containing commas, 324, 547
    quotation marks and, 342
Send, **principal parts of,** 175, 177
Sentence. *See also* Sentence fragments; Sentence parts.
Sentence(s)
    beginning with *there* or *here,* 44
    capitalization of first word, 266
    classified by purpose, 57–58
    classified by structure, 102–103
    combining sentences, 464–73
    complements and, 48–56
    complex sentences, 46, 103, 472–73, 501, 535
    compound sentences, 46, 102–103, 301, 454–55, 470–71, 500–01, 536
    compound-complex sentences, 103, 501, 536
    declarative sentences, 57, 292, 538
    definition of, 35, 446, 547
    diagramming sentences, 488–501
    exclamatory sentences, 57–58, 292–93, 538
    fused sentences, 454, 538–39
    imperative sentences, 57, 293, 540
    interrogative sentences, 57, 292, 541
    punctuation of, 292–93
    simple sentences, 102, 301, 499, 548
    stringy sentences, 477–78, 548
    varying sentence beginnings, 481–82
    varying sentence structure, 483–84
    wordy sentences, 479–80, 551
Sentence fragments
    appositive phrases, 449
    definition of, 35, 446–47, 547
    identification of, 446–47
    phrase fragments, 448–49
    prepositional phrases, 449
    series of items as, 453
    subordinate clause fragment, 450–51
    used for effect, 447
    used as writing style, 447
    verbal phrases and, 448–49
Sentence parts.
    complements, 48–56
    predicates, 37–46
    subjects, 37–46
Sentence style. *See also* Style.
    improving sentence style, 476–80
Sequence of events, verb tense and, 195–96
Series of items. *See* Items in series.

Set, **principal parts of,** 175, 183
Set, sit, 183, 548
Shall, will, 198
She, it, they, he, 243
Shone, shown, 397
Should, 198
Should of, 242
Shown, shone, 397
Simple predicates, 39. *See also* Verb(s).
Simple sentences
compound sentences distinguished from, 301
definition of, 102, 548
diagramming and, 499
Simple subjects, definition of, 38
Sing, **principal parts of,** 175, 177
Single quotation marks, 345
Single-word modifiers, varying sentence beginnings, 481–82
Sink, **principal parts of,** 177
Sit, **principal parts of,** 183
Sit, set, 183, 548
Slang, 346, 519
Sleep, **principal parts of,** 177
Slow, slowly, 216, 548
Some, somewhat, 249
Somewheres, 238
Sort of a(n), kind of a(n), 246
Sort of, kind of, 246
Sorts, types, kinds, 246
Spacing, 506, 509–14
Speak, **principal parts of,** 177
Speaking
formal speaking, 221, 346
Spelling
–cede, –ceed, –sede, 378
–ly, –ness, 380
commonly misspelled words, 405
ie and *ei,* 378
of numbers, 389–90
plurals of nouns, 385–88
prefixes, 379
pronunciation as aid to, 377
proofreading for errors, 377
rules for, 378–90
spelling notebook, 378
suffixes, 380–82
techniques for, 377–78
words often confused, 391–98
Spend, **principal parts of,** 177
Stand, **principal parts of,** 177
Standard English, 236, 519
State-of-being verbs, 17
Stationary, stationery, 397
Steal, **principal parts of,** 177
Stringy sentences, 477–78, 548

Style. *See also* Sentence style.
combining sentences, 464–73
revising stringy sentences, 477–78
revising wordy sentences, 479–80
using parallel structure, 476
varying sentence beginnings, 481–82
varying sentence structure, 483–84
Subject complements
definition of, 17, 51, 549
diagramming and, 491
linking verbs and, 51
placement of, 51–52
predicate adjectives, 52
predicate nominative, 51–52
Subject-verb agreement. *See* Agreement (subject-verb).
Subjects of sentences, 37–46
complete subjects, 37–39
compound subjects, 45–46, 118
definition of, 37, 549
double subjects, 243
finding of, 40–41
nominative case and, 147–49
simple subjects, 38
understood subjects, 36, 45, 488
Subjects of verbs
definition of, 147
in nominative case, 147
pronoun form and, 148
Subjunctive mood, 204, 549
Subordinate clauses
adjective clauses, 93–95
adverb clauses, 96–97
complements and, 49, 92
definition of, 91, 450, 549
diagramming and, 497–99
noun clauses, 99–100
object of verbs and, 54
placement of, 450–51
as sentence fragment, 450–53
uses of, 93–100
variety of sentence beginnings and, 481–82
who, whom and, 156–57
Subordinating conjunctions, 96–97, 472–73, 498
Subordination, 450–53, 472–73, 476–78, 481–84
Suffixes
definition of, 380, 549
hyphens and, 365
spelling rules for, 380–82
Superlative degree of comparison, 218–22
Suppose to, supposed to, 249
Swim, **principal parts of,** 177
Syllable
as aid to spelling, 377
definition of, 377
word division at end of line and, 365

ACKNOWLEDGMENTS

PHOTO CREDITS

Abbreviation used: (tl) top left, (tc) top center, (tr) top right, (l) left, (lc) left center, (c) center, (rc) right center, (r) right, (bl) bottom left, (bc) bottom center, (br) bottom right.

COVER: Kim Taylor/Bruce Coleman, Inc.

TABLE OF CONTENTS: Page iv, PhotoEdit; v, Image Copyright © 2003 PhotoDisc, Inc./HRW; vi, Peabody Essex Museum, Salem, Massachusetts; vii, Keren Su/Tony Stone Images; vii, Courtesy of McAllen International Museum/HRW photo by Eric Beggs; ix (tl), The Granger Collection, New York; ix (l), Michael & Patricia Fogden/CORBIS; ix (bl), Art Wolfe/Tony Stone Images; x, Jerry Jacka Photography/Courtesy of the Heard Museum, Phoenix, Arizona; xi, SuperStock; xii, George Skene/Orlando Sentinel; xiv, SuperStock; xv, © 1990 Robert A. Tyrrell; xviii, HRW Photo Research Library; xxi, Sam Dudgeon/HRW; xxii, Sam Dudgeon/HRW; xxiii, HRW Photo Research Library.

CHAPTER 1: Page 6, Stock Food Creative/Getty Images; 11, FPG International; 14, Collection of the Oakland Museum, Kahn Collection; 18, Jose Fusta Raga/The Stock Market; 21, SuperStock.

CHAPTER 2: Page 30, Nebraska State Historical Society; 36, Nebraska State Historical Society; 40, Keren Su/Tony Stone Images; 41, Image Copyright © 2001 PhotoDisc, Inc.; 42, Martin A. Levick; 47, Corbis Images; 53(cr), EyeWire, Inc./Image Club Graphics © 1998 Adobe Systems, Inc.; 53 (br), EyeWire, Inc./Image Club Graphics © 1998 Adobe Systems, Inc.; 55, Image Copyright © 2003 PhotoDisc, Inc.; 59, Tibor Bognar/The Stock Market.

CHAPTER 3: Page 67, Scala/Art Resource, NY; 69, Image Copyright © 2001 PhotoDisc, Inc.; 73, The Granger Collection, New York; 74, SuperStock; 79, AP/Wide World Photos; 80, Mark Wagner/Tony Stone Images; 83, J. Greenberg/The Image Works.

CHAPTER 4: Page 92, Bettmann/CORBIS; 98 (bl), Alain DEJEAN/Sygma; 98 (br), Ron Behrmann; 567, Rainer Hackenberg/zefa/Corbis.

CHAPTER 5: Page 117, NASA; 129, Peabody Essex Museum; 137, Alexandra Carlilel/Evele Images/Alamy; 140, Robert Hynes/HRW Photo.

CHAPTER 6: Page 147 (tr), Scala/Art Resource, NY; 147 (c), People's Republic of Congo, Northeast Region, Mahongwe Ethnic Group, Mask, Musee Barbier-Mueller, Geneva; 147 (cr) Tate Gallery, London/Art Resource, NY; 150, Park Street Photography.

CHAPTER 7: Page 182, Peter Van Steen/HRW Photo; 196, The Granger Collection, New York.

CHAPTER 8: Page 214 (tl), Courtesy of McAllen International Museum/HRW photo by Eric Beggs; 214 (cr), Courtesy of McAllen International Museum/HRW Photo by Eric Beggs; 217, Michelle Birdwell/HRW photo; 223 (cr), Jerry Jacka Photography/Courtesy of the Heard Museum, Phoenix,

Arizona; 223 (r), Jerry Jacka Photography/Courtesy of the Faust Gallery, Scottsdale, Arizona; 223 (br), Jerry Jacka Photography; 223 (bc), Jerry Jacka Photography/Courtesy of Kathleen L. and William G. Howard; 230 (br), British Museum, London/Art Resource, NY; 230 (cl) British Museum, London/Art Resource, NY.

CHAPTER 9: Page 241, Okanogan County Historical Society; 248, Cooper-Hewitt, National Design Museum, Smithsonian Institution/Art Resource, NY. Photo: Scott Hyde; 254, The Granger Collection, New York.

CHAPTER 10: Page 269 (cr) Gordon Parks/Archive Photos; 269 (bl), John Dominis/LIFE Magazine © Time Inc.; 272 (bl), James Holland/Stock Boston; 272 (bc) Photo Edit; 278, American History Museum; 283, Christopher Magadini/HRW photo by Eric Beggs.

CHAPTER 11: Page 304, Rex A. Butcher/Tony Stone Images; 305, Dave Rosenberg/Tony Stone Images; 307 (cr), Image Copyright © 2003 PhotoDisc, Inc.; 307 (r), Image Copyright © 2003 PhotoDisc, Inc.; 307 (br), Image Copyright © 2003 PhotoDisc, Inc.; 308 (tl), Michael & Patricia Fogden/CORBIS; 308 (cl), Art Wolfe/Tony Stone Images; 310, Scala/Art Resource, NY; 316, Art Resource, NY.

CHAPTER 12: Page 323, Vicki Ragan.

CHAPTER 13: Page 347, Courtesy of Emilio Aguirre/HRW photo by Eric Beggs.

CHAPTER 14: Page 372 (bl), The Granger Collection, New York; 372 (br), The Granger Collection, New York.

CHAPTER 15: Page 379, UPI/Corbis-Bettmann; 384 (tl), National Museum of American Art, Washington DC/Art Resource, NY; 384 (br), Library of Congress; 399, The Granger Collection, New York.

CHAPTER 16: Page 411, Image Copyright © 2003 PhotoDisc, Inc.; 412 (tl), Museum of the American Indian, New York/HRW Photo Research Library; 418, Classic PIO Partners; 423, © 1997 Radlund & Associates for Artville; 424, Alan Schein/The Stock Market; 434, Image Copyright © 2003 PhotoDisc, Inc.

CHAPTER 17: Page 449, Bruno Morandi/Robert Harding World Imagery/Getty Images; 450, Associated Press NASA TV; 451, Art Wolfe/Tony Stone Images; 452, Library of Congress; 455 (cl)(cr), Randal Alhadeff/HRW Photo; 456, John Elk III/Stock Boston.

CHAPTER 18: Page 464, John Lamb/Tony Stone Images; 468, Bill Nation/Sygma; 471, Will and Dent McIntyre/Tony Stone Images; 474, Giraudon/Art Resource, NY; 477, SuperStock; 480, Altrendo Nature/Getty Images; 482, A & L Sinibaldi/Tony Stone Images.